COMPUTATIONAL SYSTEMS BIOLOGY

SECOND EDITION

COMPUTATIONAL SYSTEMS BIOLOGY

SECOND EDITION

Edited by

ROLAND EILS
ANDRES KRIETE

ELSEVIER

AMSTERDAM • BOSTON • HEIDELBERG • LONDON
NEW YORK • OXFORD • PARIS • SAN DIEGO
SAN FRANCISCO • SINGAPORE • SYDNEY • TOKYO
Academic Press is an imprint of Elsevier

Academic Press is an imprint of Elsevier
525 B Street, Suite 1800, San Diego, CA 92101-4495, USA
225 Wyman Street, Waltham, MA 02451, USA
The Boulevard, Langford Lane, Kidlington, Oxford, OX5 1GB, UK
32 Jamestown Road, London, NW1 7BY, UK
Radarweg 29, PO Box 211, 1000 AE Amsterdam, The Netherlands

Library of Congress Cataloging-in-Publication Data
Computational systems biology (Kriete)
Computational systems biology / edited by Andres Kriete, Roland Eils. -- Second edition.
p. ; cm.
Includes bibliographical references and indexes.
ISBN 978-0-12-405926-9 (alk. paper)
I. Kriete, Andres, editor of compilation. II. Eils, Roland, editor of compilation. III. Title.
[DNLM: 1. Computational Biology. 2. Systems Biology. QU 26.5]
QH324.2
570.1'13--dc23

2013045039

British Library Cataloguing-in-Publication Data
A catalogue record for this book is available from the British Library.

ISBN: 978-0-12-405926-9

For information on all Academic Press publications
visit our website at store.elsevier.com

Contents

6. Gene Networks: Estimation, Modeling, and Simulation

SEIYA IMOTO, HIROSHI MATSUNO, SATORU MIYANO

7. Reconstruction of Metabolic Network from Genome Information and its Structural and Functional Analysis

HONG-WU MA, AN-PING ZENG

8. Standards, Platforms, and Applications

STANLEY GU, HERBERT SAURO

9. Databases, Standards, and Modeling Platforms for Systems Biology

JUERGEN EILS, ELENA HERZOG, BAERBEL FELDER, CHRISTIAN LAWERENZ, ROLAND EILS

10. Computational Models for Circadian Rhythms: Deterministic versus Stochastic Approaches

JEAN-CHRISTOPHE LELOUP, DIDIER GONZE, ALBERT GOLDBETER

11. Top-Down Dynamical Modeling of Molecular Regulatory Networks

REINHARD LAUBENBACHER, PEDRO MENDES

12. Discrete Gene Network Models for Understanding Multicellularity and Cell Reprogramming: From Network Structure to Attractor Landscapes Landscape

JOSEPH XU ZHOU, XIAOJIE QIU, AYMERIC FOUQUIER D'HEROUEL, SUI HUANG

13. Stochastic Simulations of Cellular Processes: From Single Cells to Colonies

JOHN COLE, MICHAEL J. HALLOCK, PIYUSH LABHSETWAR, JOSEPH R. PETERSON, JOHN E. STONE, ZAIDA LUTHEY-SCHULTEN

14. Advances in Machine Learning for Processing and Comparison of Metagenomic Data

JEAN-LUC BOUCHOT, WILLIAM L. TRIMBLE, GREGORY DITZLER, YEMIN LAN, STEVE ESSINGER, GAIL ROSEN

15. Systems Biology of Infectious Diseases and Vaccines

HELDER I NAKAYA

16. Computational Modeling and Simulation of Animal Early Embryogenesis with the MecaGen Platform

JULIEN DELILE, RENÉ DOURSAT, NADINE PEYRIÉRAS

17. Developing a Systems Biology of Aging

ANDRES KRIETE, MATHIEU CLOUTIER

18. Molecular Correlates of Morphometric Subtypes in Glioblastoma Multiforme

HANG CHANG, JU HAN, GERALD V. FONTENAY, CEMAL C. BILGIN, NANDITA NAYAK, ALEXANDER BOROWSKI, PAUL SPELLMAN, BAHRAM PARVIN

19. Applications in Cancer Research: Mathematical Models of Apoptosis

STEFAN M. KALLENBERGER, STEFAN LEGEWIE, ROLAND EILS

Contributors

Chapter 1

Roland Eils Division of Theoretical Bioinformatics (B080), German Cancer Research Center (DKFZ), Heidelberg, Germany

Department for Bioinformatics and Functional Genomics, Institute for Pharmacy and Molecular Biotechnology (IPMB) and BioQuant, Heidelberg University, Heidelberg, Germany

Andres Kriete School of Biomedical Engineering, Science and Health Systems, Drexel University, Philadelphia, PA, USA

Chapter 2

Robert B. Russell, Gordana Apic, Olga Kalinina, Leonardo Trabuco, Matthew J. Betts, Qianhao Lu CellNetworks, University of Heidelberg, Heidelberg, Germany

Chapter 3

Hans V. Westerhoff Department of Synthetic Systems Biology and Nuclear Organization, Swammerdam Institute for Life Sciences, University of Amsterdam, Amsterdam, The Netherlands

Department of Molecular Cell Physiology, Faculty of Earth and Life Sciences, VU University Amsterdam, The Netherlands

Manchester Centre for Integrative Systems Biology (MCISB), Manchester, UK

Fei He Manchester Centre for Integrative Systems Biology (MCISB), Manchester, UK

Department of Automatic Control and systems Engineering, The University of Sheffield, Sheffield, UK

Ettore Murabito Manchester Centre for Integrative Systems Biology (MCISB), Manchester, UK

Frédéric Crémazy Department of Synthetic Systems Biology and Nuclear Organization, Swammerdam Institute for Life Sciences, University of Amsterdam, Amsterdam, The Netherlands

Matteo Barberis Department of Synthetic Systems Biology and Nuclear Organization, Swammerdam Institute for Life Sciences, University of Amsterdam, Amsterdam, The Netherlands

Chapter 4

Ursula Klingmüller, Marcel Schilling, Sonja Depner, Lorenza A. D'Alessandro Division Systems Biology of Signal Transduction, German Cancer Research Center (DKFZ), Heidelberg, Germany

Chapter 5

Christina Kiel EMBL/CRG Systems Biology Research Unit, Centre for Genomic Regulation (CRG), Barcelona, Spain

Universitat Pompeu Fabra (UPF), Barcelona, Spain

Luis Serrano EMBL/CRG Systems Biology Research Unit, Centre for Genomic Regulation (CRG), Barcelona, Spain

Universitat Pompeu Fabra (UPF), Barcelona, Spain

ICREA, Barcelona, Spain

Chapter 6

Seiya Imoto Human Genome Center, Institute of Medical Science, The University of Tokyo, Minatoku, Tokyo, Japan

Hiroshi Matsuno Faculty of Science, Yamaguchi University, Yoshida, Yamaguchi, Japan

Satoru Miyano Human Genome Center, Institute of Medical Science, The University of Tokyo, Minatoku, Tokyo, Japan

Chapter 7

Hong-Wu Ma Tianjin Institute of Industrial Biotechnology, Chinese Academy of Sciences, Tianjin, P.R. China

School of Informatics, University of Edinburgh, Edinburgh, UK

An-Ping Zeng Institute of Bioprocess and Biosystems Engineering, Hamburg University of Technology, Denickestrasse, Germany

Chapter 8

Stanley Gu Department of Bioengineering, University of Washington, Seattle, WA, USA

Herbert Sauro Department of Bioengineering, University of Washington, Seattle, WA, USA

Chapter 9

Juergen Eils Division of Theoretical Bioinformat ics, German Cancer Research Center (DKFZ), Heidelberg, Germany

Elena Herzog Division of Theoretical Bioinformatics, German Cancer Research Center (DKFZ), Heidelberg, Germany

Baerbel Felder Division of Theoretical Bioinformatics, German Cancer Research Center (DKFZ), Heidelberg, Germany

Department for Bioinformatics and Functional Genomics, Institute for Pharmacy and Molecular Biotechnology (IPMB) and BioQuant, Heidelberg University, Heidelberg, Germany

Christian Lawerenz Division of Theoretical Bioinformatics, German Cancer Research Center (DKFZ), Heidelberg, Germany

Roland Eils Division of Theoretical Bioinformat ics, German Cancer Research Center (DKFZ), Heidelberg, Germany

Department for Bioinformatics and Functional Genomics, Institute for Pharmacy and Molecular Biotechnology (IPMB) and BioQuant, Heidelberg University, Heidelberg, Germany

Chapter 10

Jean-Christophe Leloup, Didier Gonze, Albert Goldbeter Unité de Chronobiologie théorique, Faculté des Sciences, Université Libre de Bruxelles, Campus Plaine, Brussels, Belgium

Chapter 11

Reinhard Laubenbacher Virginia Bioinformatics Institute, Virginia Tech, Blacksburg VA, USA

Pedro Mendes Virginia Bioinformatics Institute, Virginia Tech, Blacksburg VA, USA

School of Computer Science, The University of Manchester, Manchester, UK

Chapter 12

Joseph Xu Zhou, Xiaojie Qiu, Aymeric Fouquier d'Herouel, Sui Huang Institute for Systems Biology, Seattle, WA, USA

Chapter 13

John Cole, Mike J. Hallock, Piyush Labhsetwar, Joseph R. Peterson, John E. Stone, Zaida Luthey-Schulten University of Illinois at Urbana-Champaign, USA

Chapter 14

Jean-Luc Bouchot Department of Mathematics, Drexel University, PA, Philadelphia, USA

William L. Trimble Institute for Genomics and Systems Biology, Argonne National Laboratory, University of Chicago, Chicago, IL, USA

Gregory Ditzler Department of Electrical and Computer Engineering, Drexel University, PA, Philadelphia, USA

Yemin Lan School of Biomedical Engineering, Science and Health, Drexel University, PA, Philadelphia, USA

Steve Essinger Department of Electrical and Computer Engineering, Drexel University, PA, Philadelphia, USA

Gail Rosen Department of Electrical and Computer Engineering, Drexel University, PA, Philadelphia, USA

Chapter 15

Helder I Nakaya Department of Pathology, Emory University, Atlanta, GA, USA

Vaccine Research Center, Emory University, Atlanta, GA, USA

Department of Clinical Analyses and Toxicology, University of Sao Paulo, Sao Paulo, SP, Brazil

Chapter 16

Julien Delile Institut des Systèmes Complexes Paris Ile-de-France (ISC-PIF), CNRS, Paris, France

Neurobiology and Development Lab, Terrasse, Gif-sur-Yvette Cedex, France

René Doursat Institut des Systèmes Complexes Paris Ile-de-France (ISC-PIF), CNRS, Paris, France

School of Biomedical Engineering, Drexel University, Philadelphia, PA, USA

Nadine Peyriéras Neurobiology and Development Lab, Terrasse, Gif-sur-Yvette Cedex, France

Chapter 17

Andres Kriete School of Biomedical Engineering, Science and Health Systems, Drexel University, Bossone Research Center, Philadelphia, PA, USA

Mathieu Cloutier GERAD and Department of Chemical Engineering, Ecole Polytechnique de Montreal, Montreal, QC, Canada

Chapter 18

Hang Chang, Gerald V Fontenay, Ju Han, Nandita Nayak, Bahram Parvin, Cemal C. Bilgin Life Sciences Division, Lawrence Berkeley National Laboratory, Berkeley, CA, USA

Alexander Borowski Center for Comparative Medicine, University of California, Davis, CA, USA.

Paul Spellman Department of Biomedical Engineering, Oregon Health Sciences University, Portland, Oregon, USA

Chapter 19

Stefan M. Kallenberger Department for Bioinformatics and Functional Genomics, Division of Theoretical Bioinformatics, German Cancer Research Center (DKFZ), Institute for Pharmacy and Molecular Biotechnology (IPMB) and BioQuant, Heidelberg University, Heidelberg, Germany

Stefan Legewie Institute of Molecular Biology, Mainz, Germany

Roland Eils Department for Bioinformatics and Functional Genomics, Division of Theoretical Bioinformatics, German Cancer Research Center (DKFZ), Institute for Pharmacy and Molecular Biotechnology (IPMB) and BioQuant, Heidelberg University, Heidelberg, Germany

Preface

Computational systems biology, a term coined by Kitano in 2002, is a field that aims at a system-level understanding by modeling and analyzing biological data using computation. It is increasingly recognized that living system cannot be understood by studying individual parts, while the list of molecular components in biology is ever growing, accelerated by genome sequencing and high-throughput omics techniques. Under the guiding vision of systems biology, sophisticated computational methods help to study the interconnection of parts in order to unravel complex and networked biological phenomena, from protein interactions, pathways, networks, to whole cells and multicellular complexes. Rather than performing experimental observations alone, systems biology generates knowledge and understanding by entering a cycle of model construction, quantitative simulations, and experimental validation of model predictions, whereby a formal reasoning becomes key. This requires a collaborative input of experimental and theoretical biologists working together with system analysts, computer scientists, mathematicians, bioengineers, physicists, as well as physicians to contend creatively with the hierarchical and nonlinear nature of cellular systems.

This book has a distinct focus on computational and engineering methods related to systems biology. As such, it presents a timely, multi-authored compendium representing state-of-the-art computational technologies, standards, concepts, and methods developed in this area. If compared to the first edition published in 2005, the second edition has been specifically extended to reflect new frontiers of systems biology, including modeling of whole cells, studies of embryonic development, the immune systems, as well as aging and cancer. As in the previous edition, basics of information and data integration technologies, standards, modeling of gene, signaling and metabolic networks remain comprehensively covered. Contributions have been selected and compiled to introduce the different methods, including methods dissecting biological complexity, modeling of dynamical properties, and biocomputational perspectives.

Beside the primary authors and their respective teams who have dedicated their time to contribute to this book, the editors would like to thank numerous reviewers of individual chapters, but in particular Jan Eufinger for support of the editorial work.

It is often mentioned that biological systems in its entirety present more than a sum of its parts. To this extent, we hope that the chapters selected for this book not only give a contemporary and comprehensive overlook about the recent developments, but that this volume advances the field and encourages new strategies, interdisciplinary cooperation, and research activities.

Roland Eils and Andres Kriete
Heidelberg and Philadelphia,
September 2013

CHAPTER

1

Introducing Computational Systems Biology

Roland Eils[a,b], *Andres Kriete*[c]

[a]Division of Theoretical Bioinformatics (B080), German Cancer Research Center (DKFZ), Heidelberg, Germany

[b]Department for Bioinformatics and Functional Genomics, Institute for Pharmacy and Molecular Biotechnology (IPMB) and BioQuant, Heidelberg University, Heidelberg, Germany

[c]School of Biomedical Engineering, Science and Health Systems, Drexel University, Philadelphia, PA, USA

CONTENTS

We need to turn data into knowledge and we need a framework to do so. **S. Brenner, 2002.**

1 PROLOGUE

The multitude of the computational tools needed for systems biology research can roughly be classified into two categories: *system identification* and *behavior analysis* (Kitano 2001). In molecular biology, system identification amounts to identifying the regulatory relationships between genes, proteins, and small molecules, as well as their inherent dynamics hidden in the specific kinetic and binding parameters. System identification is arguably one of the most complicated problems in science. While behavior analysis is solely performed on a model, model construction is a process tightly connected to reality but part of an iterative process between data analysis, simulation, and experimental validation (Figure 1.1). A typical

http://dx.doi.org/10.1016/B978-0-12-405926-9.00001-0

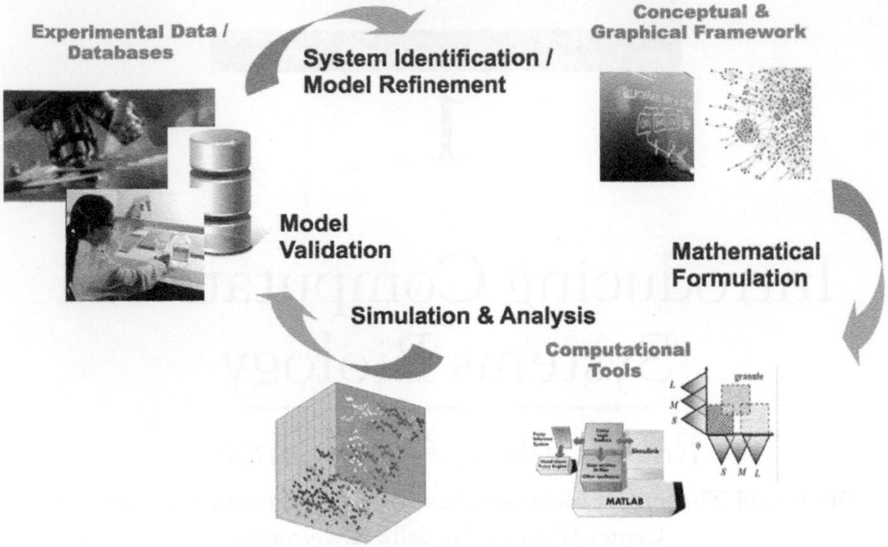

FIGURE 1.1 Key to systems biology is an iterative cycle of experimentation, model building, simulation and validation.

modeling cycle begins with a reductionist approach, creating the simplest possible model. The modeling process generates an understanding of the underlying structures, and components are represented graphically with increasing level of formalization, until they can be converted into a mathematical representation. The minimal model then grows in complexity, driven by new hypotheses that may not have been apparent from the phenomenological descriptions. Then, an experiment is designed using the biological system to test whether the model predictions agree with the experimental observations of the system behavior. The constitutive model parameters may be measured directly or may be inferred during this validation process, however, the propagation of errors through these parameters present significant challenges for the modeler. If data and predictions agree, a new experiment is designed and performed. This process continues until sufficient experimental evidence in favor of the model is collected. Once the system has been identified and a model constructed, the system behavior can be studied, for instance, by numerical integration or sensitivity analysis against external perturbations.

Although the iterative process is well defined, the amount of data to be merged into this process can be immense. The human genome project is one of the hallmarks indicating a turn from a reductionistic approach in studying biological systems at increasing level, into a discovery process using high-throughput techniques (Figure 1.2). Ongoing research increases the wealth of contemporary biological information residing in some thousand public databases providing descriptive genomics, proteomics and enzyme information, gene expression, gene variants and gene ontologies. Refined explorative tools, such as new deep sequencing, along with the emergence of new specialized -omics (metabolomics, lipidomics, pharmacogenomics) and phenotyping techniques, constantly feed into this data pool and accelerate its growth.

Given the enormous and heterogeneous amount of data, computational tools have become indispensable to mine, analyze, and connect such information. The aggregate of statistical

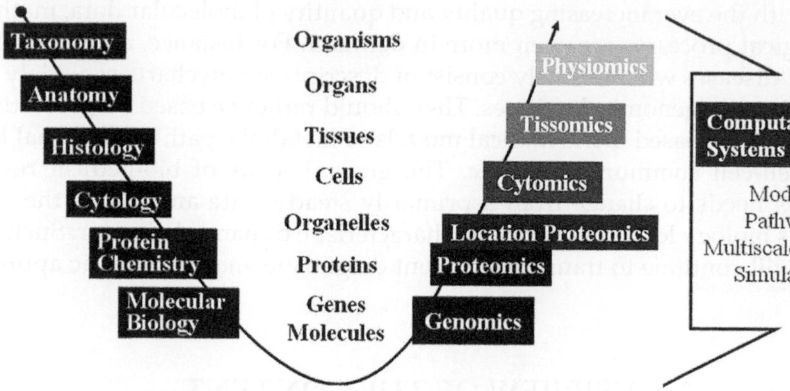

FIGURE 1.2 By the evolution of scientific disciplines in biology over time, ever-smaller structures have come into focus and more detailed questions have been asked. With the availability of high-throughput sequencing techniques in genetics a turning point was reached at the molecular basis of life. The frontiers of research extended to hypothesis-free data acquisition of biological entities, with genomics becoming the first in a growing series of "-omics" disciplines. Although functional genomics and proteomics are far from being completed, "omics" -type approaches addressing the phenotypical cellular, tissue and physiological levels constitute themselves as new scientific disciplines, filling up an otherwise sparse data space. Computational systems biology provides methodologies to combine, model, and simulate entities on diverse (horizontal) levels of biological organization, such as gene regulatory and protein networks, and between these levels by using multiscale (vertical) approaches.

bioinformatics tools to collect, store, retrieve, visualize, and analyze complex biological data has repeatedly proven useful in biological decision support and discovery. Deciphering the basic building blocks of life is a necessary step in biological research, but provides only limited knowledge in terms of understanding and predictability. In the early stages the human genome project stirred the public expectation for a rapid increase in the deciphering of disease mechanisms, more effective drug development and cure. However, it is well recognized that the battery of mechanisms involved in the proliferation of complex diseases like cancer, chronic diseases, or the development of dementias cannot be understood solely on the basis of knowing all its molecular components.

As a consequence, a lack of system level understanding of cellular dynamics has prevented a substantial increase in the number of new drugs available for treatment, drug efficacy, or eradication of any specific diseases. In contrast, pharmaceutical companies are currently lacking criteria to select the most valuable targets, R&D expenses skyrocket, and new drugs rarely hit the market and often fail in clinical trials, while physicians face an increasing wealth of information that needs to be interpreted intelligently and holistically.

Analysis of this dilemma reveals primary difficulties due to the enormous biomolecular complexity, structural and functional unknowns in a large portion of gene products and a lack of understanding of how the concert of molecular activities transfers into physiological alterations and disease. It has been long recognized that the understanding of cells as open systems, interacting with the environment, performing tasks and sustain homeostasis, or better homeodynamics (Yates 1992), requires the development of foundations for a general systems theory that started with the seminal work of Bertalanffy (Von Bertalanffy 1969).

It appears that with the ever increasing quality and quantity of molecular data, mathematical models of biological processes are even more in demand. For instance, an envisioned blueprint of complex diseases will not solely consist of descriptive flowcharts as widely found in scientific literature or in genomic databases. They should rather be based on predictive, rigorously quantitative data-based mathematical models of metabolic pathways, signal transduction cascades, cell-cell communication, etc. The general focus of biomedical research on complex diseases needs to change from a primarily steady-state analysis at the molecular level to a systems biology level capturing the characteristic dynamic behavior. Such biosimulation concepts will continue to transform current diagnostic and therapeutic approaches to medicine.

2 OVERVIEW OF THE CONTENT

This completely revised, second edition of this book presents examples selected from an increasingly diverse field of activities, covering basic key methods, development of tools, and recent applications in many complex areas of computational systems biology. In the following, we will broadly review the content of the chapters as they appear in this book, along with specific introductions and outlooks.

The first section of this book introduces essential foundations of systems biology, principles of network reconstruction based on high-throughput data with the help of engineering principles such as control theory. Robert B. Russell, Gordana Apic, Olga Kalinina, Leonardo Trabuco, Matthew J. Betts, and Qianhao Lu provide an introduction (Chapter 2) on *"Structural Systems Biology: modeling interactions and networks for systems studies."* Molecular mechanisms provide the most detailed level for a mechanistic understanding of biological complexity. The current challenges of a structural systems biology are to integrate, utilize, and extend such knowledge in conjunction with high-throughput studies. Understanding the mechanistic consequences of multiple alterations in DNA variants, protein structures, and folding are key tasks of structural bioinformatics.

Principles of protein interactions in pathways and networks are introduced by Hans V. Westerhoff, Fei He, Ettore Murabito, Frédéric Crémazy, and Matteo Barberis in Chapter 3. Their contribution is entitled *"Understanding principles of the dynamic biochemical networks of life through systems biology"* and discusses a number of basic, more recent and upcoming discoveries of network principles. The contributors review analytical procedures from flux balance in metabolic networks to measures of robustness.

In Chapter 4, Ursula Klingmüller, Marcel Schilling, Sonja Depner, and Lorenza A. D'Alessandro review the *"Biological foundations of signal transduction and aberrations in disease."* Signaling pathways process the external signals through complex cellular networks that regulate biological functions in a context-dependent manner. The authors identify the underlying biological mechanisms influential for signal transduction and introduce the mathematical tools essential to model signaling pathways and their disease aberrations in a quantitative fashion.

Further acceleration of progress in pathway reconstruction and analysis is contingent on the solution of many complexities and new requirements, revolving around the question of how high-throughput experimental techniques can help to accelerate reconstruction and simulation of signaling pathways. This is the theme of the review in Chapter 5 by Christina Kiel and Luis Serrano on the *"Complexities underlying a quantitative systems analysis of signaling networks."* Chapter 6 by Seiya Imoto, Hiroshi Matsuno, Satoru Miyano presents *"Gene networks: estimation, modeling and simulation."* The authors describe how gene networks can be reconstructed from microarray gene expression data, which is a contemporary problem. They also introduce software tools for modeling and simulating gene networks, which is based on the concept of Petri nets. The authors demonstrate the utility for the modeling and simulation of the gene network for controlling circadian rhythms.

Section 2 provides an overview of methods, mathematical tools, and examples for modeling approaches of dynamic systems. *"Standards, platforms, and applications,"* as presented by Herbert Sauro and Stanley Gu in Chapter 8, reviews the trends in developing standards indicative of increasing cooperation within the systems biology community, which emerged in recent years permitting collaborative projects and exchange of models between different software tools. *"Databases for systems biology,"* as reviewed in Chapter 9 by Juergen Eils, Elena Herzog, Baerbel Felder, Christian Lawerenz and Roland Eils provide approaches to integrate information about the responses of biological system to genetic or environmental perturbations. As researchers try to solve biological problems at the level of entire systems, the very nature of this approach requires the integration of highly divergent data types, and a tight coupling of three general areas of data generated in systems biology: experimental data, elements of biological systems, and mathematical models with the derived simulations. Chapter 10 builds on a classical mathematical modeling approach to study patterns of dynamic behaviors in biological systems. *"Computational models for circadian rhythms - deterministic versus stochastic approaches,"* Jean-Christophe Leloup, Didier Gonze and Albert Goldbeter demonstrates how feedback loops give rise to oscillatory behavior and how several results can be obtained in models which possess a minimum degree of complexity. Circadian rhythms provide a particular interesting case-study for showing how computational models can be used to address a wide range of issues extending from molecular mechanism to physiological disorders.

Reinhard Laubenbacher and Pedro Mendes review *"Top-down dynamical modeling of molecular regulatory networks,"* Chapter 11. The modeling framework discussed in this chapter considers mathematical methods addressing time-discrete dynamical systems over a finite state set applied to decipher gene regulatory networks from experimental data sets. The assumptions of final systems states are not only a useful modeling concept, but also serve an explanation of fundamental organization of cellular complexities. Chapter 12, entitled *"Multistability and multicellularity: cell fates as high-dimensional attractors of gene regulatory networks,"* by Joseph X. Zhou and Sui Huang, investigates how the high number of combinatorially possible expression configurations collapses into a few configurations characteristic of observable cell fates. These fates are proposed to be high-dimensional attractors in gene activity state space, and may help to achieve one of the most desirable goal of computational systems biology, which is the development of whole cell models. In Chapter 13 John Cole, Mike J. Hallock, Piyush Labhsetwar, Joseph R. Peterson, John E. Stone, and Zaida Luthey-Schulten review *"Whole cell modeling strategies for single cells and microbial colonies,"* taking into account spatial and time-related heterogeneities such as short-term and long-term stochastic fluctuations.

Section 3 of this book is dedicated to emerging systems biology application including modeling of complex systems and phenotypes in development, aging, health, and disease. In Chapter 14, Jean-Luc Bouchot, William Trimble, Gregory Ditzler, Yemin Lan, Steve Essinger, and Gail Rosen introduce *"Advances in machine learning for processing and comparison of metagenomic data."* The study of nucleic acid samples from different parts of the environment, reflecting the microbiome, has strongly developed in the last years and has become one of the sustained biocomputational endeavors. Identification, classification, and visualization via sophisticated computational methods are indispensable in this area. Similarly, the deciphering immune system has to deal with a large amount of data generated from high-throughput techniques reflecting the inherent complexity of the immune system. Helder I. Nakaya, in Chapter 15, reports on *"Applying systems biology to understand the immune response to infection and vaccination."* This chapter highlights recent advances and shows how systems biology can be applied to unravel novel key molecular mechanisms of immunity.

Rene Doursat, Julien Delile, and Nadine Peyrieras present *"Cell behavior to tissue deformation: computational modeling and simulation of early animal embryogenesis,"* Chapter 16. They propose a theoretical, yet realistic agent-based model and simulation platform of animal embryogenesis, to study the dynamics on multiple levels of biological organization. This contribution is an example demonstrating the value of systems biology in integrating the different phenomena involved to study complex biological process. In Chapter 17, Andres Kriete and Mathieu Cloutier present *"Developing a systems biology of aging."* The contribution reviews modeling of proximal mechanisms of aging occurring in pathways, networks, and multicellular systems, as demonstrated for Parkinson's disease. In addition, the authors reflect on evolutionary aspect of aging as a robustness tradeoff in complex biological designs.

In Chapter 18, Hang Chang, Gerald V Fontenay, Ju Han, Nandita Nayak, Alexander Borowsky, Paul Spellman, and Bahram Parvin present image-based phenotyping strategies to classify cancer phenotypes on the tissue level, entitled *"Morphometric analysis of tissue heterogeneity in Glioblastoma Multiforme."* Such work allows to associate morphological heterogeneities of cancer subtypes with molecular information to improve prognosis. In terms of a multiscale modeling approach the assessment of phenotypical changes, in cancer as well as in other diseases, will help to build bridges toward new spatiotemporal modeling approaches. Stefan M. Kallenberger, Stefan Legewie, and Roland Eils demonstrate *"Applications in cancer research: mathematical models of apoptosis"* in Chapter 19. Their contribution is focused on the mathematical modeling of cell fate decisions and its dysregulation of cell death, contributing to one of the ramifications of the complexities in cancer biology.

3 OUTLOOK

It is commonly recognized that biological multiplicity is due to progressive evolution that brought along an increasing complexity of cells and organisms over time (Adami et al. 2000). This judgement coincides with the notion that greater complexity is "better" in terms of complex adaptive systems and ability for self-organization, hence robustness (Csete and Doyle 2002 Kitano 2004). Analyzing or "reverse" engineering of this complexity and integrating results of today's scientific technologies responsible for the ubiquitous data overload are an essential part of systems biology. The goals are to conceptualize, abstract basic principles, and model biological structures from molecular to higher level of organization like cells, tissues, and organs, in order to provide insight and knowledge. The initial transition requires data cleansing and data coherency, but turning information into knowledge requires interpreting what the data actually means. Systems biology addresses this need by the development and analysis of high-resolution quantitative models that recapitulate, but more importantly predict cellular behavior in time and space and to determine physiology from the underlying molecular and cellular capacities on a multiscale (Dada and Mendes 2011). Once established, such models are indicators to the detailed understanding of biological function, the diagnosis of diseases, the identification and validation of therapeutic targets, and the design of drugs and drug therapies. Experimental techniques yielding quantitative genomic, proteomic, and metabolomic data needed for the development of such models are becoming increasingly common.

Computer representations describing the underlying mechanisms may not always be able to provide complete accuracy due to limited computational, experimental, and methodical resources. Increase in data quality and coherence, availability within integrated databases or approaches that can manage experimental variability, are less considered but may be as essential for robust growth of biological knowledge. Still, the enormous complexity of biological systems has given rise to additional cautionary remarks. First, it may well be that our models and future super-models correctly predict experimental observations, but may still prevent a deeper understanding due to complexities, non-linearities, or stochastic phenomena. This notion may initially sound quite disappointing, but is a daily experience of all those who employ modeling and simulations of large-scale phenomena. Yet, it shows the relevance of computational approaches in this area, and suggestions to link biological with computational problem solving has been suggested (Navlakha and Bar-Joseph 2011).

Systems biology should follow strict standards and conventions, and progress in theory and computational approaches will always demand new models that can provide new insights if applied to an existing body of information. Many areas, including cancer modeling, have demonstrated how models evolve over many cycles of investigation and refinement (Byrne 2010). Once established, new models can be reimplemented into existing platforms to be more broadly available. In the long run, the aim is to develop user-friendly, scalable and open-ended platforms that also handle methods for behavior analysis and model-based disease diagnosis, and support scientists in their every-day practice of decision-making and biological inquiry, as well as physicians in clinical decision support.

Systems biology has risen out of consensus in the scientific community, initially driven by visionary scientific entrepreneurs. Now, as its strength becomes obvious, it is recognized as a rapidly evolving mainstream endeavor, which requires specific educational curricula and collaboration among computational scientists, experimental and theoretical biologists, control and systems engineers, as well as practitioners in drug development and clinical research. These collaborative ties will move this field forwards toward a formal, quantitative, and predictive framework of biology.

References

Adami, C., Ofria, C., and Collier, T. C. (2000). Evolution of biological complexity. *Proc Natl Acad Sci USA* **97**:4463–4468.

Byrne, H. M. (2010). Dissecting cancer through mathematics: From the cell to the animal model. *Nat Rev Cancer* **10**:221–230.

Csete, M. E., and Doyle, J. C. (2002). Reverse engineering of biological complexity. *Science* **295**:1664–1669.
Dada, J. O., and Mendes, P. (2011). Multi-scale modelling and simulation in systems biology. *Integr Biol (Camb)* **3**:86–96.
Kitano, H. (2001). *Foundations of Systems Biology*. MIT-Press.
Kitano, H. (2004). Biological Robustness. *Nat Rev Genet* **5**:826–837.
Navlakha, S., and Bar-Joseph, Z. (2011). Algorithms in nature: The convergence of systems biology and computational thinking. *Mol Syst Biol* **7**:546.
Von Bertalanffy, L. (1969). *General Systems Theory*. George Brazillar Inc.
Yates, F. E. (1992). Order and complexity in dynamical systems: Homeodynamics as a generalized mechanics for biology. *Math and Comput Model* **19**:49–74.

CHAPTER

2

Structural Systems Biology: Modeling Interactions and Networks for Systems Studies

Robert B. Russell, Gordana Apic, Olga Kalinina, Leonardo Trabuco, Matthew J. Betts, Qianhao Lu

CellNetworks, University of Heidelberg, Heidelberg, Germany

Contents

Abstract

The best understanding of complex biological systems ultimately comes from details of the underlying atomic structures within it. In the absence of known structures of all protein complexes and interactions in a system, structural bioinformatics or modeling fill an important niche in providing predicted mechanistic information which can guide experiments, aid the interpretation of high-throughput datasets and help provide key details to model biological systems. This introductory review discusses the current state of this field and suggests how current datasets in systems studies can profit from a better integration of predicted or known structural information.

http://dx.doi.org/10.1016/B978-0-12-405926-9.00002-2

1 INTRODUCTION

We are clearly today in the era of high-throughput biology. In every area of biology—from plant sciences to human health—one increasingly sees systematic screens that identify hundreds or thousands of molecules regulated or changed in response to some stimulus or perturbation. More than ever there is a need to understand what such large sets of molecules mean when identified together in terms of system functions, and to use these data to suggest therapies, vaccines, diagnostics, herbicides, etc.

Invariably scientists wish to use the results from high-throughput experiments to unlock the underlying biological mechanism. The molecular mechanism—in the broadest sense—ultimately provides the details that give a deeper understanding of a biological process, or suggest means to perturb a system with small molecules or other agents. To address this, many efforts have been undertaken to capture systematically all of the mechanistic detail that has been captured by low-throughput experiments in the past decades. Pathway resources such as KEGG (Kotera et al. 2012) or Reactome (Croft et al. 2011) and ontological tools such as GO (Gene Ontology Consortium 2006) provide a means to state for a large set of genes, proteins, or metabolites which processes are likely being affected. These tools remain central to most high-throughput studies.

However, the ultimate understanding of a biological process comes only from a view of the actual molecular details underlying it. Specifically, the availability of multiple three-dimensional (3D) structures provides information down to the specific atoms involved in a process. Today, thanks to more than a decade of Structural Genomics driven advances in structure determination by X-ray, NMR, and electron microscopy, there are structural representatives for almost every globular domain, and the number of multi-protein complexes of known structures is also growing at an impressive rate. Concurrent advances in techniques to model protein structures by homology also means that increasingly accurate modeled structures are readily available for at least globular parts of most proteins of interest. There are also many tools for interrogating proteins structurally and increasingly these are addressing the needs of the high-throughput biologist. This chapter discusses recent advances in this broad area of Structural Systems Biology and Bioinformatics, and suggests future directions to meet new challenges of high-throughput biology.

2 A BRIEF HISTORY OF STRUCTURAL BIOINFORMATICS

Structural Bioinformatics began with the first attempts to study and predict protein structures (Blundell et al. 1987). While structure and sequences databases were small, the primary focus was the grand challenge to predict protein 3D structures from primary sequences. Methods to predict protein secondary structure or 3D structure were approached by a variety of informatics-or physics-based methods, and had mixed success until the arrival of systematic community wide assessment exercises (Critical Assessment of Structure Prediction, CASP (Moult et al. 2011)) where double-blind assessments of predictions (i.e. where the structures were unknown to both predictors and experimentalists during the predictions). These experiments identified the strengths and weaknesses of all approaches and ultimately have led to mature methods to predict secondary structure and tertiary structure either de novo or via homology modeling techniques. Today models for virtually all proteins that are modelable are now systematically available via online databases such as ModBase (Pieper et al. 2011) and Swissmodel (Kiefer et al. 2009). Structural bioinformatics now often focuses on methods that predict function of individual proteins of known structure, rather than methods that predict structure per se. For instance, numerous methods have been developed to study protein surfaces to predict functional sites using a variety of geometrical or evolutionary criteria (e.g. Aloy et al. 2001; Capra et al. 2009; Casari et al. 1995; Landgraf et al. 2001; Wilkins et al. 2012; Yang et al. 2012).

The initial genome sequencing projects produced the first large sets of genes and encoded proteins for which little information was available. Structural bioinformatics played a crucial role in identifying overall features of the genome in terms of domain distributions and combinations (e.g. Apic et al. 2001; Gerstein and Levitt 1997), a process that was greatly aided by the availability of structure classification databases (Andreeva et al. 2008; Cuff et al. 2009; Holm and Rosenström 2010). These analyses ultimately matured and were incorporated into the protein databases used today, such as Pfam (Punta et al. 2012) and CDD (Marchler-Bauer et al. 2013) and are readily visible in primary databases such as Uniprot (Wu et al. 2006) or Refseq (Pruitt et al. 2005).

3 STRUCTURAL ANALYSIS OF INTERACTION DATA

The arrival of various interaction datasets produced a new challenge for computational structural biologists. Suddenly thousands of new interactions and complexes became known with little or no structural information available. Modeling interactions is, of course, possible if one has a suitable template of known structure containing two or more interacting proteins in contact. However, early analyses of interaction data from a structural perspective highlighted the relative paucity of these interaction templates (Aloy and Russell 2002). Indeed, while solving structures for single, small, globular proteins are now a relatively straightforward process, solving experimental structures involving multiple proteins continues to be a challenge. Nevertheless, improved experimental techniques, and the increased focus on studying protein complexes in structural biology, means that there is now an exponential growth in the number of distinct interactions of known structure (Aloy and Russell 2004; Kim et al. 2006b; Tuncbag et al. 2008).

There are currently several tools that allow biologists to study interactions in three-dimensions. Early tools such as InterPReTS (Aloy and Russell 2003) and MULTIPROSPECTOR (Lu et al. 2002) were designed to rapidly assess how well homologous sequences fit onto interacting proteins with 3D structures. Systematic analysis of thousands of interactions of known 3D structure showed that sequence similar proteins retain similar interactions, and a drop in sequence similarity increases a tendency to interact differently (Aloy and Russell 2004; Kim et al. 2006b; Tuncbag et al. 2008). Analyses also showed that structural interfaces (Figure 2.1) could be used to infer details about whether or not interactions could occur simultaneously (Aloy and Russell 2006; Kim et al. 2006a) which helped the classification of protein interaction centers in terms of "party" or "date" hubs (Han et al. 2004). However, interrogation of interaction sources showed that the picture for many promiscuous proteins (in terms of interactions) is more complicated, with many having the ability to interact with multiple partners and multiple interfaces (e.g. Figure 2.2). This early work has since led to a number of databases that allow users to query interactions of known 3D structure, including 3DID (Stein

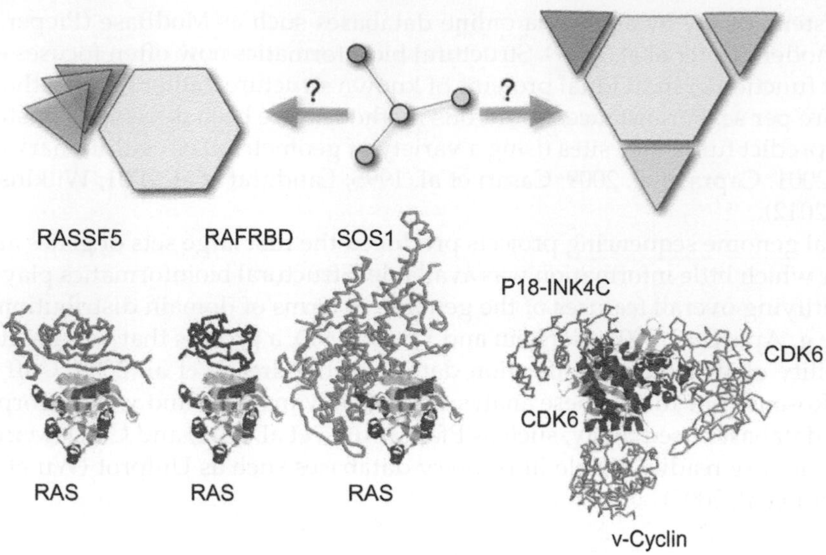

FIGURE 2.1 Structural interfaces can be used to assess whether interactions between proteins can occur simultaneously. The top of the figure shows a schematic of a protein (hexagon) that can either bind multiple proteins at one interface or simultaneously via different interfaces and that this is not obvious when looking at interaction networks alone. The bottom left of the figure shows three structures of Ras or Ras-like proteins in complex with three structurally different proteins that all bind on the same interface; the bottom right shows how the CDK6 structure can accommodate interactions with three proteins simultaneously.

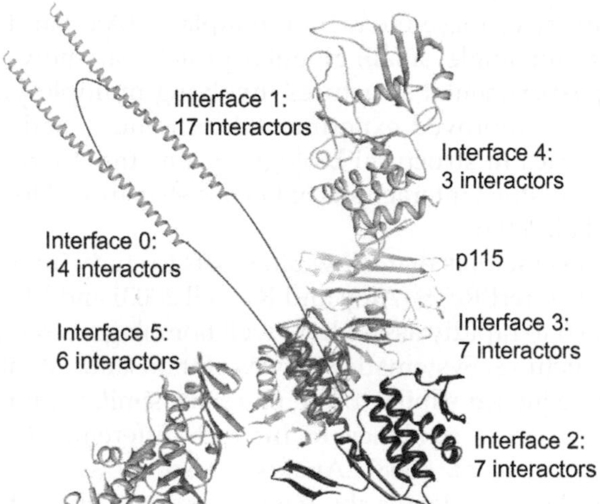

FIGURE 2.2 An example of a highly promiscuous protein (p117) uncovered during a screen of interactions within Mycoplasma pneumoniae (Kühner et al. 2009) and how it can apparently interact with multiple partners on multiple interfaces as predicted by interface modeling techniques. Protein p117 is colored in gray with the interaction partners in other colors. The number of interactors given for each interface is taken from the TAP dataset generated in the same screen.

et al. 2011), SCOPPI (Winter et al. 2006) and Interactome3D (Mosca et al. 2013). There have also been a number of applications of these tools to whole genomes to understand globally the structural repertoire of interactions and complexes present in an organism (Aloy et al. 2004; Kühner et al. 2009; Zhang et al. 2012) which has led to numerous insights into individual complexes and the nature of protein-protein interactions in general.

4 OTHER INTERACTION TYPES

Protein interactions come in many different flavors. Most of the above approaches work best when pairs of globular (i.e. folded) proteins or domains interact with one another. It has long been known that many interactions in biology do not occur in this way, but instead involve one globular protein or domain interacting with short peptide segments from other proteins. These peptide segments often show a particular pattern or motif that captures the features most responsible for binding to the globular partner. There are now several resources that capture these motifs systematically and allow users to search for motifs in query proteins (e.g. Dinkel et al. 2012). The fact that these motifs are more difficult to detect than globular segments using conventional sequence analysis tools (owing mostly to their short length) has led to various methods to identify new motif candidates (Davey et al. 2010; Neduva and Russell 2006) and most recently these approaches have been extended to methods to predict protein-peptide interactions using known 3D structures if available (Petsalaki et al. 2009).

All of this work is complementary to earlier developments on protein-protein or protein-small-molecule docking. Whereas previous docking efforts were focused on individual pairs of proteins of interest, there are now a growing number of studies whereby hundreds or thousands of pairs of proteins are docked together in an attempt either to find a handful of likely biologically meaningful docked structures (Mosca et al. 2009) or to use docking as a means to predict protein-protein interactions (Wass et al. 2011). Other efforts have attempted to use docking to combine pairwise docking methods (i.e. that attempt to dock two proteins or domains together) model higher order complexes (Inbar et al. 2005; Lasker et al. 2009) that are known from protein complex discovery experiments (Gavin et al. 2006; Guruharsha et al. 2011).

Protein-small-molecule docking is now applied in a systems-wide fashion. Specifically, virtual screening—whereby thousands of molecules can be docked simultaneously to one or often multiple proteins—is now commonplace and indeed a standard complementary approach to virtual screening (Lavecchia and Di Giovanni 2013).

5 SYSTEMS BIOLOGY APPLICATIONS

Exciting applications of structural bioinformatics techniques to systems modelling are already emerging. Structures, for example, provide a means to provide critical missing parameters for metabolic modeling processes (Gabdoulline et al. 2007; Stein et al. 2007). On a large scale, structures (experimental or modeled) can be used to identify missing substrates and products for metabolic reconstruction, which enables more accurate simulation and interpretation (Chang et al. 2013; Yus et al. 2009; Zhang et al. 2009). It is likely that these approaches will be applicable to more complex processes such as signaling or DNA repair in the future, but currently too little structural information is available and there are additional challenges to be overcome, such as the ability to reliable estimate thermodynamic or kinetic parameters for protein-protein interactions. There are various hints that this will be possible, coming from several studies that attempt to predict interaction specificity across diverse sets of proteins such as (Kiel et al. 2008).

6 NEW DATASETS-SPECIFIC PROTEIN SITES

With the advent of next generation sequencing thousands of new individual genomes of a species become available and these data are increasing at an explosive rate (Hanahan and Weinberg 2011; Xuan et al. 2012). While the previous goal was to understand the function of specific genomes or sets of proteins (i.e. a set of dysregulated genes or proteins), now one typically is presented with both a set of genes/proteins and multiple modifications within them. Therefore, these data can profit from computational predictions about the mechanistic consequences of alterations. Most tools for assessing DNA variations consider both protein sequence and structural information to some degree. For instance, tools like PolyPhen and MutationAssessor (Reva et al. 2011; Sunyaev et al. 2000) consider known or modeled structures to assess whether a mutation or variant lies in the interior or at the surface of a protein which helps to suggest how deleterious the change is likely to be, and the latter considers additional contacts to small molecules or other proteins. General principles are also emerging, for example analysis of SNPs that lie within known or predicted 3D structures shows that they tend to be on protein surfaces and to lie at protein interaction interfaces (David et al. 2012).

Other new datasets are also in need of the kind of mechanistic interpretation that struc tures can provide. Perhaps most significant among these are proteomics datasets related to the identification of post-translational modifications (PTMs) (Choudhary and Mann 2010; Pflieger et al. 2008). Here too the datasets consist of individual positions within hundreds or thousands of proteins that are often related to phenotypic differences or disease. Structural analyses of proteomic PTM datasets have found that these modifications too are enriched and protein-protein interfaces (van Noort et al. 2012) and that they show certain preferences according to type and that they tend to co-occur within interacting proteins (Minguez et al. 2012). 3D structures have also been suggested as a means to filter meaningful modification sites from possibly artifacts: it has been argued that sites known or predicted to be highly buried in a protein structure are less likely accessible to kinases and phosphatases and such sites likely need to be considered carefully in terms of their accuracy (Vandermarliere and Martens 2013).

7 CURRENT AND FUTURE NEEDS

The unifying theme to both of these types of datasets is the need to first understand as much as possible about the mechanistic consequences of mutating or modifying a particular residue in a particular protein, and then, if possible, to identify from hundreds or thousands of data-points those that are most likely to have biological consequences. Thus, beyond the analysis of individual sites within large datasets, there is an increasing need to understand an entire set of genes, proteins, or their modifications in a kind of mechanistic context.

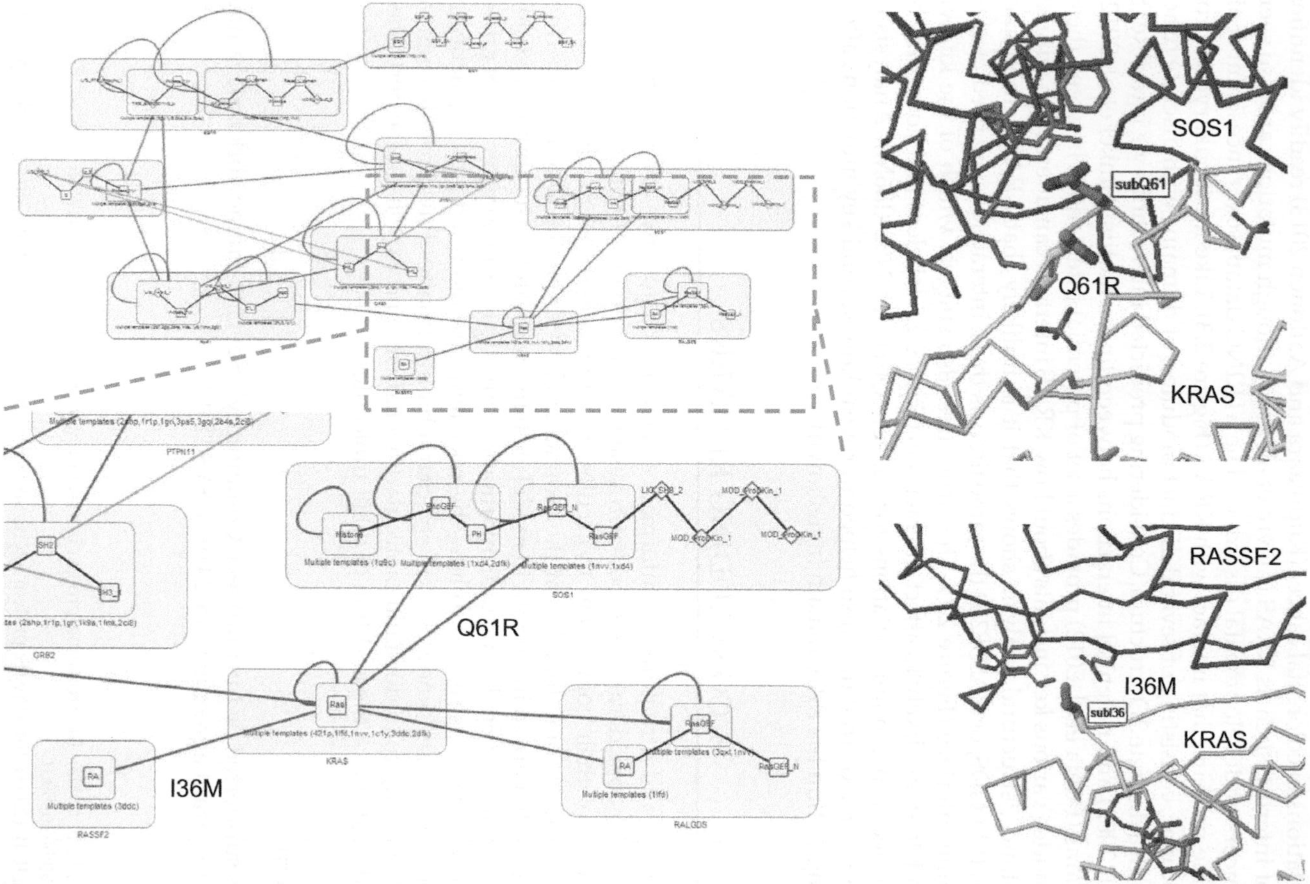

FIGURE 2.3 View of KRAS mutations in terms of known or predicted interactions between functional elements. The top of the figure shows an interaction network of KRAS and a selection of interaction partners. The inset zooms in on interactions with KRAS and various Ras-binding domain proteins. Each protein is shown a series of domains (squares) and linear motifs (diamonds) connected N- to C-terminally. Boxes around regions of the protein denote regions of protein 3D structures that are either in contact with part of another protein in the network (darker or red lines) or with themselves (circular lines connecting individual proteins). Known interactions between linear motifs and domains are also shown as yellow/lighter lines. The location of two KRAS mutations at interaction interfaces are shown to the right of the figure (For interpretation of the references to color in this figure legend, the reader is referred to the web version of this book.).

The combination of existing individual tools into a more systems-ready view of structural or mechanistic information appears to be a desirable development goal. For instance, considering data on mutations in colorectal cancer (Kilpivaara and Aaltonen 2013) readily identifies sets of proteins of interest, such as KRAS (Lièvre et al. 2006), though mutations are also seen in many other cancers or developmental disorders. The STRING database (Franceschini et al. 2013) provides nine proteins that interact with KRAS (Figure 2.3). Like most eukaryotic proteins they are modular, consisting of several distinct modules, or domains with discrete functions and often with a discrete 3D structure. Considering predicted interactions via InterPReTS (Aloy and Russell 2002) and potential interactions between linear motifs (Dinkel et al. 2012) and protein domains (Punta et al. 2012) provides a set of potential interactions between these domains that provides various key insights about how KRAS interacts can interaction with its partners. For instance, structural analysis shows that it is unlikely that KRAS can interact with SOS1, RAF1, RALGDS, or RASSF2 at the same time as these interactions are predicted to occur that the same interface (Figure 2.1). The structures also suggest which of the known mutations within KRAS are likely to affect interactions (Figure 2.3 labeled) and how some of these interactions seem to contain mutations for cancer (Q61R) or NS2 (I36M). Analysis of individual KRAS modeled structures also helped to reveal how several key mutations affect nucleotide binding within the RAS domain (not shown).

8 CONCLUDING REMARKS

Structural biology and structural bioinformatics have much to offer for systems-level studies. There is still a considerable gap between systems, assemblies or complexes that are understood in terms of their component molecules, but that lack most or all information about how the molecules come together at the atomic level or about the kinetic or thermodynamic parameters that are so important to model systems accurately. The ability to exploit and interpret known or predicted structural information quickly for these systems is of growing importance as the datasets related to how these systems are modified either genetically or via PTMs grows. Tools and know how in structural bioinformatics thus provides a great boost to anybody wishing to understand molecular mechanism and how it can be perturbed by variation, modification, or the addition of other molecules.

Acknowledgments

This work was supported by the European Community's Seventh Framework Programme FP7/2009 under the grant agreement no: 241955, SYSCILIA.

References

Aloy, P., and Russell, R. B. (2002). Interrogating protein interaction networks through structural biology. *Proc. Nat. Acad. Sci. U.S.A.* **99**:5896–5901.

Aloy, P., and Russell, R. B. (2003). InterPreTS: protein interaction prediction through tertiary structure. *Bioinformatics* **19**:161–162.

Aloy, P., and Russell, R. B. (2004). Ten thousand interactions for the molecular biologist. *Nat. Biotechnol.* **22**:1317–1321.

Aloy, P., and Russell, R. B. (2006). Structural systems biology: modelling protein interactions. *Nat. Rev. Mol. Cell Biol.* **7**:188–197.

Aloy, P., Querol, E., Aviles, F. X., and Sternberg, M. J. (2001). Automated structure-based prediction of functional sites in proteins: applications to assessing the validity of inheriting protein function from homology in genome annotation and to protein docking. *J. Mol. Biol.* **311**:395–408.

Aloy, P., Bottcher, B., Ceulemans, H., Leutwein, C., Mellwig, C., Fischer, S., Gavin, A. C., Bork, P., Superti-Furga, G., Serrano, L., et al. (2004). Structure-based assembly of protein complexes in yeast. *Science* **303**:2026–2029.

Andreeva, A., Howorth, D., Chandonia, J.-M., Brenner, S. E., Hubbard, T. J. P., Chothia, C., and Murzin, A. G. (2008). Data growth and its impact on the SCOP database: new developments. *Nucleic Acids Res.* **36**:D419–D425.

Apic, G., Gough, J., and Teichmann, S. A. (2001). Domain combinations in archaeal, eubacterial and eukaryotic proteomes. *J. Mol. Biol.* **310**:311–325.

Blundell, T. L., Sibanda, B. L., Sternberg, M. J., and Thornton, J. M. (1987). Knowledge-based prediction of protein structures and the design of novel molecules. *Nature* **326**:347–352.

Capra, J. A., Laskowski, R. A., Thornton, J. M., Singh, M., and Funkhouser, T. A. (2009). Predicting protein ligand binding sites by combining evolutionary sequence conservation and 3D structure. *PLoS Comput. Biol.* **5**:e1000585.

Casari, G., Sander, C., and Valencia, A. (1995). A method to predict functional residues in proteins. *Nat. Struct. Biol.* **2**:171–178.

Chang, R. L., Andrews, K., Kim, D., Li, Z., Godzik, A., and Palsson, B. O. (2013). Structural systems biology evaluation of metabolic thermotolerance in *Escherichia coli*. *Science* **340**:1220–1223.

Choudhary, C., and Mann, M. (2010). Decoding signalling networks by mass spectrometry-based proteomics. *Nat. Rev. Mol. Cell Biol.* **11**:427–439.

Croft, D., O'Kelly, G., Wu, G., Haw, R., Gillespie, M., Matthews, L., Caudy, M., Garapati, P., Gopinath, G., Jassal, B., et al. (2011). Reactome: a database of reactions, pathways and biological processes. *Nucleic Acids Res.* **39**:D691–D697.

Cuff, A., Redfern, O. C., Greene, L., Sillitoe, I., Lewis, T., Dibley, M., Reid, A., Pearl, F., Dallman, T., Todd, A., et al. (2009). The CATH hierarchy revisited-structural divergence in domain superfamilies and the continuity of fold space. *Structure* **17**:1051–1062 (London, England: 1993).

Davey, N. E., Haslam, N. J., Shields, D. C., and Edwards, R. J. (2010). SLiMFinder: a web server to find novel, significantly over-represented, short protein motifs. *Nucleic Acids Res.* **38**:W534–W539.

David, A., Razali, R., Wass, M. N., and Sternberg, M. J. E. (2012). Protein-protein interaction sites are hot spots for disease-associated nonsynonymous SNPs. *Hum. Mutat.* **33**:359–363.

Dinkel, H., Michael, S., Weatheritt, R. J., Davey, N. E., Van Roey, K., Altenberg, B., Toedt, G., Uyar, B., Seiler, M., Budd, A., et al. (2012). ELM–the database of eukaryotic linear motifs. *Nucleic Acids Res.* **40**:D242–D251.

Franceschini, A., Szklarczyk, D., Frankild, S., Kuhn, M., Simonovic, M., Roth, A., Lin, J., Minguez, P., Bork, P., von Mering, C., et al. (2013). STRING v9.1: protein-protein interaction networks, with increased coverage and integration. *Nucleic Acids Res.* **41**:D808–D815.

Gabdoulline, R. R., Stein, M., and Wade, R. C. (2007). qPIPSA: relating enzymatic kinetic parameters and interaction fields. *BMC Bioinformatics* **8**:373.

Gavin, A.-C., Aloy, P., Grandi, P., Krause, R., Boesche, M., Marzioch, M., Rau, C., Jensen, L. J., Bastuck, S., Dümpelfeld, B., et al. (2006). Proteome survey reveals modularity of the yeast cell machinery. *Nature* **440**:631–636.

Gene Ontology Consortium (2006). The Gene Ontology (GO) project in 2006. *Nucleic Acids Res.* **34**:D322–D326.

Gerstein, M., and Levitt, M. (1997). A structural census of the current population of protein sequences. *Proc. Nat. Acad. Sci. U.S.A.* **94**:11911–11916.

Guruharsha, K. G., Rual, J.-F., Zhai, B., Mintseris, J., Vaidya, P., Vaidya, N., Beekman, C., Wong, C., Rhee, D. Y., Cenaj, O., et al. (2011). A protein complex network of *Drosophila melanogaster*. *Cell* **147**:690–703.

Han, J.-D.J., Bertin, N., Hao, T., Goldberg, D. S., Berriz, G. F., Zhang, L. V., Dupuy, D., Walhout, A. J. M., Cusick, M. E., Roth, F. P., et al. (2004). Evidence for dynamically organized modularity in the yeast protein-protein interaction network. *Nature* **430**:88–93.

Hanahan, D., and Weinberg, R. A. (2011). Hallmarks of cancer: the next generation. *Cell* **144**:646–674.

Holm, L., and Rosenström, P. (2010). Dali server: conservation mapping in 3D. *Nucleic Acids Res.* **38**:W545–W549.

Inbar, Y., Benyamini, H., Nussinov, R., and Wolfson, H. J. (2005). Prediction of multimolecular assemblies by multiple docking. *J. Mol. Biol.* **349**:435–447.

Kiefer, F., Arnold, K., Künzli, M., Bordoli, L., and Schwede, T. (2009). The SWISS-MODEL repository and associated resources. *Nucleic Acids Res.* **37**:D387–D392.

Kiel, C., Beltrao, P., and Serrano, L. (2008). Analyzing protein interaction networks using structural information. *Annu. Rev. Biochem.* **77**:415–441.

Kilpivaara, O., and Aaltonen, L. A. (2013). Diagnostic cancer genome sequencing and the contribution of germline variants. *Science* **339**:1559–1562. (New York, N.Y.)

Kim, P. M., Lu, L. J., Xia, Y., and Gerstein, M. B. (2006a). Relating three-dimensional structures to protein networks provides evolutionary insights. *Science* **314**:1938–1941. (New York, N.Y.)

Kim, W. K., Henschel, A., Winter, C., and Schroeder, M. (2006b). The many faces of protein-protein interactions: A compendium of interface geometry. *PLoS Comput. Biol.* **2**:e124.

Kotera, M., Hirakawa, M., Tokimatsu, T., Goto, S., and Kanehisa, M. (2012). The KEGG databases and tools facilitating omics analysis: latest developments involving human diseases and pharmaceuticals. *Methods Mol. Biol.* **802**:19–39. (Clifton, N.J.)

Kühner, S., van Noort, V., Betts, M. J., Leo-Macias, A., Batisse, C., Rode, M., Yamada, T., Maier, T., Bader, S., Beltran-Alvarez, P., et al. (2009). Proteome organization in a genome-reduced bacterium. *Science* **326**:1235–1240. (New York, N.Y.)

Landgraf, R., Xenarios, I., and Eisenberg, D. (2001). Three-dimensional cluster analysis identifies interfaces and functional residue clusters in proteins. *J. Mol. Biol.* **307**:1487–1502.

Lasker, K., Topf, M., Sali, A., and Wolfson, H. J. (2009). Inferential optimization for simultaneous fitting of multiple components into a CryoEM map of their assembly. *J. Mol. Biol.* **388**:180–194.

Lavecchia, A., and Di Giovanni, C. (2013). Virtual screening strategies in drug discovery: a critical review. *Curr. Med. Chem.* **20**:2839–2860.

Lièvre, A., Bachet, J.-B., Le Corre, D., Boige, V., Landi, B., Emile, J.-F., Côté, J.-F., Tomasic, G., Penna, C., Ducreux, M., et al. (2006). KRAS mutation status is predictive of response to cetuximab therapy in colorectal cancer. *Cancer Res.* **66**:3992–3995.

Lu, L., Lu, H., and Skolnick, J. (2002). MULTIPROSPECTOR: an algorithm for the prediction of protein-protein interactions by multimeric threading. *Proteins* **49**:350–364.

Marchler-Bauer, A., Zheng, C., Chitsaz, F., Derbyshire, M. K., Geer, L. Y., Geer, R. C., Gonzales, N. R., Gwadz, M., Hurwitz, D. I., Lanczycki, C. J., et al. (2013). CDD: conserved domains and protein three-dimensional structure. *Nucleic Acids Res.* **41**:D348–D352.

Minguez, P., Parca, L., Diella, F., Mende, D. R., Kumar, R., Helmer-Citterich, M., Gavin, A.-C., van Noort, V., and Bork, P. (2012). Deciphering a global network of functionally associated post-translational modifications. *Mol. Syst. Biol.* **8**:599.

Mosca, R., Pons, C., Fernández-Recio, J., and Aloy, P. (2009). Pushing structural information into the yeast interactome by high-throughput protein docking experiments. *PLoS Comput. Biol.* **5**:e1000490.

Mosca, R., Céol, A., and Aloy, P. (2013). Interactome3D: adding structural details to protein networks. *Nat. Methods* **10**:47–53.

Moult, J., Fidelis, K., Kryshtafovych, A., and Tramontano, A. (2011). Critical assessment of methods of protein structure prediction (CASP)–round IX. *Proteins* **79**(Suppl 1):1–5.

Neduva, V., and Russell, R. B. (2006). DILIMOT: discovery of linear motifs in proteins. *Nucleic Acids Res.* **34**:W350–W355.

Van Noort, V., Seebacher, J., Bader, S., Mohammed, S., Vonkova, I., Betts, M. J., Kühner, S., Kumar, R., Maier, T., O'Flaherty, M., et al. (2012). Cross-talk between phosphorylation and lysine acetylation in a genome-reduced bacterium. *Mol. Syst. Biol.* **8**:571.

Petsalaki, E., Stark, A., García-Urdiales, E., and Russell, R. B. (2009). Accurate prediction of peptide binding sites on protein surfaces. *PLoS Comput. Biol.* **5**:e1000335.

Pflieger, D., Jünger, M. A., Müller, M., Rinner, O., Lee, H., Gehrig, P. M., Gstaiger, M., and Aebersold, R. (2008). Quantitative proteomic analysis of protein complexes: concurrent identification of interactors and their state of phosphorylation. *Mol. Cell. Proteomics* **7**:326–346.

Pieper, U., Webb, B. M., Barkan, D. T., Schneidman-Duhovny, D., Schlessinger, A., Braberg, H., Yang, Z., Meng, E. C., Pettersen, E. F., Huang, C. C., et al. (2011). ModBase, a database of annotated comparative protein structure models, and associated resources. *Nucleic Acids Res.* **39**:D465–D474.

Pruitt, K. D., Tatusova, T., and Maglott, D. R. (2005). NCBI Reference Sequence (RefSeq): a curated non-redundant sequence database of genomes, transcripts and proteins. *Nucleic Acids Res.* **33**:D501–D504.

Punta, M., Coggill, P. C., Eberhardt, R. Y., Mistry, J., Tate, J., Boursnell, C., Pang, N., Forslund, K., Ceric, G., Clements, J., et al. (2012). The Pfam protein families database. *Nucleic Acids Res.* **40**:D290–D301.

Reva, B., Antipin, Y., and Sander, C. (2011). Predicting the functional impact of protein mutations: application to cancer genomics. *Nucleic Acids Res.* **39**:e118.

Stein, A., Céol, A., and Aloy, P. (2011). 3did: identification and classification of domain-based interactions of known three-dimensional structure. *Nucleic Acids Res.* **39**:D718–D723.

Stein, M., Gabdoulline, R. R., and Wade, R. C. (2007). Bridging from molecular simulation to biochemical networks. *Curr. Opin. Struct. Biol.* **17**:166–172.

Sunyaev, S., Ramensky, V., and Bork, P. (2000). Towards a structural basis of human non-synonymous single nucleotide polymorphisms. *Trends Genet.* **16**:198–200.

Tuncbag, N., Gursoy, A., Guney, E., Nussinov, R., and Keskin, O. (2008). Architectures and functional coverage of protein-protein interfaces. *J. Mol. Biol.* **381**:785–802.

Vandermarliere, E., and Martens, L. (2013). Protein structure as a means to triage proposed PTM sites. *Proteomics* **13**:1028–1035.

Wass, M. N., Fuentes, G., Pons, C., Pazos, F., and Valencia, A. (2011). Towards the prediction of protein interaction partners using physical docking. *Mol. Syst. Biol.* **7**:469.

Wilkins, A. D., Bachman, B. J., Erdin, S., and Lichtarge, O. (2012). The use of evolutionary patterns in protein annotation. *Curr. Opin. Struct. Biol.* **22**:316–325.

Winter, C., Henschel, A., Kim, W. K., and Schroeder, M. (2006). SCOPPI: a structural classification of protein-protein interfaces. *Nucleic Acids Res.* **34**:D310–D314.

Wu, C. H., Apweiler, R., Bairoch, A., Natale, D. A., Barker, W. C., Boeckmann, B., Ferro, S., Gasteiger, E., Huang, H., Lopez, R., et al. (2006). The Universal Protein Resource (UniProt): an expanding universe of protein information. *Nucleic Acids Res.* **34**:D187–D191.

Xuan, J., Yu, Y., Qing, T., Guo, L., and Shi, L. (2012). Next-generation sequencing in the clinic: Promises and challenges. *Cancer Lett.*

Yang, H., Qureshi, R., and Sacan, A. (2012). Protein surface representation and analysis by dimension reduction. *Proteome Sci.* **10**(Suppl 1):S1.

Yus, E., Maier, T., Michalodimitrakis, K., van Noort, V., Yamada, T., Chen, W.-H., Wodke, J. A. H., Güell, M., Martínez, S., Bourgeois, R., et al. (2009). Impact of genome reduction on bacterial metabolism and its regulation. *Science* **326**:1263–1268. (New York, N.Y.)

Zhang, Q. C., Petrey, D., Deng, L., Qiang, L., Shi, Y., Thu, C. A., Bisikirska, B., Lefebvre, C., Accili, D., Hunter, T., et al. (2012). Structure-based prediction of protein-protein interactions on a genome-wide scale. *Nature* **490**:556–560.

Zhang, Y., Thiele, I., Weekes, D., Li, Z., Jaroszewski, L., Ginalski, K., Deacon, A. M., Wooley, J., Lesley, S. A., Wilson, I. A., et al. (2009). Three-dimensional structural view of the central metabolic network of *Thermotoga maritima*. *Science* **325**:1544–1549.

CHAPTER

3

Understanding Principles of the Dynamic Biochemical Networks of Life Through Systems Biology

Hans V. Westerhoff[a,b,c], *Fei He*[c,d], *Ettore Murabito*[c], *Frédéric Crémazy*[a], *Matteo Barberis*[a]

[a]Department of Synthetic Systems Biology and Nuclear Organization, Swammerdam Institute for Life Sciences, University of Amsterdam, Amsterdam, The Netherlands,
[b]Department of Molecular Cell Physiology, Faculty of Earth and Life Sciences, VU University Amsterdam, Amsterdam, The Netherlands,
[c]Manchester Centre for Integrative Systems Biology (MCISB), Manchester, UK
[d]Department of Automatic Control and systems Engineering, The University of Sheffield, Sheffield, UK

CONTENTS

Computational Systems Biology, Second Edition
http://dx.doi.org/10.1016/B978-0-12-405926-9.00003-4

Abstract

Systems Biology brings the potential to discover fundamental principles of Life that cannot be discovered by considering individual molecules. This chapter discusses a number of early, more recent, and upcoming discoveries of such network principles. These range from the balancing of fluxes through metabolic networks, the potential of those networks for truly individualized medicine, the time dependent control of fluxes and concentrations in metabolism and signal transduction, the ways in which organisms appear to regulate metabolic processes vis-à-vis limitations therein, tradeoffs in robustness and fragility, and a relation between robustness and time dependences in the cell cycle. The robustness considerations will lead to the issue whether and how evolution has been able to put in place design principles of control engineering such as infinite robustness and perfect adaptation in the hierarchical biochemical networks of cell biology.

1 PRINCIPLES BASED ON TOPOLOGY OF THE GENOME-WIDE METABOLIC NETWORK: LIMITED NUMBERS OF POSSIBLE FLUX PATTERNS

The genome-wide reconstructions of enzyme-mediated metabolic activities in various organisms have led to long lists of correspondences between genes, proteins, enzyme activities, and to implied changes in the concentrations of metabolites (Herrgård et al. 2008; Thiele et al. 2013). If any reaction activity is represented by a reaction rate v, then the list of activities may be written as a long column (or vector) of v's. For a reaction i, one may then write the change it effects in the number of Moles of any metabolite X_j by a stoichiometric number N_{ji} that is defined by the reaction chemistry:

$$\frac{dX_j}{dt} = N_{ji}\cdot v_i - \mu\cdot X_j \tag{3.1}$$

Here the final term corresponds to the dilution due to growth at the specific growth rate μ. Doing this for all reactions and generalizing to vectors and matrix this leads to:

$$\frac{dX}{dt} = N\cdot v - \mu\cdot X \tag{3.2}$$

Here v is a column of all the rates of all the reactions in the organism (i.e. one rate for every gene product at the level of enzyme or transporter) per unit intracellular volume. X is a column of all the molecule numbers (in Moles) of the metabolites in and around the organism, and N the matrix of stoichiometric coefficients of that organism. N represents all single-step catalytic capabilities of the organism. In the consensus reconstruction of the human (Thiele et al. 2013), v is a list of 7440 reactions, and X of a list 5063 metabolites, 642 of which are extracellular. N is a 5063 by 7440 matrix of numbers like 1, 2, −1, with many zero's.

N is a genome-wide culmination of molecular biochemistry. For any molecule in an organism, say molecule B, it shows from which molecules it can be made in a single step that is catalyzed by a protein encoded by the genome of the organism. It also shows into which other molecules the molecule can be converted in a single step. Although of great *biochemical* interest, this does not correspond to the solution of the *biological* question how an organism builds itself from components it takes from the environment, i.e. of how an organism recreates life from dead materials. For many components an organism cannot be built in a single step from the extracellular components.

To address this issue, systems biology is needed, i.e. some way of reflecting how the individual reactions encoded by the genome integrate their actions. Because it is genome wide, i.e. contains (in principle) all reactions encoded by the genome, matrix N has the potential to do this. N may tell us that molecule A cannot be converted in a single step to molecule B, but may be converted into a molecule C, say by reaction number 5 (i.e. $N_{A5} = -1$ and $N_{C5} = +1$, while $N_{B5} = 0$), and that molecule C can be converted to molecule B by a reaction 9 (i.e. $N_{A9} = 0$, $N_{B9} = 1$, and $N_{C9} = -1$), so that indirectly by collaboration of enzymes 5 and 9, molecule A can be converted to molecule B: networking of enzyme molecules is needed, with metabolite C as communicator (Figure 3.1). If the enzymes work intracellularly and one would start with zero B and C but with a certain amount of A, one would see that the concentration of C would build up first and that only then the concentration of B should begin to increase. If A is kept constant by external supplies, C will increase with time until it becomes constant and the rates of reactions 5 and 9 have become the same. This is called the intracellular steady state. Because the extracellular compartment is much larger, an intracellular steady state will be

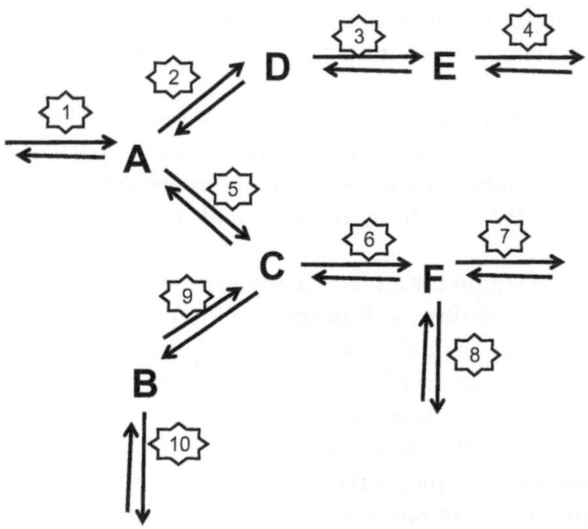

FIGURE 3.1 Example of a network described by matrix N, with molecule A converted to molecule B via equilibrium reactions.

achieved while the extracellular concentrations are still increasing or decreasing, very slowly with time.

If one divides the metabolites into m_i intracellular ones (X_i) and m_e extracellular ones (X_e), reorders the rows of matrix N such that its bottom rows make up the submatrix N_{ex} containing extracellular metabolites, one finds for the upper submatrix of N, N_{in}:

$$0 = \left(\frac{dX_i}{dt}\right)_{ss} = N_{in} \cdot v - \mu \cdot X_i \tag{3.3}$$

while:

$$\left(\frac{dX_e}{dt}\right)_{ss} = N_{ex} \cdot v \tag{3.4}$$

Most metabolites are not endpoints of a metabolic pathway, but intermediates with life times much shorter than the cell cycle time. We shall further focus on these cases and thereby be able to neglect the term containing the dilution due to growth. In cases where this does not apply, one may add the growth rate to the vector v and extend N accordingly.

At this intracellular steady state, matrix N now puts a strong constraint on all the rates because the latter have to satisfy Equation. 3.3. Only the rate vectors that are in the Kernel of N_{in}, the subspace of all the possible rate vectors, are admissible. This limitation is enormous, i.e. from the 7444 dimensional space suggested by the length of the rate vector v, the reduction is to a 7444-4421 = 3013 dimensional subspace. Clearly, the intracellular location of most enzymes and the consequent occurrence of steady state, it forces the enzymes to collaborate, to balance their fluxes, and to come to a concerted behavior that produces a steady state.

Should a chemical reaction network be created at random, then it would often not relax to a steady state. Here we use a principle of Biology, i.e. that the living organisms we study are viable and hence not subject to metabolic explosions (Teusink et al. 1998), i.e. they exhibit stationary states, and the common stationary metabolic states is the steady state (Westerhoff & Van Dam 1987).

If life harbored a single linear pathway of 7442 enzymes and two transporters, then the number of intracellular metabolites would be 7443 and the space of possible reaction rates would have been reduced from dimension 7444 to dimension 1: it is the branching of pathways that is at the basis of the remaining dimensionality of the possible rate distributions at steady state.

In actual practice only a single (or a few) steady state is obtained with a single set of rates, although the steady-state conditions still permit an incredibly high number of steady states together filling the 3013 dimensional space. The genes are however expressed to a certain level, as defined by the environment plus the parameters of the intracellular networks, which begin to define the actual vector v, whereto the intracellular metabolite concentrations adjust so that the rates v change until the steady-state condition of Equation 3.3 is met, after which the system becomes constant in time, corresponding to steady state, which corresponds to a zero dimensional space. Evolution has selected the values of all the internal parameters such that a steady state can be obtained (see above) and possibly such that the actual rates are what is optimal for the organism if the extracellular conditions correspond to conditions that reigned during evolution.

If we measure the changes in time of the extracellular metabolites, and insert these into Equation 3.4, then this gives us an additional reduction of dimensionality by 642–2271. This is now not a boundary condition imposed by a fundamental principle, but an experimental observation that could help us to estimate the intracellular behavior of the network. However, we still cannot establish what the intracellular state is: the world of possible states is still 2271 dimensional for the human metabolic map.

One approach is to determine *intra*cellular fluxes experimentally by a procedure known as flux analysis, which often employs isotopically labeled growth. Here one may deduce from the growth rate and biomass composition a great many anabolic fluxes and use these to confine the possible fluxes (Sauer 2006). All these methodologies are empirical ways to establish what the actual flux distributions are.

There are additional ways of limiting the space of possible fluxes. One is that of requiring that no single reaction runs in the direction that is uphill in terms of thermodynamics (Westerhoff & Van Dam 1987). In principle the *concentrations* of intracellular metabolites are then needed, but assuming that these are within reasonable bounds (e.g. between 0.001 and 100 mM) certain directions of reaction can be excluded. Another way is to impose that no reaction rate can become higher than the V_{max} of the enzyme that catalyzes the reaction, where the V_{max} is determined in cell extracts (Mensonides et al. 2013; and see below). These two principles merely give bounds to values of reaction rates however; they do not reduce the dimensionality of the space of rates (we define reaction rates as net fluxes through processes not as unidirectional fluxes).

A more fundamental principle is often used by what is called Flux Balance Analysis (FBA), which assumes that efficiency is maximal in terms of ATP yield, and yet another one assumes maximal biomass synthesis. We shall here discuss the former. For two parallel pathways that hydrolyze different amounts of ATP, this removes the pathways that hydrolyze most ATP. This principle has the advantages that it does not require experimental measurement if it is plainly assumed to apply and that it does reduce the dimensionality of the space of reaction rate distribution appreciably. However, this principle of optimal efficiency has been shown not to apply completely in a number of cases. Organisms such as baker's yeast for instance do not grow at maximal efficiency when glucose is present in excess (Simeonidis et al. 2010). More in general organisms do not seem to be optimized for thermodynamic efficiency or yield (Westerhoff et al. 1983). On the other hand, the effect of reducing the world of solutions to Equation 3.3, may still be largely appropriate, and the approach may be useful as a first and limited approach in some cases (Reed and Palsson, 2004) and see below.

2 PRINCIPLES BASED ON TOPOLOGY OF THE GENOME-WIDE METABOLIC NETWORK: TOWARD PERSONALIZED MEDICINE

If one is interested in whether the organism (through its matrix *N*) is actually capable of synthesizing a particular intracellular metabolite, say metabolite number 2031, one substitutes 1 for the zero at row 2031 of the zero vector at the left-hand side of Equation 3.3 and attempts to find solutions for the rate vector v. Often multiple solutions will be found. One may then ask whether metabolite number 2031 can be synthesized from a certain type of nutrition. To address this issue one should analyze the molecular composition of the nutrition, then require the rates of the transport (across the plasma membrane) reactions in v that correspond to substances that are not present in the nutrition to be nonnegative (positive being defined as outward transport), and again try to find a solution for the rate vector v that is consistent with these conditions. If such a rate vector is found then the map is consistent with producing the intracellular metabolite.

Knowledge about the DNA sequence of an individual, enables one to understand where that individual may have inactive gene products on its metabolic map. Requiring in the above computations the corresponding reaction rates (elements of rate vector v) to be zero, one may again try to find a solution for the rate vector that delivers metabolite 2031. If this is impossible for the individual then it suffers from an inborn error of metabolism. Repeating this procedure for other nutrients, then enables one to examine whether the disease can be averted by using a special diet.

By equating dX_{in}/dt to the biomass composition in terms of all molecules in the living organism, and then solving the resulting equation for the rate vector v, one may ask whether the map is able to make its complete self, and thereby scout for all possible inborn errors of metabolism at the same time.

Because of the large size of the matrix N, finding all possible solutions is computationally challenging, but finding one solution often suffices and is possible with modern algorithms.

3 INDUSTRIALLY RELEVANT APPLICATIONS OF TOPOLOGY AND OBJECTIVE-BASED MODELING

If the goal of an FBA is to identify a pattern of fluxes fulfilling the steady-state condition imposed by Equation. 3.3 under the assumption that an objective function Z representing the biological process is optimal, the task is:

$$\begin{aligned} &\text{maximize} \quad Z = \mathbf{f}^{\mathrm{T}} \cdot \mathbf{v} \\ &\text{subject to} \quad \mathbf{N} \cdot \mathbf{v} = \mathbf{0}; \quad \mathbf{v}^{\mathrm{L}} \leq \mathbf{v} \leq \mathbf{v}^{\mathrm{U}} \end{aligned} \tag{3.5}$$

where $\mathbf{v}^{\mathrm{L}}$ and $\mathbf{v}^{\mathrm{U}}$ are the lower and upper bound of the fluxes (defining the range of values that the different rates can have), and $\mathbf{f}$ is a set of coefficients defining the objective function Z in terms of a linear combination of the rates $\mathbf{v}$. Depending on the specific information we want to retrieve through FBA, Z can also represent a non-biological criterion of optimality, as we shall see below.

A promising applications of FBA is in industrial protein production. Proteins require complex systems for their synthesis that only living cells are equipped with. The complexity of these "cell factories" is far beyond that of man-made production systems and we are far from understanding their functioning in a comprehensive way. As a consequence protein production tends to be quite unpredictable. The complexity of these factories which derives from the intricate interconnectivity of its different components has to be taken into account at some level if one wants to make protein production predictable and hence be able to play with the "control knobs" of these factories to adjust the production process to our needs. The application of FBA, and more in general the adoption of the Systems Biology perspective, may help to make this process more predictable and design strategies to improve protein harvest.

Through FBA, for example, it is possible to predict the optimal pattern of internal fluxes representing the metabolic functioning of the cells cultured under specific conditions. This enables us to attempt to predict and compare the flux patterns of a control culture and a culture expressing the recombinant protein. The superposition of these patterns would provide us with a set of reactions that are either (significantly) active in both scenarios or that turn on/off when switching from one situation to the other. This set of reactions would host on the one hand the main metabolic processes common to both situations and on the other hand the main metabolic changes that cells undergo when expressing the protein. This would give us some insights on how cells redirect their metabolic trafficking in order to fulfill the new task of producing the recombinant protein.

In the scenario illustrated above one would want the flux patterns predicted through FBA for the control and recombinant cultures to be as close as possible to the real functioning of the cells. To this end a good strategy consists of including in the computational representation of the system some experimental data, such as exchange fluxes and growth rate, retrieved in the two conditions. The objective function will be then defined as the negative mismatch between the predicted and the experimental value of the quantities that have been measured:

$$Z = -\sum_i |v_i - m_i| \tag{3.6}$$

where v_i and m_i are respectively the predicted and the experimental value of the measured quantity i.

From a genetic engineering perspective a relevant question would be whether it is possible to increase the yield of the recombinant protein for a specific growth medium by diverting the internal flux toward more favorable metabolic routes. In this case one would compare the flux pattern obtained for the recombinant culture when Z is defined as in Equation 3.6 and the flux pattern obtained by setting $Z = v_r$ where v_r is the rate of the pseudo-reaction introduced in the model to represent the recombinant protein production.

Another relevant question concerns the growing medium composition. FBA could also be used to identifying the limiting nutrients and suggest alternative optimal feed design to further increase the protein production.

4 APPLICATIONS OF TOPOLOGY AND OBJECTIVE-BASED MODELING TO CANCER RESEARCH AND DRUG DISCOVERY

Drugs are designed to affect one or more specific properties of the cells needing treatment. These properties usually represent what differentiates diseased cells from their normal counterparts, or a pathogenic organism from its host. The property one chooses to affect can vary depending on the specific clinical strategy pursued. Because neoplastic cells grow and replicate at a considerably faster rate than their normal counterparts, the rationale behind many of the possible choices in cancer treatment consists of halting the proliferative potential of the malignant tissue. Indeed, traditional clinical approaches such as chemotherapy and radiotherapy aim to kill cancer cells by disrupting their replication machinery. Similarly, in drug intervention at the metabolic level, the preliminary step consists of identifying a property which characterizes the altered phenotype and which is therefore sensible to target. In this respect, constraint-based modeling approaches, and particularly FBA, can provide us with a way to identify these properties.

If the system under study is known to optimize a certain biological requirement, then that requirement might be considered as the property one may want to target in order to disrupt the metabolic phenotype of the cell. However, the identification of the biological task that the objective function should represent is not always easy. For studies involving *E. coli* metabolism, the objective function Z is usually defined to represent the yield of biomass (Reed and Palsson 2004), assuming that bacteria aim to grow as fast as possible (although this assumption does not reflect a generally valid principle in microbiology (Schuster et al. 2008). By contrast, for human cells, things are not so straightforward.

Since cancer cells grow at a much higher rate than their normal counterparts, it would seem reasonable to adopt the same approach as for *E. coli* by choosing the maximization of biomass production rate as the optimization criterion. Although this intuitive choice may seem sensible, the resulting FBA solution highlights a flux pattern which does not match with the observed characteristic of cancer metabolism (Warburg and Dickens 1931). Because of the high demand of ATP in the production of biomass, the flux pattern corresponding to the maximal yield shows the glucose uptake flux entirely entering the TCA cycle, with no lactate production. To retrieve a flux pattern highlighting the cancer metabolic features (a constitutive activation of the branch leading to lactate production and, possibly, the reduction of the flux entering the TCA cycle), the FBA problem has then to be formulated differently. A possible way to do so consists of replacing the maximal yield of biomass with a different criterion of optimality. In a recent work, Simeonidis et al. showed how an appropriate reformulation of FBA can be used to reproduce the Crabtree effect, an experimentally observed behavior whereby *Saccharomyces. cerevisiae* produces ethanol aerobically in the presence of high external glucose concentrations rather than producing biomass through the TCA cycle (Simeonidis et al. 2010) The authors hypothesized that (one of) the "driving forces" behind yeast metabolism is resource preservation (see also León et al. 2008). By minimizing the number of active reactions (and hence the number of enzymes) needed to produce a required amount of biomass, the flux patterns obtained as solutions of the FBA problem showed the characteristic switch from respiration to fermentation that occurs when the concentration of glucose in the growing medium is increased above a certain threshold. Because of the commonalities in the metabolic features of fermenting yeast and cancerous cells (Diaz-Ruiz et al. 2009), a similar argument might be applied to reproduce the constitutive metabolic changes occurring in carcinogenesis. From an FBA perspective, higher concentration of glucose in the growth medium and higher rate of glucose uptake due to over-expression of glycolytic enzymes are both implemented by increasing the upper limit of the glucose uptake flux. In both cases, the requirement of resource preservation would force the system to switch from respiration to fermentation/lactate production as soon as the glycolytic flux becomes high enough to provide the cell with the amount of ATP needed for the required production of biomass.

A related issue that FBA could address is whether cancer cells are committed to optimize different biological functions concurrently. Indeed, the enhanced replication rate of neoplastic cells, combined with a predilection for fermentation (which is not the most efficient way to produce ATP) would seem to support a multifunctional optimization hypothesis, whereby different criteria of optimization have to be satisfied simultaneously. As initially hypothesized by Gatenby and Gawlinski (1996), the production and excretion of lactic acid constitutes a way for cancer cells to compete with their normal counterpart by creating a hostile environment for normal cells. However, the fact that sometimes the TCA cycle is nevertheless active (although to a smaller extent than its normal capacity) makes evident that competing through excretion of lactate is not the only task that cancer cells try to optimize. Using a specular argument, one could say that, despite the enhanced replication rate of cancer cells, the fact that the TCA cycle is somehow hampered shows that replicating most efficiently or at the highest possible rate is not the (only) objective that drives cancer cells, or, in other words, that there are multiple goals pushing the system toward a different metabolic flux pattern. The relevance of different possible optimization criteria in the functioning of the system and their relative weights could also help to elucidate why the phenotypic traits of cancer metabolism are present to different extents in different types of cancer and in different cells in the same tumor.

There are other points that an FBA approach might help to elucidate. Knowledge of the metabolic shift occurring in tumorigenesis predominantly involves central carbon metabolism. However, the shift may extend beyond central metabolism, and remarkable metabolic differences between normal and cancer cells may lie in pathways not yet studied within the context of cancer research. A further application of FBA could highlight particularly active metabolic pathways in cancer on a genome-scale level, and identify the regions where the flux pattern differs most between cancer and normal cells. Shlomi et al. (2008) have recently used an FBA approach to describe the tissue specificity of human metabolism, where tissue-specific gene and protein expression data were integrated with a genome-scale reconstruction of the human metabolic network. Different integer values were assigned to different gene-expression states, so to distinguish among highly (1), lowly (−1), and moderately (0) expressed genes. The objective function of the FBA problem was then set to account for the differences between the activity of each reaction in the predicted pattern of fluxes and the integer representation of the corresponding experimental gene-expression level. By minimizing such an objective function, the authors were able to retrieve stoichiometrically and topologically consistent flux patterns on a genome-scale level with the maximum number of reactions whose activity was in accordance with their expression state. This study may establish a FBA-based computational approach for the genome-wide study of normal and cancer human metabolism in a tissue-specific manner.

Another interesting point FBA might address is the following. Given the selective pressure that biological systems undergo when functioning under mutual competition, it seems reasonable to assume that cancer cells fulfill their specific biological tasks in the most economical way. In other words, given the available external substrates and given a set of functionally important targets to accomplish, the cell would employ its resources most "effortlessly." From a metabolic perspective, this would translate into the employment of a minimal number of active reactions, or, more generally, a minimal employment of resources. In *E. coli*, for example, experimental results have shown that fitness increases while unused catabolic functions decrease, this reduction being beneficial and therefore favored by selection (Cooper and Lenski 2000). In the context of FBA, this "principle of minimal effort" has been used in different forms to identify the pattern of fluxes that best portraits the system functioning with respect to specific criteria of optimality (León et al. 2008; Holzhütter 2004). It should be noted however that many cancer cells appear to secrete more metabolites into their surrounding medium than what may be consistent with minimal use of their resources (Jain et al. 2012). Combinations of optimality criteria with observed flux patterns as constraints for the FBA solutions might be a strategy.

On the other hand, there exist different flux patterns that are equally optimal with respect to a certain criterion or set of criteria. Extension of FBA to find alternate optimal solutions (Lee et al. 2000) or alternate optimal patterns of fluxes (Murabito et al. 2009) have been developed. In particular, an algorithm able to find all the minimal and equally optimal flux patterns of a metabolic network with respect to a given functional task has been proposed (Murabito et al. 2009). The superposition of all minimal optimal flux patterns allows us to identify those pathways or sets of reactions that must be active in order to optimally fulfill a given function, and other sets of reactions that can be alternatively active. The application of such an approach in the context of cancer research might help to identify and predict the narrowest region of human metabolism necessary to observe the carcinogenic metabolic shift. From the perspective of developing a kinetic model of cancer metabolism, these results might also provide modelers with a concise set of reactions that can be used as a backbone for a mechanistic representation of the system under study, as well as an idea about which pathways and reactions can be reasonably neglected.

5 PRINCIPLES OF CONTROL

In biochemical networks, rates of chemical conversions or transport reactions are not just determined by the properties of the enzyme or transporter that catalyzes them, but also by properties of other components of the network. Something similar applies to the concentrations of metabolites in the network. It therefore makes sense to define the control of a rate v_i of any process in the network by the activity e_i of that same process or of any other process e_j in the network. The definition of the corresponding flux control coefficient reads as:

$$C_{e_j}^{v_i}(t) \stackrel{\text{def}}{=} \frac{\partial ln v_i}{\partial ln e_j} = \frac{\left(\frac{\partial ln v_i(t)}{\partial p_i}\right)_{\textit{in the system}}}{\left(\frac{\partial ln v_j(t=0)}{\partial p_j}\right)_{\textit{in a constant molecular environment}}} \tag{3.7}$$

This definition differs somewhat from the standard definition of the flux control coefficient (Burns et al. 1985), which is limited to the control of steady-state fluxes. Here we are more explicit about the fact that one may also define the flux control coefficient outside of steady state. This does require one to keep track of time, i.e. to be careful about defining the initial ($t = 0$) condition. The definition compares two effects that a given amount of agent p_j, that modulates the rate of process v_j specifically, may have on processes i and j (i may or may not equal j). The first is the effect agent p_j has on the rate v_i of process i when that process functions in the system. The second is the effect the same amount of the agent p_j would have on process j when the process j would be outside the system but in the same conditions, with those conditions frozen. For a network with n processes, Westerhoff (2008) has proven the general property or "law":

$$\sum_{j=1}^{n} C_{e_j}^{v_i}(t) = 1 + C_t^{v_i}(t) \tag{3.8}$$

The right-hand side is the flux control coefficient of time defined by:

$$C_t^{v_i}(t) \stackrel{\text{def}}{=} \left(\frac{\partial lnv_i}{\partial lnt}\right)_{in\ the\ system} \tag{3.9}$$

It quantifies the extent to which the rate of process i varies with time.

We first discuss the example of a signal-transduction cascade with all proteins in the inactive un-phosphorylated state, which is then confronted with a sudden activation of a receptor, the activity of which then decays slowly. The rate of phosphorylation of the target of this receptor (which we here assume to be a protein kinase) will jump from zero up to a rate that is almost constant initially, i.e. after that initial jump, the time-control coefficient of that rate will be virtually zero. As a consequence, the above law (Equation 3.8) predicts that all processes in the network together control the rate of phosphorylation of the target at a control coefficient of 1. However, since there is hardly any phosphorylated target in the beginning, none of the other processes can be active and only the first kinase (the active receptor) can control the rate of phosphorylation of its target. Consequently, that kinase will initially be in full control; a 10% activation of the kinase will produce a 10% higher degree of phosphorylation of the target at any given (short) time t after receptor activation.

Because it phosphorylates its target, the kinase will relatively quickly decrease in rate and this decrease will be quicker the more active the kinase is. Consequently, control by the kinase in the rate of phosphorylation of its target at a given moment in time will decrease fairly quickly to below 1 and the time control of the kinase reaction will become negative.

As even more of the target gets phosphorylated, its phosphatase becomes active and gains in control. Paradoxically perhaps, this control on the rate of phosphorylation of this first target is positive, as the phosphatase creates more substrate for the kinase reaction. As time proceeds, the control by the kinase will decrease further and that of the phosphatase will increase until the two add up to 1, as the time dependence control coefficient returns to zero, it steady-state value. In general both the kinase and the phosphatase control the rate of phosphorylation of their substrate.

For the concentration of any substance in the system, the time dependent control coefficients sum to zero plus the time-control coefficient:

$$\sum_{j=1}^{n} C_{e_j}^{X_k}(t) = C_t^{X_k}(t) \tag{3.10}$$

This includes the classical summation law that the sum of all control coefficients with respect to any steady-state concentration equals zero. This law is general in the absence of metabolite channeling (Kholodenko and Westerhoff 1993). The sum must also equal zero when the variation of the concentrations with time exhibits a maximum or minimum.

Hornberg et al. (2005) have used this property to prove that in the MAP kinase cascade all the phosphatases (or strictly speaking all the negatively controlling processes) together are as important for the amplitude of the ERK phosphorylation as are all the kinases together.

If instead one focuses on the time point where the ERK phosphorylation has decreased again to half its amplitude, then the time-control coefficient is negative, implying that the sum of the control by all the kinases and the control by all the phosphatases must be (equally) negative. Since the phosphatases exercise negative control and the kinases positive control, this implies that the phosphatases are more important for the concentration of Erk-PP at this time point than the kinases are. To the extent that the MAP kinase is important for transcription regulation, appreciating that transcription integrates the time dependence of Erk-PP, and accepting that the duration of Erk-PP signaling relative to its amplitude is important, Hornberg et al. (2005) concluded that the phosphatases are even more important for signal transduction than the kinases are. This conclusion was perhaps useful because much more attention had been paid to kinases that to phosphatases. Importantly also, the summation law states that all phosphatases *together* should exercise more control than all kinases together. The principle is not that the first phosphatase must exert more control than the first kinase and that these are the only two controlling enzymes. Indeed, in numerical simulations, control was distributed over all kinases and phosphatases. The biologically important conclusion is that oncogenes and tumor suppressor genes should be sought among all genes encoding kinases and all genes encoding phosphatases or regulating their expression levels, explaining why there are so many of these genes and inducing us to infer that cancer is a systems biology disease (Hornberg et al. 2006).

At the time point in which the ultimate signal (Erk-PP in the example of the MAP kinase cascade) has first increased from zero to half its amplitude, the control by time is positive, and the above summation law implies that the total control exercised by the kinases on the signal strength exceeds the total control by the phosphatases. Indeed, early on in signal transduction the kinases should be more important than the phosphatases for the concentration of the signal molecule.

Although the example is one of signal transduction, similar considerations apply to metabolic and gene-expression networks, and the above may serve to convey that, contrarily to what is often stated, control analysis and the fundamental principles that it brings, are not limited to steady state.

6 PRINCIPLES OF REGULATION

The magnitude of the flux control coefficient of a step or of the enzyme catalyzing that step, corresponds to a potential, i.e. to the effect on the flux that an activation of that step or enzyme *might* have. That magnitude does not indicate whether that step is ever activated either by the network itself, in self-regulation, or by an external influence, e.g. by an engineer (Westerhoff et al. 2009).

Regulation coefficients have been introduced to indicate how, when a process *is* actually regulated, the organism regulates it. The alternatives are regulation through metabolic interactions, through single transduction interactions leading to covalent modification of the enzyme, and through gene expression. The gene-expression regulation coefficient has been defined as the change in enzyme concentration divided by the change in flux through the enzyme, i.e. more precisely by:

$$\rho_g^i = \frac{dlne_i}{dlnv_i} \tag{3.11}$$

Here e_i is the concentration of the enzyme catalyzing the process v_i. The rate of an enzyme catalyzed reaction can often be written as the product of three factors, i.e. the enzyme concentration, the fraction ϕ_a of the enzyme that is in the covalent modification state that is active catalytically, and a factor υ_m comprising the rate's dependence on the concentrations of the substrates, the products, and the metabolic modifiers that are not binding covalently or stably. The metabolic and signal-transduction regulation coefficients are defined, respectively by:

$$\rho_m^i = \frac{dln\vartheta_{m,i}}{dlnv_i} \tag{3.12}$$

and

$$\rho_s^i = \frac{dln\varphi_{a,i}}{dlnv_i} \tag{3.13}$$

Regulation is also subject to a general principle or law: The sum of gene-expression, metabolic, and signal-transduction regulation of a metabolic rate is always the same and equal to 1 (Ter Kuile and Westerhoff 2001):

$$\rho_g^i + \rho_m^i + \rho_s^i \equiv 1 \tag{3.14}$$

7 REGULATION VERSUS CONTROL

As discussed above, regulation differs from control. Yet, it would seem that there might be connections between the two concepts. We shall limit the discussion to linear metabolic pathways. Such a pathway has a single steady-state flux, which is equal to the steady-state rates of all the reactions in the pathway. If the third step of the pathway were completely rate limiting and its expression level would be activated by 30% then the flux would also go up by 30% making its hierarchical regulation coefficient equal to 1. However, if its control on the flux were 0.2 only, then its activation by 30%, in the absence of hierarchical regulation of any of the other enzymes, would increase the flux by 6% only, so that its hierarchical regulation coefficients would equal 5. This suggests that there is some sort of reciprocity between regulation and control.

When hierarchical regulation involves more enzymes of the pathway, this reciprocity becomes pathway wide, hence again a systems property. For a linear pathway of n enzymes the reciprocity is given by the law:

$$\sum_{i=1}^{n} C_i^J \cdot \rho_h^i \equiv 1 \tag{3.15}$$

Here the hierarchical regulation coefficient ρ_h^i comprises both gene-expression and signal-transduction regulation:

$$\rho_h^i \stackrel{\text{def}}{=} \rho_g^i + \rho_s^i \tag{3.16}$$

The proof is as follows: Consider a regulation that results in a change in flux through the enzyme, $dlnv_i$. The increase in that flux may be because gene expression is increased resulting in more enzyme e_i, because the altered levels of metabolites (x) have altered the activity of the enzyme, or because signal transduction has led to activation of the enzyme ($dln\varphi_{a,i}$) by covalent modification:

$$dlnv_i = dlne_i + \frac{\partial ln\vartheta_{m,i}}{\partial lnx} \cdot dlnx + dln\varphi_{a,i} \tag{3.17}$$

With the above definition (Equation 3.11) the change in enzyme concentration relates to the change in flux through the enzyme by:

$$dlne_i = \rho_g^i \cdot dlnv_i \tag{3.18}$$

The effect of that change in activity of enzyme i on the steady-state flux through the pathway is given by:

$$(dlnJ)_{\text{as a consequence of the change in activity of } e_i} = C_{e_i}^J \cdot (dlne_i + dln\varphi_{a,i}) \tag{3.19}$$

Here the C refers to the metabolic flux control coefficient, not the hierarchical one; the metabolic pathway is allowed to relax, the gene-expression and the signal-transduction regulation are supposed to be fixed by the external world (Westerhoff 2008; Westerhoff et al. 2009). Taking into account all changes in all enzymes, the change in steady-state flux is:

$$dlnJ = \sum_{i=1}^{n} C_i^J \cdot (dlne_i + dln\varphi_{a,i}) \tag{3.20}$$

And relating the change in enzyme to the change in rate of the enzyme, and then using that flux equals rate, one obtains:

$$dlnJ = \sum_{i=1}^{n} C_i^J \cdot (\rho_g^i + \rho_s^i) \cdot dlnv_i = \sum_{i=1}^{n} C_i^J \cdot (\rho_g^i + \rho_s^i) \cdot dlnJ \tag{3.21}$$

Division by $dlnJ$ yields the law we wanted to prove.

This law implies that if there is only a single rate-limiting step in the pathway and the pathway is being regulated, the hierarchical regulation coefficient of that enzyme is always 1. It turns out that the classical paradigm of metabolic control and regulation where there was a single rate-limiting step, and where it was not even considered to make a distinction between flux-limiting step and regulated step, corresponds to one and the same special and probably rare case. When flux control is distributed and only one pathway step is regulated hierarchically, this needs not be the most rate-limiting step and the regulation coefficient equals the inverse of the control coefficient, i.e. there is much hierarchical regulation if the regulated step has little flux control.

Let us consider the example of a three step linear metabolic pathway where the first and the third step have flux control coefficients of 1/3 and 2/3, respectively, and the second step therefore a flux control coefficient of zero. The cell may decide to regulate only the first step in the pathway. This makes the hierarchical regulation coefficient of that enzyme equal 3 (Equation (15)), i.e. the cell will have to increase the concentration of enzyme three times as much as the percentage increase in flux it wishes to obtain. The fluxes through enzymes 2 and 3 would increase due to metabolic regulation only, i.e. the increase in concentration of enzyme 1 would lead to an increase in the concentration of its product, which as substrate of enzyme 2 then would push more flux through enzyme 2. In this example, the metabolic regulation coefficients of enzymes 2 and 3 are 1, while their hierarchical regulation coefficients both equal zero. In the same example, the metabolic regulation of enzyme 1 must be negative, its metabolic regulation coefficient equaling −2 (Equations 3.14 and 3.16). This reflects a strong inhibition by its product or by the substrate of the third enzyme through allosteric feedback regulation. Rossell et al. (2006) have observed such, perhaps nonintuitive aspects of regulation experimentally.

It could be more efficient for the cell to increase the concentration of the third enzyme and not to regulate the first enzyme hierarchically; then for a 10% increase in flux it would only have to increase the concentration of enzyme 3 by 15, rather than 30%. In the latter case, enzymes 1 and 2 would be regulated metabolically, again with metabolic regulation coefficients of 1.

The principles of metabolic regulation can be generalized to branched pathways, but then the meaning of some of the hierarchical regulation coefficients is less obvious.

8 ROBUSTNESS AND FRAGILITY AND APPLICATION TO THE CELL CYCLE

To survive evolution, living systems may not only require optimal performance in terms of growth rate, yield, or efficiency, they may also need to be robust against perturbations. Since living systems depend fundamentally on nonequilibrium processes (Westerhoff & Van Dam 1987; Westerhoff et al. 2009) an important issue is the robustness of an organism to the sustained perturbation of any one such process. Quinton-Tulloch et al. (2013) defined the robustness of a steady-state biological function vis-à-vis the sustained perturbation of any of its processes, as the percentage change in the activity of that process that would compromise the function by 1% only. Such a robustness is 1 for a process in isolation. Quinton-Tulloch and colleagues then calculated the robustness coefficients for fluxes in some 25 realistic models of biochemical networks. They found that virtually all robustness coefficients were much higher than the *in vitro* number of 1.

Csete and Doyle (2002) had considered robustness with respect to periodic perturbations at various frequencies and found total robustness, in the sense of robustness integrated over all frequencies, to be conserved; making a network more robust at one frequency should always reduce its robustness at different frequencies. Quinton-Tulloch et al. (2013) examined whether steady-state robustness is conserved over all processes, i.e. whether the sum of the robustness over all perturbed molecular processes in the system should always be the same. They showed that such a conservation of total robustness is *not* found. The implication is that by increasing the activity of a process and thereby increasing the robustness of a network function with respect to perturbations in that process, one may increase the total robustness of the system.

Defining fragility as the inverse of robustness, i.e. the fragility coefficient as the percentage reduction in function for a 1% reduction in the activity of a process in the system, Quinton-Tulloch et al. (2013) found that total fragility is conserved and should equal 1 if the fragility of a flux is considered. They proved this by identifying this fragility coefficient with the flux control coefficient.

We here illustrate this principle for a model of an important regulatory aspect of the yeast cell, i.e. the cell cycle. The implementation of Metabolic Control Analysis (MCA) to metabolic pathways at steady state has been frequent, successful and is well-known. MCA has also been applied to mostly metabolic oscillations, either forced or autonomous, with the yeast glycolysis oscillations synchronized by acetaldehyde as significant examples (e.g. Richard et al. 1993; Kholodenko et al. 1997; Danø et al. 2001; Reijenga et al. 2001, 2002, 2005; du Preez et al. 2012a, 2012b). The cell cycle may however be a more important oscillation, which is rarely seen as a limit cycle however. Some initial control analysis has been done, revealing again distributed control, but there has been little induction toward general principles of cell cycle. We will here briefly discuss possible developments around unsuspected relationships between robustness, fragility and time dependence.

Figure 3.2 shows a diagram underlying our dynamic model of a part of the cell cycle of *S. cerevisiae*, where activation of various mitotic kinase/cyclin (Cdk1/Clb) complexes occurs between DNA duplication (S phase) and cell division (M phase). A kinetic model describing Cdk1/Clb dynamics over time was implemented, where each kinase complex activates the next one in a linear cascade (Barberis et al. 2012). Their activation (and inactivation) occurs in a temporal fashion, and a design principle underlying the oscillatory behavior of Clb waves has been proposed (Barberis 2012).

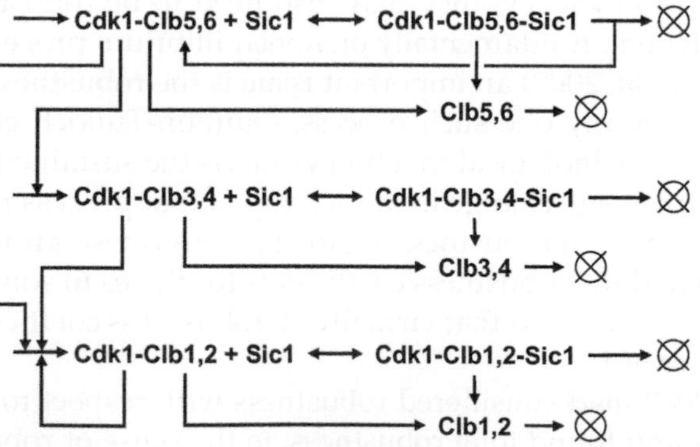

FIGURE 3.2 Signaling network describing Cdk1/Clb regulation from S to M phase of the cell cycle.

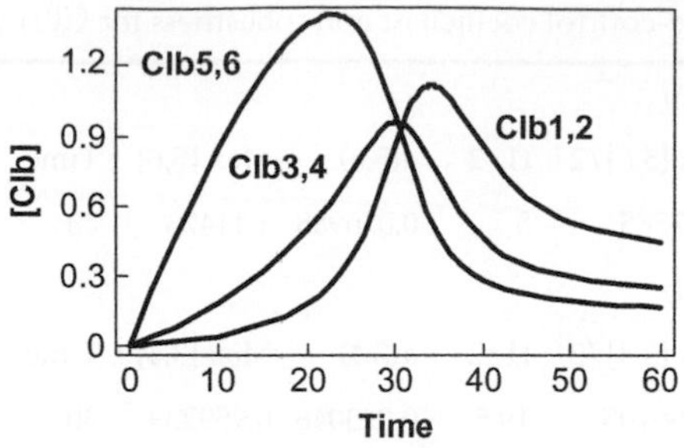

FIGURE 3.3 Computational time course of Clb cyclins couples over time.

Figure 3.3 shows that the three couples of Clb cyclins (Clb5,6, Clb3,4, and Clb1,2) undergo waves with amplitudes at different times. We shall first focus on the Clb5/6 couple and on the onset and the decay of the peak of their level. Figure 3.2 shows that Clb5/6 has a maximum at $t = 23$ and that at $t = 8$ it is hallway reaching that maximum and at $t = 31.5$ it is again halfway down. We computed the time-control coefficient Tc at those times, and this amounted to 0.87 and −4.57, respectively. We also computed the robustness R (defined as the inverse of the time-control coefficients) of the amplitude of Clb5/6 at the two halfway time points. We first computed the robustness of the Clb5/6 amplitude exercised by all processes in the network when perturbed simultaneously and equally in the same direction. The corresponding robustnesses were 1.14849 and 0.21881 (see Table 3.1).

Quinton-Tulloch et al. (2013) identified the inverse of the robustness with fragility, which in turn is equal to the control coefficient. As a consequence the above (Equation 3.10):

$$\sum_{j=1}^{n} C_{e_j}^{X_k}(t) = C_t^{X_k}(t) \tag{3.10}$$

can be reformulated as:

$$\sum_{j=1}^{n} \frac{1}{Re_{e_j}^{X_k}(t)} = C_t^{X_k}(t) \tag{3.22}$$

For this case of equal perturbations of all processes amounts to:

$$\sum_{j=1}^{n} \frac{1}{\Re_{total\ for\ equal}^{X_k}(t_{\frac{1}{2on}})} = C_t^{X_k}(t_{\frac{1}{2on}}) \tag{3.23}$$

And the same for the other time point analyzed. The last two columns in Table 3.1 confirms this computationally.

For the onset of the peak the time-control coefficient is positive. Hence the positive robustnesses must be smaller (typically those with respect to kinases perturbations) than the robustnesses with respect to the phosphatases (which are not considered explicitly in the system yet). For the decay of the peak, the inverse should be true.

TABLE 3.1 Calculation of time-control coefficient and robustness for Clb cyclins couples.

Clb5,6			α(5,6)					β(5,6)		
	Max [5,6]	Time	Max [5,6]/2	t1/2	α(5,6)	Max [5,6]	Time	Max [5,6]/2	t1/2	β(5,6)
	1,41473	23	0,707365	8	0,076988	1,41473	23	0,789371	31,5	0,11453
Clb3,4			α(3,4)					β(3,4)		
	Max [3,4]	Time	Max [3,4]/2	t1/2	α(3,4)	Max [3,4]	Time	Max [3,4]/2	t1/2	β(3,4)
	0,959239	30	0,4796195	19,5	0,023046	0,959239	30	0,60479	37	0,05489
Clb1,2			α(1,2)					β(1,2)		
	Max [1,2]	Time	Max [1,2]/2	t1/2	α(1,2)	Max [1,2]	Time	Max [1,2]/2	t1/2	β(1,2)
	1,1148	34	0,5574	27	0,094539	1,1148	34	0,780522	41,5	0,049

Tcα	Tcβ	Rα	Rβ	1/Rα	1/Rβ
Tcα(5,6)	Tcβ(5,6)	Rα(5,6)	Rβ(5,6)	Rα(5,6)	Rβ(5,6)
0,87071	4,57023	1,14849	0,21881	0,87071	4,57023
Tcα(3,4)	Tcβ(3,4)	Rα(3,4)	Rβ(3,4)	Rα(3,4)	Rβ(3,4)
0,937	3,358332	1,06723	0,29777	0,937	3,35833
Tcα(1,2)	Tcβ(1,2)	Rα(1,2)	Rβ(1,2)	Rα(1,2)	Rβ(1,2)
4,57937	2,605393	0,21837	0,38382	4,57937	2,60539

9 PERFECT ADAPTATION AND INTEGRAL CONTROL IN METABOLISM

Biochemical reaction networks can exhibit properties similar to those of control system structures in control engineering, but are they identical? The robustness of cellular adaptation to environmental conditions is often related to negative feedback control structures. For example, robust adaptations in a bacterial chemotaxis signaling network, in mammalian iron and calcium homeostasis, and in yeast osmoregulation have been interpreted as integral feedback control systems (Yi et al. 2000; El-Samad et al. 2002; Ni et al. 2009; Muzzey et al. 2009). A recent study identified the three different types of control structures used in control engineering, i.e. proportional, integral, and derivative feedback control, in regulations of energy metabolism (Cloutier and Wellstead 2010). In addition, specific nonlinear dynamics in signaling networks, such as oscillation or bi-stability, can be induced by positive feedback loops. Feed-forward control structures are also observed in gene regulatory networks (Mangan and Alon 2003), as well as in the regulation of glycolytic intermediates (Bali and Thomas 2001).

Regulation in living cells tends to occur at multiple levels simultaneously with a hierarchical structure (Westerhoff 2008). In a metabolic network the regulation of a reaction rate can be achieved by the modulation of (i) enzyme *activity* (through a substrate or product effect, through a different metabolite competing with the substrate for its binding site or through an allosteric effect), i.e. metabolic regulation, of (ii) enzyme covalent modification status as end-effect of a signal transduction pathway, or of (iii) enzyme *concentration* via gene expression, i.e. gene-expression regulation. Such multiple-level regulations correspond to different control loops in a control system. This may ensure the robustness versus perturbations at various frequencies. In engineering, an airplane wing has to be robust at high frequencies of variations of air pressures, as well as with respect to low frequency perturbations. In order to achieve this combined robustness, different control loops have to be put in place simultaneously, although a trade-off limits what one can do, in the sense that increased robustness at one frequency comes at reduced robustness at a different frequency (Csete and Doyle 2002). In systems biology, this can be illustrated through the end product feedback regulations (Goelzer et al. 2008). If the flux demand on the end product module increases rapidly, the concentration of the end product decreases rapidly. Often as a result of the allosteric effect of the penultimate metabolite directly on the first enzyme, the activity of that first enzyme increase quickly too. This metabolic control of enzyme activity is a fast actuator of the system. However, if there is a further increase in the flux demand, the first enzyme may "lose" its regulatory capacity since its activity may be approaching its maximum capacity (k_{cat}). At this stage, the system has a second "adaptation" which is slow (because the cell has to produce enzyme) but leads to increase in the concentration of the first enzyme, which then decreases the direct stimulation of the catalytic activity of the first enzyme. The regulation of the first enzyme is then bi-functional in dynamic terms (Csete and Doyle 2002): The metabolic regulation rapidly buffers against high frequency perturbations but possibly with small amplitude or capability, while the gene-expression regulation is slow to adapt but may be able to reject very large constant perturbations (Ter Kuile and Westerhoff 2001).

When interpreting metabolic and gene-expression regulation separately as specific control system structures, we identify the former more as a "proportional control" action (El-Samad et al. 2002; Yi et al. 2000) with limited range, and the latter more as an "integral control" action with potentially a wider range and acting more slowly. Mechanisms of integral control can lead to zero steady-state errors of the "controlled variable," which is not possible with proportional control mechanisms. In the latter case, the perturbation of the controlled variable has to persist for the regulation as the homeostatic regulation is proportional to the perturbation of the controlled variable (the error function). The mechanism that operates in the former case is known as "perfect adaptation" in biology when the network becomes completely robust to the environmental perturbations: here the regulation is proportional to the time integral of the error function, which persists when the error function has returned to zero. The proportional control can often provide fast control response but the corresponding adaptation would be imperfect with nonzero steady state errors.

The control engineering interpretations may be mapped onto Metabolic Control Analysis (MCA) and Hierarchical Control Analysis (HCA) (Westerhoff et al. 1990, 2009), respectively. The relatively fast metabolic regulation (proportional control) is related to the direct "elasticities" of MCA, while the slow gene-expression regulation (integral control) corresponds to the indirect "elasticities" of HCA.

Let us consider the example illustrated in Figure 3.4, which is a two-step pathway with intermediate ATP at an ADP concentration, $[ATP] = C\text{-}[ADP]$ and with the gene expression of

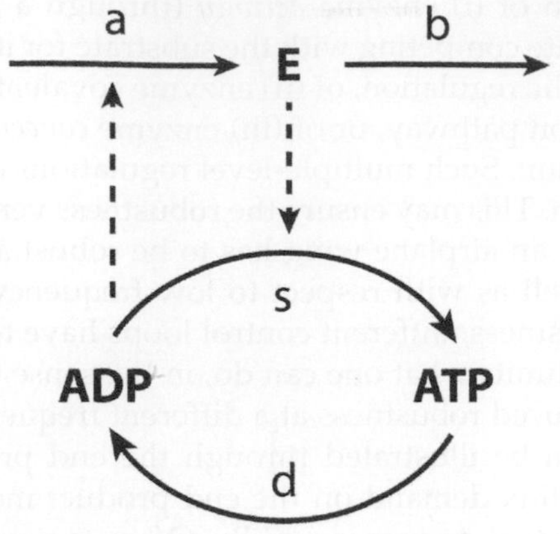

FIGURE 3.4 Illustration of ATP energy metabolism in a two-step pathway with gene-expression regulation.

the first enzyme ($E = E_s$) being increased in proportion to the concentration of ADP, which is a gene-expression regulation. The moiety conservation sum C is the sum of the concentrations of ATP and ADP and constant here because the reactions only convert the one into the other. The two-step pathway (*s* and *d*) represent supply and demand parts of a metabolic pathway (Hofmeyr 1995), and metabolic regulation is assumed to be part of these processes.

The dynamics of ADP and enzyme *E* can be described by simple kinetics:

$$\frac{d[ADP]}{dt} = -k_s \cdot E \cdot [ADP] + k_d \cdot (C - [ADP]) \tag{3.24}$$

$$\frac{dE}{dt} = k_a \cdot [ADP] - k_b \cdot E - k_0 \tag{3.25}$$

where the degradation of *E* is assumed to be a mixture of zero and first order processes. The closed-loop control system structure of the pathway can be represented in Figure 3.5.

From the control system diagram, it can be noted that the ADP concentration is the controlled variable; enzyme concentration *E* is a control output (the manipulation variable) of the

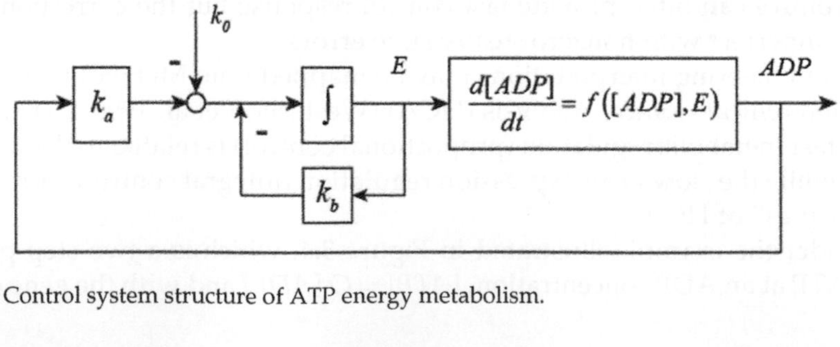

FIGURE 3.5 Control system structure of ATP energy metabolism.

gene-expression regulation control loop. When the degradation of enzyme is only zero order in terms of E (with $k_b = 0$), the gene-expression regulation becomes an ideal integral control loop, and the metabolic network can exhibit robust perfect adaptation to the external or parametric perturbations: Equation 3.25 set to zero then determines the steady level of ADP and Equation 3.24 set to zero the level of the enzyme E. This only happens when the cell population is in stationary phase, because in a dividing cell population, the enzyme level per cell would decay in a quasi first-order process. The zero order degradation rate k_0 can be treated as a reference signal to the system. The metabolic regulation is included as a part of the ADP kinetic process.

Such a control engineering insight is consistent with classical kinetic analysis and metabolic control analysis. By considering a small perturbation of k_d from its steady-state value (δk_d with δ denoting the small deviation), and reformulating the kinetics of dADP/dt and dE/dt, we have

$$\begin{aligned}\frac{d\delta ADP}{dt} &= -(k_s \cdot E_{ss} + k_d) \cdot \delta ADP - k_s \cdot ADP_{ss} \\ &\quad \cdot \int_0^{\infty} (k_a \cdot \delta ADP - k_b \cdot \delta E) \cdot dt + (C - ADP) \cdot \delta k_d\end{aligned} \tag{3.26}$$

where the subscript ss denotes the steady state value. We recognize on the right-hand side first a proportional response term, then an integral response term, and then the perturbation term. The proportional response corresponds to the direct "elasticity" of the supply and demand reactions with respect to ADP, which is a metabolic and instantaneous regulation. The integral response is related to the protein synthesis and degradation and thus to the gene-expression regulation. If $k_b = 0$, the second term corresponds to an ideal integral action. By further removing the time dependence of the change in ADP using the steady state conditions, the classical metabolic control coefficients, i.e. the control of the enzyme level by the demand reaction, and the flux control coefficient, can be obtained:

$$\begin{aligned}C^E_{k_d} &= \frac{\delta \ln E}{\delta \ln k_d} = 1 - \frac{1}{1 + \frac{k_s \cdot ([ADP]_{ss})^2}{k_d \cdot C} \cdot \frac{k_a}{k_b}} \\ C^J_{k_d} &= \frac{\delta \ln J}{\delta \ln k_d} = 1 - \frac{[ADP]_{ss}/C}{1 + \frac{k_s \cdot ([ADP]_{ss})^2}{k_d \cdot C} \cdot \frac{k_a}{k_b}}\end{aligned} \tag{3.27}$$

Both the control of enzyme level and the control of demand flux by the perturbation are equal to 1 minus a hyperbolic function of k_b. For an ideal integral control scenario with $k_b = 0$ the enzyme concentration E perfectly tracks the activity of the pathway degrading ATP, and $C^E_{k_d} = 1$. More importantly, the pathway flux perfectly tracks the perturbation in the demand flux and $C^J_{k_d} = 1$. The control of k_d on ADP is zero (Using Equation 3.25 with zero change in enzyme and zero k_b). This is the case of robust perfect adaptation. For other cases when $k_b \neq 0$, the adaptation of the pathway to the perturbation will not be perfect. Also the robustness coefficient as defined by Quinton-Tulloch et al. (2013) can be expressed

$$\Re^{ADP}_{k_d} = \frac{1}{\frac{\partial \ln [ADP]_{ss}}{\partial \ln k_d}} = \frac{k_d \cdot C + k_s \cdot ([ADP]_{ss})^2 \cdot \frac{k_a}{k_b}}{(C - [ADP]_{ss}) \cdot k_d} \tag{3.28}$$

Only when $k_b = 0$, the pathway exhibits infinite robustness ($\Re_{k_d}^{ADP} = \infty$) to the external or parametric perturbation. This example shows the consistency of control engineering and classical metabolic control analysis in understanding the adaptation of a metabolic pathway under both gene-expression and metabolic regulation.

Acknowledgments

This study was supported by the Netherlands Organization for Scientific Research NWO through the MOSES-SysMO grant, as well as by the BBSRC/EPSRC's finding of the Manchester Centre for Integrative Systems Biology (BB/F003528/1, BB/C008219/1), BBSRC's MOSES-SysMO project (BB/F003528/1), various other BBSRC projects (BB/G530225/1, BB/I004696/1, BB/I017186/1, BB/I00470X/1, BB/I004688/1, BB/J500422/1, BB/J003883/1, BB/J0200601/1), and the EU-FP7 projects SYNPOL, EC-MOAN, UNICELLSYS, ITFoM, and BioSim.

References

Bali, M., and Thomas, S. R. (2001). A modelling study of feed-forward activation in human erythrocyte glycolysis. *C. R. Acad. Sci. III* 324:185–199.

Barberis, M., Linke, C., Adrover, M. À., González-Novo, A., Lehrach, H., Krobitsch, S., Posas, F., and Klipp, E. (2012). Sic1 plays a role in timing and oscillatory behaviour of B-type cyclins. *Biotechnol. Adv.* 30:108–130.

Barberis, M. (2012). Sic1 as a timer of Clb cyclin waves in the yeast cell cycle–design principle of not just an inhibitor. *FEBS J.* 279:3386–3410.

Burns, J. A., Cornish-Bowden, A., Groen, A. K., Heinrich, R., Kacser, H., Porteous, J. W., Rapoport, S. M., Rapoport, T. A., Stucki, J. W., Tager, J. M., Wanders, R. J. A., and Westerhoff, H. V. (1985). Control analysis of metabolic systems. *Trends Biochem. Sci.* 10:16.

Cloutier, M., and Wellstead, P. (2010). The control systems structures of energy metabolism. *J. R. Soc. Interface* 7:651–665.

Cooper, V. S., and Lenski, R. E. (2000). The population genetics of ecological specialization in evolving *Escherichia coli* populations. *Nature* 407:736–739.

Csete, M. E., and Doyle, J. (2002). Reverse engineering of biological complexity. *Science* 295:1664–1669.

Danø, S., Hynne, F., De Monte, S., d'Ovidio, F., Sørensen, P. G., and Westerhoff, H. W. (2001). Synchronization of glycolytic oscillations in a yeast cell population. *Faraday Discuss.* 120:261–276.

Diaz-Ruiz, R., Uribe-Carvajal, S., Devin, A., and Rigoulet, M. (2009). Tumor cell energy metabolism and its common features with yeast metabolism. *Biochim. Biophys. Acta* 1796:252–265.

du Preez, F. B., van Niekerk, D. D., Kooi, B., Rohwer, J. M., and Snoep, J. L. (2012a). From steady-state to synchronized yeast glycolytic oscillations I: model construction. *FEBS J.* 279:2810–2822.

du Preez, F. B., van Niekerk, D. D., and Snoep, J. L. (2012b). From steady-state to synchronized yeast glycolytic oscillations II: model validation. *FEBS J.* 279:2823–2836.

El-Samad, H., Goff, J. P., and Khammash, M. (2002). Calcium homeostasis and parturient hypocalcemia: an integral feedback perspective. *J. Theor. Biol.* 214:17–29.

Gatenby, R. A., and Gawlinski, E. T. (1996). A reaction-diffusion model of cancer invasion. *Cancer Res.* 56:5745–5753.

Goelzer, A., Briki, F. B., Marin-Verstraete, I., Noirot, P., Bessieres, P., Aymerich, S., and Fromion, V. (2008). Reconstruction and analysis of the genetic and metabolic regulatory networks of the central metabolism of *Bacillus subtilis*. BMC Syst. *Biol.* 2:20.

Herrgård, M. J., Swainston, N., Dobson, P., Dunn, W. B., Arga, K. Y., Arvas, M., Blüthgen, N., Borger, S., Costenoble, E. R., Heinemann, M., Hucka, M., Li, P., Liebermeister, W., Mo, M. L., Oliveira, A. P., Petranovic, D., Pettifer, S., Simeonidis, E., Smallbone, K., Spasi, I., Weichart, D., Brent, R., Broomhead, D. S., Westerhoff, H. V., Kirdar, B., Penttilä, M., Klipp, E., Paton, N., Palsson, B. Ø., Sauer, U., Oliver, S. G., Mendes, P., Nielsen, J., and Kell, D. B. (2008). A consensus yeast metabolic network obtained from a community approach to systems biology. *Nat. Biotechnol.* 26:1155–1160.

Hofmeyr, J.-H.S. (1995). Metabolic regulation: a control analytic perspective. *J. Bioenerg. Biomembr.* 27:479–490.

Holzhütter, H. G. (2004). The principle of flux minimization and its application to estimate stationary fluxes in metabolic networks. *Eur. J. Biochem.* 271:2905–2922.

Hornberg, J. J., Bruggeman, F. J., Binder, B., Geest, C. R., Bij de Vaate, A. J. M., Lankelma, J., Heinrich, R., and Westerhoff, H. V. (2005). Principles behind the multifarious control of signal transduction. ERK phosphorylation and kinase/phosphatase control. *FEBS J.* 272:244–258.

Hornberg, J. J., Bruggeman, F. J., Westerhoff, H. V., and Lankelma, J. (2006). Cancer: A systems biology disease. *BioSystems* 83:81–90.

Jain, M., Nilsson, R., Sharma, S., Madhusudhan, N., Kitami, T., Souza, A. L., Kafri, R., Kirschner, M. W., Clish, C. B., and Mootha, V. K. (2012). Metabolite profiling identifies a key role for glycine in rapid cancer cell proliferation. *Science* 336:1040–1044.

Kholodenko, B. N., and Westerhoff, H. V. (1993). Metabolic channelling and control of the flux. *FEBS Lett.* 320:71–74.

Kholodenko, B. N., Demin, O. V., and Westerhoff, H. V. (1997). Control analysis of periodic phenomena in biological systems. *J. Phys. Chem.* 101:2070–2081.

Lee, S., Phalakornkule, C., Domach, M. M., and Grossmann, I. E. (2000). Recursive MILP model for finding all the alternate optima in LP models for metabolic networks. *Comput. Chem. Eng.* 24:711–716.

León, M. P. D., Cancela, H., and Acerenza, L. (2008). A strategy to calculate the patterns of nutrient consumption by microorganisms applying a two-level optimisation principle to reconstructed metabolic networks. *J. Biol. Phys.* 34:73–90.

Mangan, S., and Alon, U. (2003). Structure and function of the feed-forward loop network motif. *Proc. Natl. Acad. Sci. USA* 100:11980–11985.

Mensonides, F. I. C., Bakker, B. M., Cremazy, F., Messiha, H. L., Mendes, P. M., Boogerd, F. C., and Westerhoff, H. V. (2013). A new regulatory principle for in vivo biochemistry: Pleiotropic low affinity regulation by the adenine nucleotides - Illustrated for the glycolytic enzymes of Saccharomyces cerevisiae. *FEBS Lett.* **587**:2860–2867.

Murabito, E., Simeonidis, E., Smallbone, K., and Swinton, J. (2009). Capturing the essence of a metabolic network: A flux balance analysis approach. *J. Theor. Biol.* 260:445–452.

Muzzey, D., Gomez-Uribe, C. A., Mettetal, J. T., and van Oudenaarden, A. (2009). A systems-level analysis of perfect adaptation in yeast osmoregulation. *Cell* 138:160–171.

Ni, X. Y., Drengstig, T., and Ruoff, P. (2009). The control of controller: molecular mechanisms for robust perfect adaptation and temperature compensation. *Biophys. J.* 97:1244–1253.

Quinton-Tulloch, M. J., Bruggeman, F. J., Snoep, J. L., and Westerhoff, H. V. (2013). Trade-off of dynamic fragility but not of robustness in metabolic pathways *in silico*. *FEBS J.* 280:160–173.

Reed, J. L., and Palsson, B. Ø. (2004). Genome-scale in silico models of *E. coli* have multiple equivalent phenotypic states: assessment of correlated reaction subsets that comprise network states. *Genome Res.* 14:1797–1805.

Reijenga, K. A., Snoep, J. L., Diderich, J. A., van Verseveld, H. W., Westerhoff, H. V., and Teusink, B. (2001). Control of glycolytic dynamics by hexose transport in *Saccharomyces cerevisiae*. *Biophys. J.* 80:626–634.

Reijenga, K. A., van Megen, Y. M., Kooi, B. W., Bakker, B. M., Snoep, J. L., van Verseveld, H. W., and Westerhoff, H. V. (2005). Yeast glycolytic oscillations that are not controlled by a single oscillophore: a new definition of oscillophore strength. *J. Theor. Biol.* 232:385–398.

Reijenga, K. A., Westerhoff, H. V., Kholodenko, B. N., and Snoep, J. L. (2002). Control analysis for autonomously oscillating biochemical networks. *Biophys. J.* 82:99–108.

Richard, P., Teusink, B., Westerhoff, H. V., and van Dam, K. (1993). Around the growth phase transition *S. cerevisiae*'s make-up favours sustained oscillations of intracellular metabolites. *FEBS Lett.* 318:80–82.

Rossell, S., van der Weijden, C. C., Lindenbergh, A., van Tuijl, A., Francke, C., Bakker, B. M., and Westerhoff, H. V. (2006). Unraveling the complexity of flux regulation: A new method demonstrated for nutrient starvation in *Saccharomyces cerevisiae*. *Proc. Natl. Acad. Sci. USA* 103:2166–2171.

Sauer, U. (2006). Metabolic networks in motion: C-13-based flux analysis. *Mol. Syst. Biol.* 2:62.

Schuster, S., Pfeiffer, T., and Fell, D. A. (2008). Is maximization of molar yield in metabolic networks favoured by evolution?. *J. Theor. Biol.* 252:497–504.

Shlomi, T., Cabili, M. N., Herrgård, M. J., Palsson, B. Ø., and Ruppin, E. (2008). Network-based prediction of human tissue-specific metabolism. *Nat. Biotechnol.* 26:1003–1010.

Simeonidis, E., Murabito, E., Smallbone, K., and Westerhoff, H. V. (2010). Why does yeast ferment? A flux balance analysis study. *Biochem. Soc. Trans.* 38:1225–1229.

Ter Kuile, B., and Westerhoff, H. V. (2001). Transcriptome meets metabolome: hierarchical and metabolic regulation of the glycolytic pathway. *FEBS Lett.* 500:169–171.

Teusink, B., Walsh, M. C., Van Dam, K., and Westerhoff, H. V. (1998). The danger of metabolic pathways with turbo design. *Trends Biochem. Sci.* 23:162–169.

Thiele, I., Swainston, N., Fleming, R. M., Hoppe, A., Sahoo, S., Aurich, M. K., Haraldsdottir, H., Mo, M. L., Rolfsson, O., Stobbe, M. D., Thorleifsson, S. G., Agren, R., Bölling, C., Bordel, S., Chavali, A. K., Dobson, P., Dunn, W. B., Endler, L., Hala, D., Hucka, M., Hull, D., Jameson, D., Jamshidi, N., Jonsson, J. J., Juty, N., Keating, S., Nookaew, I., Le Novère, N., Malys, N., Mazein, A., Papin, J. A., Price, N. D., Selkov, E. Sr, Sigurdsson, M. I., Simeonidis, E., Sonnenschein, N., Smallbone, K., Sorokin, A., van Beek, J. H., Weichart, D., Goryanin, I., Nielsen, J., Westerhoff, H. V., Kell, D. B., Mendes, P., and Palsson, B. Ø. (2013). A community-driven global reconstruction of human metabolism. *Nat. Biotechnol.* 31:419–425.

Warburg, O., and Dickens, F. (1931). The metabolism of tumors. *Am. J. Med. Sci.* 182:123.

Westerhoff, H. V., Hellingwerf, K. J., and Van Dam, K. (1983). Thermodynamic efficiency of microbial growth is low, but optimal for maximal growth rate. *Proc. Natl. Acad. Sci. USA* 80:305–309.

Westerhoff, H. V., and Van Dam, K. (1987). *Thermodynamics and Control of Biological Free Energy Transduction*. Amsterdam: Elsevier.

Westerhoff, H. V., Aon, M. A., Van Dam, K., Cortassa, S., Kahn, D., and Van Workum, M. (1990). Dynamical and hierarchical coupling. *Biochim. Biophys. Acta* 1018:142–146.

Westerhoff, H. V. (2008). Signaling control strength. *J. Theor. Biol.* 252:555–567.

Westerhoff, H. V., Kolodkin, A., Conradie, R., Wilkinson, S. J., Bruggeman, F. J., Krab, K., van Schuppen, J. H., Hardin, H., Bakker, B. M., Moné, M. J., Rybakova, K., Eijken, M., van Leeuwen, J. P., and Snoep, J. L. (2009). Systems Biology towards Life *in silico*: mathematics of the control of living cells. J. Math. Biol. 58:7–34.

Yi, T. M., Huang, Y., Simon, M. I., and Doyle, J. (2000). Robust perfect adaptation in bacterial chemotaxis through integral feedback control. *Proc. Natl. Acad. Sci. USA* 97:4649–4653.

CHAPTER

4

Biological Foundations of Signal Transduction, Systems Biology and Aberrations in Disease

Ursula Klingmüller, Marcel Schilling, Sofia Depner, Lorenza A. D'Alessandro

Division Systems Biology of Signal Transduction, German Cancer Research Center (DKFZ), Heidelberg, Germany

CONTENTS

Abstract

Cellular communication is mediated by extracellular stimuli that bind cellular receptors and activate intracellular signaling pathways. Principal biochemical reactions used for signal transduction are protein or lipid phosphorylation, proteolytic cleavage, protein degradation and complex formation mediated by protein-protein interactions. Within the nucleus, signaling pathways regulate transcription factor activity and gene expression. Cells differ in their competence to respond to extracellular stimuli. A deeper understanding of

http://dx.doi.org/10.1016/B978-0-12-405926-9.00004-6

complex biological responses cannot be achieved by traditional approaches but requires the combination of experimental data with mathematical modeling. Following a systems biology approach, data-based mathematical models describing sub-modules of signaling pathways have been established. By combining computer simulations with experimental verification systems properties of signaling pathway including cycling behavior or threshold response could be identified. Yet, to analyze complex growth and maturation processes at a systems level and quantitatively predict the outcome of perturbations further advances in experimental and theoretical methodologies are required.

1 INTRODUCTION

Cells do not live in isolation, but have evolved mechanisms to communicate. Principal signals used are direct cell-cell contact and secreted molecules that bind to cell surface receptors. Arrays of intracellular proteins form signal transduction pathways and connect to receptors. This facilitates signal transmission from the extracellular compartment to the nucleus and thereby triggering various biological responses. A key mechanism used for signal transduction is phosphorylation due to its simplicity, flexibility, and reversibility. In the late 1970s it was discovered that the oncogene v-Src can transform cells, possesses protein kinase activity and causes an increase in tyrosine phosphorylation (Hunter and Sefton 1980). This lead to an intense hunt for the underlying mechanisms facilitating signal transduction. As a consequence many components of signaling pathways were discovered but it remained unknown how information is processed and how cellular responses are regulated.

Signaling pathways do not just process the external signals by itself but form complex cellular networks that regulate biological functions in a context-dependent manner. It became evident that to identify regulatory mechanisms and to predict the behavior of these networks, mathematical models could be very helpful. The initial attempts to model signaling were primarily based on qualitative data reflecting the possible interactions between the components and on computer simulations with ad hoc fixed parameters or parameters extracted from the literature (Fussenegger et al. 2000; Bhalla and Iyengar 1999). However these parameters frequently rely on experiments performed in different cellular settings or on *in vitro* studies. From these studies it could not be decided whether the model structure was incorrect or whether the parameters were ill chosen if the computational simulations did not fit to the experimental observations. Thus, to understand the dynamic behavior of signaling pathways at a systems level it is essential to combine mathematical model building with experiments (Kitano 2002; Eungdamrong and Iyengar 2004) and establish data-based models.

2 CONCEPTS IN SIGNAL TRANSDUCTION

2.1 The cell—structural organization

Complex organisms are highly organized assemblies of specialized cells. Despite these differences, all cells share common fundamental properties and represent a "unit" in living organisms. They are surrounded by a plasma membrane, use DNA (deoxyribonucleic acid) as their genetic material and employ the same basic mechanisms for energy metabolism.

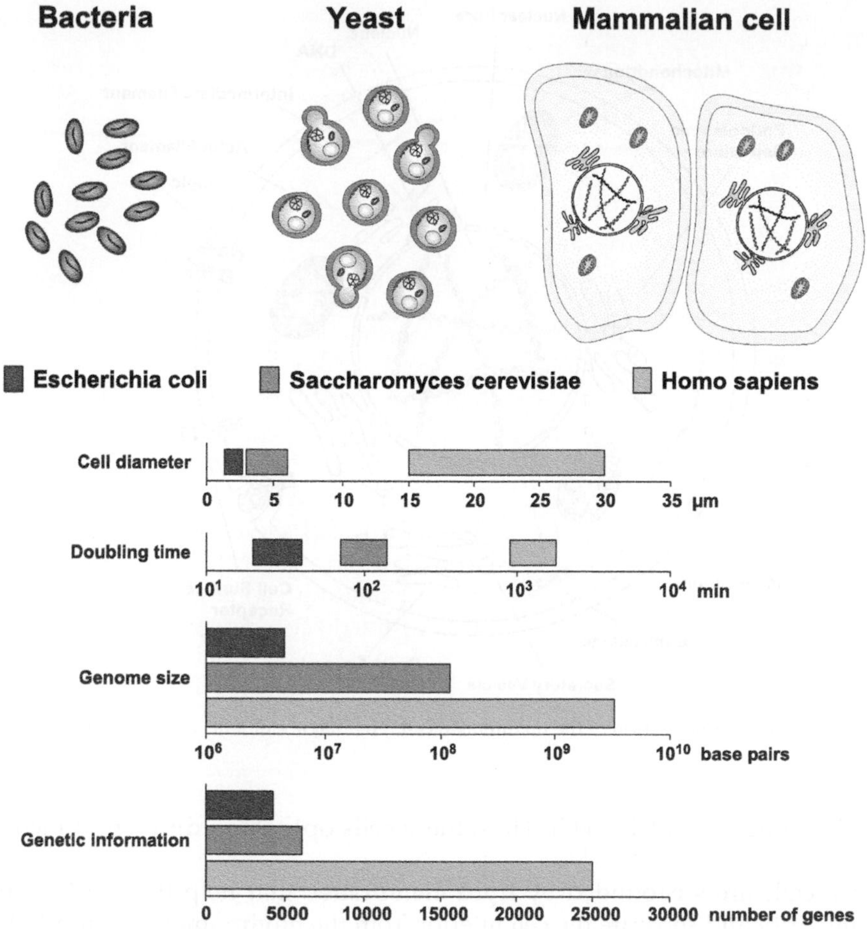

FIGURE 4.1 Structural organization and key numbers for bacteria, yeast and mammalian cells. The organizational complexity, cell diameter, average doubling time, genome size and genetic information increase in a non-linear manner.

There are two principal types of cells: The **eukaryotic cell** that participates in the formation of complex organisms and contains a nucleus, cytoplasmic organelles as well as a cytoskeleton and the anuclear **prokaryotic cell** (bacteria) that lacks these components (Figure 4.1). Additionally the cells of prokaryotic and eukaryotic organisms differ greatly in their biological properties such as size, the dimensions of genome and DNA doubling time. Prokaryotic bacteria as for example *Escherichia coli* with a diameter of 0.7–1.4 μm, a genome of roughly 5 million base pairs (bp) and 4288 genes, DNA doubling time of 20–40 min belong to the smallest cells within the living organisms. The cells of yeast that belongs to low eukaryotic organisms have a diameter of 3.0–6.0 μm, a genome of 12 million base pairs (bp), and 6034 genes with DNA doubling time of 70–140 min. In comparison, the eukaryotic mammalian cell has a diameter of 15–30 μm, a genome of 3.3 billion base pairs (bp), and 25,000 genes

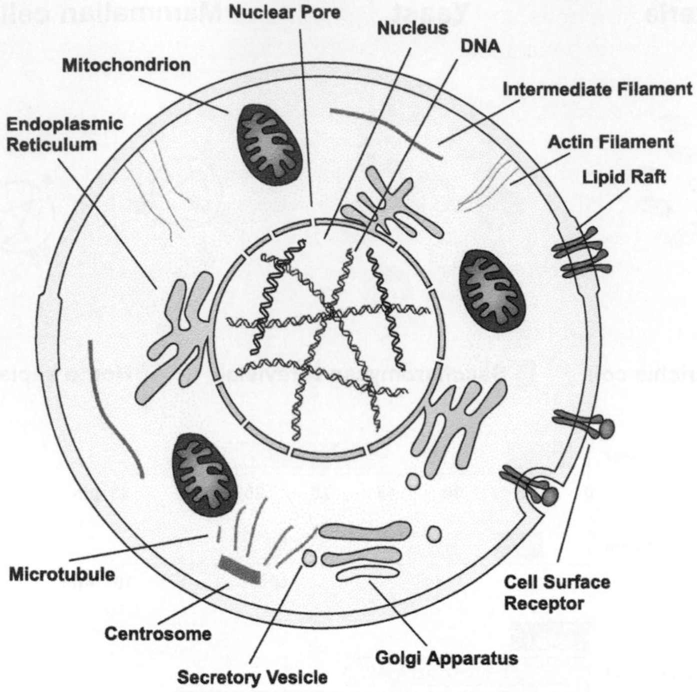

FIGURE 4.2 Structural organization of the mammalian cell. The major elements are schematically indicated.

with DNA doubling time of 15–30 h. Thus, these cells operate in different dimensions and time scales.

In general, cells are surrounded by **lipid membranes** that help the cell to maintain its shape and integrity and separate the cell interior from the environment (Figure 4.2).

Additionally, the cell membrane serves as an anchoring structure for the cytoskeleton and plays an important role in attachment of the cell to the extracellular matrix and other cells. The cell membrane consists of both lipids and proteins. The fundamental structure of the membrane is a bilayer of phospholipid molecules whose charged head groups interact with the surrounding water and whose fatty acid tails form a hydrophobic interior. In addition, the membrane of mammalian cells contains glycolipids and cholesterol that increase the rigidity. While lipids are the principal building blocks of membranes, the proteins are responsible for specific membrane functions, such as maintenance of cell-cell and cytoskeleton contact, surface recognition, transport of substances across the membrane, regulation of signaling and enzymatic activity. The cell membrane contains glycolipoprotein microdomains, termed **lipid rafts**, which function as the assembly units for signaling molecules influencing the processes of endocytosis, transcytosis, signal transduction, and receptor recycling.

In mammalian cells, membranes not only segregate the cell interior from the environment, but also surround intracellular organelles that facilitate extensive sub-cellular compartmentalization and enable mammalian cells to function efficiently. The largest double membrane-bound organelle is the **nucleus** that harbors the cell's genome (DNA), serves as a compartment for the retrieval and duplication of genetic information and functions as the site of transcription (RNA (ribonucleic acid) synthesis). Also the post-transcriptional processing of pre-messenger RNA such as RNA splicing occurs inside the nucleus and mature mRNAs are transported into the cytoplasm where the translational processes (synthesis of proteins from aminoacids) take place. Such functional compartmentalization inside the cell allows for higher levels of regulation of gene expression in mammalian cells including the selected transport of transcription factors from the cytoplasm to the nucleus.

A large network of interconnected membrane-enclosed tubules forms the **endoplasmic reticulum (ER)** and extends from the nuclear membrane throughout the cytosol. The major task of the ER is sorting of proteins destined for secretion or the plasma membrane. Polypeptide chains are translocated into the ER where protein folding and processing takes place. From the ER proteins are transported within membranous vesicles to the **Golgi apparatus**, an organelle composed of stacks of membrane-bound structures, and further delivered to the cell surface membrane or secreted. Another cell organelle present in multiple copies in the cytosol of mammalian cells are **mitochondria** in which most of the cellular ATP, used as a source of chemical energy, is generated. In addition mitochondria are involved in cellular processes such as signaling, cellular differentiation, cell death as well as the control of the cell cycle and cell growth.

Besides the membrane-enclosed organelles, a network of protein filaments extends through the cytoplasm forming the **cytoskeleton** and providing another level of organization. The cytoskeleton provides a structural framework determining the cell shape and cellular movements including transport of organelles. In contrast to the rigid implications, the cytoskeleton undergoes constant remodeling and thus reflects a highly dynamic entity. There are three principal types of protein filaments: actin filaments, intermediate filaments, and microtubules. Actin filaments are generated by head-to-tail polymerization of actin monomers forming a helical structure. Assembly and disassembly of these filaments is tightly regulated by actin binding proteins. Upon interaction with the motor protein myosin, actin filaments support a variety of movements of cells. Intermediate filaments are polymers of different proteins expressed in various cell types and possess a rope-like structure. They are not involved in cellular movement, but provide mechanical support. Microtubules are formed by reversible polymerization of tubulin in dependence of GTP hydrolysis. They are extended outward from a centrosome and the mitotic spindle formed during mitosis that is responsible for chromosomal separation. Two families of motor proteins, kinesins and dyneins, associate with microtubules and promote movement as well as positioning of organelles in the cytoplasm.

2.2 Principles of signal transduction—signal transmission from the cell surface to the nucleus

In multicellular organisms cells do not live in isolation but rely on specific mechanisms to communicate. In close proximity direct cell-cell contact is used whereas soluble ligands also permit communication over distances. But since cells are surrounded by a lipid membrane that cannot be penetrated by hydrophilic ligands such as hormones and growth factors, integral membrane proteins (receptors) in the cell membrane are essential. They bind the ligand

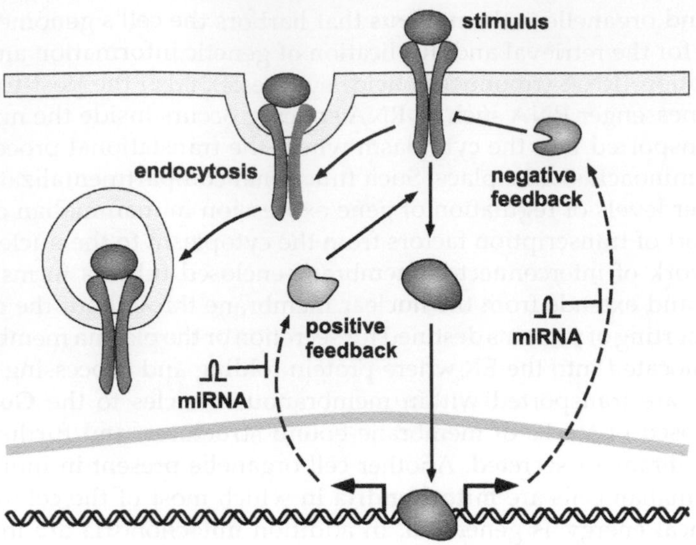

FIGURE 4.3 Concepts of signal transduction. Extracellular ligands bind to and activate cell surface receptors. This induces intracellular signaling events, often resulting in changes in gene expression. Positive or negative feedback regulators are expressed, modulating the signaling dynamics. miRNA have been reported to affect the translation of these feedback proteins, adding another layer of control. In addition, signal attenuation can be induced by endocytosis, leading to a depletion of receptor or ligand.

in the extracellular space and mediate signal transmission into the cell interior by activating specific signaling cascades. Finally, the signal is transported across the nuclear membrane and gene expression is modulated (Figure 4.3). Alternatively, hydrophobic ligands such as steroid hormones or thyroxine are transported by carrier proteins and diffuse after dissociation from the carrier into the cytosol or nucleus where they bind to specific receptors that regulate transcription of target genes.

The principal modes that are used for intracellular communication are: phosphorylation, second messengers, degradation, and complex formation.

2.2.1 *Phosphorylation*

In order to convey an intracellular signal, introduced modifications have to be transient. The most general regulatory device adopted by eukaryotic cells is protein phosphorylation since it is simple, reversible and ATP is readily available as phosphoryl donor. The key enzymes for protein phosphorylation are protein kinases that transfer a phosphoryl group from ATP to the hydroxyl group of tyrosine, serine, or threonine residues in target proteins whereas protein phosphatases counter-balance the reaction by removing phosphate groups from proteins. Reversible phosphorylation of proteins regulates nearly every aspect of cell life by increasing or decreasing the biological activity of enzymes, stabilizing or marking proteins for destruction, facilitating or inhibiting movements between subcellular compartments and initiating or disrupting protein-protein interaction. Abnormal phosphorylation is the cause or the consequence of many human diseases.

Protein kinases possess a highly conserved overall structure (Huse 2002) and operate as molecular switches: the "on"-state which represents maximal activity is highly similar in different protein kinases, whereas in the "off"-state kinases have minimal activity and adopt a conformation that is distinct for different protein kinase classes. The transition between the two states is highly regulated by phosphorylation, interaction with additional domains and/or binding of regulatory proteins.

This tight regulatory mechanism was first identified in cytoplasmic **tyrosine protein kinases** of the Src-family (Harrison 2003) that, in addition to the protein kinase domain, possess a Src-homology (SH)2 domain facilitating binding to specific phosphotyrosine residues localized within certain binding motifs and a SH3 domain mediating binding to proline rich motifs. Besides cytoplasmic tyrosine kinases several cell surface receptors possess a tyrosine kinase domain in their cytoplasmic part.

Phosphorylation on serine or threonine residues occurs much more frequently than tyrosine phosphorylation but is less inducible. The overall structure of **serine/threonine protein kinases** is very similar to tyrosine protein kinases but the regulation is mediated by additional subunits that bind second messengers or vary in their expression level (Johnson and Owen 1996). Another mode of regulation is achieved by phosphorylation or dephosphorylation on multiple residues. For example cell cycle control is performed by protein serine/threonine kinases of the cyclin-dependent kinase family that are inactive as monomers but activated by cyclin binding. Regulation of the cell cycle is achieved by synthesis and destruction of cyclines, phosphorylation of the activation loop and the ATP binding loop in the cyclin-dependent kinases and binding of an inhibitor. Counterintuitive is the regulation of the protein serine/threonine kinase glycogen synthase kinase 3 (GSK-3) that lies at the cross road of metabolism and signal transduction (Dajani et al. 2001). GSK-3 is active as kinase in the absence of signal and processively phosphorylates substrates at multiple residues that are already prephosphorylated at a C-terminal residue. Upon growth factor binding to cell surface receptors GSK-3 is phosphorylated at the N-terminus, which turns the N-terminus into a pseudosubstrate and thereby blocks the catalytic cleft of the kinase. The mitogen-activated protein (MAP) kinases form a signaling cascade consisting of an array of protein kinases (Raman 2003). These protein kinases are characterized by their ability to use protein kinases as substrate and phosphorylate them at two residues, which is required for full activation.

2.2.2 Complex formation

To ensure intracellular communication, **modular interaction domains** have evolved that recognize transient modifications (Pawson 2004). These domains fold independently, are incorporated in larger polypeptides and recognize exposed sites on their protein or lipid partners. The first modular interaction domain discovered was the SH2 domain in the N-terminus of the cytoplasmic tyrosine kinase Src. This domain comprises a block of 100 amino acids and recognizes phophotyrosine residues in conjunction with a C-terminally localized short recognition motif. Closely related is the phosphotyrosine-binding (PTB) domain that recognizes phosphotyrosine residues localized with an N-terminal NPXY motif. Less frequent are domains that specifically recognize phosphoserine/threonine residues. Best characterized are the 14.3.3 proteins that are highly abundant dimeric proteins binding phosphoserine within RXXpSXP motifs. The phosphorylation of phosphoinositides in the cellular membrane at the D3 position is recognized by pleckstrin homology domains and thereby mediates translocation of signaling proteins to the cellular membrane. Direct protein-protein interaction is mediated by several modular interaction domains such as SH3 domain that recognizes PXXP motifs. Other examples are the WW-domain that interacts with PPXY motifs and the PDZ domain that binds to ES/TDV motifs. A class of signaling molecules that is entirely composed of modular interaction domains and lack enzymatic activity are adaptor proteins or scaffolds.

2.2.3 *Proteolytic cleavage and degradation*

A common mechanism to regulate the activity of enzymes is mediated by **proteolytic cleavage** that ensures processing of hormones from larger precursor proteins, mediates activation of enzymes involved in blood coagulation or digestion or in programmed cell death. The ultimate effectors and executors of programmed cell death are caspases, a family of proteases characterized by a cysteine in the active site that cleave after an aspartic acid residue in their substrate. A large transmembrane protein that controls cell fate during development is notch. Ligand-binding is mediated by cell-cell contact and results in proteolytic cleavage of notch and translocation of the cytoplasmic domain into the nucleus.

The activity of proteins is not only controlled by synthesis and processing, but also by the rate of **degradation** that determines the life span of intracellular proteins. Whereas membrane proteins or aged organelles are primarily degraded within lysosomes, the degradation of cytosolic proteins is mediated by chemical modification of lysine residues by the addition of **ubiquitin**, a 76-residue polypeptide (Bonifacino and Weissman 1989). The process involves three consecutive steps: an ubiquitin-activating enzyme (E1) is activated by the addition of ubiquitin, ubiquitin is transferred to a cysteine residue in the ubiquitin-conjugating enzyme (E2). Finally, the peptide bond formation between ubiquitin and lysine in the target protein is catalyzed by a ubiquitin ligase (E3). These steps are repeated multiple times resulting in the formation of polyubiquitinated proteins that are recognized by the **proteasome** machinery and cleaved into short peptides.

2.2.4 *Second messenger*

Binding of ligands (first messengers) results frequently in the production of short-lived, small molecules (**second messengers**). The first identified second messenger was cyclic AMP (cAMP) that regulates the activity of protein kinase A. The binding of cAMP to the regulatory subunit results in the dissociation of the inactive tetramer and activation of the catalytic subunit. Since the binding is positively cooperative, small changes in cAMP concentration are translated into large changes of protein kinase A activity. Similarly cyclic GMP (cGMP) regulates the activity of protein kinase G and opening of rod channels. Lipid derived second messengers are diacylglycerol (DAG) that contributes to the activation of protein kinase C and inositol-1,4,5-trisphosphate (IP_3) that triggers opening of Ca^{2+} channels in the endoplasmic reticulum. The release of Ca^{2+}, another second messenger, into the cytosol facilitates binding of protein kinase C to the cell membrane and activation by DAG. Phosphoinositides phosphorylated at the D-3 position of the inositol ring structure are not cleaved but remain imbedded in the cell membrane and act as second messengers.

2.2.5 MicroRNA

Besides proteins and lipids, microRNAs act as modulators of signal transduction (Ambros 2004). They are a family of 21-25-nucleotide small non-coding RNAs produced as pri-miRNAs and processed in the nucleus by RNase III-type enzyme Drosha to form the pre-miRNAs. The pre-miRNAs translocate to the cytoplasm where they are further processed by RNase III-type enzyme Dicer into RNA duplex of 22 nucleotides, named mature miRNAs. Subsequently, the mature miRNAs bind to the complex miRISC followed by the degradation of one of the two RNA strands. The remaining RNA strand, namely miR, complexed with miRISC can bind the mRNA of the specific target gene. By repressing translation or direct degradation of the target mRNA, miRNAs can ultimately regulate gene expression in a sequence specific manner. In mammalian cells **microRNAs** are expressed in a developmentally regulated or tissue-specific manner and affect protein synthesis from their complementary target RNA. In the last years, evidences of miRNAs function in cancer were shown leading to the definition of oncogenic miRNAs, named oncomiRs (Cho 2007). An example of miRNAs involved in cancer is the mir-17-92 polycistron, which was shown to be upregulated in human B-cell lymphoma (He et al. 2005). Interestingly, the mir-17-92 cluster is located at an amplified genomic locus, the 13q13, suggesting that its upregulation is a consequence of the 13q13 amplification. Additionally, miRNAs were linked to liver disease development leading to hepatocellular carcinoma (Ura et al. 2009). miRNA expression profile was shown to differ between Hepatitis B and Hepatitis C virus related hepatocellular carcinoma progression. It has become clear that miRNAs play an important role in regulating cell functions; however the mechanism of action is still poorly understood due to the large number of putative target genes for each miRNA. Bioinformatic prediction of microRNA targets has been used to examine the function of microRNAs (Lewis et al. 2003; Rajewsky and Socci 2004) but these predictions remain to be experimentally validated.

2.3 Signaling pathways—formation of networks

2.3.1 Cell surface receptors

Receptor tyrosine kinases (Figure 4.4a) such as the epidermal growth factor receptor (EGF-R) (Schlessinger 2002) or the platelet derived growth factor receptor (PDGF-R) (Heldin 1992) are characterized by specific domains within the extracellular portion that interact with the ligand, a single transmembrane domain and a tyrosine kinase domain in part exposed to the cell interior. The tyrosine kinase activity is tightly regulated by multiple autoinhibitory mechanisms including an inhibitory conformation of the extracellular domain, the transmembrane domain, the juxtamembrane domain, and the activation loop. Ligand binding to the extracellular domain causes a conformational switch that leads to the activation of the tyrosine kinase domain.

Other cell surface receptors such as the hematopoietic **cytokine receptors** including the interleukin receptors lack enzymatic activity (D'Andrea and Fasman 1989) but couple with cytoplasmic tyrosine kinases of the Janus kinase family. Ligand binding to the cytokine receptors causes activation of the receptor-associated Janus kinase and results in tyrosine phosphorylation of the receptor on multiple tyrosine residues.

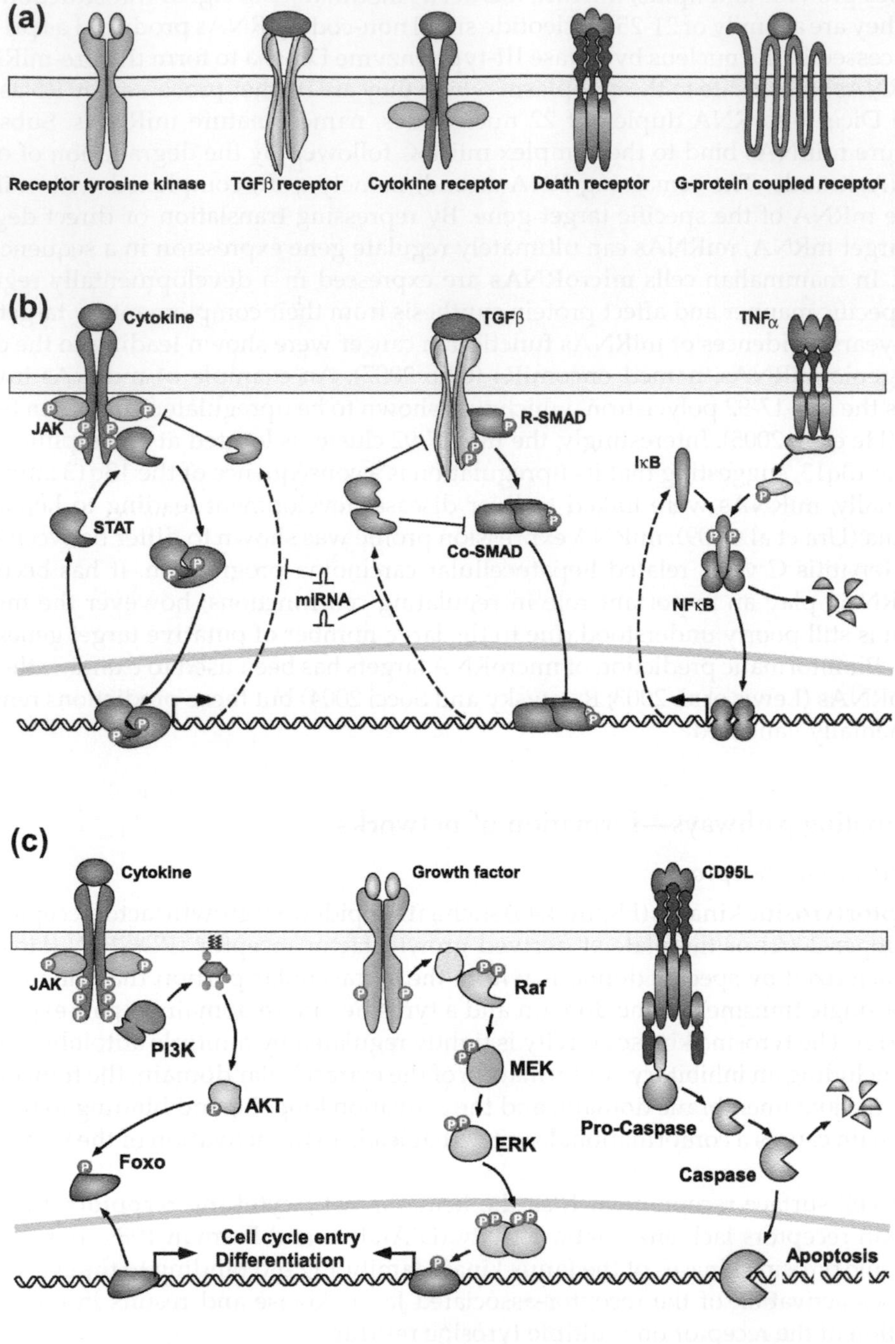
(a)
Receptor tyrosine kinase
TGFβ receptor
Cytokine receptor
Death receptor
G-protein coupled receptor
(b)
Cytokine
JAK
STAT
TGFβ
R-SMAD
Co-SMAD
miRNA
TNFα
IκB
NFκB
(c)
Cytokine
JAK
PI3K
AKT
Foxo
Growth factor
Raf
MEK
ERK
CD95L
Pro-Caspase
Caspase
Cell cycle entry
Differentiation
Apoptosis

◀ FIGURE 4.4 Signal transduction pathways in mammalian cells. (a) Examples of typical cell surface receptors. Ligand biding induces a conformational change in these receptors, transmitting the signal from the medium to the inside of the cell. (b) Feedback regulation in intracellular signaling. Latent transcription factors such as STAT, SMAD, or NFκB proteins are located in the cytoplasm in the absence of stimulation. Upon ligand binding, the STAT proteins dimerize, the SMAD family members form trimers, and the inhibitory protein IκB is phosphorylated and degraded. This allows translocation of the latent transcription factors into the nucleus and expression of target genes. Some of these genes encode negative feedback protein, leading to signal termination. miRNAs often play a role in modulation of the mRNA level of those negative feedback genes. (c) Cell fate decisions initiated by signaling pathways. Cytokine receptors as well as receptor tyrosine kinases often induce the phosphoinosited-3-kinase (PI3K) and the mitogen-activated protein kinase (MAPK) pathway. The regulatory subunit of PI3K p85 is recruited to the tyrosine phosphorylated receptor. The catalytic subunit of PI3K p110 phosphorylates phosphoinositides at the D-3 position. The product is recognized by the pleckstrin homology domain of the protein serine/threonine kinases Akt/protein kinase B and phosphoinositide-dependent kinase (PDK1), and PDK1 phosphorylates Akt resulting in full activation of Akt. Akt phosphorylates repressing transcription factors of the Foxo family, which leads to anchoring of the Foxo proteins in the cytoplasm and therefore gene expression. Activation of the MAPK cascade is initiated by recruitment of the growth factor receptor (Grb)2 associated protein to the tyrosine phosphorylated receptor. This promotes cell membrane recruitment of son-of-sevenless (SOS) guanine exchange factor, activation of Ras in the GTP bound form and membrane translocation as well as activation of the serine/threonine kinase Raf. Raf triggers phopshorylation of MEK on two serine residues and activated MEK phosphorylates the extracellular signal regulated kinase (ERK) on a tyrosine and a threonine residue. The phosphorylated ERK dimerizes, translocates to the nucleus and phosphorylates for example the transcription factor ELK which modifies the DNA binding activity of ELK. PI3 K and MAPK signaling induce cell cycle entry and differentiation in a cell-type specific manner. Binding of CD95L to death receptors induces the cleavage of pro-caspases, leading to their activation. This triggers the activation of a cascade proteinases, resulting in digestion of proteins and the cellular DNA, a process termed apoptosis. White (P) on orange indicate tyrosine phosphorylation, white (P) on green indicate serine/threonine phosphorylation.

Contrary to receptor tyrosine kinases, only one receptor serine/threonine kinase family is known (Shi and Harrison 2003). The **transforming growth factor beta (TGFβ) receptors** type I and II possess serine/threonine kinase activity in their cytoplasmic domain, which is regulated by autophosphorylation and inhibitor binding. **Death receptors** belong to the tumor necrosis factor receptor family and are trimeric cytokine receptors (Banner et al. 1993). Upon binding of ligands such as CD95L, the associated adaptor proteins determine the cellular response, such as apoptosis, inflammation or cell survival.

The large family of **G-protein coupled receptors** (Rasmussen et al. 2007) are spanning the cell membrane seven times and are activated by a diverse array of ligands include odors, pheromones and neurotransmitters. Activated receptors induce cAMP signaling or the activation of an associated G-protein.

2.3.2 *Intracellular signaling*

Intracellular proteins form signaling cascades that use the described modes for communication in order to transmit signals from the cell surface to the nucleus (Figure 4.4b,c). A rather simple and fast signaling cascade is the **JAK-STAT pathway** (Figure 4.4b, left panel) that mediates signal transduction primarily through hematopoietic cytokine receptors, but also hepta-helix receptors and receptor tyrosine kinases (Rawlings and Harrison 2004). The key enzyme of this cascade is a member of the cytoplasmic protein tyrosine kinase family of the Janus type that harbors two protein kinase domains, one catalytically active and the other with regulatory functions. Upon activation the receptor-associated Janus kinase (JAK) is activated leading to tyrosine phosphorylation of the receptor cytoplasmic domain. This mediates recruitment of signal transducer and activator of transcription (STAT) proteins to specific phosphotyrosine residues in the receptor via their SH2 domain. Then tyrosine phosphorylation of STATs occurs facilitating STAT dimerization. STAT dimers depart from the receptor and migrate to the nucleus where target gene expression is activated. Upon dephosphorylation, STATs recycle to the cytoplasm and engage in further activation cycles. Thus, by multiple consecutive activation cycles the phosphorylation level of the receptor is constantly monitored and translated into appropriate levels of target gene expression. Among the induced genes are genes encoding suppressor of cytokine signaling (SOCS) proteins that inhibit signaling through hematopoietic cytokine receptors and thereby constitute a negative feedback loop that ensures tight regulation of the JAK-STAT pathway. SOCS family members have been reported to be targets of miRNAs.

Another signaling cascade that operates very similarly is the **SMAD signaling pathway** (Figure 4.4b, middle panel) that is activated by TGFβ receptors type II and type I possessing protein serine/threonine kinase activity (Shi and Harrison 2003). Ligand binding is facilitated by the type III TGFβ receptor, a proteoglycane lacking enzymatic activity, that delivers the ligand to the type II and type I receptors. Upon oligomerization the type II receptor phosphorylates the type I receptor at the glycine/serine (GS) motif located in the juxtamembrane domain. This leads to the activation of the serine/threonine kinase activity of the type I receptor and consequently to receptor recruitment of the receptor (R) SMAD-3 and -2. The R-SMADS are serine-phosphorylated, depart from the receptor, form a trimeric complex with the common SMAD-4, translocate to the nucleus where they bind to nuclear transcription factors and activate target gene transcription including the negative regulatory SMAD7. SMAD7 has a higher affinity to the activated type I receptor and thereby displaces the R-SMADs resulting in down-modulation of the pathway. Additional regulation is ensured by the transcriptional repressors SnoN and SKI that bind to SMADs in the nucleus and form an inhibitory complex. Like in the JAK-STAT signaling cascade, negative regulators have been reported to be targeted by miRNAs.

The **NFκB signaling pathway** (Figure 4.4b, right panel) combines signal transduction through phosphorylation with complex formation and selective degradation. In the absence of signaling NFκB is sequestered by the inhibitory subunit IκB in the cytoplasm (Chung et al. 2002). Upon the activation of signal transduction through the TNF receptor 2/interleukin-1 receptor family (trimeric receptors lacking endogenous enzymatic activity connecting to trimeric TNF receptor-associated factor (TRAF)) the IκB kinase is activated and phosphorylates IκB on serine residues thereby marking the inhibitory subunit for destruction through proteasomal degradation. NFκB is released, migrates to the nucleus and activates target gene transcription.

Several signaling pathways use phosphoinositides as mediators and phosphoinositide-4,5-bisphosphate is the common precursor that is used. As part of the **canonical inositol triphosphate (IP_3) signaling cascade**, the activation of several receptors leads to phospholipase C activation resulting in cleavage of phosphoinositide-4,5-bisphosphate to DAG and IP_3. IP_3 diffuses through the cytoplasm and triggers opening of Ca^{2+} channels in the endoplasmic reticulum. The rise in cytosolic Ca^{2+} facilitates binding of protein kinase C to the membrane and activation of the protein kinase activity by DAG. In contrast the phosphoinositides modified by the **lipid kinase PI3K** (Figure 4.4c, left panel) are not cleaved and function as membrane embedded second messengers (Cantley 2002). Ligand induced receptor tyrosine phosphorylation mediates recruitment of PI3K via the SH2 domains of the regulatory subunit p85. This places the catalytic subunit p110 in proximity to substrates and results in the phosphorylation of phosphoinositide-4-phosphate and phosphoinositide-4,5-bisphosphate at the D-3 position of the inositol ring. Phosphoinositide-3,4,-bisphosphate and phosphoinositide-3,4,5,-triphosphate are recognized by the pleckstrin homology domain of two cytosolic serine/threonine kinases, the phosphoinositide-dependent kinase (PDK)1 and Akt/protein kinase B. PDK1 has a low basal activity and is fully activated by engagement of the PH domain, at the cell membrane. Mediated by the PH domain Akt is translocated to the cell membrane and requires phosphorylation by PDK1 for full activation. Multiple downstream targets have been identified for both kinases including factors involved in protein synthesis, cell survival, and metabolism.

The **MAP kinase (Raf-MEK-ERK) cascade** (Figure 4.4c, middle panel) is formed by the consecutive activation of three protein kinases (Raman 2003). The MAP kinase kinase kinase Raf is represented by three isoforms, Raf-1, B-Raf, and A-Raf, that are regulated by various inhibitory and activating phosphorylation events and phosphorylate MAP kinase kinase (MEK) at two serine residues. MEK is a dual specificity protein kinase and phosphorylates MAP kinase (ERK1 and ERK2) at a tyrosine and a threonine residue within the YPT motif which in turn activates the MAP kinases ERK1 and ERK2. The activated MAP kinases dimerize and translocate to the nucleus where they phosphorylate transcription factors such as

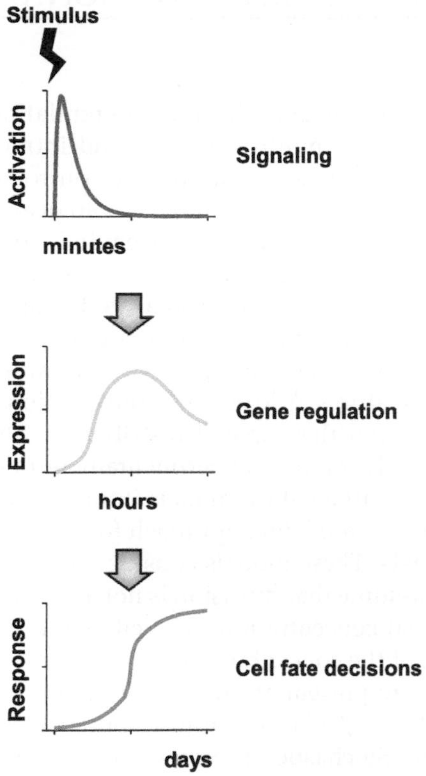

FIGURE 4.5 Time scales in cellular information processing. A stimulus with a ligand often results in fast changes in intracellular protein modifications that are detectable after a few minutes. These pathways induce gene expression, on a somewhat longer timescale ranging from minutes to hours. These genes trigger cell fate decisions that become manifest after hours or days.

ELK-1. The kinase cascade is organized by scaffold proteins and at multiple levels negative feedback loops ensure regulated activation.

Caspase apoptosis pathways are activated by binding of molecules such as CD95L to death receptors that can promote programmed cell death (apoptosis). Ligand-induced receptor trimerization facilitates the assembly of a death inducing signaling complex (DISC) leading to caspase 8 recruitment and activation. Caspase 8 is an initiator caspase that activates other caspases and thereby promotes signal amplification through the cascade.

The described signaling pathways do not operate in isolation but form complex signaling networks that regulate biological functions in a context-specific manner. These complex cellular networks integrate different signals by cellular information processing on distinct time scales. While signaling happens rather fast, target gene regulation requires several minutes to hours, while the resulting cell fate decisions become apparent after hours to days (Figure 4.5). Due to the complexity of biological responses a deeper understanding cannot be achieved by traditional approaches but requires the combination of experimental data with mathematical modeling (Schneider et al. 2012).

3 MATHEMATICAL MODELING OF SIGNALING PATHWAYS

3.1 Modeling approaches

Biological processes, such as cell growth and differentiation, are highly complex and require the coordinate regulation of multiple stimuli and intracellular signaling pathways. In the physiological context these processes are tightly controlled while in the pathological situation they are deregulated. To understand how a biological system reacts in response to alterations, it is first necessary to understand the system in its physiological context.

Although traditionally intracellular signaling pathways have been considered as independent linear cascades and their activation has been analyzed qualitatively, they are highly interconnected and their key features are timing, amplitude, and duration of signal activation. Therefore to study the activation of signaling pathways, quantitative methods are required allowing the analysis of these features. Additionally, the reaction kinetics is dependent on the concentration of the reactants and their spatial distribution. Due to this complexity, these characteristics cannot be solely determined experimentally but need to be addressed by combining experimental data with mathematical models (Eungdamrong and Iyengar 2004).

The most frequently employed modeling approach for biological systems are **deterministic** kinetic mathematical models. These models consider concentration of molecules instead of individual molecules and assume that diffusion is not a limiting factor for the reaction. For deterministic models the initial concentrations as well as the rate constants are essential to predict the dynamic changes of the concentrations.

If some molecular species are present at low concentration or the process shows random fluctuations, also referred as "noise," like gene transcription or protein translations, a **stochastic** model approach is chosen. Stochastic processes can respond to stimuli by a switch-like behavior. A non-genetic cause of cell-to-cell variability is random fluctuations of gene transcription having an impact on protein concentration and ultimately on signal transduction. In a recent study (Meyer et al. 2012) addressing at the variability in the activation of signaling pathway observed at the single cell level, a deterministic model was calibrated based on experimental data and was combined with a stochastic model in order to simulate the observed variability. "Intrinsic noise" is defined as the variability derived from fluctuations intrinsic to the signaling pathway, as for example the stochastic fluctuations of the reaction rates. On the contrary, "extrinsic noise" refers to the variability in the signaling pathway, like protein concentration level, arising from factors that are extrinsic from the signaling pathway, as for example gene expression. By combining deterministic and stochastic modeling, the work shows that the major source of the observed cell-to-cell variability arises from extrinsic noise. Signaling networks are composed of a large number of interacting components and their representation is defined by **network models**. The molecular interactions can be extracted from literature data or by high-throughput approaches when considering large networks. Examples of network models are the **logic-based models**, where dependencies among the species are defined by logic gates, as the Boolean logic of OR, AND, and NOT. The Boolean logic considers molecules in on-off state; therefore detailed dynamics and information on the amplitude of the signal are missing. However, there are different logic-based model approaches allowing the analysis of intermediate activation states (Morris et al. 2010). For example, in order to understand the alterations of signaling pathways in the tumor context, data from primary human hepatocytes and human liver cancer cell lines treated with different stimuli were compared. A discrete logical model based on literature knowledge was generated to fit the data. By this approach the activation of the immediate-early signaling pathways deregulated in hepatocellular carcinoma (HCC) was provided (Saez-Rodriguez et al. 2011).

Different from network models of signaling pathway, the dynamics of metabolic models are based on **balance equations** considering the balance of production and degradation of a compound. The model can be used for stoichiometry analysis based on the ratio of the substrate and the product of a reaction. Furthermore, flux balance analysis can be performed allowing to determine the optimal flux distribution. To increase the quality of network models, it is important that the literature data on which the models are based on is manually curated. An example is the human liver metabolism model, named HepatoNet1, that is based on biochemical data generated in human hepatocytes (Gille et al. 2010).

Detailed mechanistic insights into regulatory mechanisms of signal transduction are addressed by **dynamic pathway models** based on coupled ordinary differential equations models (ODE-based models) in which the concentration is a function of time. The biological knowledge introduced in the previous paragraph is translated into ODE-based models. These models are characterized by many parameters and are calibrated with kinetic experimental data. Due to the requirement of a large number of quantitative data, ODE-based models initially represent the core of the signaling pathway and they are developed to describe all the measured species. Additionally, parameter estimation, as discussed in more details in the next paragraph, is a major challenge requiring the application of advanced numerical methods.

In signaling pathways several molecules shuttle from one cellular compartment to the other, therefore the spatial distribution plays an important role. ODE-based model can include **compartmentalization** to approximate the spatial organization of the molecules, while partial differential equations (PDEs) are applied for a precise temporal and spatial description. Models based on PDEs have a higher complexity compared to ODE-based models and parameter estimation is extremely difficult.

The intracellular response to stimulation can vary according to the mechanisms of activation that are introduced in paragraph II. Non-covalent interactions, such as complex formation mediated by protein-protein interaction, show a linear response relationship and can be described by the law of mass action. Several signaling pathways show dimer or oligomer formation, such as Smad proteins complexes functioning as transcriptional regulator. Alternatively, when the reaction reaches saturation it follows the Michaelis-Menten kinetic resulting in hyperbolic function, as in case of phosphorylation/dephosphorylation processes. A further behavior, as for example the regulation of enzymatic activity that results from allosteric regulation and allows an increased activity in response to binding of multiple ligands, is described by a sigmoidal response representing a switch-like behavior. A well-studied example for allosteric regulation and positive cooperativity is the binding of the second messenger cAMP to the inhibitory subunit of the serine/threonine protein kinase A permitting the activation of the protein kinase in response to small local changes in cAMP.

Alternatively, the existence of positive feedback loops in which a downstream component of a signaling pathway accelerates the activity of an upstream component can lead to sigmoidal response curves. Furthermore, negative feedback loops or a certain combination of negative and positive feedback loops within signaling pathways can result in oscillatory responses. For the NFκβ signaling cascade oscillation of the nuclear localization of NFκβ in dependence of the expression of the inhibitory signaling component IκB has been observed (Nelson et al. 2004).

By applying different approaches it is possible to represent biological systems by generating large network models and further characterize them by dynamic pathway models. The described examples consider the study at single cell or population level, but when considering the interaction between different cell types, as it occurs in a tissue, these modeling approaches need to be integrated into a modeling framework allowing the description of individual cell properties and the interaction with other cells. **Single-cell-based models** allow to describe single cells and their interactions, leading to three dimensional representation of a tissue. This model has been applied to reconstruct the liver tissue based on image processing and is able simulate liver regeneration upon damage (Hoehme et al. 2010).

3.2 Signaling pathways model: parameter estimation and ODE-model analysis

Mathematical models allow to perform *in silico* simulations and to establish different hypothesis that can be experimentally tested and consequently the model can be validated. In order to perform powerful predictions, the model parameters have to be estimated and analysis of the goodness of the model fit should be performed.

The dynamic pathway models are calibrated by estimating the **model parameters** based on experimental data. To evaluate the goodness of parameter estimation, as a result of model fit, the **likelihood function** is calculated. The likelihood is the probability that the estimated parameter set corresponds to the given data. Based on the likelihood function, parameter identifiability analysis can be performed (Raue et al. 2010). This method approximates the confidence region defined as the region in the parameter space where the estimated parameters lay with a certain probability. If parameters are functionally related, for example they are formalized as product of each other, they cannot be uniquely identified leading to **structural non-identifiability**. The structural non-identifiabilities arise from the model structure and can be solved by modifying it, by adding or reducing the number of described species and by measuring different species. If a model is structurally identifiable, some parameters can still show **practical non-identifiability** when experimental data is too noisy. In this case, the parameter values show infinite confidence region; therefore the parameter cannot be identified. Practical non-identifiability can be solved by increasing the number of measurements and by measuring different species.

An additional analysis, namely **sensitivity analysis**, can be performed to evaluate if parameters of the model are sensitive to changes. The sensitivity analysis observes how the model reacts by changing the parameter values.

Parameter estimation corresponds to find the minimal distance between the model simulation and the data points. This distance, named objective function, is quantified by the sum of squared residuals and consequently the minimum of the function represents the best solution. A **local minimum** is the value of the objective function for which no smaller values exists in the near parameter space. An optimization algorithm allows exploring part of the parameter space in order to find a (local) minimum. Modeling biological systems requires an iterative process between the modeling results and the generation of new experimental data needed to better define the model, as for example, in case of non-practical identifiability. During this process new hypotheses can be tested by generating new models. When the performance of two or more models is compared, selection criteria are required. For the comparison of two models the selection can be based on statistical tests applying the null hypothesis. Several models can be compared based on their likelihood representing the goodness of the fit. The comparison requires that the number of parameters is taken into account; therefore additional selection criteria are represented by the Akaike information criterion and Bayesian information criterion penalizing for the number of free parameters. These criteria can be applied to rank models but a standard procedure for model selection has still to be established.

To obtain an identifiable model a large number of data points and experimental conditions are required, therefore experimental methods facilitating the generation of quantitative data have been developed in the last years.

3.3 Challenges for performing kinetic measurements on large scale

Important biological knowledge can be generated by data-based mathematical models, but the establishment of models critically depends on the generation of **high quality quantitative data**. The techniques that have been successfully used for data-based mathematical modeling include: (1) **Quantitative immunoblotting** combines separation of proteins according to their molecular weight with detection by specific antibodies followed by chemiluminescence-detection (Swameye et al. 2003; Bentele et al. 2004). Additionally, by quantitative immunoblotting it is possible to calculate absolute numbers, such as molecules per cell; (2) **Electrophoretic mobility shift assay** (EMSA) that enables to measure the DNA-binding capacity of proteins by mixing protein extracts with radioactively labeled DNA-probes (Hoffmann et al. 2002) and (3) **Imaging** based on fluorescently labeled proteins allows to monitor protein activation kinetics at population level (Nelson et al. 2004).

In recent years multiple new high-throughput quantitative methods for protein measurement were established: (1) **Protein array** (or protein chip) is based on antibodies immobilized on solid surface serving as capture antibodies for the analysis of proteins of interest. It allows to analyze multiple proteins and samples simultaneously but a method for reliable signal normalization is still under development; (2) **Multiplex bead-based technology** is based on microscopic beads labeled with fluorescent dye that function as solid support for antibodies. This assay allows the simultaneous quantification of about 100 different analytical parameters in a single probe; (3) **Enzyme-Linked Immunosorbent Assay** (ELISA) is based on enzyme reaction between antigen and antibody and allows the quantification and comparison of proteins, antibodies, and hormones in different probes; (4) **Quantitative proteomics** based, for example, on stable isotope labeling by amino acids in cell culture (SILAC) is a powerful mass spectrometry method. It enables to compare different samples and the determination of protein abundances. Additionally, mass spectrometry can be used to measure with high accuracy the degree of phosphorylation of target proteins by using internal standards (Hahn et al. 2013); (5) **Cell-based microarray** is based on high-throughput transfection of cDNAs or siRNAs printed on a solid surface. This method was developed to study the perturbation of the function of gene in a systematic fashion (Wu et al. 2002), however to generate quantitative data mere overexpression or disruption of function is not sufficient, but precisely identifiable expression levels must be achieved; (6) **Single cell imaging** utilizing fluorescently labeled proteins functioning as markers for cell cycle progression or apoptosis, allowing to monitor the cellular response dynamics (Sakaue-Sawano et al. 2008). Several imaging methods are applied to measure protein diffusion, protein-protein interaction, and protein activation kinetics (Spiller et al. 2010).

Systems biology is characterized by iterative cycles of experiments and modeling; consequently there is the need of data exchange between experimentalists and modelers fostering the development of databases. Additionally, these databases are extremely important since they collect all available information on a specific cell type or disease.

4 CONCLUSION

Biological systems are highly complex and the integration of experimental data with mathematical modeling is essential to unravel the underlined regulatory mechanisms. Mathematical models are calibrated on highly accurate quantitative experimental data of protein concentration, dynamic protein activation, and localization. Models are subjected to a detailed analysis, such as the identifiability analysis, in order to define if they require additional calibration on experimental data or if their structure has to be modified. Iterative cycles of model adjustments and experimental validation are required to obtain identifiable models. These models can be used to perform simulations by testing different scenario requiring subsequent experimental validation. The resulting models can be applied to explore biological conditions that cannot be addressed experimentally. To generate informative mathematical models of signaling pathways, the knowledge of the involved biochemical reactions, the concentration of the components and possibly their subcellular organization are critical. The generated data needs to be quantitative and highly accurate; therefore new methods for multiplexed protein measurements have been developed. In addition, it is important to establish quality standards for the experimental data used for parameter estimation. This will be facilitated by the development of standard operating procedures for the techniques used for data acquisition and the data-processing procedure.

The advancement in theoretical tools and quantitative techniques will determine whether systems biology will be able to fulfill the promise to decipher mechanism leading to diseases and to enhance the identification of efficient therapeutical targets.

References

Ambros, V. (2004). The functions of animal microRNAs. *Nature* **431**(7006):350–355.

Banner, D. W., D'Arcy, A., Janes, W., Gentz, R., Schoenfeld, H. J., Broger, C., Loetscher, H., and Lesslauer, W. (1993). Crystal structure of the soluble human 55 kd TNF receptor-human TNF beta complex: implications for TNF receptor activation. *Cell* **73**:431–445.

Bentele, M., Lavrik, I., Ulrich, M., Stosser, S., Heermann, D. W., Kalthoff, H., Krammer, P. H., and Eils, R. (2004). Mathematical modeling reveals threshold mechanism in CD95-induced apoptosis. *J Cell Biol.* **166**:839–851.

Bhalla, U. S., and Iyengar, R. (1999). Emergent properties of networks of biological signaling pathways. *Science* **283**:381–387.

Bonifacino, J. S., and Weissman, A. M. (1989). Ubiquitin and the control of protein fate in the secretory and endocytic pathways. *Annu. Rev. Cell Dev. Biol.* **14**:418–428.

Cantley, L. C. (2002). The phosphoinositide 3-kinase pathway. *Science* **296**(5573):1655–1657.

Cho, W. C. (2007). OncomiRs: the discovery and progress of microRNAs in cancers. *Mol. Cancer* **6**:60.

Chung, J. Y., Park, Y. C., Ye, H., and Wu, H. (2002). All TRAFs are not created equal: common and distinct molecular mechanisms of TRAF-mediated signal transduction. *J Cell Sci.* **115**(Pt 4):679–688.

Dajani, R., Fraser, E., Roe, S. M., Young, N., Good, V., Dale, T. C., and Pearl, L. H. (2001). Crystal structure of glycogen synthase kinase 3 beta: structural basis for phosphate-primed substrate specificity and autoinhibition. *Cell. Cell.* 721–723.

D'Andrea, A. D., Fasman, G. D., and Lodish, H. F. (1989). Erythropoietin receptor and interleukin-2 receptor beta chain: a new receptor family. *Cell* **58**(6):1023–1024.

Eungdamrong, N. J., and Iyengar, R. (2004). Computational approaches for modeling regulatory cellular networks. *Trends Cell Biol.* **14**:661–669.

Fussenegger, M., Bailey, J. E., and Varner, J. (2000). A mathematical model of caspase function in apoptosis. *Nat. Biotechnol.* **18**:768–774.

Gille, C., Bolling, C., Hoppe, A., Bulik, S., Hoffmann, S., Hubner, K., Karlstadt, A., Ganeshan, R., Konig, M., Rother, K., Weidlich, M., Behre, J., and Holzhutter, H. G. (2010). HepatoNet1: a comprehensive metabolic reconstruction of the human hepatocyte for the analysis of liver physiology. *Mol. Syst. Biol.* **6**:411.

Hahn, B., D'Alessandro, L. A., Depner, S., Waldow, K., Boehm, M. E., Bachmann, J., Schilling, M., Klingmuller, U., and Lehmann, W. D. (2013). Cellular ERK phospho-form profiles with conserved preference for a switch-like pattern. *J. Proteome. Res.* **12**:637–646.

Harrison, S. C. (2003). Variation on an Src-like theme. *Cell* **112**(6):737–740.

He, L., Thomson, J. M., Hemann, M. T., Hernando-Monge, E., Mu, D., Goodson, S., Powers, S., Cordon-Cardo, C., Lowe, S. W., Hannon, G. J., and Hammond, S. M. (2005). A microRNA polycistron as a potential human oncogene. *Nature* **435**:828–833.

Heldin, C. H. (1992). Structural and functional studies on platelet-derived growth factor. *EMBO J.* **11**(12):4251–4259.

Hoehme, S., Brulport, M., Bauer, A., Bedawy, E., Schormann, W., Hermes, M., Puppe, V., Gebhardt, R., Zellmer, S., Schwarz, M., Bockamp, E., Timmel, T., Hengstler, J. G., and Drasdo, D. (2010). Prediction and validation of cell alignment along microvessels as order principle to restore tissue architecture in liver regeneration. *Proc. Natl. Acad. Sci. USA* **107**:10371–10376.

Hoffmann, A., Levchenko, A., Scott, M. L., and Baltimore, D. (2002). The IkappaB-NF-kappaB signaling module: temporal control and selective gene activation. *Science* **298**:1241–1245.

Hunter, T., and Sefton, B. M. (1980). Transforming gene product of Rous sarcoma virus phosphorylates tyrosine. *Proc. Natl. Acad. Sci. USA* **77**(3):1311–1315. Related Articles, Links.

Huse, M. K. J. (2002). The conformational plasticity of protein kinases. *Cell* **109**(3):275–282.

Johnson, L. N., Noble, M. E., and Owen, D. J. (1996). Active and inactive protein kinases: structural basis for regulation. *Cell* **85**(2):149–158.

Kitano, H. (2002). Computational systems biology. *Nature* **420**:206–210.

Lewis, B. P., Shih, I. H., Jones-Rhoades, M. W., Bartel, D. P., and Burge, C. B. (2003). Prediction of mammalian microRNA targets. *Cell* **115**:787–798.

Meyer, R., D'Alessandro, L. A., Kar, S., Kramer, B., She, B., Kaschek, D., Hahn, B., Wrangborg, D., Karlsson, J., Kvarnstrom, M., Jirstrand, M., Lehmann, W. D., Timmer, J., Hofer, T., and Klingmuller, U. (2012). Heterogeneous kinetics of AKT signaling in individual cells are accounted for by variable protein concentration. *Front Physiol.* **3**:451.

Morris, M. K., Saez-Rodriguez, J., Sorger, P. K., and Lauffenburger, D. A. (2010). Logic-based models for the analysis of cell signaling networks. *Biochemistry* **49**:3216–3224.

Nelson, D. E., Ihekwaba, A. E., Elliott, M., Johnson, J. R., Gibney, C. A., Foreman, B. E., Nelson, G., See, V., Horton, C. A., Spiller, D. G., Edwards, S. W., McDowell, H. P., Unitt, J. F., Sullivan, E., Grimley, R., Benson, N., Broomhead, D., Kell, D. B., and White, M. R. (2004). Oscillations in NF-kappaB signaling control the dynamics of gene expression. *Science* **306**:704–708.

Pawson, T. (2004). Specificity in signal transduction: from phosphotyrosine-SH2 domain interactions to complex cellular systems. *Cell* **116**(2):191–203.

Rajewsky, N., and Socci, N. D. (2004). Computational identification of microRNA targets. *Dev. Biol.* **267**:529–535.

Raman, M. C., and Cobb, M. H. (2003). MAP kinase modules: many roads home. *Curr. Biol.* **13**(22):886–888.

Rasmussen, S. G., Choi, H. J., Rosenbaum, D. M., Kobilka, T. S., Thian, F. S., Edwards, P. C., Burghammer, M., Ratnala, V. R., Sanishvili, R., Fischetti, R. F., Schertler, G. F., Weis, W. I., and Kobilka, B. K. (2007). Crystal structure of the human beta2 adrenergic G-protein-coupled receptor. *Nature* **450**:383–387.

Raue, A., Becker, V., Klingmuller, U., and Timmer, J. (2010). Identifiability and observability analysis for experimental design in nonlinear dynamical models. *Chaos* **20**:045105.

Rawlings, J. S. R. K., and Harrison, D. A. (2004). The JAK/STAT signaling pathway. *J Cell Sci.* **117**(Pt 8):1281–1283.

Saez-Rodriguez, J., Alexopoulos, L. G., Zhang, M., Morris, M. K., Lauffenburger, D. A., and Sorger, P. K. (2011). Comparing signaling networks between normal and transformed hepatocytes using discrete logical models. *Cancer Res.* **71**:5400–5411.

Sakaue-Sawano, A., Kurokawa, H., Morimura, T., Hanyu, A., Hama, H., Osawa, H., Kashiwagi, S., Fukami, K., Miyata, T., Miyoshi, H., Imamura, T., Ogawa, M., Masai, H., and Miyawaki, A. (2008). Visualizing spatiotemporal dynamics of multicellular cell-cycle progression. *Cell* **132**:487–498.

Schlessinger, J. (2002). Ligand-induced, receptor-mediated dimerization and activation of EGF receptor. *Cell* **110**(6):669–672.

Schneider, A., Klingmuller, U., and Schilling, M. (2012). Short-term information processing, long-term responses: Insights by mathematical modeling of signal transduction. Early activation dynamics of key signaling mediators can be predictive for cell fate decisions. *Bioessays* **34**:542–550.

Shi, Y., and Massagué, J. (2003). Mechanisms of TGF-beta signaling from cell membrane to the nucleus. *Cell* **113**(6):685–700.

Spiller, D. G., Wood, C. D., Rand, D. A., and White, M. R. (2010). Measurement of single-cell dynamics. *Nature* **465**:736–745.

Swameye, I., Muller, T. G., Timmer, J., Sandra, O., and Klingmuller, U. (2003). Identification of nucleocytoplasmic cycling as a remote sensor in cellular signaling by databased modeling. *Proc. Natl. Acad. Sci. USA* **100**:1028–1033.

Ura, S., Honda, M., Yamashita, T., Ueda, T., Takatori, H., Nishino, R., Sunakozaka, H., Sakai, Y., Horimoto, K., and Kaneko, S. (2009). Differential microRNA expression between hepatitis B and hepatitis C leading disease progression to hepatocellular carcinoma. *Hepatology* **49**:1098–1112.

Wu, R. Z., Bailey, S. N., and Sabatini, D. M. (2002). Cell-biological applications of transfected-cell microarrays. *Trends Cell. Biol.* **12**:485–488.

CHAPTER

5

Complexities in Quantitative Systems Analysis of Signaling Networks

Christina Kiel[a,b], *Luis Serrano*[a,b,c]

[a]EMBL/CRG Systems Biology Research Unit, Centre for Genomic Regulation (CRG), Barcelona, Spain

[b]Universitat Pompeu Fabra (UPF), Barcelona, Spain

[c]ICREA, Barcelona, Spain

CONTENTS

Abstract

This chapter brings mammalian signal transduction to the center of quantitative and integrative sciences. Historically imbedded within human physiology, thanks to proteomics, interactomics, and molecular biology approaches, signaling is now far beyond the "black box" principle. However, despite the large amount of data available, we still have only limited insight into general design principles, and we lack knowledge on how cell

http://dx.doi.org/10.1016/B978-0-12-405926-9.00005-8

type-specific signaling is achieved. Here, we summarize recent efforts in elucidating cell type-specific signaling, and in particular the role of protein abundances, signaling complexes and modules. We further discuss the potential of using synthetic biology approaches to decipher signaling networks. All of this is discussed in light of complementary quantitative mathematical modeling approaches. Signaling, more than any other discipline, needs computational biology to capture the dynamic systems behavior, and to reach its final goal: to be truly predictive for both the physiological and disease perturbed cellular conditions.

1 INTRODUCTION

The exploration of mammalian cellular signal transduction dates back to the 19th century as a field of study within human physiology, in particular with the appearance of the "Cell theory," which proposed cells as the smallest units of an organism (Turner 1890). Physiology has provided a profound understanding of how ligands and receptors control responses in a given tissue or cell type. For example, today the physiological roles of epidermal growth factor receptor signaling are relatively well understood (Sibilia et al. 2007). However, physiological studies usually viewed intracellular signaling cascades as a "black box," or with only a few components, their modulation, and their arrangement into linear pathways depicted (Figure 5.1). This is for a large part due to the difficulty of studying normal physiology on a molecular level, as primary cells from human or animal tissues are difficult to obtain, laborious and troublesome in culturing, and they often lose their physiological character when cultured outside the natural organ and organism.

In parallel to the discipline of physiology, structural biology, molecular biology, imaging, and "omics" approaches have contributed to cellular signal transduction. The past and present ongoing efforts from the above-mentioned disciplines aimed/aim to go beyond the "black box" principle, to identify components, crosstalk, and to elucidate general signaling design principles. The ambitious collective goal of this struggle is the generation of quantitative predictive models that capture the dynamics of cell signaling responses. While these efforts led to the identification of general cellular design principles, such as modularity (Hartwell et al. 1999) and robustness (Kitano 2002; Stelling et al. 2004), scientists, especially physiologists, became puzzled by the many interactions that are by now described ("Are we crosstalking ourselves into general confusion?" (Dumont et al. 2001)). Considering that the above-described approaches profoundly rely on model systems, such as cell lines or reconstituted systems, which lose their physiological relevance with increasing simplification, the physiological relevance of many of the described interactions was questioned (Dumont et al. 2001). In fact, the concept of "everything does everything to everything" represents a paradox to the known specificity of signal responses in a particular cell type (Dumont et al. 2001). Cell type-specific signaling has since then caught attention. It is now viewed that despite the apparent complexity and crosstalk in signal transduction cascades as reported in the literature, not all possible signaling routes are taken in a given cell type, and that different cell types can exhibit very specific responses to the same signal. Mechanisms explaining some of the specificity of signaling outputs include scaffolds, localized signaling of proteins in cell compartments, protein abundances and competing interactions, and alternative splicing (reviewed in Kholodenko et al. (2010), Kiel and Serrano (2012)).

Signaling—more than any other scientific discipline—needs mathematical modeling tools. Fortunately, we are now approaching an era where "omics" approaches can provide quantitative data on a large scale. Thus, together with computational systems biology, signaling is

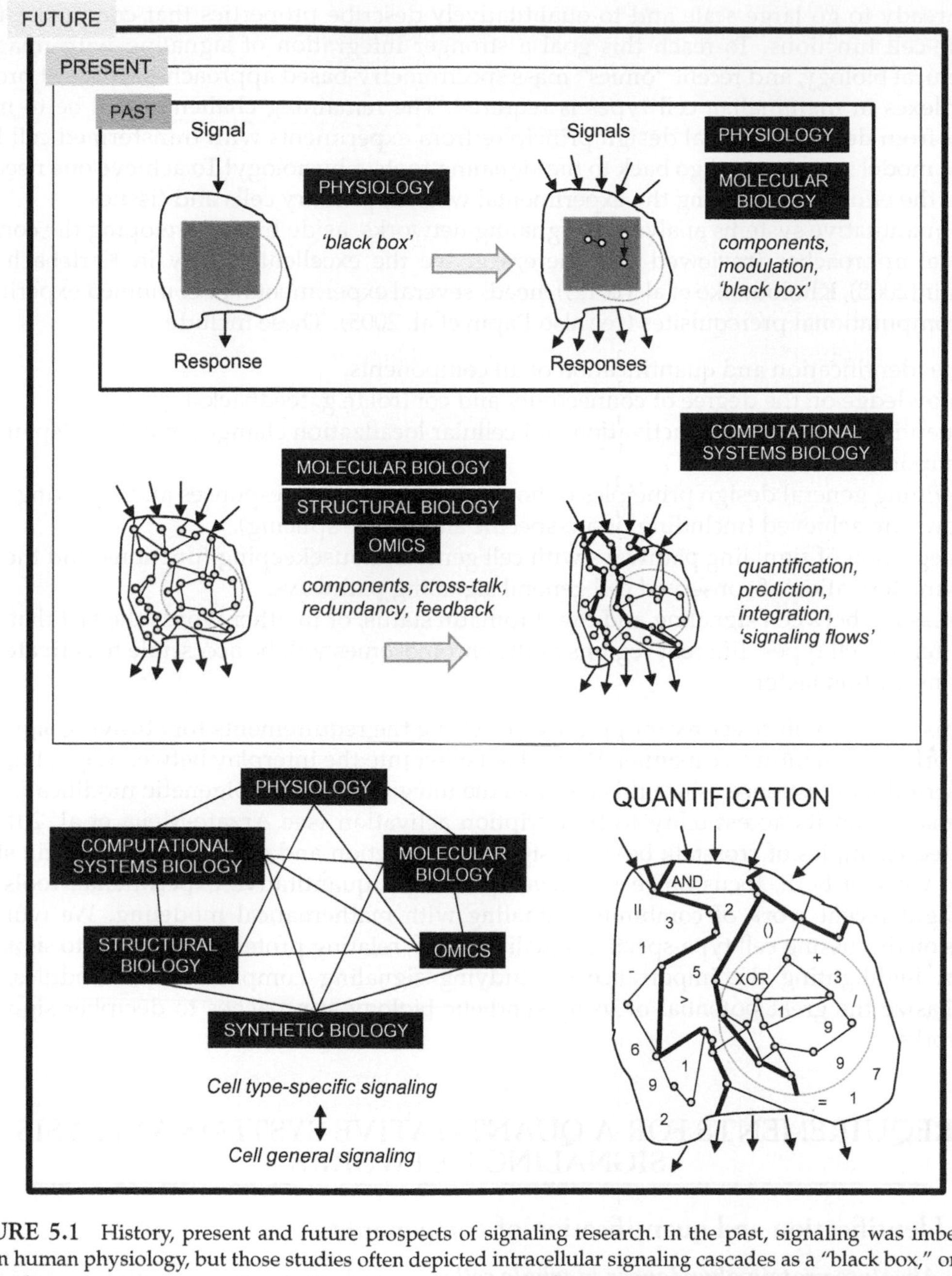

FIGURE 5.1 History, present and future prospects of signaling research. In the past, signaling was imbedded within human physiology, but those studies often depicted intracellular signaling cascades as a "black box," or with only a few components considered. Since then, structural biology, molecular biology, imaging, and "omics" approaches have contributed present research aims at identifying components, crosstalk, signaling flows, and to elaborate general signaling design principles, with a main aim to generate quantitative predictive models of cell signaling responses. In the future, we will need an even stronger connection of the different scientific disciplines to be truly predictive for both the physiological and disease perturbed cellular states.

now ready to go large scale and to quantitatively describe properties that commence from whole-cell functions. To reach this goal a stronger integration of signaling with imaging, structural biology, and recent "omics" mass spectrometry-based approaches to detect protein complexes in mammalian cell types is required. The remaining challenge will be to move away from deriving general design principles from experiments with transformed cell lines as the model systems, and go back to the signaling roots: physiology! To achieve one needs to make the effort of expanding the experimental work in primary cells and tissues.

A quantitative systems analysis of signaling networks, aside from developing the computational approaches (reviewed elsewhere; e.g. see the excellent review in Karlebach and Shamir (2008), Kholodenko et al. (2012)), needs several experimental or combined experimental/computational prerequisites (see also Papin et al. 2005). These include:

- The identification and quantification of all components.
- Knowledge on the degree of connectivity and control (e.g. feedbacks).
- Quantification of protein activation and cellular localization changes over time (spatial-temporal scales).
- Defining general design principles of how cell type-specific responses and signaling flows are achieved (including tissue-specific alternative splicing).
- Integration of signaling pathways with cell general/housekeeping functions, and the characterization of conserved cell general signaling pathways.
- Crosstalk between signaling and the chromatin status, or in other words the fact that in different cell types different regions of the chromosomes will be accessible to activated transcription factors.

This chapter will cover recent progress in setting the requirements for studying signaling networks in a quantitative manner. We will not enter into the interplay between signaling and transcriptional responses since this requires the integration with epigenetic modifications of chromatin and its accessibility to transcription activation (see Arzate-Mejia et al. 2011 for selected examples of crosstalk between signal transduction and changes in chromatin structure). We will both, focus on recent developments in quantitative experimental tools and highlight recent work of combining signaling with mathematical modeling. We will also focus on discussing cell type-specific signaling flows, relating protein abundance to signaling flows, highlighting the importance of studying signaling complexes and modules, and emphasize the great potential of using synthetic biology approaches to decipher signaling networks.

2 REQUIREMENTS FOR A QUANTITATIVE SYSTEMS ANALYSIS OF SIGNALING NETWORKS

2.1 Identification and quantification of components

2.1.1 Absolute protein abundances in whole cells

Past efforts already resulted in a near-to-complete list of signaling components (http://www.uniprot.org/; http://www.hprd.org/), and their structural analysis (http://www.rcsb.org); however estimating protein abundances in whole cells is still in its infancy. Determining absolute protein concentrations in mammalian cell lysates is challenging due to the high complexity and high dynamic range of proteins (Hortin and Sviridov 2010). Until recently, transcriptome analyses were the only (high-throughout) methods to get a rough estimate on protein expression levels. However, due to differences in translation efficiency, mRNA stability and protein stability for each component, in general the correlation between mRNA and protein is not perfect (Maier et al. 2009). While nevertheless mRNA levels could be a valid approximation when looking at changes in one cell type, e.g. during stimulation or cell differentiation, measurements of mRNA levels in different cell types or tissues do not provide a reliable value of protein abundances. In addition, transcriptomic analyses do not capture the post translational modifications (PTMs), such as phosphorylation, which are especially important in signaling cascades.

Improvements in quantitative mass spectrometry-based proteomics (Domon and Aebersold 2006) allow recently deep human proteome mapping, and enable the identification and quantification of ~10.000 proteins in different cell lines (Schwanhausser et al. 2011; Beck et al. 2011; Geiger et al. 2012). In these studies, the quantified proteins span an abundance range of seven orders of magnitude with up to 20.000.000 molecules per cell. The first study stands out, as here both the transcriptome and proteome was quantified, and using a quantitative mathematical model the first genome-scale prediction of synthesis rates of mRNAs and proteins was achieved (Schwanhausser et al. 2011).

The above mass spectrometry studies were performed in a so-called "shot gun" set up, where the aim is to detect and quantify all peptides in a tryptic cell lysate. Normally, shot gun proteomics requires extensive fractionation prior to mass spectrometry analysis. Recently, proteins were quantified in unfractionated mammalian cell lysates, using the selected reaction monitoring (SRM) mode, where selectively the peptides of interest are searched for—thus a promising alternative when analyzing single signaling pathways (Ebhardt et al. 2012). However, when comparing abundances measured in the same cell line with different instruments and using SRM or shot gun approaches numbers varied often more than 10-fold (Ebhardt et al. 2012). Moreover, recently it was shown that there is a strong bias in absolute protein quantitation depending on the protease used, even when performed on the same mass spectrometer (Peng et al. 2012). These differences were shown to be not restricted to low abundant proteins, but can differ for high abundant proteins by more than a factor of 1000, in some cases (Peng et al. 2012). Thus, to use protein abundances from large-scale efforts for mathematical modeling, until the above issues are solved, one still needs parameter optimization (see review Jaqaman and Danuser 2006), or to rely on low-throughput methods, such as quantitative western blotting.

2.1.2 Subcellular localization

Another problem is that usually whole-cell extracts are measured, which neglects an important issue that is to say cellular localization. A solution is emerging from the large-scale efforts by Uhlen and colleagues in the so-called "human protein atlas" project (http://www.proteinatlas.org/). In this antibody-based project the ambitious aim is to acquire expression profiles based on immunohistochemistry for all human proteins for a large number of human tissues, cancers and cell lines, and to measure subcellular localization in three cell types. Based on immunostaining results in the three cell types, for the 3500 human proteins analyzed so far, 92% of the proteins had similar cellular distribution (Fagerberg et al. 2011). This suggests that, to be correct for a large part, cellular distribution does not need to be analyzed in all cell types but data from one could be used for others.

2.1.3 *Posttranslational modifications*

Similar as for the absolute protein quantification, the identification of PTMs using mass spectrometry is now well advanced, with ~20.000 phosphorylation sites, 3600 acetylations, 59 methylations, and 141 α-linked-β-N-acetylglucosamin modifications (reviewed in Choudhary and Mann (2010)), and ~11.000 ubiquitinylation sites mapped in different human cell lines (Wagner et al. 2011). However, in most cases no absolute quantifications of the PTMs were made, and they are mostly used to monitor changes during an activation process, such as phosphorylation changes of downstream proteins after receptor stimulation with a ligand. Thus, for mathematical modeling we have the limitation that we cannot relate maximal phosphorylation of a protein to the respective copy number per cell. Moreover, in the immense majority of cases we do not know the functional effect of the modification, or the extent of noise (e.g. accidental modifications without a function).

2.2 Connectivity, binding constants, information processing, and feedback control

2.2.1 *Protein interactions*

The reconstruction of the connectivity of signal transduction pathways on large scale is an iterative process that includes the collection of existing biological knowledge, the characterization of interactions and their directionalities, and mathematical methods (Papin et al. 2005). Existing biological knowledge is accessible in protein protein interactions (PPI) databases such as STRING (http://string-db.org/) or Reactome (http://www.reactome.org/), a database manually curated by experts in the field, which includes reactions and directionalities, but is of lower coverage. Recently, a pipeline was described to automatically analyze online pathway and interactome databases (Cancer CellMap, GeneGo, KEGG, NCI-Pathway Interactome Database (NCI-PID), PANTHER, Reactome, I2D, and STRING) to construct high-confident prior knowledge networks, which can be used as the basis for subsequent combined experimental/mathematical modeling approaches (Kirouac et al. 2012).

2.2.2 *Binding affinities*

The characterization of interactions, such as binding affinity and kinetic rate constants, is important for parameterization in quantitative mathematical models. Usually, affinities and rate constants cannot be measured in a high-throughout fashion, and up to now a database storing these quantities with high coverage is still missing. Protein microarrays have revolutionized the possibility of accessing affinities on large scale. In the pioneering work by McBeath and colleagues, microarrays were used to measure the binding affinities of all SH2 and PTB domains in the human genome with 61 peptides representing physiological tyrosine phosphorylation sites on the four ErbB family receptors (Jones et al. 2006).

There are two potential problems of using protein microarrays to determine binding affinities between in vitro purified SH2 and SH3 domains and synthetic peptides (Jones et al. 2006). First, there are examples showing that the isolated domain can have a different binding affinity compared to the full length protein or protein complexes. For example, it has been demonstrated that the Grb2-Sos1 complex binds phosphopeptides with higher affinity (Chook et al. 1996). Second, there are several examples of multidomain proteins, which can use several of their domains to be recruited to partner proteins or the plasma membrane. For example, Sos1 can bind to the Grb2-SH3 domain using its proline-rich region, to a distal binding site in Ras (Gureasko et al. 2008), and to phospholipids in the membrane, via its PH domain. This could on one hand increase binding affinity, but also reduce noise by preventing spontaneous activation or membrane recruitment (Kholodenko 2006). In mathematical modeling approaches, implementing multidomain interactions on a mechanistic level is a fundamental problem called "combinatorial complexity" (Goldstein et al. 2004), as the number of differential equations can reach $\sim 1 \times 10^6$, even for simple signaling systems (Birtwistle et al. 2007). Recently, rule-based modeling (RBM) approaches were developed to tackle this issue (Faeder et al. 2009). RMB uses a set of binding rules between domains and binding sites and allows for the easier construction and simulations of mathematical models (e.g. RuleBender; http://rulebender.org/).

The topological arrangement of signaling networks from high-throughput data poses a major challenge. In a recent combined study, both the interaction and the directionality of interactions were addressed using yeast 2-hybrid experiments combined with a naïve Bayesian learning strategy (Vinayagam et al. 2011). In this computational method, the directionality is inferred by assuming that information flow follows the shortest path between receptors and transcription factors. Other solutions to this problem are offered from the various reverse engineering frameworks, originally developed for gene regulatory networks, which usually need perturbation data to infer the network structure (Kholodenko et al. 2002; Madar et al. 2009). Modular response analysis (MRA), an algorithm that analyses the steady-state response of a dynamic system upon perturbation (Kholodenko et al. 2002), has been successfully applied to infer topological organization in signaling networks (Gardner et al. 2003; Santos et al. 2007; Stelniec-Klotz et al. 2012). The latter work stands out as it connects the Ras signaling network to the downstream gene regulatory network, with the overall network showing high modularity and hierarchical organization (Stelniec-Klotz et al. 2012). Noteworthy, the hierarchical and modular structure is reflected in different phenotypic outputs as a result of perturbations.

2.2.3 Directionality

One of the key questions in signal transduction is to understand how specific information processing is achieved through the so-called "hour-glass" shape of many signaling pathways (Citri and Yarden 2006) (Figure 5.2). The hour-glass shape pictures that a large set of receptors (inputs) gives rise to a multitude of transcription factors (output), but this usually involves only a limited number of pathways, or even identical proteins, in-between. This issue was addressed in a combined experimental and computational quantitative manner for receptor tyrosine kinase (RTK) signaling Gordus et al. 2009. In this study it was demonstrated that at least for the upstream adaptor proteins the phosphorylation levels could be predicted using the *in vitro* affinities for receptor-docking. However, this was not possible for downstream proteins such as protein kinases, and therefore mathematical models for this part of the network will always be more challenging to predict and will always require more experimental parameterizations. In another study (Miller-Jensen et al. 2007) it was shown that the

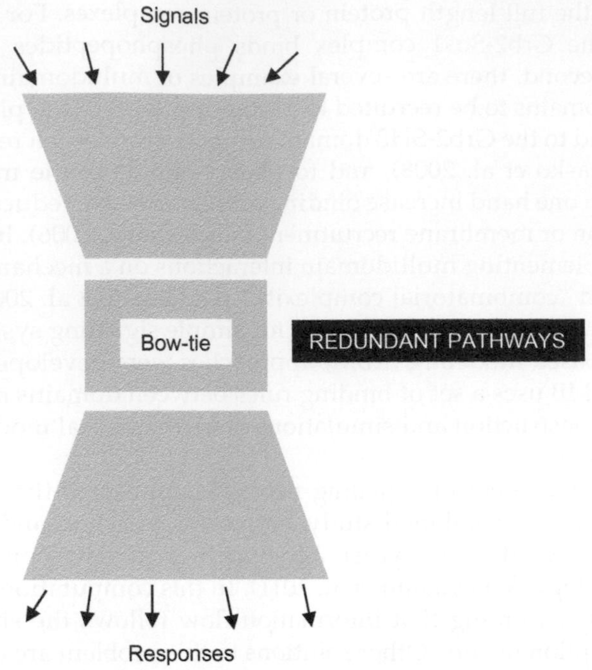

FIGURE 5.2 Schematic illustration of the "hour-glass" shape of signaling pathways. A similar figure is also depicted by Ferrell (2008). Signaling cascades of different receptors ("Stimuli") are often reused and converge into the "bow-tie" at the center, to results in various output responses. One of the key questions in signal transduction is to unravel the mechanisms of how a limited number of signaling proteins act together to coordinate a multitude of functional outputs.

phenotypic responses could be predicted based on linear correlations of a common set of downstream proteins. Together this suggests that signals in the input and output layers of the "hour-glass" shape of signaling pathways are transduced in a linear manner, while signals in the intermediate layer ("bow-tie") are processes in a non-linear way.

2.2.4 Feedback loops

Positive and negative feedback loops are crucial for suppressing noise (robustness) in biological systems by controlling the expression or activation levels of proteins (Becskei and Serrano 2000; Ferrell 2008). In accordance with this, it has been shown by computational modeling that the effect of drugs will be neutralized if the target is situated within a negative feedback loop (Kitano 2007). Later, it was confirmed experimentally that the downstream signaling output after perturbations in the Ras-Raf complex, critically depends on the—cell type-specific—underlying network topology: the signaling output is only weakly affected under conditions of strong negative feedback, whereas a strong effect is observed in a cell line with reduced negative feedback (Kiel et al. 2009) (Figure 5.3). The concept of robustness, and in particular the role of feedbacks under perturbed protein levels, were

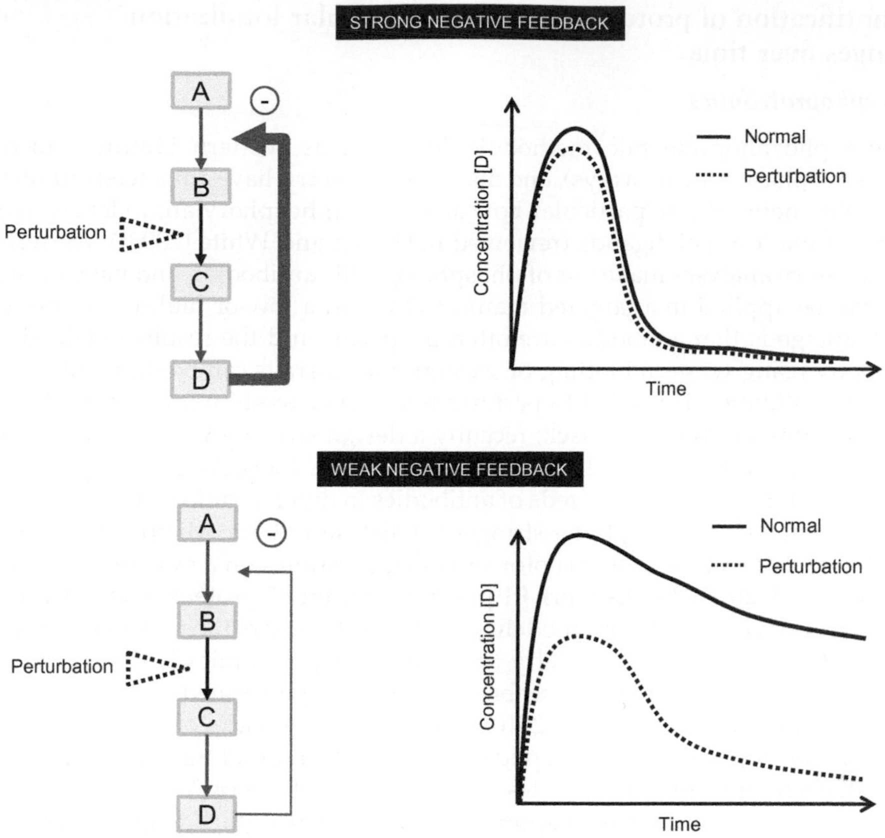

FIGURE 5.3 Schematic illustration of the effect of applying perturbations (e.g. drugs) under strong or weak negative feedback. When perturbing the interaction between proteins B and C, which are within a negative feedback initiated from protein D to upstream activation, the effect (on protein D production) is much larger in a situation with weak negative feedback.

investigated in mechanistic detail using experiments and modeling for MAPK signaling (Fritsche-Guenther et al. 2011). In this work a strong robustness of Erk phosphorylation levels against perturbations of Erk protein levels were found, and a single feedback from Erk to Raf-1 was responsible for the observed robustness. Feedback loops are difficult to detect in a systematic high-throughput manner, and are usually determined in case-by-case studies (Shin et al. 2009; Aksamitiene et al. 2010; Kolch et al. 1993). However, in a recent systematic study the negative feedback regulators in growth factor signaling were identified through large-scale profiling of protein phosphorylation and gene expression (Amit et al. 2007). Noteworthy, in this study also general and common motifs within the EGF-induced transcriptional network were identified. Sensitivity analysis (systematically altering rate constants and concentrations) can be an alternative for distinguishing the sensitive and robust parts of a network, which can inform on the feedback loops involved (Chen et al. 2009).

2.3 Quantification of protein activation and cellular localization changes over time

2.3.1 *Phosphoproteomics*

Applying phosphoproteomic methodologies, such as western blotting, microwestern arrays (reverse-phase protein arrays), and mass spectrometry, have advanced our understanding of signaling networks, in particular how activation (phosphorylation) levels change over time after stimulation with ligands (reviewed in Huang and White (2008)). Western blotting and microwestern analyses make use of phospho-specific antibodies, and have the advantage that they can be applied in a targeted manner, either in a low-or high-throughput manner. The disadvantage is that antibodies are often unspecific and the results obtained using the same antibody using western blotting or western microarrays can be different. Thus, extensive antibody validation is needed to perform microarray western for systems-level investigations. To circumvent this drawback, recently a design strategy was developed to identify high-quality antibodies to be used in microwestern arrays (Sevecka et al. 2011). The pipeline involved screening of several hundreds of antibodies in diverse biological contexts (cell types and stimuli), together with applying stringent statistical criteria. Microwestern arrays have been applied to unravel the EGF receptor signaling dynamics on a systems and quantitative level (Ciaccio et al. 2010). In this work 91 phosphosites on 67 proteins were measured at six time points and Bayesian network modeling was used to model the network connectivity.

The advantage of mass spectrometry-based phosphoproteomics is that peptide/protein modifications can be monitored in an unbiased manner, if performed in the "shot gun" mode (reviewed in Choudhary and Mann (2010)). The main drawbacks of this technique are that prior enrichment steps for phosphopeptides are needed, and that the reproducibility is often inconsistent, even on technical replicates (Wolf-Yadlin et al. 2006). Mass spectrometry in the SRM mode, in contrast, is a targeted approach and has been applied to quantify the temporal phosphorylation profiles for 222 tyrosine phosphorylated peptides after EGF treatment, with high reproducibility and a short 2 h-run time (Wolf-Yadlin et al. 2007). Thus, mass spectrometry performed in the SRM mode seems to be ideal for a targeted quantitative analysis of individual signaling networks.

2.3.2 *Single cell analysis*

Cell-to-cell variability arises in many physiological contexts, such as during development (Fortini 2009). Furthermore, protein abundances can vary and individual cells can differ in the magnitude they respond to stimuli (Spencer et al. 2009). Thus, single cell analysis is of great interest to unravel general design principles, which has been addressed by both measurements and mathematical modeling (reviewed in Kolitz and Lauffenburger (2012)). For example, recently the role of protein abundance for cellular signal processing was investigated in TRAIL-induced apoptosis (Spencer et al. 2009). Fluorescence-based flow cytometry allows the simultaneous detection of up to 12 molecules in a single cell (Hulett et al. 1969; Chattopadhyay et al. 2006). An improved version of flow cytometry is mass cytometry, which uses antibodies that are labeled with different isotopic pure metals, and allow for 34 simultaneous measurements (Bendall et al. 2011). Recently, multiplexed mass cytometry has greatly revolutionized the field, by drastically increasing the throughput, and thus allowing systems-level single cell analyses (Bodenmiller et al. 2012). This technique has a great potential, especially for preclinical testing of tissues, analyzing drugs, and their side effects. For example, it enables the quantification of signaling pathways during drug treatments from individual cells taken from biopsies.

2.3.3 *Spatial signaling through compartmentalization*

Signaling networks are highly spatially arranged (reviewed in Kholodenko (2009), Kholodenko et al. (2010)). For example, the differential localization and activity of the Ras isoforms, H-, K-, and N-Ras, regulated through posttranslational modifications, was shown to be responsible for differences in the signaling amplitude and duration (Rocks et al. 2005). Here, a novel way of signal propagation was demonstrated, where a cellular organelle, the Golgi apparatus, exhibits an "echo" of the Ras activity profile at the plasma membrane (Lorentzen et al. 2010). Interestingly, also the cell shape can control spatial-temporal signaling properties (Meyers et al. 2006). For example, experimental work and mathematical modeling have shown that the GTPase Cdc42 gets activated for the most part at the cell periphery at extending protrusions, where the surface-volume ratio is larger (Nalbant et al. 2004). In the pioneering work from Iyengar and colleagues it was shown, in a combined experimental and modeling study, how cell shape and negative feedback loops control the spatial information flow in hippocampal neurons after β-adrenergic receptor activation (Neves et al. 2008). Recently, the transient and sustained ERK activation kinetics in response to different ligands (EGF [epidermal growth factor] and HRG [heregulin] was elucidated in MCF-7 cells (Nakakuki et al. 2010). In this work the authors mechanistically elucidated using experimental and modeling approaches how a spatially distributed signaling-transcription cascade—with different interlinked feedback loops—can robustly distinguish transient and sustained ERK activation at the transcription factor level.

To model spatial cell signaling, we need to know the spatial arrangement of the pathway, the cell shape and how it affects signal propagation, and quantitative parameters on diffusion and signal propagation (Kholodenko 2009). Mathematical modeling programs that can deal with cell shape are available, e.g. the Virtual Cell simulation software (http://vcell.org/). Fluorescence microscopy methods are used to study the spatial-temporal properties of cells, and together with quantitative systems biology approaches provide the means to bridge the molecular level (protein interaction and signaling networks) with the cellular response (reviewed in Verveer and Bastiaens (2008)). In fact, high-throughput fluorescence microscopy methods have been developed for analyzing signal transduction (reviewed in Pepperkok and Ellenberg (2006)). Importantly, also fluorescence-based tools (fluorescence cross-correlation spectroscopy, FCCS) for measuring quantitative parameters of molecular interactions and oligomerization (affinities and rate constants) *in vivo* were developed (Slaughter et al. 2007). Obviously, this opens exciting possibility for quantitative mathematical modeling of spatial-temporal dynamics for larger signaling pathways. However, one of the main limitations of using fluorescence microscopy techniques is that the endogenous system is perturbed by introducing a protein with a fluorescence label. This can result in altered localization or interference with the normal endogenous signaling machinery.

2.3.4 *Spatial signaling through scaffolds*

Aside from the spatial arrangement through cellular compartments, scaffold proteins provide another way for organizing signaling networks into larger signaling complexes and thereby achieve spatial-temporal regulation (Brown and Sacks 2009). Experimentally this has been mainly demonstrated for yeast signaling, e.g. through the pioneering engineering research by Lim and colleagues, where scaffolds were engineered to redirect signaling flows (Park et al. 2003). Moreover, protein scaffolds were rewired by engineering artificial binding sites, and by introducing positive and negative feedback loops several dynamically different input-output responses were generated (Bashor et al. 2008). Recently, also the quantitative effect of the expression levels of scaffold proteins on signal transduction was investigated (Chapman and Asthagiri 2009). In some cases, scaffolds can allosterically activate their target proteins, as found for KSR that triggers Raf activation (Rajakulendran et al. 2009). In another fundamental study, it was shown that the Ste5 scaffold proteins (in *S. cerevisiae*) not only serve as an assembly platform to guide information flow, but also derive input signals and act as conformational switches to passage information flow between two distinct output responses (Zalatan et al. 2012).

Thus, as scaffolding is a common mechanism in signaling, it is crucial to identify all scaffolds and their targets, the affinity between them, the dynamics of complex assembly and disassembly, and their abundance in order to understand their role in cell signaling. However, so far systematic efforts in analyzing scaffold-target interactions, together with their localization, have not been made.

2.4 The role of protein abundances and competition for signaling flows and cell type-specific responses

2.4.1 *Mutually exclusive interactions and competition*

It is clear that a central "hub" protein in the network cannot interact with all of its partner proteins simultaneously and that some interactions are mutually exclusive (Kim et al. 2006; Kiel et al. 2011). One hypothesis is that differences in protein concentrations between cell lines could change cellular output if there is competition at a critical branching point of the network. For example, assuming an upstream protein is low abundant, the concentrations (and affinities) of competing binding partners could determine the signaling pathway taken. This idea is supported by a recent experimental study of MAPK signaling in the developing drosophila embryo, in where MAPK substrate competition was found to control gene expression (Kim et al. 2011). Knowing that proteins have diverse binding partners and many of them will use a similar binding surface (Kim et al. 2006), competitive effects are likely to be a new emerging feature of signaling pathways. The above data suggests that fine-tuned protein abundances allow for various input-output responses, and they therefore may enable the same signaling pathway to operate in different modes (depending on local concentration or activation state), or give rise to cell type-specific outputs.

The investigation of signaling complexes/machines represents another way to address the role of protein abundance variation. It is now clear that signaling cascades are imbedded into larger complexes, which can rearrange during ligand stimulation. For example, using quantitative proteomics 284 ERK-interacting proteins were identified in PC12 cells, and after ligand-induced differentiation 60 proteins dissociated from ERK (von Kriegsheim et al. 2009). In pioneering work from Pawson and colleagues the kinetics of how protein complexes assemble after stimulation was analyzed in a quantitative way using affinity purification combined with SRM analysis (Bisson et al. 2011). This was exemplified with the adaptor protein Grb2, which was shown to participate in an extraordinary high number of signaling complexes in HEK293 cells. Recently, a complete map of human cellular protein complexes was determined based on high-level chromatographic separation of Hela and HEK293 cell extracts and subsequent analysis by mass spectrometry (although, under one condition) (Havugimana et al. 2012). As this method does not perturb the endogenous system (no expression of tagged proteins or generation of stable cell lines with tagged proteins is needed), it could be ideal to investigate signaling complexes in primary cells and tissues and measure how they re-arrange during stimulation.

Advances in the systems-level quantification of proteins in different cell lines and tissues using antibody- and mass spectrometry-based proteomics showed that a high fraction of proteins were expressed in most cells and tissues (Ponten et al. 2009; Burkard et al. 2011; Geiger et al. 2012). However, using hierarchical clustering analyses, cells could still be clustered according to the histological relationships between different cell types, which suggests that cell specificity is achieved by the exact regulation of protein levels in space and time, rather than which specific proteins are expressed (Ponten et al. 2009). In agreement with this concept, it was demonstrated that somatic cell reprogramming efficiency mediated by cell fusion is dependent on the abundance of β-catenin protein levels (Lluis et al. 2008): small changes in expression levels of around fivefold had a substantial effect on the efficiency of reprogramming. In another study, the endogenous intrinsic changes in the abundance or activation of apoptosis-regulating proteins were shown to be the cause of cell-to-cell variability in apoptosis sensitivity (Spencer et al. 2009). Likewise, when mammalian MAPK cascades were analyzed insulated in yeast, altering protein concentrations or the addition of scaffold proteins could modify the strengths of the signal processing and the output response (O'Shaughnessy et al. 2011).

However, considering that there are fluctuations in protein expression levels in individual cells (Cohen et al. 2008), not surprisingly studies have demonstrated that cells have mechanisms to cope with noise (Kitano 2002; Stelling et al. 2004). For example, the steady-state phosphorylation levels of ERK were demonstrated to be robust with respect to total ERK protein level perturbations (Fritsche-Guenther et al. 2011). When endogenous protein levels were quantified in individual cells, the standard deviation of cell-to-cell variation was measured to range between 10% and 60% of the mean, and 20% of the variability was a result of differences in cell-cycle phase (Cohen et al. 2008; Frenkel-Morgenstern et al. 2010). Thus, cells have to cope with a considerable amount of protein abundance variation, and need to keep under tight control critical nodes that are sensitive to protein concentration levels in signaling pathways. The challenge lies in identifying these concentration sensitive nodes, as they may provide a means to explain the different responses in different cell lines to the same signal, if some critical proteins in the network are differentially expressed.

In summary, it will be important for the future to map those proteins that by changing their levels exhibit a strong effect on a signaling output, and to analyze if they exhibit less variability than others with minor effect. Also mathematical models should include this experimental variability and predict how it affects the result (stochastic simulations versus modeling based on ordinary differential equations).

2.4.2 Rewiring signaling through alternative splicing

Alternative splicing (different inclusion of exons) has been shown to play a significant role for cell development and differentiation, and current estimates suggest that 90% of all human genes are alternatively spliced (Wang et al. 2008). It has been shown that patterns of alternative splicing can differ in different tissues, and thus can provide another mechanism of achieving cell and tissue-specific responses (Wang et al. 2008). In fact, recently it was demonstrated that genes containing tissue-specific exons are enriched in signaling and developmental genes, and tissue-specific splicing can rewire protein interaction networks (Buljan et al. 2012). This is happening through the loss or inclusion of binding motifs and domains. For example in the Ras-ERK signaling pathway, DA-Raf1 is a splice variant of A-Raf, which contains the Ras binding domain, but lacks the kinase domain, and thereby acts as a negative regulator of the Ras pathways through competition with other, but signaling-competent, Ras effectors (Yokoyama et al. 2007). Despite the importance of rewiring signaling networks through the presence of different alternative spliced proteins, alternative splicing so far has been often neglected in signaling and modeling projects. One reason is that the large-scale identification of spliced isoforms is a challenge, as identification needs to happen on the protein level since some transcripts can degraded or they do not produce a functional protein (Lewis et al. 2003). The identification of protein isoforms resulting from alternative exon skipping needs either antibodies that are splice variant specific, or, through mass spectrometry, the selection and identification of peptides that span the splice junction.

2.5 Integration of signaling pathways with cell general/housekeeping functions

2.5.1 The core (signaling) proteome

Pioneering work from Lauffenburger and colleagues proposed that cell type-specific signaling responses emanate from the differential activation of kinases and other upstream transducers, which can generate diverse signaling responses by using similar common—in all cell types present—effectors (Miller-Jensen et al. 2007). This work suggested that not every model for each cell type requires its own in depth experiments and model training, but proposes that cell general models could be broadly applicable with just some new, cell type-specific data. Thus, a major challenge in understanding the cell's functional organization is to distinguish cell type-specific signaling mechanisms from cell general mechanisms. Different cells of higher eukaryotic organisms need to perform similar housekeeping functions and, at the same time, cell type-specific functions. This has prompted research groups to investigate the transcriptome in different organs and tissues and to integrate this data with protein interaction networks (Komurov and White 2007; Bossi and Lehner 2009). One important conclusion derived from these studies was that tissue-specific proteins often bind to core cellular proteins, and that they are more likely to be recent evolutionary innovations (Bossi and Lehner 2009). Later, also the proteome of different cell types was analyzed using various approaches. For example, mass spectrometry was employed to analyze which proteins are expressed in most/all of the tissues and cell types, and defined them as the so-called "central proteome" (Schirle et al. 2003; Burkard et al. 2011). The central proteome was found to be enriched in evolutionary conserved proteins, but no absolute protein levels were provided. Last year, mass spectroscopy analyses accomplished by Mann and colleagues determined absolute protein abundances for 11 common human cancer cell lines with high coverage (Geiger et al. 2012). Interestingly, in both studies signal transduction proteins were among the proteins of the central proteome, suggesting that a (conserved) core signaling pathway exists in all cell types, which could then dynamically connect to cell type-specific proteins. A major challenge for the future is to further define and functionally characterize such cell general and cell-specific signaling functions.

2.5.2 *Signaling modules*

Cell function is determined by a network of nodes (such as protein-protein, protein-DNA, protein-RNA, and protein-small metabolites), which describe cellular functions on a systems level in normal and perturbed/ disease states (Vidal et al. 2011). Thus, a large effort has been made in the past years to determine those interaction networks, the affinities of edges (interactions), and through which parts of the proteins (domains and linear motifs) the interactions are mediated (Lamond et al. 2012). Knowing the interaction network, its high level of crosstalk, and the multiple feedback loops is not enough to understand cell type function and specificity. In order to reduce the complexity, it is crucial to identify organizational patterns, such as protein complexes, localization, expression levels, and splice variants. The challenge lies in achieving the right balance between reductionism and necessary details. One important design principle is that despite high signaling complexity, networks can be decomposed into modules, which have independent functions (Hartwell et al. 1999; Lauffenburger 2000). The identification of signaling modules is challenging as proteins can often participate in more than one module. Therefore, modules predicted from connectivity analysis of PPI data from high-throughput data (Sharan et al. 2005; Rhrissorrakrai and Gunsalus 2011) do not necessarily reflect true functional modules. Another problem is that pathways without extensive interconnectivity can be missed in such approaches. Other approaches to identify functional and analyze modules use comparative methods to search for conserved proteins (Lin et al. 2012) or mathematical modeling approaches, such as elementary flux modes (Kaltenbach and Stelling 2012). Furthermore, transcriptional signatures have been used to deconstruct a signaling pathway into modules (Chang et al. 2009). In this work, specific modules within the Ras pathway were shown to be of different functional importance for different cancer groups.

The use of structural information, combined with the analysis of protein interaction and signaling networks, is expected to accelerate the integration of global approaches with mechanistic details, and thus help elucidate functional assemblies (reviewed in Kiel and Serrano (2012), Fraser et al. (2013)). Using three-dimensional structures of protein/domain complexes or of homologs one can distinguish between proteins/domains that interact in a compatible ("AND") way, from those that interact in a mutually exclusive ("XOR") manner (Kim et al. 2006; Yang et al. 2012). Knowing which interactions bind in a "XOR" and which in an "AND" fashion is functionally important, as demonstrated for the rhodopsin signaling networks, where competitors may dynamically connect to different modules (Kiel et al. 2011). Furthermore, structural information could be integrated into mathematical modeling approaches: in a pioneering study, geometrical fitting at the EGFR receptor was realized through a three-dimensional structural model for binding of four SH2/PID domain-containing partner proteins (Hsieh et al. 2010). Agent-based modeling was then used to analyze the effects of reaction kinetics, steric constraints, and receptor clustering. An interesting conclusion from this study was that simultaneous docking of multiple proteins is highly dependent on the stability between receptor and partner proteins. Although this seems to add an additional layer of complexity, it may help to define the functional assemblies and modules in the long-term, and provide new clues in the functional assembly of proteins.

2.5.3 Whole-cell signaling models

With respect to the integration of signaling networks with cell general and housekeeping functions, a final goal is the development of a predictive mathematical model that can integrate cell types-specific signaling flows with cell general functions and that can predict changes in response to perturbations, such as by drugs or disease mutations. The challenge is to develop mathematical methods which can cope with the complexity of several signaling pathways, crosstalks, feedbacks, multidomain or competing interactions, and three-dimensional spatial cellular localization. In addition, many uncertainties exist in parameters (i.e. affinities, rate constants) and different temporal scales have to be handled. A promising approach to cope with these difficulties was taken by Covert and colleagues, who generated a predictive whole-cell model of the small bacterium, *Mycoplasma genitalium* (Karr et al. 2012). In their approach the important novelty was to decompose molecular components and interactions into functional modules, which were modeled independently of each other and then integrated together. The advantage of such an approach is that for some modules a lot of quantitative information and in depth knowledge is available, while other processes are less understood or poorly characterized; consequently each module is modeled using the most appropriate mathematical representation (i.e. based on ordinary differential equations (ODEs), Boolean network modeling, constraint-based modeling, etc.).

3 SYNTHETIC BIOLOGY APPROACHES IN SIGNAL TRANSDUCTION

Structure-based protein design represents an important approach in engineering signaling networks, for analyzing the dynamic network behavior or elucidating general design principles of signaling networks (Kiel and Serrano 2012). For example, proteins can be designed to either eliminate interactions or to change kinetic or binding constants (Selzer et al. 2000), with the aim of probing the network properties. For example, using electrostatic steering, "mild/subtle" mutations were designed for the Ras-Raf1 complex and experimentally tested, which unraveled the different cell type-specific underlying network topologies, e.g. weak or strong negative feedback (Kiel et al. 2009). Recently, it was shown that natural disease mutations located on the protein surface forming the interface of a protein complex, may affect binding to only some of the interaction partners ("edgetic mutations" versus node removal), which provides an explanation how similar proteins can be involved in multiple diseases (Zhong et al. 2009; Wang et al. 2012). Likewise, structure-based protein design may also be used to re-design mutations of an upstream key hub protein, which specifically binds to only a subset of downstream effector molecules. This would allow measuring signaling flows through only one of many possible downstream signaling branches of an upstream hub protein to be analyzed ("branch pruning").

Synthetic biology also represents a great possibility for characterizing signaling modules, as the best proof of a proposed module is if it can function in isolation in orthogonal systems

(Collins 2012). Analyzing signaling modules and re-engineered modules in artificial environments also has great value, as mechanistic aspects are studied in isolation (reviewed in O'Shaughnessy and Sarkar (2012)). Based on pre-defined proposed modules, advances in mathematical tools can contribute to the automatic design for experimentally implementing synthetic circuits (Marchisio and Stelling 2011). Experimentally implementing synthetic networks in living systems, although still challenging, has seen great developments during the past 30 years, and a large collection of standardized building blocks is available to the community today (reviewed in Auslander and Fussenegger (2012)). An outstanding achievement with respect to synthetic design in mammalian signaling systems was the reconstitution of an artificial T-cell receptor system in a non-immune cell (James and Vale 2012). It allowed the detailed biophysical characterization of the mechanism triggering T-cell activation.

Once implemented, systems properties of the designed modules can be investigated. For example, robustness with respect to environmental changes or intracellular noise is a key property of cellular systems, and is for example achieved through back-up systems and feedback control (Kitano 2002; Stelling et al. 2004). Protein level perturbations are a means to analyze robust spots in a signaling module. Furthermore, subtle mutations can be designed to gain insight into network and feedback properties of the module. Subtle mutations in protein complexes could be those that retain a similar affinity but have compensating changes in association and dissociation rate constants (Figure 5.4). Association rate constants can be

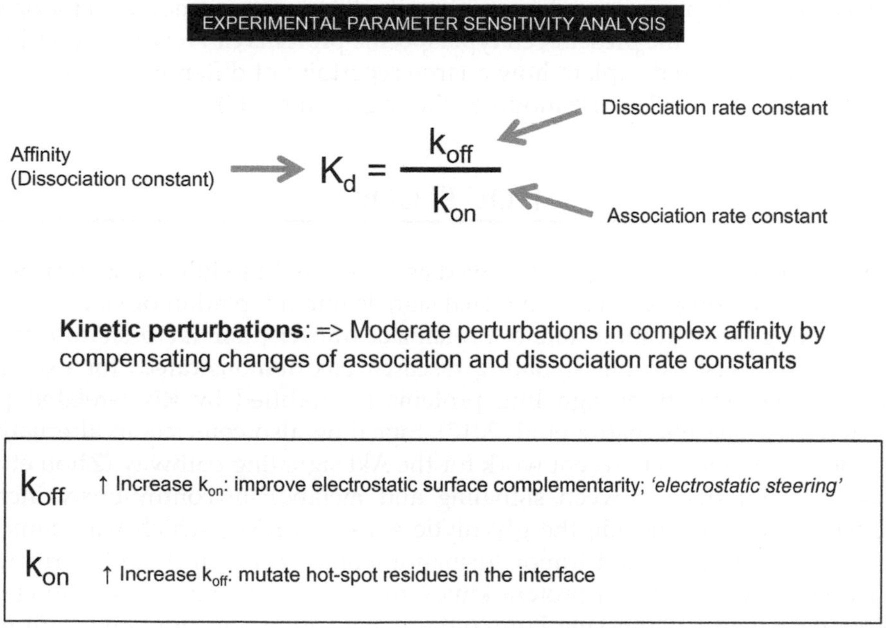
EXPERIMENTAL PARAMETER SENSITIVITY ANALYSIS
Dissociation rate constant
Affinity
(Dissociation constant)
$K_d = \frac{k_{off}}{k_{on}}$
Association rate constant
Kinetic perturbations: => Moderate perturbations in complex affinity by compensating changes of association and dissociation rate constants
k_{off} ↑ Increase k_{on}: improve electrostatic surface complementarity; *'electrostatic steering'*
k_{on} ↑ Increase k_{off}: mutate hot-spot residues in the interface

FIGURE 5.4 Illustration of the basic principle for designing kinetic perturbations. Using structure-based protein design mutations can be designed in protein complexes, which have a similar complex affinity (K_d), but different kinetic parameters (k_{on} and k_{off}). Introducing these mutated complexes in vitro (e.g. in cell lines), and quantifying signaling changes is a possibility to investigate the effect of moderate perturbations on signaling properties. It analogy to sensitivity analysis in mathematical modeling, this corresponds to an "experimental parameter sensitivity analysis."

increased by increasing the electrostatic charge complementarity at the edge of the interface (long range interactions, "electrostatic steering") (Selzer et al. 2000). Dissociation rate constants can be increased by mutating amino acid residues in the interface (short range interactions). These mutants could be used to test if a network is under kinetic control (Kiel et al. 2009). However, this type of experimental parameter sensitivity analysis needs some prior knowledge of the network, since for example strong negative feedback effects will be dampened if the modified interaction is located inside (Kiel et al. 2009). Recently, a web tool based on a program for inducing disturbances into protein interaction networks was developed, which calculates the changes in global network topology and connectivity as a function of the perturbation (Yadav and Babu 2012).

Another important aspect to analyze is how the robust and sensitive parts compare to the natural protein abundance fluctuations. In the case that a relation is found, e.g. conserved modules show a smaller protein level variation between tissues and cell lines, one would not need to test all signaling modules experimentally. Rather, one could focus on studying the variable parts and on the crosstalk between modules. Recently, an experimental network-perturbation approach was used to investigate crosstalk between signaling modules during the neutrophil polarization process (Ku et al. 2012). This work was remarkable, as a surprisingly simple circuit was identified that influenced and affected all crosstalk and signaling module interactions during the differentiation response. This suggests a mechanism of a few key (perhaps cell types-specific) proteins controlling several modules and their crosstalk. Thus, with a common basic conserved module in all cell types ("common effector processing" (Miller-Jensen et al. 2007), the present cell type-specific proteins can rewire and influence different modules, which could explain how a large repertoire of different signaling responses can be achieved using a similar core module ("hour glass model").

4 OUTLOOK

Signal transduction can no longer be viewed as an isolated discipline that aims to uncover mechanisms of converting external or internal signals into adaptation or cell fate responses, by mainly affecting the activation state of proteins or transcription factors (Yaffe and Gough 2013). In contrast, latest exciting signaling research has demonstrated, for example, how the abundance and activity of signaling proteins is modified by RNA-related processes (Guzzo et al. 2012; Rajasethupathy et al. 2012). Signaling also connects to alternative splicing in the nucleus, as shown in recent work for the Akt signaling pathway (Zhou et al. 2012). Furthermore, the interface between signaling and metabolism continuously increases in players. Recent examples include the glycolytic enzyme PKM2, which was demonstrated to induce gene transcription and tumor formation (Yang et al. 2012), and pyruvate kinase M2 which was shown to act as a protein kinase to promote transcription (Gao et al. 2012). However, so far we are still missing large datasets on combining signaling with metabolic and genomic alterations, alternative splicing, and—crucially—there is a lack of quantitative data for these integrated datasets.

This chapter has placed signal transduction at the center of cellular research. However, we could have equally placed here proteomics, genomics, transcriptomics, or interactomics. In fact, the different scientific areas such as biology, chemistry, engineering, and mathematics, are now, more than ever before, merged. Excitingly, this merging of fields is gaining ground, and at Princeton there is even a new revolutionary science curriculum, "Integrated Science" (http://www.princeton.edu/integratedscience/), which educates students in all main scientific areas, assuming that research nowadays will always span several disciplines. Mathematical modeling has a strong foundation in this curriculum, as it is unquestioned that understanding general design principles will need quantitative modeling to be truly predictive.

However, in the middle of all these integrative approaches, we should not forget about physiology, and the need to come up with ways to bridge the gap with omics. The other substantial challenge will be to find ways to systematically relate signaling changes to the chromatin status and epigenetic changes in different cell types and tissues.

References

Aksamitiene, E., Kholodenko, B. N., Kolch, W., Hoek, J. B., and Kiyatkin, A. (2010). PI3K/Akt-sensitive MEK-independent compensatory circuit of ERK activation in ER-positive PI3K-mutant T47D breast cancer cells. *Cell Signal.* **22**:1369–1378.

Amit, I., Citri, A., Shay, T., Lu, Y., Katz, M., Zhang, F., Tarcic, G., Siwak, D., Lahad, J., Jacob-Hirsch, J., Amariglio, N., Vaisman, N., Segal, E., Rechavi, G., Alon, U., Mills, G. B., Domany, E., and Yarden, Y. (2007). A module of negative feedback regulators defines growth factor signaling. *Nat. Genet.* **39**:503–512.

Arzate-Mejia, R. G., Valle-Garcia, D., and Recillas-Targa, F. (2011). Signaling epigenetics: Novel insights on cell signaling and epigenetic regulation. *IUBMB Life* **63**:881–895.

Auslander, S., and Fussenegger, M. (2012). *From gene switches to mammalian designer cells: present and future prospects.* Trends Biotechnol.

Bashor, C. J., Helman, N. C., Yan, S., and Lim, W. A. (2008). Using engineered scaffold interactions to reshape MAP kinase pathway signaling dynamics. *Science* **319**:1539–1543.

Beck, M., Schmidt, A., Malmstroem, J., Claassen, M., Ori, A., Szymborska, A., Herzog, F., Rinner, O., Ellenberg, J., and Aebersold, R. (2011). The quantitative proteome of a human cell line. *Mol. Syst. Biol.* **7**:549.

Becskei, A., and Serrano, L. (2000). Engineering stability in gene networks by autoregulation. *Nature* **405**:590–593.

Bendall, S. C., Simonds, E. F., Qiu, P., Amirel, A. D., Krutzik, P. O., Finck, R., Bruggner, R. V., Melamed, R., Trejo, A., Ornatsky, O. I., Balderas, R. S., Plevritis, S. K., Sachs, K., Pe'er, D., Tanner, S. D., and Nolan, G. P. (2011). Single-cell mass cytometry of differential immune and drug responses across a human hematopoietic continuum. *Science* **332**:687–696.

Birtwistle, M. R., Hatakeyama, M., Yumoto, N., Ogunnaike, B. A., Hoek, J. B., and Kholodenko, B. N. (2007). Ligand-dependent responses of the ErbB signaling network: experimental and modeling analyses. *Mol. Syst. Biol.* **3**:144.

Bisson, N., James, D. A., Ivosev, G., Tate, S. A., Bonner, R., Taylor, L., and Pawson, T. (2011). Selected reaction monitoring mass spectrometry reveals the dynamics of signaling through the GRB2 adaptor. *Nat. Biotechnol.* **29**:653–658.

Bodenmiller, B., Zunder, E. R., Finck, R., Chen, T. J., Savig, E. S., Bruggner, R. V., Simonds, E. F., Bendall, S. C., Sachs, K., Krutzik, P. O., and Nolan, G. P. (2012). Multiplexed mass cytometry profiling of cellular states perturbed by small-molecule regulators. *Nat. Biotechnol.* **30**:858–867.

Bossi, A., and Lehner, B. (2009). Tissue specificity and the human protein interaction network. *Mol. Syst. Biol.* **5**:260.

Brown, M. D., and Sacks, D. B. (2009). Protein scaffolds in MAP kinase signalling. *Cell Signal.* **21**:462–469.

Buljan, M., Chalancon, G., Eustermann, S., Wagner, G. P., Fuxreiter, M., Bateman, A., and Babu, M. M. (2012). Tissue-specific splicing of disordered segments that embed binding motifs rewires protein interaction networks. *Mol. Cell* **46**:871–883.

Burkard, T. R., Planyavsky, M., Kaupe, I., Breitwieser, F. P., Burckstummer, T., Bennett, K. L., Superti-Furga, G., and Colinge, J. (2011). Initial characterization of the human central proteome. *BMC Syst. Biol.* **5**:17.

Chang, J. T., Carvalho, C., Mori, S., Bild, A. H., Gatza, M. L., Wang, Q., Lucas, J. E., Potti, A., Febbo, P. G., West, M., and Nevins, J. R. (2009). A genomic strategy to elucidate modules of oncogenic pathway signaling networks. *Mol. Cell* **34**:104–114.

Chapman, S. A., and Asthagiri, A. R. (2009). Quantitative effect of scaffold abundance on signal propagation. *Mol. Syst. Biol.* **5**:313.

Chattopadhyay, P. K., Price, D. A., Harper, T. F., Betts, M. R., Yu, J., Gostick, E., Perfetto, S. P., Goepfert, P., Koup, R. A., De Rosa, S. C., Bruchez, M. P., and Roederer, M. (2006). Quantum dot semiconductor nanocrystals for immunophenotyping by polychromatic flow cytometry. *Nat. Med.* **12**:972–977.

Chen, W. W., Schoeberl, B., Jasper, P. J., Niepel, M., Nielsen, U. B., Lauffenburger, D. A., and Sorger, P. K. (2009). Input-output behavior of ErbB signaling pathways as revealed by a mass action model trained against dynamic data. *Mol. Syst. Biol.* **5**:239.

Chook, Y. M., Gish, G. D., Kay, C. M., Pai, E. F., and Pawson, T. (1996). The Grb2-mSos1 complex binds phosphopeptides with higher affinity than Grb2. *J. Biol. Chem.* **271**:30472–30478.

Choudhary, C., and Mann, M. (2010). Decoding signalling networks by mass spectrometry-based proteomics. *Nat. Rev. Mol. Cell Biol.* **11**:427–439.

Ciaccio, M. F., Wagner, J. P., Chuu, C. P., Lauffenburger, D. A., and Jones, R. B. (2010). Systems analysis of EGF receptor signaling dynamics with microwestern arrays. *Nat. Methods* **7**:148–155.

Citri, A., and Yarden, Y. (2006). EGF-ERBB signalling: towards the systems level. *Nat. Rev. Mol. Cell Biol.* **7**:505–516.

Cohen, A. A., Geva-Zatorsky, N., Eden, E., Frenkel-Morgenstern, M., Issaeva, I., Sigal, A., Milo, R., Cohen-Saidon, C., Liron, Y., Kam, Z., Cohen, L., Danon, T., Perzov, N., and Alon, U. (2008). Dynamic proteomics of individual cancer cells in response to a drug. *Science* **322**:1511–1516.

Collins, J. (2012). Synthetic Biology: Bits and pieces come to life. *Nature* **483**:S8–S10.

Domon, B., and Aebersold, R. (2006). Mass spectrometry and protein analysis. *Science* **312**:212–217.

Dumont, J. E., Pecasse, F., and Maenhaut, C. (2001). Crosstalk and specificity in signalling. Are we crosstalking ourselves into general confusion?. *Cell Signal.* **13**:457–463.

Ebhardt, H. A., Sabido, E., Huttenhain, R., Collins, B., and Aebersold, R. (2012). Range of protein detection by selected/multiple reaction monitoring mass spectrometry in an unfractionated human cell culture lysate. *Proteomics* **12**:1185–1193.

Faeder, J. R., Blinov, M. L., and Hlavacek, W. S. (2009). Rule-based modeling of biochemical systems with BioNetGen. *Methods Mol. Biol.* **500**:113–167.

Fagerberg, L., Stadler, C., Skogs, M., Hjelmare, M., Jonasson, K., Wiking, M., Abergh, A., Uhlen, M., and Lundberg, E. (2011). Mapping the subcellular protein distribution in three human cell lines. *J. Proteome Res.* **10**:3766–3777.

Ferrell, J. E. Jr., (2008). Feedback regulation of opposing enzymes generates robust, all-or-none bistable responses. *Curr. Biol.* **18**:R244–R245.

Fortini, M. E. (2009). Notch signaling: the core pathway and its posttranslational regulation. *Dev. Cell* **16**:633–647.

Fraser, J. S., Gross, J. D., and Krogan, N. J. (2013). From systems to structure: bridging networks and mechanism. *Mol. Cell* **49**:222–231.

Frenkel-Morgenstern, M., Cohen, A. A., Geva-Zatorsky, N., Eden, E., Prilusky, J., Issaeva, I., Sigal, A., Cohen-Saidon, C., Liron, Y., Cohen, L., Danon, T., Perzov, N., and Alon, U. (2010). Dynamic Proteomics: a database for dynamics and localizations of endogenous fluorescently-tagged proteins in living human cells. *Nucleic Acids Res.* **38**:D508–D512.

Fritsche-Guenther, R., Witzel, F., Sieber, A., Herr, R., Schmidt, N., Braun, S., Brummer, T., Sers, C., and Bluthgen, N. (2011). Strong negative feedback from Erk to Raf confers robustness to MAPK signalling. *Mol. Syst. Biol.* **7**:489.

Gao, X., Wang, H., Yang, J. J., Liu, X., and Liu, Z. R. (2012). Pyruvate kinase M2 regulates gene transcription by acting as a protein kinase. *Mol. Cell* **45**:598–609.

Gardner, T. S., di Bernardo, D., Lorenz, D., and Collins, J. J. (2003). Inferring genetic networks and identifying compound mode of action via expression profiling. *Science* **301**:102–105.

Geiger, T., Wehner, A., Schaab, C., Cox, J., and Mann, M. (2012). Comparative proteomic analysis of eleven common cell lines reveals ubiquitous but varying expression of most proteins. *Mol. Cell Proteomics* **11** M111 014050

Goldstein, B., Faeder, J. R., and Hlavacek, W. S. (2004). Mathematical and computational models of immune-receptor signalling. *Nat. Rev. Immunol.* **4**:445–456.

Gordus, A., Krall, J. A., Beyer, E. M., Kaushansky, A., Wolf-Yadlin, A., Sevecka, M., Chang, B. H., Rush, J., and MacBeath, G. (2009). Linear combinations of docking affinities explain quantitative differences in RTK signaling. *Mol. Syst. Biol.* **5**:235.

Gureasko, J., Galush, W. J., Boykevisch, S., Sondermann, H., Bar-Sagi, D., Groves, J. T., and Kuriyan, J. (2008). Membrane-dependent signal integration by the Ras activator Son of sevenless. *Nat. Struct. Mol. Biol.* **15**:452–461.

Guzzo, C. M., Berndsen, C. E., Zhu, J., Gupta, V., Datta, A., Greenberg, R. A., Wolberger, C., and Matunis, M. J. (2012). RNF4-dependent hybrid SUMO-ubiquitin chains are signals for RAP80 and thereby mediate the recruitment of BRCA1 to sites of DNA damage. *Sci. Signal.* **5**:ra88.

Hartwell, L. H., Hopfield, J. J., Leibler, S., and Murray, A. W. (1999). From molecular to modular cell biology. *Nature* **402**:C47–C52.

Havugimana, P. C., Hart, G. T., Nepusz, T., Yang, H., Turinsky, A. L., Li, Z., Wang, P. I., Boutz, D. R., Fong, V., Phanse, S., Babu, M., Craig, S. A., Hu, P., Wan, C., Vlasblom, J., Dar, V. U., Bezginov, A., Clark, G. W., Wu, G. C., Wodak, S. J., Tillier, E. R., Paccanaro, A., Marcotte, E. M., and Emili, A. (2012). A census of human soluble protein complexes. *Cell* **150**:1068–1081.

Hortin, G. L., and Sviridov, D. (2010). The dynamic range problem in the analysis of the plasma proteome. *J. Proteomics* **73**:629–636.

Hsieh, M. Y., Yang, S., Raymond-Stinz, M. A., Edwards, J. S., and Wilson, B. S. (2010). Spatio-temporal modeling of signaling protein recruitment to EGFR. *BMC Syst. Biol.* **4**:57.

Huang, P. H., and White, F. M. (2008). Phosphoproteomics: unraveling the signaling web. *Mol. Cell* **31**:777–781.

Hulett, H. R., Bonner, W. A., Barrett, J., and Herzenberg, L. A. (1969). Cell sorting: automated separation of mammalian cells as a function of intracellular fluorescence. *Science* **166**:747–749.

James, J. R., and Vale, R. D. (2012). Biophysical mechanism of T-cell receptor triggering in a reconstituted system. *Nature* **487**:64–69.

Jaqaman, K., and Danuser, G. (2006). Linking data to models: data regression. *Nat. Rev. Mol. Cell Biol.* **7**:813–819.

Jones, R. B., Gordus, A., Krall, J. A., and MacBeath, G. (2006). A quantitative protein interaction network for the ErbB receptors using protein microarrays. *Nature* **439**:168–174.

Kaltenbach, H. M., and Stelling, J. (2012). Modular analysis of biological networks. *Adv. Exp. Med. Biol.* **736**:3–17.

Karlebach, G., and Shamir, R. (2008). Modelling and analysis of gene regulatory networks. *Nat. Rev. Mol. Cell Biol.* **9**:770–780.

Karr, J. R., Sanghvi, J. C., Macklin, D. N., Gutschow, M. V., Jacobs, J. M., Bolival, B. Jr., Assad-Garcia, N., Glass, J. I., and Covert, M. W. (2012). A whole-cell computational model predicts phenotype from genotype. *Cell* **150**:389–401.

Kholodenko, B. N. (2006). Cell-signalling dynamics in time and space. *Nat. Rev. Mol. Cell Biol.* **7**:165–176.

Kholodenko, B. N. (2009). Spatially distributed cell signalling. *FEBS Lett.* **583**:4006–4012.

Kholodenko, B. N., Kiyatkin, A., Bruggeman, F. J., Sontag, E., Westerhoff, H. V., and Hoek, J. B. (2002). Untangling the wires: a strategy to trace functional interactions in signaling and gene networks. *Proc. Natl. Acad. Sci. USA* **99**:12841–12846.

Kholodenko, B. N., Hancock, J. F., and Kolch, W. (2010). Signalling ballet in space and time. *Nat. Rev. Mol. Cell Biol.* **11**:414–426.

Kholodenko, B., Yaffe, M. B., and Kolch, W. (2012). Computational approaches for analyzing information flow in biological networks. *Sci. Signal.* **5**:re1.

Kiel, C., and Serrano, L. (2009). Cell type-specific importance of ras-c-raf complex association rate constants for MAPK signaling. *Sci. Signal.* **2**:ra38.

Kiel, C., and Serrano, L. (2012). Structural data in synthetic biology approaches for studying general design principles of cellular signaling networks. *Structure* **20**:1806–1813.

Kiel, C., and Serrano, L. (2012). Challenges ahead in signal transduction: MAPK as an example. *Curr. Opin. Biotechnol.* **23**:305–314.

Kiel, C., Vogt, A., Campagna, A., Chatr-aryamontri, A., Swiatek-de Lange, M., Beer, M., Bolz, S., Mack, A. F., Kinkl, N., Cesareni, G., Serrano, L., and Ueffing, M. (2011). Structural and functional protein network analyses predict novel signaling functions for rhodopsin. *Mol. Syst. Biol.* **7**:551.

Kim, P. M., Lu, L. J., Xia, Y., and Gerstein, M. B. (2006). Relating three-dimensional structures to protein networks provides evolutionary insights. *Science* **314**:1938–1941.

Kim, Y., Paroush, Z., Nairz, K., Hafen, E., Jimenez, G., and Shvartsman, S. Y. (2011). Substrate-dependent control of MAPK phosphorylation in vivo. *Mol. Syst. Biol.* **7**:467.

Kirouac, D. C., Saez-Rodriguez, J., Swantek, J., Burke, J. M., Lauffenburger, D. A., and Sorger, P. K. (2012). Creating and analyzing pathway and protein interaction compendia for modelling signal transduction networks. *BMC Syst. Biol.* **6**:29.

Kitano, H. (2002). Computational systems biology. *Nature* **420**:206–210.

Kitano, H. (2007). A robustness-based approach to systems-oriented drug design. *Nat. Rev. Drug Discov.* **6**:202–210.

Kolch, W., Heidecker, G., Kochs, G., Hummel, R., Vahidi, H., Mischak, H., Finkenzeller, G., Marme, D., and Rapp, U. R. (1993). Protein kinase C alpha activates RAF-1 by direct phosphorylation. *Nature* **364**:249–252.

Kolitz, S. E., and Lauffenburger, D. A. (2012). Measurement and Modeling of Signaling at the Single-Cell Level. *Biochemistry*

Komurov, K., and White, M. (2007). Revealing static and dynamic modular architecture of the eukaryotic protein interaction network. *Mol. Syst. Biol.* **3**:110.

Ku, C. J., Wang, Y., Weiner, O. D., Altschuler, S. J., and Wu, L. F. (2012). Network crosstalk dynamically changes during neutrophil polarization. *Cell* **149**:1073–1083.

Lamond, A. I., Uhlen, M., Horning, S., Makarov, A., Robinson, C. V., Serrano, L., Hartl, F. U., Baumeister, W., Werenskiold, A. K., Andersen, J. S., Vorm, O., Linial, M., Aebersold, R., and Mann, M. (2012). Advancing cell biology through proteomics in space and time (PROSPECTS). *Mol. Cell Proteomics* **11** O112 017731

Lauffenburger, D. A. (2000). Cell signaling pathways as control modules: complexity for simplicity?. *Proc. Natl. Acad. Sci. USA* **97**:5031–5033.

Lewis, B. P., Green, R. E., and Brenner, S. E. (2003). Evidence for the widespread coupling of alternative splicing and nonsense-mediated mRNA decay in humans. *Proc. Natl. Acad. Sci. USA* **100**:189–192.

Lin, C. Y., Lin, Y. W., Yu, S. W., Lo, Y. S., and Yang, J. M. (2012). MoNetFamily: a web server to infer homologous modules and module-module interaction networks in vertebrates. *Nucleic Acids Res.* **40**:W263–W270.

Lluis, F., Pedone, E., Pepe, S., and Cosma, M. P. (2008). Periodic activation of Wnt/beta-catenin signaling enhances somatic cell reprogramming mediated by cell fusion. *Cell Stem Cell* **3**:493–507.

Lorentzen, A., Kinkhabwala, A., Rocks, O., Vartak, N., and Bastiaens, P. I. (2010). Regulation of Ras localization by acylation enables a mode of intracellular signal propagation. *Sci. Signal.* **3**:ra68.

Madar, A., Greenfield, A., Ostrer, H., Vanden-Eijnden, E., and Bonneau, R. (2009). The Inferelator 2.0: a scalable framework for reconstruction of dynamic regulatory network models. *Conf. Proc. IEEE Eng. Med. Biol. Soc.* **2009**:5448–5451.

Maier, T., Guell, M., and Serrano, L. (2009). Correlation of mRNA and protein in complex biological samples. *FEBS Lett.* **583**:3966–3973.

Marchisio, M. A., and Stelling, J. (2011). Automatic design of digital synthetic gene circuits. *PLoS Comput. Biol.* **7**:e1001083.

Meyers, J., Craig, J., and Odde, D. J. (2006). Potential for control of signaling pathways via cell size and shape. *Curr. Biol.* **16**:1685–1693.

Miller-Jensen, K., Janes, K. A., Brugge, J. S., and Lauffenburger, D. A. (2007). Common effector processing mediates cell-specific responses to stimuli. *Nature* **448**:604–608.

Nakakuki, T., Birtwistle, M. R., Saeki, Y., Yumoto, N., Ide, K., Nagashima, T., Brusch, L., Ogunnaike, B. A., Okada-Hatakeyama, M., and Kholodenko, B. N. (2010). Ligand-specific c-Fos expression emerges from the spatiotemporal control of ErbB network dynamics. *Cell* **141**:884–896.

Nalbant, P., Hodgson, L., Kraynov, V., Toutchkine, A., and Hahn, K. M. (2004). Activation of endogenous Cdc42 visualized in living cells. *Science* **305**:1615–1619.

Neves, S. R., Tsokas, P., Sarkar, A., Grace, E. A., Rangamani, P., Taubenfeld, S. M., Alberini, C. M., Schaff, J. C., Blitzer, R. D., Moraru, I. I., and Iyengar, R. (2008). Cell shape and negative links in regulatory motifs together control spatial information flow in signaling networks. *Cell* **133**:666–680.

O'Shaughnessy, E. C., and Sarkar, C. A. (2012). Analyzing and engineering cell signaling modules with synthetic biology. *Curr. Opin. Biotechnol.* **23**:785–790.

O'Shaughnessy, E. C., Palani, S., Collins, J. J., and Sarkar, C. A. (2011). Tunable signal processing in synthetic MAP kinase cascades. *Cell* **144**:119–131.

Papin, J. A., Hunter, T., Palsson, B. O., and Subramaniam, S. (2005). Reconstruction of cellular signalling networks and analysis of their properties. *Nat. Rev. Mol. Cell Biol.* **6**:99–111.

Park, S. H., Zarrinpar, A., and Lim, W. A. (2003). Rewiring MAP kinase pathways using alternative scaffold assembly mechanisms. *Science* **299**:1061–1064.

Peng, M., Taouatas, N., Cappadona, S., van Breukelen, B., Mohammed, S., Scholten, A., and Heck, A. J. (2012). Protease bias in absolute protein quantitation. *Nat. Methods* **9**:524–525.

Pepperkok, R., and Ellenberg, J. (2006). High-throughput fluorescence microscopy for systems biology. *Nat. Rev. Mol. Cell Biol.* **7**:690–696.

Ponten, F., Gry, M., Fagerberg, L., Lundberg, E., Asplund, A., Berglund, L., Oksvold, P., Bjorling, E., Hober, S., Kampf, C., Navani, S., Nilsson, P., Ottosson, J., Persson, A., Wernerus, H., Wester, K., and Uhlen, M. (2009). A global view of protein expression in human cells, tissues, and organs. *Mol. Syst. Biol.* **5**:337.

Rajakulendran, T., Sahmi, M., Lefrancois, M., Sicheri, F., and Therrien, M. (2009). A dimerization-dependent mechanism drives RAF catalytic activation. *Nature* **461**:542–545.

Rajasethupathy, P., Antonov, I., Sheridan, R., Frey, S., Sander, C., Tuschl, T., and Kandel, E. R. (2012). A role for neuronal piRNAs in the epigenetic control of memory-related synaptic plasticity. *Cell* **149**:693–707.

Rhrissorrakrai, K., and Gunsalus, K. C. (2011). MINE: module identification in networks. *BMC Bioinformatics* **12**:192.

Rocks, O., Peyker, A., Kahms, M., Verveer, P. J., Koerner, C., Lumbierres, M., Kuhlmann, J., Waldmann, H., Wittinghofer, A., and Bastiaens, P. I. (2005). An acylation cycle regulates localization and activity of palmitoylated Ras isoforms. *Science* **307**:1746–1752.

Santos, S. D., Verveer, P. J., and Bastiaens, P. I. (2007). Growth factor-induced MAPK network topology shapes Erk response determining PC-12 cell fate. *Nat. Cell Biol.* **9**:324–330.

Schirle, M., Heurtier, M. A., and Kuster, B. (2003). Profiling core proteomes of human cell lines by one-dimensional PAGE and liquid chromatography-tandem mass spectrometry. *Mol. Cell Proteomics* **2**:1297–1305.

Schwanhausser, B., Busse, D., Li, N., Dittmar, G., Schuchhardt, J., Wolf, J., Chen, W., and Selbach, M. (2011). Global quantification of mammalian gene expression control. *Nature* **473**:337–342.

Selzer, T., Albeck, S., and Schreiber, G. (2000). Rational design of faster associating and tighter binding protein complexes. *Nat. Struct. Biol.* **7**:537–541.

Sevecka, M., Wolf-Yadlin, A., and MacBeath, G. (2011). Lysate microarrays enable high-throughput, quantitative investigations of cellular signaling. *Mol. Cell Proteomics* **10** M110 005363

Sharan, R., Suthram, S., Kelley, R. M., Kuhn, T., McCuine, S., Uetz, P., Sittler, T., Karp, R. M., and Ideker, T. (2005). Conserved patterns of protein interaction in multiple species. *Proc. Natl. Acad. Sci. USA* **102**:1974–1979.

Shin, S. Y., Rath, O., Choo, S. M., Fee, F., McFerran, B., Kolch, W., and Cho, K. H. (2009). Positive- and negative-feedback regulations coordinate the dynamic behavior of the Ras-Raf-MEK-ERK signal transduction pathway. *J. Cell Sci.* **122**:425–435.

Sibilia, M., Kroismayr, R., Lichtenberger, B. M., Natarajan, A., Hecking, M., and Holcmann, M. (2007). The epidermal growth factor receptor: from development to tumorigenesis. *Differentiation* **75**:770–787.

Slaughter, B. D., Schwartz, J. W., and Li, R. (2007). Mapping dynamic protein interactions in MAP kinase signaling using live-cell fluorescence fluctuation spectroscopy and imaging. *Proc. Natl. Acad. Sci. USA* **104**:20320–20325.

Spencer, S. L., Gaudet, S., Albeck, J. G., Burke, J. M., and Sorger, P. K. (2009). Non-genetic origins of cell-to-cell variability in TRAIL-induced apoptosis. *Nature* **459**:428–432.

Stelling, J., Sauer, U., Szallasi, Z., Doyle, F. J. 3rd, and Doyle, J. (2004). Robustness of cellular functions. *Cell* **118**:675–685.

Stelniec-Klotz, I., Legewie, S., Tchernitsa, O., Witzel, F., Klinger, B., Sers, C., Herzel, H., Bluthgen, N., and Schafer, R. (2012). Reverse engineering a hierarchical regulatory network downstream of oncogenic KRAS. *Mol. Syst. Biol.* **8**:601.

Turner, W. (1890). The cell theory, past and present. *J. Anat. Physiol.* **24**:253–287.

Verveer, P. J., and Bastiaens, P. I. (2008). Quantitative microscopy and systems biology: seeing the whole picture. *Histochem. Cell Biol.* **130**:833–843.

Vidal, M., Cusick, M. E., and Barabasi, A. L. (2011). Interactome networks and human disease. *Cell* **144**:986–998.

Vinayagam, A., Stelzl, U., Foulle, R., Plassmann, S., Zenkner, M., Timm, J., Assmus, H. E., Andrade-Navarro, M. A., and Wanker, E. E. (2011). A directed protein interaction network for investigating intracellular signal transduction. *Sci. Signal.* **4**:rs8.

von Kriegsheim, A., Baiocchi, D., Birtwistle, M., Sumpton, D., Bienvenut, W., Morrice, N., Yamada, K., Lamond, A., Kalna, G., Orton, R., Gilbert, D., and Kolch, W. (2009). Cell fate decisions are specified by the dynamic ERK interactome. *Nat. Cell Biol.* **11**:1458–1464.

Wagner, S. A., Beli, P., Weinert, B. T., Nielsen, M. L., Cox, J., Mann, M., and Choudhary, C. (2011). A proteome-wide, quantitative survey of in vivo ubiquitylation sites reveals widespread regulatory roles. *Mol. Cell Proteomics* **10** M111 013284

Wang, E. T., Sandberg, R., Luo, S., Khrebtukova, I., Zhang, L., Mayr, C., Kingsmore, S. F., Schroth, G. P., and Burge, C. B. (2008). Alternative isoform regulation in human tissue transcriptomes. *Nature* **456**:470–476.

Wang, X., Wei, X., Thijssen, B., Das, J., Lipkin, S. M., and Yu, H. (2012). Three-dimensional reconstruction of protein networks provides insight into human genetic disease. *Nat. Biotechnol.* **30**:159–164.

Wolf-Yadlin, A., Kumar, N., Zhang, Y., Hautaniemi, S., Zaman, M., Kim, H. D., Grantcharova, V., Lauffenburger, D. A., and White, F. M. (2006). Effects of HER2 overexpression on cell signaling networks governing proliferation and migration. *Mol. Syst. Biol.* **2**:54.

Wolf-Yadlin, A., Hautaniemi, S., Lauffenburger, D. A., and White, F. M. (2007). Multiple reaction monitoring for robust quantitative proteomic analysis of cellular signaling networks. *Proc. Natl. Acad. Sci. USA* **104**:5860–5865.

Yadav, G., and Babu, S. (2012). NEXCADE: perturbation analysis for complex networks. *PLoS One* **7**:e41827.

Yaffe, M. B., and Gough, N. R. (2013). 2012: signaling breakthroughs of the year. *Sci. Signal.* **6**:eg1.

Yang, J. S., Campagna, A., Delgado, J., Vanhee, P., Serrano, L. & Kiel, C. (2012). SAPIN: Structural Analysis for Protein Interaction Networks. *Bioinformatics*.

Yang, W., Xia, Y., Hawke, D., Li, X., Liang, J., Xing, D., Aldape, K., Hunter, T., Alfred Yung, W. K., and Lu, Z. (2012). PKM2 phosphorylates histone H3 and promotes gene transcription and tumorigenesis. *Cell* **150**:685–696.

Yokoyama, T., Takano, K., Yoshida, A., Katada, F., Sun, P., Takenawa, T., Andoh, T., and Endo, T. (2007). DA-Raf1, a competent intrinsic dominant-negative antagonist of the Ras-ERK pathway, is required for myogenic differentiation. *J. Cell Biol.* **177**:781–793.

Zalatan, J. G., Coyle, S. M., Rajan, S., Sidhu, S. S., and Lim, W. A. (2012). Conformational control of the Ste5 scaffold protein insulates against MAP kinase misactivation. *Science* **337**:1218–1222.

Zhong, Q., Simonis, N., Li, Q. R., Charloteaux, B., Heuze, F., Klitgord, N., Tam, S., Yu, H., Venkatesan, K., Mou, D., Swearingen, V., Yildirim, M. A., Yan, H., Dricot, A., Szeto, D., Lin, C., Hao, T., Fan, C., Milstein, S., Dupuy, D., Brasseur, R., Hill, D. E., Cusick, M. E., and Vidal, M. (2009). Edgetic perturbation models of human inherited disorders. *Mol. Syst. Biol.* **5**:321.

Zhou, Z., Qiu, J., Liu, W., Zhou, Y., Plocinik, R. M., Li, H., Hu, Q., Ghosh, G., Adams, J. A., Rosenfeld, M. G., and Fu, X. D. (2012). The Akt-SRPK-SR axis constitutes a major pathway in transducing EGF signaling to regulate alternative splicing in the nucleus. *Mol. Cell* **47**:422–433.

CHAPTER

6

Gene Networks: Estimation, Modeling, and Simulation

Seiya Imoto[a], *Hiroshi Matsuno*[b], *Satoru Miyano*[a]

[a]Human Genome Center, Institute of Medical Science, The University of Tokyo, Minatoku, Tokyo, Japan

[b]Faculty of Science, Yamaguchi University, Yoshida, Yamaguchi, Japan

CONTENTS

Abstract

This chapter describes the computational methods for estimating, modeling, and simulating biological systems. It also presents two approaches to understand biological systems and describes a method and a software tool developed by our research group. Bayesian network is a mathematical model for representing causal relationships among random variables by using conditional probabilities. The conditional probabilities describe the parent-child relationships and can be viewed as an extension of the deterministic models like Boolean networks. This model is suited for modeling qualitative relations between genes and allows mathematical

http://dx.doi.org/10.1016/B978-0-12-405926-9.00006-X

and algorithmic analyses. We also devised a method to infer a gene network in terms of a linear system of differential equations from time-course gene expression data. A software tool is developed based on Petri net to modeling and simulation of gene networks. With this software tool, various models have been constructed and its utility has been demonstrated in practice.

1 INTRODUCTION

Advances in measurement technology have enabled us to obtain genome-wide biological data production ranging from DNA sequences to data from developmental biology. The computational developmental stages to bridge this infra-data and the understanding of life from a systems perspective is presented below (Figure 6.1) together with the requisite milestones. In this post-genomic research direction, gene networks will play a central role in the first stage of development. In particular, computational methods for estimating, modeling, and simulating biological systems are becoming more important. Here we present our computational strategy by giving an overview of our recent contributions in computational systems biology.

The first step is "how to create gene network information" from data. For this direction, we have developed computational methods for estimating gene networks from microarray gene expression data obtained from various perturbations such as gene disruptions, shocks, etc. One of the most promising methods is the Bayesian network model, where genes are regarded as random variables. The discrete Bayesian network model was first applied to gene network modeling by Friedman et al. (2000), where gene expression levels are categorized into +1,0, and −1. Inspired by this strategy, we developed methods which can process continuous numerical data and automatically detect linear and even nonlinear relationships between genes (Imoto et al. 2002; Imoto et al. 2003a,b). We employ a nonparametric regression for capturing nonlinear relationships between genes and derived a new criterion called BNRC (Bayesian network and Nonlinear Regression Criterion) for choosing the best networks in general situations. In order to resolve the acyclicity restriction of Bayesian network model, the dynamic Bayesian network with nonparametric regression for time-course gene expression data has been also devised (Kim et al. 2003, 2004).

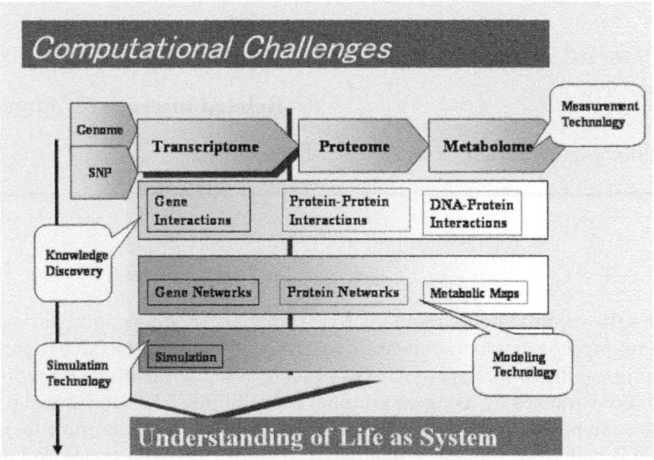

FIGURE 6.1 Genome-wide data and computational issues towards understanding of life.

Naturally, the sole use of microarray data has limitations for gene network estimation. For improving the biological accuracy of estimated gene networks, we have created a general framework by extending this method so that it can employ other genome-wide biological information such as sequence information on promoter regions, protein-protein interactions, protein-DNA interactions, localization information, subcelluar localization, and literature. Computational experiments were conducted with yeast and human gene expression data and they show that cascades of gene regulations were effectively extracted from the data (Imoto et al. 2004, 2006; Nariai et al. 2004; Tamada et al. 2003).

The problem of finding an optimal Bayesian network is known to be NP-hard. The brute force method employing all computing resources in the world would even require time exceeding the lifetime of the solar system for finding an optimal Bayesian network of 30 genes from 100 microarray datasets. Our approach has made it possible to find optimal and near optimal Bayesian networks with respect to the BNRC score in a reasonable time and has provided an evidence of the biological rationality in this computational approach (Kojima et al. 2010; Ott et al. 2004; Ott and Miyano 2003; Ott et al. 2005; Perrier et al. 2008; Tamada et al. 2011).

The second step is "how to model and simulate gene networks" with data and biological knowledge. An important challenge is a creation of a software platform with which scientists in systems biology can model and simulate dynamic causal interactions and processes in the cell, such as gene regulation, metabolic pathways, and signal transduction cascades. There have been pioneering attempts and an accumulation of knowledge in this area, e.g. simulation tools (Gepasi, E-Cell, BioSPICE) and pathway databases (KEGG, BioCyc). We have also developed a software tool, Genomic Object Net for pathway modeling and simulation (Nagasaki et al. 2003; Doi et al. 2003; Matsuno et al. 2003; Matsuno et al. 2000). As its architecture, we defined a notion called Hybrid Functional Petri Net with extension (HFPNe) which is a graphical programming language for describing concurrent processes. We show how computational systems biology can be explored with computational modeling and simulation through an example of a gene network for mammalian circadian rhythms (Matsuno et al. 2005).

2 GENE NETWORK ESTIMATION FROM MICROARRAY GENE EXPRESSION DATA

2.1 Bayesian networks and nonparametric regression

In this section, we introduce Bayesian network and nonparametric regression for estimating gene networks form microarray gene expression data.

2.1.1 Introduction of Bayesian network

Bayesian network is a mathematical model for representing causal relationships among random variables by using conditional probabilities. In the context of Bayesian network, we assume that there is a directed acyclic graph (DAG), denoted by G, as a relationship among random variables. In the gene network estimation based on Bayesian networks, a gene is regarded as a random variable and shown as a node. Let $X_i (i = 1, \ldots, p)$ be a discrete random variable that takes a value from $\{u_1, \ldots, u_m\}$. If there is a directed edge e_{ij} from X_j to X_i, we call X_j a parent of X_i. Also, we define $Pa(X_i) \subset \{X_1, \ldots, X_p\}$ as the set of parents of X_i in G. In the DAG G, the random variable X_i only depends on its direct parents $Pa(X_i)$ and is independent of other variables, i.e. this offers the first order *Markov property* to the relationship among variables described by G. Using the DAG G and its Markov property, the joint probability of all random variables can be decomposed as the product of conditional probabilities:

$$P(X_1, \ldots, X_p) = \prod_{j=1}^{p} P(X_j | Pa(X_j)) \tag{6.1}$$

Since X_j is a discrete variable, the probabilities $\theta_{jkl} = P(X_j = u_k | Pa(X_j) = \boldsymbol{u}_{jl})$ ($j = 1, \ldots, p$ $k = 1, \ldots, m$; $l = 1, \ldots, m^{|Pa(X_j)|}$) are parameters, where $\boldsymbol{u}_{jl}$ is the lth entry of the state table of parents of X_j and $|Pa(X_j)|$ is the number of parents of X_j. For example, for $|Pa(X_j)| = 2$, we have $\boldsymbol{u}_{j1} = (u_1, u_1)$, $\boldsymbol{u}_{j2} = (u_1, u_2)$ and so on. In this case, we can assume that $X_j | Pa(X_j) = \boldsymbol{u}_{jl}$ follows the multinomial distribution with probabilities $\theta_{j1l}, \ldots, \theta_{jml}$ (Friedman and Goldszmidt 1998).

The conditional probabilities $P(X_j | Pa(X_j))$ describe the parent-child relationships and can be viewed as an extension of the deterministic models like Boolean networks (Somogyi and Sniegoski, 1996). If we know the true structure of G *a priori*, from Eq. (6.1), we can construct the joint probability function by estimating each conditional probability. However, in the gene network estimation, the true G is not known and we have to estimate based on the observed data. This problem can be considered as a statistical model selection problem. We describe a graph selection criterion in Section 2.1.3.

Since gene expression data take continuous variables, some discretization methods are required for using the Bayesian networks based on the discrete random variables described above. However, the discretization lead to information loss, and the number of categories and the threshold values are parameters to be optimized. Hence, a modification of Bayesian networks in order to handle continuous variables is an important problem in the gene network estimation problem. A possible solution of this problem is given by using the nonparametric regression introduced in the next section.

2.1.2 Introduction of nonparametric regression

Suppose that we have n sets of data $\boldsymbol{X}_n = \{\boldsymbol{x}_1, \ldots, \boldsymbol{x}_n\}$ of p-dimensional random variable vector $\boldsymbol{X} = (X_1, \ldots, X_p)^t$, where $\boldsymbol{x}_i = (x_{i1}, \ldots, x_{ip})^t$ corresponds to the vector of p gene expression values measured by the ith microarray. Here $\boldsymbol{a}^t$ represents the transpose of $\boldsymbol{a}$. Using the data $\boldsymbol{X}_n$, we can rewrite Eq. (6.1) using densities instead of the probabilistic measure:

$$f(\boldsymbol{x}_1, \ldots, \boldsymbol{x}_n | \boldsymbol{\theta}, G) = \prod_{i=1}^{n} \prod_{j=1}^{p} f_j(x_{ij} | \boldsymbol{p}_{ij}, \boldsymbol{\theta}_j) \tag{6.2}$$

where $\boldsymbol{\theta} = (\boldsymbol{\theta}_1^t, \ldots, \boldsymbol{\theta}_p^t)^t$ is the parameter vector and $\boldsymbol{p}_{ij}$ is the expression value vector of parents of X_j measured by ith microarray. The construction of the conditional probability $f_j(x_{ij} | \boldsymbol{p}_{ij}, \boldsymbol{\theta}_j)$ is equivalent to the problem of the fitting regression model to the data $\{(x_{ij}, \boldsymbol{p}_{ij});\ i = 1, \ldots, n\}$ by $x_{ij} = m_j(\boldsymbol{p}_{ij}) + \varepsilon_{ij}$, where $m_j(\cdot)$ is a smooth function from $\mathrm{R}^{|Pa(X_j)|}$ to R and ε_{ij} ($i = 1, \ldots, n$) are independently and normally distributed with mean 0 and variance σ_j^2. If we set the function $m_j(\cdot)$ by $m_j(\boldsymbol{p}_{ij}) = \beta_0 + \boldsymbol{\beta}^t \boldsymbol{p}_{ij}$, where β_0 and $\boldsymbol{\beta} = (\beta_1, \ldots, \beta_{|Pa(X_j)|})^t$ are parameters, we have a linear regression model to capture the relationship between x_{ij} and $\boldsymbol{p}_{ij}$ (Friedman et al. 2000). However, this model assumes the relationships between variables are linear, and it is unsuitable to extract effective information from complex phenomena. To capture even nonlinear dependencies, Imoto et al. (2003a,b) proposed the use of the *nonparametric additive regression model* (Hastie and Tibshirani, 1990) of the form

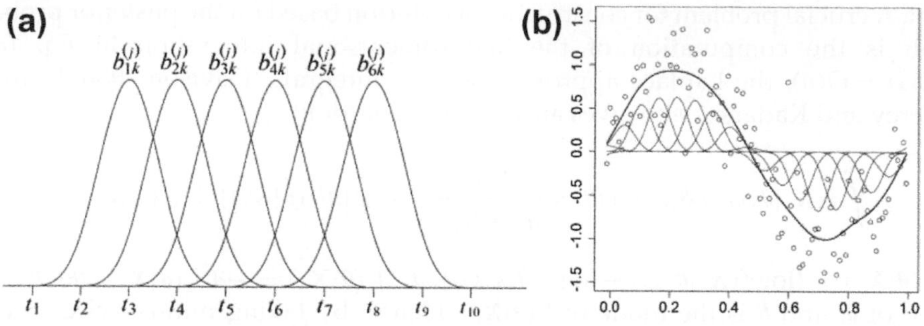

FIGURE 6.2 Example of *B*-splines. (a) Example of 6 *B*-splines of degree 3. The knots are equally spaced. (b) The fitted curve to simulated data: The thin curves are *B*-splines that are weighted by coefficients and the thick curve is the smoothed estimate that is obtained by the linear combination of the weighted *B*-splines.

$$x_{ij} = m_{j,1}(p_{i,1}^{(j)}) + \cdots + m_{j,|Pa(X_j)|}(p_{i,|Pa(X_j)|}^{(j)}) + \varepsilon_{ij} \tag{6.3}$$

where $m_{j,k}(\cdot)$ $(k = 1, \ldots, |Pa(X_j)|)$ are smooth functions from R to R and $\boldsymbol{p}_{ij} = (p_{i,1}^{(j)}, \ldots, p_{i,|Pa(X_j)|}^{(j)})^t$. We construct $m_{j,k}(\cdot)$ by the basis function expansion method with *B-splines* (de Boor 1978; Imoto and Konishi 2003): $m_{j,k}(p) = \sum_{s=1}^{M_{jk}} \gamma_{sk}^{(j)} b_{sk}^{(j)}(p)$, where $\gamma_{sk}^{(j)}$ $(s = 1, \ldots, M_{jk})$ are parameters, $\{b_{1k}^{(j)}(\cdot), \ldots, b_{M_{jk}k}^{(j)}(\cdot)\}$ is the prescribed set of *B*-splines, and M_{jk} is the number of *B*-splines. Figure 6.2 shows an example of *B*-splines ($M_{jk} = 6$) of degree 3. t_d $(d = 1, \ldots, 10)$ are called knots. By using nonparametric regression with *B*-splines, we can capture even nonlinear dependencies.

2.1.3 *Bayesian networks for modeling gene networks*

In this section, we describe a method for estimating gene networks from gene expression data using Bayesian networks and nonparametric regression. By combining Eqs. (6.2) and (6.3), we have a Bayesian network model with *B*-spline nonparametric regression of the form

$$f(\boldsymbol{X}_n|\boldsymbol{\theta}, G) = \prod_{i=1}^{n}\prod_{j=1}^{p} \frac{1}{(2\pi\sigma_j^2)^{1/2}} \exp\left\{-\frac{(x_{ij} - \sum_k \sum_s \gamma_{sk}^{(j)} b_{sk}^{(j)}(p_{ik}^{(j)}))^2}{2\sigma_j^2}\right\} \tag{6.4}$$

Once we set a graph, the statistical model based on Eq. (6.4) can by estimated by a suitable procedure. However, the problem that still remains to be solved is how we can choose the optimal graph, which gives the best approximation of the system underlying the data. We construct a criterion for evaluating a graph based on our model from Bayes approach, that is the maximization of the posterior probability of the graph. The *posterior probability* of the graph $P(G|\boldsymbol{X}_n)$ is written by $P(G|\boldsymbol{X}_n) = p(\boldsymbol{X}_n|G)P(G)/p(\boldsymbol{X}_n) \propto p(\boldsymbol{X}_n|G)P(G)$, where $P(G)$ is the *prior probability* of the graph and $p(\boldsymbol{X}_n)$ is the *normalizing constant* and not related to the graph selection. The likelihood $p(\boldsymbol{X}_n|G)$ is obtained by marginalizing the joint density $p(\boldsymbol{X}_n, \boldsymbol{\theta}|G)$ against $\boldsymbol{\theta}$ and given by

$$p(\boldsymbol{X}_n|G) = \int f(\boldsymbol{X}_n, \boldsymbol{\theta}|G)d\boldsymbol{\theta} = \int f(\boldsymbol{X}_n|\boldsymbol{\theta}, G)p(\boldsymbol{\theta}|\boldsymbol{\lambda}, G)d\boldsymbol{\theta} \tag{6.5}$$

where $p(\boldsymbol{\theta}|\boldsymbol{\lambda}, G)$ is the prior distribution on the parameter $\boldsymbol{\theta}$ and $\boldsymbol{\lambda}$ is the hyperparameter vector. Under the Bayes approach, we can choose the optimal graph such that $P(G|\boldsymbol{X}_n)$ is maximum. A crucial problem for constructing a criterion based on the posterior probability of the graph is the computation of the high-dimensional integration in Eq. (6.5). For $\log p(\boldsymbol{\theta}|\boldsymbol{\lambda}, G) = O(n)$, the Laplace approximation for integrals (Davison 1986; Konishi et al. 2004; Tinerey and Kadane 1986) gives an analytical solution:

$$\int f(\mathbf{X}_n|\boldsymbol{\theta}, G)p(\boldsymbol{\theta}|\boldsymbol{\lambda}, G)d\boldsymbol{\theta} = \frac{(2\pi/n)^{r/2}}{|J_\lambda(\hat{\boldsymbol{\theta}}|\mathbf{X}_n)|^{1/2}} \exp\{nl_\lambda(\hat{\boldsymbol{\theta}}|\mathbf{X}_n)\}\{1 + O_p(n^{-1})\} \tag{6.6}$$

where $l_\lambda(\boldsymbol{\theta}|\mathbf{X}_n) = \{\log f(\mathbf{X}_n|\boldsymbol{\theta}, G) + \log p(\boldsymbol{\theta}|\boldsymbol{\lambda}, G)\}/n$, $J_\lambda(\boldsymbol{\theta}|\mathbf{X}_n) = -\partial^2 l_\lambda(\boldsymbol{\theta}|\mathbf{X}_n)/\partial\boldsymbol{\theta}\partial\boldsymbol{\theta}^t$, r is the dimension of $\boldsymbol{\theta}$, and $\hat{\boldsymbol{\theta}}$ is the mode of $l_\lambda(\boldsymbol{\theta}|\mathbf{X}_n)$. Hence, by taking minus twice logarithm of $P(G|\mathbf{X}_n)$ and substituting Eqs. (6.5) and (6.6) into $P(G|\mathbf{X}_n)$, Imoto et al. (2002) derived a criterion named BNRC (*Bayesian network and Nonparametric Regression Criterion*) for choosing the optimal graph:

$$\mathrm{BNRC}(G) = -2\log P(G) - r\log(2\pi/n) + \log|J_\lambda(\hat{\boldsymbol{\theta}}|\mathbf{X}_n)| - 2nl_\lambda(\hat{\boldsymbol{\theta}}|\mathbf{X}_n) \tag{6.7}$$

The optimal graph $\hat{G}$ is chosen such that the criterion Eq. (6.7) is minimal. Imoto et al. (2003a,b) also extended to results of Imoto et al. (2002) to handle the *nonparametric heteroscedastic regression*. In practice the value of BNRC(G) defined in Eq. (6.7) can be computed by the sum of the local scores, $\mathrm{BNRC}(G) = \sum_{j=1}^{p} \mathrm{BNRC}_j$, where BNRC_j is defined by the approximation of

$$-2\log P_j(G) \int \prod_{i=1}^{n} f_j(x_{ij}|\boldsymbol{p}_{ij}, \boldsymbol{\theta}_j)p_j(\boldsymbol{\theta}_j|\boldsymbol{\lambda}_j)d\boldsymbol{\theta}_j$$

obtained by the Laplace approximation. Here, we assume $p(\boldsymbol{\theta}|\boldsymbol{\lambda}, G) = \prod_{j=1}^{p} p_j(\boldsymbol{\theta}_j|\boldsymbol{\lambda}_j)$ and $P_j(G)$ is called the prior probability for the jth local structure defined by the jth variable and its direct parents. Note that $P(G) = \prod_{j=1}^{p} P_j(G)$ holds.

In the Bayesian network literature (Chickering 1996; Ott 2004), it is shown that determining the optimal network is an NP-hard problem. When we focus on gene networks with the small number of genes such as 30 or 40, we can find the optimal graph structure by using a suitable algorithm (Ott et al. 2004). However, for larger number of genes, we employ a heuristic strategy such as a greedy hill-climbing algorithm to learn graph structure. The details of model learning are described in Section 3.3.

3 ADVANCED METHODS FOR GENE NETWORK ESTIMATION

3.1 Multisource biological information for estimating gene networks

Other than microarray data, there are several information that are useful for estimating gene networks. In this section, we describe methods for combining gene expression data and other biological information such as binding site information, protein-protein interaction data to estimate gene networks.

3.1.1 *General framework*

The main drawback for the gene network construction from microarray data is that while the gene network contains a large number of genes, the information contained in gene expression data is limited by the number of microarrays, their quality, the experimental design, noise, and measurement errors. Therefore, estimated gene networks contain some incorrect gene regulations, which cannot be evaluated from a biological viewpoint. In particular, it is difficult to determine the direction of gene regulation using gene expression data only. Hence, the use of biological knowledge, including protein-protein and protein-DNA interactions, sequences of the binding site of the genes controlled by transcription regulators, literature, and so on, are considered to be a key for microarray data analysis (Hartemink et al. 2002; Imoto et al. 2004).

Imoto et al. (2004) provided a general framework for combining microarray data and biological knowledge aimed at estimating a gene network by using a Bayesian network model. The criterion BNRC(G) in Eq. (6.7) contains two quantities: the prior probability $P(G)$ of the graph, and the marginal likelihood of the data $p(\boldsymbol{X}_n|G)$. The marginal likelihood shows the fitness of the model to the gene expression data. The biological knowledge can then be used as the prior probability of the graph. Suppose that the biological knowledge is represented as the matrix $\boldsymbol{A} = (a_{ij})$, where if we know gene$_i$ regulates gene$_j$, we set $a_{ij} = 1$, otherwise $a_{ij} = 2$. Using the information of $\boldsymbol{A}$, we put a value $\zeta_{a_{ij}}$ on the edge e_{ij}. Note that $\zeta_1 < \zeta_2$ holds. The prior probability of the graph G can be expressed as

$$P(G) = \frac{1}{Z} \exp\left(- \sum_{i,j:\ e_{ij} \in G} \zeta_{a_{ij}} \right) \tag{6.8}$$

where Z is the normalizing constant. In Imoto et al. (2004), ζ_1 and ζ_2 are optimized by the proposed criterion. This prior probability puts a higher probability to a graph that is consistent with the information in $\boldsymbol{A}$.

Recently, more information can be used as priors for gene network estimation simultaneously. Such information is sometimes obtained as continuous and/or discrete. To integrate such multisource prior information, Imoto et al. (2006) proposed a prior probability of the graph as follows: Let $z_{ij}^{(k)}$ represents the kth prior information of the edge e_{ij}. Using the adjacent matrix $E = \{\tilde{e}_{ij}\}_{1 \leqslant i,j \leqslant p}$, where $\tilde{e}_{ij} = 1$ for $e_{ij} \in G$ or 0 for otherwise, we assume the Bernoulli distribution on $\tilde{e}_{ij}$ having probabilistic function

$$p(\tilde{e}_{ij}) = \pi_{ij}^{\tilde{e}_{ij}} (1 - \pi_{ij})^{1 - \tilde{e}_{ij}}$$

where $\pi_{ij} = p(\tilde{e}_{ij} = 1)$. For constructing π_{ij}, we use the logistic model

$$\pi_{ij} = \frac{1}{1 + exp(-\eta_{ij})}$$

with a linear predictor $\eta_{ij} = \sum_{k=1}^{K} w_k(z_{ij}^{(k)} - c_k)$, where w_k and c_k $(k = 1, \cdots, K)$ are weight and baseline parameters, respectively. We then define a prior probability of the graph based on prior information $z_{ij}^{(k)}$ $(k = 1, \cdots, K; 1 \leqslant i, j \leqslant p)$ by

$$P(G) = \prod_i \prod_j p(\tilde{e}_{ij})$$

3.1.2 *Promoter regions*

It is known that the regulation of genes is realized by transcription factors (TFs), which are important subsets of proteins that transcribe mRNAs from DNAs. Genes that a specific TF regulates, contain a binding consensus motif called the transcription factor binding site, located in the upstream regions of the genes. Tamada et al. (2003) provided a statistical method for estimating gene networks and detecting promoter elements simultaneously. Suppose that a gene g in the network is a transcription factor. If the children of g are directly regulated by g, then they may share a consensus motif in their upstream DNA sequences. By detecting a consensus motif from a set of genes, which have been selected based on the structure of the network, we can correct the network by repairing misdirected edges and/or adding direct edges from g, based on the existence of the motif. The algorithm for simultaneous estimation of a gene network and detection of binding site is as follows:

Step 1. Estimate a gene network from microarray data alone using Bayesian network model.

Step 2. For each gene g, let D_g be the set of child and grand-child genes of g. Genes with $|D_g| \geqslant 4$ are considered as TFs, and search for motifs in D_g.

Step 3. For each TF, based on the result of the motif detection:

- **(A)** If a parent of the TF contains the motif, we reverse the edge and make it a direct child.
- **(B)** If a grand-child of the TF contains the motif, we add an edge and make it a direct child. We also embed this information into Eq. (6.8).

Step 4. Estimate a gene network again along with the motif information.

Step 5. Continue Step 2 through 4 until the network does not change.

For the motif detection method used in Step 2, Tamada et al. (2003) used a method called *string pattern regression* (Bannai et al. 2002) that employs the *substring pattern class* as the motif model.

3.1.3 *Protein-protein interactions*

Nariai et al. (2004) proposed the use of protein-protein interaction data for refining gene networks estimated by microarray gene expression data. When a gene is regulated by a protein complex, it is natural that a protein complex is considered as a direct parent. Therefore, Nariai et al. (2004) proposed the use of virtual nodes corresponding to protein complexes in the Bayesian networks. The virtual nodes corresponding protein complexes are created by the principal component analysis and the proposed criterion can be used to decide whether we make a protein complex. The information of the protein-protein interaction data can be converted into the prior probability of the graph. If gene$_i$ and gene$_j$ show the protein-protein

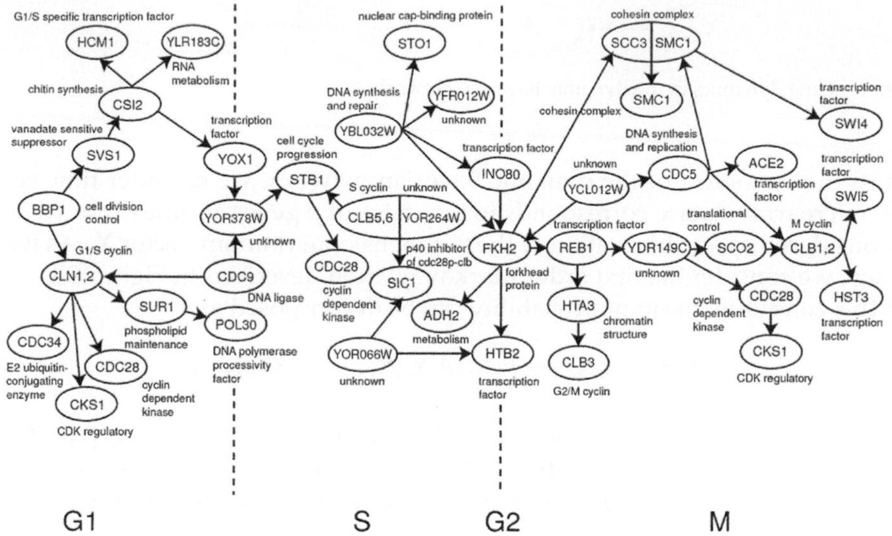

FIGURE 6.3 Cell cycle gene network estimated by using "phase" information together with microarray data and protein-protein interactions. The ellipses that has more than two genes are estimated protein complexes.

interaction, we set $a_{ij} = a_{ji} = 1$ in A. Figure 6.3 is a part of result of Nariai et al. (2004). This method enables us not only to refine gene networks but also to find unknown protein complexes.

3.1.4 *Single gene knock-down*

Imoto et al. (2006) constructed prior probability of the graph based on single gene knock-down gene expression data. They used 400 microarray gene expression data of single gene knock-down by siRNA in human endothelial cell (HUVEC). Also, time-series gene expression profiles of HUVEC dosed by Fenofibrate, anti-hyperlipidaemia drug, were measured to elucidate drug response gene networks in HUVEC against Fenofibrate. Dynamic Bayesian network estimated a dynamic network of HUVEC genes affected by dosing Fenofibrate and this graph structure was also used as prior information. Therefore, two types of prior information were integrated to the 400 gene knock-down microarray data and a gene network that is a candidate pathway strongly affected by Fenofibrate was estimated by Bayesian network and nonparametric regression method. They discussed the position of PPARa that is the target of Fenofibrate in the estimated gene network and found 21 lipid metabolism-related genes and 11 molecules previously identified experimentally to be related to PPARa. Imoto et al. (2006); Tamada et al. (2009) and Araki et al. (2009) provide the details of the results.

3.2 Dynamic Bayesian networks

A shortcoming of the Bayesian networks is that this model cannot construct cyclic networks, while a real gene regulation mechanism has cyclic regulations. Recently, the use of the *dynamic Bayesian networks* has been proposed for constructing a gene network with cyclic

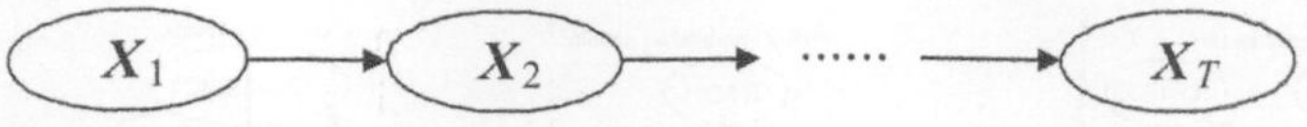

FIGURE 6.4 Time dynamics in the dynamic Bayesian networks.

regulations. In the context of the dynamic Bayesian network, we consider time series data, i.e. the tth microarray data $\mathbf{x}_t$ corresponds to the states of p genes at time t ($t = 1,\ldots,T$). Note that $\mathbf{x}_t$ is considered as an observation of the p-dimensional random vector $\mathbf{X}_t$. As for the time dependency, we consider the first order Markov relation described in Figure 6.4.

Under this condition, the joint probability can be decomposed as

$$P(\mathbf{X}_1,\ldots,\mathbf{X}_T) = P(\mathbf{X}_1)P(\mathbf{X}_2|\mathbf{X}_1)\cdots P(\mathbf{X}_T|\mathbf{X}_{T-1}) \tag{6.9}$$

The gene regulations can be modeled through the construction of $P(\mathbf{X}_t|\mathbf{X}_{t-1})$ for $t = 2,\ldots,T$. The network structure is assumed to be stable through all time points. The conditional probability $P(\mathbf{X}_t|\mathbf{X}_{t-1})$ can also be decomposed into the product of conditional probabilities of each gene given its parents

$$P(\mathbf{X}_t|\mathbf{X}_{t-1}) = \prod_{j=1}^{p} P(X_{tj}|Pa(X_j)_{t-1}) \tag{6.10}$$

where $Pa(X_j)_{t-1}$ is the set of random variables corresponding to the parent genes of jth gene at time $t-1$. By combining Eqs. (6.9) and (6.10), we have the decomposition:

$$P(\mathbf{X}_1,\ldots,\mathbf{X}_T) = P(\mathbf{X}_1)\prod_{t=2}^{T}\prod_{j=1}^{p} P(X_{tj}|Pa(X_j)_{t-1}) \tag{6.11}$$

From Eq. (6.11), the extension the dynamic Bayesian networks to handle continuous variable, the detection of nonlinear relationships by using nonparametric regression, and the construction of a graph selection criterion based on the Bayes approach can be done in the same way as the Bayesian networks in Section 2.1. The details of the combination of the dynamic Bayesian networks with the nonparametric regression are described in Kim et al. (2003, 2004).

3.3 Searching optimal Bayesian networks

Finding optimal Bayesian networks is computationally hard. Potentially, we need to search the space of directed acyclic graphs of n vertices whose size c_n is approximately (Robinson 1973):

$$c_n = \frac{n!\cdot 2^{\frac{n}{2}\cdot(n-1)}}{r\cdot z^n};\; r \approx 0.57436;\; z \approx 1.4881$$

From this formula we can see that there are roughly $2.34 \cdot 10^{72}$ networks with 20 vertices and $2.71 \cdot 10^{158}$ for 30 vertices. This complexity does not allow us any brute force approach even with a supercomputer system. Furthermore, without obtaining the optimal Bayesian networks, we cannot have any right insight that Bayesian network model can really extract biologically meaningful regulatory information from microarray gene expression data. Thus we face with two issues. The first issue is how to cope with this complexity and the second is the search for optimal Bayesian networks and their biological evaluation.

3.3.1 *Greedy heuristics for searching Bayesian networks*

Some heuristic approached have been employed for this search problem, e.g. greedy algorithms (Heckerman et al. 1995; Friedman et al. 2000; Imoto et al. 2002), simulated annealing (Hartemink et al., 2002), and genetic algorithms (van Someren et al. 2002).

The greedy hill climbing algorithm due to Heckerman et al. (1995) is shown below as a typical example, where n is the number of repeats. The greedy algorithm algorithm assumes a score function for solutions. It starts from some initial solution and successively improves the solution by selecting the modification from the space of possible modifications, which yields the best score. When no improvement is found, then the algorithm terminates with the currently best solution. Some ideas should be employed for the choice of the initial solution and for the choice of the space of possible modifications. Biologically reasonable locally optimal Bayesian networks of several hundreds genes are reported (Imoto et al. 2002, 2003; Tamada et al. 2003; Nariai et al. 2004).

Greedy Hill Climbing (Heckerman et al. 1995)

Step 1. Initialize the network as the empty network.
Step 2. Randomly select a permutation $\pi : \{1,\ldots,|X|\} \to X$.
Step 3. For all $i = 1,\ldots,|X|$,do the following two steps:
- **(A)** Compute the changes of the score when adding a new parent for$\pi(i)$or removing or reversing the edge of a parent gene of $\pi(i)$.
- **(B)** Select the modification among the modifications which improve the score most without violating the acyclicity condition.

Step 4. Repeat **Step 3** until the score does not improve.
Step 5. Repeat **Steps 1** through **Step 4** for n times and return the best solution found in these iterations.

3.3.2 *Optimal search for Bayesian networks*

BNRC score can be decomposed to an additive form $\mathrm{BNRC}(G) = \sum_{j=1}^{p} \mathrm{BNRC}_j$as shown in Section 2.1.2. We will formulate this optimization problem in an abstract way: For a finite set X (of genes), we call a function $s : X \times 2^X \to R$ a *score function* for X. Then for a DAG $G = (X, E)$, we define the score of X by $\mathrm{score}(G) = \sum_{g\in X} s(g, Pa(g))$.. This corresponds to Eq. (6.7) and its decomposition as above. The problem is to find the best network $G = (X, E)$ which attains the optimal score. In the case of the BNRC score, the problem is defined as a minimization problem. Furthermore, it is noted in Ott (2004) tha the case for the MDL score (Friedman and Goldszmidt 1998) is also formulated as a minimization problem while the case for the BDe score (Cooper and Herskovits 1992; Friedman and Goldszmidt 1998; Heckerman et al. 1995) is defined as a maximization problem.

Ott et al. (2004) have devised an algorithm which can find optimal Bayesian networks of size up to 25 or so if a supercomputer such as SUN FIRE 15K with 96CPUs 900MHz each is used. The algorithm decomposes the search space into subspaces and employs the dynamic programming technique for finding the right subspace as well as for determining the optimal solution in the subspace. In order to describe the algorithm, several notations shall be introduced as follows: For a gene g in X and a subset $A \subseteq X$, $F(g, A) = \min_{B\subseteq A} s(g, B)$ gives the optimal choice of parents for g if the parents are selected from A. An order on a subset $A \subseteq X$ is given as a permutation $\pi : \{1, \ldots, |A|\} \rightarrow A$. We denote by Π^A the set of all permutations on A. We denote the subnetwork of $G = (X, E)$ restricted to A by $G(A) = (A, E(A))$. For a permutation $\pi \in \Pi^A$, we say that $G(A)$ is π-*linear* if $\pi^{-1}(g) < \pi^{-1}(h)$ holds for all $(g, h) \in E(A)$. The idea of the algorithm is to decompose the set of all DAGs on A into subsets of π-linear DAGs for all $\pi \in \Pi^A$. Then we divide the problem into (6.1) to find the subspace of the search space that contains the optimal network and (6.2) to find the optimal network within the selected subspace. We denote $Q^A(\pi) = \sum_{g \in A} F(g, \{h \in A | \pi^{-1}(h) < \pi^{-1}(g)\})$. Then we find the best π-linear network for any given permutation by F and Q. The optimal network can be found by finding the optimal permutation, which yields the global minimum, which is given by $M(A) = \arg\min_{\pi \in \Pi^A} Q^A(\pi)$. Then the whole algorithm is described as follows:

Algorithm for Finding Optimal Bayesian Network (Ott et al. 2004)

Step 1. Compute $F(g, \phi) = s(g, \phi)$ for all $g \in X$.
Step 2. For all $g \in X$ and all $A \subseteq X - \{g\}$ with $A \neq \phi$,
compute $F(g, A)$ as $\min\{s(g, A), \min_{a \in A} F(g, A - \{a\})\}$.
Step 3. Set $M(\phi) = \phi$.
Step 4. For all $A \subseteq X$ with $A \neq \phi$, execute the following steps:
(A) Compute$g^* = \arg\min_{g \in A}(F(g, A - \{g\}) + Q^{A-\{g\}}(M(A - \{g\})))$.
(B) For all $1 \leqslant i < |A|$, set $M(A)(i) := M(A - \{g^*\})(i)$ and $M(A)(|A|) := g^*$.
Step 5. Return $Q^G(M(G))$.

Theorem (Ott et al. 2004). *Optimal Bayesian networks can be found using* $(\frac{|X|}{2} + 1) \cdot 2^{|X|}$ *dynamic programming steps, where X is a set of genes.*

A rigorous proof is required to show the correctness of this algorithm that can be found in Ott et al. (2004). Furthermore, with some biologically reasonable constraints on the networks, we can obtain a much faster algorithm (Ott and Miyano 2003). By computing optimal Bayesian networks of small size and evaluating them, it is reported that optimal Bayesian networks are not necessarily biologically optimal. However by combining optimal to near optimal Bayesian networks thoroughly, we can extract biologically more accurate information from microarray gene expression data (Ott et al. 2004; Ott and Miyano 2003; Ott et al. 2005).

To improve the feasibility of the optimal search, parallelization of the algorithm is a possible way. Tamada et al. (2011) proposed a parallel algorithm for optimal search for Bayesian networks, called ParaOS algorithm. The main feature of this algorithm is that it guarantees that the amount of intermediate results that are required to be shared redundantly among independently split calculations is minimal. In other words, our algorithm guarantees that minimal communications are required between independent parallel processors. Because of this advantage, our algorithm can be easily parallelized, and, in practice, it can run very efficiently on massively parallel computers with several hundreds of processors. They succeeded in estimating the largest optimal Bayesian network search attempted thus far on a 32-node network with 256 processors.

3.3.3 *Constraint optimal search for Bayesian networks*

Recently, Perrier et al. (2008) considered a constraint search space called super-structure (SS) and an optimal search of Bayesian networks on SS. A super-structure is defined as an undirected graph and the score-based search is performed so that the skeleton of the resulting network become a sub-graph of the given SS. Perrier et al. (2008) theorized this idea and proposed a constraint optimal search (COS) algorithm. They showed that COS can be applied to larger networks than optimal search (with an average degree around 2.1, graphs having 1.6 times more nodes could be considered). Furthermore, by using a sound super-structure, COS can learn more accurate graphs than unconstrained optima.

Definition (Perrier et al. 2008). An undirected graph $S = (X, E_S)$ is said to be a super-structure of a DAG $G = (X, E)$, if the skeleton of G, $G_0 = (X, E_0)$ is a subgraph of S (i.e. $E_0 \subseteq E$). We say that S contains the skeleton of G.

Let $N(g)$ be the neighborhood of a variable g in S, i.e., the set of nodes connected to g in S. The constraint optimal search algorithm can be obtained by replacing $X - \{g\}$ in Step 2 of optimal search algorithm by $N(g)$. Perrier et al. (2008) empirically showed the resulting networks from COS have higher accuracy than those from other heuristic algorithms. However, even for a sparse super-structure, i.e. the average degree of the super-structure is around 2, COS is feasible for networks with 50 nodes or so. It is important for gene network estimation to improve the feasibility of COS.

Kojima et al. (2010) proposed an extended constraint optimal search, ECOS, by dividing given super-structure into several clusters and run COS on each cluster. An intuitive way is to perform this strategy for all patterns of the direction of edges that connect between clusters and select the network that has the best score. However, by performing COS to each cluster separately, it is possible to occur a cycle that passes several clusters; the final network cannot be guaranteed as a DAG. For keeping acyclicity assumption, Kojima et al. (2010) proposed the concept of ancestral constraints (ACs) and derived an optimal algorithm satisfying a given set of ACs. The necessary and sufficient sets of ACs for finding an optimal network under a super-structure were also theoretically derived. ECOS can estimate optimal Bayesian networks with several hundred nodes when the average degree of the super-structure is around 4.

4 PETRI NET BASED MODELING OF GENE NETWORKS

4.1 Hybrid functional petri nets for modeling gene networks

4.1.1 Hybrid functional petri net

Petri net is a graphical programming language for modeling concurrent systems which has been mainly used to model artificial systems such as manufacturing systems and communication protocols. From the first attempt by Reddy et al. (1993), several types of Petri nets including stochastic Petri net (Goss et al. 1998) and colored Petri net (Genrich et al. 2001) have been employed to model biological pathways. On the other hand, biological pathways can be observed as hybrid systems, e.g. protein concentration dynamics behaves continuously being coupled with discrete switches; protein production is switched on or off depending on the expression levels of other genes, i.e. presence or absence of other proteins in sufficient concentration. Based on this observation, we proposed *hybrid functional Petri net* (HFPN) (Matsuno et al. 2003) and its extension called *hybrid functional Petri net with extension* (HFPNe) (Nagasaki et al. 2003; Nagasaki et al. 2004; Nagasaki et al. 2005) for modeling biological pathways and developed the HFPNe based simulation software called "Genomic Object Net" (GON) (Genomic Object Net). With GON, we have modeled and simulated many biological pathways including the gene switch mechanism of lambda phage (Matsuno et al. 2000), the signal transduction pathway for apoptosis induced by the protein Fas (Matsuno et al. 2003), and the glycolytic pathway in *E.coli* with the lac operon gene regulatory mechanism (Doi et al. 2004), alternative splicing, frame shifting, Huntington's disease model, p53 modifications (Nagasaki et al. 2004). Since Genomic Object Net equips a biology-oriented GUI, modeling of very complex biological processes with HFPNe can be performed in a simply way. Since the purpose of this chapter is to show that the notion of Peri net has a high affinity to biological process modeling, we deal only with HFPN and will not touch HFPNe. For further details, we refer to Nagasaki et al. (2005). Various modeling methods and biological pathway models have been developed with these modeling concepts (Doi et al. 2006; Li et al. 2006; Matsuno et al. 2006; Li et al. 2007; Mito et al. 2008; Li et al. 2009; Li et al. 2010; Miwa et al. 2010a,b; Matsuno et al. 2011; Li et al. 2011). After our development of GON, we have developed an XML named Cell System Markup Language (CSML) and an ontology Cell System Ontology (CSO) (http://www.csml.org/) for biological pathways (Jeong et al. 2007; Jeong et al. 2011a; Jeong et al. 2011b). Based on these concepts, GON is renewed and is now released as Cell Illustrator 5.0 (https://www.cellillustrator.com/) (Nagasaki et al. 2010). We also developed a pathway database with Cell Illustrator (Nagasaki et al. 2011).

Generally, biological molecular interactions are explained with pictures representing molecules (e.g. genes, mRNAs, proteins, and protein complexes) and arrows representing interactions of these molecules such as activation and repression. To model these interactions mathematically, differential equations have been commonly used. However, in this modeling process, we have to make redundant efforts to reconstruct a system of differential equations from the biological interaction map. Modeling with HFPN allows us to construct a computational model for simulation without taking such a redundant effort. That is, an HFPN model is directly constructed from the map of biological pathway. Thereafter, parameters of reactions such as the transcription speeds of genes and degradation rates of proteins are going to be tuned so that input/output concentration behaviors of substances such as mRNAs and proteins are matched to biological facts obtained from experiments or written in the literature. Since the HFPN based modeling method follows the graphical pictures of biological pathways, the constructed HFPN model can be readily understood without getting into mathematical consideration.

Petri net (Reisig 1985) is a network consisting of *place*, *transition*, *arc*, and *token*. A place can hold tokens as its content. A transition has arcs coming from places and arcs going out from the transition to some places. A transition with these arcs defines a firing rule in terms of the contents of the places where the arcs are attached. *Hybrid Petri net* (HPN) (Alla and David 1998) has two kinds of places *discrete place* and *continuous place* and two kinds of transitions *discrete transition* and *continuous transition*. A discrete place and a discrete transition are the same notions as used in the traditional discrete Petri net. A continuous place can hold a nonnegative real number as its content. A continuous transition fires continuously at the speed of a parameter assigned at the continuous transition. The graphical notations of a discrete transition, a discrete place, a continuous transition, and a continuous place are shown in Figure 6.5, together with three types of arcs. A specific value is assigned to each arc as a weight. When a *normal arc* is attached to a discrete/continuous transition, w tokens are transferred through the normal arc, in either of normal arcs coming from places or going out to places. An *inhibitory arc* with weight w enables the transition to fire only if the content of the place at the

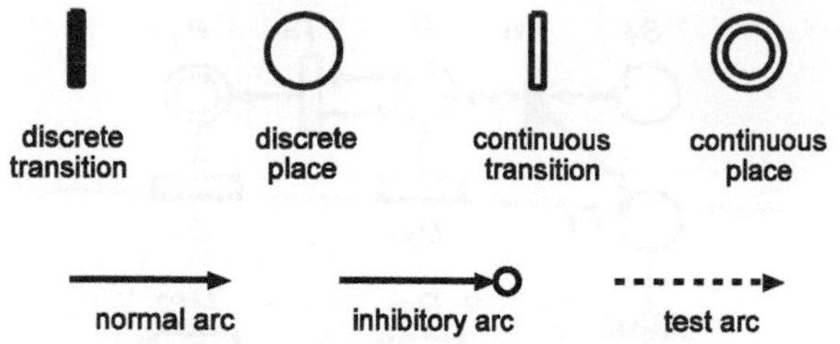

FIGURE 6.5 Elements of hybrid (functional) Petri net.

source of the arc is less than or equal to w. For example, an inhibitory arc can be used to represent repressive activity in gene regulation. A *test arc* does not consume any content of the place at the source of the arc by firing. For example, a test arc can be used to represent enzyme activity, since the enzyme itself is not consumed.

Hybrid dynamic net (HDN) (Drath, 1998) has a similar structure to the HPN, using the same kinds of places and transitions as the HPN. The main difference between HPN and HDN is the firing rule of continuous transition. As we can see from the explanation about HPN above, for a continuous transition of HPN, the different amounts of tokens can be flowed through the two types of arcs, coming from/going out the continuous transition. In contrast, the definition of HDN does not allow transferring different amount through these two types of arcs. However, HDN has the following firing feature of continuous transition which HPN does not have; "the speed of continuous transition of HDN can be given as a function of values in the places."

From the above discussion, we can see that each of HPN and HDN has its own feature for the firing mechanism of continuous transition. As a matter of fact, both of these features of HPN and HDN are essentially required for modeling common biological reactions. This motivated us to define the notion of *hybrid functional Petri net* (HFPN) (Matsuno et al 2003) which includes both of these features of HPN and HDN. Moreover, HFPN has the third feature for arcs, that is, a function of values of the places can be assigned to any arc. This feature was originated from the *functional Petri net* (Hofestädt and Thelen 1998) which was introduced in order to realize the calculation of dynamic biological catalytic process on Petri net based biological pathway modeling. The formal definition of the HFPN is given in Nagasaki et al. (2004) and Nagasaki et al. (2005).

4.1.2 A model of operon with HFPN

Figure 6.6 shows a hybrid Petri net model of an operon which has two genes. Discrete place S_1 (S_2), discrete transition TR_1 (TR_2), continuous places R_1 (R_2) and P_1 (P_2), and continuous transitions TP_1 (TP_2), DR_1 (DR_2), and DP_1 (DP_2) constitute the first gene (the second gene) in the operon. Discrete place F_1 is used to represent transaction of transcription from the first gene to the second gene. At discrete transition T_{R1} (T_{R2}), the parameter which reflects time for transcription of the first gene (the second gene) is assigned, and at discrete transition T_{12}, time for RNA polymerase to traverse the gap between the first and the second genes is assigned. For continuous transitions, parameter at T_{P1} (T_{P2}) represents translation rate of the first gene (the second gene), parameters at D_{R1} and D_{P1} (D_{R2} and D_{P2}) represent degradation rates of mRNA and protein of the first (the second) gene, respectively.

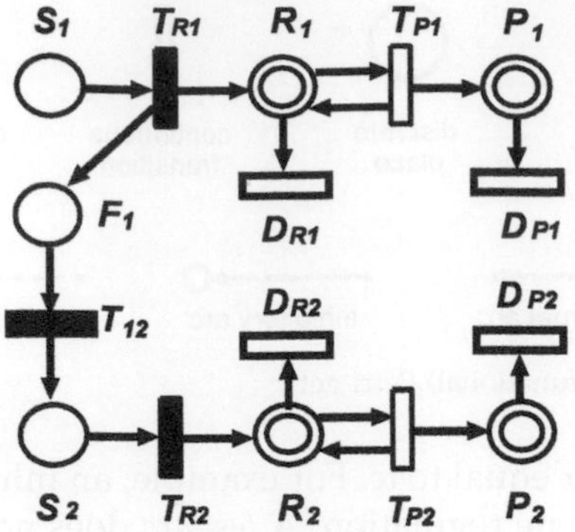

FIGURE 6.6 HFPN model of operon constituted by two genes.

Initially, only discrete place S_1 has one token. This reflects the situation in which RNA polymerase binds at the promoter of the operon. Just after the transcription of the first gene (the second gene) is finished, the amount of continuous place R_1 (R_2) increases by the weight assigned at the arc from the transition T_{R1} (T_{R2}) to the place R_1 (R_2). In the speed of parameter at continuous transition T_{P1} (T_{P2}), the amount of continuous place P_1 (P_2) is increased by the weight at the arc from the transition T_{P1} (T_{P2}), which reflects the translation rate of the first gene (the second gene). Note that, in order to represent the fact that mRNA is not consumed by translation, two arcs are described in both directions between the place R_1 (R_2) and the transition T_{P1} (T_{P2}). This can be also represented by one test arc from R_1 (R_2) to T_{P1} (T_{P2}). Continuous transitions D_{R1} and D_{P1} (D_{R2} and D_{P2}) without outgoing arc are used to represent degradation of mRNA and protein of the first gene (the second gene).

4.2 Modeling gene network for circadian rhythms

This section explains an example of modeling and simulation analysis by following Matsuno et al. (2005) and shows a computational strategy with a simulation tool for systems biology.

4.2.1 Mammalian circadian genetic control mechanism

Molecular clocks reside within suprachiasmatic nucleus cells. Each molecular circadian clock is a negative feedback loop of the gene transcription and its translation into protein. The loop includes several genes and their protein products. In case of mammals, three period genes *Per1*, *Per2*, and *Per3* and two Cryptochrome genes *Cry1* and *Cry2* comprise the negative limb, while *Clock* and *Bmal1* (*Bmal*) genes constitute positive limb of the feedback loop in the molecular circadian clock. In order to simplify the model and gain the insight of each interaction path, we deal with two group of genes (*Per1*, *Per2*, and *Per3* genes) and (*Cry1* and *Cry2* genes) as *Per* and *Cry*, respectively.

Mammalian circadian genetic control mechanism is composed of two interlocked negative feedback loops. PER and CRY proteins collaborate in the regulation of their own expression, assembling in PER-TIM complexes that permit nuclear translocation, inactivation of *Per* and *Cry* transcription in cycling negative feedback loop. At the same time, the PER-TIM complex inactivates the expression of *Rev-Erb* gene. Proteins of Bmal and Clock form heterodimers that activate *Per*, *Cry*, and *Rev-Erb* transcriptions. The *Bmal* gene is inactivated by REV-ERB protein in nucleus. The genes except the gene *Clock* are rhythmically expressed in around 24 hours according to these molecular interactions of genes and their products.

4.2.2 HFPN model

In the present model, *Per* and *Cry* genes and their protein products constitute the first major circadian feedback loop. The second loop is composed of the *Clock* and *Bmal* genes and their protein products. These two pathways are connected by the interaction including *Rev-Erb* and its product. Expression of *Rev-Erb* was accelerated by the PER/CRY dimmers and REV-ERB protein suppresses transcription of *Bmal* gene. Figure 6.7 is an HFPN model of mammalian circadian gene mechanism. In the HFPN, symbols of places and transitions were changed to pictures, which were depicted according to the corresponding biological reactions. These changes are meaningless in mathematical sense, but meaningful in biological sense. With only these changes of Petri net symbols to biological pictures, we can make the whole biological pathway described in Petri net more biologically intuitive.

This HFPN model was described according to the following simple rules. To each substance such as mRNA and protein, a continuous place is assigned. To each transition, a function of the style such as $mX/10$ is assigned, which defines the speed of the corresponding reaction. For example, the translation speed of PER protein is controlled by the formula $m1/5$, where $m1$ is the concentration of *Per* mRNA. This reflects the biological observation that the reaction speed of transcription is changed depending on the concentration of *Per* mRNA. Complex forming rate is given as a formula of the style such as $mX*mY/10$. For example, the formula $m2*m4/10$ is assigned to the continuous transition as the complex forming rate of the proteins PER ($m2$) and CRY ($m4$). Continuous transitions without outgoing arcs are used for representing natural degradation rates of mRNAs, proteins, and protein complexes.

After constructing an HFPN of the biological mechanism to be modeled, parameters of transition speed and initial values of places have to be tuned based on the biological knowledge and/or the facts described in biological literature. In general, many trial and error processes are required until appropriate parameters for simulation are determined. Since GON provides the GUI specially designed for biological modeling, we can perform these processes very easily and smoothly.

4.2.3 Inconsistency discovered by simulation

We carried out simulations of the HFPN model in Figure 6.7 with GON. This model produces periodic oscillations of mRNA and protein concentrations as shown in Figure 6.8. We made some modifications on this HFPN model for checking mutant behaviors including *Per* gene disruption (by removing the normal arc going into the place PER) and preventing *Cry* gene from transcription (by removing the test arc going into the transition attached to the place mCry). The resulting behavior of these modifications corresponded well to the facts in the biological literature (Reppert et al, 2001; Sehgal 2004). However, at the same time, we found the following inconsistency with the biological observation in Figure 6.8.

- In Figure 6.8, the *Bmal* mRNA peaks at almost the same time as the peaks of *Cry* and *Per* mRNAs. However, it is biologically known that the peak of *Bmal* mRNA is located in almost the center of two peaks of *Cry* or *Per* mRNA.

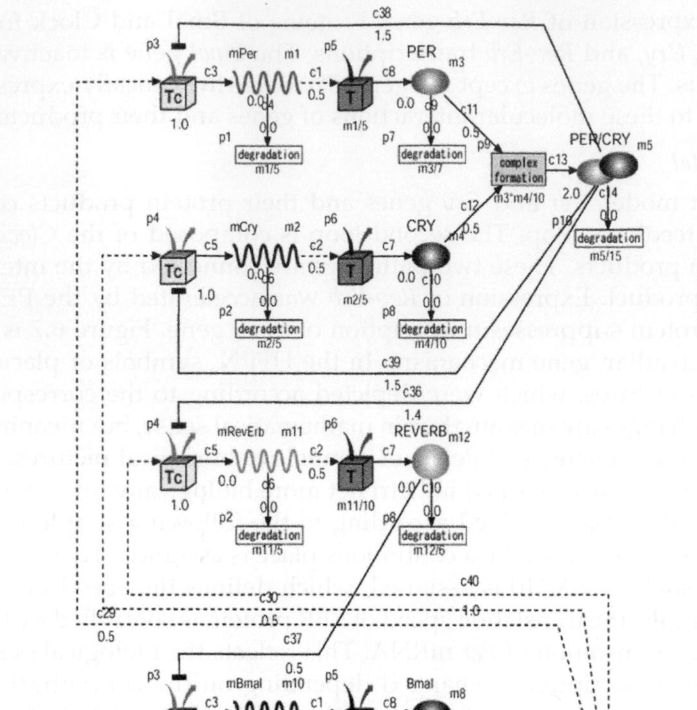

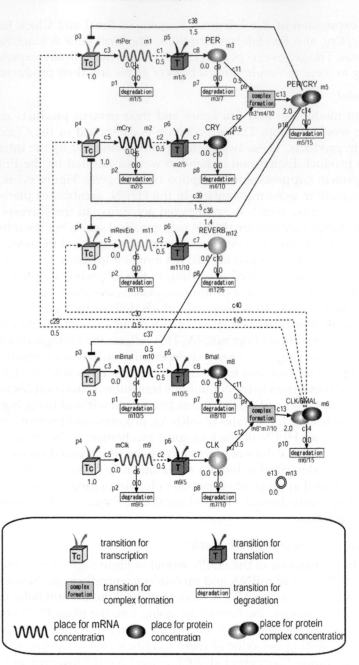

FIGURE 6.7 HFPN model of circadian gene regulatory mechanism in mammals. Places and transitions of HFPN have been changed to pictures which were depicted according to biological reactions.

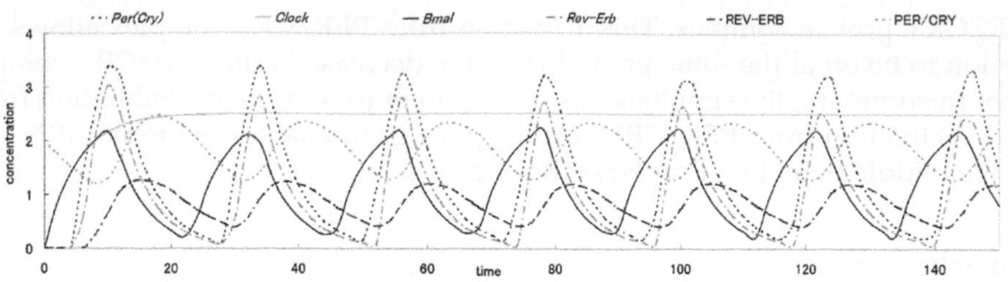

FIGURE 6.8 Simulation result of the HFPN model in Figure 6.7, where dark solid line is *Bmal* mRNA, dark dotted line is *cry* and *per* mRNAs, pale dot-dash-line is *Rev-Erb* mRNA, pale solid line is *Clock* mRNA, pale dotted line is PER/CRY complex, and dark dot-dash-line is REV-ERB protein.

4.2.4 *A new interaction resolves the inconsistency*

Circadian clock mechanisms have been examined in many living organisms such as cyanobacteria, fruit fly, and mouse (Sassone-Corsi 2003; Sehgal 2004; Reppert and Weaver, 2001). Especially, many investigations have been made on fruit fly (*Drosophila melanogaster*) and it is known that it has a similar circadian gene regulatory mechanism to the one in mouse. Then, in order to fix the inconsistency pointed out in the previous section, we compared these two circadian mechanisms. Consequently, we noticed that a path in *Drosophila* circadian mechanism has not been identified in that of mouse.

- PER/TIM complex activates the gene *dClock*, where TIM (timeless) is a protein of *Drosophila* which works in place of CRY, and *dClock* is a gene of *Drosophila* which corresponds to *Bmal*.

We conducted simulation again on the modified HFPN model in which the above hypothetical path was incorporated by adding the test arc from the place PER/CRY to the transition p3 from which the normal arc connects to the place mBmal. Figure 6.9 shows the result of simulation. This figure shows that the inconsistency is resolved by introducing this hypothetical path. Recall that, in the original model, the transcription switch of gene *Bmal* was controlled only by inhibition from the REV-ERB protein. In contrast, in the new model, this transcription is controlled not only the inhibition from the REV-ERB but also the activation

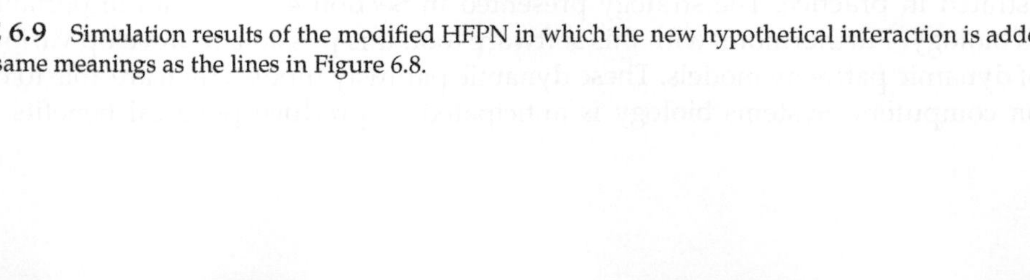

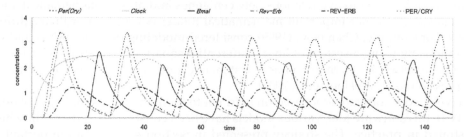

FIGURE 6.9 Simulation results of the modified HFPN in which the new hypothetical interaction is added. Lines have the same meanings as the lines in Figure 6.8.

from PER/CRY protein complex. This activation from PER/CRY complex allows the *Bmal* transcription to be off at the some point during the decrease in the PER/CRY complex concentration. In summary, the simultaneous operation of two reactions "inhibition from REV-ERB" and "activation from PER/CRY" on the gene *Bmal* enables the *Bmal* mRNA peak to locate at the middle point two *Cry* (*Per*) mRNA peaks.

4.3 Remarks

Genomic Object Net (GON) is a biosimulation tool developed by inheriting the tradition of the researches on Petri nets. Many Petri net tools have been developed by researchers in concurrent technology (Petri net tools). These Petri net tools so far developed generally have user-friendly GUIs which allows us to describe complex concurrent systems very easily and smoothly. GON inherits this feature of Petri net, enabling to describe and manipulate biological pathway naturally even for biologists who are not familiar with mathematical description and programming language.

In this section, we explained how gene networks can be described by HFPN with the example of the circadian genetic control mechanism in mammals, and demonstrated that computer simulations make it possible to observe behaviors of gene networks more systematically, being able to suggest new regulatory interactions which have not been found with only viewing the gene network as a map.

5 CONCLUSION

In the understanding of complex biological systems, computational methods, software tools, and biological databases should be extensively developed and employed. This chapter presented two approaches to understand biological systems and described a method and a software tool developed by our research group.

We devised a Bayesian network model with nonparametric regression to extract gene network information from microarray data, and developed a series of computational methods based on this approach. It should be briefly mentioned that there are other gene network models and analysis methods. The simplest model is the Boolean network model (Somogyi and Sniegoski 1996; Liang et al. 1998; Akutsu et al. 1999; Akutsu et al. 2003). This model is suited for modeling qualitative relations between genes and allows mathematical and algorithmic analyses. Another important mathematical model is based on ordinary differential equations. For example, Chen et al. (1999) considered modeling of both mRNA and protein concentrations by using a system of linear differential equations. We also devised a method to infer a gene network in terms of a linear system of differential equations from time-course gene expression data (de Hoon et al. 2003).

We developed a software tool based on Petri net to modeling and simulation of gene networks. With this software tool, various models have been constructed and its utility has been demonstrated in practice. The strategy presented in Section 4 will be an important key to systems biology. Furthermore, with this software tool, it is possible to develop various databases of dynamic pathway models. These dynamic pathway models then are able to be simulated on computers. Systems biology is anticipated to produce practical benefits such as biomedical applications, solutions for environmental problems, etc. As an example of this , we have succeeded in discovering a drug target gene by analyzing gene networks constructed from gene expression profile data. This gene expression profile data was based on gene disruptions or knock-down and drug doses (Imoto et al. 2003a,b; Savoie et al., 2003; Imoto et al. 2006). This example suggests that systems biology will lead to a new paradigm for target selection by employing computational modeling of gene networks.

6 RELATED INTERNET RESOURCES

BioCyc. http://www.biocyc.org/.
BioSPICE. http://www.biospice.org/
E-Cell. http://www.e-cell.org/.
Cell Illustrator. https://www.cellillustrator.com/.
Cell System Ontology (CSO). http://www.csml.org/.
Gepasi. http://www.gepasi.org/.
KEGG. http://www.genome.ad.jp/.
Petri net tools. http://www.informatik.uni-hamburg.de/TGI/PetriNets/.

Acknowledgments

The authors would like to thank our colleagues and collaborators Hideo Bannai, Michiel de Hoon, Atsushi Doi, Takao Goto, Sunyong Kim, Satoru Kuhara, Masao Nagasaki, Naoki Nariai, Sascha Ott, Christopher J. Savoie, Yoshinori Tamada, and Kousuke Tashiro. Especially, Hiroshi Matsuno would like to thank Professer Shin-Ichi T. Inouye who guided him to the construction of circadian genetic control mechanism in mammals and gave him many useful and suggestive comments for simulations.

References

Akutsu, T., Kuhara, S., Maruyama, O., and Miyano, S. (2003). Identification of genetic networks by strategic gene disruptions and gene overexpressions under a Boolean model. *Theoretical Computer Science* **298**(1):235–251.

Akutsu, T., Miyano, S., and Kuhara, S. (1999). Identification of genetic networks from a small number of gene expression patterns under the Boolean network model. *Pacific Symp. Biocomput.* **4**:17–28.

Alla, H., and David, R. (1998). Continuous and hybrid Petri nets. *J. Circ. Syst. Comp.* **8**:159–188.

Araki, H., Tamada, Y., Imoto, S., Dunmore, B., Sanders, D., Humphrey, S., Nagasaki, M., Doi, A., Nakanishi, Y., Yasuda, K., Tomiyasu, Y., Tashiro, K., Print, C., Charnock-Jones, D. S., Kuhara, S., and Miyano, S. (2009). Analysis of PPAR alpha-dependent and PPAR alpha-independent transcript regulation following fenofibrate treatment of human endothelial cells. *Angiogenesis* **12**(3):221–229.

Bannai, H., Inenaga, S., Shinohara, A., Takeda, M., and Miyano, S. (2002). A string pattern regression algorithm and its application to pattern discovery in long introns. *Genome Informatics* **13**:3–11.

Chen, T., He, H. L., and Church, G. M. (1999). Modeling gene expression with differential equations. *Pacific Symp. Biocomput.* **4**:29–40.

Chickering, D. M. (1996). Learning Bayesian networks is NP-complete. In (D. Fisher, and H.-J. Lenz, eds.), *"Learning from Data: Artificial Intelligence and Statistics V"*, pp. 121–130. Springer-Verlag.

Cooper, G. F., and Herskovits, E. (1992). A Bayesian method for the induction of probabilistic networks from data. *Machine Learning* **9**:309–347.

Davison, A. C. (1986). Approximate predictive likelihood. *Biometrika* **73**:323–332.

De Boor, C. (1978). *A Practical Guide to Splines*. Berlin: Springer-Verlag.

De Hoon, M., Imoto, S., Kobayashi, K., Ogasawara, N., and Miyano, S. (2003). Inferring gene regulatory networks from time-ordered gene expression data of *Bacillus subtilis* using differential equations. *Pacific Symp. Biocomput.* 8:17–28.

Doi, A., Fujita, S., Matsuno, H., Nagasaki, M., and Miyano, S. (2004). Constructing biological pathway models with hybrid functional Petri nets. *Silico Biology* **4**(3):271–291.

Doi, A., Nagasaki, M., Matsuno, H., and Miyano, S. (2006). Simulation based validation of the p53 transcriptional activity with hybrid functional Petri net. *Silico Biology* **6**(1–2):1–13.

Drath, R. (1998). Hybrid object nets: an object oriented concept for modeling complex hybrid systems. In *Proc. Hybrid Dynamical Systems, 3rd International Confernce on Automation of Mixed Processes, ADPM'98*, pp. 437–442.

Friedman, N., and Goldszmidt, M. (1998). Learning Bayesian networks with local structure. In (M. I. Jordan (Ed.), *"Learning in Graphical Models"*, pp. 421–459. Kluwer Academic Publishers.

Friedman, N., Linial, M., Nachman, I., and Pe'er, D. (2000). Using Bayesian networks to analyze expression data. *J. Comput. Biol.* **7**:601–620.

Genrich, H., Kuffner, R., and Voss, K. (2001). Executable Petri net models for the analysis of metabolic pathways. *International J. Software Tools for Technology Transfer* **3**(4):394–404.

Goss, P. J. E., and Peccoud, J. (1998). Quantitative modeling of stochastic systems in molecular biology by using Stochastic Petri nets. *Proc. Natl. Acad. Sci. USA* **95**:6750–6755.

Hartemink, A. J., Gifford, D. K., Jaakkola, T. S., and Young, R. A. (2002). Combining location and expression data for principled discovery of genetic regulatory networkmodels. *Pacific Symp. Biocomput.* **7**:437–449.

Hastie, T., and Tibshirani, R. (1990). *Generalized Additive Models*. London: Chapman & Hall.

Heckerman, D., Geiger, D., and Chickering, D. M. (1995). Learning Bayesian networks: the combination of knowledge and statistical data. *Machine Learning* **20**:197–243.

Hofestädt, R., and Thelen, S. (1998). Quantitative modeling of biochemical networks. *In Silico Biology* **1**:39–53.

Imoto, S., Goto, T., and Miyano, S. (2002). Estimation of genetic networks and functional structures between genes by using Bayesian network and nonparametric regression. *Pacific Symp. Biocomput.* **7**:175–186.

Imoto, S., Higuchi, T., Goto, T., Tashiro, K., Kuhara, S., and Miyano, S. (2004). Combining microarrays and biological knowledge for estimating gene networks via Bayesian networks. *J. Bioinform. Comp. Biol.* **2**:77–98.

Imoto, S., Kim, S., Goto, T., Aburatani, S., Tashiro, K., Kuhara, S., and Miyano, S. (2003a). Bayesian network and nonparametric heteroscedastic regression for nonlinear modeling of genetic network. *J. Bioinform. Comp. Biol.* 1:231–252.

Imoto, S., and Konishi, S. (2003). Selection of smoothing parameters in *B*-spline nonparametric regression models using information criteria. *Ann. Inst. Statist. Math.* **55**:671–687.

Imoto, S., Savoie, C. J., Aburatani, S., Kim, S., Tashiro, K., Kuhara, S., and Miyano, S. (2003b). Use of gene networks for identifying and validating drug targets. *J. Bioinform. Comp. Biol.* **1**(3):459–474.

Imoto, S., Tamada, Y., Araki, H., Yasuda, K., Print, C. G., Charnock-Jones, S. D., Sanders, D., Savoie, C. J., Tashiro, K., Kuhara, S., and Miyano, S. (2006). Computational strategy for discovering druggable gene networks from genome-wide RNA expression profiles, *Pacific Symp. Biocomput.* **11**:559–571.

Jeong, E., Nagasaki, M., Saito, A., and Miyano, S. (2007). Cell System Ontology: Representation for modeling, visualizing, and simulating biological pathways. *In Silico Biology* **7**:0055.

Jeong, E., Nagasaki, M., Ikeda, E., Saito, A., and Miyano, S. (2011a). CSO validator: improving manual curation workflow for biological pathways. *Bioinformatics* **27**(17):2471–2472.

Jeong, E., Nagasaki, M., Ueno, K., and Miyano, S. (2011b). Ontology-based instance data validation for high-quality curated biological pathways. *BMC Bioinformatics* **12**(Suppl 1):S8.

Kim, S., Imoto, S., and Miyano, S. (2003). Inferring gene networks from time series microarray data using dynamic Bayesian networks. *Brief. Bioinform.* **4**:228–235.

Kim, S., Imoto, S., and Miyano, S. (2004). Dynamic Bayesian network and nonparametric regression for nonlinear modeling of gene networks from time series gene expression data. *Biosystems* **75**:57–65.

Kojima, K., Perrier, E., Imoto, S., and Miyano, S. (2010). Optimal search on clustered structural constraint for learning Bayesian network structure. *Journal of Machine Learning Research* **11**:285–310.

Konishi, S., Ando, T., and Imoto, S. (2004). Bayesian information criteria and smoothing parameter selection in radial basis function networks. *Biometrika* **91**:27–43.

Li, C., Ge, Q.-W., Nakata, M., Matsuno, H., and Miyano, S. (2007). Modeling and simulation of signal transductions in an apoptosis pathway by using timed Petri nets. *J. Biosciences* **32**(1):113–125.

Li, C., Nagasaki, M., and Miyano, S. (2011). Online model checking approach based parameter estimation to a neuronal fate decision simulation model in Caenorhabditis elegans with hybrid functional Petri net with extension. *Molecular BioSystems* **7**(5):1576–1592.

Li, C., Nagasaki, M., Saito, A., and Miyano, S. (2010). Time-dependent structural transformation analysis to high-level Petri net model with active state transition diagram. *BMC Systems Biology* **4**:39.

Li, C., Nagasaki, M., Ueno, K., and Miyano, S. (2009). Simulation-based model checking approach to cell fate specification during *Caenorhabditis elegans* vulval development by hybrid functional Petri net with extension. *BMC Systems Biology* **3**:42.

Li, C., Suzuki, S., Ge, Q.-W., Nakata, M., Matsuno, H., and Miyano, S. (2006). Structural modeling and analysis of signaling pathways based on petri nets. *J. Bioinform. Comput. Biol.* **4**(5):1119–1140.

Liang, S., Fuhrman, S., and Somogyi, R. (1998). REVEAL, a general reverse engineering algorithm for inference of genetic network architectures. *Pacific Symp. Biocomput.* **3**:18–29.

Matsuno, H., Doi, A., Nagasaki, M., and Miyano, S. (2000). Hybrid Petri net representation of gene regulatory network. *Pac. Symp. Biocomput* **5**:341–352.

Matsuno, H., Inouye, S. T., Okitsu, Y., Fujii, Y., and Miyano, S. (2005). A new regulatory interaction suggested by simulations for circadian genetic control mechanism in mammals. In (Y. P. Chen, and L. Wong, eds.), *"Proc. 3rd Asia-Pacific Conf. Bioinformatics"*, pp. 171–180. Imperial College Press.

Matsuno, H., Li, C., and Miyano, S. ((2006). Petri net based description for systematic understanding of biological pathways. *IEICE Trans. Fundamentals* **E89-A**(11):3166–3174.

Matsuno, H., Nagasaki, M., and Miyano, S. (2011). Hybrid Petri net based modeling for biological pathway simulation. *Natural Computing* **10**(3):1099–1120.

Matsuno, H., Tanaka, Y., Aoshima, H., Doi, A., Matsui, M., and Miyano, S. (2003). Biopathways representation and simulation on hybrid functional Petri net. *Silico Biology* **3**(3):389–404.

Mito, N., Ikegami, Y., Matsuno, H., Miyano, S., and Inouye, S. (2008). Simulation analysis for the effect of light-dark cycle on the entrainment in circadian rhythm. *Genome Informatics* **21**:212–223.

Miwa, Y., Li, C., Ge, Q.-W., Matsuno, H., and Miyano, S. (2010a). On determining delay time of transitions for Petri net based signaling pathways by introducing stochastic decision rules. *In Silico Biology* **10**:0004.

Miwa, Y., Murakami, Y., Ge, Q.-W., Li, C., Matsuno, H., and Miyano, S. (2010b). Delay time determination for the timed Petri net model of a signaling pathway based on its structural information. *IEICE Trans. Fundamentals of Electronics, Communications and Computer Sciences* **E93-A**(12):2717–2729.

Nagasaki, M., Doi, A., Matsuno, H., and Miyano, S. (2003). Genomic Object Net I: a platform for modeling and simulating biopathways. *Applied Bioinformatics* **2**(3):181–184.

Nagasaki, M., Doi, A., Matsuno, H., and Miyano, S. (2004). A versatile Petri net based architecture for modeling and simulation of complex biological processes. *Genome Informatics* **15**(1):180–197.

Nagasaki, M., Doi, A., Matsuno, H., and Miyano, S. (2005). Computational modeling of biological processes with Petri net based architecture. In (Y. P. Chen (Ed.), *"Bioinformatics Technologies"*, pp. 179–242. Springer-Verlag.

Nagasaki, M., Saito, A., Jeong, E., Li, C., Kojima, K., Ikeda, E., and Miyano, S. (2010). Cell Illustrator 4.0: A computational platform for systems biology. *In Silico Biology* **10**:0002.

Nagasaki, M., Saito, A., Fujita, A., Tremmel, G., Ueno, K., Ikeda, E., Jeong, E., and Miyano, S. (2011). Systems biology model repository for macrophage pathway simulation. *Bioinformatics* **27**(11):1591–1593.

Nariai, N., Kim, S., Imoto, S., and Miyano, S. (2004). Using protein-protein interactions for refining gene networks estimated from microarray data by Bayesian networks. *Pacific Symp. Biocomput.* **9**:336–347.

Ott, S., and Miyano, S. (2003). Finding optimal gene networks using biological constraints. *Genome Informatics* **14**:124–133.

Ott, S., Imoto, S., and Miyano, S. (2004). Finding optimal models for small gene networks. *Pacific Symp. Biocomput.* **9**:557–567.

Ott, S., Hansen, A., Kim, S.-Y., and Miyano, S. (2005). Superiority of network motifs over optimal networks and an application to the revelation of gene network evolution. *Bioinformatics* **21**:227–238.

Perrier, E., Imoto, S., and Miyano, S. (2008). Finding optimal Bayesian network given a super-structure. *Journal of Machine Learning Research* **9**:2251–2286.

Reddy, V. N., Mavrovouniotis, M. L., and Liebman, M. N. (1993). Petri net representations in metabolic pathways. In *"Proc. First International Conference on Intelligent Systems for Molecular Biology (ISMB '93)"*, pp. 328–336. AAAI Press.

Reisig, W. (1985). *Petri Nets*. Berlin: Springer-Verlag.

Reppert, S. M., and Weaver, D. R. (2001). Molecular analysis of mammalian circadian rhythms. *Annual Review of Physiology* **63**:647–676.

Robinson, R. W. (1973). Counting labeled acyclic digraphs. In (F. Hrary (Ed.), *New Directions in the Theory of Graphs*, pp. 239–273. New York: Academic Press.

Sassone-Corsi, P. (2003). *Novartis Foundation Symposium 253*. John Wiley and Sons, Hoboken, NJ: Molecular Clocks and Light Signaling.

Sehgal, A. (2004). *Molecular Biology of Circadian Rhythms*. Hoboken, NJ: John Wiley and Sons.

Somogyi, R., and Sniegoski, C. A. (1996). Modeling the complexity of genetic networks: Understanding multigene and pleiotropic regulation. *Complexity* **1**:45–63.

Tamada, Y., Araki, H., Imoto, S., Nagasaki, M., Doi, A., Nakinishi, Y., Tomiyasu, Y., Yasuda, K., Dunmore, B., Sanders, D., Humphries, S., Print, C., Charnock-Jones, D. S., Tashiro, K., Kuhara, S., and Miyano, S. (2009). Unraveling dynamic activities of autoacine pathways that control drug-response transcriptome networks, *Pacific Symp. Biocomput*. **14**:251–263.

Tamada, Y., Imoto, S., and Miyano, S. (2011). Parallel algorithm for learning optimal Bayesian network structure. *Journal of Machine Learning Reseach* **12**:2437–2459.

Tamada, Y., Kim, S., Bannai, H., Imoto, S., Tashiro, K., Kuhara, S., and Miyano, S. (2003). Estimating gene networks from gene expression data by combining Bayesian network model with promoter element detection. *Bioinformatics* **19**(Suppl. 2):ii227–ii236.

Tinerey, L., and Kadane, J. B. (1986). Accurate approximations for posterior moments and marginal densities. *J. Am. Stat. Assoc*. **81**:82–86.

Van Someren, E. P., Wessels, L. F. A., Backer, E., and Reinders, M. J. T. (2002). Genetic network modeling. *Pharmacogenomics* **3**:507–525.

CHAPTER

7

Reconstruction of Metabolic Network from Genome Information and its Structural and Functional Analysis

Hong-Wu Ma[a, b], *An-Ping Zeng*[c]

[a]Tianjin Institute of Industrial Biotechnology, Chinese Academy of Sciences, Tianjin, P.R. China

[b]School of Informatics, University of Edinburgh, Edinburgh, UK,

[c]Institute of Bioprocess and Biosystems Engineering, Hamburg University of Technology, Denickestrasse, Germany

CONTENTS

http://dx.doi.org/10.1016/B978-0-12-405926-9.00007-1

Abstract

Understanding the complex interactions among cellular components (genes, proteins and metabolites) at a network level is a key issue in systems biology. In this chapter, we give an overview of metabolic network reconstruction from genome information and its structural analysis. First, two approaches for genome scale metabolic network reconstruction: high throughput reconstruction and high quality reconstruction, are discussed. Then the various means for mathematical representation of metabolic networks are explained, with particular emphasis on the problem arising from currency metabolites. Several topological features of metabolic network such as the power law connection degree distribution and the "bow-tie" global connectivity structure are explained in detail. In the last section, we discuss the different types of methods for network decomposition which can be used to identify somehow structurally and functionally independent modules in a complex network. This allows us to understand the functional organization of metabolic network from a modular perspective.

1 INTRODUCTION

One of the key issues in systems biology is to decipher the metabolic and regulatory networks involved in cellular processes. The rapid development in genome sequencing and functional genomics studies provide a large amount of information on the constituents (genes, mRNA, proteins/enzymes, and metabolites) of these biological networks and their activities in different organisms and under different environmental conditions. This makes it feasible to understand cell physiology and to compare different organisms at a system level. To this end, the reconstruction and analysis of genome-wide metabolic network is of particular importance since it ultimately determines the metabolic activities and thus the physiology of cells. In fact, the study of genome-scale metabolic network has gained much attention in past years (Jeong et al. 2000; Wagner and Fell 2001; Ravasz et al. 2002; Almaas et al. 2004; Covert et al. 2004; Hatzimanikatis et al. 2004). In this chapter, we first illustrate the major approaches and available databases for the reconstruction of genome-scale metabolic network. We then introduce the different means of mathematical representation of metabolic network. Subsequently, methods for the structural and functional analysis of metabolic network are explained and discussed. Emphases are put on methods which are based on graph theory and found useful in deciphering the global organization principle and the local, modular hierarchical structure of metabolic network.

2 RECONSTRUCTION OF GENOME SCALE METABOLIC NETWORKS

2.1 Computational genome-based metabolic network reconstruction

The general method for genome-based metabolic network reconstruction is depicted in Figure 7.1. An important step in the reconstruction process is to obtain the gene-enzyme and enzyme-reaction relationships. For organisms whose genome annotation information is available in public databases, we can extract the gene-enzyme (represented as EC numbers) relationships directly from databases such as Entrez gene and Uniprot. This can be easily done by using bioinformatics tools like SRS (srs.ebi.ac.uk) without the need of programming.

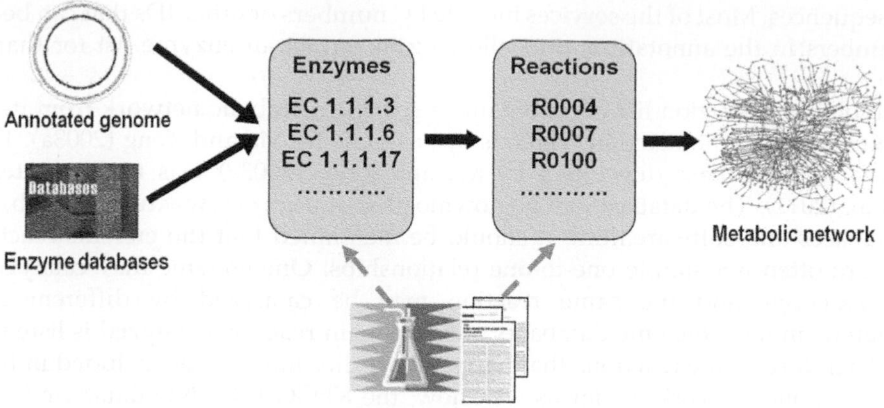

FIGURE 7.1 The reconstruction of metabolic network from genome information. The high/throughput reconstruction method (shown by the solid arrows) directly extracts information from enzyme or genome databases to obtain a list of reactions which are included in the metabolic network of one organism. The high quality metabolic network reconstruction also adds new enzymes or reactions from biological experiments or literature (shown by the dashed arrows) besides those from databases.

Normally less than one-third of the genes in a genome are coding for metabolic enzymes. Therefore this process is basically a data extraction process: extract the enzyme coding genes and acquire their corresponding EC numbers. There is also a high-throughput metabolic network reconstruction approach which simultaneously reconstruct networks for many organisms by utilizing the specific enzyme databases such as Brenda (Schomburg et al. 2004), KEGG (Kanehisa et al. 2004) and ExPASy enzyme nomenclature database (Gasteiger et al. 2003). These databases collect all enzyme genes from gene/protein databases and organize the data based on enzymes. For each enzyme all the corresponding genes in different organisms are listed in these databases. Therefore, it is easy to obtain the lists of enzymes for all the organisms in the database at one time. This is especially useful for large-scale comparative analysis of metabolic networks which will be discussed later in the chapter.

An alternative approach is to reconstruct the metabolic network for a specific organism directly from its genome annotation information. Based on sequence similarity or protein domain (motif) analysis, many genes are annotated as enzymes. Then from the annotation information we can directly get an enzyme list for the organism. This method is especially useful for newly sequenced organisms the information of which has not yet been included in the enzyme databases. From this method one may get more enzymes for a specific organism than that from enzyme databases because the enzyme databases often only include the well-annotated enzyme genes. There are also several automatic genome annotation services available, such as IMG/ER (Integrated Microbial Genome Expert Review system) from the Joint Genome Institute (Markowitz et al. 2008), the National Microbial Pathogen Data Resource's RAST (Rapid Annotation using Subsystems Technology) server (Aziz et al. 2008), KAAS (KEGG Automatic Annotation Server) (Moriya et al. 2007) and University of Maryland's IGS (Institute for Genome Sciences) annotation engine (http://ae.igs.umaryland.edu/cgi/). These services can greatly reduce the cost and human efforts needed for annotating new genome sequences. Most of the services include EC numbers or other IDs that can be mapped to EC numbers in the annotation, thus allowing to extract an enzyme list for that specific organism.

We can obtain a reaction list of an organism specific metabolic network from its enzyme list based on the enzyme-reaction relationships as done by Ma and Zeng (2003a). The gene-enzyme-reaction database developed by Ma and Zeng (2003a) was further extended by Stelzer et al. (2011). The database can be downloaded at http://www.tuhh.de/ibb/publications/databases-and-software.html. It should be mentioned that the enzyme-reaction relationships are often not simple one-to-one relationships. One enzyme may catalyze several different reactions and the same reaction may be catalyzed by different enzymes. Unfortunately, in most enzyme databases only the main reaction catalyzed is listed for each enzyme. Therefore, some reactions that happen in reality may not be included in the reconstructed metabolic network. So far as we know, the KEGG LIGAND database is the most complete metabolic reaction database(Goto et al., 2002). It includes nearly 10,000 enzyme catalyzed or nonenzyme catalyzed biochemical reactions. Most of the known reactions catalyzed by a specific enzyme are listed, thus allowing for the reconstruction of more complete metabolic networks.

2.2 High quality metabolic network reconstruction

The metabolic network reconstruction methods described above are based on enzyme and reaction databases and can be called high-throughput reconstruction because it only makes use of information available from databases. This allows an automatic programming-based approach to reconstruct networks for several organisms at one time. The general workflow of this reconstruction method is summarized in Figure 7.1 (the solid arrows). The high-throughput methods are necessary for comparative analysis of large-scale metabolic networks. However, there is a trade-off between the high productivity and the high quality. For example, the networks reconstructed in such a high-throughput way may be not complete or contain errors due to following reasons:

(1) There are some nonenzyme catalyzed reactions occurring spontaneously in metabolic network. These reactions should be added to the reactions lists obtained from genome information to avoid artificial missing links in the reconstructed metabolic network.

(2) Many enzymes have incomplete EC numbers like 1.2.-.- in the genome annotation databases. Such incomplete EC numbers appear in almost all KEGG metabolic maps and their corresponding reactions cannot be obtained correctly through the EC numbers. To address this problem, people need to develop a set of new IDs for these unclear enzymes to correctly map a reaction to a gene. For example, KO (KEGG Orthology) IDs could be used to generate a reaction list based on the reaction-KO and gene-KO relationships (Mao et al. 2005). A comparison of the reconstructed *Escherichia coli* metabolic networks from the EC number-based method and the KO-based method is shown in Figure 7.2. Surprisingly, more reactions using the EC-based method were obtained (Figure 7.2a). We found that many of the EC-unique reactions are general reactions which are not in any pathway map, such as R00391 (Acyl-CoA + Acetyl-CoA =

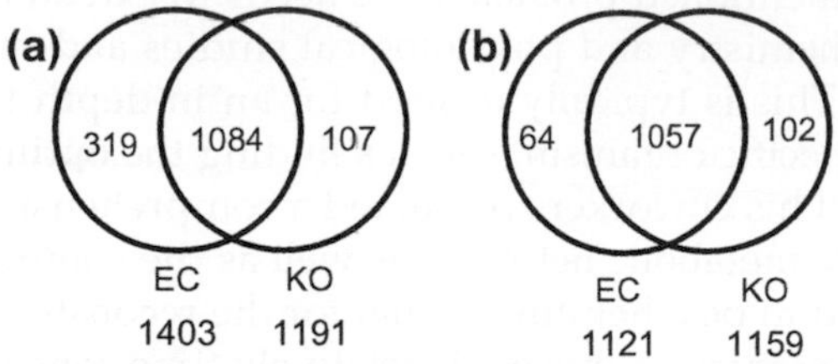

FIGURE 7.2 Comparison of the *E. coli* metabolic networks reconstructed based on EC number or KEGG Orthology. (a) For all reactions; (b) for reactions in the pathway maps.

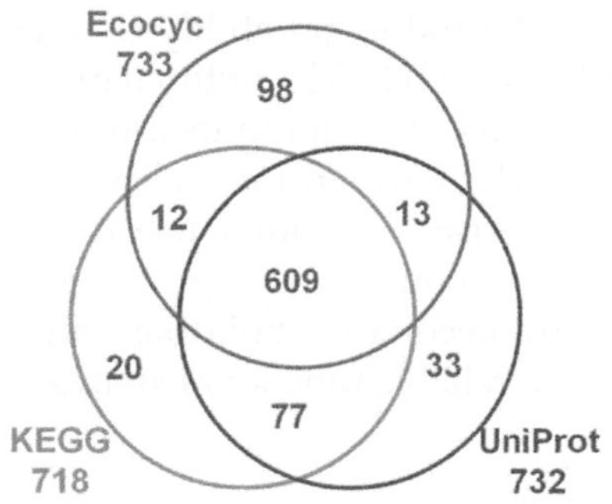

FIGURE 7.3 Comparison of EC numbers for *E. coli* from three different databases.

CoA + 3-Oxoacyl-CoA). The corresponding genes for this reaction in *E. coli* are b2342 and b3845 that are assigned to K00632 and EC 2.3.1.16. However, only EC 2.3.1.16 is related to R00391 while K00632 is only related to the specific reactions. If we consider only the reactions included in the pathway maps, the KO-based network would include more reactions (Figure 2b), especially many new reactions corresponding to incomplete EC numbers. To get a more complete network, the reactions obtained from both methods should be integrated.

(3) Many enzymes for which the reactions catalyzed have been experimentally determined are not found in any fully sequenced genomes. Actually half of the enzymes (EC numbers) in KEGG database do not have coding genes found in any fully sequenced organism. The reason for this may be that the functions of a large part of the genes in a genome are unknown. For this reason, (Karp 2004) called for an Enzyme Genomics Initiative to find coding sequences for these enzymes.

(4) The enzyme annotation information from databases may be wrong and inconsistent across databases. This is true even for *E. coli*, one of the best studied model organisms. Figure 7.3 shows the comparison of EC numbers for *E. coli* from three commonly used databases: KEGG, Uniprot and Entrez Gene. Altogether we obtained 862 EC numbers from the three database but only 609 (70%) are common in all three. The inconsistent part needs careful investigation based on information from literature to determine the correct ones.

To address the above-mentioned problems one needs to extend and validate the network with reactions from biochemistry and physiological studies and inferred from literature as illustrated in Figure 7.1. This is typically desired for an in-depth functional analysis of the metabolic network of a specific organism, such as finding the optimal pathways by flux balance analysis. Palsson and his coworkers presented a comprehensive protocol for building a high quality genome-scale metabolic network, as well as the common trials and tribulations step by step which proved to be a helpful manual for the reconstruction (Thiele and Palsson 2010). However, this reconstruction process is relatively time consuming and requires many nonstandardized manual examination processes. Therefore, metabolic networks reconstructed by different research groups for the same organism are often different. For example, three groups have published four different metabolic networks for *Pseudomonas putida*, an organism known for its high PHA production ability (Nogales et al. 2008; Puchalka et al. 2008; Sohn et al. 2010; Oberhardt et al. 2011). The optimal growth rates calculated varies from 0.42 to 1.17 h^{-1} even the glucose and oxygen inputs are set the same, indicating big difference among these metabolic networks. Furthermore, it is very difficult to compare these manually reconstructed networks because they often use different metabolite names in the reactions but not use consistent compound IDs (e.g., the KEGG compound ID). Therefore strict quality control processes are needed for building "high quality" metabolic networks whose quality is high enough for a reliable functional analysis.

3 MATHEMATICAL REPRESENTATION OF METABOLIC NETWORKS

A proper mathematical representation of the large number of reactions obtained for a specific organism is necessary for any structural analysis of metabolic network. Two approaches are generally used: the stoichiometric matrix and the connectivity graph (Figure 7.4). In the stoichiometric representation, the rows and columns of the so-called stoichiometry matrix represent reactions and metabolites respectively. A cell with a nonzero value in the matrix represents the stoichiometric coefficient of the corresponding metabolite in the corresponding reaction. A positive value means that it is a product while a negative value indicates a substrate. The stoichiometric representation is a full representation of the network structure. Several quantitative analysis methods have been developed based on the stoichiometric matrix of metabolic network such as flux balance analysis, elementary flux mode analysis and extreme pathway analysis(Schuster et al. 1999; Price et al. 2002; Klamt and Stelling 2003). A high quality metabolic network is often required for these stoichiometric matrix-based methods. So far, over 100 high quality metabolic networks have been published and most of them are available from the GSMNDB database (http://synbio.tju.edu.cn/GSMNDB/).

3.1 Graph representation of metabolic networks

In contrast to the stoichiometric representation, graph representation is a simplified way to represent the metabolic network. As shown in Figure 7.4, two types of graphs can be generated from a metabolic network: namely metabolite graph in which the nodes are metabolites and the links are reactions and reaction graph in which the nodes are reactions and two

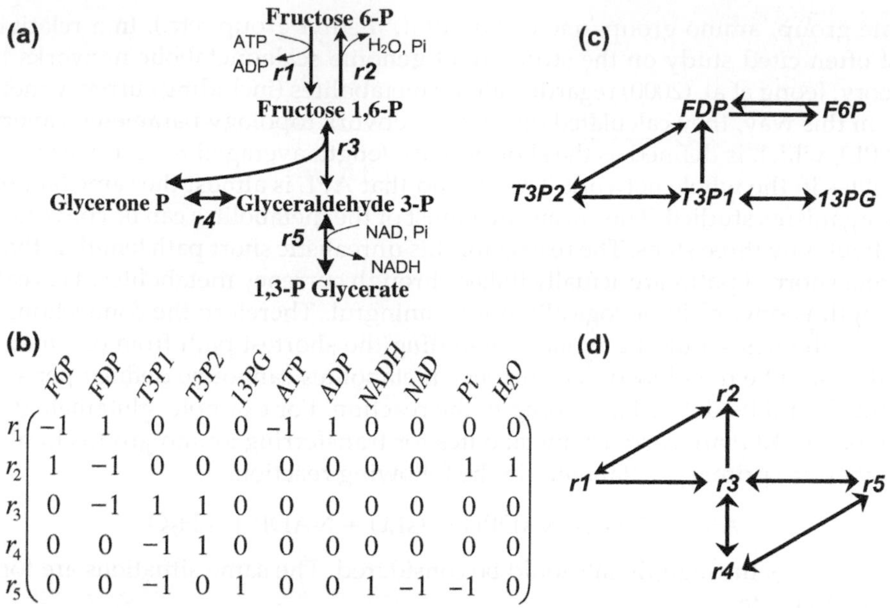

FIGURE 7.4 Mathematical representation of metabolic networks. (a) The upper part of the glycolysis pathway; (b) the stoichiometric matrix of the pathway; (c) the metabolite graph representation of the pathway; (d) the reaction graph representation of the pathway. Metabolite abbreviations: F6P, Fructose 6-phosphate; FDP, Fructose 1,6-phosphate; T3P1, 3-phosphate glyceraldehyde; T3P2, glycerone phosphate; 13PG, 1,3-Phosphoglycerate.

reactions are linked if a metabolite is the substrate of one reaction and the product of another production. The metabolite graph is similar to the classical way of metabolic pathway illustration in biochemistry textbooks and thus often used in structural analysis of metabolic network. Considering that many reactions are irreversible, many links in the graph are directed (called arcs in graph theory, correspondingly the undirected links are called edges), resulting in a directed graph. Compared with the stoichiometric representation, the graph representation is more suitable for visualization and structural analysis of large-scale metabolic networks. However, we should keep in mind that the graph representation is a simplified way of network representation which loses some information such as stoichiometric coefficients of reactions. A reaction often has several links in the graph (sometimes in very different parts) because most reactions have multiple substrates and products. On the other hand, one link in the graph may represent several different reactions. Therefore, a reverse step to map a link to its corresponding reaction(s) is required when providing biological interpretation for the results from graph analysis of metabolic network.

3.2 Currency metabolites in graph representation of metabolic networks

An important issue in graph representation of metabolic network is how to deal with the currency metabolites such as H_2O, CO_2, ATP, etc. (Ma and Zeng 2003a). Currency metabolites are normally used as carriers for transferring electrons and certain functional groups (phosphate group, amino group, one carbon unit, methyl group, etc.). In a relatively early and most often cited study on the structure of genome scale metabolic networks based on graph theory, Jeong et al. (2000) regarded all the metabolites (including currency metabolites) as nodes. In this way, they calculated one of the network topology parameters, average path length (APL), which is defined as the shortest path length averaged for every connected pair of metabolites in the whole network. They found that APL is almost the same (about 3.2) for all the 43 organisms studied. This means that most of the metabolites can be converted to each other in about only three steps. The reason for this unrealistic short path length is that most of the apparent shortest paths are actually linked through currency metabolites. This calculation of path length is obviously biologically not meaningful. Therefore the connections through currency metabolites should be avoided in finding the shortest path from one metabolite to another. It should be mentioned that currency metabolites cannot be defined per se by compounds but should be defined according to the reaction. For example, glutamate (GLU) and 2-oxoglutarate (AKG) are currency metabolites for transferring amino groups in many reactions, but they are primary metabolites in the following reaction:

$$\mathrm{AKG} + \mathrm{NH_3} + \mathrm{NADPH} = \mathrm{GLU} + \mathrm{NADP} + +\mathrm{H_2O}$$

The connections through them should be considered. The same situations are for NADH, NAD+, and ATP, etc.

From the above discussion we can see that it is difficult to remove the connections through currency metabolites automatically by a program. Therefore, in a previous study (Ma and Zeng 2003a) we manually checked the reactions that appear in the KEGG metabolic maps and added corresponding connections one by one. In this way, the reaction-connection relationships can be more accurately obtained and used to generate metabolite graphs from the lists of reactions of different organisms. As an example, Figure 7.5 depicts the two graphs (with and without connections through currency metabolites) for the reconstructed metabolic network of *Streptococcus pneumonia*. It can be seen that the one without currency metabolites is more realistic and more amendable for analysis. In contrast, the true network structure in the graph with currency metabolites is masked by the large number of links through currency metabolites. Therefore, the removal of connections through currency metabolites is an essential step to draw biologically meaningful conclusions from graph analysis of metabolic networks.

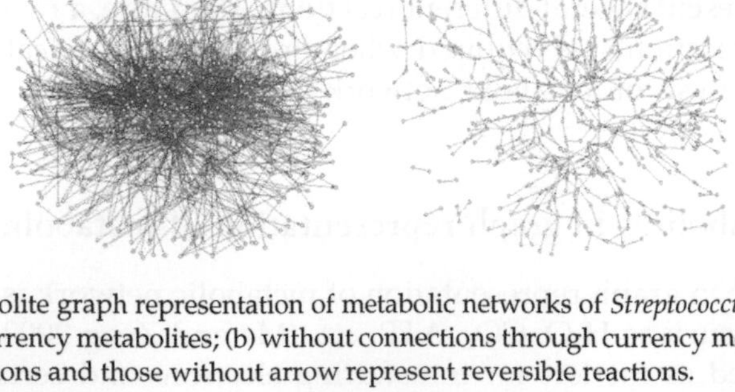

FIGURE 7.5 The metabolite graph representation of metabolic networks of *Streptococcus pneumoniae*. (a) Including the connections through currency metabolites; (b) without connections through currency metabolites. Links with arrow represent irreversible reactions and those without arrow represent reversible reactions.

In a similar way, KEGG developed the RPAIR database (Kotera et al. 2004). KEGG RPAIR is a derived database containing biochemical structure transformation patterns for substrate–product pairs (reactant pairs) in KEGG reactions. The substrate–product pairs are classified into different types such as "main," "trans". Only the "main" rpairs will be considered in the generation of a graph. However, there are many rpairs involving currency metabolites, especially CO_2. Therefore the metabolite graph obtained from Rpair database often has more links that that from our manually created metabolite connection database.

Arita (2003) proposed a different approach called atomic reconstruction of metabolism for graph representation of metabolic networks. In this approach, the atomic flow in a metabolic reaction is traced and a substrate is only connected to the product(s) which contains at least one atom from it. An example is shown here for the reaction:

$$\text{ATP} + \text{D-Glucose} = \text{ATP} + \text{D-Glucose 6-phosphate}$$

In this reaction, the link from D-glucose to ADP is not included in the graph because there is no atomic flow between these two metabolites. However, all the other three links (ATP to ADP, ATP to D-glucose 6-phosphate, D-glucose to D-glucose 6-phosphate) are included in the resulted graph. Therefore, though this approach can avoid certain connections through currency metabolites, there are still biologically not meaningful connections in the graph.

4 STRUCTURAL ANALYSIS OF METABOLIC NETWORKS

4.1 Degree distribution and average path length

An important structure characteristic of metabolic network and many other complex networks is the power law degree distribution: namely most of the nodes in the network have a low connection degree, while few nodes have a very high connection degree(Jeong et al. 2000; Strogatz 2001;Wolf et al. 2002; Bray 2003). The high degree nodes dominate the network structure and are called hubs of the network. Most of the nodes are connected through the hubs by a relatively short path and the average path length is insensitive to the network scale. Therefore this kind of network is called scale free network in several studies(Strogatz 2001). Both metabolite and reaction graphs (with or without connections through currency metabolites) were found to follow the power law degree distribution, implying that they both are scale free networks (Jeong et al. 2000; Ma and Zeng 2003a). However, the hubs identified for the two graphs are very different. Most of the hub metabolites in the metabolite graph with currency metabolites are currency metabolites like H_2O, ATP, ADP, etc due to their frequent appearance in many reactions. Excluding these currency metabolites one normally find several major primary metabolites as hubs. These include glycerate-3-phosphate, pyruvate, D-fructose-6-phosphate and D-glyceraldehyde-3-phosphate which are intermediates in the glycolysis pathway; D-ribose-5-phosphate and D-xylulose-5-phosphate which are intermediates in the pentose phosphate pathway; acetyl-CoA which is the metabolite linking glycolysis pathway, citric acid cycle, and fatty acid synthesis pathway; 5-phospho-D-ribose 1-diphosphate which is the precursor for purine and histidine synthesis; L-glutamate and L-aspartate, two important amino acids which are directly produced from precursors in citrate acid cycle

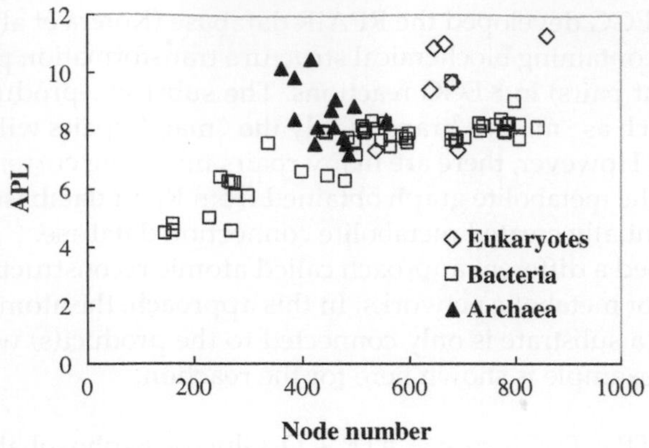

FIGURE 7.6 The calculated average path length for the metabolic networks of fully sequenced organisms.

and can be converted to many other amino acids. These metabolites are in the central metabolic network across organisms and thus are the true hubs in the organization of metabolic networks.

One feature of the scale free network is the invariable average path length (APL) with the increasing network size. This phenomenon has been found by Jeong et al. (2000) in the metabolite graphs with currency metabolites (about 3.2 for all the 43 studied organisms). However, for metabolite graphs without currency metabolites, much longer and variable path lengths are obtained as shown in Figure 7.6. Generally APL has a trend to increase with the network scale. Furthermore, quantitative differences exist among the three domains of organisms, namely the metabolic networks of eukaryotes and archaea generally have a longer APL than those of bacteria. The average APL values for networks of these three domains of organisms are 9.57, 8.50, and 7.22 respectively. This result indicates that there are true structure differences between the metabolic networks of different organisms which can only be revealed by removing the connection through currency metabolites.

4.2 Network global connectivity: the "bow-tie" structure

The scale free property revealed by the power law connection degree distribution is regarded as an important finding in the study of complex networks and has been found in many different types of networks(Jeong et al. 2000; Strogatz 2001). However, this property only reflects one aspect of the network structure. Actually it only shows the local connectivity of a network but does not tell us anything about the global network structure. For example, both networks in Figure 7.7 show a power law degree distribution. However, the left network is a fully connected one whereas the right one consists of several disconnected subgraphs. Therefore, new method(s) and parameter(s) are needed to investigate the global network connectivity. In graph theory, the number and sizes of connected components are used to represent network connectivity. A connected component of a network is defined as a maximal subset of nodes such that for any pair of nodes *u* and *v* in the subset there is a path from u to v

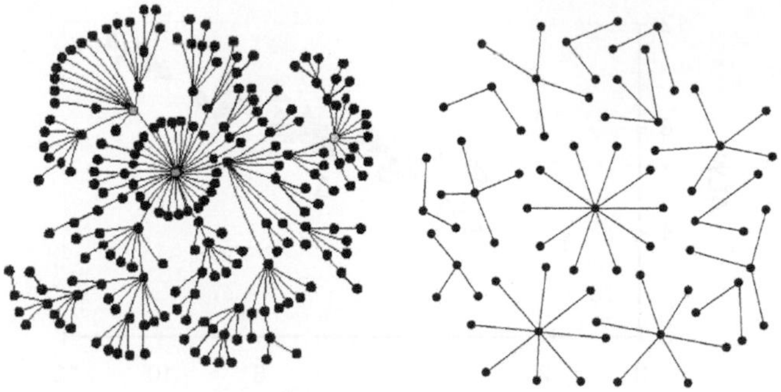

FIGURE 7.7 Two simple network examples to show the limitation of connection degree distribution. Both networks show power law degree distributions, but have apparently different network connectivity.

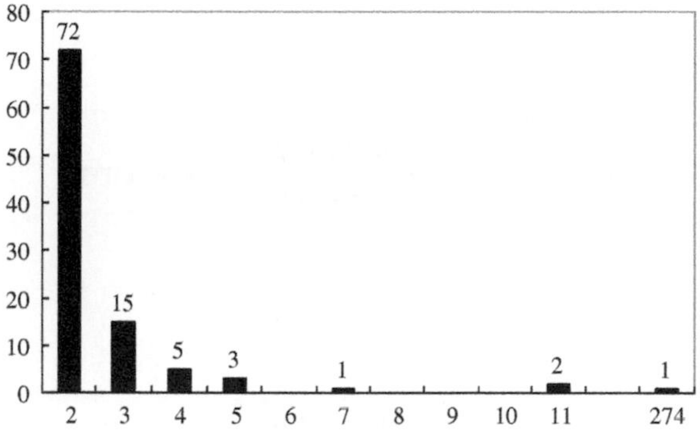

FIGURE 7.8 The distribution of the size of the strongly connected components in the metabolic network of *E. coli*.

(Batagelj and Mrvar 1998). Depending on whether the edge direction is considered or not, the connected components can be classified as strongly connected components and weakly connected components. Metabolic networks are directed graphs as many reactions are irreversible. Therefore we calculated the strongly connected components and the size distribution of the strongly connected components in the metabolic network of *E. coli* is shown in Figure 7.8. It can be seen that the largest component is much bigger than other components and thus is called the "giant strong component (GSC)." (Ma and Zeng, 2003b)

The giant strong component forms the backbone of a metabolic network. We found that the GSC follows a similar power law connection degree distribution as the whole network. Furthermore, the average path length of the whole network (ALW) was found to be determined by that of the GSC (ALG) as depicted in Figure 7.9. Because of the large scale, it is often difficult to achieve a comprehensive understanding of biological features of genome-based metabolic networks. Certain forms of reduction or classification of the whole network are desired to make the network more amenable to functional analysis. The most important part of the network, GSC, normally contains less than one-third of the nodes of the whole network but conserves the main features of the whole network. Most of the metabolic branch points and thus most of the key nodes for metabolic flux control are located in GSC. For example, the

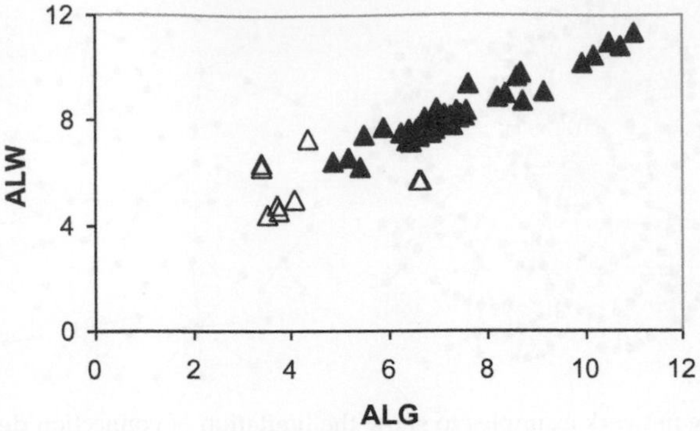

FIGURE 7.9 The relationship between the average path length of the whole network and that of the GSC.

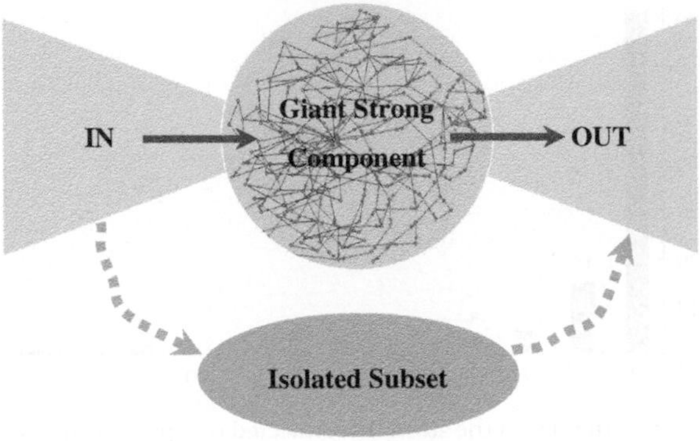

FIGURE 7.10 The "bow-tie" connectivity structure of metabolic networks.

whole metabolic network of *Streptococcus pneumoniae* consists of 486 metabolites, while its GSC contains only 87 metabolites, making it much easy for visually examination or kinetic model development. Therefore one may focus on the GSC when studying the flux distribution and its regulation in metabolic network. This can largely simplify the analysis process.

Another two concepts used for connectivity analysis in graph theory are output domain (number of reachable nodes from a node) and input domain (number of nodes which can reach a node) for all the nodes in the network. We found that the output domain for the nodes in GSC are larger than the number of nodes in GSC, implying that there is a subset of metabolites can be produced from metabolites in the GSC but cannot be used for synthesis of metabolits in GSC. We called this subset of nodes the OUT subset. Similarly, there is also an IN subset in which all the metabolites can be converted to metabolites in the GSC. All the other metabolites which are not connected with metabolites in the GSC form an isolated subset (IS). In this way, we obtained a "bow-tie" connectivity structure of metabolic networks as shown in Figure 7.10. This bow-tie connectivity structure was found in the metabolic networks of all other organisms studied. The "bow-tie" structure has also been found in the web page graph in which web pages represent nodes and hyperlinks represent links(Broder et al. 2000).

The discovery of the "bow-tie" structure in different kinds of networks implies that it is a common structure in large-scale networks. Organization as a "bow-tie" may be important for the complex system to be robust under variable and undetermined environments(Csete and Doyle 2004; Kitano 2004).

5 FROM NETWORK TO MODULES

For large-scale metabolic networks such as that of *E. coli,* even the GSC is still quite complex for obtaining a functional overview from the structure. In this case, a top-down approach to decompose it into relatively independent functional subsets or modules is often necessary for further biological functional analysis (Bray 2003). Modules in a network are groups of vertices within which connections are dense but between which they are sparser. Various network decomposition methods have been developed for the identification of modules in complex networks. Those decomposition methods can be classified into two groups. One group of methods are called agglomerative methods (Girvan and Newman 2002) which try to construct a similarity measure for finding the closely related nodes in a network and then successively combining the nodes together until all the nodes are in one big cluster. This combining process is often represented as a clustering tree and functional modules can be obtained by cutting the tree at a level. Another group of network decomposition methods are called divisive methods which have been developed based on how to effectively break down the network (network robustness analysis). These methods try to find the nodes or edges which are likely between modules, thus removal of those nodes/edges is likely to break down the network into separated modules.

5.1 Network decomposition based on clustering tree

The traditional and straightforward methods for detecting modules in complex networks are based on hierarchical clustering. A common feature of these methods is that a clustering tree is constructed by defining a distance (dissimilarity) measurement between each pair of nodes in the network. Then cutting the tree at any level gives the modular organization structure. Two important issues in these methods are: (1) how to define the distance between two nodes; (2) where to cut the tree. Different distance measurements and different cutting levels will generate different modules.

The distance measure should reflect how closely connected the nodes are. Therefore the path length between two nodes can be directly used as a distance measure (Rives and Galitski 2003; Ma et al. 2004a,b). It should be noted that in a directed network the path length from node A to node B is often not the same as that from B to A. The smaller of the two path lengths can be used as the distance between A and B. This method was used by Ma et al. (2004) to calculate the distance between two reactions in a metabolic network. However, a directed network may be not fully connected, namely there may be no path from A to B and from B to A. Therefore this method may only be used for the giant strongly connected component (GSC) in a network as shown in the paper by Ma et al. (2004). To extend the applicability of the method, a directed graph may be regarded as an undirected graph for the calculation of the distance between two nodes. In most cases, the neglect of the direction of the links in detecting the modular structure is acceptable.

Besides the path length-based distance measurement, many other measures have been proposed for use with the hierarchical clustering algorithms. Ravasz et al. (2002) have proposed a similarity measure based on topological overlap between two metabolites in a metabolic network. A topological overlap of 1 between substrates *i* and *j* implies that they are connected to the same set of substrates, whereas a 0 value indicates that *i* and *j* do not link to common substrates. The metabolites that are part of highly integrated modules have a high topological overlap with their neighbors. In contrast, a metabolite is not likely to link to the same set of metabolites with another metabolite in a different module. Another definition is based on the number of independent paths between vertices (Girvan and Newman 2002). Two paths that connect the same pair of vertices are said to be node-independent if they share none of the same vertices other than their initial and final vertices. Similarly, two paths are edge-independent if they share none of the same edges. It is known that the number of independent paths between two vertices in a graph is equal to the minimum number of vertices (edges) that must be removed to disconnect the two vertices (Girvan and Newman 2002). Thus it is more likely that the two vertices are in the same module if the number of independent paths between them is high. A feature of the modular structure lies in the dense intermodule connections and sparse intramodule connections. From this point of view, the number of independent paths is a measure of the similarity between two vertices rather than the dissimilarity as calculated based on path lengths. Numbers of independent paths can be computed quickly by using polynomial-time "max-flow" algorithms such as the augmenting path algorithm (Girvan and Newman 2002).

Once a distance measure is defined for the nodes in a network, a distance matrix for the network can be calculated where the number in the *i*th row *j*th column is the distance between the *i*th and *j*th nodes. Standard distance based clustering algorithms can then be used for the classification tree construction. The first step is to determine which two nodes to merge in a cluster. Usually, we choose to merge the two closest nodes according to the distance measure. Then we need to calculate the distance between the new cluster (including the two merged nodes) and the other nodes. Repeating these two steps will progressively merge all the nodes in one cluster and the tree is reconstructed based on the order of merging nodes during the process. Different algorithms may use different methods to calculate the distance between merged clusters. The frequently used one in network decomposition is the average linkage clustering algorithm which uses the mean distance between nodes of each cluster as the distance between the two clusters.

The clustering tree is a natural way to represent the hierarchical organization of a network. However, to obtain well-defined modules we need to decide at which level the tree should be cut. Unfortunately up to now there is still no golden quantitative criterion to decide how to properly cut the tree. Quite often cutting the tree at a fixed level often leads to uneven module size distribution: a few very large modules and many small modules (even modules with just one node). To overcome this problem, it may be necessary to cut the tree at different levels. Ma et al. (2004) proposed a bottom-up method to identify the modules from the tree structure. First, all the branches with ten or more nodes in the tree were identified as preliminary modules, then these modules were extended to include nodes in the neighbor branches. Whether a neighbor branch should be grouped into a preliminary module is decided based on two criteria: (1) the

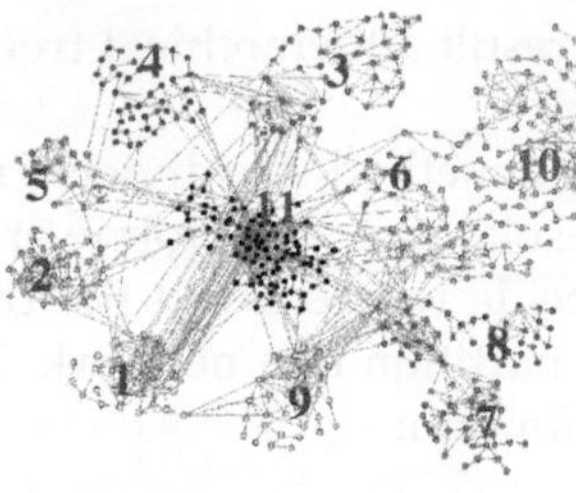

FIGURE 7.11 Functional modules in the metabolic network of *E. coli* obtained by network decomposition.

neighbor branch should have more links with the preliminary module than other modules; (2) investigating the biological function of the nodes in the neighbor branch and move those with closely related function to the preliminary module. After this step, a major part of the nodes can be assigned to a number of modules, whereas there are still some nodes which cannot be grouped into any of the preliminary modules. These nodes were assigned to a new module which is often in the central position in the whole network. Thus, this method leads to a core/periphery structure for the modular organization of the network as shown in Figure 7.11.

5.2 Network decomposition based on network break-down

In contrast to the clustering tree method, the divisive method try to find the nodes or edges which are likely between modules, thus removal of those nodes/edges can break down the network into separated modules. As a general method, Girvan and Newman proposed to use edge betweenness centrality to find the most lethal edges in the network and progressively removed them (Girvan and Newman 2002). They defined the edge betweenness of an edge as the number of shortest paths between pairs of vertices that run along it. If a network contains modules loosely connected by a few intergroup edges, then all shortest paths between different modules must go along one of these few edges. Thus, the edges connecting modules will have high edge betweenness. By removing these edges, the network can be separated into groups and so the underlying modular structure can be revealed. The proposed method includes the following steps: (1) Calculate the betweenness for all edges in the network. (2). Remove the edge with the highest betweenness. (3) Recalculate betweennesses for all edges affected by the removal. (4) Repeat from step 2 until the network is broken down into a proper number of separated groups. It should be noted that the removal of one edge may break down a network into two or may not. Therefore for a network with many intramodule connections, a large number of high betweenness edges may need to be removed before separated modules are revealed.

A modified version of the Girvan-Newman algorithm was used by Holme et al (2003) to decompose metabolic networks. They represented the metabolic network as a bipartite graph (both metabolites and reactions are regarded as nodes and all metabolite nodes are separated by reaction nodes). Instead of removing edges with high betweenness, they removed reaction nodes in the order of their scaled betweenness centrality. Considering that several metabolites can involved in one and the same reaction, they scaled the reaction betweenness centrality as $c = CB(r)/k_{in}(r)$, where $CB(r)$ is the calculated original betweenness centrality, $k_{in}(r)$ is the number of metabolites linked with reaction r. Then the high betweenness reaction nodes were iteratively removed and as a result a hierarchical tree showing the modular organization of the network was constructed.

Similar to the clustering tree-based method, the divisive methods may also lead to uneven distribution of modules and many isolated nodes(Holme et al. 2003). A quantitative measure of modularity might be used to decide where to cut the tree or how many edges or nodes should be removed to get the best partition in a network. Newman and Girvan (2004) proposed the following modularity definition:

$$Q = \sum_i (e_{ii} - a_i^2) = \sum_i \left[\frac{l_i}{L} - \left(\frac{d_i}{2L} \right)^2 \right]$$

Where e_{ii} is the fraction of links between nodes in module i, calculated as the number of links (l_i) in the module divided by the total number of links (L) in the network, a_i is an item showing the effect of intramodule connectivity which is calculated as the sum of degrees of the nodes in module i (d_i) normalized by the sum of degrees in the whole network (which equals to twice the number of the links). Different partitions of a network have different modularity values. Therefore modularity can be used as a criterion to find the best partition of a network which maximizes the modularity. The modularity change after removing different numbers of high betweenness edges in an example network is shown in Figure 7. 12. It can be seen that the modularity Q reaches the highest level when a certain number of edges are removed and then decreases when more edges are removed as the network is broken into many small modules. Therefore based on modularity the best decomposition of a network can be determined.

Based on the quantitative measure of modularity, people have developed new network decomposition methods solely based on maximizing modularity. As a true global optimization of modularity is computationally very costly, Newman (2004) developed a fast algorithm which progressively increases the modularity until a maximal value is reached. The algorithm starts with a state in which each vertex is the sole member of a community and then successively joins linked communities together in pairs. At each step, the joined pair which results in the greatest increase (or smallest decrease) in Q is chosen. The join process is repeated until Q is maximized and the modular organization structure obtained at that point would be regarded as the best partition of the network. Guimera and Nunes Amaral (2005) developed a simulated annealing method for network decomposition. Simulated annealing is a stochastic optimization technique that enables people to find "low-cost" configuration

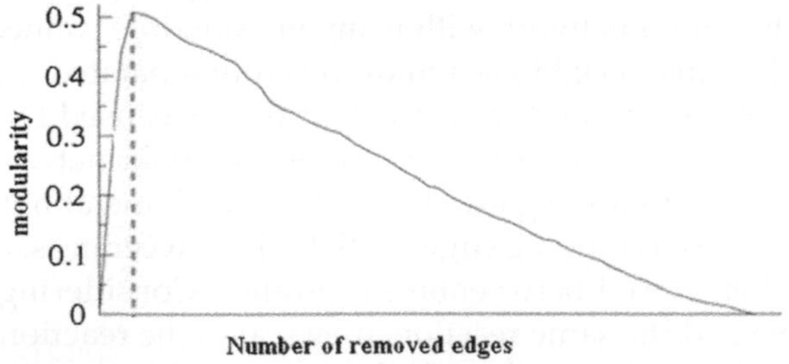

FIGURE 7.12 Modularity change after successively removing high betweenness edges in a network.

without getting trapped in "high-cost" local optimization. This method has been used in several studies for the decomposition of metabolic networks (Guimera and Nunes Amaral 2005; Zhao et al. 2006). However, as simulated annealing is a probability based method, different runs can still generate slightly different decomposition results. Mainly the nodes at the boundary of the modules are affected. Generally the result from this method is more robust than the Newman-method and a better decomposition with higher modularity can be obtained.

6 CONCLUDING REMARK

One of the goals of systems biology is to develop theoretical models to describe and predict cellular behavior at whole system level. The structural and functional analysis of genome-based metabolic networks described in this chapter represents one step toward this goal. The macroscopic structure of the metabolic network (scale free, bow-tie, modular organization) which can only be uncovered by analysis of the network as a whole represent certain system level principles governing the organization of interacting cellular components (enzymes and metabolites). Though these structure properties still merely give a static picture of the metabolic network, they can serve as a basis or blueprint for analyzing dynamic behavior of the network, the next necessary and more demanding step in network analysis. To this end, the metabolic network model needs to be further extended. In particular, transcriptional regulatory interactions should be integrated into the metabolic network. Most of the metabolic genes are regulated by one or more transcriptional factors and are activated/repressed under different environmental conditions. Therefore by integrating the regulatory relationships one may predict which reactions (pathways) are activated or repressed under given environmental conditions. One of the challenges in this endeavor is to establish genome-scale regulatory networks. So far our knowledge on regulatory interactions at genome level is still limited to a few model organisms such as *E. coli* (Salgado et al., 2004;Ma et al., 2004a) and *Saccharomyces cerevisiae* (Luscombe et al., 2004). The integration of functional genomic data such as those from transcriptomic, proteomic and metabolomic analyses is also essential for functional and dynamic analysis of metabolic network. These high-throughput technologies provide means to measure the expression or concentration levels of gene, protein and metabolites for the whole system. Combined with bioinformatics and systems biology tools this wealth of data may allow us to reconstruct integrated metabolic and regulatory networks at different molecular levels and to understand their system level interactions in the near future.

References

Almaas, E., Kovacs, B., Vicsek, T., Oltvai, Z. N., and Barabasi, A. L. (2004). Global organization of metabolic fluxes in the bacterium *Escherichia coli*. *Nature* **427**:839–843.

Arita, M. (2003). In silico atomic tracing by substrate-product relationships in *Escherichia coli* intermediary metabolism. *Genome Res.* **13**:2455–2466.

Aziz, R., Bartels, D., Best, A., DeJongh, M., Disz, T., Edwards, R., Formsma, K., Gerdes, S., Glass, E., Kubal, M., et al. (2008). The RAST server: Rapid Annotations using Subsystems Technology. *BMC Genomics* **9**(1):75.

Batagelj, V., and Mrvar, A. (1998). Pajek – program for large network analysis. *Connections* **21**:47–57.

Bray, D. (2003). Molecular networks: The top-down view. *Science* **301**:1864–1865.

Broder, A., Kumar, R., Maghoul, F., Raghavan, P., Rajagopalan, S., Stata, R., Tomkins, A., and Wiener, J. (2000). Graph structure in the Web. *Comput. Networks* **33**:309–320.

Covert, M. W., Knight, E. M., Reed, J. L., Herrgard, M. J., and Palsson, B. O. (2004). Integrating high-throughput and computational data elucidates bacterial networks. *Nature* **429**:92–96.

Csete, M., and Doyle, J. (2004). Bow ties, metabolism and disease. *Trends Biotechnol.* **22**:446–450.

Gasteiger, E., Gattiker, A., Hoogland, C., Ivanyi, I., Appel, R. D., and Bairoch, A. (2003). ExPASy: The proteomics server for in-depth protein knowledge and analysis. *Nucl. Acids. Res.* **31**:3784–3788.

Girvan, M., and Newman, M. E. J. (2002). Community structure in social and biological networks. *Proc. Natl. Acad. Sci. USA* **99**(12):7821–7826.

Goto, S., Okuno, Y., Hattori, M., Nishioka, T., and Kanehisa, M. (2002). LIGAND: Database of chemical compounds and reactions in biological pathways. *Nucl. Acids Res.* **30**:402–404.

Guimera, R., and Nunes Amaral, L. A. (2005). Functional cartography of complex metabolic networks. *Nature* **433**:895–900.

Hatzimanikatis, V., Li, C., Ionita, J. A., and Broadbelt, L. J. (2004). Metabolic networks: Enzyme function and metabolite structure. *Curr. Opin. Struct. Biol.* **14**:300–306.

Holme, P., Huss, M., et al. (2003). Subnetwork hierarchies of biochemical pathways. *Bioinformatics* **19**:532–538.

Jeong, H., Tombor, B., Albert, R., Oltvai, Z. N., and Barabasi, A. L. (2000). The large-scale organization of metabolic networks. *Nature* **407**:651–654.

Kanehisa, M., Goto, S., Kawashima, S., Okuno, Y., and Hattori, M. (2004). The KEGG resource for deciphering the genome. *Nucl. Acids Res.* **32**:D277–D280.

Karp, P. (2004). Call for an enzyme genomics initiative. *Genome Biol.* **5**:401.

Kitano, H. (2004). Biological robustness. *Nat. Rev. Genet.* **5**:826–837.

Klamt, S., and Stelling, J. (2003). Two approaches for metabolic pathway analysis?. *Trends Biotechnol.* **21**:64–69.

Kotera, M., Hattori, M., Oh, M. A., et al. (2004). Rpair: A reactant-pair database representing chemical changes in enzymatic reactions. *Genome Inform.* **15**:62.

Luscombe, N. M., Babu, M. M., Yu, H., Snyder, M., Teichmann, S. A., and Gerstein, M. (2004). Genomic analysis of regulatory network dynamics reveals large topological changes. *Nature* **431**:308–312.

Ma, H. W., and Zeng, A. P. (2003a). Reconstruction of metabolic networks from genome data and analysis of their global structure for various organisms. *Bioinformatics* **19**:270–277.

Ma, H. W., and Zeng, A. P. (2003b). The connectivity structure, giant strong component and centrality of metabolic networks. *Bioinformatics* **19**:1423–1430.

Ma, H. W., Kumar, B., Ditges, U., Gunzer, F., Buer, J., and Zeng, A. P. (2004a). An extended transcriptional regulatory network of *Escherichia coli* and analysis of its hierarchical structure and network motifs. *Nucl. Acids Res.* **32**:6643–6649.

Ma, H. W., Zhao, X. M., Yuan, Y. J., and Zeng, A. P. (2004b). Decomposition of metabolic network based on the global connectivity structure of reaction graph. *Bioinformatics* **20**:1870–1876.

Mao, X., Cai, T., Olyarchuk, J. G., and Wei, L. (2005). Automated genome annotation and pathway identification using the KEGG Orthology (KO) as a controlled vocabulary. *Bioinformatics* **21**(19):3787–3793.

Markowitz, V. M., Szeto, E., Palaniappan, K., Grechkin, Y., Chu, K., Chen, I. M., Dubchak, I., Anderson, I., Lykidis, A., Mavromatis, K., et al. (2008). The integrated microbial genomes (IMG) system in 2007: Data content and analysis tool extensions. *Nucl. Acids Res.* **36**(Database issue):D528–D533.

Moriya, Y., Itoh, M., Okuda, S., Yoshizawa, A. C., and Kanehisa, M. (2007). KAAS: An automatic genome annotation and pathway reconstruction server. *Nucl. Acids Res.* **35**(suppl 2):W182–W185.

Newman, M. E. (2004). Fast algorithm for detecting community structure in networks. *Phys. Rev. E Stat. Nonlin. Soft Matter Phys.* **69**(6 Pt 2):066133.

Newman, M. E., and Girvan, M. (2004). Finding and evaluating community structure in networks. *Phys. Rev. E Stat. Nonlin. Soft Matter Phys.* **69**(2 Pt 2):026113.

Nogales, J., Palsson, B. Ø., and Thiele, I. (2008). A genome-scale metabolic reconstruction of *Pseudomonas putida* KT2440: iJN746 as a cell factory. *BMC Syst. Biol.* **2**(1):79.

Oberhardt, M. A., Puchałka, J., dos Santos, V. A. M., and Papin, J. A. (2011). Reconciliation of genome-scale metabolic reconstructions for comparative systems analysis. *PLoS comput. Biol.* **7**(3):e1001116.

Price, N. D., Papin, J. A., and Palsson, B. B. (2002). Determination of redundancy and systems properties of the metabolic network of *helicobacter pylori* using genome-scale extreme pathway analysis. *Genome Res.* **12**:760–769.

Puchałka, J., Oberhardt, M. A., Godinho, M., Bielecka, A., Regenhardt, D., Timmis, K. N., and dos Santos, V. A. M. (2008). Genome-scale reconstruction and analysis of the *Pseudomonas putida* KT2440 metabolic network facilitates applications in biotechnology. *PLoS Comput. Biol.* **4**(10):e1000210.

Ravasz, E., Somera, A. L., Mongru, D. A., Oltvai, Z. N., and Barabasi, A. L. (2002). Hierarchical organization of modularity in metabolic networks. *Science* **297**:1551–1555.

Rives, A. W., and Galitski, T. (2003). Modular organization of cellular networks. *Proc. Natl. Acad. Sci. USA* **100**(3):1128–1133.

Salgado, H., Gama-Castro, S., Martinez-Antonio, A., Diaz-Peredo, E., Sanchez-Solano, F., Peralta-Gil, M., Garcia-Alonso, D., Jimenez-Jacinto, V., Santos-Zavaleta, A., Bonavides-Martinez, C., and Collado-Vides, J. (2004). RegulonDB (version 4.0): Transcriptional regulation, operon organization and growth conditions in *Escherichia coli* K-12. *Nucl. Acids Res.* **32**(Database issue):D303–D306.

Schomburg, I., Chang, A., Ebeling, C., Gremse, M., Heldt, C., Huhn, G., and Schomburg, D. (2004). BRENDA, the enzyme database: Updates and major new developments. *Nucl. Acids Res.* **32**:D431–D433.

Schuster, S., Dandekar, T., and Fell, D. A. (1999). Detection of elementary flux modes in biochemical networks: A promising tool for pathway analysis and metabolic engineering. *Trends Biotechnol.* **17**:53–60.

Sohn, S. B., Kim, T. Y., Park, J. M., and Lee, S. Y. (2010). In silico genome-scale metabolic analysis of *Pseudomonas putida* KT2440 for polyhydroxyalkanoate synthesis, degradation of aromatics and anaerobic survival. *Biotechnol. J.* **5**(7):739–750.

Stelzer, M. J., Sun, J., Zeng, A. P., Kamphans, T., and Fekete, S. (2011). An extended bioreaction database that significantly improves reconstruction and analysis of genome-scale metabolic networks. *Integrative Biol.* **3**:1071–1086.

Strogatz, S. H. (2001). Exploring complex networks. *Nature* **410**:268–276.

Thiele, I., and Palsson, B. Ø. (2010). A protocol for generating a high-quality genome-scale metabolic reconstruction. *Nat. protocols* **5**(1):93–121.

Wagner, A., and Fell, D. A. (2001). The small world inside large metabolic networks. *Proc. R. Soc. Lond B Biol. Sci.* **268**:1803–1810.

Wolf, Y. I., Karev, G., and Koonin, E. V. (2002). Scale-free networks in biology: New insights into the fundamentals of evolution?. *Bioessays* **24**:105–109.

Zhao, J., Yu, H., et al. (2006). Hierarchical modularity of nested bow-ties in metabolic networks. *BMC Bioinformatics* **7**(1):386.

CHAPTER

8

Standards, Platforms, and Applications

Stanley Gu, Herbert Sauro

Department of Bioengineering, University of Washington, Seattle, WA, USA

CONTENTS

Abstract

With the sequencing of the human genome, it has become apparent that systems biology, the understanding of cellular networks through dynamical analysis is becoming an important part of research for mainstream biologists. One of the indicative trends to emerge in recent years is the development of model interchange standards that permit biologists to easily exchange dynamical models between different software tools. This chapter describes the current and rising standards in systems biology that facilitate knowledge management and physiological model exchange. In addition, software platforms that implement these standards and enables the reuse of software code are discussed. Finally, the range of possible computational applications is described, highlighting the most commonly used and emerging tools in the field.

http://dx.doi.org/10.1016/B978-0-12-405926-9.00008-3

1 INTRODUCTION

Although computational systems biology may seem to be a recent field of endeavor, its origins can be traced as far back as the 1920s and 1930s (Wright 1929). During this period it was already believed by some that genes were responsible in some way for specifying enzymes. It was also around this time that glycolysis, the first metabolic pathway, was being elucidated and the beginnings of the idea that enzymes formed linked sequences called pathways. It is even more remarkable therefore that given the infancy of these concepts, Sewall Wright should attempt to give a physiological explanation for the occurrence of genetic dominance and recessivity (Wright 1934). Wright argued that the explanation for the origin of dominance lay with the properties of catalytic networks, and laid out an initial mathematical theory which described the properties of enzyme networks.[1] In the 1940s, as the first digital computers were being built, pioneering individuals such as Garfinkel, Higgins, and Chance began investigating the possibility of modeling the subtle behavior of biochemical pathways. Even before the advent of the digital computer, the same group had been using analog computers to model simple biochemical pathways for almost 15 years (Garfinkel et al. 1961; Higgins 1959; Chance 1943).

Since the work of the pioneers in the 1950s, there have been many small groups that have continued this line of inquiry and that together laid the foundation for many of the techniques and theory that we use today and take for granted, in contemporary systems biology. It should be noted that there is a large body of literature, particularly in the Journal of Theoretical Biology, dating back fifty years that many newcomers to the field will find useful to consider.

1.1 What is systems biology?

There are many conflicting opinions today on what exactly systems biology is. Historically the answer seems clear. The chief aim of systems biology is to understand how individual proteins, metabolites, and genes contribute quantitatively to the phenotypic response. Lee Hood, president of the Institute of Systems Biology in Seattle, US, defines it similarly as "the identification of the elements in a system and the analysis of their interrelationships to explain the emergent properties of the system." Even so, some believe systems biology to be concerned with the collection of high-throughput data while others consider the elucidation of protein-protein networks and gene networks to be its hallmark. Certainly, both are vital prerequisites for understanding systems but neither alone can offer great *insight* into how networks operate dynamically.

Systems biology is the natural progression of classical molecular biology from a descriptive to a quantitative science and is concerned with the dynamic response of biological networks.

[1] This early work later became significant during the development of metabolic control analysis (Kacser and Burns 1981).

1.2 Statement of problem

Building models is not an entirely new approach to biology. If one examines any text book on molecular biology or biochemistry, virtually every page has a diagram of a model. These models, which are often termed cartoon-based models, represent the culmination of years of painstaking research; they serve as repositories of accepted doctrine and the starting point for the generation of new hypotheses. There are, however, limits to what can be done with these models, their predictive value tends to be poor, and the ability to reason using qualitative models is limited. In other sciences these limitations are avoided through the use of quantitative models, models which are described not just pictorially but also mathematically. Quantitative models by their nature have much better predictive value compared to qualitative models, but their real usefulness stems from the capacity to carry out precise reasoning with them.

1.3 Quantitative approaches

There is a wide range of mathematical representations that one can use to build quantitative models, the choice of approach depending on the type of biological question, the accessibility of experimental data and the tractability of the mathematics. Probably the most successful and widely used kind of model are those based on differential equations (both ordinary and partial). These models assume a continuum of concentrations and rates. In reality of course, cellular systems are discrete at the molecular level, however, since the numbers of molecules is very large, the continuum approximation turns out to be very good. When the number of molecules drops to below a certain threshold the continuum model can break down and in these cases one must revert to stochastic simulation. The disadvantage of a stochastic simulation is that all the analytical methods available for continuous models no longer apply. One should therefore only use stochastic simulation if it is necessary and not in cases where an ODE-based model adequately describes the data. This problem highlights the need to develop a new set of mathematical approaches in order to understand the dynamics of stochastic systems. There are other approaches, which include boolean, Bayesian, formal logic and connectivity studies but these have yet to show any overwhelming advantage over continuum-based models.

This chapter will be primarily concerned with models based on differential equations and to a lesser extent stochastic equations.

List of modeling representations

Boolean: One of the simplest possible modeling techniques is to represent a network using Boolean logic (deJong 2002). This approach has been used to model gene networks.

Ordinary differential equations (ODEs): This is the most common and arguably most useful representation. Although based on a continuum model, ODE models have proved to be excellent descriptions of many biological systems. Another advantage to using ODEs is the wide range of analytical and numerical methods that are available. The analytical methods in particular provide a means to gain a deeper insight into the workings of the model.

Deterministic hybrid: A deterministic hybrid model is one which combines a continuous model (e.g. ODE model) with discrete events. These models are notoriously difficult to solve efficiently and require carefully crafted numerical solvers. The events can occur either in the state variables or parameters and can be time dependent or independent. A simple example involves the division of a cell into two daughter cells. This event can be treated as a discrete event which occurs when the volume of the cell reaches some preset value at which point the volume halves.

Differential-algebraic equations (DAEs): Sometimes a model requires constraints on the variables during the solution of the ODEs. Such a situation is often termed a DAE system. The simplest constraints are mass conservation constraints, however these are linear and can be handled efficiently and easily using simple assignment equations (see Equation 8.2). DAE solvers need only be used when the constraints are nonlinear.

Partial differential equations (PDEs): Whereas simple ODEs model well stirred reactors, PDEs can be used model heterogeneous spatial models.

Stochastic: At the molecular level concentrations are discrete, but as long as the concentrations levels are sufficiently high, the continuous model is perfectly adequate. When concentrations fall below approximately one hundred molecules in the volume considered (e.g. the cell or compartment) one has to consider using stochastic modeling. The great disadvantage in this approach is that one looses almost all the analytical methods that are available for continuous models, as a result stochastic models are much more difficult to interpret.

1.3.1 Quantitative models based on differential equations

It is probably fair to say that most of the successful models to be found in the literature are based on ordinary differential equations. Many researchers will express these models using the following equation:

$$\frac{d\boldsymbol{S}}{dt} = \boldsymbol{N}\boldsymbol{v}(\boldsymbol{S}(\boldsymbol{p}), \boldsymbol{p}) \tag{8.1}$$

where $\boldsymbol{S}$ is the vector of molecular species concentrations, $\boldsymbol{N}$, the stoichiometry matrix; $\boldsymbol{v}$ the rate vector and $\boldsymbol{p}$ a vector of parameters which can influence the evolution of the system. Real cellular networks have an additional property that is particularly characteristic of biological networks, this is the presence of so-called moiety conserved cycles. Depending on the time-scale of a study, there will be molecular subgroups conserved during the evolution of a network, these are termed *conserved moieties*; (Reich and Selkov 1981). The total amount of a particular moiety in a network is time invariant and is determined solely by the initial conditions imposed on the system.[2]

[2] There are rare cases when a conservation relationship arises out of a non-moiety cycle. This does not affect the mathematics but only the physical interpretation of the relationship. For example, $A \rightarrow B + C$; $B + C \rightarrow D$ has the conservation, $B - C = \text{constant}$.

In metabolism, conserved cycles act as common conveyors of energy (ATP) or reducing power (NAD); in signaling pathways they occur as protein phosphorylation states while in genetic networks, they occur as bound and unbound protein states to DNA. These conserved cycles will often have a profound effect on the network behavior and it is important that they be properly considered in computational models.

From the full set of molecular species in a model, it is customary to divide the set into two groups, the dependent (S_d) and independent set (S_i). This division is dependent entirely on the number and kind of conserved cycles in the network. If there aren't any conserved cycles in a model then the dependent set is empty and the size of the independent set equals the number of molecular species in the model. For details on how to compute S_d and S_i the reader should consult Sauro and Ingalls (2004) or refer to Box 8.1 in this chapter. In many cases it is vital that this separation into dependent and independent species be made. For simple time course simulations the separation is not so important, but for most other analyses it is critical and for stiff integration methods highly desirable. The reason is that many numerical methods, including the stiff integrators, employ a measure called the Jacobian matrix as part of the numerical calculation. If the separation is not carried out, the Jacobian becomes singular and thereby rendering most analyses (e.g. steady-state location, bifurcation analysis, certain optimization methods and sensitivity methods, etc.) numerically unstable if not impossible. Even when carrying out simple time course simulations, the separation is also useful because it enables the number of differential equations to be reduced in number and thereby improve computational efficiency.

Equation 8.1 is therefore better expressed as:

$$\begin{aligned} \boldsymbol{S}_d &= \boldsymbol{L}_0 \boldsymbol{S}_i + \boldsymbol{T} \\ \frac{d\boldsymbol{S}_i}{dt} &= \boldsymbol{N}_R \boldsymbol{v}(\boldsymbol{S}_i(\boldsymbol{p}), \boldsymbol{S}_d, \boldsymbol{p}) \end{aligned} \tag{8.2}$$

In these equations, $\boldsymbol{S}_i$ is the vector of independent species, $\boldsymbol{S}_d$, the vector of dependent species, $\boldsymbol{L}_0$ the link matrix, $\boldsymbol{T}$ the total mass vector, $\boldsymbol{N}_R$ the reduced stoichiometry matrix, $\boldsymbol{v}$ the rate vector, and $\boldsymbol{p}$ the vector of parameters. Equation 8.2 constitutes the most general expression of an ODE-based temporal model (Hofmeyr 2001; Heinrich and Schuster 1996). The symbolism used in Equation 8.2 is the standard notation used by many in the systems biology community.

Although mathematically, reaction-based models are given by Equations 8.1 and 8.2, many researchers are more familiar with expressing models in the form of a reaction scheme. For example, the following describes part of glycolysis:

```
Glucose-6-P -> Fructose-6-Phosphate
Fructose-6-Phosphate + ATP -> Fructose-1-6-Bisphosphate + ADP
Fructose-1-6-Bisphosphate -> DHAP + GAP
```

For brevity, the rates laws that accompany each reaction have been left out. Such notation is well understood by biologists. It is not straightforward however to convert this representation to the representation given by Equation 8.2. However, many software tools will permit users to enter models as a list of reactions and then automatically generate the mathematical model (Sauro and Fell 1991; Sauro 2000; Sauro et al. 2003).

Box 8.1 Reaction Network Consider the simple reaction network shown on the left below:

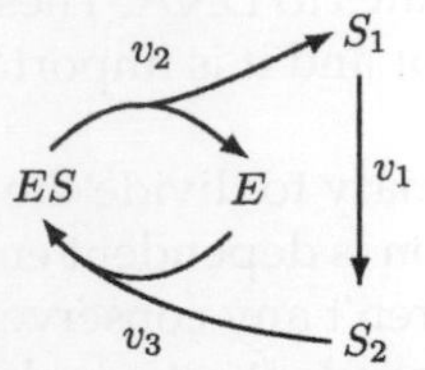

$$\begin{array}{c} \\ ES \\ S_1 \\ S_2 \\ E \end{array} \begin{array}{c} \begin{array}{ccc} v_1 & v_2 & v_3 \end{array} \\ \begin{bmatrix} 0 & -1 & 1 \\ -1 & 1 & 0 \\ 1 & 0 & -1 \\ 0 & 1 & -1 \end{bmatrix} \end{array}$$

The **stoichiometry matrix** for this network is shown to the right. This network possesses two conserved cycles given by the constraints: $S_1 + S_2 + ES = T_1$ and $E + ES = T_2$. The set of independent species includes: $\{ES, S_1\}$ and the set of dependent species $\{E, S_2\}$.

The L_0 matrix can be shown to be:

$$L_0 = \begin{bmatrix} -1 & -1 \\ -1 & 0 \end{bmatrix}$$

The complete set of equations for this model is therefore:

$$\begin{bmatrix} S_2 \\ E \end{bmatrix} = \begin{bmatrix} -1 & -1 \\ -1 & 0 \end{bmatrix} \begin{bmatrix} ES \\ S_1 \end{bmatrix} + \begin{bmatrix} T_1 \\ T_2 \end{bmatrix}$$

$$\begin{bmatrix} dES/dt \\ dS_1/dt \end{bmatrix} = \begin{bmatrix} 0 & -1 & 1 \\ -1 & 1 & 0 \end{bmatrix} \begin{bmatrix} v_1 \\ v_2 \\ v_3 \end{bmatrix}$$

Note that even though there appears to be four variables in this system, there are in fact only two independent variables, $\{ES, S_1\}$, and hence only two differential equations and two linear constraints.

2 STANDARDS

A standard is defined as a uniform set of specifications applied toward an activity or product that encourages interoperation and cooperation. Ideally, a standard is clearly and unambiguously defined and while remaining easy to interpret and implement. In the modern world, standards have been applied to nearly everything from electronics cables and audio formats to paper sizes and telephone numbers. In the field of systems biology, the desire to facilitate interoperability and reuse of computational models and data was the motivation for developing standardized digital annotations and representations.

2.1 Minimum information (MI)

At the turn of the millennium, with the sequencing of the human genome and the rise of DNA microarray technologies, standards development for systems biology reached its first major milestone. Given increasingly large and complex experiments involving numerous biological samples and different experimental conditions, researchers within the DNA microarray community quickly realized that if one was to make sense of the results from any such analysis, a new way of storing and retrieving this complex information was needed. Scientists struggled to coordinate the outputs of different software platforms, identify the ancillary information needed to interpret results, and define the data necessary to enable reproduction of results. Through discussions between interested members of the community, public presentations, and workshop meetings, the Microarray Gene Expression Data (MGED) Society outlined the Minimum Information About a Microarray Experiment (MIAME) specification (Brazma 2001) and Microarray Gene Expression Markup Language (MAGE-ML) (Spellman et al. 2002). As we will discuss in the following sections, in many ways, this has become the prototype (Quackenbush 2006) for subsequent data annotation guidelines in systems biology.

The early success of MIAME and its widespread adoption led to the development of many domain-specific extensions and variations. MIAME is now accompanied by a myriad of "minimum information" reporting standards groups that cover practically every corner of the biomedical field (Standard operating procedures 2006). The Minimum Reporting Guidelines for Biological and Biomedical Investigations (MIBBI) (Taylor et al. 2008) project has arisen as a comprehensive source of these reporting "checklists." MIBBI maintains a web-based and freely accessible resource for minimum information standards (http://www.mibbi.org/), providing access to existing checklists, complementary data formats, controlled vocabularies, tools, and databases. This resource thereby enhances both transparency and accessibility of experimental results to the wider bioscience community.

2.1.1 Minimum information required in the annotation of models (MIRIAM)

Extending beyond the laboratory, the Minimum Information Requested In the Annotation of biochemical Models (MIRIAM) standard (Novere et al. 2005; Le Novère 2006) was developed for describing quantitative models of biochemical systems and bring together the new standards in computational systems biology, SBML and CellML (both are which discussed later in this chapter). By unifying different modeling sub-domain standards under the same requisites, and thus ensuring that models are easily testable, reproducible, and comparable, the utility of quantitative modeling may be enhanced for the benefit of biomedical research. However, the ultimate impact of these standards depends on their adoption throughout the community and the number of software tools that are developed to facilitate its use (more issues that we will discuss later in this chapter).

Traditionally, a challenge that MIRIAM faces is that encoded models in scientific publications or online are not in a standard format. And, of those that are encoded in a standard format, many actually fail compliance and validation tests developed for the standards. Failures may occur for a variety of reasons, ranging from minor syntactic errors to significant conceptual problems. Further semantic inaccuracies may lie within the model structure. With models that are not annotated, users are faced with ambiguous reaction specifications, such as species "A" and "B" producing "C".

Thus, to address these quality issues, MIRIAM comprises of the following guidelines:

Reference correspondence.

- The model must be encoded in a public, standardized, machine-readable format (SBML, CellML, GENESIS, …).
- The model must comply with the standard in which it is encoded.
- The model must be clearly related to a single reference description. If a model is composed from different parts, there should still be a description of the derived/combined model.
- The encoded model structure must reflect the biological processes described by the reference description.
- The model must be instantiable in a simulation: all quantitative attributes must be defined, including initial conditions.
- When instantiated, the model must be able to reproduce all results given in the reference description within an epsilon (algorithms, round-up errors).

Attribution annotation.

- The model has to be named.
- A citation to the reference description must be provided (complete citation, unique identifier, unambiguous URL). The citation should identify the authors of the model.
- The name and contact information for model creators must be provided.
- The date and time of model creation and last modification should be specified. A history is useful but not required.
- The model should be linked to a precise statement about the terms of it's distribution. MIRIAM does not require "freedom of use" or "no cost."

External resource annotation.

- The annotation must unambiguously relate a piece of knowledge to a model constituent.
- The referenced information should be described using a triplet {collection, identifier, qualifier}:
- The annotation should be written as a Uniform Resource Identifier (URI).
- The identifier should be considered within the context of the framework of the collection.
- Collection namespace and identifier are combined into a single URI, such as: http://identifiers.org/collection/identifier. For example: http://identifiers.org/uniprot/P62158.
- Qualifiers (optional) should refine the link between the model constituent and the piece of knowledge: "has a," "is version of," "is homolog to," etc.
- The community has to agree upon a set of standard valid URIs. A database and the associated API (Web Services) have been developed at the EBI to provide the generation and interpretation of URIs.

MIRIAM applies these guidelines to a wide range of quantitative models, which may use a variety of different mathematical representations, such as ODE, PDE, or DAEs. However, the ultimate test is to compare simulation results from a model representation with the reference description of the model.

2.1.2 *Minimum information about a simulation experiment (MIASE)*

While the MIRIAM guidelines promote the inclusion of many crucial pieces of information within a computational model, it is vague about the advanced numerical algorithms and modeling workflows that are used in a modern computational setting. Without this information on the model context in which the original simulations were performed, reproducibility of the model results is still ambiguous. Thus, the Minimum Information About a Simulation Experiment (MIASE) guidelines (Waltemath et al. 2011) describe the minimal set of information that a model description must provide regarding the implementation of its simulation. This includes the list of models that were used, any modifications that were made, simulation procedures that were applied, and how the raw numerical results were processed to produce the final output.

The MIASE guidelines are comprised of the following:

All models used in the experiment must be identified, accessible, and fully described.

- The description of the simulation experiment must be provided together with the models necessary for the experiment, or with a precise and unambiguous way of accessing those models.
- The models required for the simulations must be provided with all governing equations, parameter values, and necessary conditions (initial state and/or boundary conditions). If a model is not encoded in a standard format, then the model code must be made available to the user.
- If a model is not encoded in an open format or code, its full description must be provided, sufficient to re-implement it.
- Any modification of a model (pre-processing) required before the execution of a step of the simulation experiment must be described.

A precise description of the simulation steps and other procedures used by the experiment must be provided.

- All simulation steps must be clearly described, including the simulation algorithms to be used, the models on which to apply each simulation, the order of the simulation steps, and the data processing to be done between the simulation steps.
- All information needed for the correct implementation of the necessary simulation steps must be included, through precise descriptions, or references to unambiguous information sources.
- If a simulation step is performed using a computer program for which source code is not available, all information needed to reproduce the simulation, and not only repeat it, must be provided, including the algorithms used by the original software and any information necessary to implement them, such as the discretization and integration methods.
- If it is known that a simulation step will produce different results when performed in a different simulation environment or on a different computational platform, an explanation of how the model has to be run with the specified environment/platform in order to achieve the purpose of the experiment must be given.

All information necessary to obtain the desired numerical results must be provided.

- All post-processing steps applied on the raw numerical results of simulation steps in order to generate the final results have to be described in detail. That includes the identification of data to process, the order in which changes were applied, and the nature of changes.
- If the expected insights depend on the relation between different results, such as a plot of one against another, the results to be compared have to be specified.

By providing the information specified by these guidelines, modelers can be reasonably assured that the simulation experiment corresponds with those of the original authors. Thus, as adoption of MIASE spreads, the quality of scientific reporting will increase, and collaborative efforts in computational modeling and simulation of biological systems is encouraged.

2.2 Ontologies

The value of any kind of data is greatly enhanced when it can be easily integrated and interpreted by other systems or third parties. Toward this goal, the MIRIAM and MIASE guidelines state that a model's constituents and simulation procedure must be unambiguously annotated. Thus, a common language is necessary for different models to describe the same physical entity or biological process. One approach is through the annotation of multiple bodies of data using common controlled and structured vocabularies or "ontologies."

For example, one successful biomedical ontology is the Gene Ontology (GO) (Smith 2005). GO defines specific gene products across different species. All terms are organized in a hierarchical structure, where there are three main branches: biological process, cellular component, or molecular functions. GO terms have been used in millions of annotations relating to gene products described in protein databases.

2.2.1 *Open biomedical ontologies (OBO)*

The success of the ontology approach has led to dizzying number of different ontologies, the sheer number which may create an obstacle to integration. OBO (http://obofoundry.org) (Smith et al. 2007) was created in 2001 to address this issue by serving as an umbrella body for the developers of life-science ontologies. The key principles behind OBO ontologies are that they must be *open* and *orthogonal*. Ontologies within OBO are *open* in the sense that its usage should be available without any constraints, and new applications may build upon OBO without restriction. Ontologies within OBO are *orthogonal* such that vocabulary is non-overlapping with other ontologies.

2.2.2 *Model annotations*

One of the ways that modelers directly interact with ontologies is through the annotations within a model. This section will present an overview of the major components of the model and some of the most commonly used external resources and controlled vocabularies used for annotating them.

MODEL METADATA

In the model metadata, the information for what the model is describing, a number of different ontologies may be used. In biological pathway models, Reactome (http://www.reactome.org/ReactomeGWT/entrypoint.html) (Joshi-Tope et al. 2005) and KEGG Pathway (http://www.genome.jp/kegg/) (Ogata et al. 1999) are comprehensive, human-curated, pathway databases that are often referenced. Information regarding the taxonomy of the biological pathway can be referenced in the UniProt Taxonomy database (http://www.uniprot.org/) (Bairoch 2005).

MATHEMATICS

When describing the mathematics in a model, the Systems Biology Ontology (SBO) (http://www.ebi.ac.uk/sbo/main/) (Le Novère 2006) is a recently developed vocabulary used for specifying the roles of biochemical species, parameters, kinetic laws, and other model components in relation to a systems biology model. For instance, SBO annotations can denote the substrate, products, and Michaelis-Menten constant in a model. GO and Reactome may also be used to describe what biological process a kinetic rate law is describing.

PHYSICAL ENTITIES

When it comes to describing the biophysical constituents, or species, in a model, several different ontologies can be referenced, sometimes in combination. GO and UniProt are often referenced for annotating proteins, and KEGG and ChEBI (http://www.ebi.ac.uk/chebi/) (Degtyarenko et al. 2008) may be used for annotating small molecules and chemical compounds that are related to biological processes.

2.2.3 *Simulation experiment annotations*

Ontologies for describing simulation procedure and numerical results are relatively newer than the previously described model annotations, and is currently an active field of work and new changes. The Kinetic Simulation of Algorithm Ontology (KiSAO) (http://biomodels.net/kisao/) is currently being developed to describe the precise numerical steps and procedures taken in a simulation experiment. When looking at the numerical output of a simulation experiment, the Terminology for the Description of Dynamics (TEDDY) (http://www.ebi.ac.uk/compneur-srv/teddy/) (Courtot et al. 2011) is being designed to describe the observed dynamical behavior in a simulation.

2.3 Physiological models

In these following sections, the most popular and influential standards for encoding and exchanging physiological models will be discussed. The relative merits of each format will be surveyed and compared. But first, why are model standards useful?

Over the years, there has been an ever increasing list of wide ranging cellular models published in the literature. For most of scientific publishing history, each author has a particular notation that they use to publish the model. Some authors will publish the model as a reaction scheme (see the example in Section 1.3.1), much like the notation given in scheme. Others will itemize the actual mathematical representation in the form of a list of differential equations. Some authors do not publish the model at all but provide the model as supplementary information. Until recently, there has been no way to publish models in a standard format. Without a standard format it has proved very difficult if not impossible in many cases to implement and use published models without considerable effort.

Thus, as a result of this serious issue, a number of groups set out to gather community support to develop a standard that model developers would be happy to use. There was an early effort in 1998 by the BTK (BioThermoKinetics) group to standardize on a practical format for exchanging models between Gepasi (Mendes 1993) and SCAMP (Sauro and Fell 1991), both tools were widely used at the time. Around the same time, bioengineers at the University of Auckland began investigating the role that Extensible Markup Language (XML) (Harold and Means 2001) could play in defining a standard for exchanging computational models in order to reduce errors that appeared frequently in published models. From the Auckland team emerged CellML (Lloyd et al. 2004). Members from the BTK group subsequently took their experience and contributed significantly to the other major model exchange standard, called SBML (Hucka et al. 2003).

2.3.1 *CellML*

CellML (Lloyd et al. 2004) represents cellular models using a mathematical description similar to Equation 8.2. CellML also has provisions for metadata annotations to allow MIRIAM compliance. In addition, CellML represents entities using a component-based approach where relationships between components are represented by connections. In many ways CellML represents a literal translation of the mathematical equations, except that the relationship between dependent and independent species is implied rather than explicit. The literal translation of the mathematics however goes much further, in fact the representation that CellML uses is very reminiscent of the way an engineer might wire up an analog computer to solve the equations (though without specifying the integrators). As a result CellML is very general and in principle could probably represent any system that has a mathematical description (and not just the kind indicated by Equation 8.1). CellML is also very precise in that every item in a model is defined explicitly. However, the generality and explicit nature of CellML also results in increased complexity especially for software developers. Another side effect of the increased complexity is that models that are represented using CellML tend to be quite large. On average, a sample from the CellML repository (http://models.cellml.org/cellml) indicates that each reaction in a model requires about 5 kilobytes of storage.

Owing to the complexity of CellML, one unfortunate side effect is that there are substantially fewer tools which can read and write CellML compared to SBML. The CellML team (http://cellml.sourceforge.net/) also provides their own software tools to third-party developers, including the CellML API (http://cellml-api.sourceforge.net/), which is a library much like libSBML (discussed later in Section 2.3.2) that allows software developers to read and write CellML models.

2.3.2 *Systems biology markup language (SBML)*

SBML was developed in 2000 at Caltech, Pasadena, as a result of funding received from the Japanese ERATO program. Both CellML and SBML are today viewed as the main standards for exchanging cellular network models. There are however fundamental differences between the approaches that CellML and SBML take in the way models are represented.

Whereas CellML attempts to be highly comprehensive, SBML was designed to meet the immediate needs of the modeling community and is therefore more focused on a particular problem set. One result of this is that the standard is much simpler and much less verbose. Like CellML, SBML is based on XML, however unlike CellML, it takes a different approach to representing cellular models. The way SBML represents models closely maps the way existing modeling packages represent models. Whereas CellML represents models as a mathematical wiring diagram, SBML represents models as a list of chemical transformations. Since every process in a biological cells can ultimately be broken down into one or more chemical transformations this was the natural representation to use. However SBML does not have generalized elements such as components and connections, SBML employs specific elements to represent spatial compartments, molecular species, and chemical transformations. In addition to these, SBML also has provision for rules which can be used to represent constraints, derived values and general math which for one reason or another cannot be transformed into a chemical scheme. Like CellML, the dependent and independent species are implied.

The development of SBML is stratified in order to organize architectural changes and versioning. Major editions of SBML are termed Levels and represent substantial changes to the composition and structure of the language. Models defined in lower Levels of SBML can always be represented in higher Levels, though some translation may be necessary. The converse (from higher Level to lower Level) is sometimes also possible, though not guaranteed. The Levels remain distinct; a valid SBML Level 1 document is not a valid SBML Level 2 document. Minor revisions of SBML are termed Versions and constitute changes within a level to correct, adjust, and refine language features. Finally, specification documents inevitably require minor editorial changes as its users discover errors and ambiguities. Such problems are corrected in new Releases of a given SBML specification.

EXTENSIBILITY

It was realized early on by the authors of SBML that as systems biology developed there would be pressure from the community to make additional functionality available in SBML. To address this issue, SBML has a formal means for adding extensions in the form of annotations. There now exist a number of annotations that are used by software developers. Some of these address issues such as providing visualization information to allow software tools to render the model in some meaningful way (two examples of these will be given in a later section). Other extensions provide a means to store information necessary for flux balance analysis or to provide information for stochastic simulations. Ultimately some of the extensions will most likely be folded into the official SBML standard. This mechanism, a sort of Darwinian evolution, permits the most important and popular requests to be made part of SBML. It makes the process of SBML evolution more transparent and permits users to be more involved in the development of SBML.

The current generation of SBML, Level 3 (http://sbml.org/Documents/Specifications#SBML_Level_3_Packages) (Hucka et al. 2010), is modular in the sense of having a defined core set of features and optional packages adding features on top of the core. This modular approach means that models can declare which feature-sets they use, and likewise, software tools can declare which packages they support. It also means that the development of SBML Level 3 can proceed in a concurrent manner, where each module is developed relatively independently.

SBML Level 3 package development is today an ongoing activity, with packages being created to extend SBML in many areas that its core functionality does not directly support. Examples include models whose species have structure and/or state variables, models with spatially non-homogeneous compartments and spatially dependent processes, and models in which species and processes refer to qualitative entities and processes rather than quantitative ones.

SBML DEVELOPMENT TOOLS

Early on in the development of SBML, the original authors decided to provide software tools almost immediately for the community. Since XML at the time was not well understood by many software developers the provision of such assistance was crucial. In hindsight, this is probably one reason why SBML has become a popular standard. Initially the original authors provided a simple library for the Windows platform since the bulk of biology based users tend to be Windows users. Today this library is still used by a number of tools including Gepasi, Jarnac, and JDesigner (discussed later). With the growing popularity of SBML, the community has since developed a comprehensive cross platform tool libSBML (http://sbml.sourceforge.org) which is now the recommended SBML toolkit to use. LibSBML was developed in C/C++, with bindings to a number of different languages, for maximum portability.

PRACTICAL CONSIDERATIONS

Whereas CellML is very general, SBML is more specific, as result, the storage requirement for SBML is much less. It takes on average roughly 1.5 kilobytes to store a single chemical transformation in SBML Level 2 (compared to 5 kilobytes for CellML). Interestingly it only takes roughly 50–100 bytes to store single transformations in raw binary format where there is minimal extraneous syntax. Some readers may feel that with todays cheap storage technologies, that discussions on storage requirements is unnecessary. Indeed for small models it is not an issue. However, in future very large models are likely to be developed. There is, for example a serious attempt (http://www.physiome.org) now underway to model in the long-term entire organs and even whole organisms. The amount of information in these cases is huge and the question of efficient storage is not so trivial. Obviously XML is highly compressible and large models can be stored in this way. However, inefficient storage also increases the time taken to manipulate the models. Furthermore, in a modeling environment, model authors tend to generate hundreds of variants while developing the model. For a large model this clearly would generate huge amounts of XML-based data. One of the things that has yet to be addressed by either standard is the how model variants can be efficiently stored.

USAGE

Both SBML and CellML have been taken up by many software developers and implemented in their software. Over the past decade, SBML has become the *de facto* standard for systems biology models. As December 2012, 251 different software packages are officially listed on the SBML Software Guide (http://sbml.org/SBML_Software_Guide). In addition,

SBML is the official model interchange format for the SBW project (http://sys-bio.org/), the international *E. coli* alliance, and the receptor tyrosine kinase consortium.

2.3.3 NeuroML

Paralleling efforts in SBML and CellML in molecular pathway and cell physiology modeling, NeuroML (Goddard et al. 2001) provides a common data format for defining and exchanging descriptions of neuronal cell networks. Level 1 (MorphML), Level 2 (ChannelML), and Level 3 (NetworkML) describe neuronal systems to different levels of biological granularity.

A number of software of packages are written to work with NeuroML, NEURON (Carnevale and Hines 2006), GENESIS (Bower et al. 1995), MOOSE (Ray and Bhalla 2008), NEST (Diesmann and Gewaltig 2001), and PSICS (Cannon et al. 2010). These different environments were successfully able to reproduce the same model simulation (including a reconstruction of the 3D structure of a neural pathway) (Gleeson 2010), using NeuroML as the exchange format.

There are also recent efforts to convert NeuroML into SBML (Keating and Novère 2012), which may allow NeuroML models and modelers access to the vast library of SBML compliant software tools.

2.4 Simulation

The share and reuse of biological models are primary challenges in the field of computational biology. While the previous discussed model exchange formats address issues of reproducing the structural components of the model, there are still missing elements in the computational procedure to unambiguously generate or reproduce relevant simulation results. This section will cover several standards that implement the MIASE guidelines and enable the transmission and sharing of simulation experimental procedures and results

2.4.1 Simulation experiment description markup language (SED-ML)

SED-ML (http://sed-ml.org/) (Köhn and Le Novere 2008) is an XML format that enables the storage and exchange of part of the information required to implement the MIASE guidelines. It covers information about the simulation settings, including information about the models, changes on them, simulation settings applied to the models and output definitions. SED-ML is independent of the formats used to encode the models as long as they are expressed in XML, and it is independent of the software tools used to run the simulations. The community believes that providing detailed information about simulation recipes will highly improve the efficient use of existing models, encoded in widely accept formats of model structure, such as SBML and CellML.

2.4.2 Systems biology results markup language (SBRML)

SBRML (http://www.comp-sys-bio.org/SBRML) (Dada 2010) is another standardization effort that essentially associates a model with one or more datasets. Each dataset is represented as a series of values associated with the model variables. SBRML and SED-ML are complementary. While the main purpose of SBRML is to encode the simulation results, or even experimental data and the context in which it was obtained, SED-ML is used as a more detailed description of the operations that generate simulation results. This means that a SED-ML document can be used to describe the specific operations that led to the data contained in an SBRML document.

2.4.3 Numerical markup language (NuML)

NuML (http://code.google.com/p/numl/) aims to standardize the exchange of numerical results, and is planned to be used by SED-ML and SBRML. NuML is designed to support any type of numerical result through the powerful coupling of ontology terms with one or more result components. Ontology terms reference external resources that define the vocabulary and terms used to describe the results in the NuML file. The results of the NuML file contain two principle components, a description of the results and the results themselves. Further details can be found by consulting the NuML specification (http://numl.googlecode.com/svn/trunk/numl-spec-l1v1.pdf).

2.5 Visualization

Circuit diagrams and Unified Modeling Language diagrams are just two examples of standard visual languages that help accelerate work by promoting regularity, removing ambiguity, and enabling software tool support for communication of complex information. Ironically, despite having one of the highest ratios of graphical to textual information, biology still lacks standard graphical notations. The recent deluge of biological knowledge makes addressing this deficit a pressing concern. For many users, the ability to visualize models and to build models using visual tools is an important feature. There are currently a number of visualization formats that are in common use. One of the earliest, most comprehensive, and freely available formats is the molecular interaction maps developed by Kohn (1999) and more recently by Mirit Aladjem (Kohn et al. 2002). The Kohn format emerged from the need to represent complex signaling networks in a compact way. Unlike metabolic networks, signaling networks can be extremely complex with multiple protein states and interactions and therefore an alternative and more concise approach is desirable.

Kitano (2003) took a traditional approach where different molecular entities (such as proteins, ions, transporters, etc.) have particular pictorial representations. The software tool CellDesigner (Funahashi et al. 2003), which will be discussed later in this chapter, implemented this proposed format.

2.5.1 Systems biology graphical notation (SBGN)

SBGN (http://www.sbgn.org/) (Le Novère et al. 2009) has arisen in recent years as one of the most widely supported and comprehensive visual languages, developed by a community of biochemists, modelers, and computer scientists. SBGN consists of three complementary languages: process diagram, entity relationship diagram, and activity flow diagram. Together they enable scientists to represent networks of biochemical interactions in a standard, unambiguous way. The process diagram draws its inspiration from process-style notations, borrowing ideas from the work of Kitano. In contrast, the entity relationship diagram is based on a large extent on Kohn's notation. The SBGN activity flow diagram depicts only the cascade of activity, thus making the notation most similar to the representations often used in the current literature to describe signaling pathways.

SBGN-ML

While SBGN defines how biological information should be visualized, it does not specify how the mapping should be stored electronically. SBGN-ML (http://www.sbgn.org/LibSBGN/Exchange_Format) (Le Novere, 2010) is a dedicated file format that can be used to store and transfer the information necessary for software to faithfully render the corresponding SBGN diagram. The software library libSBGN (http://www.sbgn.org/SBGN_Software/LibSBGN) complements the file format. It consists of two parallel implementations (van Iersel et al. 2012) in Java and C++, which can be easily ported to different programming languages.

The plugin cySBGN (http://www.ebi.ac.uk/saezrodriguez/cysbgn/) (Goncalves and Saez-Rodriguez 2013), through use of libSBGN and SBGN-ML, allows SBGN diagrams to be imported, modified, and analyzed within Cytoscape (http://www.cytoscape.org/), a popular network visualizer. Coupled with the cySBML (http://sourceforge.net/projects/cysbml/) (König et al. 2012) plugin, which allows SBML models to be imported into Cytoscape, SBGN maps can be generated from SBML models directly.

2.6 Other standards

Apart from the mentioned model interchange formats, there are many other mediums for representing models. This section will briefly cover several additional formats.

2.6.1 Human readable formats

In addition to visualization approaches and the use of XML to represent models, there has been a long tradition in the field to describe models using human readable text-based formats. Indeed the very first simulator BIOSSIM, (Garfinkel 1968), allowed a user to describe a model using a list of reaction schemes. Variants of this have been employed by a number of simulators since, including, SCAMP (Sauro and Fell 1991), Jarnac (Sauro 2000), E-Cell (Tomita et al. 1999), and more recently PySCeS (Olivier et al. 2004). Being able to represent models in a human readable format offers many advantages, including, conciseness, easily understood and manipulated using a simple editor, flexible, portable, and above all extremely easy to include commenting and annotation.

JARNAC

Jarnac (Sauro 2000; Bergmann and Sauro 2006) (also described later as part of the Jarnac modeling platform) implements two languages, a biochemical descriptive language which allows users to enter models as reaction schemes (similar to a SCAMP script) and a second language, the model control language which is a full featured scripting language that can be used to manipulate and analyze a model. The main advantage of Jarnac over other tools is that models can be very rapidly built and modeled.

MATHEMATICAL MODELING LANGUAGE (MML)

MML is a text-based format that is the primary form of model representations in the JSim platform (Raymond et al. 2003) (discussed in Section 4.1.4). Unlike SBML and CellML which are based on XML, MML uses its own a C-styled language for model declaration. MML models are often expressed generally in terms of mathematical equations, any mixture of ordinary and partial differential equations, implicit equations, integrations, discrete events, and even external programming code, such as Java, C, or MATLAB. One feature that sets MML apart from other modeling languages is its awareness of physical units when run through JSim's MML compiler (Chizeck et al. 2009).

PYSCES

PySCeS is a console-based application written in the Python (http://www.python.org) programming language that runs on all major computing platforms (Olivier et al. 2004). Although users interact with PySCeS via Python scripts, many of the underlying numerical capabilities are provided by well established C/C++ or FORTRAN-based numerical libraries through the SciPy package (Olivier et al. 2002). While it is possible to build models directly in Python using SciPy, PySCeS was written by team experienced with biochemical modeling to provide a high-level modeling interface that saves the modeler from needing to work with low-level numerical algorithms.

SBML-SHORTHAND

The SBML community has also developed a human readable script called SBML-shorthand (Gillespie et al. 2006). This notation maps directly onto SBML but is much easier to hand write compared to SBML. The shorthand is also much less verbose and uses infix to represent expressions rather than MathML.

ANTIMONY

Antimony (http://antimony.sourceforge.net/main.html) (Smith et al. 2009) is a more recent scripting language that combines the relative simplicity of languages like Jarnac, PySCeS, and SBML-shorthand with the modularity of languages like little-b (http://www.littleb.org/), without forcing the modeler learn a general programming language. Antimony-formatted files may be read by other software packages, like PySCeS using the libAntimony library. Furthermore, Antimony to SBML converters extend Antimony's usefulness by allowing users to convert their modules into a form usable with the vast number of SBML-compliant software.

2.6.2 Biological pathway exchange (BioPAX)

BioPAX (http://www.biopax.org/) (Demir et al. 2010; Strömbäck and Lambrix 2005) is another proposed standard based on XML. BioPAX aims to integrate many of the incompatible pathway related databases (such as BioCYC, BIND, WIT, aMAZE, KEGG, and others) so that data from any one of these databases can be easily interchanged. In future it should be possible to extract data from many of the pathway databases and integrate the data directly into SBML (or CellML) via BioPAX. The BioPAX group proposes to embed BioPAX elements onto SBML or CellML for unambiguous identification of substances (metabolites, enzymes) and reactions. However, it is possible for to convert, or map, from SBML to BioPAX (http://www.ebi.ac.uk/compneur-srv/sbml/converters/SBMLtoBioPax.html).

2.7 Model databases

High-throughput experimental techniques have led to the population of web-accessible databases with vast amounts of biological data. Mathematical models of biological systems are playing an essential role in the interpretation of this data. The scientific community now faces the challenge of the mathematical models themselves becoming increasingly complex and numerous. There is a need for centralized databases to store all these models in standard formats to make them easily accessible and reusable by the research community. Publishing the models in a standard format, concurrent with the submission of a written paper, will eliminate many of the errors introduced into the model during the publication process.

2.7.1 BioModels

BioModels Database (http://www.ebi.ac.uk/biomodels/) (Le Novere et al. 2006) is one largest open- access databases in systems biology. Part of the international initiative BioModels.net, BioModels provides access to peer-reviewed and published models. Each model is manually curated by the database maintainers to verify that it corresponds to the reference publication and gives the expected numerical results. Curators also annotate the components of the models with terms from controlled vocabularies (Taxonomy, Gene Ontology, ChEBI, etc.) and links to other databases (UniProt, KEGG, Reactome, etc.). This annotation is a crucial feature of BioModels Database in that it permits the unambiguous identification of molecular species or reactions and enables effective search algorithms in finding model and model components of interest. As of December 2012, the database contains 142,973 models, comprising of 923 models published in literature, of which roughly half are manually curated by BioModels, and 142,050 models automatically generated from the Path2Models project (http://code.google.com/p/path2models/), an effort aimed at automatically converting biological pathway databases (such as KEGG) into corresponding SBML models.

2.7.2 CellML repository

The CellML Model Repository (http://www.cellml.org/models) (Lloyd et al. 2008; Beard 2009) is a similar effort, which contains hundreds of biochemical pathway models that have been described in peer-reviewed publications. CellML and the CellML Model Repository are part of the IUPS Physiome Project effort to create a virtual physiological human (Hunter et al. 2005). The explicit representation of modularity, together with the flexible nature of the CellML language which allows the description of a diverse range of cellular and subcellular systems.

The CellML Model Repository contains over 330 freely available, quantitative models of biological processes taken from the peer-reviewed literature. In contrast with other databases, such as BioModels, which focus on specific areas such as systems biology pathway models or computational neuroscience, the CellML Model Repository contains models describing a wide range of biological processes, including: signal transduction pathways, metabolic pathways, electrophysiology, immunology, the cell cycle, muscle contraction and mechanical models and constitutive laws. This wide scope exemplifies CellML's ability to describe much of the biochemistry, electrophysiology, and mechanics of the intracellular environment. Lumped parameter models dealing with systems physiology (e.g. blood pressure control, fluid retention, electrolyte balance, endocrine function, etc.) are also within the scope of CellML.

2.7.3 *JSim repository*

The JSim (discussed in Section 4.1.4) group provides a repository of 370 freely-accessible MML models (http://www.physiome.org/jsim/db/). These may be either downloaded to the desktop as JSim project files, or directly simulated in the web browser using the JSim Java applet.

2.7.4 *JWS Online*

JWS Online (http://jjj.biochem.sun.ac.za/) (Olivier and Snoep 2004) is a repository of kinetic models, describing biological systems, which can be interactively run and interrogated over the Internet. As of December 2012, JWS Online contains 131 models, downloadable to SBML, while also providing a web browser interface to a simulation server.

PHYSIOME REPOSITORY

The Physiome Model Repository (http://www.cellml.org/tools/pmr) (Yu et al. 2011) is an offshoot of the CellML repository, which is unique in that it allows users to make their own copies of CellML and keep track of model changes using a distributed version control system, Mercurial (O'Sullivan 2007). One of the primary goals of this platform is to facilitate collaboration between several researchers, a common occurence during model development.

3 FUTURE CONSIDERATIONS

With the success of Minimum Information guidelines and standardized representations of biological models, quantitative modeling has surged in popularity. However, the ever-growing number of published dynamic models published also presents a significant challenge in terms of model reuse and integration. While there is currently no agreed upon way to merge smaller submodels into larger models, MIRIAM and MIASE annotations enable model composition software to make use of the semantic information and enable algorithms parse through models, or parts of models, of interest to the user. Recent efforts in this arena include semanticSBML (Krause et al. 2010), SemSim (Neal et al. 2009), and the SBML Reaction Finder (Neal and Sauro 2012).

4 PLATFORMS

This section will focus on the different modeling and simulation platforms that are available, which implement the systems biology standards highlighted in the previous section. While this section is certainly not an exhaustive list of all modeling platforms, highly influential or previously mentioned software packages will be discussed.

The first systems biology simulation package, BIOSIM, was written in the 1960s (Garfinkel 1968). Especially in recent years, there has been a boom of software applications for the systems biology community. While, most software projects have ended development over the years, for a variety of reasons, such as lack of funding or maintainers, there are still far too many different modeling platforms to possibly be covered in this chapter. Thus, in this section will highlight specific software tools that have had a significant impact on the community, or some unique features that set them aside.

Furthermore, discussion will be focused specifically on modeling and simulation tools, and not more advanced analytical techniques, such as metabolic flux balance analysis. For more detailed discussion on flux balance software, please refer to a recent review (Copeland 2012) and a very comprehensive listing of SBML compatible software provided by the SBML consortium (http://sbml.org/SBML_Software_Guide/SBML_Software_Matrix).

4.1 Modeling

On the whole, many of these applications provide very similar functionality. The distinguishing feature among them is how easy they are to install and use. The more mature applications tend to be easier to install and have a much richer repertoire of functionality. Many of the applications are simple wrappers around standard ODE or Gillespie solvers and provide a simple means to load models and run time courses. Some of the applications fall by the wayside because the author has lost interest or funding has stopped. It is important therefore that what ever tool one uses, that the ability to export and import a recognized standard (or at least a documented format) such as SBML and/or CellML be available.

4.1.1 CellDesigner

CellDesigner (http://www.celldesigner.org/) (Funahashi 2003; Funahashi et al. 2008) is a structured diagram editor for drawing gene-regulatory and biochemical networks. Networks are drawn based on the process diagram, with graphical notation system that influenced the development of SBGN, and are stored using the Systems Biology Markup Language (SBML), a standard for representing models of biochemical and gene-regulatory networks. CellDesigner supports simulation and parameter scanning through a selection of different simulation engines, SBML ODE Solver, COPASI, or SBW.

4.1.2 Jarnac

Jarnac (Sauro 2000; Bergmann and Sauro 2006) is a rapid prototyping script-based tool that was developed as a successor to SCAMP (Sauro and Fell 1991). It is distributed as part of the Systems Biology Workbench which makes installation a on-click affair. Jarnac was developed in the late 1990s before the advent of portable GUI toolkits which explains why it only runs under Windows although it runs well under Wine (Windows emulator) thus permitting it to run under Linux. Visually, Jarnac has two main windows, a console where commands can be issued and results returned and an editor where control scripts and models can be developed. The application also has a plotting window which is used when graphing commands are issued (see Figure 8.1).

From our experience with using many simulation tools over the years, Jarnac probably offers the fastest development time for model building of any tool. Models can also be imported or exported as SBML. Like COPASI and PySCeS, Jarnac offers many analysis capabilities including extensive support for metabolic control analysis, structural analysis of networks, and stochastic simulation. It has no explicit support for parameter fitting but this is easily remedied by transferring a model directly to a tool such as COPASI via SBW.

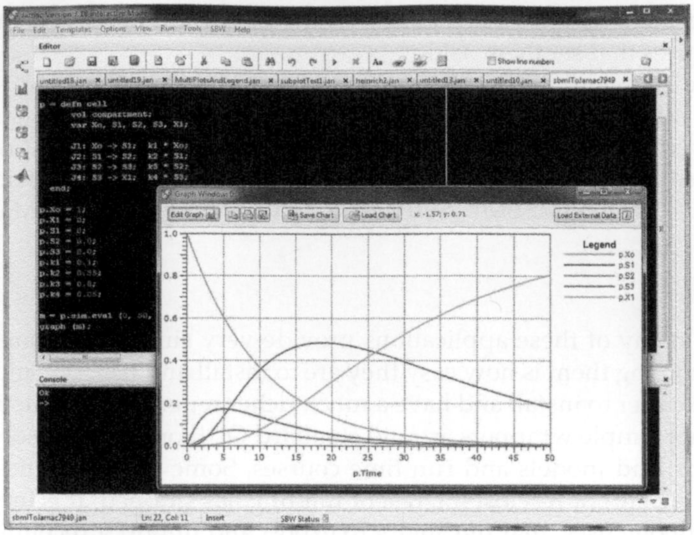

FIGURE 8.1 User interface for Jarnac.

4.1.3 JDesigner

JDesigner (Sauro et al. 2003; Bergmann et al. 2006) is open source (BSD license) and runs under Windows. It requires SBW to enable simulation capabilities. With SBW, models can be constructed using JDesigner and seamlessly transferred to other tools such as COPASI or any other SBW enabled tools. Unlike CellDesigner, JDesigner takes a minimal approach to representing networks. CellDesigner has twelve node types (plus variants) and six different transition types. JDesigner in contrast has one node type, one generic reaction type, and two regulatory types. All networks can be constructed from these four basic types. This minimal approach reflects the fact that the underlying models are the same regardless of the molecules or reaction types. Thus protein network models and metabolic models are indistinguishable at the mathematical level. Although JDesigner has only a limited number of types, nodes, reactions, and membranes can be modified visually to change colors, shapes, etc. Moreover, nodes can be decorated with covalent sites and multimeric structures. JDesigner uses fully adjustable multi-bezier arcs to generate reactions and regulatory arcs and has a variety of export formats that allow camera-ready copy to be generated for publications (see Figure 8.2 as an example). Models are stored in native SBML with specific open access annotations to store the visual information.

4.1.4 JSim

JSim (Raymond et al. 2003) is a Java-based simulation system for building quantitative numeric models and analyzing them with respect to experimental reference data. JSim was

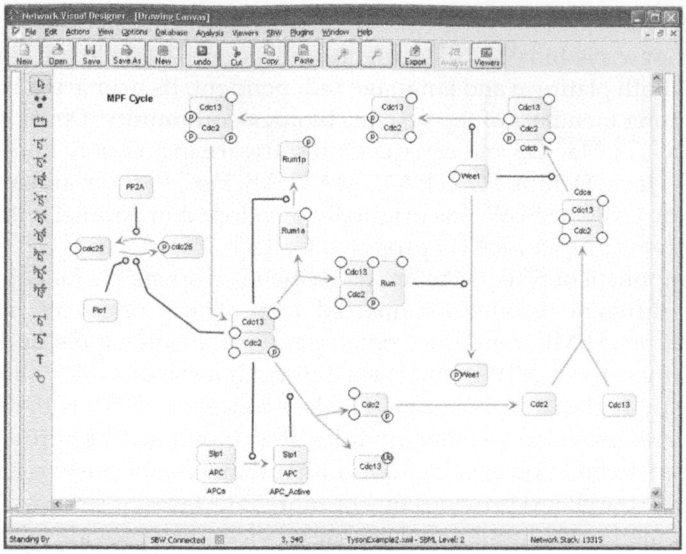

FIGURE 8.2 Example of JDesigner's visual format.

developed primarily for generating model solutions for use in designing experiments and analyzing data in physiological and biochemical studies, but its computational engine is general and equally applicable to solving equations in physics, chemistry, and mechanics. JSim has been under development at the National Simulation Resource for Mass Transport and Metabolism (NSR) since 1999. JSim uses a model specification language, MML (for Mathematical Modeling Language) which supports ordinary and partial differential equations, implicit equations, integrals, summations, discrete events, and allows calls to external procedures. JSim's compiler translates MML into Java code in which the numeric results are calculated. Within the JSim GUI users adjust parameter values, initiate model runs, plot data, and perform behavioral analysis, sensitivity analysis, parameter optimization for curve fitting. Alternatively one can use JSim's command line interfaces (jsbatch and jsfim). JSim source code, binaries (for Windows, Macintosh and Linux), and documentation are available free for non-commercial use at http://physiome.org/.

4.1.5 PySCeS

While PySCeS has already been mentioned earlier as a human readable format for expressing biological models, the software package warrants mention again as a full-featured modeling platform that can be used interactively and as a library. along with its scripted model description language, PySCeS is SBML compatible, and provides a full set of simulation tools, including stoichiometric, simulation, steady state, metabolic control, and Eigen analysis. Two- and three-dimensional graphing is also made available through utilizing additional Python libraries.

4.1.6 Systems biology workbench (SBW)

SBW (http://www.sys-bio.org) (Bergmann and Sauro 2006) is an extensible software framework that is both platform and language independent. Its primary purpose is to encourage code reuse among members of the systems biology community. Developers can run SBW on Linux, Windows, or Mac OS and can develop software in a variety of different languages including C/C++, Java, Delphi, FORTRAN, MATLAB, Perl, Python, and any .NET language (e.g. Visual Basic or C#). The SBW was originally developed in parallel with SBML as part of the Symbiotic Systems Project ERATO project at Caltech, Pasadena.

The central component of SBW is the broker, which is responsible for coordinating interactions among the different resources connected to it. These resources include simulation engines, model editors, SBML translators, databases, visualization tools, and a variety of analysis packages. All modules in SBW connect via defined interfaces, which allows any one of the modules to be easily replaced if necessary. The key concept in SBW is that any new module may exploit resources provided by other modules; this dramatically improves productivity by allowing developers to build on existing tools rather than continuously reinvent.

An SBW module (the client) provides one or more interfaces or services. Each service provides one or more methods. Modules register the services they provide with the SBW Broker. The module optionally places each service it provides into a category. By convention, a category is a group of services from one or more modules that have a common set of methods.

One of the key advantages of SBW is its language and OS neutrality. At a stroke this eliminates the irrational language and operating systems wars that often plague software development. In addition to providing support for multiple languages there is also the facility to automatically generate web services from any SBW module.

4.1.7 VCell

The Virtual Cell (VCell; http://vcell.org/) (Loew and Schaff 2001; Moraru et al. 2008) is a client/server-based tool that specializes in three-dimensional whole cell simulations. It is unique in that it provides a framework for not only modeling biochemical networks but also electrophysiological, and transport phenomena while at the same time considering the subcellular localization of the molecules that take part in them. This localization can take the form of a three-dimensional arbitrarily shaped cell, where the molecular species might be heterogeneously distributed. In addition, the geometry of the cell, including the locations and shapes of subcellular organelles, can be imported directly from microscope images. VCell is written in Java but has numerical analysis carried out by C/C++ and FORTRAN coded software to improve performance. Currently, modeling must be carried out using the client/server model which necessitates a connection to the internet. In addition models are generally stored on the VCell remote server rather than the clients desktop. This operating model is not always agreeable to users and as a result the VCell team are reorganizing the software so that it can also be run as a stand-alone application on a researchers machine. The VCell team has incorporated the BioNetGen (Blinov 2004) network generator which allows models to be specified in a rule-based manner. VCell is also one of the few tools that can both import and export SBML and CellML. This feature could in principle be used to translate between SBML and CellML models.

4.1.8 *Other modeling tools*

Several other modeling tools will be mentioned in this section but with shorter descriptions. Some basic information on which platforms this software is available on and a URL to find more information will be provided.

BIONETGEN (BLINOV 2004)

Tool for rule-based modeling of biochemical systems. In rule-based models, molecules and their complexes are represented using graphs, and their consequent interactions will cause rewiring of the graph based on rules. Originally, it was developed to study the problem of combinatorial complexity of signal transduction systems, such as antibody receptor binding.

- Open source; Linux, Mac OS, Microsoft Windows
- http://bionetgen.org/index.php/Main_Page

GEPASI (MENDES 1993)

This is forms-based application was one of the first simulation platforms written for the PC. The tool is particularly adept at carrying out optimizations of ODE-based models to data.

- Closed source; Microsoft Windows
- http://www.gepasi.org/

iBioSim (MYERS ET AL. 2009)

Tool for the design and analysis of genetic circuits, with applications to both systems and synthetic biology. Models can be constructed manually or imported from various databases and then analyzed with a variety of ODE and stochastic simulators.

- Open source; Linux, Mac OS, Microsoft Windows
- (http://www.async.ece.utah.edu/iBioSim/)

JigCell (VASS ET AL. 2004, 2006)

A suite of computational tools with graphical user interfaces that includes model building, simulation, and parameter estimation. A unique feature of JigCell is its display of data and simulation experiments in a spreadsheet format and run in batch mode.

- Closed source; Linux, Mac OS, Microsoft Windows
- http://jigcell.cs.vt.edu/

ProMot (MIRSCHEL ET AL. 2009)

Short for "process modeling tool," this is a software package for simulating and manipulating models. Some key features are its support of modular models, modeling libraries, its own modeling language MDL, and graphical capabilities.

- Open source; Linux, Microsoft Windows
- http://www.mpi-magdeburg.mpg.de/projects/promot

SBSI (ADAMS ET AL. 2013)

Provides fitting of model parameters to experimental data, especially on models with oscillatory components, as well as standard model editing and simulation capabilities.

- Open source; Linux, Mac OS, Microsoft Windows
- http://www.sbsi.ed.ac.uk/

WinSCAMP (SAURO AND FELL 1991; SAURO 1993)

A script-based GUI application, which like Gepasi has a long tradition. Specialized for time course, steady state and metabolic control analysis of ODE-based models.

- Source available upon request; Windows
- http://sbw.kgi.edu/software/winscamp.htm

4.2 Simulation engines libraries

Simulation and modeling is one of the standard approaches to understanding complex biochemical processes. Therefore, there is a growing need for software tools that allow access to diverse simulation and modeling methods as well as support for the usage of these methods. These software libraries should be compatible, e.g. via file standards, platform independent and user friendly to avoid time-consuming conversions and learning procedures. In addition, the software should be actively maintained and updated by its authors.

This section will cover some of the most widely used, open source, simulation libraries that many modeling platforms depend on for computation. These libraries all support the simulation of SBML models, and have been validated against an online suite of SBML test cases (http://sbml.org/Facilities/Online_SBML_Test_Suite) provided by the SBML consortium.

4.2.1 COPASI

COPASI (Hoops et al. 2006) (http://www.copasi.org/tiki-view_articles.php) is the successor to Gepasi and comes in two versions: a graphical and a command line interface. The command line version is designed for batch jobs where a graphical user interface is unnecessary and where runs can be carried out without human supervision. COPASI uses its own file format to store models, however like all the tools discussed here, it can import and export SBML. One of its undoubted strengths is optimization and parameter fitting which it inherited from its predecessor. It has a unique ability to optimize on a great variety of different criteria including metrics such as eigenvalues, transient times, etc. This makes COPASI extremely flexible for optimization problems. Installation is very simple and entails using a one-click installer. Although the source code to COPASI is available and can be freely used for research purposes in academia, owing to the way in which the development of COPASI was funded there are restrictions on commercial use.

The graphical user interface is based on a menu/dialog approach, much like its immediate predecessor, Gepasi. COPASI has capabilities to simulate deterministic as well as stochastic models and includes a wide range of analyzes. It correctly takes into account conservation laws and has very good support for metabolic control analysis amongst other things. COPASI is without doubt one of the better simulators available. Although the user interface is graphical, it does, due to its particular design, require some effort to master but with the availability of the COPASI the source code, there is the opportunity to provide alternative user interfaces. Finally, there is a version that has an SBW interface (Systems Biology Workbench) which allows SBW enabled tools access to COPASI's functionality (currently available at http://sys-bio.org/).

SimpleCOPASI

SimpleCOPASI (http://code.google.com/p/copasi-simple-api/) is a C interface to the C++ COPASI library. The core functionality of reading, writing, simulating, and numerical analysis of SBML models is retained from COPASI. In addition, Antimony scripts can be used to load models. The structural library (http://libstruct.sourceforge.net/) is also included within this library for analyzing the stoichiometric networks.

4.2.2 LibSBMLSim

LibSBMLSim (http://fun.bio.keio.ac.jp/software/libsbmlsim/) is a relatively newer simulation library and available on Unix and Windows based operating systems. It features a number of explicit and implicit ODE solvers and a relatively straightforward interface for producing simulation results from an SBML input file. However, compared to the other simulators in this chapter that have been around longer, the API contains fewer features. As of this writing, there are no functions for steady state analysis (useful for flux balance analysis) and single time step simulations (useful for real-time and interactive simulations).

LibSBMLSim is written in C which makes it "portable" in the sense that it is relatively easy to port to a wide variety of different programming languages and environments through the use of the SWIG software tool (http://swig.org/). Indeed, this feature of C to serve as a least common denominator of sorts is an attractive reason systems biology software developers to program into expand the reach of their software to a user base that runs numerous different computing environments.

4.2.3 RoadRunner

RoadRunner is a powerful and portable simulation engine that was originally written in C# for SBW but is now available as a C/C++ library that can be called from other tools. RoadRunner works by generating C files containing the equations for the model from a loaded SBML file. The C file is compiled and linked at runtime into roadRunner. This results in improved performance when compared with traditional interpreter models. RoadRunner uses the integrator CVODE and NLEQ for steady-state analysis (Cohen and Hindmarsh 1996). To further speed up the simulation, the model is separated into a system of independent and dependent variables. This separation process is described in detail in Vallabhajosyula et al. (2006). RoadRunner supports a threaded model where multiple models can be simulated simultaneously on multi-core machines. In addition roadRunner has a plugin interface that allows additional functionality to be added by a third-party. Most notable are the optimization plugins. At its core, roadRunner has the capacity to carry out time course simulations, compute the steady state, carry out sensitivity analysis together with all the usual coefficients as defined in metabolic control analysis (Hofmeyr 2001). RoadRunner can also linearize the

SBML model and perform a frequency analysis on the model. RoadRunner is available at http://code.google.com/p/roadrunnerlib/ and can be compiled on Linux and Windows. Developers can access functionality either via the C API or a Python interface. COPASI and SBML ODE Solver may also be used as simulation engines alongside RoadRunner within SBW (Bergmann and Sauro 2008).

4.2.4 SBMLSimulator

SBMLsimulator (http://www.cogsys.cs.uni-tuebingen.de/software/SBMLsimulator/) (Dräger et al. 2011) is a simulation library and accompanying GUI that is implemented in Java. In particular, the Java developer community benefits greatly from Java software to ease the ability to implement third party dependencies. Analogous to the way COPASI and RoadRunner are built from libSBML (C/C++), SBMLsimulator depends on JSBML, an SBML document manipulation library written entirely in Java (http://sbml.org/Software/JSBML).

4.3 MATLAB

MATLAB (http://www.mathworks.com/products/matlab/) is one of the most widely used numerical platforms in science and engineering. MATLAB contains excellent numerical and data analysis methods useful for systems biology. Many add-ons, referred to as "toolboxes" are available commercially or open-source to extend the functionality of MATLAB.

4.3.1 SimBiology

MathWorks offers a specialized toolbox called SimBiology (http://www.mathworks.com/products/simbiology/) which offers many useful capabilities. SimBiology provides graphical and programmatic tools to model, simulate, and analyze dynamic biological systems. SimBiology also includes a library of common pharmacokinetic/pharmacodynamic models. Users may use a graphical block diagram editor for building models, or directly import existing SBML models. Models within SimBiology can then use MATLABs powerful scripting interface and extensive set of built-in ODE and stochastic solvers for simulation.

4.3.2 Systems biology toolbox (SBToolBox2) and PottersWheel

SBToolBox2 (http://www.sbtoolbox2.org/main.php) (Schmidt and Jirstrand 2006) is a very extensive, open-source, MATLAB tool box developed by Henning Schmidt. The tool box has a wide range of capabilities. In addition, PottersWheel (Maiwald and Timmer 2008), is a very comprehensive parameter fitting tool that works well with the SBToolBox2 but can also be used alone. In a number of cases it is better than COPASIs capabilities particularly in the area of generating nonlinear confidence limits on parameter fits and analyzing the resulting fit. The experimental data input formats are also very flexible. The tool provides a number of optimization algorithms including genetic and simulated annealing approaches.

4.3.3 SBMLToolbox

SBMLToolbox (http://sbml.org/Software/SBMLToolbox) (Keating 2006) is an open source MATLAB toolbox developed by the SBML Team. SBMLToolbox ports functionality from libSBML into MATLAB, by creating MATLAB structures that mirror the functionality of libSBML. SBMLToolbox is also compatible with Octave (http://www.gnu.org/software/octave/), a free and open source computing environment that is similar to MATLAB.

4.3.4 SBML to MATLAB translation

It is also possible to export SBML models into MATLAB scripts without the need for any additional toolboxes. SBML2MATLAB (http://sysbio-online.org/sbml2matlab/) is a cross-platform tool for performing such conversions. The SBML model structures and mathematics are mapped to MATLAB functions and structures, allowing users to easily manipulate the models through additional MATLAB scripting. SBML2MATLAB has also been integrated as a standalone web application that provides a user friendly interface for using SBML2MATLAB without any need for installing software.

In addition, a web application for viewing, editing, and simulating SBML models is also actively being developed (http://sysbio-online.org) which would allow modelers work on any platform that supports a web browser, circumvent the need to install any software, and not be limited by the local computer hardware power by performing computationally intensive calculations on a remote server.

5 APPLICATIONS

This section will provide an overview for some of the different computational techniques and applications that are used with quantitative models in systems biology.

5.1 Model analysis

As a user, one of the most important aspects that is considered is the range of techniques that are available for analyzing a model. The purpose of building a model is not simply to generate a predictive tool, if that was solely the case, than one could probably use empirical statistical techniques or machine learning approaches rather than the mechanistic models discussed in this chapter. An additional important role of model building is to also gain a deeper understanding into the properties of the model and to how the structure of the model leads it to behave the way it does. In order to answer these kinds of questions one needs techniques that can interrogate the model in a variety of different ways.

The list below outlines some of the most important techniques that are available for analyzing models. Without these techniques, a model will often be as difficult to understand as the real system it attempts to model; the application of these techniques is therefore important.

Approach and Description

Connectionist Theory: Connectivity studies are centered around the search for patterns in the way cellular networks are physically connected (Barabási and Oltvai 2004)

Structural Analysis: There are a wide range of useful techniques which focus on the properties of the networks that depend on the mass conservation properties of networks. These include, conservation analysis, flux balance, and elementary mode analysis (Heinrich and Schuster 1996).

Cellular Control Analysis: CCA (also known as metabolic control analysis) is a powerful technique for analyzing the propagation of perturbations through a network. There exists a very large literature describing applications and theory (Fell 1997).

Frequency Analysis: Closely related to CCA is the analysis of how signals propagate through a network (Sauro and Ingalls et al. 2004; Rao et al. 2004).

Bifurcation Analysis: Bifurcation analysis is concerned with the study of how the qualitative behavior of steady-state solutions change with fluctuations in the model parameters (Tyson et al. 2001).

All these techniques are extremely useful in gaining insight into how a model operates. The connectionist and structural analyses focus on the network properties of the model. They do not explicitly consider the dynamics of the model but rather how the network connectivity sets the stage for generating the dynamics of the model. The last three techniques, CCA, frequency analysis, and bifurcation analysis focus on the dynamical aspects of a model and are crucial to gaining a deep insight into the model (Bakker 1997; Tyson et al. 2001).

5.2 Model fitting and validation

An important activity in systems biology modeling is the need to fit experimental data to models. While the scope of this chapter does not permit covering this topic to any great detail, as time series data from microarray, proteomic, and metabolomic data becomes more readily available, the need to fit models to experimental data will become more acute. There are a number of issues related to this topic, one such concern is the nature of the data that is generated by many of the current experimental techniques. In particular, most current techniques generate normalized data, that is absolute values are not given. This poses a number of problems to a fitting algorithm, since the underlying model is in terms of absolute quantities. A number of solutions are potentially available, however none are entirely satisfactory and, ultimately, the models generated by normalized data will may only be capable of reproducing trends in the data. Whether such models will have great predictive value is open to question and much research remains to be done in this area.

Another issue is the intensive computations that are required to fit even a moderately sized model. One of the necessary requirements for fitting a model is estimating the confidence limits on the fitted parameters and the range of parameter space which describes the experimental data. This information is crucial to determine the validity of the model and can be used to design additional experiments to either refute the model or increase the precision of the model parameters. As a result of these requirements, computing a global optimization can take a considerable time. For example, in a recent study, Vijay Chickarmane[3] estimated that the time required to fit a model of approximately three hundred parameters would be of the

[3] Personal correspondence.

order of seven years on a normal desktop computer. Luckily, global optimization can be easily parallelized given a suitable optimizer (for example a genetic algorithm-based optimizer) and the computation time can be reduced by hosting the problem on a cluster machine. Chickarmane estimates that using a one thousand node cluster, the optimization of a three hundred parameter model can be reduced to approximately two days of computation time. Such a computation can be easily set up using SBW. A single node on the cluster would act as the primary optimizer; this node in turn would farm out the time consuming simulation computations to the remaining nodes on the computer. For very large models, Grid computing (Abbas 2004) may be very appropriate for solving this kind of problem.

6 FUTURE PROSPECTS AND CONCLUSION

The systems biology field has been developing rapidly in recent years but much remains to be done. One of the most useful developments must undoubtedly go to the development of standards, such as SBML and CellML. Indeed one of the highest impact systems biology journals, Molecular Systems Biology, has stipulated that SBML is the preferred format for contributing models. Furthermore, as models are being increasingly better annotated with standardized vocabularies, an exciting horizon for the future of systems biology models is their improved modularity and ease of reuse.

The other area that has received a lot of attention in recent years is the development of tools for systems biology. To avoid the problem of stagnating software projects that may have a short lifetime, the development of reusable software is a potential solution. Examples of reusable software are extensible frameworks, such as SBW, and suites of open-source libraries that can carry out specific functionality. An example of this is libSBML which enables other developers to concentrate on unique features, such as graphical interface or simulation capability, rather than waste unnecessary effort developing their own SBML parser. In terms of other possible libraries, examples include, open-source Gillespie based stochastic solvers and ODE solvers. Further more, hybrid methods combining continuous and stochastic methods is a pressing need at the current time. Many biological systems interface noisy sensory apparatus (e.g. ligand binding to the surface of a cell membrane) to internal continuous analog networks (Sauro and Kholodenko 2004). In addition to the core solvers, there is also need for scalable analysis tools, particularly bifurcation and sensitivity analysis tools. On the model validation front, much remains to be done, particularly the relationship between model validation and how this can direct future experimentation. This leads onto the development of new methods and algorithms for analyzing the complex networks in particular methods should be developed to modularize large networks since understanding an entire network is virtually impossible without some recourse to a hierarchical modularization.

In conclusion, while there is certainly much to be done in this field, it is a very exciting time for systems biology and the role that standards and software platforms will play. The development of standards and their adoption in the community have accelerated drastically over the years. Furthermore, the tremendous efforts of many systems biology groups worldwide have made available an unprecedented number of resources and tools for building, sharing, and publishing models. We believe that more modular designs will accelerate the development of standards (Hucka et al. 2010), and promote the re-usability of models, or parts of models (Neal and Sauro 2012). Furthermore, recent advancements in cloud computing and web technologies could potentially lead to many exciting and novel approaches in addressing the current challenges in computational systems biology.

7 RECOMMENDED RESOURCES

Three main web sources which are of interest to readers of this chapter include:

http://www.cellml.org: This is the main CellML site. It has a very rich set of models expressed in CellML including specifications for the standard and pointers to software toolkits.

http://www.sbml.org: This is the main SBML site. The site as ample documentation, examples illustrating how SBML is and should be used. In addition is has a rich set of software tools, in particular libSBML, which allows developers to easily add SBML support to their tools.

http://www.sys-bio.org: This is the main SBW (Systems Biology Workbench) site. The latest versions for SBW, developer documentation, example models, screen shots, user guides can be obtained from this site. A link to the main sourceforge site is given where all the source code for SBW is made available.

Acknowledgments

This publication was made possible by Grant No. GM081070 from the National Institute for General Medical Sciences (NIGMS) at the National Institutes of Health. Its contents are solely the responsibility of the authors and do not necessarily represent the official views of NIGMS. We would also like to thank Maxwell Neal for his help and expertise on biomedical ontologies.

References

Abbas, A. (2004). *Grid Computing: A Practical Guide to Technology and Applications*. Firewall Media.

Adams, R. et al. (2013). SBSI: An extensible distributed software infrastructure for parameter estimation in systems biology. *Bioinformatics*

Bairoch, A. et al. (2005). The universal protein resource (UniProt). *Nucleic Acids Res.* **33**(suppl 1):D154–D159.

Bakker, B. M. et al. (1997). Glycolysis in bloodstream form *Trypanosoma brucei* can be understood in terms of the kinetics of the glycolytic enzymes. *J. Biol. Chem.* **272**:3207–3215.

Barabási, A. L., and Oltvai, Z. N. (2004). Network biology: Understanding the cell's functional organization. *Nat. Rev. Genet.* **5**(2):101–113.

Beard, D. A. et al. (2009). CellML metadata standards, associated tools and repositories. *Philos. Trans. R. Soc. A: Math. Phys. Eng. Sci.* **367**(1895):1845–1867.

Bergmann, F. T., and Sauro, H. M. (2006). SBW-a modular framework for systems biology. In *Proceedings of the 38th Conference on Winter simulation. Winter Simulation Conference*, pp. 1637–1645.

Bergmann, F. T., and Sauro, H. M. (2008). Comparing simulation results of SBML capable simulators. *Bioinformatics* **24**(17):1963–1965.

Bergmann, F. T., Vallabhajosyula, R. R., and Sauro, H. M. (October 2006). Computational tools for modeling protein networks. *Curr. Proteomics* **3**(17):181–197.http://www.ingentaconnect.com/content/ben/cp/2006/00000003/

Blinov, M. L. et al. (2004). BioNetGen: Software for rule-based modeling of signal transduction based on the interactions of molecular domains. *Bioinformatics* **20**(17):3289–3291.

Bower, J. M., Beeman, D., and Wylde, A. M. (1995). *The book of GENESIS: Exploring realistic neural models with the GEneral NEural SImulation System*. New York: Telos.

Brazma, A. et al. (2001). Minimum information about a microarray experiment (MIAME)-toward standards for microarray data. *Nat. Genet.* **29**(4):365–372.

Cannon, R. C., O'Donnell, C., and Nolan, M. F. (2010). Stochastic ion channel gating in dendritic neurons: Morphology dependence and probabilistic synaptic activation of dendritic spikes. *PLoS Comput. Biol.* **6**(8):e1000886.

Carnevale, N. T., and Hines, M. L. (2006). *The NEURON Book*. Cambridge University Press.

Chance, B. (1943). The kinetics of the enzyme-substrate compound of peroxidase. *J. Biol. Chem.* **151**:553–577.

Chizeck, H. J., Butterworth, E., and Bassingthwaighte, J. B. (2009). Error detection and unit conversion. *Eng. Med. Biol. Mag. IEEE* **28**(3):50–58.

Cohen, S. D., Hindmarsh, A. C., et al. (1996). CVODE, a stiff/nonstiff ODE solver in C. *Comput. Phys.* **10**(2):138–143.

Copeland, W. B. et al. (2012). Computational tools for metabolic engineering. *Metab. Eng.*

Courtot, M. et al. (2011). Controlled vocabularies and semantics in systems biology. *Mol. Syst. Biol.* **7**(1)

Dada, J. O. et al. (2010). SBRML: A markup language for associating systems biology data with models. *Bioinformatics* **26**(7):932–938.

Degtyarenko, K. et al. (2008). ChEBI: A database and ontology for chemical entities of biological interest. *Nucleic Acids Res.* **36**(suppl 1):D344–D350.

deJong, H. (2002). Modeling and simulation of genetic regulatory systems: A literature review. *J. Comput. Biol.* **9**:67–103.

Demir, E. et al. (2010). The BioPAX community standard for pathway data sharing. *Nat. Biotechnol.* **28**(9):935–942.

Diesmann, M., and Gewaltig, M. O. (2001). NEST: An environment for neural systems simulations. *Forschung und Wissenschaftliches Rechnen, Beiträge zum Heinz-Billing-Preis* **58**:43–70.

Dräger, A. et al. (2011). JSBML: A flexible Java library for working with SBML. *Bioinformatics* **27**(15):2167–2168.

Fell, D. A. (1997). *Understanding the Control of Metabolism*. London: Portland Press.

Funahashi, A. et al. (2003). Cell Designer: A process diagram editor for gene-regulatory and biochemical networks. *BIOSILICO* **1**:159–162.

Funahashi, A. et al. (2003). Cell Designer: A process diagram editor for gene-regulatory and biochemical networks. *BIOSILICO* **1**(5):159–162.

Funahashi, A. (2008). CellDesigner 3.5: A versatile modeling tool for biochemical networks. *Proc. IEEE* **96**(8):1254–1265.

Garfinkel, D. (1968). A machine-independent language for the simulation of complex chemical and biochemical systems. *Comput. Biomed. Res.* **2**:31–44.

Garfinkel, D., Rutledge, J. D., and Higgins, J. J. (1961). Simulation and analysis of biochemical systems: I. Representation of chemical kinetics. *Commun. ACM* **4**(12):559–562.

Gillespie, C. S. et al. (2006). Tools for the SBML community. *Bioinformatics* **22**(5):628–629.

Gleeson, P. et al. (2010). NeuroML: A language for describing data driven models of neurons and networks with a high degree of biological detail. *PLoS Comput. Biol.* **6**(6):e1000815.

Goddard, Nigel H. et al. (2001). Towards NeuroML: Model description methods for collaborative modelling in neuroscience. *Philos. Trans. R. Soc.*

Goncalves, E. J. V., Saez-Rodriguez, J., et al. (2013). CySBGN: A cytoscape plugin to integrate SBGN maps. *BMC Bioinform.* **14**(1):17.

Harold, E. R., and Means, E. S. (2001). XML in a Nutshell.

Heinrich, R., and Schuster, S. (1996). *The Regulation of Cellular Systems*. Chapman and Hall.

Higgins, J. J. (1959). Kinetic properties of sequential enzyme systems. PhD thesis. University of Pennsylvania, 1959.

Hofmeyr, J.-H. S. (2001). Metabolic control analysis in a nutshell. In *Proceedings of the Second International Conference on Systems Biology*. Caltech.

Hoops, S. et al. (2006). COPASI - a complex pathway simulator. *Bioinformatics* **22**(24):3067–3074.

Hucka, M. et al. (2003). The systems biology markup language (SBML): A medium for representation and exchange of biochemical network models. *Bioinformatics* **19**:524–531.

Hucka, M., et al. (2010). The Systems Biology Markup Language (SBML): Language Specification for Level 3 Version.

Hunter, P. et al. (2005). Integration from proteins to organs: The IUPS Physiome Project. *Mech. Ageing Dev.* **126**(1):187.

Joshi-Tope, G. et al. (2005). Reactome: A knowledgebase of biological pathways. *Nucleic Acids Res.* **33**(suppl 1):D428 –D432.

Kacser, H., and Burns, J. A. (1981). The molecular basis of dominance. *Genetics* **97**:1149–1160.

Keating, S. M. et al. (2006). SBMLToolbox: An SBML toolbox for MATLAB users. *Bioinformatics* **22**(10):1275–1277.

Keating, S. M., and Novère, N. (2012). Encoding neuronal models in SBML. *Comput. Syst. Neurobiol.* 459–488.

Kitano, H. (2003). A graphical notation for biochemical networks. *BIOSILICO* **1**:169–176.

Kohn, Kurt W. (1999). Molecular interaction map of the mammalian cell cycle control and DNA repair systems. *Mol. Biol. Cell* **10**(8):2703–2734.http://www.molbiolcell.org/content/10/8/2703.abstract

Kohn, K. W. et al. (2004). *Cell Cycle Control: Molecular Interaction Map*. London: Nature Publishing Group (c) 2002 Macmillan Publishers Ltd. pp. 457–474.

Köhn, D., and Le Novere, N. (2008). SED-ML–an XML format for the implementation of the MIASE guidelines. In *Computational Methods in Systems Biology*, pp. 176–190. Springer.

König, M., Dräger, A., and Holzhütter, H. G. (2012). CySBML: A Cytoscape plugin for SBML. *Bioinformatics* **28**(18):2402–2403.

Krause, F. et al. (2010). Annotation and merging of SBML models with semanticSBML. *Bioinformatics* **26**(3):421–422.

Le Novère, N. (2006). Model storage, exchange and integration. *BMC Neurosci.* **7**(suppl 1):S11.

Le Novere, N. et al. (2006). BioModels database: A free, centralized database of curated, published, quantitative kinetic models of biochemical and cellular systems. *Nucleic Acids Res.* **34**(suppl 1):D689–D691.

Le Novère, N. et al. (2009). The systems biology graphical notation. *Nat. Biotechnol.* **27**(8):735–741.

Le Novere, N. (2010). Report on the status of SBGN ER and proposed extensions.

Lloyd, C. M. et al. (2008). The CellML model repository. *Bioinformatics* **24**(18):2122–2123.

Lloyd, C. M., Halstead, M. D., and Nielsen, P. F. (2004). CellML: Its future, present and past. *Prog. Biophys. Mol. Biol.* **85**:433–450.

Loew, L. M., and Schaff, J. C. (2001). The Virtual Cell: A software environment for computational cell biology. *Trends Biotechnol.* **19**:401–406.

Maiwald, T., and Timmer, J. (2008). Dynamical modeling and multi-experiment fitting with PottersWheel. *Bioinformatics* **24**(18):2037–2043.

Mendes, P. (1993). GEPASI: A software package for modelling the dynamics, steady states and control of biochemical and other systems. *Comput. Appl. Biosci.* **9**:563–571.

Mirschel, S. et al. (2009). PROMOTE: Modular modeling for systems biology. *Bioinformatics* **25**(5):687–689.

Moraru, I. I. et al. (2008). Virtual cell modelling and simulation software environment. *Syst. Biol. IET* **2**(5):352–362.

Myers, C. J. et al. (2009). iBioSim: A tool for the analysis and design of genetic circuits. *Bioinformatics* **25**(21):2848–2849.

Neal, M. L. et al. (2009). Advances in semantic representation for multiscale biosimulation: A case study in merging models. In *Pacific Symposium on Biocomputing*, pp. 304. NIH Public Access.

Neal, M. L., and Sauro, H. M. (2012). SBML Reaction Finder: Retrieve and extract specific reactions from the BioModels database.

Novere, N. L. et al. (2005). Minimum information requested in the annotation of biochemical models (MIRIAM). *Nat. Biotechnol.* **23**(12):1509–1515.

Ogata, H. et al. (1999). KEGG: Kyoto encyclopedia of genes and genomes. *Nucleic Acids Res.* **27**(1):29–34.

Olivier, B. G., and Snoep, J. L. (2004). Web-based kinetic modelling using JWS Online. *Bioinformatics* **20**(13):2143–2144.

Olivier, B. G., Rohwer, J. M., and Hofmeyr, J. H. S. (2002). Modelling cellular processes with Python and Scipy. *Mol. Biol. Rep.* **29**(1):249–254.

Olivier, B. G., Rohwer, J. M., and Hofmeyr, J. H. S. (2004). Modelling cellular systems with PySCeS. *Bioinformatics*

O'Sullivan, B. (2007). Distributed revision control with Mercurial. *Mercurial project*

Quackenbush, J. (2006). Standardizing the standards. *Mol. Syst. Biol.* **2**(1)

Rao, C. V., Sauro, H. M., and Arkin, A. P. (2004). Putting the control in metabolic control analysis. In *7th International Symposium on Dynamics and Control of Process Systems, DYCOPS*, Vol. 7.

Ray, S., and Bhalla, U. S. (2008). PyMOOSE: Interoperable scripting in Python for MOOSE. *Front. Neuroinformatics* **2**(6):1–16.

Raymond, G. M., Butterworth, E., and Bassingthwaighte, J. B. (2003). JSIM: Free software package for teaching physiological modeling and research. *Exp. Biol.* **280**:102–107.

Reich, J. G., and Selkov, E. E. (1981). *Energy Metabolism of the Cell*. London: Academic Press.

Sauro, H. M. (1993). SCAMP: A general-purpose simulator and metabolic control analysis program. *Comput. Appl. Biosci. CABIOS* **9**(4):441–450.

Sauro, H. M. (2000). Jarnac: A system for interactive metabolic analysis. In (J-H. S. Hofmeyr, J. M. Rohwer, and J. L. Snoep, eds.), *Animating the Cellular Map: Proceedings of the 9th International Meeting on BioThermoKinetics*. Stellenbosch University Press. isbn: ISBN 0-7972-0776-7

Sauro, H. M. et al. (2003). Next generation simulation tools: The systems biology workbench and BioSPICE integration. *OMICS* **7**(4):355–372.

Sauro, H. M., and Fell, D. A. (1991). SCAMP: A metabolic simulator and control analysis program. *Math. Comput. Model.* **15**:15–28.

Sauro, H. M., and Ingalls, B. (2004). Conservation analysis in biochemical networks: Computational issues for software writers. *Biophys. Chem.* **109**:1–15.

Sauro, H. M., Ingalls, B., et al. (2004). Conservation analysis in biochemical networks: Computational issues for software writers. *Biophys. Chem.* **109**(1):1.

Sauro, H. M., and Kholodenko, B. N. (2004). Quantitative analysis of signaling networks. *Prog. Biophys. Mol. Biol.* **86**(1):5–43.

Schmidt, H., and Jirstrand, M. (2006). Systems Biology Toolbox for MATLAB: A computational platform for research in systems biology. *Bioinformatics* **22**(4):514–515.

Smith, B. et al. (2005). Relations in biomedical ontologies. *Genome Biol.* **6**(5):R46.

Smith, B. et al. (2007). The OBO Foundry: Coordinated evolution of ontologies to support biomedical data integration. *Nat. Biotechnol.* **25**(11):1251–1255.

Smith, L. P. et al. (2009). Antimony: A modular model definition language. *Bioinformatics* **25**(18):2452–2454.

Spellman, P. et al. (2002). Design and implementation of microarray gene expression markup language (MAGE-ML). *Genome Biol.* **3**(9) research0046

Nature Publishing Group (2006). Standard operating procedures: Is biological research ready for the new wave of data-reporting standards currently under development? *Nat. Biotechnol.* **24**:1299.

Strömbäck, L., and Lambrix, P. (2005). Representations of molecular pathways: An evaluation of SBML, PSI MI and BioPAX. *Bioinformatics* **21**(24):4401–4407.

Taylor, C. F. et al. (2008). Promoting coherent minimum reporting guidelines for biological and biomedical investigations: The MIBBI project. *Nat. Biotechnol.* **26**(8):889–896.

Tomita, M. et al. (1999). E-CELL: Software environment for whole-cell simulation. *Bioinformatics* **15**:72–84.

Tyson, J. J., Chen, K., and Novak, B. (2001). Network dynamics and cell physiology. *Nat. Rev. Mol. Cell Biol.* **2**:908–916.

Vallabhajosyula, R. R., Chickarmane, V., and Sauro, H. M. (2006). Conservation analysis of large biochemical networks. *Bioinformatics* **22**(3):346–353.

van Iersel, M. P. et al. (2012). Software support for SBGN maps: SBGN-ML and LibSBGN. *Bioinformatics* **28**(15):2016–2021.

Vass, M. et al. (2004). The JigCell model builder and run manager. *Bioinformatics* **20**(18):3680–3681.

Vass, M. T. et al. (2006). The JigCell model builder: A spreadsheet interface for creating biochemical reaction network models. *Comput. Biol. and Bioinform. IEEE/ACM Trans.* **3**(2):155–164.

Waltemath, D. et al. (2011). Minimum information about a simulation experiment (MIASE). *PLoS Comput. Biol.* **7**(4):e1001122.

Wright, S. (1929). Fisher's theory of dominance. *Am. Nat.* **63**:274–279.

Wright, S. (1934). Physiological and evolutionary theories of dominance. *Am. Nat.* **68**:24–53.

Yu, T. et al. (2011). The physiome model repository 2. *Bioinformatics* **27**(5):743–744.

CHAPTER

9

Databases, Standards, and Modeling Platforms for Systems Biology

Juergen Eils[a], *Elena Herzog*[a], *Baerbel Felder* [a,b], *Christian Lawerenz*[a], *Roland Eils* [a,b]

[a]**Division of Theoretical Bioinformatics, German Cancer Research Center (DKFZ), Heidelberg, Germany**

[b]**Department for Bioinformatics and Functional Genomics, Institute for Pharmacy and Molecular Biotechnology (IPMB) and BioQuant, Heidelberg University, Heidelberg, Germany**

CONTENTS

Computational Systems Biology, Second Edition
http://dx.doi.org/10.1016/B978-0-12-405926-9.00009-5

Abstract

Systems biology combines experimental and computational research to facilitate understanding of complex biological processes. In this chapter we describe data repositories, data standards, modeling, and visualization tools as prerequisites for systems biology research in order to help us to better study and understand biological processes. In addition, we propose improvements of these tools providing an example application (JUMMP) developed in our laboratory. We suggest that flexibility, interoperability, and modularity of novel applications contribute to better acceptance and further development of these tools. We also emphasize that having flexible and extendable standards describing complex and incomplete biological data allow new discoveries to be incorporated in a seamless way into systems biology tools. Overall, we discuss here advances, challenges and perspectives of data, and other platforms in systems biology which we believe will continue to make an impact on biomedical research.

1 INTRODUCTION

The ultimate goal of systems biology approaches is to facilitate understanding of complex biological processes as well as to investigate each step in these processes. Knowledge of these processes might allow us to predict changes in behavior when normal conditions are perturbed. This knowledge is obtained from different sources and it is typically collected in scientific publications. As a lot of knowledge has been accumulated in the last 10 years, not least due to novel experimental technologies producing massive amounts of data, finding and analyzing such data is becoming more and more challenging. There is a wide gap between the data generated from experimental research and the ability to analyze it. The amount of data, *per se*, does not contribute to knowledge itself, rather, we need to have readily available tools to explore these vast amounts of data. Even though we are dealing with complex biological processes, we need simple rules and thorough biological understanding to generate models describing these processes.

Acquisition of new knowledge is very laborious and requires a deep understanding of how biological systems function as well as the knowledge of best suited experimental methods to be applied to investigate these systems. The underlying biological mechanisms are highly complex and it is, therefore, challenging, if at all possible, to represent them as a set of mathematical expressions which are ultimately combined into models. Traditionally, such mechanisms are investigated by experimental scientists and described by a set of biological, chemical, and physical rules. These rules can be translated into mathematical equations and combined in mathematical models. Therefore, systems biology approaches integrate experimental and computational research to explain complex biological mechanisms. These models can help experimental scientists, for instance, to validate hypotheses and to reduce cost and time of experimental work. Additionally, mathematical models can produce novel hypotheses for ambiguous experimental observations, which have then to be confirmed again by experimentalists. Therefore, close collaborations of wet lab and *in silico* lab researchers are recognized as highly beneficial and resulted in the establishment of many excellent systems biology centers contributing toward a deeper understanding of complex biological systems and processes.

Recently, the amount of computational models and modeling programs has increased, enabling us to extract highly unstructured information of biological processes from the scientific literature, annotate it more accurately and represent it in a more structured way in systems biology databases. These advances have been facilitated by recently developed systems biology standards, repositories to store computational models, and modeling programs. Successful examples of these databases are BioModels, Brenda and Transpath. Additionally, these databases can link to external resources such as UniProt, Pubmed and to non-kinetic and non-quantitative biological pathway databases such as KEGG, Reactome, and others.

2 PATHWAY DATABASES

Pathway databases store information about the kinetics and topology of a reaction network, which is needed for modeling biochemical reactions based on experimental data. In the following section, we present well-established databases (see Table 9.1) in this area. A common feature of all these platforms is an interface to systems biology data standard formats for mathematical models such as SBML (Systems Biology Markup Language), SBGN (Systems Biology Graphical Notation), BioPAX (Biological Pathways Exchange), and others.

2.1 KEGG database

One of the most renowned databases integrating genomic, chemical, and network information is KEGG (Kyoto Encyclopedia of Genes and Genomes). Initiated in 1995 as part of the Japanese Human Genome Program, the KEGG resource has been established to help understanding higher-order functions and utilities of the biological system, such as the cell or parts of it. KEGG pathways focus on metabolism, signaling/information processing, and human diseases. There are approximately 229 human pathways annotating more than 5900 human genes in the latest free-access KEGG version. KEGG has a restricted access since 2011. Several linked databases (e.g. KEGG GENES, KEGG LIGAND, KEGG PATHWAY, KEGG BRITE) and associated software tools allow modeling and simulation of biological processes as well as

TABLE 9.1 Pathway databases.

Database	URL
KEGG	http://www.genome.jp/kegg
KEGG GENES	http://www.genome.jp/kegg/genes.html
KEGG LIGAND	http://www.genome.jp/ligand
KEGG PATHWAY	http://www.genome.jp/kegg/pathway.html
KEGG BRITE	http://www.genome.jp/kegg/brite.html
Reactome	http://www.reactome.org
Brenda	http://www.brenda-enzymes.org
Panther	http://www.pantherdb.org/pathway

for browsing and data retrieval. Gene expression data can be mapped to metabolic pathways from KEGG to identify significantly deregulated biological processes in cancer and other diseases. (Schramm et al. 2010; Lewis et al. 2010). KEGG PATHWAY output formats can be processed and converted to standardized community pathway formats like SBML and BioPAX (Wrzodek et al. 2013). Also, there have been efforts to bring KEGG data to the new mobile technologies like tablet computers (iPathCaseKEGG) (Johnson et al. 2013) for easy browsing of data and interactive visualization.

2.2 Reactome database

The Reactome database generalizes the concept of a reaction, where entities include nucleic acids, small molecules, proteins, and macromolecular complexes. This concept allows the description of various biological processes including signaling, metabolism, transcriptional regulation, and others in a single format. Functional interactions are derived from both Reactome reactions and other pathway databases (KEGG, Panther, etc.) (Croft et al. 2011). Since Reactome is an open-source database, all data and software are freely available for download. Interaction, reaction, and pathway data are provided as downloadable flat, MySQL, BioPAX, and SBML files. Often, a specific scope is covered by the databases, e.g. metabolic pathways, signal transduction cascades, gene regulatory networks, or a selection of these. Reactome holds more than 1100 pathways/functional gene sets for humans.

2.3 BRENDA database

The enzyme data portal BRENDA (BRaunschweig ENzyme DAtabase) is one of the main information sources of functional biochemical and molecular enzyme data. Available online since 1998, BRENDA contains 2.7 million manually annotated functional data like enzyme-catalyzed reactions, kinetic data for catalysis and enzyme inhibition, enzyme stability, purification, crystallization, or mutations, as well as the largest collection of enzyme names and synonyms. Similar to other pathway databases, enzyme kinetic data can be obtained via an SBML output (Schomburg et al. 2013).

2.4 PANTHER database

Another source for network modeling is PANTHER Pathways, a branch of the PANTHER protein family database, providing tools for functional analysis of lists of genes or proteins. The current release of PANTHER Pathways includes more than 170 pathways. To support other pathway analysis and modeling tools, PANTHER Pathways can be downloaded in three major pathway exchange formats: SBML, SBGN-ML, and BioPAX.

3 MODEL DATABASES

The previous chapter has shown how wet-lab approaches can be translated into modeling approaches by transferring biological pathways into mathematical descriptions. However, this shows just the feasibility of mathematical and *in silico* methodologies, but not

TABLE 9.2 Model databases.

Database	URL
BioModels	http://www.ebi.ac.uk/biomodels-main
CellML	http://en.wikipedia.org/wiki/CellML
JUMMP	https://bitbucket.org/jummp
SABIO-RK	http://sabio.h-its.org
SYSMO-SEEK	https://seeks.sysmo-db.org

the mathematical approach itself. From the *in silico* point of view, mathematical methods to describe biological behavior are more reflected in pure modeling databases. A first approach has been already very extensively outlined by these authors in the prior edition of this book (Kriete and Eils 2005). Among others, two major data repositories, the BioModels database and the cellML data repository (see Table 9.2) will be described in detail below.

3.1 BioModels database

In contrast to the above-mentioned biological pathways databases, BioModels database stores quantitative models of biochemical and cellular systems, which include both kinetic data and network information (Li et al. 2010; Le Novere et al. 2006). BioModels is not only a repository for computational models of biological systems, but also allows searching and retrieving models. These models are highly curated and integrated with external resources due to extensive annotation processes improving models' search and subsequent retrieval results. Quantitative models are encoded in SBML files, while metadata are stored separately in a MySQL database. There are various tools for converting SBML to other standards, for example, CellML (Cell Markup Language) for greater interoperability and usability of the model. During model submission, numerous consistency checks are performed and manual curating is applied. Mathematical expression validity is performed using MathML (Math Markup Language). There are two branches in the BioModels database pipeline, containing curated and non-curated models. Curated models are tested and simulated using COPASI (COmplex PAthway SImulator) and SBML ODESolver to be able to reproduce the results using experimental parameters described in the original publication. It is important to check the model for reproducibility and consistency as well as independence of the software application. The curated models require compliance with MIRIAM (Minimum Information Required in the Annotation of Models). Currently, 390 published curated models are provided in the BioModels database as well as 373 non-curated models. The BioModels database has become a benchmark for different simulation systems. It is also used to cluster various models depending on their annotation differences. Model submission, in particular, to the BioModels database is now recommended by many publishers. The main BioModels database is hosted at EMBL-EBI, UK, one mirror exists at Caltech, USA. To allow unambiguous identification of the elements in any model, it is important to annotate its elements and link these elements to external reference sources. For instance, BioModels Database has links to external databases such as KEGG and REACTOME described above.

3.2 CellML database

Another model repository database, CellML, follows a similar approach to the BioModels repository. However, CellML is more known as a comprehensive exchange standard designed to facilitate distribution and reuse of reference descriptions of any mathematical model. The CellML language is very similar to SMBL. Both CellML and SMBL standards are XML-based exchange formats for describing cellular models. CellML is a general standard for cellular biological function but SMBL focuses more on pathway and reaction models. SBML, the mostly accepted and used standard, will be described in detail below.

3.3 JUMMP database

JUMMP (JUst a Model Management Platform) is a modular software infrastructure for the collaborative development and management of biochemical models. Since the code running BioModels database is highly dependent on the EBI infrastructure, it is not possible to install it on other sites. However, systems biology groups outside EBI are interested in finding an integrated solution for storing, displaying, and manipulating XML-based bio-mathematical models. JUMMP has been developed to replace the existing BioModels database application, enabling local installations, and supporting different XML dialects developed by the SBML community. Currently, only SBML is implemented in JUMMP and, as a result, it is a more general solution compared to BioModels. JUMMP has a modern modular software architecture following the model-view-controller pattern, separating the view part from database and logic, allowing extension and adaptation of the software in many directions. Additionally to the features supported by BioModels, JUMMP provides a set of new features. One of the newly developed features is the enhanced search functionality. This enhanced search is a plugin encapsulating all functionality, which is used programmatically by a well-defined interface. The search captures metadata available for XML models on which it is run and stores the metadata in its own database, which is a modern NoSQL database, supporting more flexible functionality in terms of storing and querying data. This search functionality was implemented by a collaboration partner from the University of Rostock (Henkel et al. 2010), clearly indicating a well-designed modular and flexible software. It is therefore possible to extend JUMMP and contribute to its development in a distributed manner. JUMMP is an open-source project. Its freely accessible code is hosted on Bitbucket, a web-based hosting service for software projects. Not only JUMMP's source code will be open source, but also all integrated tools. In addition, one can choose MySQL or PostgreSQL as a database engine, adjustable via graphical "admin user interface." Once the development of JUMMP's functionality is completed, it is envisaged to substitute the original BioModels database instance at the EBI's site.

3.4 SABIO-RK database

An important factor in the development of mathematical models in systems biology is knowledge of kinetics parameters. This information can be extracted from literature, but they are hard to find. For this reason, the SABIO-RK (System for the Analysis of Biochemical Pathways-Reaction Kinetics) has been set up as a web-accessible database storing comprehensive information about biochemical reactions and their kinetic properties. Its major goal is to support modelers and wet-lab scientists in understanding and analyzing complex biochemical networks. All data are manually curated and annotated to achieve maximum correctness and consistency within the database. SABIO-RK can be accessed via web-based user interfaces or automatically via web services that allow direct data access by other tools. Both interfaces support the export of data together with its annotations in SBML, e.g. for import in modeling tools (Wittig et al. 2012).

3.5 SysMO-SEEK database

Originally designed to support the SysMO (Systems Biology of Microorganisms) consortium, SysMO-SEEK is a platform developed for sharing and exchange of data, models, and processes in systems biology (Wolstencroft et al. 2011). Since research in systems biology is often multidisciplinary, involving many groups in different locations generating heterogeneous data, efforts must be taken to facilitate sharing of experimental data and the resulting mathematical models. To bring together various data both from wet-lab experimentalists and modelers, SysMo-SEEK has developed its own model format JERM (Just Enough Results Model), which includes the minimal information on how to find and interpret stored data.

4 SYSTEMS BIOLOGY STANDARDS

Storage of data in a database and exchange of data between different software always require standardized data exchange formats. Conveniently, they are formalized by an XML structure as this allows the data to be defined by a set of machine-readable rules. Models written in description languages such as CellML or, in particular, SBML have become a popular solution in the field of computational modeling and systems biology. The two above described model repositories CellML database and BioModels are both constructed on XML standards. Furthermore, there are other standards, e.g. BioPAX and SBGN, for visualization of models and pathways as well as SED-ML (Simulation Experiment Description Markup Language) for describing simulation experiments. SBML is mainly used by the systems biology community for network simulation and by modeling tools. SBGN-ML captures the layout information and is used by any SBGN compliant tools for visual representation of the networks. BioPAX captures detailed biochemical reaction information of any pathways, and is used by database developers and tools. (Mi et al. 2013). The list of available standards mentioned above is not exhaustive but highlights the most important and popular standards describing a diversity of computational models, simulations, and visualizations. Therefore, we will illustrate in detail how these important systems biology standards (see Table 3) are used in the field of computational system biology.

4.1 CellML standard

CellML is an open-source XML-based standard for defining mathematical models of cellular functions. CellML 1.0 was the first specification generated in 2000 and it has introduced

TABLE 9.3 Systems biology standards.

Standards	URL
CellML	http://www.cellml.org
SBML	http://www.sbml.org
libSBML	http://sbml.org/Software/libSBML
JSBML	http://sbml.org/Software/JSBML
BioPAX	http://www.biopax.org
SBGN	http://www.sbgn.org/LibSBGN
SED-ML	http://sysbioapps.dyndns.org/SED-ML%20Web%20Tools
MathML	http://www.w3.org/Math
MIRIAM	http://www.ebi.ac.uk/miriam/main

some biochemistry-specific elements for describing the role of variables in a reaction model. The extension, CellML 1.1 has been created in 2003 and added the ability to import components and units. Additionally, CellML has been extended with several metadata specifications. The metadata can be used to complement models with a variety of additional information such as related references, authorship information, and other information. Furthermore, some basic metadata concerning simulation and visualization can be included.

Within CellML an ordinary differential equation (ODE) solving scheme description language based on XML has been designed in combination with a code generation system for simulations of biological functions. In order to fully simulate a model, boundary conditions and ODE solving schemes have been combined. The CellML-based approach has been designed as a two-stage methodology. In the first stage, the system generates a set of equations associating the physiological model variable values at a certain time. The second stage generates the simulation code for the model. This approach enables the construction of code generation modules that can support composite sets of formulas (Punzalan et al. 2012).

4.2 SBML standard

CellML as well as SBML are using Content MathML to provide unambiguous semantics of the mathematical relationships of biochemical models. In particular, the fact that every variable has associated physical units enables automatic check of equations for dimensional consistency. CellML and SBML have been adapted to the same subset of MathML operators. Therefore, the two modeling languages are comparable in their ability to express mathematical relationships and there is a considerable degree of overlap. In contrast to the more generic approach of CellML, SBML is intended for use in describing reaction pathway models and biochemical reactions.

Stochastic- and differential equations-based approaches are typically used in systems biology to describe the dynamics of the biological behavior. SBML, the second XML approach with its software-independent format, has a long standing tradition in the systems biology community. SMBL comprises, similar to CellML, the differential equation-based approach. The focus of SBML and CellML is quantitative modeling and dynamic simulation of models.

The development of the SBML Level 1 (Hucka et al. 2003) and SBML Level 2 (Finney and Hucka 2003) standards was essential for the current SBML Level 3 (Hucka and Le Novere 2010). In SBML Level 2 the reflection of the formulas has changed from free text to the usage of MathML as well as the consideration of RDF-based controlled annotation scheme. SBML Level 3 is divided into a core area that is called SBML core and an extension area where additional Level 3 packages can be created to provide specific, optional features. SBML *core* exclusively describes quantitative processes such as reactions and is slightly extending the SBML Level 2 functionality. However, in contrast to Level 2, the structure of SBML Level 3 is now modular and allows successive inclusion of newly developed work packages. The SBML Development Process for SBML Level 3 for work packages defines two stages: a proposal stage, and a specification development stage. In google docs a spreadsheet table (https://docs.google.com/spreadsheet/ccc?key=0ApbKgxVhXxVydG15WXlIT0JacHhwc0FPemV6bE1aQXc#gid=0) is available that reflects the actual state of the specification status. One example of work package is the SBML qualitative (*qual*) models extension, where it is possible to describe relations in SBML. This extension includes Boolean networks, logical models, and some Petri nets as the most used qualitative formalisms in biology. As ODEs are commonly used for describing time dependent processes, relations to spatial constraints are typically represented by Partial Differential Equations (PDE). Support for PDEs is proposed in the *spatial* work package. Both work packages proposals, *spatial*, and *qual*, are currently under review. There are currently several other proposals available. Until now, some proposed work packages e.g. *comp* for the composition of a new model from existing ones or *fbc* for representing flux balanced based models have been accepted and approved.

4.2.1 LibSBML programming library

LibSBML is a free, open-source, portable, and user-friendly programming library for reading, writing, manipulating, translating, and validating SBML files and data streams. This library can be embedded in applications that are compatible with SBML. The principle behind libSBML is that it is more convenient and efficient for developers to start with a higher-level API tailored specifically to SBML and its distinctive features than it is to start with a plain XML parser library. It is written in ISO standard C++ and provides interfaces for the C and C++ programming languages, which are implemented natively. Wrapper technologies exist in libSBML for the C#, Java, Perl, Python, and Ruby programming languages.

4.2.2 JSBML library

JSBML (Java SBML) is a community-driven project to develop a pure Java library for reading, writing, and manipulating SBML files and data streams and an alternative to the C++ code-based interface provided in libSBML (Drager et al. 2011). LibSBML as well as JSBML support all levels and versions of SBML with common API classes and methods. They provide facilities for manipulating mathematical formulas in both text-string format and MathML format, perform validation of XML and SBML at the time of parsing files and data streams, verify the correctness of models, offer support for dimensional analysis and unit checking and create and manipulate SBML annotations and notes. Application programming interface (API) exists for libSBML for the two approved SBML 3 extensions such as *fbc* and *qual*. APIs to the latest Level 3 extensions in JSBML are still under development.

4.3 BioPAX language

Besides providing APIs for the usage of the SBML standard in external applications, it's also desirable to support the community with standards for graphical visualization of models and pathways. The biological pathway exchange language BioPAX enables development of pathway visualization from databases and it is a standard language to represent biological pathways at the molecular and cellular level. The BioPAX specification concentrates mainly on visualization and qualitative analysis of pathway maps. BioPAX describes reactions and relations and captures detailed biochemical reaction information of the pathway and is used by database developers and tools (Buchel et al. 2012).

4.4 SBGN language

SBGN is yet another graphical description format. It captures the layout information and is used by any SBGN compliant tool for visual and representation of the pathways. Both, BioPax as well as SBGN, are providing converters to SBML.

4.5 Summary

The systems biology standardization community organizes two annual meetings: "Annual COMBINE forum" and "HARMONY" hackathon. Harmony hackathons focus on development of software, standards, and infrastructure, whereas COMBINE is typically a workshop-style meeting with oral presentations and posters sessions. The development and maintenance of the SBML and CellML standards as well as the BioModels and JUMMP databases, are core topics in these meetings. The systems biology researchers are working together at these meetings to coordinate and to promote close interaction and interoperability between the databases, the tools, and the adapted standards.

However, the development of standards mostly by programmers is one issue, the application and the usage of these standards in the research community is another. When a proposed standard becomes widely accepted by the scientific community, as a consequence, it requires additional efforts from scientists to adapt and transform their data into this common standard/format. In general, such efforts do not produce any measurable scientific impact at least in the beginning. Further, these efforts are time and cost consuming. However, benefits of standardization become evident as time passes by. There has been a huge progress in standards development, maturity, and usage in systems biology research. This progress is best reflected in the successful usage of these standards in a lot of software tools.

5 SIMULATION AND MODELING PLATFORMS

The above described system biology modeling standards, in particular, the well-established SBML format as well as recently developed standards for experimental data (kinetic, metabolomics, proteomics) are the basic requirement for systems biology databases. However, not only repositories and standards are the basic pre-requisites but also how easily these standards can be used in modeling tool boxes. The acceptance and usage of the standards is demonstrated

TABLE 9.4 Simulation and modeling platforms

Platform	URL
COPASI	http://www.copasi.org/tiki-view_articles.php
SYCAMORE	http://sycamore.eml.org/sycamore
JWS Online	http://jjj.biochem.sun.ac.za
CellDesigner	http://www.celldesigner.org
Cytoscape	http://www.cytoscape.org

in ever growing system biology modeling applications. The SBML project claims, for instance, that more than 250 simulations and modeling platforms have already integrated their standards. We will describe some of the modeling tools (see Table 9.4) in the next section.

5.1 COPASI

COPASI (COmplex PAthway SImulator) provides both a Graphical User Interface (CopasiUI) and a command line version (CopasiSE) containing only a calculation engine (Hoops et al. 2006). It offers a choice of different simulation methods: Gillespie's stochastic simulation methods, deterministic methods based on solving ordinary differential equations (ODEs) and a combination of both or hybrid methods (Mendes et al. 2009). COPASI supports models in the SBML standard and can simulate their behavior using the above-mentioned methods. COPASI enables semi-automatic comparisons of kinetic parameters and units from two sources, thus preventing a common source of errors. In addition, COPASI provides simple but flexible plotting tools and output files. The software also provides an estimation of model performance in comparison to the experimental data. Last but not least, the software is available for almost all major operating systems.

COPASI has been successfully integrated in a number of other modeling software such as EPISIM and SYCAMORE. EPISIM is a multiscaled tissue modeling and simulation workflow integrating SBML-based quantitative models with cell behavioral (CBM) models (Sütterlin et al. 2013). EPISIM combines graphical multiscale CBM modeling and COPASI simulation of the imported SBML models extracted from the earlier described BioModels database.

5.2 SYCAMORE

SYCAMORE is a web-browser-based application that integrates and provides an access to a number of biochemical modeling tools and methods such as SABIO-RK, BRENDA, and COPASI (Weidemann et al. 2008). SYCAMORE allows to build, view, analyze, and refine kinetic models, as well as to readily perform simulations. For example, kinetic data can be selected from SABIO-RK for a model of interest. SYCAMORE is intended to support and guide biologists in the initial stage of model set-up, whereas COPASI is recommended for expert simulations.

5.3 JWS Online

JWS Online (Olivier and Snoep 2004) is a web-based tool for simulation and storage of kinetic models using ODE methods. JWS supports the SBML format and links to various model databases such as BioModels and SABIO-RK allowing direct access and model exchange. SBML files are used to start an online simulation and the simulation parameters can be entered via a web interface. A local usage of the JWS on any other platform can be easily realized by just installing a Java Web Start program.

5.4 CellDesigner

CellDesigner is a popular modeling tool of biochemical networks (Funahashi et al. 2003). There are various possibilities to create and represent biochemical network diagrams, all of them having been extensively discussed by several systems biology groups (Kitano et al. 2005; Kohn et al. 2006). The graphical representation of process diagrams describing biological networks ranging from only a few to several hundred molecular interactions is undoubtedly a helpful visualization tool which prompted development and usage of standard notation for diagrams such as SBGN (Le Novere et al. 2009). Moreover, these diagrams can be translated into SBML and data exchange with other SBML compliant applications is possible. CellDesigner also integrates with COPASI, SBML ODE Solver, and Systems Biology Workbench (SBW) tools for model simulations.

5.5 Cytoscape

Another visualization tool for system biology focusing on large-scale biomolecular interaction networks is Cytoscape. Cytoscape supports many standards including BioPAX and SMBL. Cytoscape has a remarkable number of available plug-ins (ca. 190) to support specific features (Shannon et al. 2003). This indicates flexible extension to the core application of Cytoscape. Cytoscape functions as a web-client and annotation of the network can be extracted from other publicly available databases.

6 CONCLUSION

The overwhelming amount of experimental data as well as multidisciplinary nature of expert knowledge in systems biology prompted a number of systems biology groups to redesign comprehensive computational modeling software in order to hide the technical complexity of models and simulation tools. The huge application of standards and comprehensive usage of databases and tools in the field of systems biology demonstrates very clearly the high acceptance of these efforts in the community. There are of course drawbacks of these approaches such as less expert knowledge and less flexible programming frameworks. However, these approaches reach wider research communities and contribute much more successfully to the advance of knowledge in the systems biology community .

7 OUTLOOK

While we have described gradual maturity of systems biology standards and successful usage of systems biology tools in solving biological questions, there are, however, a few challenges that must be addressed. These challenges have been partially described by Steven D. Buckingham (Buckingham 2007). In addition to the improvement of model data representation, storage and integration with other online resources, there is a need for better linkage with experimental data. Also, we have to allow models to be more modular, hence, more flexible to cover a wide spectrum of possible combinations of molecules/pathways affecting each other. The other missing parameter is the inclusion of spatial characteristics such as the representation of molecules in space. For example, the SMBL format does not represent spatial information but CellML has extended this representation through a separate FieldML language and it might be that the two languages will eventually merge (Christie et al. 2009). Furthermore, the annotation of experiments on the one hand and models on the other hand is similar in nature. However, the underlying experimental and theoretical methods are quite different and the integration of both has just begun in spite of a decade of development of systems biology approaches. Prominent examples are the integration of both methodologies at a very high level in the SysMO-SEEK and the possibilities of interconnecting some of the above-described databases. It is expected that the number of systems biology approaches will grow and so their acceptance and usage to complement and support experimental methods. This requires efforts and dedication from both computational and experimental communities. We still need to learn more how best to integrate data from disparate sources, how to transfer knowledge from simple simulation systems to explain higher cellular/biological processes, and how to link experimental data to computational models.

References

Buchel, F., Wrzodek, C., Mittag, F., Drager, A., Eichner, J., Rodriguez, N., Le Novere, N., and Zell, A. (2012). Qualitative translation of relations from BioPAX to SBML qual. *Bioinformatics* **28**:2648–2653.

Buckingham, S. D. (2007). To build a better model. *Nat. Methods* **4**:367–374.

Christie, G. R., Nielsen, P. M., Blackett, S. A., Bradley, C. P., and Hunter, P. J. (2009). FieldML: Concepts and implementation. *Philos.Trans. A Math. Phys. Eng. Sci.* **367**:1869–1884.

Croft, D., O'Kelly, G., Wu, G., Haw, R., Gillespie, M., Matthews, L., Caudy, M., Garapati, P., Gopinath, G., Jassal, B., Jupe, S., Kalatskaya, I., Mahajan, S., May, B., Ndegwa, N., Schmidt, E., Shamovsky, V., Yung, C., Birney, E., Hermjakob, H., D'Eustachio, P., and Stein, L. (2011). Reactome: A database of reactions, pathways and biological processes. *Nucleic Acids Res.* **39**:D691–D697.

Drager, A., Rodriguez, N., Dumousseau, M., Dorr, A., Wrzodek, C., Le Novere, N., Zell, A., and Hucka, M. (2011). JSBML: A flexible Java library for working with SBML. *Bioinformatics* **27**:2167–2168.

Finney, A., and Hucka, M. (2003). Systems biology markup language: Level 2 and beyond. *Biochem. Soc. Trans.* **31**:1472–1473.

Funahashi, A., Morohashi, M., Kitano, H., and Tanimura, N. (2003). Cell Designer: A process diagram editor for gene-regulatory and biochemical networks. *BIOSILICO* **1**:159–162.

Henkel, R., Endler, L., Peters, A., Le Novere, N., and Waltemath, D. (2010). Ranked retrieval of computational biology models. *BMC Bioinformatics* **11**:423.

Hoops, S., Sahle, S., Gauges, R., Lee, C., Pahle, J., Simus, N., Singhal, M., Xu, L., Mendes, P., and Kummer, U. (2006). COPASI–a COmplex PAthway SImulator. *Bioinformatics* **22**:3067–3074.

Hucka, M., and Le Novere, N. (2010). Software that goes with the flow in systems biology. *BMC Biol.* **8**:140.

Hucka, M., Finney, A., Sauro, H. M., Bolouri, H., Doyle, J. C., Kitano, H., Arkin, A. P., Bornstein, B. J., Bray, D., Cornish-Bowden, A., Cuellar, A. A., Dronov, S., Gilles, E. D., Ginkel, M., Gor, V., Goryanin II, Hedley, W. J.,

Hodgman, T. C., Hofmeyr, J. H., Hunter, P. J., Juty, N. S., Kasberger, J. L., Kremling, A., Kummer, U., Le Novere, N., Loew, L. M., Lucio, D., Mendes, P., Minch, E., Mjolsness, E. D., Nakayama, Y., Nelson, M. R., Nielsen, P. F., Sakurada, T., Schaff, J. C., Shapiro, B. E., Shimizu, T. S., Spence, H. D., Stelling, J., Takahashi, K., Tomita, M., Wagner, J., and Wang, J. (2003). The systems biology markup language. *Bioinformatics* 19. 2003/03/04 edit

Johnson, S., Qi, X., Cicek, A. E., and Ozsoyoglu, G. (2013). iPathCaseKEGG: An iPad interface for KEGG metabolic pathways. *Health Info. Sci. Syst.* **1**:4.

Kitano, H., Funahashi, A., Matsuoka, Y., and Oda, K. (2005). Using process diagrams for the graphical representation of biological networks. *Nat. Biotechnol.* **23**:961–966.

Kohn, K. W., Aladjem, M. I., Kim, S., Weinstein, J. N., and Pommier, Y. (2006). Depicting combinatorial complexity with the molecular interaction map notation. *Mol. Syst. Biol.* **2**:51.

Kriete, A., and Eils, R. (2005). *Computational Systems Biology*. (1st edit). San Diego: Academic Press.

Le Novere, N., Bornstein, B., Broicher, A., Courtot, M., Donizelli, M., Dharuri, H., Li, L., Sauro, H., Schilstra, M., Shapiro, B., Snoep, J., and Hucka, M. (2006). BioModels Database: A free, centralized database of curated, published, quantitative kinetic models of biochemical and cellular systems. *Nucleic Acids Res.* **34**:D689–D691.

Le Novere, N., Hucka, M., Mi, H., Moodie, S., Schreiber, F., Sorokin, A., Demir, E., Wegner, K., Aladjem, M. I., Wimalaratne, S. M., Bergman, F. T., Gauges, R., Ghazal, P., Kawaji, H., Li, L., Matsuoka, Y., Villeger, A., Boyd, S. E., Calzone, L., Courtot, M., Dogrusoz, U., Freeman, T. C., Funahashi, A., Ghosh, S., Jouraku, A., Kim, S., Kolpakov, F., Luna, A., Sahle, S., Schmidt, E., Watterson, S., Wu, G., Goryanin, I., Kell, D. B., Sander, C., Sauro, H., Snoep, J. L., Kohn, K., and Kitano, H. (2009). The systems biology graphical notation. *Nat. Biotechnol.* **27**:735–741.

Lewis, N. E., Schramm, G., Bordbar, A., Schellenberger, J., Andersen, M. P., Cheng, J. K., Patel, N., Yee, A., Lewis, R. A., Eils, R., Konig, R., and Palsson, B. O. (2010). Large-scale in silico modeling of metabolic interactions between cell types in the human brain. *Nat. Biotechnol.* **28**:1279–1285.

Li, C., Donizelli, M., Rodriguez, N., Dharuri, H., Endler, L., Chelliah, V., Li, L., He, E., Henry, A., Stefan, M. I., Snoep, J. L., Hucka, M., Le Novere, N., and Laibe, C. (2010). BioModels Database: An enhanced, curated and annotated resource for published quantitative kinetic models. *BMC Syst. Biol.* **4**:92.

Mendes, P., Hoops, S., Sahle, S., Gauges, R., Dada, J., and Kummer, U. (2009). Computational modeling of biochemical networks using COPASI. *Methods Mol. Biol.* **500**:17–59.

Mi, H., Muruganujan, A., and Thomas, P. D. (2013). PANTHER in 2013: Modeling the evolution of gene function, and other gene attributes, in the context of phylogenetic trees. *Nucleic Acids Res.* **41**:D377–D386.

Olivier, B. G., and Snoep, J. L. (2004). Web-based kinetic modelling using JWS Online. *Bioinformatics* **20**:2143–2144.

Punzalan, F. R., Yamashita, Y., Soejima, N., Kawabata, M., Shimayoshi, T., Kuwabara, H., Kunieda, Y., and Amano, A. (2012). A CellML simulation compiler and code generator using ODE solving schemes. *Source Code Biol. Med.* **7**:11.

Schomburg, I., Chang, A., Placzek, S., Söhngen, C., Rother, M., Lang, M., Munaretto, C., Ulas, S., Stelzer, M., Grote, A., Scheer, M., and Schomburg, D. (2013). BRENDA in 2013: Integrated reactions, kinetic data, enzyme function data, improved disease classification: New options and contents in BRENDA. *Nucleic Acids Res.* **41**:D764 –D772.

Schramm, G., Wiesberg, S., Diessl, N., Kranz, A. L., Sagulenko, V., Oswald, M., Reinelt, G., Westermann, F., Eils, R., and Konig, R. (2010). PathWave: Discovering patterns of differentially regulated enzymes in metabolic pathways. *Bioinformatics* **26**:1225–1231.

Shannon, P., Markiel, A., Ozier, O., Baliga, N. S., Wang, J. T., Ramage, D., Amin, N., Schwikowski, B., and Ideker, T. (2003). Cytoscape: A software environment for integrated models of biomolecular interaction networks. *Genome Res.* **13**:2498–2504.

Sütterlin, T., Kolb, C., Dickhaus, H., Jäger, D., and Grabe, N. (2013). Bridging the scales: Semantic integration of quantitative SBML in graphical multi-cellular models and simulations with EPISIM and COPASI. *Bioinformatics* **29**:223–229.

Weidemann, A., Richter, S., Stein, M., Sahle, S., Gauges, R., Gabdoulline, R., Surovtsova, I., Semmelrock, N., Besson, B., Rojas, I., Wade, R., and Kummer, U. (2008). SYCAMORE–a systems biology computational analysis and modeling research environment. *Bioinformatics* **24**:1463–1464.

Wittig, U., Kania, R., Golebiewski, M., Rey, M., Shi, L., Jong, L., Algaa, E., Weidemann, A., Sauer-Danzwith, H., Mir, S., Krebs, O., Bittkowski, M., Wetsch, E., Rojas, I., and Muller, W. (2012). SABIO-RK–database for biochemical reaction kinetics. *Nucleic Acids Res.* **40**:D790–D796.

Wolstencroft, K., Owen, S., du Preez, F., Krebs, O., Mueller, W., Goble, C., and Snoep, J. L. (2011). The SEEK: A platform for sharing data and models in systems biology. *Methods Enzymol.* **500**:629–655.

Wrzodek, C., Buchel, F., Ruff, M., Drager, A., and Zell, A. (2013). Precise generation of systems biology models from KEGG pathways. *BMC Syst. Biol.* **7**:15.

CHAPTER

10

Computational Models for Circadian Rhythms: Deterministic versus Stochastic Approaches

Jean-Christophe Leloup, Didier Gonze, Albert Goldbeter

Unité de Chronobiologie théorique, Faculté des Sciences, Université Libre de Bruxelles, Brussels, Belgium

CONTENTS

http://dx.doi.org/10.1016/B978-0-12-405926-9.00010-1

Abstract

Circadian rhythms originate from intertwined feedback processes in genetic regulatory networks. Computational models of increasing complexity have been proposed for the molecular mechanism of these rhythms, which occur spontaneously with a period on the order of 24 h. We show that deterministic models for circadian rhythms in *Drosophila* account for a variety of dynamical properties, such as phase shifting or long-term suppression by light pulses and entrainment by light/dark cycles. Stochastic versions of these models allow us to examine how molecular noise affects the emergence and robustness of circadian oscillations. Finally, we present a deterministic model for the mammalian circadian clock and use it to address the dynamical bases of physiological disorders of the sleep/wake cycle in humans.

1 INTRODUCTION: THE COMPUTATIONAL BIOLOGY OF CIRCADIAN RHYTHMS

Most living organisms have developed the capability of generating autonomously sustained oscillations with a period close to 24 h. The function of these so-called *circadian rhythms* is to allow the organisms to adapt their physiology to the natural alternation of day and night. Circadian rhythms are endogenous because they can occur in constant environmental conditions (e.g. constant darkness). During the last two decades, experimental studies have shed much light on the molecular mechanism of circadian rhythms, which represents a longstanding problem in biology (Dibner et al. 2010; Ukai and Ueda 2010; Zhang and Kay 2010; Merrow and Brunner 2011; Baker et al. 2012). In all eukaryotic organisms investigated so far, the molecular mechanism of circadian oscillations relies on the negative feedback exerted by a clock protein on the expression of its gene (Hardin et al. 1990; Glossop et al. 1999; Lee et al. 2000; Alabadi et al. 2001; Reppert and Weaver 2002).

Even before details were known about their molecular origin, abstract mathematical models were used to probe the dynamic properties of circadian rhythms. A popular model of this type was provided by the van der Pol equations, which were originally proposed for sustained oscillations in electrical circuits. Thus, the van der Pol oscillator has been used for more than three decades for modeling circadian rhythms (e.g. to account for phase shifts of these rhythms by light pulses (Jewett and Kronauer 1998)). Another application involving this model pertains to modeling the enhanced fitness due to the resonance of circadian rhythms with the external light/dark cycle in cyanobacteria (Gonze et al. 2002c).

However, now that the molecular mechanism of circadian rhythms has largely been uncovered, mathematical models based on experimental observations have been proposed. Taking the form of a system of coupled ordinary differential equations, these deterministic models predict that in a certain range of parameter values the genetic regulatory network at the core of the clock mechanism can produce sustained oscillations of the limit cycle type. Deterministic models for circadian rhythms were first proposed for *Drosophila* and *Neurospora* (Goldbeter 1995, 1996; Leloup and Goldbeter 1998; Leloup et al. 1999; Smolen et al. 2001; Ueda et al. 2001), and later for mammals (Forger and Peskin 2003; Leloup and Goldbeter 2003, 2004; Becker-Weimann et al. 2004; Mirsky et al. 2009; Kim and Forger 2012). The first model showing in a biochemical context that oscillations can originate from negative feedback was due to Goodwin (1965). Modified versions of the Goodwin model are still being used to probe properties of circadian rhythms in organisms such as *Neurospora* (Ruoff et al. 2001). In this chapter we will focus on models which rely on more detailed molecular mechanisms.

One limitation of deterministic models is that they do not take into consideration the fact that the number of molecules involved in the regulatory mechanism within the rhythm-producing cells may be small as observed, for example, in *Neurospora* (Merrow et al. 1997). At low concentrations of protein or messenger RNA molecules, molecular fluctuations are likely to have a marked impact on circadian oscillations (Barkai and Leibler, 2000). To assess the effect of molecular noise, it is necessary to resort to a stochastic approach. Comparing the predictions of deterministic and stochastic models for circadian rhythms shows that robust circadian oscillations can be observed even when the maximum number of mRNA and protein molecules is of the order of some tens and hundreds, respectively (Gonze et al. 2002a, 2002b, 2004a).

The goal of this chapter is to present an overview of deterministic and stochastic models for circadian rhythms. We will begin by presenting (in Section 2) deterministic models for circadian oscillations of the PER protein and its mRNA in *Drosophila*. A core model will be presented, which also provides a useful model for circadian rhythms in *Neurospora*. This model for *Drosophila* circadian rhythms will be extended to take into account the role of the TIM protein and the control of circadian behavior by light.

In Section 3, we consider stochastic versions of these models. We examine how molecular noise affects the emergence of circadian oscillations and determine the influence of a variety of factors, such as number of protein and mRNA molecules, degree of cooperativity of repression, distance from bifurcation point, and rate constants characterizing the binding of the repressor protein to the gene. Two types of stochastic models are presented: one involves a fully detailed description of individual reaction steps, whereas a second relies on a non-developed description of nonlinear kinetic steps. Both types of models yield largely similar results. The study of stochastic models for circadian oscillations will allow us to characterize the domain of validity of deterministic models for circadian rhythms.

In Section 4 we return to deterministic approaches and present a model for the mammalian circadian clock. We use this model to address the molecular bases of disorders of the sleep/wake cycle in humans, which are associated with dysfunctions of the clock. Computational models can thus be applied to investigating not only the molecular mechanism of circadian rhythms but also the origin of associated physiological disorders. As discussed in Section 5, the example of circadian rhythms illustrates how more and more complex models have been presented over the years to account for new experimental observations. We consider the need for such an increase in complexity of computational models for circadian rhythms, and the added insights these complex models provide for a better understanding of circadian behavior.

2 MODELING THE *DROSOPHILA* CIRCADIAN CLOCK

2.1 Overview of experimental observations

Some of the most remarkable advances in elucidating the molecular basis of circadian rhythms have been made in mutants of the fly *Drosophila* (Konopka 1979; Hall and Rosbash 1988; Baylies et al. 1993; Dunlap 1993), in which circadian rhythms affect the rest/activity cycle and the daily eclosion peaks of pupae. Both rhythms persist in constant darkness or temperature (Pittendrigh 1960). The classic work of Konopka and Benzer (1971) yielded *Drosophila* flies altered in their circadian system, owing to mutations in a single gene called *per* (for "period"). Four phenotypes were characterized: the wild type (per^{+}) has a free running period of activity and eclosion close to 24 h; short-period mutants (*per*^{s}) have a period close to 19 h; in long-period mutants (*per*^{l}), the periodicity increases up to 29 h; and arrhythmic mutants (*per*^{0}) have lost the circadian pattern of eclosion or activity (Konopka and Benzer 1971; Konopka 1979). Interestingly, whereas in the wild type the period remains independent of temperature—a property known as temperature compensation, which is common to all circadian rhythms (Pittendrigh 1960)—the mutants *per*^{l} and *per*^{s} have lost this property (Konopka et al. 1989). In contrast to the wild type, the period of their activity rhythm respectively increases and decreases with temperature. Accounting for temperature compensation of circadian rhythms remains an important challenge for computational biology.

A breakthrough for the mechanism of circadian rhythms in *Drosophila* was the finding (Hardin et al. 1990, 1992) that *per* mRNA is produced in a circadian manner. This periodic variation is accompanied by a circadian rhythm in the degree of abundance of PER. The peak in *per* mRNA precedes the peak in PER by 4–8 h (Zerr et al. 1990; Zeng et al. 1994). On the basis of this observation, Hardin et al. (1990, 1992) suggested that the *Drosophila* circadian rhythm results from a negative feedback exerted by the PER protein on the synthesis of the *per* mRNA. Post-translational modification of PER is also involved in the mechanism of circadian oscillations. Experimental evidence indeed indicates that PER is multiply phosphorylated (Edery et al. 1994). It appears that PER phosphorylation plays a role in the circadian oscillatory mechanism, by controlling the nuclear localization of PER and/or its degradation (Grima et al. 2002; Ko et al. 2002).

Overexpression of PER in *Drosophila* eyes represses *per* transcription and suppresses circadian rhythmicity in these cells, without affecting circadian oscillations in other *per*-expressing cells in the brain or the circadian rhythm in locomotor activity. This work shows that the action of PER on transcription is intracellular, and suggests that "each *per*-expressing cell contains an autonomous oscillator of which the *per* feedback loop is a component" (Zeng et al. 1994). Such a mechanism, based on negative autoregulation of transcription, has also been found in *Neurospora* (Aronson et al. 1994). The current view is that negative autoregulation of gene expression by a clock protein represents a unified mechanism for the generation of circadian rhythmicity in a wide variety of experimental systems (Dunlap 1999; Young and Kay 2001).

2.2 A core deterministic model for circadian oscillations of the PER protein and its mRNA

A first model for circadian oscillations in the *Drosophila* PER protein and its mRNA is based on multiple phosphorylation of PER and on the inhibition of *per* transcription by a phosphorylated form of the protein (Goldbeter 1995). This model, schematized in Figure 10.1a, can be viewed as a minimal core model because it takes into account a limited number of phosphorylated residues of PER. The model also applies to oscillations of FRQ and *frq* mRNA in *Neurospora*.

In the model, the *per* gene is first expressed in the nucleus and transcribed into *per* messenger RNA (mRNA). The latter is transported into the cytosol, where it is translated into the PER protein, P_0, and degraded. The PER protein undergoes multiple phosphorylation, from P_0 into P_1 and from P_1 into P_2. These modifications, catalyzed by a protein kinase, are reverted by a phosphatase. The fully phosphorylated form of the protein is marked up for degradation and transported into the nucleus in a reversible manner. The nuclear form of the protein (P_N) represses the transcription of the gene.

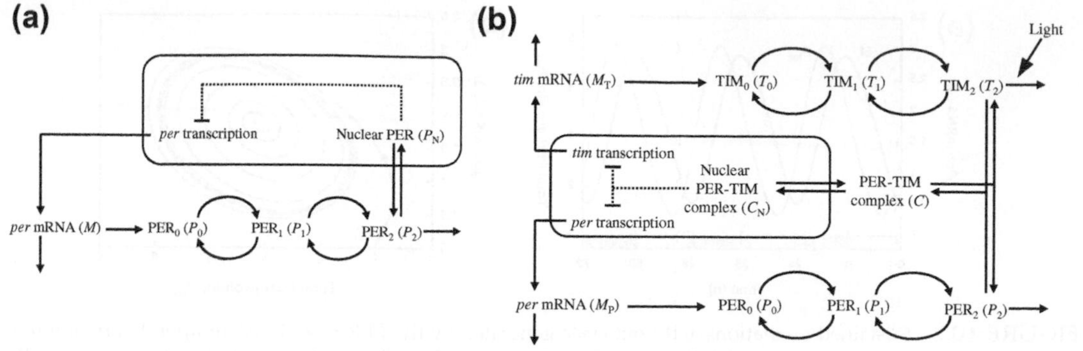

FIGURE 10.1 Schemes of the models for circadian oscillations in *Drosophila*. (a) The PER model is based on the sole negative regulation exerted by the PER protein on the expression of its gene (Goldbeter 1995). (b) The PER-TIM model incorporates the *tim* gene and its product, which forms a complex with the PER protein. This model is based on the negative regulation exerted by the PER-TIM complex on the expression of the *per* and *tim* genes. The effect of light is to increase the rate of TIM degradation (Leloup and Goldbeter 1998).

In the model, we consider two successive phosphorylations of PER, which is the minimal implementation of multiple phosphorylation. A single phosphorylation step would yield similar results. In fact, sustained oscillations can occur in the absence of phosphorylation, as shown by the study of a three-variable model representing an even simpler model for circadian oscillations (Leloup et al. 1999; Gonze and Goldbeter 2000; Gonze et al. 2000). We nevertheless focus on a model that includes multiple phosphorylation, because this process contributes to the mechanism of circadian oscillations by introducing a delay in the negative feedback loop.

In the model, the temporal variation of the concentrations of mRNA (M) and of the various forms of the regulatory protein—cytosolic (P_0, P_1, P_2) or nuclear (P_N)—is governed by the following system of kinetic equations (see Goldbeter 1995, 1996 for further details):

$$
\begin{aligned}
\frac{dM}{dt} &= v_s \frac{K_I^n}{K_I^n + P_N^n} - v_m \frac{M}{K_m + M}, \\
\frac{dP_0}{dt} &= k_s M - v_1 \frac{P_0}{K_1 + P_0} + v_2 \frac{P_1}{K_2 + P_1} \\
\frac{dP_1}{dt} &= v_1 \frac{P_0}{K_1 + P_0} - v_2 \frac{P_1}{K_2 + P_1} - v_3 \frac{P_1}{K_3 + P_1} + v_4 \frac{P_2}{K_4 + P_2} \\
\frac{dP_2}{dt} &= v_3 \frac{P_1}{K_3 + P_1} - v_4 \frac{P_2}{K_4 + P_2} - v_d \frac{P_2}{K_d + P_2} - k_1 P_2 + k_2 P_N \\
\frac{dP_N}{dt} &= k_1 P_2 - k_2 P_N
\end{aligned}
\tag{10.1}
$$

In these equations, the phosphorylation and dephosphorylation terms (with maximum rates v_1, v_3, and v_2, v_4, respectively)—as well as the degradation terms for mRNA and fully phosphorylated PER protein (with maximum rates v_m and v_d, respectively)—are all of Michaelian form corresponding to non-cooperative enzyme kinetics. The repression term

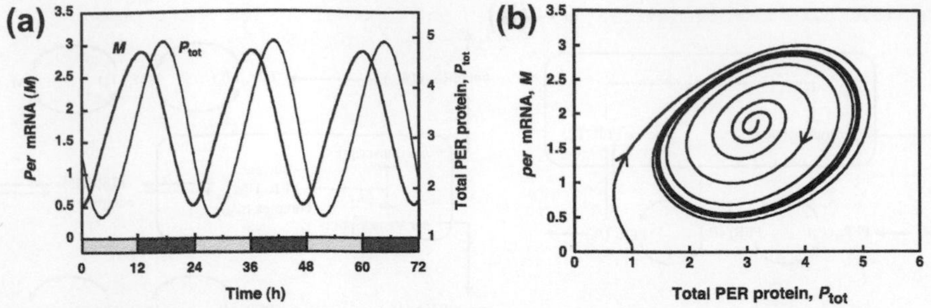

FIGURE 10.2 Sustained oscillations and limit cycle generated by the PER model. (A) Temporal variation in *per* mRNA (M) and in the total amount of PER protein (P_{tot}). (B) Sustained oscillations in total PER protein and *per* mRNA (expressed in nM) correspond to the evolution toward a limit cycle when the system's trajectory is projected onto the (M, P_{tot}) plane. Starting from two different initial conditions, the system reaches a unique closed curve characterized by a period and amplitude that are fixed for the given set of parameter values. The curves have been obtained by numerical integration of Equations (10.1). Parameter values are $v_s = 0.76$ nM h^{-1}, $v_m = 0.65$ nM h^{-1}, $k_s = 0.38$ h^{-1}, $v_d = 0.95$ nM h^{-1}, $k_1 = 1.9$ h^{-1}, $k_2 = 1.3$ h^{-1}, $K_I = 1$ nM, $K_d = 0.2$ nM, $K_1 = K_2 = K_3 = K_4 = 2$ nM, $n = 4$, $V_1 = 3.2$ nM h^{-1}, $V_2 = 1.58$ nM h^{-1}, $V_3 = 5$ nM h^{-1}, and $V_4 = 2.5$ nM h^{-1}. Initial conditions are $M = 0.1$ nM, $P_0 = P_1 = P_2 = P_N = 0.25$ nM ($P_{tot} = 1$ nM), $M = 1.9$ nM, and $P_0 = P_1 = P_2 = P_N = 0.8$ nM ($P_{tot} = 3.2$ nM) (see Goldbeter 1995, 1996).

takes the form of a Hill equation characterized by the Hill coefficient n. Repression by P_N becomes steeper and steeper as the degree of cooperativity n increases above unity. Although higher cooperativity favors the occurrence of sustained oscillations, periodic behavior can also be obtained for $n = 1$ (i.e. in the absence of cooperativity in repression).

For an appropriate set of parameter values, the model accounts for the occurrence of sustained oscillations in continuous darkness (Figure 10.2a). When plotting the time evolution of one variable (e.g. *per* mRNA (M)) as a function of another variable (e.g. the total amount of PER protein (P_{tot})), these oscillations correspond in such a phase plane to the evolution toward a closed curve, known as a limit cycle (Figure 10.2b). This name stems from the fact that the same closed trajectory is reached regardless of initial conditions, as illustrated in Figure 10.2b. In addition to accounting for the circadian rhythms in mRNA and for protein level, the model shows how variations in parameters such as the rate of degradation of PER or the rate of its translocation into the nucleus may change the period of the oscillations, or even suppress rhythmic behavior (Goldbeter 1995, 1996).

When the model based on PER alone was proposed, the way light affects circadian rhythms in *Drosophila* was still unknown. In 1996, a series of papers showed, concomitantly, that a second protein—TIM (for TIMELESS)—forms a complex with PER, and that light acts by inducing degradation of TIM (Hunter-Ensor et al. 1996; Lee et al. 1996; Myers et al. 1996; Zeng et al. 1996). These observations paved the way for the construction of a more detailed computational model incorporating the formation of a PER-TIM complex as well as the enhancement of TIM degradation during the light phase.

2.3 A ten-variable deterministic model for circadian oscillations in *Drosophila*

The ten-variable model for circadian oscillations of the PER and TIM proteins and of *per* and *tim* mRNAs in *Drosophila* (Leloup and Goldbeter 1998; Leloup et al. 1999) is schematized in Figure 10.1b. The mechanism is based on the negative feedback exerted by the complex between the nuclear PER and TIM proteins on the expression of their genes. For each of these proteins, transcription, translation, and multiple phosphorylation are treated as in the PER model of Figure 10.1a. The fully phosphorylated proteins PER and TIM are marked up for degradation, and form a complex that is transported into the nucleus in a reversible manner. The nuclear form of the PER-TIM complex represses the transcription of the *per* and *tim* genes.

Recent experiments indicate that repression is in fact of indirect nature: a complex between two activators, the CLOCK and CYC proteins, promotes the expression of the *per* and *tim* genes. The PER-TIM complex prevents this activation by forming a complex with CLOCK and CYC (Darlington et al. 1998; Rutila et al. 1998; Lee et al. 1999). We return to the effect of such an indirect negative feedback in Section 4, restricting the present discussion to the PER-TIM model. In this model, the variables are the concentrations of the mRNAs (M_P and M_T), the various forms of the PER and TIM proteins (P_0, P_1, P_2, T_0, T_1, T_2), and the cytosolic (C) and nuclear (C_N) forms of the PER-TIM complex. The temporal evolution of the concentration variables is governed by the following system of 10 kinetic equations (see Leloup and Goldbeter (1998) and Leloup et al. (1999) for further details):

$$
\begin{aligned}
\frac{dM_P}{dt} &= v_{sP}\frac{K_{IP}{}^n}{K_{IP}{}^n + C_N{}^n} - v_{mP}\frac{M_P}{K_{mP} + M_P} - k_d M_P \\
\frac{dP_0}{dt} &= k_{sP}M_P - V_{1P}\frac{P_0}{K_{1P} + P_0} + V_{2P}\frac{P_1}{K_{2P} + P_1} - k_d P_0 \\
\frac{dP_1}{dt} &= V_{1P}\frac{P_0}{K_{1P} + P_0} - V_{2P}\frac{P_1}{K_{2P} + P_1} - V_{3P}\frac{P_1}{K_{3P} + P_1} + V_{4P}\frac{P_2}{K_{4P} + P_2} - k_d P_1 \\
\frac{dP_2}{dt} &= V_{3P}\frac{P_1}{K_{3P} + P_1} - V_{4P}\frac{P_2}{K_{4P} + P_2} - k_3P_2T_2 + k_4C - v_{dP}\frac{P_2}{K_{dP} + P_2} - k_d P_2 \\
\frac{dM_T}{dt} &= v_{sT}\frac{K_{IT}{}^n}{K_{IT}{}^n + C_N{}^n} - v_{mT}\frac{M_T}{K_{mT} + M_T} - k_d M_T \\
\frac{dT_0}{dt} &= k_{sT}M_T - V_{1T}\frac{T_0}{K_{1T} + T_0} + V_{2T}\frac{T_1}{K_{2T} + T_1} - k_d T_0 \\
\frac{dT_1}{dt} &= V_{1T}\frac{T_0}{K_{1T} + T_0} - V_{2T}\frac{T_1}{K_{2T} + T_1} - V_{3T}\frac{T_1}{K_{3T} + T_1} + V_{4T}\frac{T_2}{K_{4T} + T_2} - k_d T_1 \\
\frac{dT_2}{dt} &= V_{3T}\frac{T_1}{K_{3T} + T_1} - V_{4T}\frac{T_2}{K_{4T} + T_2} - k_3P_2T_2 + k_4C - v_{dT}\frac{T_2}{K_{dT} + T_2} - k_d T_2 \\
\frac{dC}{dt} &= k_3P_2T_2 - k_4C - k_1C + k_2C_N - k_{dC}C \\
\frac{dC_N}{dt} &= k_1C - k_2C_N - k_{dN}C_N
\end{aligned}
\tag{10.2}
$$

These equations correspond to one particular version in a family of possible models, which differ by details of the molecular implementation of the feedback mechanism. Thus, rather than considering the formation of a complex between the fully phosphorylated forms of PER and TIM the complex could be made also (or instead) between the non-phosphorylated or mono-phosphorylated forms of the proteins. These other versions of the basal model yield largely similar results.

The various terms appearing in Equations (10.2) are similar to those of Equations (10.1). We have added non-specific degradation terms, characterized by the rate constants k_d, k_{dC}, and k_{dN}. These linear terms are generally of negligible magnitude, and are not essential for oscillations. Their inclusion ensures the existence of a steady state when the specific protein degradation processes are inhibited. In Equations (10.2), parameter v_{dT} represents the maximum value of the TIM degradation rate. This is the light-sensitive parameter, which will be set to a constant low value during continuous darkness, and to a constant high value during continuous light. In a light/dark cycle, v_{dT} will vary in a square-wave manner between these two extreme values. The square-wave corresponds well to laboratory conditions under which light varies in an all-or-none manner. The natural variation of light is of course smoother, and other waveforms should be considered to address the effect of variations of luminosity under natural light/dark cycles.

Much as the PER model, the model based on the formation of the PER-TIM complex can account for sustained autonomous oscillations originating from negative autoregulatory feedback. Now, however, we may address the dynamic behavior of the model in various lighting conditions, by incorporating suitable changes in parameter v_{dT}. Thus, as illustrated in Figure 10.3, sustained oscillations can occur in continuous darkness (DD), but damped oscillations occur in conditions corresponding to continuous light (LL), as observed in *Drosophila* (Qiu and Hardin 1996). In LL, the light-sensitive parameter was chosen so that it takes a high value corresponding to a stable steady state. The disappearance of oscillations can be explained intuitively: because of enhanced degradation, the TIM protein cannot reach a level allowing effective repression by the PER-TIM complex. Oscillations observed in DD with a period close to 24 h can be entrained by a 12:12 LD cycle (12 h of light followed by 12 h of darkness). Experimentally, there exists a window of entrainment, ranging typically from 21 to 28 h (Moore-Ede et al. 1982).

The PER-TIM model allows us to compare theoretical predictions with experimental observations in a variety of cases. A first comparison pertains to entrainment by LD cycles of varying photoperiod. As shown by the experiments of Qiu and Hardin (1996), the peak in *per* mRNA always follows the transition from the L to the D phase by about 4 h. A similar result is obtained in the PER-TIM model (Figure 10.4). The lag after the L to D transition appears to be the same regardless of the duration of the light phase, because the level of TIM has decreased to a minimum value at the end of the L phase, and the time required for the PER-TIM complex to accumulate during the dark phase above the threshold for repression remains unchanged.

Another key comparison pertains to the phase shifts induced by light pulses in continuous darkness. Depending on the phase at which these perturbations are made, circadian oscillations can be either advanced or delayed. Alternatively, no phase shift may occur. These data yield a phase response curve (PRC) when the phase shift is plotted as a function of the phase of perturbation. The PRC is an important tool in the study of circadian rhythms. We may simulate the effect of light pulses in the PER-TIM model by transiently increasing the maximum rate of TIM degradation, v_{dT}. Unperturbed oscillations of fully phosphorylated TIM (T_2) are shown in Figure 10.5a, where the vertical line through the fourth peak will serve as reference for determining phase shifts triggered by transient perturbations.

As shown in Figure 10.5b, when the perturbation is applied during the rising phase of TIM a phase delay is observed. In contrast, a phase advance occurs when the perturbation is made

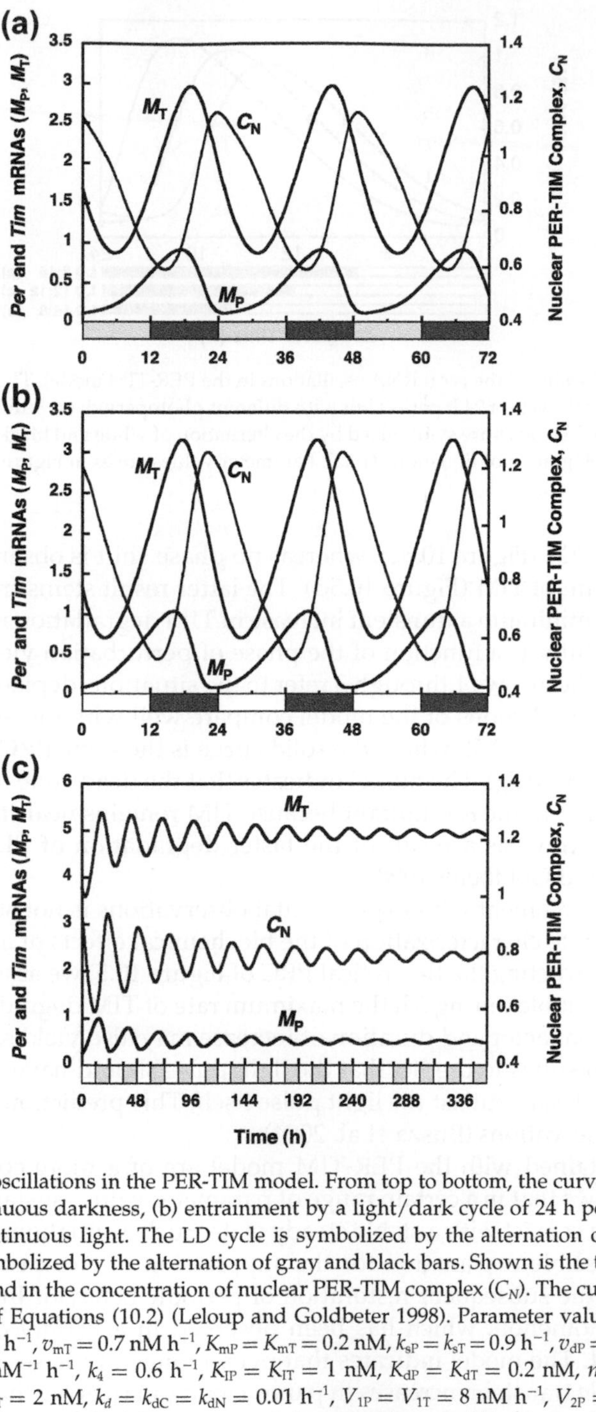

FIGURE 10.3 Circadian oscillations in the PER-TIM model. From top to bottom, the curves correspond to (a) sustained oscillations in continuous darkness, (b) entrainment by a light/dark cycle of 24 h period (12:12 LD), and (c) damped oscillations in continuous light. The LD cycle is symbolized by the alternation of white and black bars. Continuous darkness is symbolized by the alternation of gray and black bars. Shown is the temporal variation in *per* and *tim* mRNAs (M_P, M_T) and in the concentration of nuclear PER-TIM complex (C_N). The curves have been obtained by numerical integration of Equations (10.2) (Leloup and Goldbeter 1998). Parameter values are $v_{sP} = 0.8$ nM h^{-1}, $v_{sT} = 1$ nM h^{-1}, $v_{mP} = 0.8$ nM h^{-1}, $v_{mT} = 0.7$ nM h^{-1}, $K_{mP} = K_{mT} = 0.2$ nM, $k_{sP} = k_{sT} = 0.9$ h^{-1}, $v_{dP} = v_{dT} = 2$ nM h^{-1}, $k1 = 1.2$ h^{-1}, $k2 = 0.2$ h^{-1}, $k_3 = 1.2$ nM^{-1} h^{-1}, $k_4 = 0.6$ h^{-1}, $K_{IP} = K_{IT} = 1$ nM, $K_{dP} = K_{dT} = 0.2$ nM, $n = 4$, $K_{1P} = K_{1T} = K_{2P} = K_{2T} = K_{3P} = K_{3T} = K_{4P} = K_{4T} = 2$ nM, $k_d = k_{dC} = k_{dN} = 0.01$ h^{-1}, $V_{1P} = V_{1T} = 8$ nM h^{-1}, $V_{2P} = V_{2T} = 1$ nM h^{-1}, $V_{3P} = V_{3T} = 8$ nM h^{-1}, and $V_{4P} = V_{4T} = 1$ nM h^{-1}. Parameter v_{dT} is increased from 2 nM h^{-1} in the dark phase to 5 nM h^{-1} in the light phase (Leloup and Goldbeter 1998).

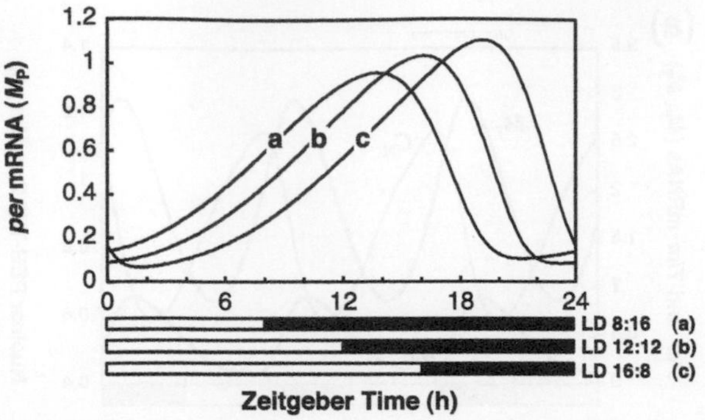

FIGURE 10.4 Phase locking of the *per* mRNA oscillations in the PER-TIM model. The three curves correspond to entrainment by a light/dark cycle of 24 h period but with different photoperiod: (a) 8:16 LD cycle, (b) 12:12 LD cycle, and (c) 16:8 LD cycle. The LD cycles are symbolized by the alternation of white and black bars. The curves have been obtained by numerical integration of Equations (10.2). Parameter values are as in Figure 10.3.

at the maximum of TIM (Figure 10.5c), whereas no phase shift is observed when the pulse is given at the minimum of TIM (Figure 10.5d). The latter result stems from the fact that when TIM is already at its minimum a transient increase in TIM degradation remains without effect. Plotting the phase shifts as a function of the phase of perturbation yields the PRC shown in Figure 10.5e, where the arrows 1 through 3 refer to the situations depicted in panels B through D, respectively. The predictions of the model compare well with the experimental PRC both for wild-type flies (Figure 10.5f, where the solid curve is the same PRC as in panel E) and for the per^s mutant (Figure 10.5g). The model indicates that the dead zone in which no phase shift occurs is nearly absent in the per^s mutant because TIM remains near its minimum for a relatively much shorter time, as a result of the faster degradation of PER in this mutant (see Figure 6 in Leloup and Goldbeter 1998).

Obtaining good agreement with experimental observations is not straightforward, as this requires an appropriate characterization of the biochemical effects of a light pulse on the circadian clock. In constructing the theoretical PRC of Figure 10.5, we assumed that the effect of the light pulse is to double during 3 h the maximum rate of TIM degradation. Other combinations of multiplication factor and duration of increase may also yield satisfactory agreement. The interest of this result is to predict that the light pulse should have long-lasting biochemical consequences that may outlast the light pulse itself. This prediction is in fact corroborated by experimental observations (Busza et al. 2004).

Other results obtained with the PER-TIM model are of a more counterintuitive nature. First, the model shows that in a certain range of parameter values sustained oscillations of the limit cycle type may coexist with a stable steady state. Such a situation, known as hard excitation, provides a possible explanation for the suppression of circadian rhythms by a single light pulse and for the subsequent restoration of periodic behavior by a second such pulse. This puzzling phenomenon, which has been observed in a variety of organisms, remains largely unexplained. The model indicates that over a range of phases corresponding to TIM increase in *Drosophila* transient increases in parameter v_{dT} may bring the system from the limit cycle into the basin of attraction of the stable steady state. A second pulse in v_{dT} may then

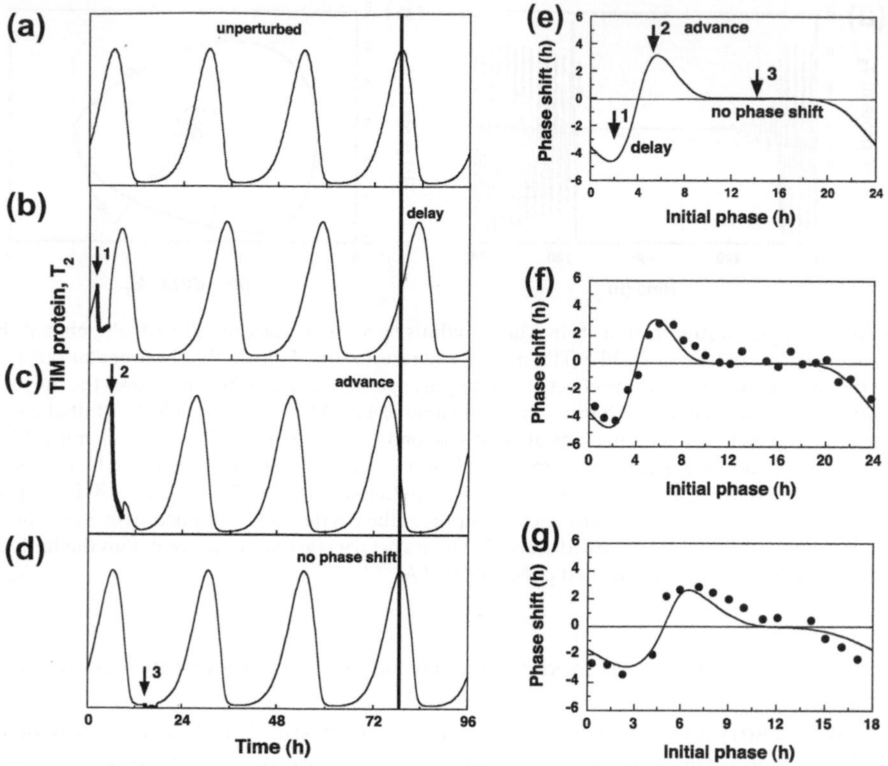

FIGURE 10.5 Phase shifting by a light pulse: Comparison with experiments. (a) Unperturbed oscillations of phosphorylated TIM (T2). The vertical line through the fourth peak serves as reference for determining phases shifts. (b–d) Transient perturbations at three different phases of the oscillations, producing, respectively, a phase delay, a phase advance, or an absence of phase shift. The arrows mark the beginning of the light pulse and the thick lines indicate both the duration and the effect of this perturbation (see following). (e) Phase response curve (PRC) obtained by plotting the phase shift as a function of the phase at which the perturbation is applied. The perturbation takes the form of a 3 h twofold increase in TIM maximum degradation rate (v_{dT}), triggered by the light pulse. (F and G) PRCs obtained theoretically (solid lines) for the wild type (panel F) and for the *per*^{s} mutant (panel G) in *Drosophila*. The theoretical predictions compare well with the experimental observations (dots) based on data obtained by Konopka and Orr using a 1-min light pulse (redrawn from Figure 2 of Hall and Rosbash 1987). The oscillations of the TIM protein (panels A through D) and the PRCs (panels E through G) have been obtained by numerical integration of Equations (10.2) (Leloup and Goldbeter 1998). Parameter values are listed in Figure 2 of Leloup and Goldbeter (1998). For the PRCs, the zero phase is chosen, as in the experiments (Hall and Rosbash 1987), so that the minimum in *per* mRNA occurs after 12 h.

bring back the oscillations (Figure 10.6a). Suppression is only possible over a finite portion of the limit cycle, as shown in Figure 10.6b. The characteristics (duration and amplitude) of the suppressing pulse change with the phase of perturbation in this domain (Leloup and Goldbeter 2001). In contrast, a single critical perturbation suppressing the rhythm exists in the situation described by Winfree (1980), wherein the stable limit cycle surrounds an unstable steady state. However, suppression is only transient in that case. The coexistence between a stable steady state and a stable limit cycle (illustrated in Figure 10.6a) is by no means

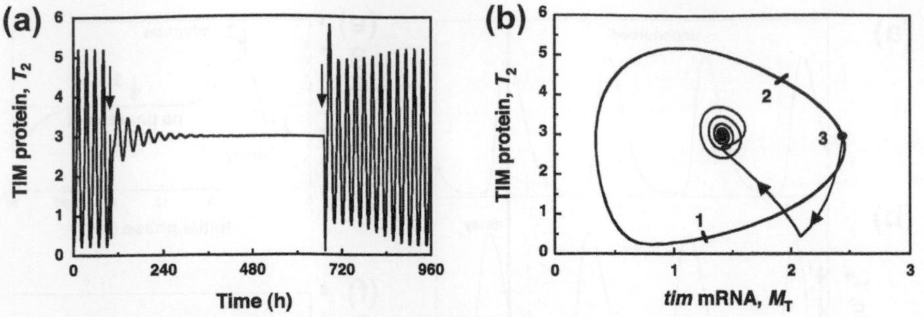

FIGURE 10.6 Long-term suppression of circadian rhythms by a single pulse of light. (A) Permanent rhythm suppression by a single pulse of light in the PER-TIM model, and restoration of the rhythm by a similar pulse. At the time indicated by the first arrow, to mimic the effect of a light pulse parameter v_{dT}, which measures the maximum rate of TIM degradation, is increased during 2 h from the basal value of 1.3 nM h^{-1} up to 4.0 nM h^{-1}. Initial conditions correspond to point 3 in panel B. At the time indicated by a second arrow, a similar change in v_{dT}, mimicking a second light pulse, is initiated, and the system returns to the oscillatory regime. The curve is obtained by numerical integration of Equations (10.2) for the parameter values of Figure 4 in Leloup and Goldbeter (2001). (B) Light pulses, translated into transient increases in v_{dT}, can permanently suppress the rhythm when applied over a portion of the limit cycle bounded by the two black bars marked 1 and 2. The trajectory starting from point 3 on the limit cycle corresponds to the rhythm suppression by the first pulse in panel A.

uncommon, but a computational model is clearly needed to predict the occurrence of such a phenomenon.

We were at first surprised to observe that the deterministic PER-TIM model was also capable of producing chaotic behavior in constant environmental conditions (e.g. continuous darkness, Leloup and Goldbeter 1999). Such autonomous chaos has previously been shown to originate from the interplay between two instability generating mechanisms (e.g. two feedback loops, each of which may produce sustained oscillations Goldbeter 1996). Here, the model contains but a single negative feedback loop, exerted by the PER-TIM complex. However, the formation of this complex involves two branches leading to the synthesis of PER and TIM. Chaos occurs in a relatively small parameter domain when a dynamical imbalance arises between the synthesis and degradation of the PER and TIM proteins or their mRNAs. Non-autonomous chaos can also be found in models for circadian rhythms, as a result of the periodic forcing of the circadian clock by light/dark cycles. The theoretical study indicates that the occurrence of such non-autonomous chaos is favored by the square-wave nature of LD cycles: the domain of entrainment indeed enlarges at the expense of the domain of chaos when the waveform of the LD cycle progressively changes from square wave to sinusoidal (Gonze and Goldbeter 2000).

Another use of the PER and PER-TIM models for circadian oscillations in *Drosophila* is to address the dynamical bases of temperature compensation (i.e. the relative independence of the period of circadian oscillations with respect to temperature (see Section 2.1)). The analysis of the models supports the view (Ruoff and Rensing 1996) that temperature compensation originates from a balance between two opposing tendencies: the acceleration of some reactions with temperature tends to increase the period, whereas the acceleration of other reactions tends to lower it (Leloup and Goldbeter 1997). When the balance is lost (as a result of a mutation), temperature compensation fails to occur, as observed in long- and short-period *Drosophila* mutants.

This discussion shows how useful deterministic models of moderate complexity may prove for the study of circadian rhythms. However, the question arises as to the validity of these computational models when the numbers of molecules involved in the oscillatory mechanism are small, as may occur for proteins and mRNAs in cellular conditions. Then, deterministic models may reach their limits, and it becomes necessary to resort to stochastic approaches. We shall now examine how stochastic models may account for the emergence of circadian rhythms, and will turn thereafter to more complex deterministic models proposed for the mammalian circadian clock.

3 STOCHASTIC MODELS FOR CIRCADIAN RHYTHMS

3.1 Core molecular model for circadian oscillations

To illustrate the stochastic approach to modeling circadian rhythms, it will be useful to resort to a relatively simple model for circadian oscillations. The model examined in Section 2.1 and schematized in Figure 10.1a provides a core model for circadian rhythms based on the negative feedback exerted by a protein (which is referred to in the following as clock protein) on the expression of its gene. As previously indicated, this model applies to circadian oscillations of the PER protein and *per* mRNA in *Drosophila*, and to the case of *Neurospora* (Leloup et al. 1999; Gonze et al. 2000) for which circadian rhythms originate from the negative feedback exerted by the FRQ protein on the expression of its gene (Aronson et al. 1994; Lee et al. 2000). The core model contains five variables and is described by Equations (10.1). When the effect of light is incorporated—as was done for the PER-TIM model discussed in Section 2.2—this model accounts for the occurrence of sustained oscillations in continuous darkness, phase shifting by light pulses, and entrainment by light/dark cycles. The model shown in Figure 10.1a will thus serve as a convenient core model for testing the effect of molecular noise on circadian oscillations. An even simpler model (governed by a set of three kinetic equations) is obtained when disregarding multiple phosphorylation of the clock protein (Leloup et al. 1999; Gonze et al. 2000). The following discussion pertains to the five-variable model, which includes PER reversible phosphorylation.

3.2 Molecular noise in the fully developed stochastic version of the core model

The decrease in the total number (N) of molecules in a system of chemical reactions is accompanied by a rise in the amplitude of fluctuations around the state predicted by the deterministic evolution of this chemical system. These fluctuations, which reflect intrinsic molecular noise, can be taken into account by describing the chemical reaction system as a birth-and-death stochastic process governed by a master equation (Nicolis and Prigogine 1977). In a given reaction step, molecules of participating species are either produced (birth) or consumed (death). At each step is associated a transition probability proportional to the numbers of molecules of involved chemical species and to the chemical rate constant of the corresponding deterministic model.

To implement such a master equation approach to stochastic chemical dynamics, Gillespie (1976, 1977) introduced a rigorous numerical algorithm. In addition to other approaches (Morton-Firth and Bray 1998), this method of the Monte Carlo type is widely used to determine the effect of molecular noise on the dynamics of chemical (Baras et al. 1990; Baras 1997), biochemical (McAdams and Arkin 1997), or genetic (Arkin et al. 1998) systems. The Gillespie method associates a probability with each reaction. At each time step the algorithm stochastically determines the reaction that takes place according to its probability, as well as the time interval to the next reaction. The numbers of molecules of the different reacting species as well as the probabilities are updated at each time step. In this approach (Gillespie 1976, 1977), a parameter denoted Ω permits the modulation of the number of molecules present in the system.

To assess the effect of molecular noise on circadian oscillations, we have used the Gillespie method to perform stochastic simulations of the core deterministic model governed by Equations (10.1). When the degree of cooperativity of repression—given by the Hill coefficient n in Equations (10.1)—is equal to 4, the core mechanism can be decomposed in 30 elementary steps, as indicated in Table 10.1. A probability of occurrence, proportional to the deterministic rate constant, is associated with each of these individual steps. This approach rests on the analysis of a fully developed stochastic version of the core model for circadian oscillations. In the following we will show that an alternative (more compact) approach—in which the nonlinear functions in Equations (10.1) are not decomposed into elementary steps—yields largely similar results.

TABLE 10.1 Decomposition of the deterministic model into elementary reaction steps.

Reaction number	Reaction step	Probability of reaction
1	$G + P_N \xrightarrow{a_1} GP_N$	$w_1 = a_1 \times G \times P_N/\Omega$
2	$GP_N \xrightarrow{d_1} G + P_N$	$w_2 = d_1 \times GP_N$
3	$GP_N + P_N \xrightarrow{a_2} GP_{N2}$	$w_3 = a_2 \times GP_N \times P_N/\Omega$
4	$GP_{N2} \xrightarrow{d_2} GP_N + P_N$	$w_4 = d_2 \times GP_{N2}$
5	$GP_{N2} + P_N \xrightarrow{a_3} GP_{N3}$	$w_5 = a_3 \times GP_{N2} \times P_N/\Omega$
6	$GP_{N3} + \xrightarrow{d_3} GP_{N2} + P_N$	$w_6 = d_3 \times GP_{N3}$
7	$GP_{N3} + P_N \xrightarrow{a_4} GP_{N4}$	$w_7 = a_4 \times GP_{N3} \times P_N/\Omega$
8	$GP_{N4} + \xrightarrow{d_4} GP_{N3} + P_N$	$w_8 = d_4 \times GP_{N4}$
9	$[G, GP_N, GP_{N2}, GP_{N3}] \xrightarrow{V_s} M$	$w_9 = v_s \times (G + GP_N + GP_{N2} + GP_{N3})$
10	$M + E_m \xrightarrow{k_{m1}} C_m$	$w_{10} = k_{m1} \times M \times E_m/\Omega$
11	$C_m \xrightarrow{k_{m2}} M + E_m$	$w_{11} = k_{m2} \times C_m$
12	$C_m \xrightarrow{k_{m3}} E_m$	$w_{12} = k_{m3} \times C_m$
13	$M \xrightarrow{k_s} M + P_0$	$w_{13} = k_s \times M$

Continued

TABLE 10.1 Decomposition of the deterministic model into elementary reaction steps.

Reaction number	Reaction step	Probability of reaction
14	$P_0 + E_1 \xrightarrow{k_{11}} C_1$	$w_{14} = k_{11} \times P_0 \times E_1/\Omega$
15	$C_1 \xrightarrow{k_{12}} P_0 + E_1$	$w_{15} = k_{12} \times C_1$
16	$C_1 \xrightarrow{k_{13}} P_1 + E_1$	$w_{16} = k_{13} \times C_1$
17	$P_1 + E_2 \xrightarrow{k_{21}} C_2$	$w_{17} = k_{21} \times P_1 \times E_2/\Omega$
18	$C_2 \xrightarrow{k_{22}} P_1 + E_2$	$w_{18} = k_{22} \times C_2$
19	$C_2 \xrightarrow{k_{23}} P_0 + E_2$	$w_{19} = k_{23} \times C_2$
20	$P_1 + E_3 \xrightarrow{k_{31}} C_3$	$w_{20} = k_{31} \times P_1 \times E_3/\Omega$
21	$C_3 \xrightarrow{k_{32}} P_1 + E_3$	$w_{21} = k_{32} \times C_3$
22	$C_3 \xrightarrow{k_{33}} P_2 + E_3$	$w_{22} = k_{33} \times C_3$
23	$P_2 + E_4 \xrightarrow{k_{41}} C_4$	$w_{23} = k_{41} \times P_2 \times E_4/\Omega$
24	$C_4 \xrightarrow{k_{42}} P_2 + E_4$	$w_{24} = k_{42} \times C_4$
25	$C_4 \xrightarrow{k_{43}} P_1 + E_4$	$w_{25} = k_{43} \times C_4$
26	$P_2 + E_d \xrightarrow{k_{d1}} C_d$	$w_{26} = k_{d1} \times P_2 \times E_d/\Omega$
27	$C_d \xrightarrow{k_{d2}} P_2 + E_d$	$w_{27} = k_{d2} \times C_d$
28	$C_d \xrightarrow{k_{d3}} E_d$	$w_{28} = k_{d3} \times C_d$
29	$P_2 \xrightarrow{k_1} P_N$	$w_{29} = k_1 \times P_2$
30	$P_N \xrightarrow{k_2} P_2$	$w_{30} = k_2 \times P_N$

3.3 Robustness of circadian oscillations with respect to molecular noise

The first result obtained with the fully developed stochastic version of the core model for circadian rhythms is that it is also capable of producing sustained oscillations in conditions of continuous darkness. These oscillations correspond to the evolution toward a limit cycle, which is shown in the right-hand panels of Figure 10.7b as a projection onto the (M, P_N) plane. For comparison, the deterministic oscillations and the corresponding limit cycle are shown in Figure 10.7a. The effect of molecular noise is merely to induce variability in the maxima of the oscillations. This is reflected by the noisy appearance of the limit cycle and a thickening of its upper portion linking the maximum in mRNA with the maximum in nuclear (or total) clock protein. The noisy stochastic limit cycle surrounds the deterministic limit cycle (shown as the closed white curve in the lower right-hand panel in Figure 10.7b) obtained by numerical integration of Equations (10.1) in corresponding conditions (Gonze et al. 2002a, 2002b).

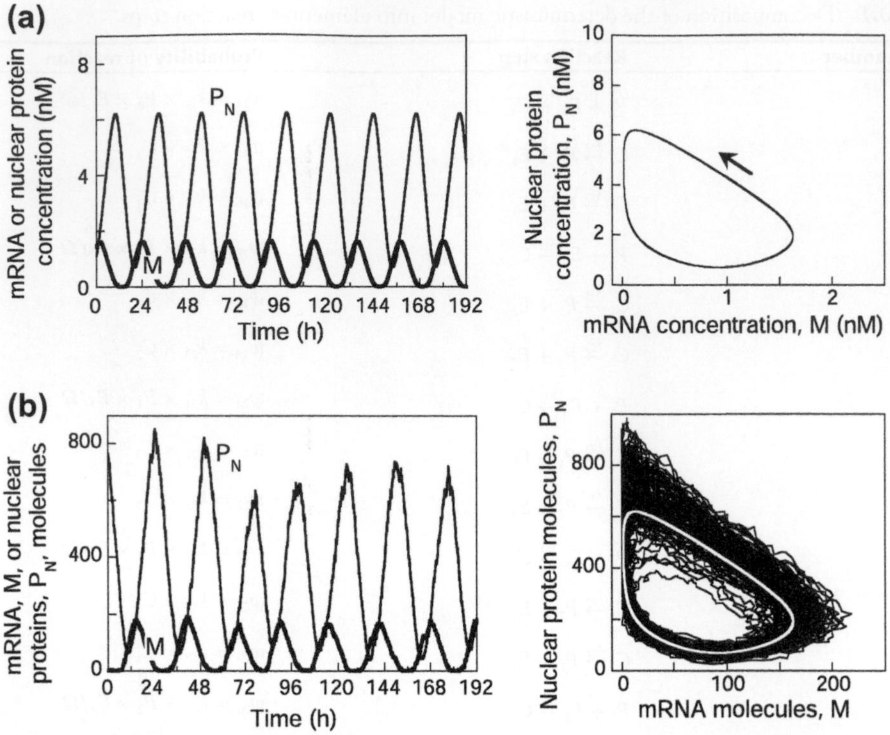

FIGURE 10.7 Deterministic versus stochastic simulations of the core model for circadian oscillations (schematized in Figure 10.1a). (a) Oscillations obtained in the absence of noise for the deterministic model governed by Equations (10.1). Sustained oscillations of mRNA (*M*) and nuclear clock protein (P_N) in the left-hand panel correspond to the evolution toward a limit cycle shown as a projection onto the (M, P_N) plane in the right-hand panel. (b) Oscillations generated by the stochastic version of the core model in the presence of noise, for $\Omega = 100$ and $n = 4$. The data, expressed in numbers of molecules of mRNA and of nuclear clock protein, are obtained by stochastic simulations of the detailed reaction system (Table 10.1) corresponding to the deterministic version of the core model. In the lower right-hand panel, the white curve corresponds to the deterministic limit cycle. The latter is surrounded by the stochastic trajectory which takes the form of a noisy limit cycle.

To assess the robustness of circadian oscillations at low numbers of molecules, we performed stochastic simulations for decreasing values of Ω. For $\Omega = 500$, the number of mRNA molecules varies in the range 0–1,000, whereas the numbers of nuclear and total clock protein molecules oscillate in the ranges 200–4,000 and 800–8,000, respectively (see left-hand panel in Figure 10.8a). The results in Figure 10.8 show that as Ω decreases progressively from the value of 500 down to a value of 100 or 50 robust circadian oscillations continue to occur in continuous darkness. The number of mRNA molecules oscillates from 0 to 200 or 0 to 120, whereas the number of nuclear clock protein molecules oscillates in the range 20–800 or 10–600. For these smaller values of Ω, the limit cycles are more noisy but the period histograms calculated for some 1,200 successive cycles indicate that the distribution remains narrow with a mean free running period μ close to a circadian value. The standard deviation σ remains small with respect to the mean period but slightly increases as the number of molecules diminishes.

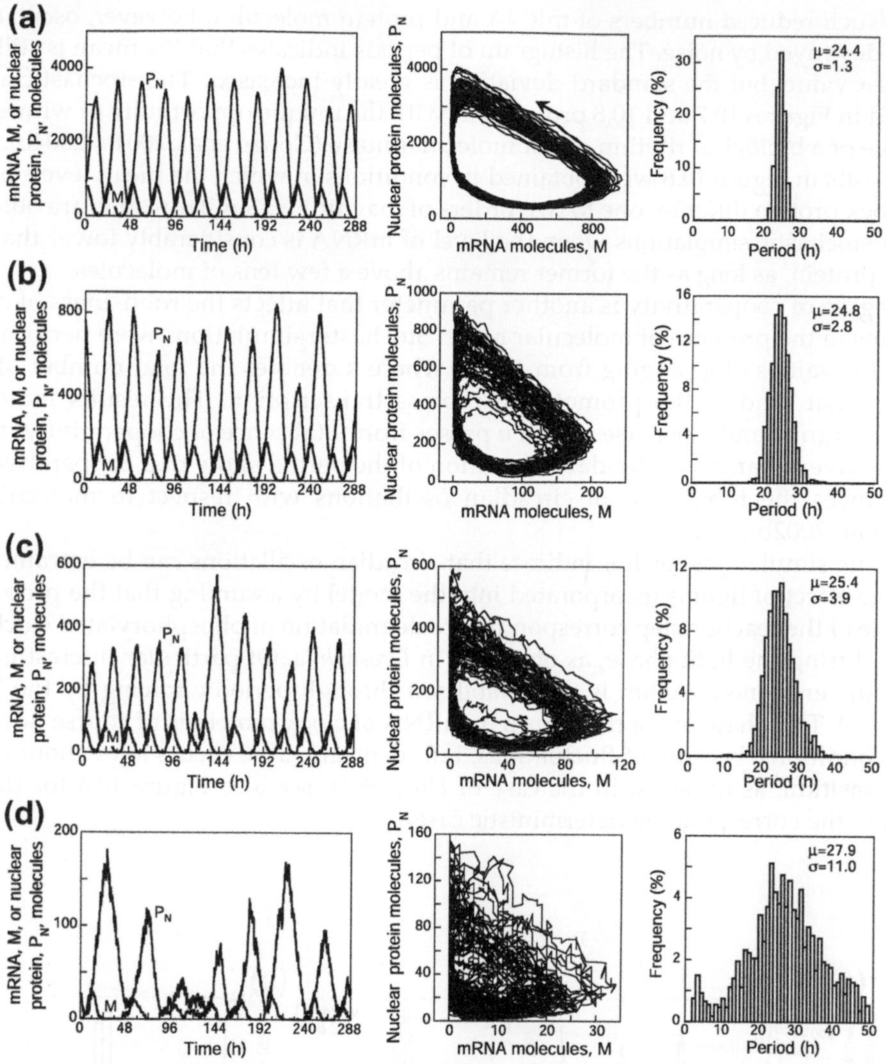

FIGURE 10.8 Effect of number of molecules on the robustness of circadian oscillations. Shown in rows a through d are the oscillations in the numbers of molecules of mRNA and nuclear clock protein, the projection of the corresponding limit cycle, and the histogram of periods of 1,200 successive cycles, for Ω varying from 500 (a), to 100 (b), 50 (c), and 10 (d). The curves are obtained by stochastic simulations of the core model (Table 10.1), for $n = 4$ (other parameters are listed in Table 10.2 where "mol" stands for "molecule"). For period histograms, the period was determined as the time interval separating two successive upward crossings of the mean level of mRNA or clock protein. In b and c, the decrease in the numbers of mRNA and protein molecules still permits robust circadian oscillations (see histograms where the mean value (μ) and standard deviation (σ) of the period are indicated in h), whereas at still lower numbers of molecules (d) noise begins to obliterate rhythmic behavior (Gonze et al. 2002b).

A further decrease in the number of molecules (e.g. down to $\Omega = 10$) will eventually obliterate circadian rhythmicity, and the latter is overcome by noise (Figure 10.8d). At such a low value of Ω, highly irregular oscillations occur, during which the number of mRNA molecules varies from 0 to 30 and the number of nuclear protein molecules oscillates in the range 5–160.

Even for such reduced numbers of mRNA and protein molecules, however, oscillations are not fully destroyed by noise. The histogram of periods indicates that the mean is still close to a circadian value, but the standard deviation is greatly increased. The stochastic approach illustrated in Figures 10.7 and 10.8 provides us with the unique opportunity of witnessing the emergence of a biological rhythm out of molecular noise (Gonze et al. 2004a, 2004b).

The results in Figure 10.8 were obtained in conditions in which the mean levels of mRNA and of clock protein differ by one to two orders of magnitude. Similar results are obtained by means of stochastic simulations when the level of mRNA is considerably lower than that of the clock protein, as long as the former remains above a few tens of molecules.

The degree of cooperativity is another parameter that affects the robustness of circadian oscillations in the presence of molecular noise. Stochastic simulations were performed with $\Omega = 100$ for values of n ranging from 1 to 4, where n denotes the total number of protein molecules that bind to the promoter to repress transcription. The results indicate that robustness significantly increases when n passes from 1 (absence of cooperativity) to values of 2 and above. Changes in standard deviation of the period show that cooperative repression enhances the robustness of circadian oscillations with respect to molecular noise (Gonze et al. 2002b).

Stochastic simulations further indicate that circadian oscillations can be entrained by LD cycles. The effect of light is incorporated into the model by assuming that the probability of occurrence of the reaction step corresponding to degradation of phosphorylated clock protein increases during the light phase, as observed in *Drosophila*. Of particular interest is that the phase of the entrained rhythm is then stabilized through periodic forcing by the LD cycle (Figure 10.9). The phase of the maximum in mRNA of clock protein is of course not constant in these conditions, because of fluctuations, but its mean value occurs a few hours after the L-to-D transition, as observed in the case of *Drosophila* (see also Figure 10.4 for the results obtained in the corresponding deterministic case).

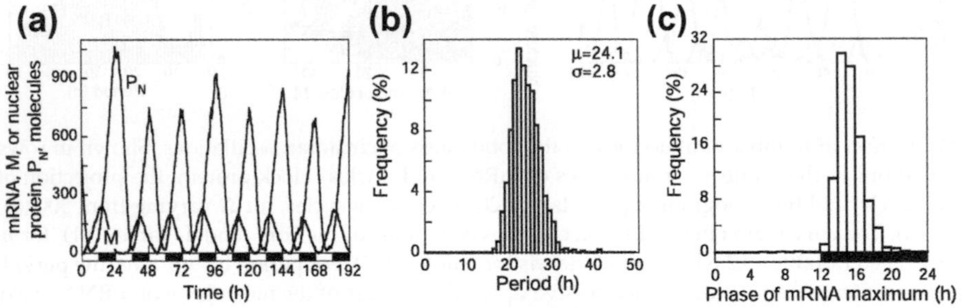

FIGURE 10.9 Effect of molecular noise on circadian oscillations under conditions of periodic forcing by a light/dark cycle. The data are obtained for $\Omega = 100$ and $n = 4$. (a) Circadian oscillations in the numbers of mRNA and nuclear clock protein molecules. (b) Histogram of periods with mean value (μ) and standard deviation (σ) indicated in h. (c) Histogram of the time corresponding to the maximum number of mRNA molecules over a period. Periodic forcing is achieved by doubling during each light phase the value ascribed during the dark phase to the parameter (k_{d3}) measuring the probability of the protein degradation step (Table 10.1). Histograms are determined for some 1,200 successive cycles (Gonze et al. 2002b).

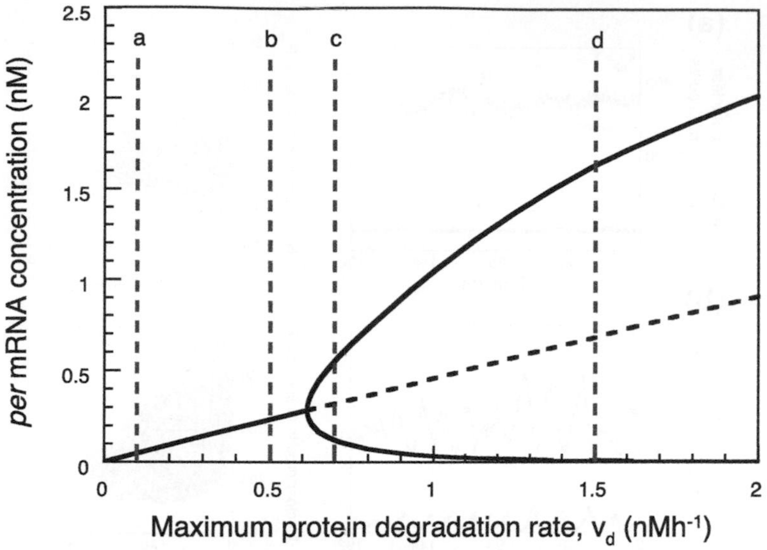

FIGURE 10.10 Bifurcation diagram showing the onset of sustained oscillations in the deterministic core model for circadian rhythms, as a function of parameter v_d (which measures the maximum rate of protein degradation). The curve shows the steady-state level of *per* mRNA, stable (solid line), or unstable (dashed line), as well as the maximum and minimum concentration of *per* mRNA in the course of sustained circadian oscillations. The diagram is established by means of the program AUTO (Doedel 1981) applied to Equations (10.1). Parameter values are given in Table 10.2 (Gonze et al. 2002a).

Additional factors influence the robustness of circadian oscillations with respect to molecular noise. Among these are the distance from a bifurcation point, and the magnitude of the rate constants characterizing binding of the repressor to the gene. To illustrate the first aspect, it is useful to consider the bifurcation diagram showing the onset of sustained oscillations as a function of a control parameter such as the maximum rate of clock protein degradation, v_d (Figure 10.10). This diagram, obtained for the core deterministic model of Figure 10.1a governed by Equations (10.1), shows that as v_d is progressively increased from a low initial value the system at first settles in a stable non-oscillatory state before sustained oscillations of the limit cycle type arise when v_d exceeds a critical value. The amplitude of the oscillations progressively increases as the value of v_d moves away from this bifurcation point. We now select four increasing values of v_d located well below (a) or just below (b) the bifurcation value, and just above (c) or well beyond (d) it. Stochastic simulations performed for a given value of Ω with the fully developed version of the core model indicate (Figure 10.11) that circadian oscillations become less sensitive to molecular noise as the system moves away from the bifurcation point, well into the domain of periodic behavior.

Finally, among the kinetic parameters that govern the probability of occurrence of the various individual steps listed in Table 10.1 few have as much influence on the robustness of circadian oscillations as the rate constants characterizing the successive binding of repressor molecules to the gene promoter of the clock protein. In the case of cooperative binding of four repressor molecules, we have to consider four successive steps of association and dissociation

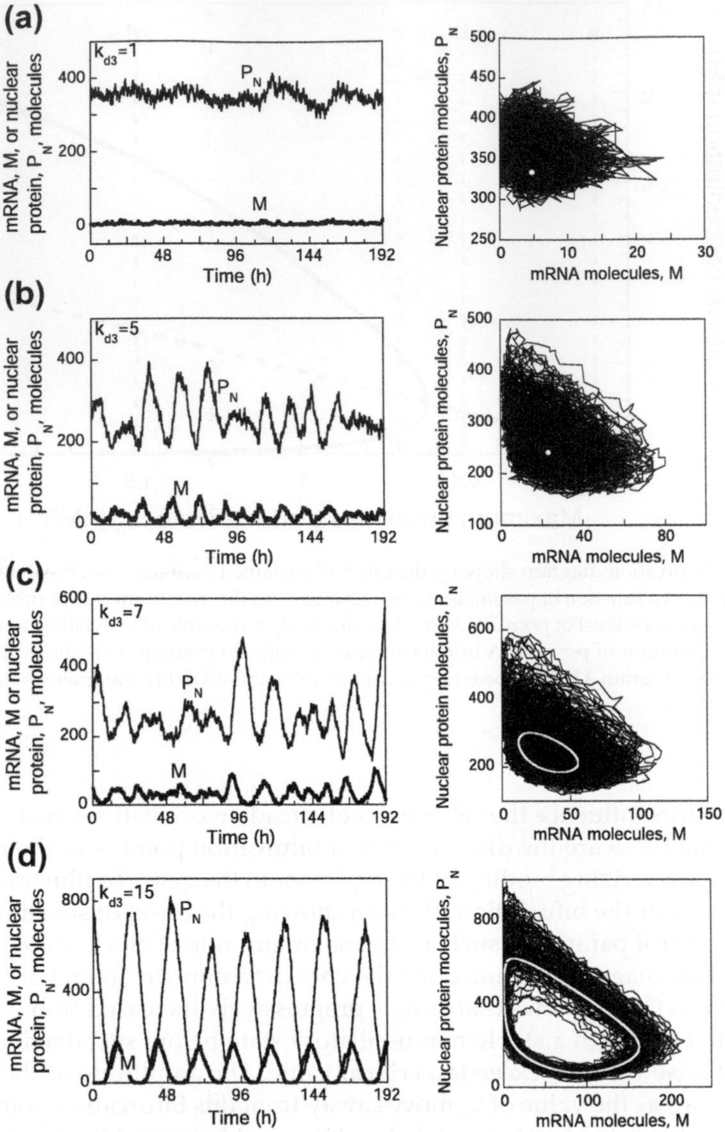

FIGURE 10.11 Effect of the proximity from a bifurcation point on the effect of molecular noise in the stochastic model for circadian rhythms. The different panels are established for the four increasing values of parameter k_{d3} corresponding to the v_d values shown in Figure 10.10: 0.1 (a), 0.5 (b), 0.7 (c), and 1.5 (d). The values of k_{d3} listed in the left panels, are expressed here in molecules per h. The right-hand panels show the evolution in the phase plane, whereas the left-hand panels represent the corresponding temporal evolution of the number of *per* mRNA and nuclear PER molecules. (a) Fluctuations around a stable steady state. (b) Fluctuations around a stable steady-state close to the bifurcation point. Damped oscillations occur in these conditions when the system is displaced from the stable steady state. In a and b, the white dot in the right-hand panel represents the stable steady-state predicted by the deterministic version of the model in corresponding conditions. (c) Oscillations observed close to the bifurcation point. (d) Oscillations observed further from the bifurcation point, well into the domain of sustained oscillations. In c and d, the thick white curve in the right-hand panel represents the limit cycle predicted by the deterministic version of the model governed by Equations (10.1), in corresponding conditions. The smaller amplitude of the limit cycle in c as compared to the limit cycle in d is associated with an increased influence of molecular noise. The curves are obtained by means of the Gillespie algorithm applied to the model of Table 10.1 (Gonze et al. 2002a).

characterized by the rate constants a_i and d_i (i = 1, ... 4) (see steps 1 through 8 in Table 10.1). It will be useful to divide these rate constants by a scaling parameter γ to assess their influence on the robustness of circadian rhythms with respect to molecular noise. An increase in γ will thus correspond to a decrease in the rate constants a_i and d_i.

In Figure 10.12 are shown the results of stochastic simulations of the core model for $\gamma = 1$ (a), $\gamma = 100$ (b), and $\gamma = 1{,}000$ (c). As γ increases up to 100 and 1,000, oscillations with larger and larger amplitude and increasing variability of the period are observed. The oscillations obtained for $\gamma = 1$ are much more regular. To clarify the nature of this phenomenon, we

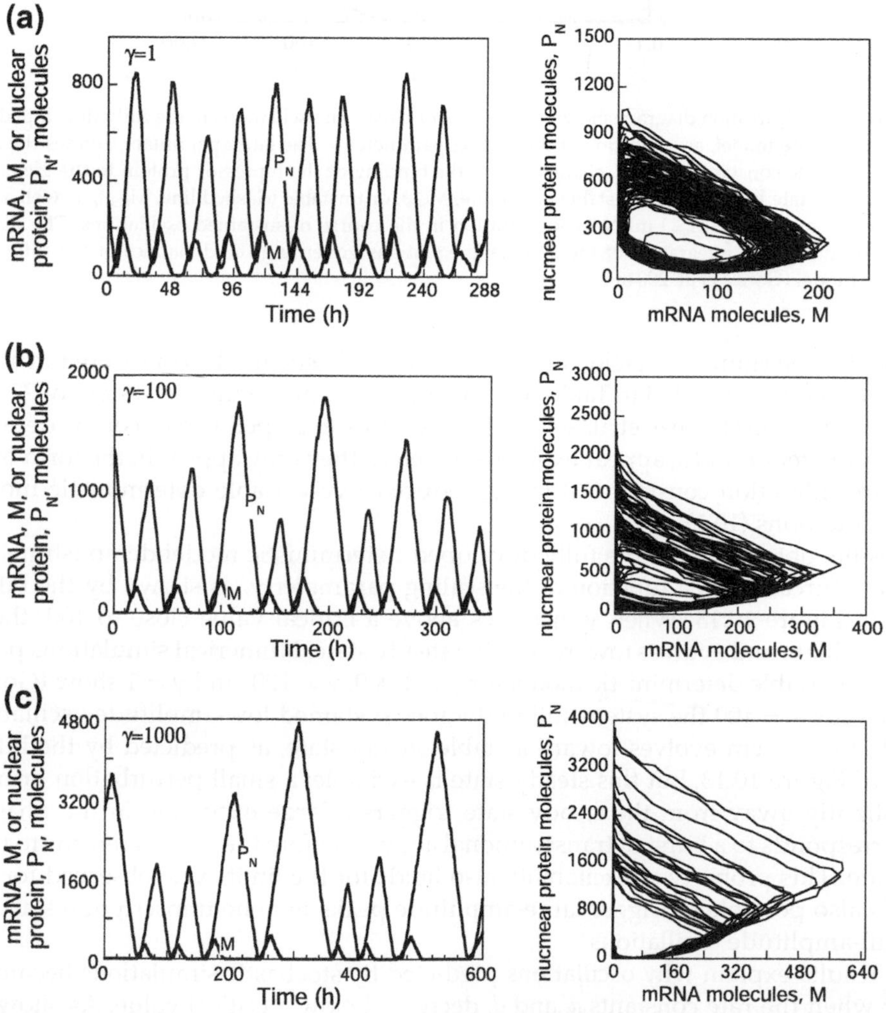

FIGURE 10.12 Irregular time series and trajectory in the phase space obtained by stochastic simulations of the core model for circadian rhythms for $\gamma = 1$ (a), $\gamma = 100$ (b), and $\gamma = 1{,}000$ (c). The curves were obtained for the model of Table 10.1, with $\Omega = 100$. Other parameter values are given in Table 10.2. The results should be compared with the bifurcation diagram established in Figure 10.13 as a function of γ for the corresponding fully developed version of the deterministic model. This diagram predicts that the steady state is stable and excitable for $\gamma = 100$ and 1,000, whereas sustained oscillations occur for $\gamma = 1$ when the steady state is unstable (Gonze et al. 2004a).

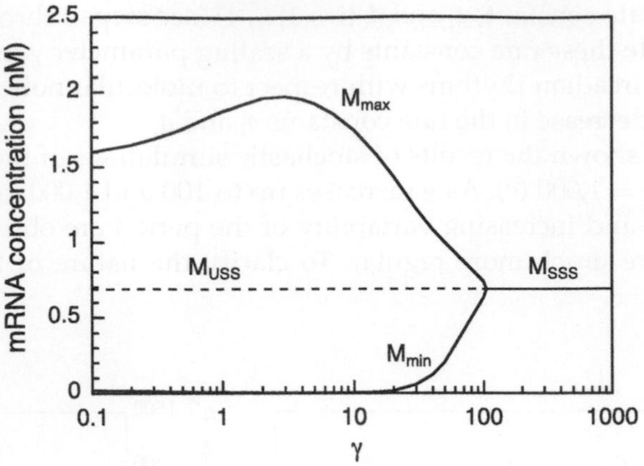

FIGURE 10.13 Bifurcation diagram showing the onset of circadian oscillations in the fully developed version of the deterministic core model, as a function of the scaling parameter γ. The latter parameter divides the association and dissociation rate constants a_i and d_i characterizing the binding of the repressor protein to the gene. The curve shows the steady-state level of mRNA, stable (solid line, M_{SSS}), or unstable (dashed line, M_{USS}), as well as the maximum (M_{max}) and minimum (M_{min}) mRNA concentration in the course of sustained oscillations. The diagram was determined by numerical integration of the 22 kinetic equations governing the dynamics of the fully developed deterministic model (Gonze et al. 2004a).

examined the deterministic version of the detailed stochastic model considered in Table 10.1. To the 30 reaction steps listed in Table 10.1 corresponds a deterministic system of 22 ordinary differential equations (Gonze et al. 2004a). In this fully developed version of the deterministic model, parameters a_i and d_i appear explicitly, whereas they only appear in the form of a single equilibrium inhibition constant (K_I) in the reduced five-variable deterministic model governed by Equations (10.1).

The results obtained with the fully developed deterministic model demonstrate the existence of a bifurcation as a function of the scaling parameter γ, as shown by the bifurcation diagram in Figure 10.13. When γ increases above a critical value close to 100, the system ceases to oscillate and evolves toward a stable steady state. Numerical simulations performed with the 22-variable deterministic model for $\gamma = 1{,}000$, $\gamma = 100$, and $\gamma = 1$ show (Gonze et al. 2004a) that for $\gamma = 100$ the system still undergoes sustained low-amplitude oscillations. For $\gamma = 1{,}000$, the system evolves toward a stable steady state, as predicted by the bifurcation diagram of Figure 10.13, but this steady state is excitable: a small perturbation bringing the system slightly away from the steady state triggers a large excursion in the phase space, which corresponds to a burst of transcriptional activity, before the system returns to the stable steady state. This property of excitability also holds for the limit cycle observed for $\gamma = 100$. Thus, it is also possible to trigger large-amplitude peaks in gene transcription starting from such small-amplitude oscillations.

These results explain why oscillations predicted by stochastic simulations become highly irregular when the rate constants a_i and d_i decrease below a critical value. As shown by the study of the corresponding detailed deterministic model, such irregular oscillations reflect repetitive noise-induced large excursions away from a stable excitable steady state or from a small-amplitude limit cycle close to the bifurcation point. The values of the bimolecular rate constants a_i used by Barkai and Leibler (2000) for simulating the circadian models of Figure 10.1a and b were probably below the critical value corresponding to sustained oscillations, which may explain their failure to obtain robust circadian oscillations in these models. When γ decreases (i.e. when the values of parameters a_i and d_i increase)— as in the case considered in Figure 10.8, which corresponds to $\gamma = 1$—the oscillations become more regular and more robust, because the system operates well into the domain of sustained large-amplitude oscillations. The high values of parameters a_i and d_i corresponding to $\gamma = 1$ are of the order of those determined experimentally (Gonze et al. 2002b). Similar results showing that the oscillations become more robust when the rates of binding and unbinding to DNA increase were obtained by Forger and Peskin (2005) in stochastic simulations of a model for the mammalian circadian clock.

TABLE 10.2 Parameter values for stochastic simulations.

Reaction steps	Parameter values
Steps 1–8	For $n = 4$: $a_1 = \Omega$ mol^{-1} h^{-1}, $d_1 = (160 \times \Omega)$ h^{-1}, $a_2 = (10 \times \Omega)$ mol^{-1} h^{-1}, $d_2 = (100 \times \Omega)$ h^{-1}, $a_3 = (100 \times \Omega)$ mol^{-1} h^{-1}, $d_3 = (10 \times \Omega)$ h^{-1}, $a_4 = (100 \times \Omega)$ mol^{-1} h^{-1}, $d_4 = (10 \times \Omega)$ h^{-1} For $n = 3$: $a_1 = \Omega$ mol^{-1} h^{-1}, $d_1 = (80 \times \Omega)$ h^{-1}, $a_2 = (100 \times \Omega)$ mol^{-1} h^{-1}, $d_2 = (100 \times \Omega)$ h^{-1}, $a_3 = (100 \times \Omega)$ mol^{-1} h^{-1}, $d_3 = \Omega$ h^{-1} For $n = 2$: $a_1 = \Omega$ mol^{-1} h^{-1}, $d_1 = (40 \times \Omega)$ h^{-1}, $a_2 = (100 \times \Omega)$ mol^{-1} h^{-1}, $d_2 = (10 \times \Omega)$ h^{1} For $n = 1$: $a_1 = (10 \times \Omega)$ mol^{-1} h^{-1}, $d_1 = (20 \times \Omega)$ h^{-1}
Step 9	$V_s = (0.5 \times \Omega)$ mol h^{-1}
Steps 10–12	$k_{m1} = 165$ mol^{-1} h^{-1}, $k_{m2} = 30$ h^{-1}, $k_{m3} = 3$ h^{-1}, $E_{m\,tot} = E_m + C_m = (0.1 \times \Omega)$ mol
Steps 13	$k_s = 2.0$ h^{-1}
Steps 14–16	$k_{11} = 146.6$ mol^{-1} h^{-1}, $k_{12} = 200$ h^{-1}, $k_{13} = 20$ h^{-1}, $E_{1\,tot} = E_1 + C_1 = (0.3 \times \Omega)$ mol
Steps 17–19	$k_{21} = 82.5$ mol^{-1} h^{-1}, $k_{22} = 150$ h^{-1}, $k_{23} = 15$ h^{-1}, $E_{2\,tot} = E_2 + C_2 = (0.2 \times \Omega)$ mol
Steps 20–22	$k_{31} = 146.6$ mol^{-1} h^{-1}, $k_{32} = 200$ h^{-1}, $k_{33} = 20$ h^{-1}, $E_{3\,tot} = E_3 + C_3 = (0.3 \times \Omega)$ mol
Steps 23–25	$k_{41} = 82.5$ mol^{-1} h^{-1}, $k_{42} = 150$ h^{-1}, $k_{43} = 15$ h^{-1}, $E_{4\,tot} = E_4 + C_4 = (0.2 \times \Omega)$ mol
Steps 26–28	$k_{d1} = 1650$ mol^{-1} h^{-1}, $k_{d2} = 150$ h^{-1}, $k_{d3} = 15$ h^{-1}, $E_{d\,tot} = E_d + C_d = (0.1 \times \Omega)$ mol
Steps 29–30	$k_1 = 2.0$ h^{-1}, $k_2 = 1.0$ h^{-1}

3.4 Non-developed stochastic models for circadian rhythms

The nonlinear terms appearing in the kinetic Equations (10.1) of the deterministic core model do not correspond to single reaction steps. These terms rather represent compact kinetic expressions obtained after application of quasi-steady-state hypotheses on enzyme-substrate or gene-repressor complexes. The resulting expressions are of the Michaelis-Menten type for enzyme reaction rates, or of the Hill type for cooperative binding of the repressor to the gene promoter. In the fully developed stochastic version of the core model, all reactions were decomposed into elementary steps (see Table 10.1).

Alternatively, we may resort to a simpler approach in which we attribute to each linear or nonlinear term of the kinetic equations a probability of occurrence of the corresponding reaction step (Gonze et al. 2002a). Then, in contrast to the treatment presented previously for the fully developed stochastic version we do not decompose the binding of the repressor P_N to the gene promoter into successive elementary steps, and rather retain the Hill function description for cooperative repression. A similar approach is taken for describing degradation of

TABLE 10.3 Non-developed stochastic version of the PER-TIM model for circadian rhythms [Gonze et al. 2003].

Reaction number	Reaction step	Probability of reaction
1	$\xrightarrow{V_{sP}} Mp$	$w_1 = (V_{sP} \times \Omega)\frac{(K_{IP}\times\Omega)^n}{(K_{IP}\times\Omega)^n + C_N^n}$
2	$M_p \xrightarrow{V_{mP}}$	$w_2 = (V_{mP} \times \Omega)\frac{M_p}{(K_{mP}\times\Omega)+M_p}$
3	$M_p \xrightarrow{k_{sP}} M_p + P_0$	$w_3 = k_{sP} \times M_p$
4	$P_0 \xrightarrow{V_{1P}} P_1$	$w_4 = (V_{1P} \times \Omega)\frac{P_0}{(K_{1P}\times\Omega)+P_0}$
5	$P_1 \xrightarrow{V_{2P}} P_0$	$w_5 = (V_{2P} \times \Omega)\frac{P_1}{(K_{2P}\times\Omega)+P_1}$
6	$P_1 \xrightarrow{V_{3P}} P_2$	$w_6 = (V_{3P} \times \Omega)\frac{P_1}{(K_{3P}\times\Omega)+P_1}$
7	$P_2 \xrightarrow{V_{4P}} P_1$	$w_7 = (V_{4P} \times \Omega)\frac{P_2}{(K_{4P}\times\Omega)+P_2}$
8	$P_2 + T_2 \xrightarrow{k_3} C$	$w_8 = k_3 \times P_2 \times T_2/\Omega$
9	$C \xrightarrow{k_4} P_2 + T_2$	$w_9 = k_4 \times C$
10	$P_2 \xrightarrow{V_{dP}}$	$w_{10} = (V_{dP} \times \Omega)\frac{P_2}{(K_{dP}\times\Omega)+P_2}$
11	$\xrightarrow{V_{sT}} M_T$	$w_{11} = (V_{sT} \times \Omega)\frac{(K_{IT}\times\Omega)^n}{(K_{IT}\times\Omega)^n + C_N^n}$
12	$M_T \xrightarrow{V_{mT}}$	$w_{12} = (V_{mT} \times \Omega)\frac{M_T}{(K_{mT}\times\Omega)+M_T}$
13	$M_T \xrightarrow{k_{sT}} M_T + T_0$	$w_{13} = k_{sT} \times M_T$
14	$T_0 \xrightarrow{V_{1T}} T_1$	$w_{14} = (V_{1T} \times \Omega)\frac{T_0}{(K_{1T}\times\Omega)+T_0}$
15	$T_1 \xrightarrow{V_{2T}} T_0$	$w_{15} = (V_{2T} \times \Omega)\frac{T_1}{(K_{2T}\times\Omega)+T_1}$
16	$T_1 \xrightarrow{V_{3T}} T_2$	$w_{16} = (V_{3T} \times \Omega)\frac{T_1}{(K_{3T}\times\Omega)+T_1}$
17	$T_2 \xrightarrow{V_{4T}} T_1$	$w_{17} = (V_{4T} \times \Omega)\frac{T_2}{(K_{4T}\times\Omega)+T_2}$

Continued

TABLE 10.3 Non-developed stochastic version of the PER-TIM model for circadian rhythms [Gonze et al. 2003].

Reaction number	Reaction step	Probability of reaction
18	$T_2 \xrightarrow{V_{dT}}$	$w_{18} = (V_{dT} \times \Omega)\frac{T_2}{(K_{dT} \times \Omega) + T_2}$
19	$C \xrightarrow{k_1} C_N$	$w_{19} = k_1 \times C$
20	$C_N \xrightarrow{k_2} C$	$w_{20} = k_2 \times C_N$
21	$M_p \xrightarrow{k_d}$	$w_{21} = k_d \times M_p$
22	$P_0 \xrightarrow{k_d}$	$w_{22} = k_d \times P_0$
23	$P_1 \xrightarrow{k_d}$	$w_{23} = k_d \times P_1$
24	$P_2 \xrightarrow{k_d}$	$w_{24} = k_d \times P_2$
25	$M_T \xrightarrow{k_d}$	$w_{25} = k_d \times M_T$
26	$T_0 \xrightarrow{k_d}$	$w_{26} = k_d \times T_0$
27	$T_1 \xrightarrow{k_d}$	$w_{27} = k_d \times T_1$
28	$T_2 \xrightarrow{k_d}$	$w_{28} = k_d \times T_2$
29	$C \xrightarrow{k_{dC}}$	$w_{29} = k_{dC} \times C$
30	$C_N \xrightarrow{k_{dN}}$	$w_{30} = k_{dN} \times C_N$

mRNA, translation of mRNA into protein, phosphorylation, or dephosphorylation reactions, and enzymatic degradation of fully phosphorylated clock protein and its reversible transport into and out of the nucleus. Some of these steps are of the Michaelian type, whereas others correspond to linear kinetics.

The comparison of stochastic simulations performed with the fully developed and non-developed versions of the core model showed that the two versions yield largely similar results (Gonze et al. 2002a). On the basis of these findings, a non-developed stochastic version of the ten-variable deterministic model governed by Equations (10.2), incorporating the formation of the PER-TIM complex, was considered. This version corresponds to a set of 30 reaction steps (listed in Table 10.3). Stochastic simulations show how sustained oscillations occur in this model under conditions corresponding to continuous darkness. As for the core model considered previously, the robustness of the oscillations is enhanced when the number of protein and mRNA molecules increases.

A conspicuous property of the ten-variable deterministic PER-TIM model for circadian rhythms in *Drosophila* is that it can produce autonomous chaotic behavior in a restricted domain in parameter space (see Section 2.3). It was therefore interesting to check whether stochastic simulations were capable of reproducing this mode of dynamic behavior, which corresponds to the evolution to a strange attractor in the phase space. As shown in Figure 10.14, the strange attractor obtained by numerical integration of the deterministic Equations (10.2) can be recovered in corresponding conditions by simulations of the non-developed version of the stochastic model of Table 10.3. Here again, as illustrated in Figure 10.14, the larger

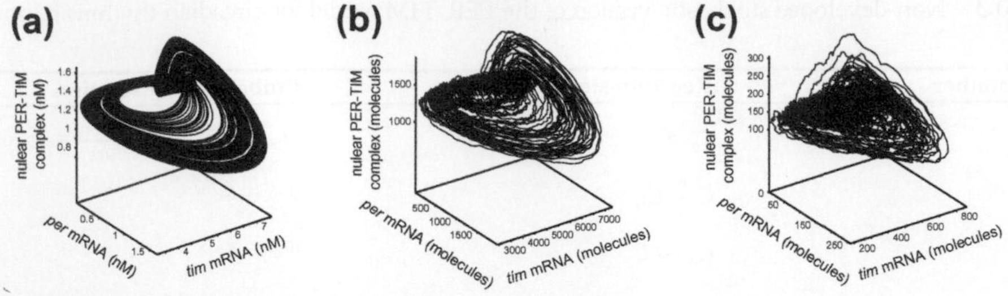

FIGURE 10.14 Effect of molecular noise on autonomous chaos. (a) Strange attractor corresponding to chaotic oscillations in the deterministic PER-TIM model for circadian rhythms. (b and c) Progressive dissolution of the strange attractor in the presence of molecular noise, for $\Omega = 1{,}000$ and 100, respectively. The curve in *a* is obtained by numerical integration of Equations (10.2). In panels b and c, the curves are obtained by means of the Gillespie algorithm applied to the non-developed stochastic version of the PER-TIM model listed in Table 10.3 (Gonze et al. 2003).

the number of molecules of mRNAs and proteins involved in the oscillatory mechanism the closer the noisy stochastic trajectory is from the deterministic chaotic attractor.

The results obtained with stochastic models help to clarify the limits of validity of deterministic models for circadian oscillations. It appears that the deterministic approach provides a faithful picture as long as the number of molecules involved in the oscillatory mechanism exceeds a few tens or hundreds of molecules. Above this range, the larger the number of molecules the closer the stochastic trajectory from that predicted by the deterministic model.

4 MODELING THE MAMMALIAN CIRCADIAN CLOCK

The molecular mechanism of circadian rhythms in mammals resembles that brought to light for *Drosophila*. In this organism, the negative feedback exerted by the PER-TIM complex is of an indirect rather than direct nature (Glossop et al. 1999). Thus, the transcription of the *per* and *tim* genes is triggered by a complex formed by the activators CYC and CLOCK. Binding of the PER-TIM complex to CYC and CLOCK prevents the activation of *per* and *tim* expression (Lee et al. 1999). In mammals the situation resembles that observed in *Drosophila*, but it is the CRY protein that forms a regulatory complex with a PER protein (Shearman et al. 2000; Reppert and Weaver 2002). Several forms of these proteins exist (PER1, PER2, PER3, CRY1, and CRY2). The complex CLOCK-BMAL1, formed by the products of the *Clock* and *Bmal1* genes, activates *Per* and *Cry* transcription. As in *Drosophila*, the PER-CRY complex inhibits the expression of the *Per* and *Cry* genes in an indirect manner, by binding to the complex CLOCK-BMAL1 (Lee et al. 2001; Reppert and Weaver 2002).

The mechanism of circadian rhythms in *Drosophila* and mammals thus relies on interlocked negative and positive feedback loops. In addition to the negative regulation of gene expression described previously, indirect positive regulation is involved. In *Drosophila*, the PER-TIM complex de-represses the transcription of *Clock* by binding to CLOCK, which exerts a negative autoregulation on the expression of its gene (Bae et al. 1998) via the product of the *vri* gene (Blau and Young 1999). In mammals, likewise, *Bmal1* expression is subjected to negative autoregulation by BMAL1, via the product of the *Rev-Erbα* gene (Preitner et al. 2002). The PER-CRY complex enhances *Bmal1* expression in an indirect manner (Reppert and Weaver 2002) by binding to CLOCK-BMAL1 and thereby decreasing the transcription of the *Rev-Erbα* gene (Preitner et al. 2002).

Models based on intertwined positive and negative regulatory loops have been proposed for *Drosophila* (Smolen et al. 2001; Ueda et al. 2001) and mammals (Forger and Peskin 2003, 2005; Leloup and Goldbeter 2003, 2004; Becker-Weimann et al. 2004; Mirsky et al. 2009; Kim and Forger 2012). We shall focus here on the model proposed for the mammalian circadian clock, as it allows us to address the molecular dynamical bases of disorders of the human sleep/wake cycle associated with dysfunctions of the circadian clock.

4.1 Toward a detailed computational model for the mammalian circadian clock

The model for the mammalian circadian clock is schematized in Figure 10.15, both in a compact (A) and in a detailed manner (B). It describes the regulatory interactions between

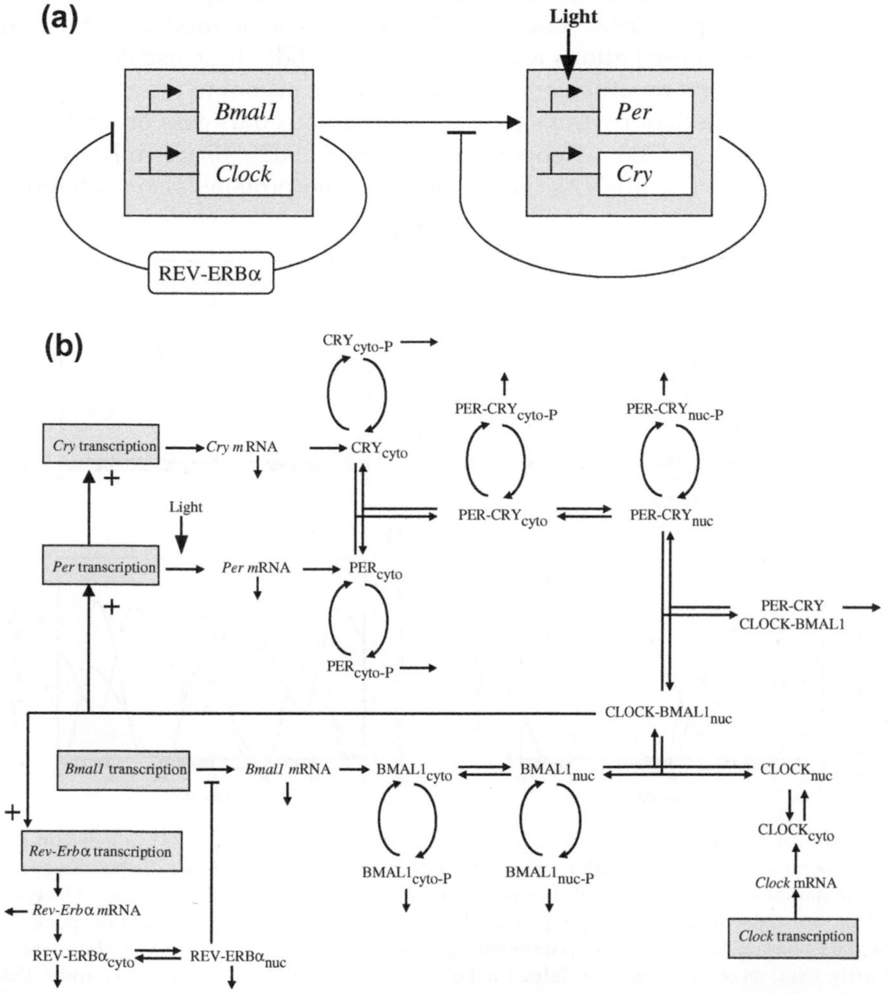

FIGURE 10.15 Model for the mammalian circadian clock involving interlocked negative and positive regulations of the *Per*, *Cry*, and *Bmal1* genes by their protein products. (a) Synthetic scheme of the model with the positive limb involving BMAL1-CLOCK and the negative limb involving PER-CRY. (b) Developed model for the mammalian clock (Leloup and Goldbeter 2003). The effect of light is to increase the rate of expression of the *Per* gene.

the products of the *Per*, *Cry*, *Bmal1*, and *Clock* genes. For simplicity, we do not distinguish between the *Per1*, *Per2*, and *Per3* genes and represent them in the model by a single *Per* gene. Similarly, *Cry1* and *Cry2* are represented by a single *Cry* gene. Moreover, as the *Clock* mRNA and its product (the CLOCK protein) are constitutively high in comparison to *Bmal1* mRNA and BMAL1 protein, they are considered in the model as parameters rather than variables.

We shall treat the regulatory effect of BMAL1 on *Bmal1* expression as a direct negative autoregulation. We have shown (Leloup and Goldbeter 2003) that similar conclusions are reached in an extended model in which the action of the REV-ERBα protein in the indirect negative feedback exerted by BMAL1 on the expression of its gene is considered explicitly. The version of the model without REV-ERBα is governed by a set of 16 kinetic equations (Leloup and Goldbeter 2003, 2004), whereas three more equations are needed in the extended model that incorporates the Rev-Erbα mRNA and the Rev-Erbα protein (Leloup and Goldbeter 2003).

In a certain range of parameter values, the 16- or 19-variable model for the mammalian clock produces sustained oscillations with a circadian period. These oscillations are endogenous, in that they occur for parameter values that remain constant in time, in agreement with the observation that circadian rhythms persist in continuous darkness or light. As observed experimentally (Lee et al. 2001; Reppert and Weaver 2002), *Bmal1* mRNA oscillates in antiphase with *Per* and *Cry* mRNAs (Figure 10.16a). The proteins also undergo antiphase

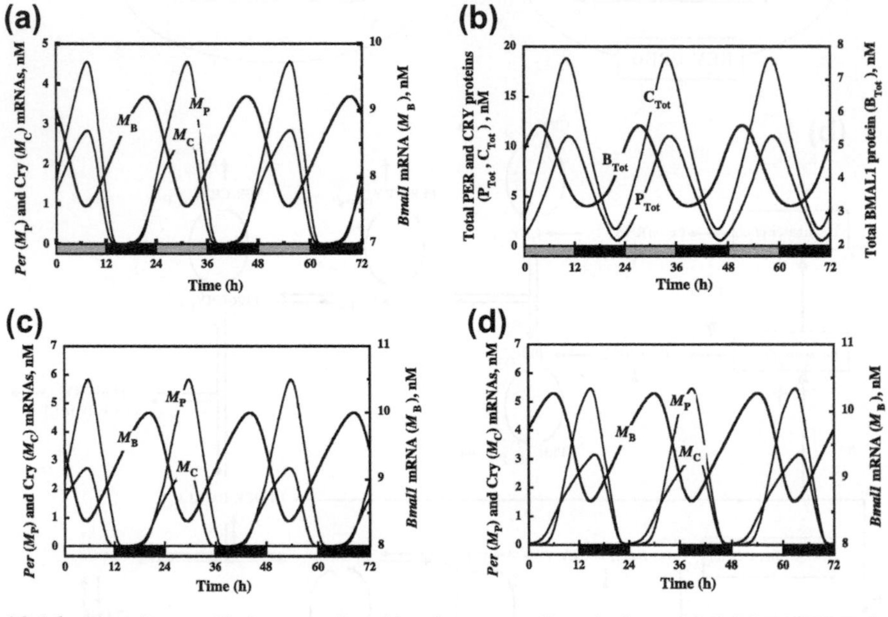

FIGURE 10.16 Circadian oscillations predicted by the mammalian clock model. (a) In constant darkness, the mRNA of *Bmal1* oscillates in antiphase with respect to the mRNAs of *Per* and *Cry*. (b) Corresponding protein oscillations in constant darkness. (c) Oscillations of the mRNAs after entrainment by 24 h light/dark (LD) cycles. The peak in *Per* mRNA occurs in the middle of the light phase. (d) Oscillations are delayed by 9 h and the peak in *Per* mRNA occurs in the dark phase when the value of parameter K_{AC} is decreased from 0.6 to 0.4 nM. Other parameter values correspond to the basal set of values listed in Table 1 in Leloup and Goldbeter (2003). In panels c and d, the maximum value of the rate of *Per* expression, v_{sP}, varies in a square-wave manner so that it remains at a constant low value of 1.5 nM h^{-1} during the 12-h-dark phase (black rectangle), and is raised up to the high value of 1.8 nM h^{-1} during the 12-h light phase (white rectangle). The curves have been obtained by numerical integration of Equations 1 through 16 of the model without REV-ERBα (listed, together with parameter values, by Leloup and Goldbeter 2003).

oscillations and follow their mRNAs by a few hours (Figure 10.16b). Because most parameter values remain to be determined experimentally—as for the case of *Drosophila* (see Figures 10.2 and 10.3)—these oscillations were obtained for a semi-arbitrary choice of parameter values in a physiological range so as to yield a period of oscillations in continuous darkness (DD) close to 24 h.

To probe for entrainment of the circadian clock by LD cycles, we must incorporate the effect of light on *Per* expression. In continuous darkness, the maximum rate of *Per* expression, v_{sP}, remains at a low constant value. In LD, this rate varies periodically (e.g. as a square wave, going from a constant low value during the dark phase up to a higher constant value v_{sPmax} during the light phase). In such conditions, entrainment by a 12:12 LD cycle (12 h of light followed by 12 h of darkness) can be obtained over an appropriate range of v_{sPmax} values (Leloup and Goldbeter 2003).

Interestingly, the phase of oscillations entrained in LD is particularly sensitive to changes in parameters that control the level of CRY protein and *Cry* mRNA. This was shown for parameter K_{AC} (the equilibrium constant describing the activating effect of CLOCK-BMAL1 on *Cry* expression) and for parameter v_{mC}, which measures the maximum rate of degradation of *Cry* mRNA. An example of such a situation is illustrated in Figure 10.16d, where the only difference with respect to Figure 10.16c is a change in parameter K_{AC}. The autonomous period in DD is 23.85 h and 23.55 h in Figure 10.16c and d, respectively, whereas the phase of *Per* mRNA is delayed by about 9 h in the latter case—so that *Per* mRNA reaches its maximum during the D phase instead of peaking in the L phase. This result is counterintuitive, in that we expect the maximum in *Per* mRNA to occur in phase L, because *Per* expression is enhanced by light. The virtue of the computational model is to alert us to the possibility that the phase of oscillations in LD may be highly labile, with the peak in *Per* mRNA shifting well into the D phase as a result of a small change in a light-insensitive parameter.

4.2 Multiple sources for oscillations in the circadian regulatory network

The genetic regulatory network underlying circadian rhythms contains intertwined positive and negative feedback loops. In view of the complexity of these regulatory interactions, it should not be a surprise that more than one mechanism in the network may give rise to sustained oscillations. Evidence pointing to the existence of a second oscillatory mechanism (Leloup and Goldbeter 2003, 2004) stems from the fact that sustained oscillations generally disappear in the absence of PER protein (Figure 10.17a). However, even in such conditions sustained oscillations may occur with a period that is not necessarily circadian (Figure 10.17b). This second oscillator is based on the negative autoregulation exerted by BMAL1 on the expression of its gene, via the *Rev-Erbα* gene (see Figure 10.15).

Experimental observations so far suggest that if a second oscillator exists in the circadian regulatory network it does not manifest itself in producing rhythmic behavior. Thus, *mPer1/mPer2* (Zheng et al. 2001) or *mCry1/mCry2* (Van der Horst et al. 1999) double-knockout mice are arrhythmic. In some conditions, however, an extended light pulse can restore rhythmic behavior in a low proportion of *mPer1/mPer2* double-knockout mice (Bae and Weaver, 2007).

In the absence of the negative feedback exerted by BMAL1 on the expression of its gene, oscillations can still originate from the PER-CRY negative feedback loop involving BMAL1. This result holds with the observation that circadian oscillations occur in the absence of REV-ERBα in mice (Preitner et al. 2002). Preventing altogether the synthesis of BMAL1 suppresses oscillations, because BMAL1 is involved in the mechanism of the two oscillators described previously.

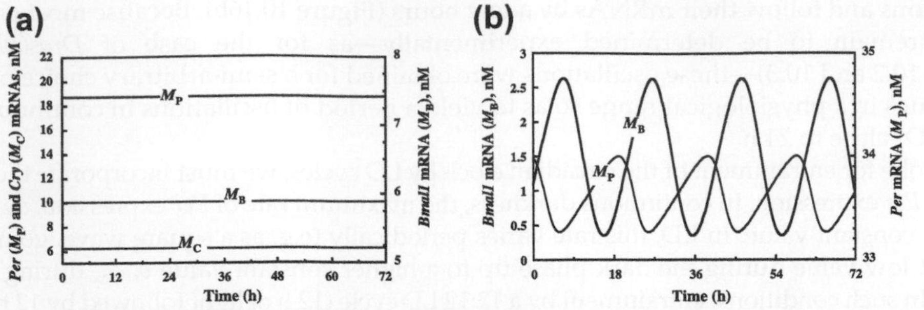

FIGURE 10.17 Multiple sources of oscillatory behavior in the genetic regulatory network controlling circadian rhythms. (a) Oscillations shown in Figure 10.16a-b disappear in the absence of PER protein synthesis ($k_{sP} = 0$). The curves show the asymptotic stable steady state reached after transients have subsided. (b) Sustained oscillations can nevertheless be restored when choosing a slightly different set of parameter values, even though $k_{sP} = 0$ (Leloup and Goldbeter 2003). The fact that oscillations can occur in the absence of PER protein indicates the existence of another oscillatory mechanism, which relies only on CLOCK-BMAL1 negative autoregulation (see scheme in Figure 10.15a).

4.3 Sensitivity analysis of the computational model for circadian rhythms

To assess the sensitivity of circadian oscillatory behavior to changes in parameter values, we determined for each parameter (one at a time) the range of values producing sustained oscillations (as well as the variation of the period over this range) while keeping the other parameters set to their basal values (Leloup and Goldbeter 2004; for an alternative sensitivity analysis, see Stelling et al. 2004). Such a sensitivity analysis was performed by constructing a series of bifurcation diagrams for four different sets of basal parameter values, each yielding circadian oscillations. Parameter set 1 was chosen so that oscillations disappear in the absence of PER protein or in the absence of negative autoregulation by BMAL1. Parameter set 2 corresponds to a situation in which oscillations can occur in the absence of PER, as a result of the negative autoregulation of BMAL1. Parameter set 3 corresponds to a situation in which circadian oscillations can occur in the absence of negative autoregulation by BMAL1. Finally, parameter set 4 was selected because oscillations can occur in the absence of PER or in the absence of negative autoregulation of BMAL1. On the basis of this analysis we may distinguish between two types of sensitivity: the first relates to the size of the oscillatory domain and the other to the influence on the period.

For some parameters the range of values producing sustained oscillations is quite narrow, less than one order of magnitude, whereas for other parameters it is much larger and extends over several orders of magnitude. The largest variation in period, by a factor close to 3, is observed for parameters that measure, respectively, the entry of the PER-CRY complex into the nucleus, and the formation of the inactive complex between PER-CRY and CLOCK-BMAL1 in the nucleus. For some sets of parameter values, the period may vary significantly (by a factor close to 2) over the oscillatory domain, whereas for other sets of parameter values the change in period as a function of this parameter may be reduced. Parameters for which the range of values yielding oscillations is narrowest are mainly those linked to BMAL1 and its mRNA. On the basis of these results, we may conclude that parameters affecting the level of BMAL1 possess the narrowest range of values producing sustained oscillations, whereas the period is most affected by the parameters measuring the entry of the PER-CRY complex into the nucleus and the formation of the inactive complex between PER-CRY and CLOCK-BMAL1.

4.4 From molecular mechanism to physiological disorders

The computational model for circadian oscillations in mammals provides us with the unique opportunity to address not only the molecular mechanism of a key biological rhythm but the dynamical bases of physiological disorders resulting from perturbations of the human circadian clock. Several disorders of the sleep/wake cycle are indeed associated with dysfunctions of the circadian clock in humans. In the familial advanced sleep/phase syndrome (FASPS), the phase of the sleep/wake cycle in LD is advanced by several hours, as a result of a decreased rate of PER phosphorylation (Toh et al. 2001). In a family in which FASPS is present over five generations, those affected by the syndrome tend to go to sleep around 7:30 p.m. and awake around 4:30 a.m. Moreover, in a patient affected by FASPS the period of the circadian clock in DD was reduced down to 23.5 h from a normal mean value of 24.4 h (Jones et al. 1999).

The phase advance characteristic of FASPS can be accounted for by the model as a result of a decrease in parameter V_{phos}, which measures the maximum rate of PER phosphorylation by the protein kinase CK1ε. As in clinical observations (Jones et al. 1999), the advance of the phase in LD then accompanies a decrease in autonomous period as the phosphorylation rate decreases (Leloup and Goldbeter 2003). Such a decrease in period in DD can be observed over parts of the bifurcation diagram established as a function of V_{phos} (see Figure 10.18a). The

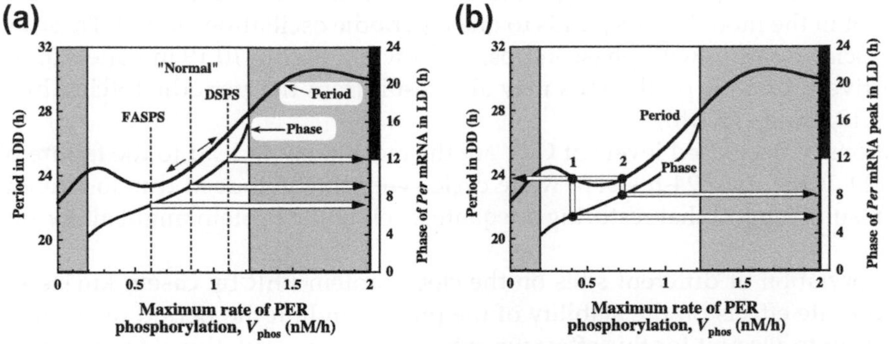

FIGURE 10.18 Relating the mammalian clock model to syndromes associated with disorders of the sleep/wake cycle in humans (Leloup and Goldbeter 2003). (a) Effect of the maximum rate of PER phosphorylation on the free running period in DD and on the phase of the oscillations in LD. The phase corresponds to the time (in h) at which the maximum in *Per* mRNA occurs after the onset of the L phase. Decreasing (increasing) the rate of phosphorylation of the PER protein, V_{phos}, with respect to the "normal" situation can produce a phase advance (delay) as well as a decrease (increase) in free running period that accounts for the phase shift observed in the familial advanced sleep phase syndrome (FASPS) or the delayed sleep phase syndrome (DSPS). (b) Situations 1 and 2 show that different values of the control parameter can produce different phases after entrainment, even though they correspond to the same free running period in DD. The gray areas on the left and right in the two panels refer to absence of entrainment (see Figure 10.19).

model could be used similarly to address the delayed sleep phase syndrome, which is the mirror physiological disorder of the sleep/wake cycle and appears to be associated with increased rate of PER phosphorylation (Ebisawa et al. 2001; Archer et al. 2003). The bifurcation diagram of Figure 10.18a indicates that an increase in V_{phos} may correspond to a delayed phase of the sleep/wake cycle in LD, and to an increase in the autonomous period of circadian oscillations in DD. An interesting prediction arising from Figure 10.18b is that two distinct values of V_{phos} may yield the same period in DD and different phases upon entrainment in LD.

For a long time the model for the mammalian circadian clock placed us in a quandary, as the model failed to account for the most conspicuous property of circadian rhythms, namely, their entrainment by LD cycles. There is generally a range of parameter values in which entrainment occurs (see panels a and b in Figure 10.19), but we failed to find any such range when the light-sensitive parameter (the maximum rate of *Per* expression) was made to vary in a square-wave manner. Regardless of the magnitude of the periodic variation, entrainment did not occur. We then realized that the level of CRY protein was critical for entrainment by LD cycles. When the level of CRY remains too low, free PER builds up during successive light phases, as there is not enough CRY with which to form a complex. Consequently, entrainment fails to occur (Leloup and Goldbeter 2003). It was sufficient to raise the level of CRY—by increasing the rate of CRY synthesis or the rate of *Cry* expression, or by decreasing the rate of degradation of either CRY or *Cry* mRNA—for entrainment to occur.

If entrainment failure is so easy to obtain in the model, could it be that a corresponding syndrome exists in human physiology? The answer is yes: there is a condition known as non-24-h sleep/wake syndrome (Richardson and Malin 1996), in which the time at which the subject goes to sleep is drifting every day. This slow drift is sometimes accompanied by "jumps" in the phase ϕ of the sleep/wake cycle in LD conditions. During such jumps, ϕ rapidly traverses one phase of the LD cycle in a few days, and slowly drifts across the other phase of the LD cycle during a much longer time (on the order of several weeks). The absence of entrainment in the model corresponds to quasi-periodic oscillations in LD. These oscillations can be associated or not with phase jumps, as shown in Figure 10.19 in panels (e)-(f) and (c)-(d) respectively. Chaotic oscillations may also result from the periodic forcing by LD cycles (Figure 10.19, panels (g)-(h)).

Conditions of decreased levels of CRY are the most likely to lead to the failure of entrainment in LD. If the non- 24-h sleep/wake cycle syndrome is indeed due to altered levels of CRY, the results suggest that restoring adequate levels of the protein might allow entrainment to occur.

Phosphorylation of different sites on the clock protein PER by casein kinase I (CKI) can lead to opposite effects on the stability of the protein and on the period of circadian oscillations. In order to account for this effect we extended our computational model by incorporating two distinct phosphorylations of PER by CKI (Leloup and Goldbeter 2011). On the basis of experimental observations (Gallego et al. 2006; Xu et al. 2007) we considered that phosphorylation at one site (denoted PER-P1) enhances the rate of degradation of the protein and decreases the period, while phosphorylation at another site (PER-P2) stabilizes the protein, enhances the transcription of the *Per* gene, and increases the period (see Figure 1 and the Appendix in Leloup and Goldbeter (2011)). The model also incorporates an additional phosphorylation of PER by the glycogen synthase kinase 3, GSK3. The extended model accounts for observations pertaining to the FASPS in which the period is shortened and the phase of

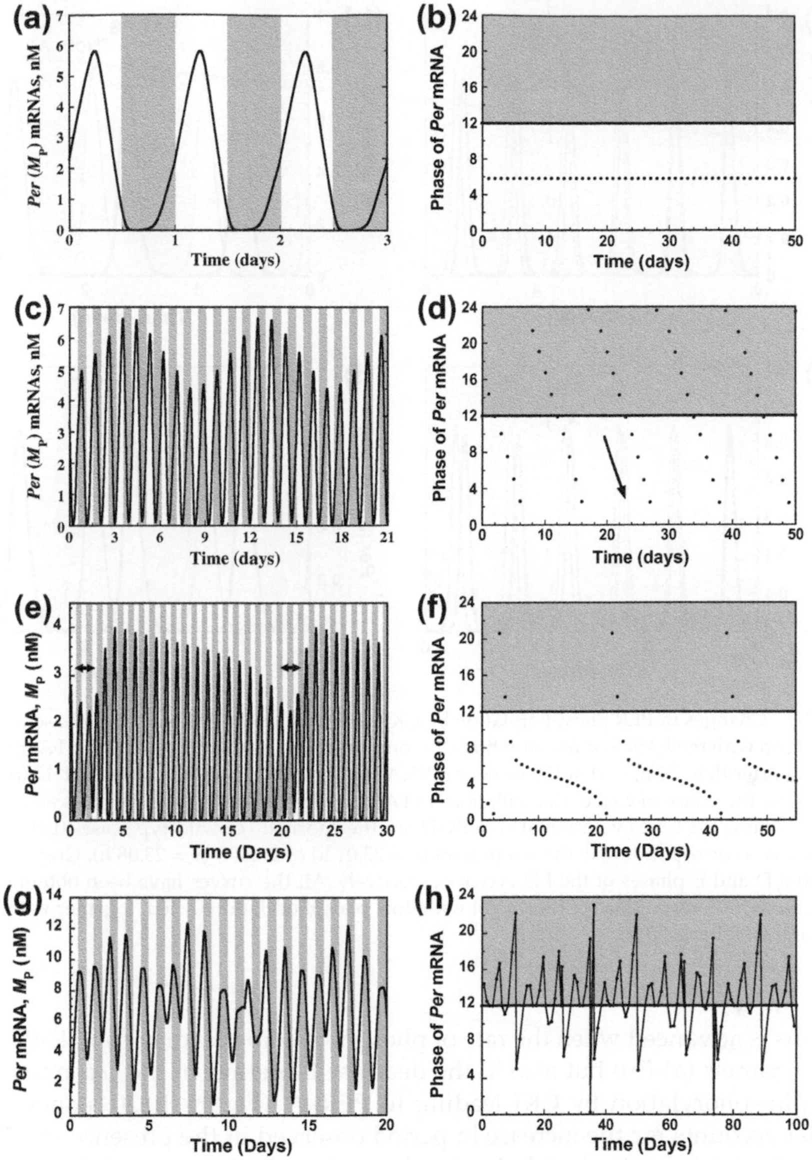

FIGURE 10.19 Entrainment or absence of entrainment by the 24 h light-dark cycle. On the left column are shown the oscillations of *Per* mRNA (M_P). On the right column the phase of the peak of *Per* mRNA (dots) is represented as a function of time. The phase of the circadian oscillations does not always lock to a constant value with respect to the 24-h LD cycle, in contrast to what occurs in the case of entrainment (a-b). Lack of entrainment can lead to quasi-periodic behavior (c-d), which is sometimes accompanied by phase jumps (e-f) corresponding to slow drifts of the phase followed by rapid progression through the L or D phase (horizontal arrows). Such quasi-periodic behavior is often associated with the non-24-h sleep/wake cycle syndrome. Chaotic behavior (g-h) can also be observed as a result of forcing by the LD cycle. Gray and white columns represent the D and L phases of the LD cycles, respectively. Parameter values for panels a-b, c-d, e-f, and g-h are as in Figures 4A-B, 4C-D, 5A-B, and 5C-D of Leloup and Goldbeter (2008), respectively.

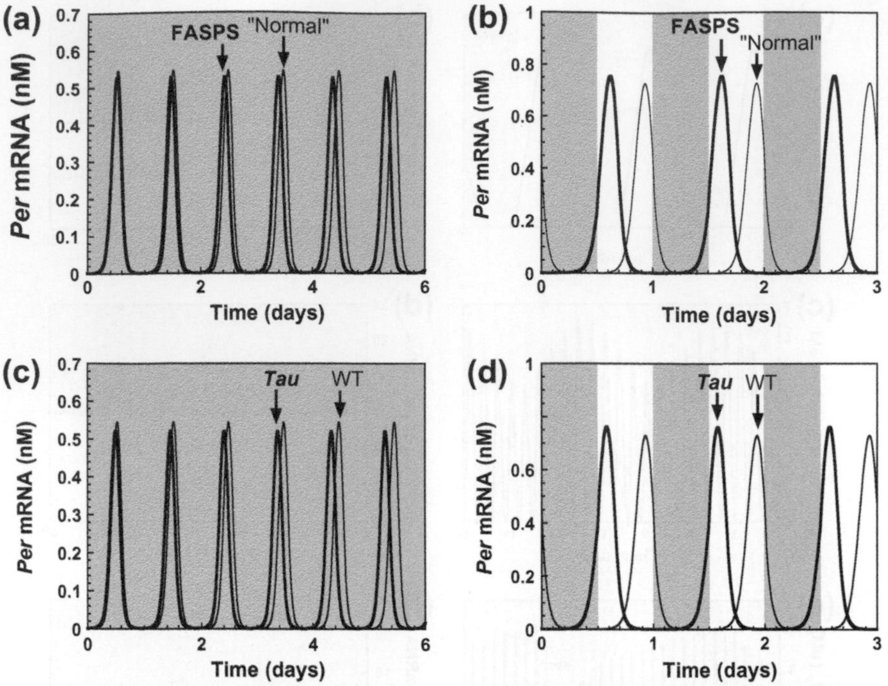

FIGURE 10.20 Changes in PER phosphorylation by CKI lead to changes in period and phase of circadian oscillations: Comparison with the FASPS or *Tau* mutations. In constant darkness (DD), the period in FASPS (a) and the *Tau* mutants (c) are shorter than 24 h, so that the peak of mRNA is progressively shifted to the left. During entrainment by a 12:12 LD cycle, the phase of circadian oscillations in FASPS (b) and the *Tau* mutants (d) is advanced by several hours. The curves show the time evolution of *Per* mRNA for the "normal" or wild-type cases (period $\tau = 23.65$ h in DD) and for the cases corresponding to the *Tau* mutant ($\tau = 23.01$ h) or FASPS ($\tau = 23.08$ h). Gray and white rectangles represent the D and L phases of the LD cycles, respectively. All the curves have been obtained by numerical integration of Equations 1 through 20 of the model with dual phosphorylation (listed, together with parameter values, in Leloup and Goldbeter 2011).

the oscillations is advanced when the rate of phosphorylation leading to PER-P2 is decreased (Figure 10.20, panels (a)-(b)) but also to the decrease in period in the *Tau* mutant due to an increase in phosphorylation by CKI leading to PER-P1 (Figure 10.20, panels (c)-(d)). The model further accounts for the increase in period observed in the presence of CKI inhibitors that decrease the rate of phosphorylation leading to both PER-P1 and PER-P2.

5 CONCLUSIONS

Remarkable advances have been made during the last two decades in unraveling the molecular bases of circadian rhythms—first in *Drosophila* and *Neurospora*, and more recently in cyanobacteria, plants, and mammals. Based on experimentally determined mechanisms, computational models of increasing complexity have been proposed for these rhythms.

As reviewed in this chapter, computational approaches throw light on the precise conditions in which circadian oscillations occur as a result of genetic regulation. The models also account for a variety of properties of circadian rhythms, such as phase shifting or long-term suppression by light pulses, entrainment by light/dark cycles, and temperature compensation.

When the numbers of molecules of protein or mRNA involved in the oscillatory mechanism are very low, it becomes necessary to resort to stochastic approaches. We have shown by means of stochastic simulations that coherent sustained oscillations emerge from molecular noise in the genetic regulatory network as soon as the maximum numbers of mRNA and clock protein molecules are in the tens and hundreds, respectively. At higher numbers of molecules, the stochastic models yield results that are largely similar to the predictions of the corresponding deterministic models. The latter therefore provide a useful representation of circadian oscillatory behavior over a wide range of conditions.

Among the factors that contribute to the robustness of circadian rhythms with respect to molecular noise are the degree of cooperativity of repression, the distance from a bifurcation point, and the rate constants measuring the binding of the repressor to the gene. All models considered here pertain to the onset of circadian rhythms at the cellular level. The intercellular coupling of oscillatory cells—for example, in the suprachiasmatic nuclei (SCN), which represent the central circadian pacemaker in mammals (Kunz and Achermann 2003; Gonze et al. 2005)—may further contribute to the robustness of circadian rhythms.

The model for the mammalian circadian clock describes the self-sustained oscillations produced in SCN cells. Peripheral tissues such as liver, kidney, or skeletal muscle also display circadian rhythms, with a phase in LD that differs from that observed for SCN rhythms (Reppert and Weaver 2002). Peripheral oscillators are also self-sustained and cell-autonomous (Yoo et al. 2004; Dibner et al. 2010) but, in constant conditions, peripheral rhythms often show damped oscillations unless they are driven by periodic signals received from the SCN (Brown et al. 2002). Our model can readily account for the generation of circadian rhythms in individual cells in these peripheral organs. The phase difference could easily be accounted for by tuning some kinetic parameter values, and the damping observed at the level of the tissues can be explained by the loss of intercellular coupling due to the dissociation from the SCN, which normally synchronizes rhythms in peripheral tissues.

We have used the case of circadian rhythms to show how more and more complex computational models must be considered to accommodate the accelerating flux of new experimental observations. A question that arises naturally is whether such an ever-increasing complexity of the models is really needed. It appears that as with geographical maps a balance must be found between the necessity of including the most relevant details and the desire to not become lost in a too meticulous description, because the model might quickly become so complex that its detailed numerical study would become highly cumbersome.

An example of molecular detail that has to be incorporated is the phosphorylation of the PER protein: even if sustained oscillations are possible, in principle, in the absence of PER covalent modification the phosphorylation step is needed not only to account for the effect of mutations in the protein kinase that phosphorylates PER but also to account for some disorders of the sleep/wake cycle in humans related to altered PER phosphorylation. Moreover, as described in this chapter, several results can only be obtained in models that possess a minimum degree of complexity. Thus, autonomous chaos was obtained in the ten-variable model for circadian rhythms in *Drosophila* incorporating the formation of a PER-TIM complex, but not in the five-variable model based on PER alone. In the mammalian clock model, incorporation of additional feedback loops brought to light the possibility of multiple sources of oscillatory behavior.

Finally, circadian rhythms provide a case in point for showing how computational models can be used to address a wide range of issues, extending from molecular mechanism to physiological disorders, including jet lag (Leloup and Goldbeter 2013). Identifying the origin of dysfunctions and predicting ways of obviating them in metabolic or genetic regulatory networks on the basis of numerical simulations presents a key challenge for computational biology.

Acknowledgments

This work was supported by grants 3.4607.99 and 3.4636.04 from the Fonds de la Recherche Scientifique Médicale (F.R.S.M., Belgium), DARPA-AFRL grant F30602-02-0554, and the BIOSIM Network of Excellence within the FP6 Program of the European Union. J.-C. L. is Research Associate (F.N.R.S., Belgium). The initial version of this chapter was prepared while A. G. held a Chaire Internationale de Recherche Blaise Pascal de l'Etat et de la Région d'Ile-de-France, gérée par la Fondation de l'Ecole Normale Supérieure at the University of Paris Sud-Orsay (France), in the Institute of Genetics and Microbiology directed by Professor Michel Jacquet, whose hospitality is gratefully acknowledged.

References

Alabadi, D., Oyama, T., Yanovsky, M. J., Harmon, F. G., Mas, P., and Kay, S. A. (2001). Reciprocal regulation between TOC1 and LHY/CCA1 within the Arabidopsis circadian clock. *Science* **293**:880–883.

Archer, S. N., Robilliard, D. L., Skene, D. J., Smits, M., Williams, A., Arendt, J., and von Schantz, M. (2003). A length polymorphism in the circadian clock gene *Per3* is linked to delayed sleep phase syndrome and extreme diurnal preference. *Sleep* **26**:413–415.

Arkin, A., Ross, J., and McAdams, H. H. (1998). Stochastic kinetic analysis of developmental pathway bifurcation in phage lambda-infected *Escherichia coli* cells. *Genetics* **149**:1633–1648.

Aronson, B. D., Johnson, K. A., Loros, J. J., and Dunlap, J. C. (1994). Negative feedback defining a circadian clock: Autoregulation of the clock gene frequency. *Science* **263**:1578–1584.

Bae, K., and Weaver, D. R. (2007). Transient, light-induced rhythmicity in mPER-deficient mice. *J. Biol. Rhythms* **22**:85–88.

Bae, K., Lee, C., Sidote, D., Chuang, K.-Y., and Edery, I. (1998). Circadian regulation of a *Drosophila* homolog of the mammalian *Clock* gene: PER and TIM function as positive regulators. *Mol. Cell Biol.* **18**:6142–6151.

Baker, C. L., Loros, J. J., and Dunlap, J. C. (2012). The circadian clock of *Neurospora crassa*. *FEMS Microbiol. Rev.* **36**:95–110.

Baras, F. (1997). Stochastic analysis of limit cycle behavior. In (L. Schimansky-Geier, and T. Poeschel, eds.), *Stochastic Dynamics: Lecture Notes in Physics*, pp. 167–178. Berlin: Springer.

Baras, F., Pearson, J. E., and Mansour, M. M. (1990). Microscopic simulation of chemical oscillations inhomogeneous systems. *J. Chem. Phys.* **93**:5747–5750.

Barkai, N., and Leibler, S. (2000). Circadian clocks limited by noise. *Nature* 403 267–268.

Baylies, M. K., Weiner, L., Vosshall, L. B., Saez, L., and Young, M. W. (1993). Genetic, molecular, and cellular studies of the *per* locus and its products in *Drosophila melanogaster*. In (M. W. Young (Ed.), *Molecular Genetics of Biological Rhythms*, pp. 123–153. New-York: Marcel Dekker.

Becker-Weimann, S., Wolf, J., Herzel, H., and Kramer, A. (2004). Modeling feedback loops of the mammalian circadian oscillator. *Biophys. J.* **87**:3023–3034.

Blau, J., and Young, M. W. (1999). Cycling vrille expression is required for a functional *Drosophila* clock. *Cell* **99**:661–671.

Brown, S., Zumbrunn, G., Fleury-Olela, F., Preitner, N., and Schibler, U. (2002). Rhythms of mammalian body temperature can sustain peripheral circadian clocks. *Curr. Biol.* **12**:1574–1583.

Busza, A., Emery-Le, M., Rosbash, M., and Emery, P. (2004). Roles of the two *Drosophila* CRYPTOCHROME structural domains in circadian photoreception. *Science* **304**:1503–1506.

Darlington, T. K., Wager-Smith, K., Ceriani, M. F., Staknis, D., Gekakis, N., Steeves, T. D. L., Weitz, C. J., Takahashi, J. S., and Kay, S. A. (1998). Closing the circadian loop: CLOCK- induced transcription of its own inhibitors *per* and *tim*. *Science* **280**:1599–1603.

Dibner, C., Schibler, U., and Albrecht, U. (2010). The mammalian circadian timing system: Organization and coordination of central and peripheral clocks. *Annu. Rev. Physiol.* **72**:517–549.

Doedel, E. J. (1981). AUTO: A program for the automatic bifurcation analysis of autonomous systems. *Cong. Numer.* **30**:265–384.

Dunlap, J. C. (1993). Genetic analysis of circadian clocks. *Annu. Rev. Physiol.* **55**:683–728.

Dunlap, J. C. (1999). Molecular bases for circadian clocks. *Cell* **96**:271–290.

Ebisawa, T., Uchiyama, M., Kajimura, N., Mishima, K., Kamei, Y., Katoh, M., Watanabe, T., Sekimoto, M., Shibui, K., Kim, K., et al. (2001). Association of structural polymorphisms in the human *period3* gene with delayed sleep phase syndrome. *EMBO Rep.* **2**:342–346.

Edery, I., Zwiebel, L. J., Dembinska, M. E., and Rosbash, M. (1994). Temporal phosphorylation of the *Drosophila* period protein. *Proc. Natl. Acad. Sci. USA* **91**:2260–2264.

Forger, D. B., and Peskin, C. S. (2003). A detailed predictive model of the mammalian circadian clock. *Proc. Natl. Acad. Sci. USA* **100**:14806–14811.

Forger, D. B., and Peskin, C. S. (2005). Stochastic simulation of the mammalian circadian clock. *Proc. Natl. Acad. Sci. USA* **102**:321–324.

Gallego, M., Eide, E. J., Woolf, M. F., Virshup, D. M., and Forger, D. B. (2006). An opposite role for tau in circadian rhythms revealed by mathematical modeling. *Proc. Natl. Acad. Sci. USA* **103**:10618–10623.

Gillespie, D. T. (1976). A general method for numerically simulating the stochastic time evolution of coupled chemical reactions. *J. Comput. Phys.* **22**:403–434.

Gillespie, D. T. (1977). Exact stochastic simulation of coupled chemical reactions. *J. Phys. Chem.* **81**:2340–2361.

Glossop, N. R. J., Lyons, L. C., and Hardin, P. E. (1999). Interlocked feedback loops within the *Drosophila* circadian oscillator. *Science* **286**:766–768.

Goldbeter, A. (1995). A model for circadian oscillations in the *Drosophila* period protein (PER). *Proc. R. Soc. London Ser. B* **261**:319–324.

Goldbeter, A. (1996). *Biochemical Oscillations and Cellular Rhythms: The Molecular Bases of Periodic and Chaotic Behavior*. Cambridge UK: Cambridge University Press.

Gonze, D., and Goldbeter, A. (2000). Entrainment versus chaos in a model for a circadian oscillator driven by light-dark cycles. *J. Stat. Phys.* **101**:649–663.

Gonze, D., Leloup, J.-C., and Goldbeter, A. (2000). Theoretical models for circadian rhythms in *Neurospora* and *Drosophila*. *C R Acad. Sci. III* **323**(323):57–67.

Gonze, D., Halloy, J., and Goldbeter, A. (2002a). Deterministic versus stochastic models for circadian rhythms. *J. Biol. Phys.* **28**:637–653.

Gonze, D., Halloy, J., and Goldbeter, A. (2002b). Robustness of circadian rhythms with respect to molecular noise. *Proc. Natl. Acad. Sci. USA* **99**:673–678.

Gonze, D., Roussel, M. R., and Glodbeter, A. (2002c). A Model for the enhancement of fitness in cyanobacteria based on resonance of a circadian oscillator with the external light-dark cycle. *J. Theor. Biol.* **214**:577–597.

Gonze, D., Halloy, J., Leloup, J.-C., and Goldbeter, A. (2003). Stochastic models for circadian rhythms: Effect of molecular noise on periodic and chaotic behaviour. *C R Biol* **326**:189–203.

Gonze, D., Halloy, J., and Goldbeter, A. (2004a). Emergence of coherent oscillations in stochastic models for circadian rhythms. *Physica A* **342**:221–233.

Gonze, D., Halloy, J., and Goldbeter, A. (2004b). Stochastic models for circadian oscillations: Emergence of a biological rhythm. *Int. J. Quantum Chem.* **98**:228–238.

Gonze, D., Bernard, S., Waltermann, C., Kramer, A., and Herzel, H. (2005). Spontaneous synchronization of coupled circadian oscillators. *Biophys. J.* **89**:120–129.

Goodwin, B. C. (1965). Oscillatory behavior in enzymatic control processes. *Adv. Enzyme Regul.* **3**:425–438.

Grima, B., Lamouroux, A., Chelot, E., Papin, C., Limbourg-Bouchon, B., and Rouyer, F. (2002). The F-box protein Slimb controls the levels of clock proteins period and timeless. *Nature* **420**:178–182.

Hall, J. C., and Rosbash, M. (1987). Genes and biological rhythms. *Trends Genet.* **3**:185–191.

Hall, J. C., and Rosbash, M. (1988). Mutations and molecules influencing biological rhythms. *Annu. Rev. Neurosci.* **11**:373–393.

Hardin, P. E., Hall, J. C., and Rosbash, M. (1990). Feedback of the *Drosophila* period gene product on circadian cycling of its messenger RNA levels. *Nature* **343**:536–540.

Hardin, P. E., Hall, J. C., and Rosbash, M. (1992). Circadian oscillations in period gene mRNA levels are transcriptionally regulated. *Proc. Natl. Acad. Sci. USA* **89**:11711–11715.

Hunter-Ensor, M., Ousley, A., and Sehgal, A. (1996). Regulation of the *Drosophila* protein timeless suggests a mechanism for resetting the circadian clock by light. *Cell* **84**:677–685.

Jewett, M. E., and Kronauer, R. E. (1998). Refinement of a limit cycle oscillator model of the effects of light on the human circadian pacemaker. *J. Theor. Biol.* **192**:455–465.

Jones, C. R., Campbell, S. S., Zone, S. E., Cooper, F., DeSano, A., Murphy, P. J., Jones, B., Czajkowski, L., and Ptacek, L. J. (1999). Familial advanced sleep-phase syndrome: A short-period circadian rhythm variant in humans. *Nat. Med.* **5**:1062–1065.

Kim, J. K., and Forger, D. B. (2012). A mechanism for robust circadian timekeeping via stoichiometric balance. *Mol. Syst. Biol.* **8**:630.

Ko, H. W., Jiang, J., and Edery, I. (2002). Role for Slimb in the degradation of *Drosophila* Period protein phosphorylated by doubletime. *Nature* **420**:673–678.

Konopka, R. J. (1979). Genetic dissection of the *Drosophila* circadian system. *Fed. Proc.* **38**:2602–2605.

Konopka, R. J., and Benzer, S. (1971). Clock mutants of *Drosophila melanogaster*. *Proc. Natl. Acad. Sci. USA* **68**:2112–2116.

Konopka, R. J., Pittendrigh, C., and Orr, D. (1989). Reciprocal behaviour associated with altered homeostasis and photosensitivity of *Drosophila* clock mutants. *J. Neurosci.* **6**:1–10.

Kunz, H., and Achermann, P. (2003). Simulation of circadian rhythm generation in the suprachiasmatic nucleus with locally coupled self-sustained oscillators. *J. Theor. Biol.* **224**:63–78.

Lee, C., Parikh, V., Itsukaichi, T., Bae, K., and Edery, I. (1996). Resetting the *Drosophila* clock by photic regulation of PER and a PER-TIM complex. *Science* **271**:1740–1744.

Lee, C., Bae, K., and Edery, I. (1999). PER and TIM inhibit the DNA binding activity of a *Drosophila* CLOCK-CYC/dBMAL1 heterodimer without disrupting formation of the heterodimer: A basis for circadian transcription. *Mol. Cell. Biol.* **19**:5316–5325.

Lee, C., Etchegaray, J. P., Cagampang, F. R., Loudon, A. S., and Reppert, S. M. (2001). Post-translational mechanisms regulate the mammalian circadian clock. *Cell* **107**:855–867.

Lee, K., Loros, J. J., and Dunlap, J. C. (2000). Interconnected feedback loops in the *Neurospora* circadian system. *Science* **289**:107–110.

Leloup, J.-C., and Goldbeter, A. (1997). Temperature compensation of circadian rhythms: Control of the period in a model for circadian oscillations of the PER protein in *Drosophila*. *Chronobiol. Int.* **14**:511–520.

Leloup, J.-C., and Goldbeter, A. (1998). A model for circadian rhythms in *Drosophila* incorporating the formation of a complex between the PER and TIM proteins. *J. Biol. Rhythms* **13**:70–87.

Leloup, J.-C., and Goldbeter, A. (1999). Chaos and birhythmicity in a model for circadian oscillations of the PER and TIM proteins in *Drosophila*. *J. Theor. Biol.* **198**:445–459.

Leloup, J.-C., and Goldbeter, A. (2001). A molecular explanation for the long-term suppression of circadian rhythms by a single light pulse. *Am. J. Physiol. Regul. Integrat. Comp. Physiol.* **280**:R1206–R1212.

Leloup, J.-C., and Goldbeter, A. (2003). Toward a detailed computational model for the mammalian circadian clock. *Proc. Natl. Acad. Sci. USA* **100**:7051–7056.

Leloup, J.-C., and Goldbeter, A. (2004). Modeling the mammalian circadian clock: Sensitivity analysis and multiplicity of oscillatory mechanisms. *J. Theor. Biol.* **230**:541–562.

Leloup, J.-C., and Goldbeter, A. (2008). Modeling the circadian clock: From molecular mechanism to physiological disorders. *BioEssays* **30**:590–600.

Leloup, J.-C., and Goldbeter, A. (2011). Modelling the dual role of *Per* phosphorylation and its effect on the period and phase of the mammalian circadian clock. *IET Syst. Biol.* **5**:44–49.

Leloup, J.-C., and Goldbeter, A. (2013). Critical phase shifts slow down circadian clock recovery : Implications for jet lag. *J. Theor. Biol.* **333**:47–57.

Leloup, J.-C., Gonze, D., and Goldbeter, A. (1999). Limit cycle models for circadian rhythms based on transcriptional regulation in *Neurospora* and *Drosophila*. *J. Biol. Rhythms* **14**:433–448.

McAdams, H. H., and Arkin, A. (1997). Stochastic mechanisms in gene expression. *Proc. Natl. Acad. Sci. USA* **94**:814–819.

Merrow, M., and Brunner, M. (eds.) (2011). Special Issue: Circadian rhythms. FEBS Lett. 585:1383–1502.

Merrow, M., Garceau, N. Y., and Dunlap, J. C. (1997). Dissection of a circadian oscillation into discrete domains. *Proc. Natl. Acad. Sci. USA* **94**:3877–3882.

Mirsky, H. P., Liu, A. C., Welsh, D. K., Kay, S. A., and Doyle, F. J. 3rd, (2009). A model of the cell-autonomous mammalian circadian clock. *Proc. Natl. Acad. Sci. USA* **106**:11107–11112.

Moore-Ede, M. C., Sulzman, F. M., and Fuller, C. A. (1982). *The Clocks That Time Us: Physiology of the Circadian Timing System*. Cambridge, MA: Harvard University Press.

Morton-Firth, C. J., and Bray, D. (1998). Predicting temporal fluctuations in an intracellular signalling pathway. *J. Theor. Biol.* **192**:117–128.

Myers, M. P., Wager-Smith, K., Rothenfluh-Hilfiker, A., and Young, M. W. (1996). Light-induced degradation of TIMELESS and entrainment of the *Drosophila* circadian clock. *Science* **271**:1736–1740.

Nicolis, G., and Prigogine, I. (1977). *Self-Organization in Nonequilibrium Systems: From Dissipative Structures to Order through Fluctuations*. New York: Wiley.

Pittendrigh, C. S. (1960). Circadian rhythms and the circadian organization of living systems. *Cold Spring Harbor Symp. Quant. Biol.* **25**:159–184.

Preitner, N., Damiola, F., Lopez-Molina, L., Zakany, J., Duboule, D., Albrecht, U., and Schibler, U. (2002). The orphan nuclear receptor REV-ERBalpha controls circadian transcription within the positive limb of the mammalian circadian oscillator. *Cell* **110**:251–260.

Qiu, J., and Hardin, P. E. (1996). *Per* mRNA cycling is locked to lights-off under photoperiodic conditions that support circadian feedback loop function. *Mol. Cell Biol.* **16**:4182–4188.

Reppert, S., and Weaver, D. (2002). Coordination of circadian timing in mammals. *Nature* **418**:935–941.

Richardson, G. S., and Malin, H. V. (1996). Circadian rhythm sleep disorders: Pathophysiology and treatment. *J. Clin. Neurophysiol.* **13**:17–31.

Ruoff, P., and Rensing, L. (1996). The temperature-compensated Goodwin model simulates many circadian clock properties. *J. Theor. Biol.* **179**:275–285.

Ruoff, P., Vinsjevik, M., Monnerjahn, C., and Rensing, L. (2001). The Goodwin model: Simulating the effect of light pulses on the circadian sporulation rhythm of *Neurospora crassa*. *J. Theor. Biol.* **209**:29–42.

Rutila, J. E., Suri, V., Le, M., So, W. V., Rosbash, M., and Hall, J. C. (1998). CYCLE is a second bHLH-PAS clock protein essential for circadian rhythmicity and transcription of *Drosophila period* and *timeless*. *Cell* **93**:805–814.

Shearman, L. P., Sriram, S., Weaver, D. R., Maywood, E. S., Chaves, I., Zheng, B., Kume, K., Lee, C. C., van der Horst, G. T., Hastings, M. H., and Reppert, S. M. (2000). Interacting molecular loops in the mammalian circadian clock. *Science* **288**:1013–1019.

Smolen, P., Baxter, D. A., and Byrne, J. H. (2001). Modeling circadian oscillations with interlocking positive and negative feedback loops. *J. Neurosci.* **21**:6644–6656.

Stelling, J., Gilles, E. D., and Doyle, F. J. 3rd, (2004). Robustness properties of circadian clock architectures. *Proc. Natl. Acad. Sci. USA* **101**:13210–13215.

Toh, K. L., Jones, C. R., He, Y., Eide, E. J., Hinz, W. A., Virshup, D. M., Ptacek, L. J., and Fu, Y.-H. (2001). An *hPer2* phosphorylation site mutation in familial advanced sleep-phase syndrome. *Science* **291**:1040–1043.

Ueda, H. R., Hagiwara, M., and Kitano, H. (2001). Robust oscillations within the interlocked feedback model of *Drosophila* circadian rhythm. *J. Theor. Biol.* **210**:401–406.

Ukai, H., and Ueda, H. R. (2010). Systems biology of mammalian circadian clocks. *Annu. Rev. Physiol.* **72**:579–603.

van der Horst, G. T., Muijtjens, M., Kobayashi, K., Takano, R., Kanno, S., Takao, M., de Wit, J., Verkerk, A., Eker, A. P., van Leenen, D., et al. (1999). Mammalian *Cry1* and *Cry2* are essential for maintenance of circadian rhythms. *Nature* **398**:627–630.

Winfree, A. T. (1980). *The Geometry of Biological Time*. New York: Springer.

Xu, Y., Toh, K. L., Jones, C. R., Shin, J. Y., Fu, Y. H., and Ptacek, J. L. (2007). Modeling of human circadian mutation yields insights into clock regulation by PER2. *Cell* **128**:59–70.

Yoo, S. H., Yamazaki, S., Lowrey, P. L., Shimomura, K., Ko, C. H., Buhr, E. D., Siepka, S. M., Hong, H. K., Oh, W. J., Yoo, O. J., Menaker, M., and Takahashi, J. S. (2004). PERIOD2: LUCIFERASE real-time reporting of circadian dynamics reveals persistent circadian oscillations in mouse peripheral tissues. *Proc. Natl. Acad. Sci. USA* **101**:5339–5346.

Young, M. W., and Kay, S. A. (2001). Time zones: A comparative genetics of circadian clocks. *Nat. Rev. Genet.* **2**:702–715.

Zeng, H., Hardin, P. E., and Rosbash, M. (1994). Constitutive overexpression of the *Drosophila period* protein inhibits *period* mRNA cycling. *EMBO J.* **13**:3590–3598.

Zeng, H., Qian, Z., Myers, M. P., and Rosbash, M. (1996). A light-entrainment mechanism for the *Drosophila* circadian clock. *Nature* **380**:129–135.

Zerr, D. M., Hall, J. C., Rosbash, M., and Siwicki, K. K. (1990). Circadian fluctuations of period protein immunoreactivity in the CNS and the visual system of *Drosophila*. *J. Neurosci.* **10**:2749–2762.

Zhang, E. E., and Kay, S. A. (2010). Clocks not winding down: Unravelling circadian networks. *Nat. Rev. Mol. Cell. Biol.* **11**:764–776.

Zheng, B., Albrecht, U., Kaasik, K., Sage, M., Lu, W., Vaishnav, S., Li, Q., Sun, Z. S., Eichele, G., Bradley, A., and Lee, C. C. (2001). Nonredundant roles of the *mPer1* and *mPer2* genes in the mammalian circadian clock. *Cell* **105**:683–694.

CHAPTER

11

Top-Down Dynamical Modeling of Molecular Regulatory Networks

Reinhard Laubenbacher[a], *Pedro Mendes*[a,b]

[a]Virginia Bioinformatics Institute, Virginia Tech, Blacksburg VA, USA

[b]School of Computer Science, The University of Manchester, Manchester, UK

CONTENTS

Abstract

Mathematical and statistical network modeling is an important step toward uncovering the organizational principles and dynamic behavior of biological networks. This chapter focuses on methods to construct discrete dynamic models of gene regulatory networks from experimental data sets, also sometimes referred to as top-down modeling or reverse engineering. Time-discrete dynamical systems models have long been used in biology, particularly in population dynamics. The models mainly focused on here are also assumed to have a finite set of possible states for each variable. That is, the modeling framework discussed in this chapter is that of time-discrete dynamical systems over a finite state set.

Computational Systems Biology, Second Edition
http://dx.doi.org/10.1016/B978-0-12-405926-9.00011-3

1 INTRODUCTION

"The advent of functional genomics has enabled the molecular biosciences to come a long way towards characterizing the molecular constituents of life. Yet, the challenge for biology overall is to understand how organisms function. By discovering how function arises in dynamic interactions, systems biology addresses the missing links between molecules and physiology" (Bruggeman and Westerhoff 2007).

Thus, an important step in a successful systems biology approach is an understanding of the *dynamics* exhibited by the molecular interaction networks that control cellular function. While the natural language for static networks of molecules, such as gene regulatory or protein-protein interaction networks, is graph theory, so the natural language for dynamic models is a mathematical description of the molecular network as a dynamical system. Depending on the specific network to be modeled and the quantity and quality of available information, several different modeling frameworks are available. Discrete models, such as Boolean networks, provide a coarse, discrete-time, high-level view of the mechanisms that drive the time evolution of network nodes, such as a model of the budding yeast cell cycle in Hong et al. (2012). Systems of ordinary or partial differential equations give a potentially quantitative description of the network as a time-continuous system of continuously varying concentrations, such as a biochemical reaction network (Chifman et al. 2012). Dynamic Bayesian networks are an example of statistics-based models, such as a model of the immune response to influenza in Dimitrakopoulou et al. (2011). Each of these model types has its own advantages and disadvantages, and its own limits of applicability. The problem then is to construct models of networks of interest from available information. This chapter treats a method that allows the construction of time- and state-discrete dynamic models from time course data.

We will focus primarily on time-discrete models, whose variables also take on (finitely many) discrete values. Furthermore, we will restrict ourselves to deterministic models, although stochastic discrete models are well studied and have been used successfully (Pahle 2009). We will also discuss the relationship between discrete and continuous models and how they can be combined to improve the model construction process. Top-down modeling, otherwise known as reverse engineering, or network inference, refers to the process of inferring dynamic models from experimental measurements of all the network nodes at a given time or in the form of a time course. In its "pure" form, it does not incorporate any prior information, such as regulatory network interactions that have been reported in the literature, in order not to bias the discovery process. There are several methods, however, that can take into account *a priori* information of different kinds, and which will facilitate the inference. In contrast, so-called bottom-up modeling begins with a list of network nodes and available information about their interactions. Typically, experimental data are then used to estimate particular parameter choices for the model. One may view top-down modeling as a special case of bottom-up modeling, in which one chooses a generic model that contains all possible network interactions, with unknown parameters representing the strength of the interactions, and experimental data are used to estimate all the parameters in the model.

The problem of top-down modeling is one of the central problems in systems biology, and this research area is very active. One focal point for the area is provided by the *Dialogue for Reverse Engineering Assessment and Methods* (DREAM) (Dimitrakopoulou et al. 2011). This annual competition, in its 8th year at the time of this writing, provides data sets and gold standards against which to compare inferred models. Most current methods are designed to infer a static model from a given data set, in the form of a graph, with genes as nodes and either directed or undirected edges (Faith et al. 2007; Haury et al. 2012; Kuffner et al. 2012; Wang et al. 2010; Vignes et al. 2011). Depending on the method, an edge indicates either a causal regulatory relationship or a correlation of expression values, based on criteria such as covariance or mutual information. Some methods aim to infer dynamic models directly, such as Kramer et al. (2009), Madar et al. (2010), Porreca et al. (2010). It is clear that substantially more data, including time course data, is required to reverse engineer a dynamic model that captures the correct time evolution of the system rather than simply the absence or presence of interactions.

2 TOP-DOWN MODELING

Traditionally, models of molecular regulatory systems in cells have been created bottom-up, where the model is constructed piece-by-piece by adding new components and characterizing their interactions with other molecules in the model. This process requires that the molecular interactions have been well characterized, usually through quantitative numerical values for kinetic parameters (typically through *in vitro* procedures). Note that the construction of such models is biased toward molecular components that have already been associated with the phenomenon. Still, modeling can be of great help in this bottom-up process, by revealing whether the current knowledge about the system is able to replicate its *in vivo* behavior. There are many good examples of this process, going back decades. Teusink et al. (2000) have built a comprehensive model of yeast glycolysis based on detailed kinetics of 15 enzymes of carbohydrate catabolism. Arkin et al. (1998) studied stochastic switching between lysis and lysogeny in a model of lambda phage infection. In a landmark paper, Bray et al. (1993) studied the regulation of chemotactic swimming of *E. coli* cells, correlating the model to the phenotypes of dozens of mutants. Ashall et al. (2009) studied the NFκB signalling pathway. For an example of bottom-up modeling of a problem involving spatial distributions of signaling molecules, we refer to a study of calcium waves in neuroblastoma cells in Fink et al. (2000). Finally, a recent example presents a Boolean network models of the cell cycle regulatory network in budding yeast (Hong et al. 2012).

Bottom-up modeling is essentially a process of synthesis by which models of isolated cellular components (enzymes, etc.) are merged to become part of a larger model. Note that without applying other steps, models built bottom-up are mechanistic, i.e., they represent one level of organization with all of the details of the level below. For example, the model of ethanol catabolism mentioned above contains details of enzyme action of each of its 15 component enzymes.

This modeling approach is well suited to complement experimental approaches in biochemistry and molecular biology, since models thus created can serve to validate the mechanisms determined *in vitro* by attempting to simulate the behaviors of intact cells. While this approach has been dominant in cellular modeling, it does not scale very well to larger scale studies, since it requires that proteins be purified and studied in isolation. This is not a practical endeavor due to its large scale, but especially because a large number of proteins act on small molecules that are not available in purified form, as would be required for *in vitro* studies.

Modern systems biology approaches are characterized by large-scale molecular profiling and *in vivo* experiments (or if not truly *in vivo*, at least carried out with intact cells). Technologies such as transcript profiling with microarrays or RNA sequencing, protein profiling with mass spectrometry, and metabolite profiling with chromatography and mass spectrometry, produce measurements that are large-scale characterizations of the state of the biological material probed. Other new large-scale technologies, such as next generation sequencing, are also able to uncover groups of molecules that interact (bind), allowing inference of interaction networks. All of these experimental methods are data rich, and it has been recognized for some time (see, e.g., (Brenner 1997; Kell 2004; Loomis and Sternberg 1995)) that modeling is necessary to transform these data into knowledge. A new modeling approach is needed to best suit large-scale profiling experiments. Such a top-down approach will start with little knowledge about the system, capturing at first only a coarse-grained image of the system with only a few variables. Then, through cycles of simulation and experiment, the number of variables in the model is increased. At each iteration, novel experiments will be suggested by simulations of the model, which, when carried out, will provide data to improve the model further, leading to a higher resolution in terms of mechanisms.

While the processes of bottom-up and top-down modeling are distinct, both have as an objective the identification of molecular mechanisms responsible for cell behavior. The main difference between the two is that the construction of top-down models is biased by the data of the large-scale profiles, while bottom-up models are biased by the pre-existing knowledge of particular molecules and mechanisms.

Note that while top-down modeling makes use of genome-wide profiling data, it is conceptually very different from other genome-wide data analysis approaches. Top-down modeling needs data produced in experiments that lend themselves to the approach; most likely those designed with that purpose in mind. One should not expect that a random combination of arbitrary molecular snapshots would be of much use for the top-down modeling process. Sometimes they may serve some purpose (e.g. variable selection) but overall, top-down modeling requires perturbation experiments that are carried out with appropriate controls. In the face of modern experimental research methods, the development of an effective top-down modeling strategy is crucial. In addition, we believe that a combination of top-down and bottom-up approaches will eventually have to be used. An example of a step in this direction is the apoptosis model in Bentele et al. (2004).

3 DISCRETE MODELS

Some of the time- and state-discrete (deterministic) models commonly used in systems biology can be specified as follows. Suppose we have variables $x_1, \ldots, x_n$, representing mRNA or protein concentrations in a particular biological context. Each of these variables is assumed to take values in a finite set X. (The framework can be easily generalized to allow each variable x_i to take values in a different finite set X_i; see (Veliz-Cuba et al. 2010).) Let

$$f = (f_1, \ldots, f_n) : X^n \to X^n$$

be a function described in terms of "coordinate functions" $f_i: X^n \to X$ for each variable x_i. The description also includes the specification of an update scheme, such as synchronous or asynchronous computation of the change of the individual variables. With this information, f is a time- and state-discrete dynamical system.

Boolean networks can clearly be viewed in this way, with $X = \{0, 1\}$, and the f_i given by the Boolean rules assigned to the individual network nodes. It was shown in Veliz-Cuba et al. (2010) that logical models and bounded Petri nets can also be represented in this way. The same applies to certain types of agent-based models (Hinkelmann et al. 2011).

Thus, discrete models can be viewed as set functions on finite sets. For the purpose of construction, analysis, and use of discrete models, the lack of a rich mathematical structure is a hindrance, akin to Euclidean geometry carried out with ruler and compass. It was the introduction of the Cartesian coordinate system that imposed an algebraic structure on space and gave geometers access to the tools of solving systems of algebraic equations over the real numbers in order to answer geometric questions such as whether a given line and a given circle intersect and where. And it is this algebraic structure that provides the foundation for a large body of tools for the construction and analysis of differential equations models. We can implement a very similar strategy here. Imposing a coordinate system on a line is equivalent to mapping the line onto the algebraic structure of the real numbers, with its addition and multiplication; analogously for higher dimensional spaces. In our setting, this amounts to imposing an algebraic structure, with addition and multiplication, on the finite set X in which our variables take their values. However, this is not always possible, only in the case where the cardinality of X is a power of a prime number. We will make this assumption from now on. To distinguish the set X from the set X together with algebraic structure, we will denote the latter by K and refer to it as a *finite field*. We explain below how this can always be achieved without changing model properties.

Consider now one of the coordinate (set) functions $f_i: K^n \to K$ of a model $f: K^n \to K^n$. The algebraic structure on K propagates to the description of f_i which can be described as a polynomial function in the variables $x_1, \ldots, x_n$, with coefficients in K (see, e.g., Lidl and Niederreiter 1997, p. 369). Thus, the model f can be specified by a collection of n polynomial functions, which we shall refer to as a *polynomial dynamical system*. As an example, consider $K = \{0, 1\}$, with addition and multiplication modulo 2, that is, $1 + 1 = 0$. The set function $g: K^2 \to K$, given by $g(0,0) = g(0,1) = g(1, 0) = 0$, and $g(1,1) = 1$, can be expressed as the polynomial function $g(x,y) = x \cdot y$. Furthermore, g is also equal to the Boolean function $x \wedge y$. More generally, there is a one-to-one correspondence between Boolean functions and polynomial functions, using the dictionary $x \vee y = x + y + xy$, and $\neg x = x + 1$. Consequently, any model $f: \{0, 1\}^n \to \{0, 1\}^n$, specified as a set function, is in fact a Boolean network or, equivalently, a polynomial dynamical system.

What do we gain from the additional algebraic structure and the polynomial viewpoint? We have now access to all the theoretical and computational tools from algebra and algebraic geometry. In particular, over the last two decades, the field of computer algebra has emerged with powerful software implementations of a wide range of algorithms for symbolic computation. Among a host of available software packages, the top-down modeling approaches described below are implemented in the open source computer algebra package Macaulay2 (Grayson and Stillman, 1992). As mentioned above, it was shown in Veliz-Cuba et al. (2010), Hinkelmann et al. (2011) that other types of discrete models can be translated into polynomial dynamical systems over a finite field. This makes the polynomial framework widely applicable, and allows the easy comparison of different model types.

We now address the issue of how restrictive the assumption is that the set X of variable states is actually a finite field. Suppose that we are given a model $f : X^n \to X^n$, and suppose that the set X contains four possible states, which we shall call 0, 1, 2, 3. We now add an extra state, "4," to obtain a total of five states, a prime number. Now, we can turn this extended state set X' into an algebraic structure with addition and multiplication similar to the real numbers, by using addition and multiplication of integers modulo 5. (We could do the same thing on the original set X, but then we would obtain undesirable properties such as "$2{\cdot}2 = 4 = 0$" in addition modulo 4. The fact that this phenomenon doesn't occur if X has a prime number of states simply follows from the fact that prime numbers cannot be factored.) The resulting structure is called a *field*, in this case a *finite field*. To distinguish X together with this structure, we shall call it K instead. To extend f to a model $g : K^n \to K^n$, we can simply specify that the value of g on any state that contains a "4" is the same as the value of f on the state obtained by replacing the "4" by a "3." The extended model can easily be reduced again to the original, since the new threshold that defines "4" is not "active," in the sense that it does not alter the action of the network nodes. Thus, the restriction that X should have a certain number of states can easily be accomplished in practice. Furthermore, the same approach allows the freedom of having a different set of states X_i for each variable x_i.

4 DISCRETE METHODS FOR TOP-DOWN MODELING

Given the model setting described in the previous section, the basic top-down modeling problem is as follows. Suppose we are given sequences of experimentally measured network states (in the form of one or more time courses):

$$\begin{gathered}\boldsymbol{s}_1 = (s_{11}, s_{21}, \ldots, s_{n1}), \ldots, \boldsymbol{s}_m = (s_{1m}, \ldots, s_{nm})\\ \boldsymbol{t}_1 = (t_{11}, t_{21}, \ldots, t_{n1}), \ldots, \boldsymbol{t}_r = (t_{1r}, \ldots, t_{nr}))\\ \ldots\end{gathered}$$

These satisfy the property that, if the unknown transition function of the network is f, then

$$\begin{aligned} f(\boldsymbol{s}_i) &= \boldsymbol{s}_{i+1}, \quad \text{for } i = 1, \ldots, m-1 \ldots\\ f(\boldsymbol{t}_j) &= \boldsymbol{t}_{j+1}, \quad \text{for } j = 1, \ldots, r-1 \ldots\\ &\ldots\end{aligned}$$

Typically, there will be more than one possible choice. In fact, unless **all** state transitions of the system are specified, there will always be more than one model that fits the given data set. Since this much information is hardly ever available in practice, any top-down modeling method has to choose from a large set of possible models. The criterion used is basically some sort of Occam's Razor principle to choose the simplest model(s), based on some definition of "simple" appropriate for the situation. In many cases, the core of each method is a search algorithm that examines the space of possible models to find those "simplest" ones. For some methods, the search space is reduced by making additional assumptions, for instance, that the number of regulatory inputs for each node is limited (Gardner et al. 2003). Without additional mathematical structure that comes with the search space only heuristic search methods are possible. We will see below how the assumption that we are dealing with dynamical systems over finite fields can provide such additional mathematical structure and, consequently, additional mathematical tools for top-down modeling.

The basic approach was first published in Laubenbacher and Stigler (2004). The model(s) $f: K^n \rightarrow K^n$ we are searching for is determined by its coordinate functions $f_i : K^n \rightarrow K$. We can reverse engineer each coordinate function independently and thus reconstruct the system one variable at a time. The strategy of the method is to first compute the space of all systems that are consistent with the given time series data. This is done in a way quite similar to the method of determining all solutions to a nonhomogeneous system of linear equations. There, one first computes a particular solution $\boldsymbol{a}$ heuristically. Then one computes the null space of the system, that is, the vector space V of solutions to the corresponding homogeneous linear system. The space V is described by a vector space basis, that is, a set of vectors with cardinality the dimension of the space, so that every vector in V is given as a linear combination of this finite set of vectors, which avoids enumeration of the entire set V. Finally, the set of all solutions to the nonhomogeneous system is given by the set of points $\boldsymbol{a} + V = \{\boldsymbol{a} + \boldsymbol{v} \mid \boldsymbol{v} \in V\}$.

Once the set of models for a given data set is described in this way, the method in Laubenbacher and Stigler (2004) then chooses a particular system $f = (f_1,\ldots,f_n)$ that satisfies the following property:

Minimality: For each i, f_i is minimal in the sense that there is no nonzero polynomial g such that $f = h + g$ and g is identically equal to zero on the given time points. That is, we exclude terms in the polynomials f_i that vanish identically on the data. In other words, we do not include interactions in the model that are not manifested in the given dataset.

Suppose that f_i and f_i' are two models that fit the given dataset. Then $f_i(\mathbf{x}) = f_i'(\mathbf{x})$ for all data points $\mathbf{x}$. That is, $(f_i - f_i')(\mathbf{x}) = 0$ for all $\mathbf{x}$. Therefore, the set of all such models can be described as $f_i + I$, where f_i is a particular model and I is the set of all models that vanish identically on the given dataset. (This approach can also be viewed as a discrete analog of the ODE modeling method described in Yeung et al. (2002).) Thus, we need to compute f_i and I.

The particular solution f_i can be computed using a standard formula for Lagrange interpolation (see (Laubenbacher and Stigler 2004) for details). To compute a set of polynomials that generate I, analogous to a basis for the nullspace V, we use mathematical algorithms from computer algebra based on the theory of Groebner bases (Cox et al. 1997). What allows us to do this is the fact that the set of polynomials that vanish on a given data set has the algebraic structure of an *ideal* in the algebraic system $K[x_1,\ldots,x_n]$ of all polynomials in n variables with coefficients in K. These algorithms are implemented using the computer algebra system *Macaulay2*. An important aspect of this computation is that the set of all possible models is described not by enumeration, but in terms of a small set of generators, similar to describing a vector space by giving a basis for it. The algorithm to select the simplest model from the set $f_i + I$ uses another fundamental procedure in computer algebra, that of dividing a polynomial by all polynomials in the ideal I.

One can prove that there is in fact a unique simplest model to choose. However, the algorithm in Laubenbacher and Stigler (2004) depends on an up-front choice of a total ordering of the variables $x_1,\ldots, x_n$. This choice has the effect that the algorithm uses the "cheapest" (smallest in this ordering) variables preferentially. On the one hand, this feature allows the incorporation of biological knowledge in the case where certain interactions are already known. But, on the other hand, it arbitrarily biases the model output in the case where such information is absent.

In (Laubenbacher and Stigler 2004), several variable orders were used and common terms in the polynomial models for each order were extracted in order to circumvent this problem. We briefly describe the validation of this approach. In the absence of a published large multistate discrete model the authors used a Boolean model instead. The goal of this validation is not to make statements about the Boolean model and its validity, but rather to test how well the polynomial method is able to recover the model. In (Albert and Othmer 2003) a Boolean model for a well-characterized network of segment polarity genes in *Drosophila melanogaster* was presented. The network, consisting of five genes and 16 gene products, is responsible for pattern formation in the *Drosophila* embryo. The network is a ring of 12 interconnected cells, in which the genes are expressed in patterns resembling stripes. The genes represented in the model are *wingless, engrailed, hedgehog, patched,* and *cubitus interruptus*.

The proposed model is a collection of 21 Boolean functions, representing the genes and proteins in the network. Each function governs the state transitions of a single compound. Below are four of the functions, defined in the model:

$$
\begin{aligned}
f_6 &= hh_i^{t+1} = EN_i^t \wedge \neg CIR_i^t \\
f_7 &= HH_i^{t+1} = hh_i^t \\
f_8 &= ptc_i^{t+1} = CIA_i^{t+1} \wedge \neg EN_i^{t+1} \wedge \neg CIR_i^{t+1} \\
f_9 &= PTC_i^{t+1} = ptc_i^t \vee (PTC_i^t \wedge \neg HH_{i-1}{}^t \wedge \neg HH_{i+1}{}^t)
\end{aligned}
$$

Representing each of the molecular species by a variable, the Boolean functions may be translated into the following polynomial functions:

$$
\begin{aligned}
f_6 &= x_5(x_{15}+1), \\
f_7 &= x_6, \\
f_8 &= x_{13}\left((x_{11}+x_{20}+x_{11}x_{20})+x_{21}+(x_{11}+x_{20}+x_{11}x_{20})\,x_{21}\right) \\
&\quad (x_4+1)\,(x_{13}\,(x_{11}+1)\,(x_{20}+1)\,(x_{21}+1)+1) \\
f_9 &= x_8+x_9\,(x_{18}+1)\,(x_{19}+1)+x_8x_9\,(x_{18}+1)\,(x_{19}+1)
\end{aligned}
$$

Treating this Boolean model as "reality," wildtype and simulated knock-out experiments were generated, creating "knock-outs" by setting the function representing the gene to be knocked out equal to 0.

Not surprisingly, algorithm performance improved greatly with knock-out data rather than just wild-type data. The algorithm is able to reconstruct approximately 84% of the interactions in the Boolean model, versus 32% when only wildtype data were used. Furthermore, it correctly identified 92% of the additive interactions and 10% of the nonadditive interactions, whereas none of the nonadditive interactions were identified in the model constructed with only wildtype data.

In (Jarrah et al. 2007), a computational method was proposed, based on the algorithm in Laubenbacher and Stigler (2004), to find all minimal wiring diagrams, so that there exists a polynomial dynamical system with the exact same variable dependencies, which fits the given data set. Here, a wiring diagram is *minimal,* if there is no other wiring diagram with the same property, whose edges are a proper subset of the edges of the given wiring diagram. It uses an encoding of the information in the data as an algebraic object, which can then be analyzed by tools from computer algebra. To be precise, suppose we are looking at models

$$f = (f_1, \ldots, f_n) : K^n \to K^n$$

Where K is an appropriately chosen finite field, with variables $x_1, \ldots, x_n$. And suppose we are given a collection of state transitions $\mathbf{s} \to \mathbf{t}$, that is, any model f that fits the data set will have the property that $f(\mathbf{s}) = \mathbf{t}$. Now focus on a single coordinate i, so that the condition becomes $f_i(\mathbf{s}) = t$, with $t \in K$. We bin together the data points $\mathbf{s}$, depending on where they get mapped to. That is, consider the sets $P_a = \{\mathbf{s} \mid f(\mathbf{s}) = a$, for all f that fit the data$\}$, for all $a \in K$.

The basic idea behind the approach in Jarrah et al. (2007) is that, if we are given 2 system states $\mathbf{s}$ and $\mathbf{t}$, then a coordinate function f_i which takes on different values on these must contain some of the variables corresponding to coordinates in which $\mathbf{s}$ and $\mathbf{t}$ differ. This difference can be encoded in a monomial $m(\mathbf{s}, \mathbf{t}) = x_i \cdot x_j \cdot x_k \cdots$, which contains all those variables corresponding to coordinates in which $\mathbf{s}$ and $\mathbf{t}$ differ. We now collect together into a set M all those monomials $m(\mathbf{s}, \mathbf{t})$ for which $\mathbf{s} \in P_a$ and $t \in P_b$, and $a \neq b$, that is, $\mathbf{s}$ and $\mathbf{t}$ have different images under all possible ith coordinate functions. The space of all possible ith coordinate functions for models that fit the given data can then be described as

$$\{f \in K[x_1, \ldots, x_n] \mid f(\mathbf{s}) = a \text{ for all } \mathbf{s} \in P_a, \text{and for all } a \in K\}$$

We can now generate what is called an *ideal* in the collection of all polynomials $K[x_1, \ldots, x_n]$. The ideal I consists of all linear combinations of monomials in M with coefficients in K, multiplied by arbitrary polynomials. (This is the analog of a vector subspace of a vector space, with the monomials as the analog of a basis.) It turns out that the ideal I contains all the needed information about the minimal wiring diagrams (for variable x_i) that are consistent with the given data set.

To extract this information, we need to compute what is called the *primary decomposition* of I. This is the analog of the decomposition of a positive integer into a product of powers of prime numbers. It was known already to Euclid that such a decomposition exists and is unique. The concept of an ideal, such as I, began in number theory as the notion of an ideal number. It was shown in several contexts, such as the polynomial context $K[x_1, \ldots, x_n]$, that one can generalize the notion of a decomposition into prime numbers. In $K[x_1, \ldots, x_n]$, one can show that each ideal can be expressed as an intersection of ideals that are powers of prime ideals (suitably defined). Each of these prime ideals turns out to be generated (in the same way as I) by a subcollection of the variables x_i. We call those prime ideals minimal whose generating variables are not contained in the set of generating variables for another prime ideal in this decomposition.

The main result in Jarrah et al. (2007) is that the collection of minimal wiring diagrams is in one-to-one correspondence with the set of minimal primes in the primary decomposition of I. Furthermore, a suite of likelihood scores was defined that allows further selection of minimal wiring diagrams. Algorithms for computing primary decompositions are implemented in several computer algebra software packages, and are readily available for top-down modeling.

A useful freely available web tool for top-down modeling using the framework described here is *Polynome* (Dimitrova et al. 2011). This tool has several algorithms available for model inference from experimental data. While *Polynome* in its entirety constructs only Boolean models, all the algorithms available for the construction of deterministic models choose the appropriate number of model variable states based on the individual data set input. Another useful web tool for the analysis and simulation of discrete models is *ADAM (Analysis of Dynamic Algebraic Models)* (Hinkelmann et al. 2011). Both packages make use of the open source computer algebra package *Macaulay2*.

The method in Laubenbacher and Stigler (2004) has been significantly improved upon in Veliz-Cuba and Laubenbacher (2012). In Laubenbacher and Stigler 2004 no restriction was imposed on the type of logical rules/polynomial functions that could appear in the models. However, in typical gene regulatory networks, the causal interactions can be classified as either activations or inhibitions. The capability to use only monotone increasing or decreasing functions in top-down modeling has been added in Veliz-Cuba and Laubenbacher (2012), with a primary focus on an improved algorithm to infer the wiring diagram of a network, rather than a dynamic model. It also uses concepts and algorithms from computational algebraic geometry to an even greater extent. We briefly describe this approach here. The setting is quite general, with variable x_i taking values in a set X_i, which we represent as $\{0, 1, \ldots, m_i\} = [0, m_i]$. We further assume that X_i is ordered, with the natural ordering $0 < 1 < \ldots < m_i$. The coordinate function f_i then has the form

$$f_i : [0, m_1] \times [0, m_2] \times \cdots \times [0, m_n] \rightarrow [0, m_i]$$

With the natural ordering of the state sets, we can now define, in the obvious way, monotone increasing and decreasing functions. Those will be the only ones considered by the top-down modeling algorithm. In this way, edges in the wiring diagram can be designated as positive (activation) or negative (inhibition). Such functions are also known as *unate.* The basic idea behind the algorithm is a generalization of the primary decomposition approach in Jarrah et al. (2007) by encoding the requirement that regulatory relationships should have a sign attached to it into the definition of an analog to the ideal *I*. With this generalization, all minimal signed wiring diagrams can again be computed by finding the minimal prime ideals in the primary decomposition of this ideal. It is shown that this modified version of the algorithm exhibits greatly increased performance over the algorithm in Jarrah et al. (2007).

It is worth noting that these algorithms represent excellent examples of how the introduction of additional mathematical structure can give access to powerful theoretical results and computational approaches. In this case, the set of models that fit a given data set was endowed with algebraic structure, which allowed the authors to apply the concept of a primary decomposition, and the computational tool of symbolic algorithms implemented in existing computer algebra programs, to the selection of suitable wiring diagrams. Note that the input, as well as the output of the method only carries set-theoretic information, and the algebra is introduced as a sort of "black box" computational device.

5 DATA DISCRETIZATION

One drawback of any discrete modeling framework is that it requires the discretization, or categorization, of the experimental data to be used. There are many possible ways to do that, and different choices may result in different discretized data sets. The goal is to optimize

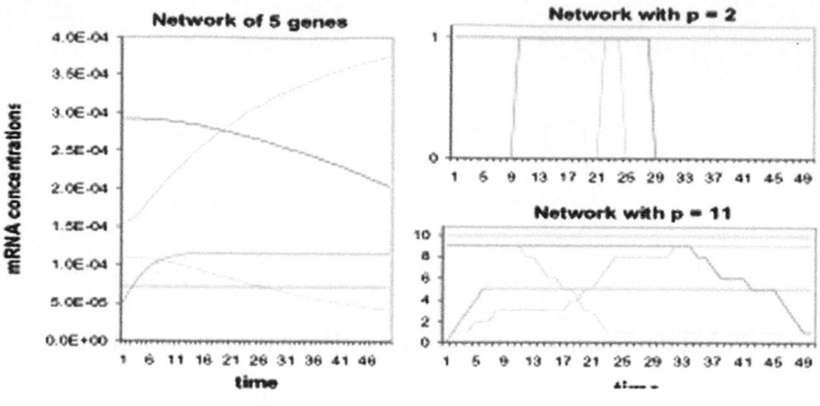

FIGURE 11.1 Different levels of data discretization.

between a small number of possible states, in order to limit the size of the model search space, and a sufficiently good resolution of the data to preserve key dynamic features. Figure 11.1 shows mRNA concentrations of a gene regulatory network simulated with the biochemical network simulator Gepasi (Mendes 1993; Mendes 1997) on the left. The right side of Figure 11.1 shows two different discretizations, one Boolean, the other allowing 11 possible states.

This example makes it is clear that in many cases a finer data discretization is needed in order for a model to capture the essential dynamic features contained in a multivariate dataset. It is well understood that gene regulation relies on a delicate balance of transcription factors (Werner et al. 2003) that is not easily captured with an ON/OFF scheme. The algorithm in Dimitrova et al. (2010) is intended to optimize between a small number of variable states and faithfulness to the continuous data. We illustrate it in the example below.

Consider the simulated gene regulatory network in Figure 11.2 with five genes, whose wiring diagram is given in Figure 11.2a. The network was generated with the artificial gene network system AGN (Mendes et al. 2003). After simulating the network with the biochemical network simulator Gepasi (Mendes 1993, 1997), one finds that it has the positive stable steady state (1.99006, 1.99006, 0.000024814, 0.997525, 1.99994). From the model we generated 6 time series, each of length 20, including one wild-type time series, and five deletion mutant time series. The discretization algorithm in Dimitrova et al. (2010) chooses the number system $X = \{0, 1, 2, 3, 4\}$, consisting of five different states for the combined data set. After using the multivariate interpolation algorithm we obtain a "best" polynomial model f: $X^5 \rightarrow X^5$ in five variables. Its phase space consists of a directed graph whose nodes are the 5^5 possible states for the five variables, and there is a directed edge from state $\boldsymbol{a}$ to state $\boldsymbol{b}$ if $f(\boldsymbol{a}) = \boldsymbol{b}$. The model also has a fixed point, like the continuous "real world" system. Figure 11.2c shows a particular initialization of the network, simulated in Gepasi, reaching the above steady state. Figure 11.2d shows a sample of the time series obtained by initializing the discrete model f with the discretization of this initialization. It converges to the discretization (4, 4, 0, 4, 2) of the steady state above.

This example illustrates the fact that the discrete model f exhibits the same qualitative dynamics as the continuous model we started with. Figure 11.2b shows the wiring diagram of the discrete model obtained with our algorithm. The main point of this example is to

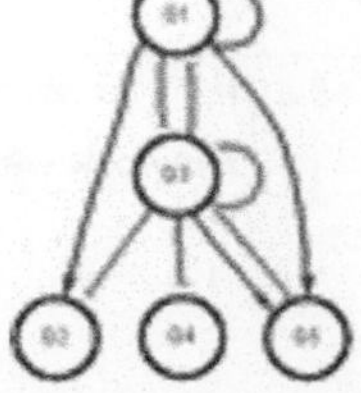

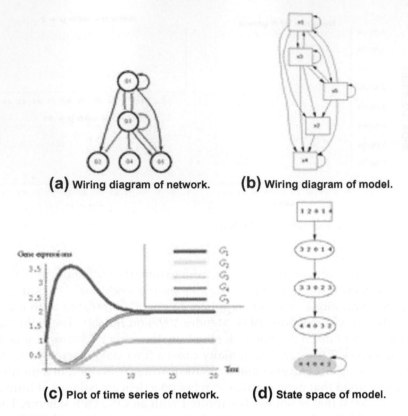

(a) Wiring diagram of network.

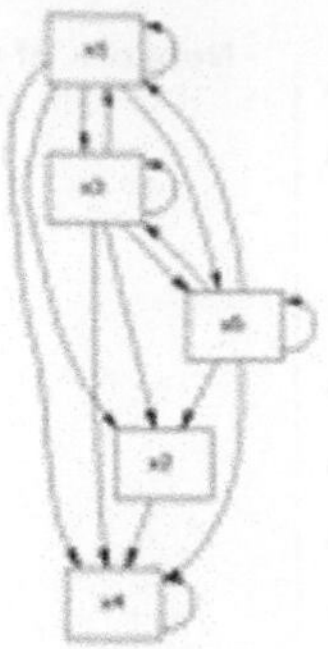

(b) Wiring diagram of model.

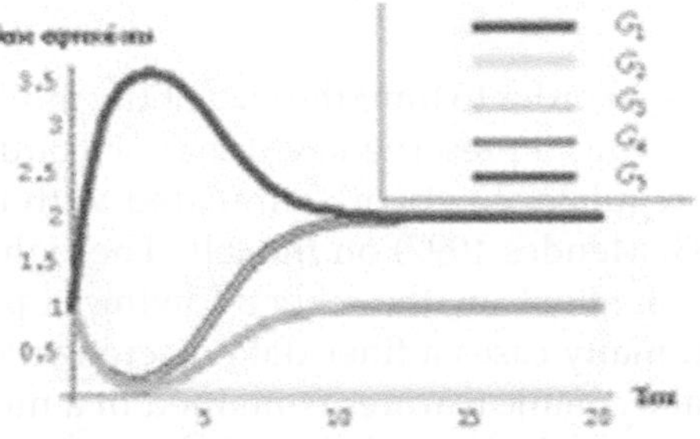

(c) Plot of time series of network.

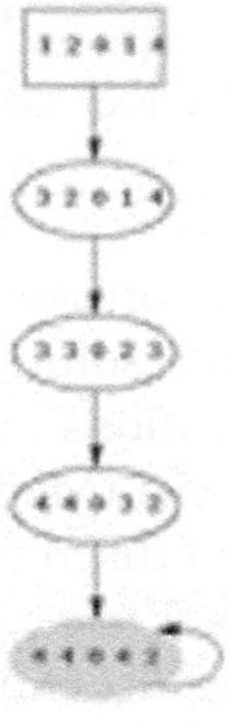

(d) State space of model.

FIGURE 11.2 Graphs of a network and its associated models.

demonstrate that our discretization method preserves the essential dynamic features of the continuous system representing "reality" in this case, and our interpolation algorithm chooses a model that reflects these dynamic features as well as most of the causal dependencies among the variables.

6 RELATIONSHIP BETWEEN DISCRETE AND CONTINUOUS TOP-DOWN MODELING

It has been argued in Cantone et al. (2009) and elsewhere that it might be advantageous to combine different top-down modeling methods to improve algorithm performance. In this section we provide an example involving the modeling method in Jarrah et al. (2007), described above, taken from Stigler et al. (in press). There, an algorithm named DICORE (DIscrete and COntinuous Reverse Engineering) is presented, that combines the polynomial method with a top-down modeling method based on a system of linear ordinary differential equations. Several existing methods take the approach of estimating parameters in a generic linear ODE system, e.g., (Gardner et al. 2003). The general set-up in Stigler et al. (in press) is to consider a network with n genes and p perturbations and assume that the network dynamics can be approximated by a system of linear ordinary differential equations (ODE) of the form:

$$\begin{aligned} dx_i/dt &= \sum_k a_{k,i}x_k + \sum_l b_{l,i}\, p_l + e_i \\ dp_j/dt &= \sum_k a_{k,j+n}x_k \end{aligned} \tag{11.1}$$

with $1 \le i, k \le n$ and $1 \le j, l \le p$. The variable x_i represents the expression level of gene i, p_l is the magnitude of perturbation l (which could be a concentration of an inhibitor), $a_{k,i}$ is the effect of gene k on gene i, $a_{k,j+n}$ is the effect of gene k on perturbation j, b_{li} is the direct effect caused by perturbation p_l on x_i, and e_i is associated with the basal rate of expression of x_i. Given this general form, the main task is to determine the coefficients, or parameters, of the terms on the right-hand sides of the ODEs by fitting them to experimental time course data. The positive parameters then provide activation edges in the wiring diagram and the negative ones inhibition edges. For n genes and p perturbations one thus has to fit $n(n+p+1) + pn$ parameters, a computationally expensive task as n gets even moderately large. In order to make the problem tractable, different methods make assumptions, such as a small upper bound on the number of variables that provide input to a given variable, e.g. (Gardner et al. 2003), which is based on biological assumptions that do not always hold. The approach in Stigler et al. (in press) is to instead use a preprocessing step that helps reduce the number of nonzero parameters to be fit.

Recall that the algorithm in Jarrah et al. (2007) has as output a collection of minimal wiring diagrams that received the highest score using a particular scoring method. We now take the union of all the edges in all these wiring diagrams. The resulting consensus network will then be biased toward false positives, that is, edges/regulatory relationships that are actually not present in the network. We now assume that those edges not present in the consensus network are in fact absent in the network. Consequently, we can set the corresponding parameters in the ODE system (Bruggeman and Westerhoff 2007) equal to 0, thereby reducing the number of parameters to be estimated, typically quite significantly in practice. In (Stigler et al. in press), the resulting smaller ODE system is then fitted to data using the software package COPASI (Hoops et al. 2006), with its built-in particle swarm parameter estimation algorithm. The combined method, DICORE, is then applied to a data set generated by the authors, consisting of DNA microarray data from wildtype and knockout mutant time courses, measuring the response of *Saccharomyces cerevisiae* to oxidative stress induced by treatment with cumene hydroperoxide. It is shown that DICORE outperforms several other well-established top-down modeling methods.

7 TOWARD A MATHEMATICAL THEORY OF BIOLOGICAL SYSTEM IDENTIFICATION

The basic inverse problem we face in modeling biochemical networks is common in engineering and applied mathematics, known as system identification. Our goal is to make a phenomenological (and, ultimately, mechanistic) mathematical model of a multivariate system which we can observe as well as perturb, and about which we may have partial knowledge. The major challenges, compared to typical engineered systems, are that the system is very often high dimensional, often strongly nonlinear, the number of observations is small in comparison to the dimension, and the information we have about the systems is very limited. The basic procedure is to choose an appropriate modeling framework, use one or more time courses of observations to identify some or all possible models within this framework and choose "the best" one from the space of possible models. For engineered systems there is a well-developed mathematical theory that helps in this process. (An important application is to developing controllers for systems.) In particular, there is a theory of system identifiability, which provides criteria for how good a given data set is for the system identification process; see, e.g., (Ljung 1999) for a comprehensive treatment of system identification.

No corresponding mathematical theory exists yet for the identification of biological systems. In particular, there is no good understanding about the appropriate experimental design for a particular modeling framework, which provides good data sets for top-down modeling. The most commonly studied type of systematic perturbation still focuses on single genes in regulatory networks (Ideker et al. 2000; Karp et al. 1999; Rung et al. 2002; Shmulevich et al. 2002; Tegner et al. 2003). Genetical genomics provides another possible approach (Jansen 2003). Studies of the quantity of data needed were done in Krupa (2002). The study of appropriate experimental designs for different modeling methods must be part of a long-term systems biology modeling program.

8 CONCLUSION

We have discussed some top-down modeling methods resulting in time-discrete dynamical system models over finite state sets. They serve to provide high-level information about systems that can be used as constraints for the construction of low-level models, either top-down or bottom-up. Our method using polynomial dynamical systems over finite fields has the advantageous feature that its mathematical underpinning provides access to a variety of mathematical algorithms and symbolic computation software. Other modeling approaches have other advantages, such as the capability of asynchronous update or the incorporation of discrete as well as continuous variables. The choice of what method to use in a particular case will depend on the type of data and information available. For instance, the incorporation of asynchronous update is only feasible computationally with prior biological information on the pathways to be modeled.

The methods discussed here also provide a mathematical basis for the investigation of questions like "goodness" measures on datasets. Ultimately, the performance of a top-down modeling method cannot be properly evaluated unless we understand what types of input data are required for optimal performance. That is, "the data must fit the model." Experimental data sets suitable for the different modeling methods are still difficult to obtain, and the biochemical networks producing the data are typically too poorly understood to truly test modeling performance.

We believe that the field of system identification can serve as a blueprint for a mathematical top-down modeling program in systems biology. Based on a well-defined collection of model classes, from high-level statistical models down to ODE and PDE models, such a program must include the development of appropriate system identification methods for each model class and quality measures on data sets that can be used to develop confidence measures for the resulting models. The ongoing DREAM program, referenced earlier, is already making a very important contribution to this effort.

Acknowledgments

This work was partially supported by NIH Grant RO1 GM068947-01. The authors thank E. Dimitrova, A. Jarrah, D. Potter, B. Stigler, J. Tyson, and P. Vera-Licona for help in preparing this manuscript.

References

Albert, R., and Othmer, H. G. (2003). The topology of the regulatory interactions predicts the expression pattern of the segment polarity genes in Drosophila melanogaster. *J. Theor. Biol.* **223**(1):1–18.

Arkin, A., Ross, J., and McAdams, H. H. (1998). Stochastic kinetic analysis of developmental pathway bifurcation in phage lambda-infected *Escherichia coli* cells. *Genetics* **149**(4):1633–1648.

Ashall, L., Horton, C., Nelson, D., Paszek, P., Harper, C., Sillitoe, K., et al. (2009). Pulsatile stimulation determines timing and specificity of NF-kappaB-dependent transcription. *Science* **324**:242–246.

Bentele, M., Lavrik, I., Ulrich, M., Stoesser, S., Heermann, D. W., Kalthoff, H., et al. (2004). Mathematical modeling reveals threshold mechanism in CD95-induced apoptosis. *J. Cell Biol.* **166**(6):839–851.

Bray, D., Bourret, R. B., and Simon, M. I. (1993). Computer simulation of the phosphorylation cascade controlling bacterial chemotaxis. *Mol. Biol. Cell* **4**(5):469–482.

Brenner, S. (1997). *Loose Ends*. London: Current Biology. p. 73

Bruggeman, F. J., and Westerhoff, H. V. (2007). The nature of systems biology. *Trends Microbiol.* **15**(1):45–50.

Cantone, I., Marucci, L., Iorio, F., Ricci, M. A., Belcastro, V., Bansal, M., et al. (2009). A yeast synthetic network for in vivo assessment of reverse-engineering and modeling approaches. *Cell* **137**(1):172–181. Epub 2009/03/31

Chifman, J., Kniss, A., Neupane, P., Williams, I., Leung, B., Deng, Z., et al. (2012). The core control system of intracellular iron homeostasis: a mathematical model. *J. Theor. Biol.* **300**:91–99.

Cox, D., Little, J., and O'Shea, D. (1997). *Ideals, varieties, and algorithms*. (2nd ed.). New York: Springer Verlag.

Dimitrakopoulou, K., Tsimpouris, C., Papadopoulos, G., Pommerenke, C., Wilk, E., Sgarbas, K. N., et al. (2011). Dynamic gene network reconstruction from gene expression data in mice after influenza A (H1N1) infection. *J. Clin. Bioinform.* **1**

Dimitrova, E. S., Licona, M. P. V., McGee, J., and Laubenbacher, R. (2010). Discretization of time series data. *J. Comput. Biol.* **17**(6):853–868.

Dimitrova, E., García-Puente, L. D., Hinkelmann, F., Jarrah, A. S., Laubenbacher, R., Stigler, B., et al. (2011). Parameter estimation for Boolean models of biological networks. *Theor. Comput. Sci.* **412**(26):2816–2826.

Faith, J. J., Hayete, B., Thaden, J. T., Mogno, I., Wierzbowski, J., Cottarel, G., et al. (2007). Large-scale mapping and validation of *Escherichia coli* transcriptional regulation from a compendium of expression profiles. *PLoS Biol.* **5**(1):e8. Epub 2007/01/12

Fink, C. C., Slepchenko, B., Moraru, I. I., Watras, J., Schaff, J. C., and Loew, L. M. (2000). An image-based model of calcium waves in differentiated neuroblastoma cells. *Biophys. J.* **79**(1):163–183.

Gardner, T. S., di Bernardo, D., Lorenz, D., and Collins, J. J. (2003). Inferring genetic networks and identifying compound mode of action via expression profiling. *Science* **301**(5629):102–105.

Grayson D, Stillman M. Macaulay2, a software system for research in algebraic geometry; 1992–2003. Available from: http://www.math.uiuc.edu/Macaulay2.

Haury, A. C., Mordelet, F., Vera-Licona, P., and Vert, J. P. (2012). TIGRESS: Trustful Inference of Gene REgulation using Stability Selection. *BMC Syst. Biol.* **6**(1):145. Epub 2012/11/24

Hinkelmann, F., Murrugarra, D., Jarrah, A. S., and Laubenbacher, R. (2011). A mathematical framework for agent based models of complex biological networks. *Bull. Math. Biol.* **73**(7):1583–1602. Epub 2010/09/30

Hinkelmann, F., Brandon, M., Guang, B., McNeill, R., Blekherman, G., Veliz-Cuba, A., et al. (2011). ADAM: analysis of discrete models of biological systems using computer algebra. *BMC Bioinform.* **12**Hinkelmann, F., Brandon,

M., Guang, B., McNeill, R., Blekherman, G., Veliz-Cuba, A., et al. (2011). ADAM: analysis of discrete models of biological systems using computer algebra. *BMC Bioinform.* **12**

Hong, C., Lee, M., Kim, D., Cho, K.-H., and Shin, I. (2012). A checkpoints capturing timing-robust Boolean model of the budding yeast cell cycle regulatory network. *BMC Syst. Biol.* **6**(1)

Hoops, S., Sahle, S., Gauges, R., Lee, C., Pahle, J., Simus, N., et al. (2006). COPASI - a COmplex PAthway SImulator. *Bioinformatics* **22**:3067–3074.

Ideker, T. E., Thorsson, V., and Karp, R. M. (2000). Discovery of regulatory interactions through perturbation: inference and experimental design. *Pac. Sym. Biocomput.* **5**:305–316.

Jansen, R. C. (2003). Studying complex biological systems using multifactorial perturbation. *Nat. Rev. Genet.* **4**:145–151.

Jarrah, A. S., Laubenbacher, R., Stigler, B., and Stillman, M. (2007). Reverse-engineering of polynomial dynamical systems. *Adv. Appl. Math.* **39**(4):477–489.

Karp RM, Stoughton R, Yeung K. Algorithms for Choosing Differential Gene Expression Experiments. RECOMB99. 1999.

Kell, D. B. (2004). Metabolomics and systems biology: making sense of the soup. *Curr. Opin. Microbiol.* **7**(3):296–307.

Kramer, N., Schafer, J., and Boulesteix, A. L. (2009). Regularized estimation of large-scale gene association networks using graphical Gaussian models. *BMC Bioinform.* **10**:384. Epub 2009/11/26

Krupa, B. (2002). On the number of experiments required to find the causal structure of complex systems. *J. Theor. Biol.* **219**(2):257–267.

Kuffner, R., Petri, T., Tavakkolkhah, P., Windhager, L., and Zimmer, R. (2012). Inferring gene regulatory networks by ANOVA. *Bioinformatics* **28**(10):1376–1382. Epub 2012/04/03

Laubenbacher, R., and Stigler, B. (2004). A computational algebra approach to the reverse-engineering of gene regulatory networks. *J. Theor. Biol.* **229**:523–537.

Lidl, R., and Niederreiter, H. (1997). *Finite fields.* (2nd ed.). New York: Cambridge University Press.

Ljung, L. (1999). *System identification; Theory for the user.* (2nd ed.). Upper Saddle River, NJ: Prentice Hall.

Loomis, W. F., and Sternberg, P. W. (1995). Genetic networks. *Science* **269**(5224):649.

Madar, A., Greenfield, A., Vanden-Eijnden, E., and Bonneau, R. (2010). DREAM3: network inference using dynamic context likelihood of relatedness and the inferelator. *PLoS One* **5**(3):e9803. Epub 2010/03/27

Mendes, P. (1993). GEPASI: a software package for modelling the dynamics, steady states and control of biochemical and other systems. *Comput. Appl. Biosci.* **9**(5):563–571.

Mendes, P. (1997). Biochemistry by numbers: simulation of biochemical pathways with Gepasi 3. *Trends Biochem. Sci.* **22**:361–363.

Mendes, P., Sha, W., and Ye, K. (2003). Artificial gene networks for objective comparison of analysis algorithms. *Bioinformatics* **19**(Suppl. 2):ii122–ii129.

Pahle, J. (2009). Biochemical simulations: stochastic, approximate stochastic and hybrid approaches. *Brief. Bioinform.* **10**(1):53–64.

Porreca, R., Cinquemani, E., Lygeros, J., and Ferrari-Trecate, G. (2010). Identification of genetic network dynamics with unate structure. *Bioinformatics* **26**(9):1239–1245. Epub 2010/03/23

Rung, J., Schlitt, T., Brazma, A., Freivalds, K., and Vilo, J. (2002). Building and analysing genome-wide gene disruption networks. *Bioinformatics* **18**(Suppl. 2):S202–S210.

Shmulevich, I., Dougherty, E. R., and Zhang, W. (2002). Gene perturbation and intervention in probabilistic Boolean networks. *Bioinformatics* **18**(10):1319–1331.

Stigler B, Camacho D, Martins A, Sha W, Dimitrova E, Vera Licona P, et al. Reverse engineering a yeast oxidative stress response network, in press.

Tegner, J., Yeung, M. K., Hasty, J., and Collins, J. J. (2003). Reverse engineering gene networks: integrating genetic perturbations with dynamical modeling. *Proc. Natl. Acad. Sci. USA* **100**(10):5944–5949.

Teusink, B., Passarge, J., Reijenga, C. A., Esgalhado, E., van der Weijden, C. C., Schepper, M., et al. (2000). Can yeast glycolysis be understood in terms of in vitro kinetics of the constituent enzymes?. *Test. Biochem. Eur. J. Biochem.* **267**(17):5313–5329.

Veliz-Cuba, A., and Laubenbacher, R. (2012). On the computation of fixed points in Boolean networks. *J. Appl. Math. Comput.* **39**(1–2):145–153.

Veliz-Cuba, A., Jarrah, A. S., and Laubenbacher, R. (2010). Polynomial algebra of discrete models in systems biology. *Bioinformatics* **26**(13):1637–1643.

Vignes, M., Vandel, J., Allouche, D., Ramadan-Alban, N., Cierco-Ayrolles, C., Schiex, T., et al. (2011). Gene regulatory network reconstruction using Bayesian networks, the Dantzig Selector, the Lasso and their meta-analysis. *PLoS One* **6**(12):e29165. Epub 2012/01/05

Wang, H., Qian, L., and Dougherty, E. (2010). Inference of gene regulatory networks using S-system: a unified approach. *IET Syst. Biol.* **4**(2):145–156. Epub 2010/03/18

Werner, T., Fessele, S., Maier, H., and Nelson, P. J. (2003). Computer modeling of promoter organization as a tool to study transcriptional coregulation. *FASEB J.: Official pub. Federation Am. Soc. Exp. Biol.* **17**(10):1228–1237. Epub 2003/07/02

Yeung, M. K., Tegner, J., and Collins, J. J. (2002). Reverse engineering gene networks using singular value decomposition and robust regression. *Proc. Natl. Acad. Sci. USA* **99**(9):6163–6168.

CHAPTER

12

Discrete Gene Network Models for Understanding Multicellularity and Cell Reprogramming: From Network Structure to Attractor Landscapes Landscape

Joseph Xu Zhou, Xiaojie Qiu, Aymeric Fouquier d'Herouel, Sui Huang

Institute for Systems Biology, Seattle, WA, USA

CONTENTS

Computational Systems Biology, Second Edition
http://dx.doi.org/10.1016/B978-0-12-405926-9.00012-5

Abstract

In this chapter, we introduced the basic concepts of cell attractors and showed that Waddington's metaphoric epigenetic landscape has a formal basis in the attractor landscape. This conceptual framework helps to understand core properties of cell differentiation and ultimately, multicellularity. Specifically, we developed the concept of relative stability of network states on the epigenetic landscape, thus providing the elevation in the landscape picture a formal, quantifiable basis. We proposed methods to quantify the relative stability of attractor states in discrete gene networks models. We show in two examples that even with incomplete information about network structures, the use of Boolean networks can capture the essential outlines of cell fate dynamics and more importantly, permit the estimation of relative stability and the attractor transition barriers. These measures hold great promise for the rational design of the perturbation protocols for cell reprogramming in regenerative medicine. As the knowledge of the structure of GRNs for the development of various tissues will undoubtedly increase in the next decade, the utilization of such network information for therapeutic reprogramming may benefit from the concepts developed here.

1 INTRODUCTION

A characteristic for multicellular organisms is the propensity of their cells to differentiate into functionally distinct *cell types*, such as a nerve cell, a skin cell, etc., although they all share the very same genome. A cell type represents a discretely distinct phenotypic state. A phenotypic state refers to any functional state with a cell type's lineage, such as the immature stem-cell sate, a proliferative, quiescent, apoptotic, activated, migratory, senescent or the mature, differentiated state. Each such state exhibits a biological function in the tissue and can in a first approximation be characterized by the expression status of a cell state-defining set of genes. This set contains both regulators as well as effector genes that perform the state-specific functions. For example, red blood cell's capacity to transport oxygen depend on the expression of the hemoglobin genes, but also on the expression (at least in its precursor) of the regulatory protein GATA1, a transcription factor that stimulates differentiation of blood stem cells into the red blood cell lineage. More generally, a cell state, of which a differentiated cell type is the most prosaic representation, is defined by the expression status across all the 23,000 or so gene loci in the human genome which is manifest (with some modification) as the cellular abundance of transcripts and proteins of the respective loci. Here we refer to such genome-wide gene expression pattern as "*gene expression state*" or simply "state", of a cell. Since the gene expression pattern is imposed by the dynamics of the gene regulatory network, a cell state is in this discussion equivalent to a network state.

More specifically, the discreteness of the biologically observable functional states, as listed above, have been explained by theorists by the fact that they correspond to ***attractor states***, distinct naturally emerging stable states of the gene regulatory network (GRN) that coordinate gene expression across the genome and that will be the central topic of this chapter.

It is because functional cell phenotypes are manifestations of attractor states that biologists can readily speak of ***transitions*** of cells from one state to another. Then, these transitions between different phenotypic states, or in the most extreme case, the switch from one cell type to another, as recently popularized by "reprogramming", is the in essence embodied by the change from one gene expression state to another, and thus, involved the coordinated change in the expression status of the genes across the genome.

Historically, in cell and molecular biology, the formalism of states, attractor states and transitions between them however have not been the concepts in which cell phenotype changes have been portrayed. With the tradition in the mind-set of *ad hoc* molecular causality, cell phenotype switching has typically been explained by so-called "signal transduction", mediated by cascades of biochemical events, typically protein-protein interactions, that link an extracellular signal (e.g. a growth factor binding to a cell receptor) to the alteration of expression of regulatory genes that in turn control the expression of those proteins necessary to implement the new cell fate. This molecular biology framework has driven the elucidation of countless signal transduction pathways and gene regulatory interactions which in turn has brought great insight into the material foundation of cell fate regulation.

But this pathway-centric biology, in ceaseless quest for linear-causal relationships between biomolecule and phenotypic traits, has limitations for a formal treatment of cell phenotype change. At closer inspection the very notion of an independently acting and thus cleanly defined *pathway* does not hold: Massive cross-talks take place between the various pathways (Bouvier 1990). One "pathway" can perform different tasks due to the interactions with many others, depending on the cellular context. For example, the WNT pathway can maintain the stemness state of pancreas cells and while it triggers cell differentiation of skin cells (Murtaugh 2008; Larue and Delmas 2006). With the arrival in mainstream biology of "systems thinking" and of theories of complex dynamical systems, originating in the late 1960s (Kauffman 1993; Von Bertalanffy 1956) the notion of distinct pathways that embody a causation eventually has begun to fade (but still persists) as the concept of a gene regulatory network (GRN) with various network states began to gain a foothold. The GRN is the network that consists of the web of regulatory interactions among all the genes that regulate each other (or at least, are being regulated). It is in this sense, that systems biology has been initially called "network biology" by those to which such systems thinking was new Marcotte 2001).

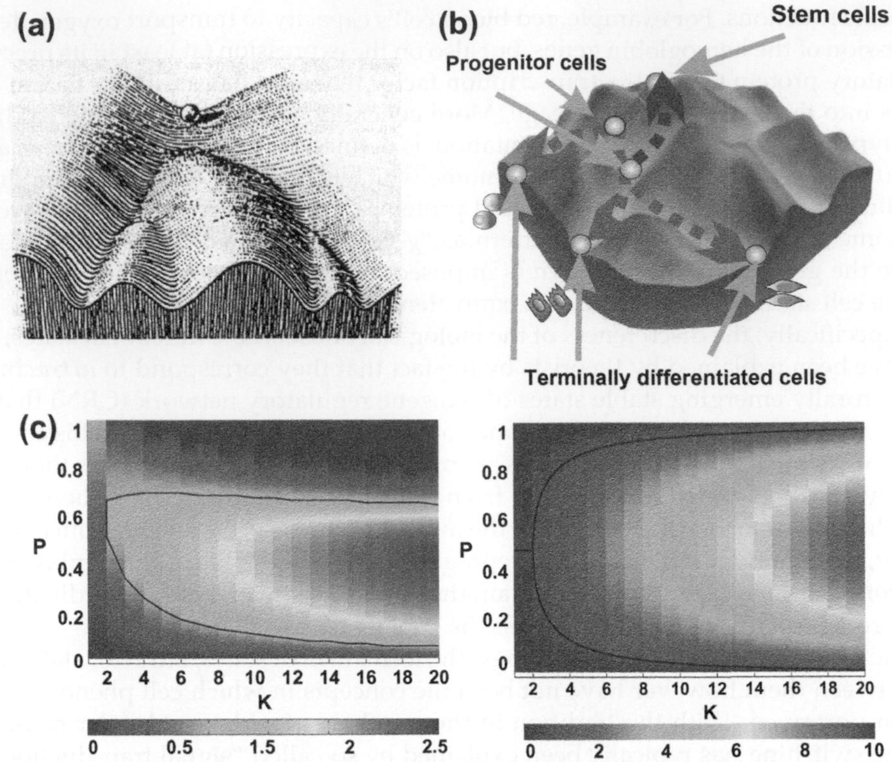

FIGURE 12.1 (a) Waddington's "Epigenetic Landscape", captures the discrete nature of cell fate decision. Reprinted from C.F. Waddinton "The strategy of the Gene" (1957). (b) A schematic quasi-potential landscape that is computed from the normal decomposition of the driving forces defined in GRN (Zhou et. al. 2012). The high-dimensional state space is projected to a two-dimensional plane, the elevation representing the quasi-potential associated to every state. The landscape captures the global dynamics and permits the comparison of attractors (cavities). The downhill movement of the green ball represents the differentiation process. The metastable quality of progenitor cells is reflected in the higher "altitude" of such states, illustrating the inherent potential to further differentiate. Red trajectories illustrate cell lineage determination in normal development; the blue trajectory represents a putative path taken by artificial reprogramming. (c) The heatmap of the ensemble sensitivity of threshold network and random Boolean network with the same range of input degree *K* and positive output probability *p*. **LEFT PANEL.** The heatmap of the ensemble sensitivity of the threshold networks. **RIGHT PANEL.** The heatmap of the ensemble sensitivity of the random Boolean networks.

From a broader perspective, the central questions on multicellularity that were rarely addressed in the pathway-centric picture are: Why do different cell types have distinct and stable gene expression patterns albeit carrying identical genomes? Why is the gene expression pattern characteristic of cell types robust (self-sustaining) in a noisy environment? What are the driving forces and the obstacles associated with the transition from one cell type to another? Ever since the first nuclear transfer experiment in the 1950s and various cell reprogramming experiments later (Gurdon et al. 1958), it has been, against prevailing orthodoxy, increasingly realized that every cell type possess certain phenotype plasticity in that it can be reprogrammed into another cell type. Actually, why not—given that all cells possess the same genome (Huang 2009)? The most extreme example of reprogramming is of course *in vitro* "back-conversions" of fibroblast cells (or many other differentiated cells) to embryonic cell like pluripotent cells, now commonly referred to as induced pluripotent stem(iPS) cells, or of fibroblast cells to neurons and cardiomyocytes etc. (Takahashi and Yamanaka 2006; Graf 2011)

A useful principle to frame these observations within one single concept has been articulated by the embryologist Conrad Hal Waddington in the 1950s (Waddington 1957). He introduced the intuitive and at that time purely metaphoric concept of an "epigenetic landscape", shown in Figure 12.1, to illustrate the fact that cells are forced by external influences toward distinct (quasi-)discretely separated cell fates, much like a marble is forced by gravitation to roll along a given path downhill into pre-existing valleys of the landscape. If such rolling down represents development (as Waddington intended his metaphor to do), then reprogramming would correspond to jumping from one valley to another—in fact an extension of his metaphor now widely used by contemporary biologists without further formal thought (Zhou and Melton 2008). But since each cell fate is associated with a distinct gene expression profile, the latter must also exhibit discrete states that can change into one another through (quasi-)discontinuous transitions—as predicted by the idea that the valleys are attractor states of the gene regulatory network (Huang 2012).

In this chapter, we review the hypothesis that cell types are the attractors in a high-dimensional gene expression state space and present some experimental evidences. A small (low-dimensional) genetic circuit is then used to explain how distinct phenotypes can arise from its dynamics, a requisite for differentiation and multicellularity. We use two widely employed simplifying models, Boolean networks and threshold networks, to computationally implement GRNs and analyze their sensitivity, criticality, and other architecture-dynamics relationships. The concepts of "relative stability" and "global ordering" of network states, which are essential for understanding the spontaneity (directionality) the cell differentiation, will be established in the framework of Boolean networks and threshold networks by using a transition matrix. To demonstrate the modeling process, we discuss two biological problems: differentiation and reprogramming of the central nervous system and of pancreas cells.

2 GENE REGULATORY NETWORKS AND CELL TYPES: ATTRACTORS IN A DYNAMICAL SYSTEM

The molecular processes that take place inside cells and drive their behavior can be modeled in the framework of *dynamical systems theory*. In the following sections, we illustrate the connection between key concepts of the theory and central questions of cell differentiation and multicellularity. For a general and comprehensive introduction to the topic, we refer the reader to (Huang 2009; Huang et al. 2005).

2.1 Beyond linear pathways: Cell types as high-dimensional attractors

How does a fertilized egg cell differentiate into distinct cell types with different functions and morphology? The commitment of a pluripotent or a multipotent stem cell to a cell lineage is generally thought to be initiated by the activation of a "master" transcription factor (TF) that is specialized to promote that respective cell type (Smith et al. 2007; Oliveri and Davidson 2004a; Oliveri and Davidson 2004b; Oliveri et al. 2002). These master regulators control sets of "downstream" or "target" genes that perform tissue-specific functions. But how are the master TFs regulated *themselves*?

A commonly invoked "controller of the controller" is the epigenetic machinery of gene regulation, consisting mainly of DNA methylation and a series of covalent histone modification occurred after cell differentiation, which open the chromatin in which the genomic DNA is packaged, such that the promoter regions of gene loci become accessible to master TFs mentioned (Goldberg et al. 2007). Epigenetic control is also used to explain the stabilization of gene expression patterns which in turn would enable cells to maintain the same phenotype during their lifetime, even across cell divisions. This explanation of the control of the controller of course is a brainchild of the aforementioned traditions of linear pathway thinking that reigns in molecular biology and seeks proximate causation. In addition to the epistemic fallacy or circular argumentation (who controls the controller, and so on…?), one concrete problem is that epigenetic modifications of DNA and histones are dynamic and reversible (Kubicek and Jenuwein 2004) and above all, the enzymes that write the epigenetic marks are agnostic of gene loci and depend on TFs to recruit them to the appropriate genes. They are thus more likely to be a consequence of cell differentiation than the cause of it, since their placement and maintenance is tightly controlled by other factors. These observations suggest that epigenetic modifications are secondary to the regulation of cell differentiation by transcription factors, (please see supplementary file in (Huang 2012)). Thus, the ultimate carrier of responsibility for orchestrating gene expression pattern is the gene regulatory network—which in turn is the natural embodiment of interdependence between the various gene loci, the essence behind patterns of gene expression.

How does a single GRN allow produce the distinct phenotypic cell states or cell types? Since a cell state is associated with a distinct gene expression pattern, let us play briefly with the numbers. Humans have about 23,000 genes in their genome (Southan 2004), of which roughly 3000 are TFs (or other regulators that control specific sets of targets, such as miRNAs) (Vaquerizas et al. 2009). This would combinatorically allow in principle for an immense number of different expression patterns: if only each gene could be in the ON ('1') and OFF ('0') state, such a binary system would display $2^{3000} \approx 10^{1000}$ states. Yet, instead of this continuum of gene expression patterns we have finite number, perhaps in the order of thousands, of different biologically observable cell states that represent quasi-discrete entities. Moreover, gene expression is intrinsically noisy (Swain et al. 2002) yet, the cell type defining gene expression patterns remain stable in presence of noise-induced fluctuations of gene expression.

The reason for the collapse of the vast number potential gene expression patterns and the extremely smaller number of realized ones lies obviously in the interdependence of expression of individual genes embodied by the GRN (which in turn is specified by the genomic sequence). The specific mutual dependence of gene expression dictated by the GRN can be modeled as a complex dynamical system- which we will explain in more detail using simple gene circuits. It suffices to say here that because genes are not expressed independently but instead their expression depends on other genes in a fashion specified by the GRN, the cell is not "free" to realize any possible gene expression configuration. The majority of combinations are in a regulatory sense not possible, very unlikely to be realized. The degree to which a gene expression pattern is allowed or not determines its stability. This relationship between the stability of a gene expression pattern and the GRN structure is at the core of formal concepts of the epigenetic landscape explained in this chapter.

This constraint on the realization of gene expression patterns in the high-dimensional gene expression space imposed by the GRN leads to attractor states, which are stable, stationary gene expression states among the set of all possible gene expression configurations and have been now studied in the past decade as the basis for the existence of discrete cell phenotypes (Kauffman 1969). The attractor property stem from the fact that these states appear to be self-stabilizing: similar states (state space neighbors) are unstable and overtime, move ("are attracted") to the attractor state. The existence of multiple (thousands) of attractors within a system (the GRN of a given genome) is an extreme manifestation of the elementary phenomenon of *multistability* which occurs in non-linear dynamical systems.

2.2 Experimental evidences for high-dimensional attractors and attractor transitions

Recent progress in high-throughput technology, such as microarray analysis (Maskos and Southern 1992) and more recently, RNAseq (Mortazavi et al. 2008) allows researchers to monitor the whole transcriptome (cellular abundance of expressed transcripts across the genome) as a surrogate for the activation of the gene loci, thus, in essence to measure cell states. Early measurements of transcriptomes have shown that gene expression is indeed coordinated across the whole genome and generates apparently stable, reproducible, and discretely distinct expression patterns that correspond to cell types (Hsiao et al. 2001; Perou et al. 2000). The high-dimensional robustness is evidently suggested by the fact that cells reliably integrate multiple simultaneous and often conflicting and non-specific signals to produce very same cell phenotypes (Huang and Ingber 2000). The actual demonstration of the attractor property was provided by perturbation experiments: human promyelocytic HL60 cells differentiate in response to a wide array of chemicals. When differentiation to neutrophils was triggered by treatment with either all-trans retinoic acid or dimethylsulfoxide and their transcriptome trajectories are compared, it was observed that gene expression patterns for the two treatments first diverged drastically and then, at least with respect to 70% of the observed gene expression state space dimensions, converged again when cells in both treatments reached the state of mature neutrophils (Huang et al. 2005b). This experiment indicated that cells follow perturbation specific "differentiation paths" to transition from one cell state to another but also that there exist multiple alternative paths for doing so. More generally, cell phenotype changes represent attractor state transitions in a multiattractor system.

This idea of a cell type as a high-dimensional attractors and of cell type change as attractor transition inherently suggest the potential that any cell type could in principle be converted to any other one (Kauffman 1993). Hence from the dynamical systems perspective it is not surprising that cell types can be reprogrammed. Cell types are no longer viewed as terminally fixed phenotypes as was once the dogma in developmental biology. The question now is not *whether* but how a cell type can be converted to another. Here, too as we will see that the landscape concept will be useful.

In the first experiment of cell reprogramming Gurdon demonstrated in 1950s that a somatic cell in frog could achieve pluripotency, that is, converted to embryonic-like state, by nuclear

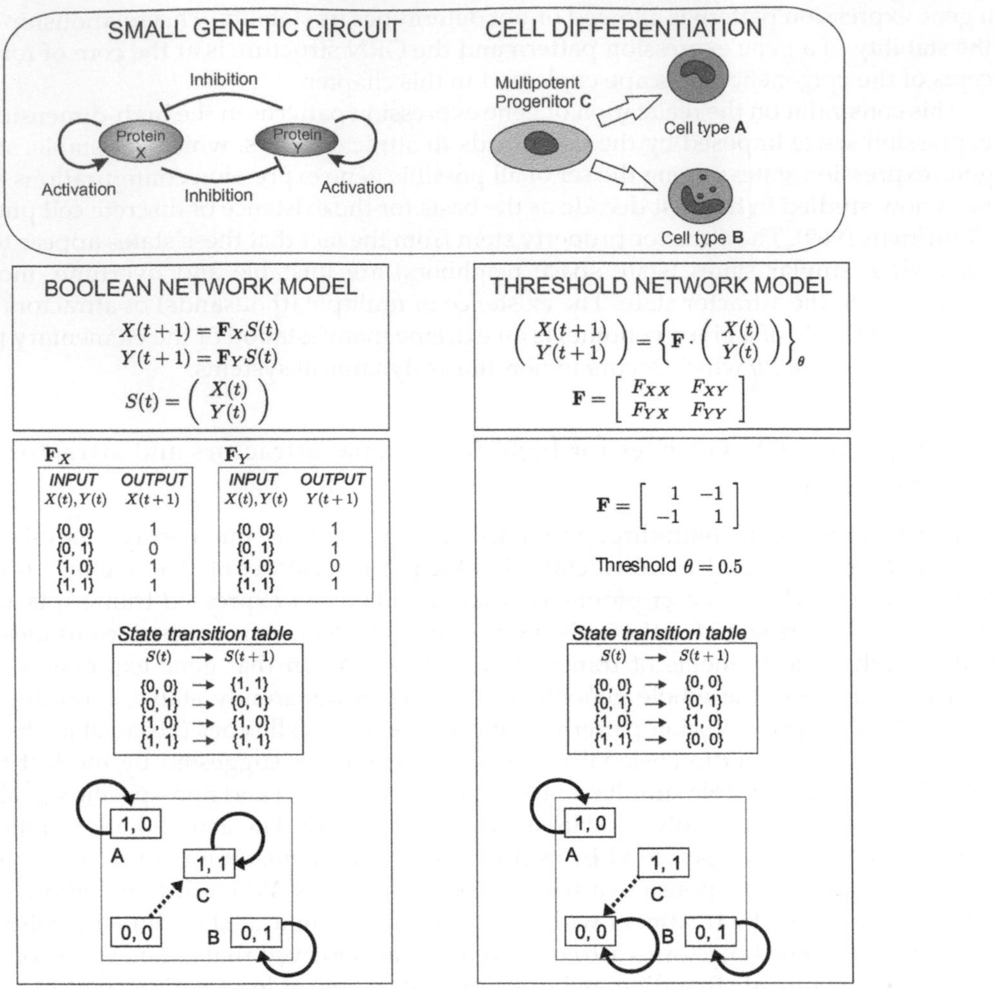

FIGURE 12.2 **UPPER BOX.** Small gene regulatory circuit and differentiation pathway. Genes X and Y inhibit each other and activate themselves. The cell fate behavior regulated by this circuit is shown on the right: Commitment of a multipotent precursor cell C into two differentiated cells, A and B. Below, two models of the underlying gene regulatory network. **LEFT COLUMN.** Discrete variable (Boolean network) model. The model captures how the stable steady states (attractors) arise from the network dynamics. The values of the variables X and Y at discrete time t are given by Boolean functions, F_X and F_Y, respectively, of the corresponding set of input genes at time t is equivalent to the entire state of the network, $S(t)$. Below, the truth tables for the Boolean functions. The entire dynamics can be represented in the state transition table, which can be depicted as a state transition graph (bottom). In this particular case, the basins of attractions consist of only the attractor state itself. Arrows represent the "trajectories" indicating which transition a given state (rectangular box) undergoes when updating the network by executing the Boolean functions. Stable states (point attractors) update into themselves. **RIGHT COLUMN.** Threshold network model. This panel demonstrated that the same GRN is modeled by threshold network model. Rather than an updating function, threshold network uses a regulatory strength matrix $[F_{xx}, F_{xy}; F_{yx}, F_{yy}]$ to represent the gene regulation rules. The activation is represented as 1, the inhibition is represented as -1. The total dynamics of the network can be described by the state transition table in the middle. In this example, the threshold network produces two stable steady states (attractors) as the Boolean model: (1,0), (0,1). However, the third attractor is (0,0) instead of (1,1). This is caused by the equally weighted influence from the inputs, which usually make threshold network more stable.

transfer which exposed the genome of an intestinal cell to the set of TFs present in egg cells thereby "rebooting" the GRN into an embryonic state. (Gurdon et al. 1958). Graf pioneered reprogramming of blood cells in the 1980s (Graf 2011) by overexpressing master regulator TFs. Cell reprogramming research reached a pinnacle when Yamanaka in the 2006 succeeded in converting fibroblasts to iPS cells. It has since been shown that almost every cell types can be reprogrammed back to an embryonic stem cell-like state with different efficiency (Mali and Cheng 2012). In light of iPS cell reprogramming, the study of trans-differentiation between differentiated cell types has gained new momentum. For example, fibroblast cells are directly reprogrammed to functioning neuronal cells by overexpressing *Ascl1, Brn2, Myt1, Olig1,* and *Zic1*; Pancreas exocrine cells are reprogrammed to endocrine insulin-secreting beta cells by overexpressing *Pdx1, Ngn3,* and *MafA* (Zhou et al. 2008). Fibroblast cells are reprogrammed into fully functioning cardiomyocyte-like cells by overexpressing *Gata4, Mef2c,* and *Tbx5* (Efe et al. 2011).

The cell reprogramming experiments confirm the biochemical notion that epigenetic modifications are dynamic, as discussed above. To those who rely on epigenetic modifications as the explanation of stability of gene expression status, and hence of the genome-wide gene expression patterns, it may be astonishing to observe that cells maintain their new states after manipulation that induced the reprogramming, i.e. the ectopically expressed genes or the small molecules, are shut off or withdrawn. This self-enforcing property, the persistence of a new state after a transient perturbation that causes it, is an elementary property that attractors naturally confer.

2.3 Multistability in a small genetic circuit that govern differentiation

If all the cells of an organism have the same genome and a particular cell type is an attractor state of a GRN defined by the expression pattern, then multicellularity entails a multistable dynamics which the GRN offers. While the high-dimensional attractors arise in complex systems of thousands of genes, multistability has long been studied in small gene "networks" of a few genes, here referred to as "gene circuits". As early as 1948 Max Delbrück suggested that bistable systems (the simplest case of multistability) in a two-metabolite network with discontinuous transitions between the two steady states could explain differentiation into two cell types. Monod and Jacob discussed "cross-feedback" systems with multiple steady states in the context of differentiation (Monod and Jacob 1961). Thomas showed that the minimum circuit for bistability must contain at least one positive feedback (Thomas 1978).

Here we introduce a small but real biological system as a pedagogical example to illustrate the basic principles. A small circuit of gene regulation determines the cell lineage of hematopoietic progenitor cells. Figure 12.2 shows a circuit consisting of two genes, X and Y, which exhibit a self-activation and cross-inhibition of each other. While the dynamical systems approach would be to formulate this system as a set of ordinary differential equations we would like here for didactical reasons use discrete value networks. The details will be introduced in Section 3, but here we demonstrate what to expect.

The first question is how to represent the dynamics from this particular network architecture and derive the attractor states. In a Boolean network model (as explained in Section 3) let the Boolean variables for the two genes be X and Y. The Boolean functions associated with each gene are shown as look-up tables in Figure 12.2. If we "run the dynamics", by

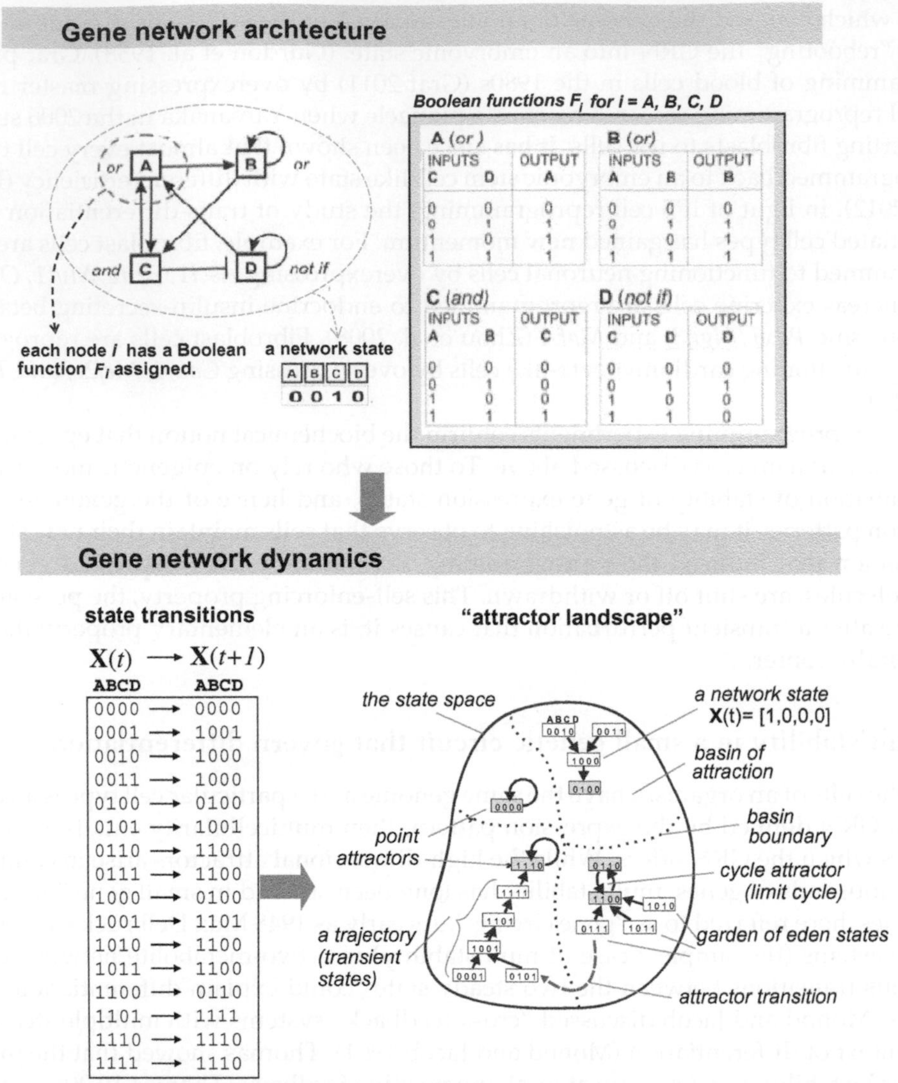

Gene network archtecture
Boolean functions F_i for i = A, B, C, D
or
or
and
not if
each node i has a Boolean function F_i assigned.
a network state
A B C D
0 0 1 0
A (or)
INPUTS C D | OUTPUT A
0 0 | 0
0 1 | 1
1 0 | 1
1 1 | 1
B (or)
INPUTS A B | OUTPUT B
0 0 | 0
0 1 | 1
1 0 | 1
1 1 | 1
C (and)
INPUTS A B | OUTPUT C
0 0 | 0
0 1 | 0
1 0 | 0
1 1 | 1
D (not if)
INPUTS C D | OUTPUT D
0 0 | 0
0 1 | 1
1 0 | 0
1 1 | 0
Gene network dynamics
state transitions
X(t) → X(t+1)
ABCD ABCD
0000 → 0000
0001 → 1001
0010 → 1000
0011 → 1000
0100 → 0100
0101 → 1001
0110 → 1100
0111 → 1100
1000 → 0100
1001 → 1101
1010 → 1100
1011 → 1100
1100 → 0110
1101 → 1111
1110 → 1110
1111 → 1110
"attractor landscape"
the state space
a network state
X(t)= [1,0,0,0]
basin of attraction
basin boundary
point attractors
cycle attractor (limit cycle)
garden of eden states
a trajectory (transient states)
attractor transition

FIGURE 12.3 From architecture to dynamics of gene networks. **UPPER PANEL.** Interaction graph of a simple four-gene network and truth-tables corresponding to Boolean functions implemented by each gene. The network state summarizes values of each gene (on/one or off/zero) as a vector. **LOWER PANEL.** The choice of Boolean functions implies specific state transition table. Visualizing relationships between individual states in a state transition graph reveals the attractor landscape, a discrete version of the potential landscape of Figure 12.1.

updating the variables as imposed by the Boolean functions, we will see that the model generates stationary states that are updated to themselves. These are attractor states because from whatever initial state the system starts from, the circuit will end up in one of these three attractor states. The two attractor states $A = (X_A, X_B) = (1, 0)$ (with gene X highly expressed and Y lowly expressed) and $B = (X_B, Y_B) = (0, 1)$ (low X and high Y) correspond the configuration in which one gene dominates and suppresses the other. This is intuitively plausible from the cross-inhibition of two genes. The third attractor with $C = (X_C, Y_C) = (1, 1)$ represents the pattern in which both X and Y are equally active. A biological example for such a circuit is one in which $X = PU.1$ and $Y = GATA1$, the two master regulators in the blood's common multipotent progenitor cell (CMP) that determine the two respective cell lineages, macrophage/monocyte and megakaryocyte/erythrocyte, corresponding to attractors A and B (Orkin and Zon 2008; Huang et al. 2007): In fact these two lineages exhibit the reciprocal gene expression pattern, ($PU.1 \gg GATA1$) and ($PU.1 \ll GATA1$) respectively. Their common precursor cells can be viewed as a cell type, hence as an attractor, C, and indeed is characterized by the "balanced" expression pattern ($PU.1 \approx GATA1$). Experimental overexpression of TF *PU.1* leads to suppression of *GATA.1* and to the macrophage/monocyte lineage whereas overexpression of *GATA.1* causes the suppression of *PU.1* and promotes differentiation to the megakaryocyte/erythrocyte precursor cells (Graf 2002). Similarly, loss of *GATA.1* gene will push the cell to the lineage of macrophage/monocyte (Galloway et al. 2005).

Figure 12.3 shows a larger gene network of 4 genes that gives rise to 4 attractors in the state space comprising of 2^4 states to illustrate the terminology used. We now move from this qualitative description of attractor states in the dynamics of GRN and its biological significance to the formal description using discrete-value network models.

3 BOOLEAN NETWORKS FOR MULTICELLULARITY

Broadly, network dynamics of GRNs that control cell phenotypes, notably cell types, have been studied using either *continuous* or *discrete* models. This dichotomy refers to the representation of the modeled variable x_i, which represents the expression level of gene i or equivalently, node i of the network of m genes. Unlike in biophysical models of the process of gene expression per se, here one typically does not distinguish between transcription and translation but focus on the network-wide (genome-wide) *configuration* of the expression status of all its nodes, the genes i which corresponds to the biologists' notion of "gene expression pattern" or "profile." Concretely, x_i can be a binary (rarely, ternary) or a continuous variable and molecularly can represent any of the following: the activation status of gene locus i, measured by the detection of bound RNA polymerase or the presence of transcripts of gene i, or the abundance of its encoded protein, or its activity, etc.). In a first approximation and focusing on integrated dynamics we can neglect these distinctions.

Continuous models include ordinary differentiation equations (ODEs), partial differentiation equations (PDEs), and stochastic differentiation equations (SDEs). Discrete models include Markov chains models, Boolean Network models, threshold network etc. Continuous models are generally thought to be the "gold standard" in the quantitative description of network dynamics but come at a price for it requires knowledge of the network architecture down to quantitative details, notably, the functional form of interactions between genes and the values of associated parameters. But this level of detail may not be needed for global dynamics of networks depend to a great extent on the structure of the network than the exact values of interaction parameters (Brown et al. 2004), notably if one is interested in classes of "typical dynamics" associated with particular ensembles of networks(Kauffman 1993). In fact, studies using discrete networks have offered great insights in this respect. Representing a biological network as discrete networks only requires the kind of information about network topology and qualitative regulatory relationships that resemble the conclusions of experimental investigation in molecular biology of gene control, and hence is more readily available. But in turn such discrete models permit computationally efficient analysis of the dynamics and thus they are ideal for capturing the elementary qualitative and intrinsic relationship between architecture of a network and its dynamic properties. Specifically discrete network models permit the simulation of large ensembles of networks and of large-scale networks (=containing high number of nodes) needed for this type of questions. Therefore, in this chapter, we will use discrete networks, and focus on Boolean networks to build a general framework to model the multi-cellularity. We then briefly discuss alternative discrete network, threshold networks which are enjoy wide usage in modeling GRN dynamics.

3.1 Boolean Network: The basic formalism

A Boolean network has defined structure, consisting of m nodes and directed edges that connect all nodes to a graph (see Figure 12.3 for overview). When used to model a GRN, each node i represents one gene and its value, the variable x_i represents the state of gene expression of gene i as explained above: either 1 (gene being expressed) or 0 (gene not being expressed). Time is also discretized, and in the simplest case, the gene variables x_i are updated synchronously, i.e. there is a central clock. The edges represent gene regulatory interactions and the direction, e.g. from node A to node B, signifies that gene A activates or inhibits the expression of gene B. In a Boolean network has m genes (nodes), the state vector $\mathbf{X} = (x_1, x_2, \ldots, x_m)$ represents the gene expression state. Each node is assigned a Boolean function F_i which determines its *output* value x_i at time $t + 1$ given the values of the genes (*inputs*) that regulate gene x_i at time t, as shown in Figure 12.2. More generally, the Boolean function F_i actually takes care of the connectivity of the nodes and maps the current state of the network $\mathbf{X}(t)$ into the value $\mathbf{X}(t + 1)$—the expression status of genes at time $t + 1$. Thus, the gene expression state at the next time step is determined by the recursive equation:

$$\mathbf{X}^{t+1} = \mathbf{F}(\mathbf{X}^t) \tag{12.1}$$

where $\mathbf{X}^t$ is the m-dimensional binary state vector at the time step t, for example $(1, 0, 0, \ldots, 0, 1)_n$. Jointly, set Boolean functions F_1 for gene x_i or $\mathbf{F}(\mathbf{X})$ determine the next state $X(t + 1)$ given the current state $\mathbf{X}(t)$ and are often defined as a Boolean lookup-table, as shown in Figures 12.2 and 12.3.

Long-term behavior—attractors. The long-term network dynamics, starting from an initial state $\mathbf{X}(t{=}0)$ has three possible outcomes and have been studied extensively with regard to architecture classes (Wang et al. 2012). Briefly, the first situation is the aforementioned case when the network evolves to a stable state $X^* := X^{t+1} = X^t$ that updates into itself. Such states are the fixed points or ***point attractors***. The second situation is that the network cycles on a finite sequence of states—a ***cycle attractor*** (the discrete equivalent of the limit cycle in continuous systems)—often referred to as "state cycle" in the older literature. Since the state space is finite, soon or later the evolving state vector $\mathbf{X}$ will, if not trapped in a point attractor, encounter a previously occupied state, and since the model is deterministic—it will follow the same trajectory as the previous encounter and will stay on the cycle. The third case is an extreme form of the latter: a network may not converge to a point or a cycle before visiting all states of the state space. In other words, we have a cycle attractor whose trajectory visits all possible configurations X of the state space. This scenario is the equivalent of a chaotic behavior (Matache and Heidel 2004). Given that the state space can be very large for biological GRN (2^m states, thus for 1000 genes, the chaotic attractor would have a period of $2^{1000} \approx 10^{300}$ states). Such trajectories are not necessarily recognized as a cycle when one monitors the dynamics for only a limited time interval. The network seems to wander aimlessly ("chaotically") in state space. Finally, of note, is that (deterministic) discrete networks do not have unstable fixed points encountered in continuous systems.

In biology, stable steady states or attractor states (=point attractors, often "point" is dropped for simplicity) are more relevant than cycles because they represent robust cell types in homeostasis. (The abundance of cycle attractors found in earlier work on Boolean networks is largely due to the artificial synchronization of updating rules (Greil et al. 2007).

The attractor landscape. The set of network states that converge to the same attractor (point or cycling attractor) form the ***basin of attraction*** of that attractor. Because there are no unstable steady states or manifolds as in continuous systems, attractors (and their basins) are disjoint entities and the state space is compartmentalized by imaginary "attractor boundaries"—see Figure 12.3. The entire dynamics of discrete networks can be depicted as a *state transition diagram*—the equivalent of flow fields in continuous system—in which the trajectories from the initial states are depicted, revealing the basins of attractions and associated attractors. We call such representation the attractor landscape of the network. An example is shown in Figure 12.3).

The study of Boolean networks, has for a long tradition, championed by Stuart Kauffman (Kauffman 1993; Kauffman 2004), operated not at the level of individual networks but of statistical /ensembles of Boolean networks defined by particular architectural properties and focused on the general properties of such attractor landscapes and their relationship to features in the network architecture (Aldana-Gonzalez et al. 2003). These studies, not further elaborated here, divide Boolean network ensembles into three broad "regimes", the ordered, critical, and chaotic regime with respect to the dynamical behavior (discussed below).

Finding the attractor states. Given a defined Boolean network (topology of the network graph and Boolean functions of all nodes), how can we find all attractors (point or cycle), or determine that it is chaotic? A straightforward way is to exhaustively evaluate the dynamics, initiating the system at each state X, until either a point attractor or a cycle attractor is reached. This will obviously run into a problem when there is a chaotic attractor or any "near chaotic" attractor that is, a cycle attractor whose period encompasses a large number of states that approaches $T=2^m$: In a large network this would demand a long computing time to verify the cycle for large networks. Another more formal method is to transform a Boolean network to a Markov model, which will be elaborated in the Section 5.2. The third method is to use a new mathematical tool called *half-tensor product* in which a new linear algebra is invented to analyze the dynamics of the original Boolean network model (Cheng et al. 2011).

Assigning Boolean functions. Since the Boolean functions control the network dynamics, and cell fate behavior displays a particular type of attractor landscape, the next question is: How can we choose the set of appropriate Boolean functions such that the ensuing networks dynamics mimics cell fate behavior? It has been proposed by Kauffman, on the background of the aforementioned characterization of Boolean network ensembles as ordered, chaotic and critical, that, for a variety of reasons (Aldana-Gonzalez et al. 2003; Kauffman 2004), cells are in the critical regime. Kauffman had showed that Boolean functions that belong to the class of "canalyzing functions" shift the dynamics from the chaotic to the critical regime.

A ***canalyzing*** Boolean function is a function in which at least the value of one input (1, 0) fully determines ("canalyzes") the value of the ouput., e.g. if that input is 1, the output of the regulated gene is 1, if the input is 0, the output is 0—no matter the value of the other input(s). In other words, this can also be seen as the property that the value of some inputs "don't matter" in determining the output. (Kauffman et al. 2003). Later Kauffman extended this concept. If Gene A, B, C are the inputs, they may follow a certain order of canalizing activity: e.g., changing the input of C does not change the output when A, B take certain values. Changing the input of B does not change the output when A takes certain m values. Such behavior is called "***nested canalizing***." The presence of canalizing Boolean functions implies that genes have less effective upstream regulators than it appears on the network diagram which improves the robustness of the networks and pushes the networks more to the ordered regime.

A related property of Boolean functions will be needed in conjunction with a biologically relevant dynamics. Since gene regulation is either activating or inhibiting, the ***unate function*** is used to capture the monotonic properties of the Boolean functions (Jarrah et al. 2007). A Boolean function $F(x_1, x_2, \ldots, x_n)$ is said to be positive unate in x_i if for all $x_j (i \neq j)$.

$$F(x_1, x_2, \ldots, x_{i-1}, 1, x_{i+1}, \ldots, x_n) \geq F(x_1, x_2, \ldots, x_{i-1,}, 0, x_{i+1}, \ldots, x_n) \tag{12.2}$$

Similarly, $\mathbf{F}(x_1, x_2, \ldots, x_n)$ is called negative unate if

$$F(x_1, x_2, \ldots, x_{i-1}, 0, x_{i+1}, \ldots, x_n) \geq F(x_1, x_2, \ldots, x_{i-1}, 1, x_{i+1}, \ldots, x_n) \tag{12.3}$$

Here we use the positive unateness to represent the activation while negative unateness to represent the inhibition. For a Boolean function, the positive unateness means that the "on" state of input gene x_i will be passed to the regulated gene, whose state can be "on" only when input gene x_i is "on". A given gene cannot be "on" when its input gene x_i is "off". This sign compatiblity will plays an important role in determining the ordering of cell attractors, which would be elaborated in Section 8.

3.2 Threshold Network—basic formalisms

While the Boolean Network is a simple model for GRN dynamics and has been extensively studied as a theoretical model class, it is in general difficult to define the Boolean functions for a real biological network. The threshold network, or alternatively Hopfield network (Hopfield 1984), originally proposed for modeling neuronal networks, is a discrete network with a simple updating rule that avoid this problem. A gene i's expression level $x_i(t)$ at time t is determined by its n upstream regulators $\mathbf{R} = [r_1, r_2, \ldots, r_n]$ whose gene expression level constitutes a vector $\mathbf{E}_\mathbf{R}(t)$ and whose individual *regulatory strengths* over gene i are represented by vector $\mathbf{A}_i = [a_{i1}, a_{i2}, \ldots, a_{in}]$. We assume that these regulators $\mathbf{R}$ have independent actions on the target gene. To "binarize" the output that is the gene expression level $x_i(t)$ one further assumes that the target gene i is turned on when the sum of the expression values of its regulators exceed certain threshold θ_i. The threshold function **F** of the gene expression $x_i(t+1)$ is thus determined by the following equation:

$$x_i(t+1) = F_i(\mathbf{A}_i, \mathbf{E_R}(t), x_i(t), \theta_i) = \mathbf{A}_i.\mathbf{E_R}(t)$$
$$= \begin{cases} 1, & \sum_j a_{ij} \cdot E_{r_i} > \theta_i, \\ x_i(t), \ \sum_j a_{ij} \cdot E_{r_i} = \theta_i, & j \in 1 \dots N \\ 0, & \sum_j a_{ij} \cdot E_{r_i} < \theta_i \end{cases} \tag{12.4}$$

Here θ_i is the threshold, which can be either an integer or a fraction. When the sum of all regulator's regulation strength $\mathbf{A}_i$ multiplied by their current gene expression level $\mathbf{E}_{\mathbf{R}i}(t)$ is larger (smaller) than the threshold θ_i, the target gene's expression level at the next time point, $x_i(t+1)$, is 1(0). One way to deal with the case when the sum equals to θ_i, is to set $x_i(t+1)$ to keep the value $x_i(t)$ it had in previous time step's value. Thus, the network dynamics is governed by:

$$\mathbf{X}(t+1) = \mathbf{F}(\mathbf{A}, \mathbf{E}_R(t), \mathbf{X}(t), \theta) \tag{12.5}$$

In general, the elements of the regulation strength matrix **A** can take any real value to indicate the different strengths of different regulators. Similar to the Boolean network, with the updating of the states of the network through the Equation (12.5) the network will settle in fixed-point, cycle or chaotic attractors. An example is shown in Figure 12.2 (right column).

4 DYNAMICS OF LARGE ENSEMBLE OF NETWORKS

The small circuits used as example above are actually embedded in a much larger network which encompasses the TF in the genome—or about 3,000 genes (nodes) for mammals. But because this genome-wide network is modular (Cordell 2009), and overall, the GRN are sparse networks (Huang and Kauffman 2009), modeling of small circuits have been fairly successful in predicting network dynamics in cell fate control (Huang et al. 2007) As we have seen in Section 2.2., experimental work shows the existence of attractors in large networks of thousands of genes—so large that even when using discrete models, they cannot be comprehended at the level of explicit modeling of individual instance as we may be accustomed to from the study of dynamical systems. Thus, instead of examining specific instances, the statistical approach has offered much insight: The use of discrete models has facilitated the study of entire statistical ensembles characterized by some architectural parameters but otherwise *randomly* wired networks, to understand classes of behaviors. We have briefly mentioned the ordered, critical, and chaotic regimes above (Section 3) to which we now return to.

4.1 Sensitivity and Criticality in Boolean Network and threshold network

An important measure for the dynamical characteristics of an ensemble of random networks is the "order parameter", now referred to as ***sensitivity S***—a quantity that is related to the Lyapunov exponent in continuous systems (Shmulevich and Kauffman 2004) and determines to which dynamical regime (ordered, critical, and chaotic) an ensemble of Boolean networks belong. It reflects the average network dynamics in terms of divergence or convergence of nearby trajectories following small perturbations. Several methods have been developed to describe the sensitivity of random Boolean networks. The classical numerical method is based on the Derrida plot (Derrida and Pomeau 1986) which in essence determines the ratio of the (normalized) Hamming distance between two randomly chooses states at time t to that at time $t+1$: $S = H(t+1)/H(t)$ [in the limit of small Hamming distances i.e. the initial slope in the Derrida curve in which all the $H(t+1)$ values is plotted against all the corresponding $H(t)$ value, see e.g. (Derrida and Pomeau 1986). If S is larger than 1, on average, trajectories diverge, and the network ensemble is unstable (in the chaotic regime). If the S is smaller than 1, it is a stable (in the ordered regime) (Kauffman 1993). If $S = 1$, it indicates that the networks of the respective ensemble are in a critical region, between order and chaos, when trajectories on average neither converge nor diverge. With respect to the attractor landscape, ordered networks contain typically just one or a small number of large attractors basins whose size is in the scale of the state space whereas chaotic networks consist of a small number (in the extreme case, just one) cycle attractors—a trajectory that visits (almost) every possible network configuration with a period length (measured as number of states) that is in the scale of the state space size. This causes the network to appear to wander without rule in state space when observed over a short time window. Alternatively, a large number of attractors with tiny basins will also produce high sensitivity because the disjoint attractors prevent convergence. Kaufmann postulated early on that biological networks are at or near the critical regime, poised between chaos and order—for which there is accumulating indirect evidence (Nykter et al. 2008a). Networks in this regime exhibit many still counterintuitive properties, such as maximal information processing capacity (Nykter et al. 2008b) and have been suggested to unite network robustness and evolvability (Torres-Sosa et al. 2012; Balleza et al. 2008).

In this body of work based on the ensemble approach to relate classes of architectures with the dynamical regime, Kauffman investigated the Kp model (Shmulevich and Kauffman 2004), which consists of a large ensemble of random Boolean networks with the architecture parameters K, the input degree for each node ("homogeneous networks"), m and p, the probability for the Boolean function to have positive output in average. For these networks the average sensitivity S is determined directly by these network parameters, in the following way: (Shmulevich and Kauffman 2004; Balleza et al. 2008; Kauffman et al. 2003) .

$$S = 2Kp(1-p) \tag{12.6}$$

This was further developed to a sensitivity measure applied on a single Boolean Network although it still presents mean value for an ensemble of random networks (Shmulevich and Kauffman 2004).

Unlike the case of Boolean networks, for the analogous homogenous threshold network there is to date no exact, closed-form formula to calculate the sensitivity. However, an approximation formula has been proposed (Zanudo et al. 2011). Based on it we compared the sensitivity between these two discrete network models. We found that the chaotic region in the threshold is much narrower than that of the Boolean network, as shown in Figure 12.1c. This implies that threshold networks are in general more ordered than the Boolean network which may be a consequence of the additive update functions as opposed to the nonlinear Boolean functions.

4.2 Architecture features of large networks

Paradoxically, it was only long after and independent of the work of Kauffman on the rich generic dynamics of large random gene regulatory networks that interest in biomolecular networks has begun to take off—stimulated by systems biology; but it was directed at a much more elementary aspect of networks, namely their architecture. In this more recent independent development, the availability of data for real molecular networks in biology and man-made systems has triggered a flurry of study of complex, irregular network topologies as static graphs, focusing on the topology. This burgeoning field was also stimulated by earlier studies of social networks (Amaral et al. 2000; Barabási and Albert 1999; Watts and Strogatz 1998). We are now only entering the era where these two fields, network dynamics and topology, are beginning to merge. Below we summarize some of the interesting architecture features and their significance for network dynamics:

(1) The average connectivity per node K. Initial studies on Boolean networks by Kauffman assumed a homogenous distribution of K. It was found that $K =$ networks are in the ordered/critical regime (Kauffman 1993). Above a critical K_c value (which depends on other parameters) networks behave chaotically. Analysis of continuous, linearized models also suggest that in general, sparsity of connections is more likely to promote ordered dynamics—or stability (May 1972) .

(2) The distribution of K_i over the individual network genes, i. Recent work on the topology of complex networks in general and of molecular networks in particular has revealed that many "evolved" networks, i.e. where N grew over time by addition of new elements and connections, such as the protein-protein interaction networks, appear to have a connectivity distribution that approximates a power-law (Barabási and Albert 1999). Such networks have no characteristic average value of K(sampling of larger number of nodes N will lead to larger "average" K values) and are hence said to be "scale-free". Analysis of scale-free Boolean networks suggest that this property favors a behavior in the ordered regime for a given value of the parameters K and p (Aldana and Cluzel 2003; Fox and Hill 2001).

(3) There are many global and local topological features of complex networks defined in graph theory terms that appear to be interesting with regard to the behavioral regime of the network dynamics because they were found to be enriched in genome-wide molecular networks when compared to a set of randomly generated null-hypothesis networks that were constrained to exhibit more elementary topological features. These features include:

- Centrality measures to identify most important nodes in the network, proportion of genes with high betweeness value(Joy et al. 2005; Amaral et al. 2000)
- small-worldness, cliquishness, modularity, and hierarchy of network (Amaral et al. 2000; Ravasz et al. 2002; Watts and Strogatz 1998)
- frequency and distribution of local network motifs that are enriched in real networks, such as feed-forward loops in bacteria (Milo et al. 2004; Shen-Orr et al. 2002)

The influence of these topology features on the global dynamic behavior remains to be studied.

5 DEVELOPMENT OF MULTICELLULARITY: RELATIVE STABILITY OF STATES AND GLOBAL ORDERING

If network topology and dynamics are the two major aspects of network that have been investigated, we now introduce a third layer of property that is not yet widely appreciated but gains particular relevance when networks and the attractor landscape are used to model development of the cell-type diversity during Metazoa development.

Not only must the GRNs that governs the development of multiple cell types exhibit multistable dynamics (to produce and maintain the different gene expression profiles representing each cells-type) but also the developing zygote and later, embryonic cells, must be able to reliably access other cell type attractors through a well-defined order. The GRNs that govern development has long been suggested to face the trade-off between stability of attractors but also flexibility: intrinisc noise or extrinsic signal must be able to trigger an exit from attractors and entry into well–specified new attractors. It is then clear that attractors cannot be too stable, yet they must exist to confer endurance of cell indentities. Hence the idea that real GRNs must operate in or near the critical regime to deal with the trade-off.

But modeling development also exposes another much more fundamental issue: the relative stability of attractors in a multistable system—which has not been much appreciated because attractors are identified locally (return after small perturbations) and separately both in the realm of continuous and discrete networks. With the need to consider transitions between attractor, we need to take the integrative approach for which the concept of the attractor landscape plays a central role. With the notion of relative stability, we add a layer of information to the thus far "flat" attractor landscape: we map a quantity into each state that helps us to predict the direction of noise-driven attractor transition between two adjacent attractor states. Moreover, with the quantity of relative attractor stability we will be able to compare all the attractor at a global scale and ask whether there is a "global gradient"—as envisioned by Waddington in his epigenetic landscape as a "slope". A global comparison would enforce the *order* in which attractors are (transiently) occupied during development, because in a spontaneous, noise-driven system, transitions will preferentially move from a less stable to a more stable attractor, thereby establishing the arrow of development" (directionality of developmental processes as trajectory across many attractor states).

5.1 Noise-driven attractor transitions expose their relative stability

Spontaneous transitions between attractors are driven by the stochastic fluctuations of the gene expression values x_i due to molecular noise in the cell (Swain et al. 2002b; Elowitz et al. 2002), Thus, to define relative stability among attractor we need to first ask: how robust are the attractors against the noise, what magnitude of perturbation causes an exit from an attractor? And how do we quantitative this? One way to quantify the stability of attractors against noise is to calculate the probabilities of noise-induced transition between them. In a Boolean network with m nodes and k attractors, let's suppose a probabilistic bit switch (either $0->1$, or $1->0$) at gene locus x_i due to gene expression noise occurs with probability η.

We now observe where the perturbed (attractor) state will go following the Boolean rules: It can either return to the original attractor state or settled into another attractor. If we perform such one-bit-flip perturbation systematically for all the genes in all attractors and record the transition probabilities between any two attractors (Kauffman 1993), we obtain a noise-induced transition matrix, which could be used to estimate the robustness of attractors against noise (Álvarez-Buylla et al. 2008).

Calculating the robustness by sampling random bit-flipping usually requires large number of (time-consuming) sampling to reach acceptable accuracy. This problem can be avoided by using a Markov matrix approach as described in the next section.

5.2 The Markov model approach

The Markov model is one of the simplest models for studying the dynamics of stochastic processes. It assumes that the next state (at $t + 1$) is only influenced by the current state (at t). In using the Markov model to represent the Boolean network, variable values are discrete in both time and (state) space. We then introduce probabilities for the occupation of a state s_i and for the transitions between two states s_i, s_j. The m genes in the GRN can produce 2^m states $S = (s_1, s_2, \ldots, s_k)$, $k = 2^m$ and the *occupation* probability of these 2^m states corresponds to a 2^m-dimensional probability distribution vector $p = (p_1, p_2, \ldots, p_k)$, $k = 2^m$. The dynamics of the probability p_i at state s_i follows the master equation in the continuous form.

$$\frac{dp_i}{dt} = \sum_j T_{ij}p_j - T_{ji}p_i \tag{12.7}$$

It can be intuitively understood as the change of probability distribution at state s_i increases by the sum of all other state s_j transitioning to state s_i and decrease by sum of state s_i transitioning to all other states s_j. The matrix form of the Markov model in the discrete time steps:

$$\mathbf{p}^{t+1} = \mathbf{T}_{p^t} = \begin{bmatrix} T_{11} & \ldots & T_{1K} \\ \vdots & \ddots & \vdots \\ T_{k1} & \cdots & T_{kk} \end{bmatrix} \begin{pmatrix} p_1 \\ \vdots \\ p_k \end{pmatrix} \tag{12.8}$$

p^{t+1}, p^t are the distribution probability of occupancy of the 2^m states at time step $t + 1$, and the current time step t, respectively. The elements of the Markov matrix $\mathbf{T}_{ij}(2^m \times 2^m)$ are the probabilities of *transition* from state s_j to state s_i Since the jth column represents the probability from state s_i to all other states, according to the conservation principle, each column of transition matrix $\mathbf{T}$ sums up to 1. The dynamics of the Markov model is entirely determined by $\mathbf{T}$. The steady-states of the distribution probability are calculated from the eigenvalue analysis, $\lambda p^* = \mathbf{T}p^*$. When the eigenvalues $\lambda_i = 1$, the steady-state distribution is the corresponding eigenvector $\mathbf{p}^*$. If the eigenvector p^* only has one non-zero element, then the network has point attractors. If the eigenvector $\mathbf{p}^*$ has w non-zero elements with $1 < w < 2^m$, then the network has limit cycles (cycle attractors). If the eigenvector $\mathbf{p}^*$ has 2^m non-zero elements, every state goes every other state, then the network dynamics is chaotic.

5.3 Mapping between Boolean network and Markov chain model

How can a Boolean network model be transformed to a Markov model? First we list all possible states of a m-node Boolean network model in a 2^m dimensional probability distribution vector **p**. It is a 2^m dimensional vector with each element with m-bit length binary code $(0100\ldots10011)_m$. Then the transition probabilities from these 2^m states to the any other states are calculated as $\mathbf{T}_{ij}$, $(i = 1, \ldots, 2^m, j = 1, \ldots, 2^m)$. For example, for the toggle switch (Figure 12.2) between two genes (x, y) with cross-inhibition and self-activation, the Boolean network can be specified by

$$\begin{cases} x^{t+1} = x^t \wedge \neg(x^t \wedge y^t) \\ y^{t+1} = y^t \wedge \neg(x^t \wedge y^t) \end{cases} \tag{12.9}$$

And produces $2^m = 4$ states. We construct a state distribution vector $\mathbf{p} = (p_1, p_2, p_3, p_4)$. P_i is the occupation probability of each of the four states: $s_1 = (0, 0)$; $s_2 = (0, 1)$; $s_3 = (1, 0)$; $s_4 = (1, 1)$. According to the Boolean rule, the corresponding Markov matrix $\boldsymbol{T}$ is (here we define the transition from the jth column to the ith row):

$$T = \begin{pmatrix} 0 & 0 & 0 & 0 \\ 0 & 1 & 0 & 0 \\ 0 & 0 & 1 & 0 \\ 1 & 0 & 0 & 1 \end{pmatrix} \tag{12.10}$$

In this example the Markov matrix $\boldsymbol{T}$ has three eigenvectors with $\lambda_i = 1$, $(i = 1, 2, 3)$. The corresponding steady states $\mathbf{p}^*$ are (1, 0, 0, 0), (0, 1, 0, 0), (0, 0, 1, 0) and three corresponding point attractors are $s_1 = (0, 1)$; $s_2 = (1, 0)$; $s_3 = (1, 1)$.

Although the two methods are mathematically identical, Markov models have some practical advantages over Boolean network models. The complete set of point and cycle attractors can be easily identified from the eigenvalue analysis of the Markov matrix while Boolean network models depend on exhaustive sampling of all possible states as the initial states to find all attractors. It is also easier to calculate the relative stability of attractors against the noise, as we will see, than in the Boolean network formalism. However, Markov models have their drawbacks. Since in the Markov model we have to enumerate all possible states in a matrix, for m nodes $(m > 40)$, it becomes difficult to store and perform eigenvalue analysis on such a large matrix.

5.4 Markov matrix: noise-induced transitions and relative stability

The relative stabilities of attractors have no meaning in the deterministic Markov model since no transitions can happen between two attracting basins. The notion of a relative stability of the attractors exists only if noise is considered—which makes the Markov matrix ergodic, i.e. the network can reach every state from every state.

In a GRN with m genes, where each state in the Markov model is a m-bit binary vector, and η is the probability of randomly flipping one bit, a perturbation matrix **P** can be constructed using the Hamming distance between two states s_i, s_j, $d = ||s_i - s_j||$.(Shmulevich et al. 2002)

$$\mathbf{P}_{ij} = \begin{cases} C_d^m \eta^d (1-\eta)^{m-d} & (i \neq j) \\ 0 & (i = j) \end{cases} \tag{12.11}$$

where C_d^n are binomial coefficients, which guarantee that each column sums up to1—$(1-\eta)^m$. The perturbed Markov model is constructed by adding the perturbation matrix **P** back to the Markov matrix:

$$\tilde{\mathbf{T}} = (1-\eta)^m \mathbf{T} + \mathbf{P} \tag{12.12}$$

The equation for the dynamics of this noisy system is

$$\mathbf{p}^{t+1} = \tilde{\mathbf{T}}_{\mathbf{p}^t} \tag{12.13}$$

Since **T** is a Markov matrix, each column adds up to one. With a normalizing coefficient, we can construct make sure that $\tilde{\mathbf{T}}$ satisfies the conservation principle, i.e. each column adds up to one. This guarantees that there exists one and only one steady-state probability distribution $\mathbf{p}^*$(Strang 2003).

With the noise-induced transition, the original deterministic Boolean network is transformed into a probabilistic one. How can we now measure the relative stabilities of different attractors? Here we present three measurements: steady states probability distribution $\mathbf{p}^*$, mean first passage time (MFPT), and transition barriers from the least action principle (LAP).

5.5 Three measures for the relative stability of the cell states

5.5.1 Steady-state probability distribution p^*

The perturbed Markov model constructed above always converges to $\mathbf{p}^*$, which can be directly calculated from Equation (13). $\mathbf{p}^*$ is usually a non-equilibrium steady state, i.e. there exist circular (or "non-gradient") driving forces, since a gene regulatory network represents an open (non-conserved) system far from thermodynamic equilibrium. When circular driving forces are negligible compared to the "gradient forces" which drive a state toward point attractors, the ***quasi-potential*** $U \sim -ln(\mathbf{p}^*)$ can be used to measure the relative stability. If U at one attractor is higher than U at another, this attractor is less stable than the other, and *vice versa*. However, if the circular driving force is in the scale of the gradient force, $U \sim -ln(\mathbf{p}^*)$ will not be an accurate measure for relative stability. When circular driving forces are large, the dynamical system has no global ordering defined by U because the gradient $-\frac{\partial U}{\partial x}$ is no longer a driving force. Since the major portion of the state space in chaotic network is part of the huge chaotic cycle attractor whereas in ordered network it is occupied by the basins of attraction of point attractors, we can expect that in ordered networks the steady-state distribution p* behaves more like a potential function that represents the relative stability.

In any case with the introduction of the steady state of probability distribution $\mathbf{p}^*$ and the Boltzmann-inspired interpretation of it as a kind of potential $U \sim -ln(\mathbf{p}^*)$ we map into each state an energy-like quantity that warrants the notion of a landscape in which the elevation and slopes captures the dynamics—as envisioned by Waddington. This connects his epigenetic landscape metaphor to network formalism. But, as explained above the simple idea of using a steady-state distribution is not universally valid to predict state transitions. Thus we consider other formalisms.

5.5.2 *Mean First Passage Time (MFPT)*

In an ergodic dynamic system every state can visit any other state. A transition barrier, epitomizing the ease for transitioning from attractor A to B however offers a notion of relative stability. How do we formalize the ease of transitions? We can find all possible paths passing from state s_i to state s_j the first time, which vary from 1 step, 2 step s, ..., k steps. We can take the average number of time steps of all possible transition paths τ_{ij} as the measure for the transition barrier between two states s_i and state s_i. How to calculate the mean first passage time M_{ij} from the perturbed Markov matrix T? Let $f_{ij}^{(1)} := \mathbb{P}[M_{ij} = k]$, for $k = 1, 2, \ldots$, we have the equations:

$$
\begin{aligned}
p_{ij}^{(1)} &= f_{ij}^{(1)} \\
p_{ij}^{(2)} &= f_{ij}^{(2)} + f_{ij}^{(1)} \cdot p_{ij}^{(1)} \\
&\vdots \\
p_{ij}^{(n)} &= f_{ij}^{(n)} + f_{ij}^{(n-1)} \cdot p_{jj}^{(1)} + f_{ij}^{(n-2)} \cdot p_{jj}^{(2)} + \cdots + f_{ij}^{(1)} \cdot p_{jj}^{(n-1)}
\end{aligned}
\tag{12.14}
$$

It can be computed recursively with the equation

$$
f_{ij}^{(n)} = p_{ij}^{(n)} - \sum_{k=1}^{n-1} f_{ij}^{(n-k)} \cdot p_{jj}^{(k)}, \quad n = 1, 2, \ldots \tag{12.15}
$$

The mean first passage time M_{ij} is then calculated as

$$
M_{ij} = 1 + \sum_{k \neq j} \tilde{T}_{ik} M_{kj} \tag{12.16}
$$

The shorter the time M_{ij}, the higher is the transition probability between the two states s_i and state s_j. There exists a particular distribution of time steps required for the transition from state s_i to state s_j. The mean first passage time (MFPT) is the mean value of this distribution. However, a cell does not take the path with the mean value passage time to make the transition. It takes the most probable path to make the transition between two attractors (Zhou et al. 2012). If the distribution of time steps is narrow, MFPT is a reasonable measure for the transition barrier. However, if the distribution is wide, MFPT is only a rough approximation. A different measure of transition to reflect the shortest path of the transition is then needed.

5.5.3 *Least Action Principle (LAP)*

We can measure the barrier of the transition by finding the "least action path" (LAP) and estimating the probability of the transition through this path. In plain words, the LAP is the path that incurs the least effort to be mounted during the transition against the force produced by the gene regulatory interactions that are responsible in driving the network to attractor states in the first place. How to find the least action path? According to the *Freidlin-Wentzell* large variation theory (Freidlin and Wentzell 2012), for a continuous dynamic system $\dot{x} = \mathbf{G}(x)$, we can calculate the least action function along the transition path as the following:

$$V_{i,j} = min\frac{1}{2}\int_{t_i}^{t_j} \|\dot{x} = \mathbf{G}(x)\|^2 dt \tag{12.17}$$

Then it can be shown that the probability of transition along this path is

$$P_{i->j} = c_1 Exp\left(\frac{-V_{i,j}}{\epsilon^2}\right) \tag{12.18}$$

where ϵ represents the noise level. c_i is a constant coefficient. For a Markov model with discrete dynamic $x^{t+1} = \mathbf{F}(x^t)$, we can derive an analogous least action function V as follows:

$$x^{t+1} = \mathbf{F}(x^t) \tag{12.19}$$

$$\frac{1}{\Delta t}(x^{t+1} - x^t) = \frac{1}{\Delta t}(\mathbf{F}(x^t) - x^t) \tag{12.20}$$

$$\dot{x} = \frac{\mathbf{F} - \mathbf{I}}{\Delta t}(x^t) \tag{12.21}$$

Comparing Equation (17) with Equation (21), we have . Then we derive the least action function for the discrete network as:

$$\begin{aligned} V_{i,j} &= min\frac{1}{2}\sum_{t_i}^{t_j} \|\dot{x} - \frac{F - I}{\Delta t}x^t\|^2 \Delta t \\ &= min\frac{1}{2}\sum_{t_i}^{t_j} \|\frac{1}{\Delta t}(x^{t+1} - x^t) - \frac{F - I}{\Delta t}x^t\|^2 \Delta t \\ &= min\frac{1}{2}\sum_{t_i}^{t_j} \|x^{t+1} - F(x^t)\|^2 \end{aligned} \tag{12.22}$$

The least action function $V_{i,j}$ can be intuitively understood as follows: The Hamming distance between the current state and the state following the updating according to the Boolean rules are calculated and summed up along all possible paths from state s_i to s_j in the state transition graph. Since a Boolean network has a discrete-valued state space with disjoint attracting basins, we only allow an arbitrary path to be taken between the state at the edge of each attracting basin—so-called Garden of Eden (GOE) states (see Figure 12.3) that have no precursor state and thus represent the borders of attractors (Wuensche 1998). If a state is within an attracting basin, it has to climb up to the edge of the attracting basins, i.e. to a GOE, before it can reach other attractors. Different GOEs have different least action to make the last step to another attracting basin before the "free fall". This last step is also counted in the V to make sure the total path sum of the least action in the minimum among all possible paths. The smallest value V to any of the paths to the other attractor is used as the measure for the transition barrier. The smaller is the least action function $V_{i,j}$, the easier is the transition from state s_i to s_j.The above formula applies to deterministic Boolean networks. With the perturbation matrix **P**, which is the next state according to the probabilistic Boolean function, i.e. $\mathbf{F}(x^t)$ is no longer unique. Instead, it will represent several states with different probabilities. We can define the least action function $V_{i,j}$ for the probabilistic Boolean Network as follows:

$$V_{i,j} = min\frac{1}{2}\sum_{t_i}^{t_j} \|\mathrm{x}^{t+1} - \mathbf{F}(\mathrm{x}^t)\|_\epsilon^2 \tag{12.23}$$

Here a new norm of the distance between two states $\| \|_\epsilon$ is defined as

$$\|\mathrm{x}^{t+1} - \mathbf{F}(\mathrm{x}^t)\|_\epsilon = \sum_i \tilde{T}_{ij}\|\mathrm{x}_j^{t+1} - \mathrm{x}_i^t\| \tag{12.24}$$

where x_j^{t+1} is the next state in a prescribed path, and x_i^t are all possible states following the probabilistic Boolean rule applied on the current state. $\tilde{T}_{ij}$ is the perturbed Markov matrix as defined in Section 5.4. This means that the action function is the weighted sum of Hamming distances between the prescribed state and all possible next state according the probabilistic Boolean rules.

We have now presented three measures for the transition barrier or relative stability between attractors which can be used for a global ordering of the attractors in different circumstances. The first, the steady-state distribution $\mathbf{p}^*$ can be used for a system with relatively small non-gradient driving forces. The second, MFPT can be used for those systems where the time step distribution for all transition paths is narrowly distributed. Finally, the least action principle can be used if the first exit time is the dominant term for the transition time.

5.6 Mathematical definition of consistent global ordering and sensitivity analysis

Cell differentiation process during development is a largely (spontaneously) irreversible process: the zygote robustly reaches other cell types in a predetermined order. This predestined behavior requires that the gene regulatory network is not only near critical (to balance robustness with flexibility), but also that it has a *consistent* global ordering of the relative stabilities of all cell attractors so that a meaningful global developmental gradient in the attractor landscape is produced which ensures a robust and efficient development. By consistent we mean that in the directed graph where each vertex is an attractor state and the directed links represent the asymmetric (spontaneous) attractor transitions, there is little, or ideally, no non-transitive (circular) structure. Based on the relative stabilities of different cell states introduced above, here a mathematical formula is proposed to define a consistent global ordering of all attractors in the GRN.

Suppose that we have a relative stability matrix **M**, which reflects the transition barrier between any two states, based on either the mean first passage time (MFPT) or least action principle (LAP), we can define a global ordering as following. First, a net transition rate $d_{i,j}$ is defined

$$d_{ij} = \frac{1}{M_{ij}} - \frac{1}{M_{ji}} \tag{12.25}$$

If $d_{i,j} > 0$, this implies that s_i is more stable than s_j. This relationship is extended to m attractors. A permutation of m integers is defined as $\pi = \pi_1, \ldots, \pi_i, \ldots, \pi_m$, $\pi_i = 1, 2, \ldots, m$.

$$\begin{aligned}
d_{\pi_1\pi_2} \cdot d_{\pi_1\pi_3} > 0, \ldots, d_{\pi_1\pi_2} \cdot d_{\pi_1\pi_j} > 0 \ldots, d_{\pi_1\pi_2} \cdot d_{\pi_1\pi_m} > 0 \\
d_{\pi_2\pi_3} \cdot d_{\pi_2\pi_4} > 0, \ldots, d_{\pi_2\pi_3} \cdot d_{\pi_2\pi_j} > 0 \ldots, d_{\pi_2\pi_3} \cdot d_{\pi_2\pi_m} > 0 \\
\vdots \\
d_{\pi_i\pi_j} \cdot d_{\pi_i\pi_{j+1}} > 0 \ldots, d_{\pi_i\pi_j} \cdot d_{\pi_i\pi_m} > 0 \\
\vdots \\
d_{\pi_{m-1}\pi_{m-2}} \cdot d_{\pi_{m-1}\pi_m} > 0
\end{aligned} \tag{12.26}$$

If the relationship above is satisfied, then the permutation $\pi = \pi_1, \ldots, \pi_i, \ldots, \pi_m$ defines a globally consistent ordering for m states with respect to their relative stability, that is, there exists a non-local reference system akin to a gradient in conserved systems. The net probability flows between all attractors follow the order defined by the permutation π.

6 BOOLEAN NETWORK MODEL OF NEURON CELL DIFFERENTIATION AND REPROGRAMMING

We now apply the concepts of relative stability in the attractor landscape of discrete network models to two examples of cell lineage development: brain and pancreas.

6.1 Background of central nervous system development

The hundreds of cell types and subtypes in the central nervous system (CNS) can be divided in the three major types: the *neurons* (the large family of the actual "brain cells") and the two glia cells (support cells), *astrocyte* and *oligodendrocytes*. The glia cells comprise the major part of the cerebral cortex. Neurons have essentially no or very low regenerative capacity and much hope has been put in reprogramming non-neural cells into neurons for the treatment of neurodegenerative disease and dementia. Therefore understanding the attractor landscape of neuronal development is important for its application in the regenerative medicine.

The differentiation of a common CNS progenitor cell ("brain stem cell") into these three major cell lineages of the CNS follows a typical hierarchical binary branching scheme: the CNS precursor cells first differentiate into neurons and glial progenitors cells. Subsequently these glial progenitors differentiate into the *astrocyte* and the *oligodendrocytes* (Ravin et al. 2008). As in the example discussed in the introduction for blood, pairs of cross-inhibitory transcription factors govern the binary branching process, such as *Mash1-Hes5* and *Scl-Olig2*. Based on literature reports, we have constructed a minimal regulatory network ($m = 11$ nodes) for this differentiation process, whose network topology is shown in Figure 12.4b.

6.2 Boolean network model for CNS Development

With the topology at hand we next need to assign Boolean functions to the nodes. Based on an extensive literature review on the participating TFs and how they regulate the nerve cell differentiation (Bertrand et al. 2002), we assigned a putative Boolean function for each gene in the network. Modeling the regulation of a given gene by its regulators using a Boolean function is not straightforward because the required knowledge of molecular mechanisms of input integration at promoter regions is scarce. For the potentially up to $k = 11$ inputs of this network at each gene the number of possible Boolean functions is huge: $2^{2^{11}} \sim 10^{617}$. Thus we defined principles for establishing the Boolean functions based on known rudimentary regulatory relationships as follows:

- If gene A is positively (negatively) regulated by gene B, we set B (or B) in Gene A's Boolean update rule. For example, Mash1 is negatively regulated by Hes5, hence the Hes5 in Mash1's Boolean function.
- If gene A and gene B influence gene C dependently (independently), we set A $\wedge$ (or $\vee$) B in gene C's Boolean update rule. Taking Mash1 again as an example, it is influenced by both Pax6 and Hes5 dependently, hence the Pax6 $\wedge$ Hes5 is used as Mash1's Boolean function.

The detailed Boolean functions for all eleven genes are shown in Table 12.1.

Running the dynamics. Once the Boolean functions for the updating have been assigned, we "ran" the Boolean network using the Boolean network simulation package DDLab (Wuensche, 2010) and obtained the attractor states. The attractor states and their corresponding Boolean network states are shown in detail in Table 12.2. All network states flow into either point attractors or limit cycles, as shown in Figure 12.4c. This representation is a state transition diagram showing the attractor landscape as in Figure 12.3. Here each dot represents a state. An individual "circle" consisting of many network states connected by lines (= state updating) display the basins of attraction for the attractor state at its center. In our case, analysis of the specific configuration of gene expression of the attractors revealed that the four largest basins correspond to the *CNS precursor*, the *neuron*, the *astrocyte*, and the *oligodendrocyte*. Thus the attractors emanating from the Boolean dynamics recovered the cell type-specific gene expression patterns solely based on the information put into the network architecture and Boolean functions. For instance, because attractor 2 expresses the neuron marker genes *Tuj1*, *Brn2/Zic1* and *Mash1* (in the "$x_i = 1$" state), it represents the neuron.

The remaining smaller basins (basin 3, 5, 6) cannot be assigned a known cell type based on their gene expression patterns. But their very existence point to an important phenomenon and an associated conjecture: The presence of "unused attractors" that arise in the network to

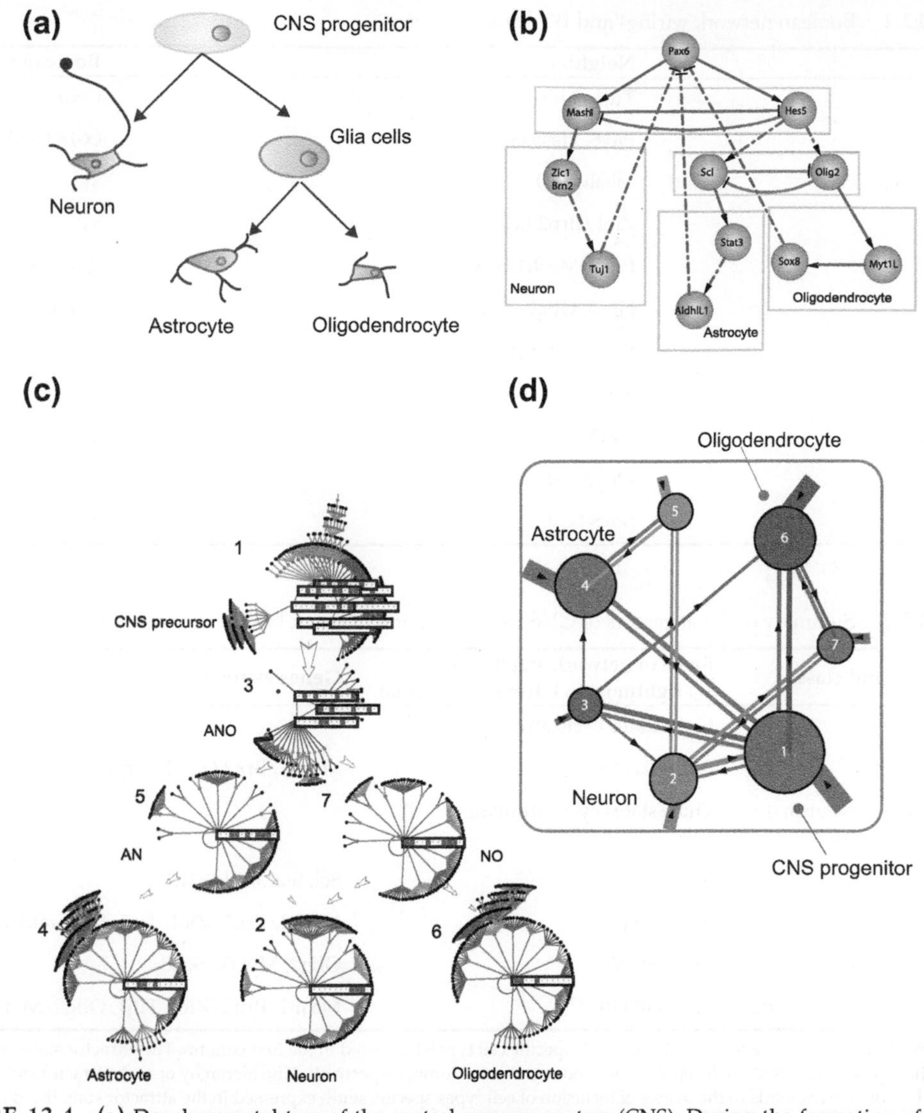

FIGURE 12.4 (a) Developmental tree of the central nervous system (CNS). During the formation of the CNS, neuronal stem cells can differentiate into *neurons* or *glial precursors*. The latter can further differentiate into either *astrocytes* or *oligodendrocytes*. (b) Curated minimal network used to model the developmental process. The network mainly consists of a cascade of two mutual inhibitor pairs: the first (*Mash1-Hes5*) determines the commitment to *neurons* or *glia*; the second (*Scl-Olig2*) determines the commitment to *astrocytes* or *oligodendrocytes*. Solid and dashed lines represent experimentally confirmed and predicted interactions, respectively. (c) Attracting landscape of the CNS developmental network. Numbers refer to the all cell types listed in Table 12.2. The hierarchy of each attractor (including its basin of attraction) corresponds to the degree of inclusion of cell types specific genes expressed in the attractor state listed in the last row. For example, the genes expression in attractor 3 includes all three cell types (*astrocyte, neuron, oligodendrocyte*) specific genes and is termed as ANO attractor. A: *astrocyte*, N: *neuron*, O: *oligodendrocyte*. (d) Transition graph between different cell attractors in the presence of noise. The probability of transitions, indicated by the thickness of the edge between two nodes, is calculated based on random switch of a single gene in one attractor. The size of a node is proportional to the size of the corresponding attracting basin.

TABLE 12.1 Boolean network wirings and Boolean functions.

Genes	Neighbors	Boolean function
Pax6 (x_1)	Tuj1, Aldh1L1, Sox8 (x_4, x_9, x_{11})	$(\neg x_4) \wedge (\neg x_9) \wedge (\neg x_{11})$
Mash1 (x_2)	Pax6, Hes5 (x_1, x_5)	$(x_1) \wedge (\neg x_5)$
Zic1/Brn2 (x_3)	Mash1 (x_2)	x_2
Tuj1 (x_4)	Zic1/Brn2 (x_3)	x_3
Hes5 (x_5)	Pax6, Mash1 (x_1, x_2)	$(x_1) \wedge (\neg x_2)$
Scl (x_6)	Hes5, Olig2 (x_5, x_7)	$(x_5) \wedge (\neg x_7)$
Olig2 (x_7)	Hes5, Scl (x_5, x_6)	$x_5 \wedge (\neg x_6)$
Stat3 (x_8)	Scl (x_6)	x_6
Aldh1L1 (x_9)	Stat3 (x_8)	x_8
Myt1L (x_{10})	Olig2 (x_7)	x_7
Sox8 (x_{11})	Sox8 (x_{11})	x_{10}

TABLE 12.2 Summary of the attractors of CNS developmental network by synchronous Boolean functions.

Attractor no. and class	Boolean network state($x_1 \rightarrow x_{11}$: rightmost to leftmost elements)	Genes expressed
1, CNS precursor	Eight states cycle attractors	–
2, Neuron	00000001110	Mash1, Brn2/Zic 1, Tuj 1
3, Astrocyte + Neuron + Oligodendrocyte	Three states cycle attractor	–
4, Astrocyte	00110100000	Scl, Stat3, Aldh1L1
5, Neuron + Astrocyte	00110101110	Mash1, Brn2/Zic1, Tuj1, Scl, Stat3, Aldh1L1
Oligodendrocyte	11001000000	Olig2, Myt1L, Sox8
Neuron + Oligodendrocyte	11001001110	Mash1, Brn2/Zic1, Tuj1, Olig2, Myt1L, Sox8

Each attractor is assigned into a (or a combination of) specific cell type(s), as listed in the first column. The attractor states and the corresponding genes expressed are listed in the second and third column, respectively. The hierarchy of each attractor (including its basin of attraction) corresponds to the degree of inclusion of cell types specific states expressed in the attractor state listed in the last row. For example, the genes expression in attractor 3 includes all three cell types (*astrocyte, neuron, oligodendrocyte*) specific genes and is termed as ANO attractor. A: *astrocyte*, N: *neuron*, O: *oligodendrocyte*.

attractor landscape. There may be too many constraints for producing networks that precisely only contain the "desired" attractors such that excess attractors represent an unwanted but necessary "side-effect." It has been proposed that such unoccupied attractors represent cancerous states: Lurking in the dark regions of gene expression space, they may become occupied in response to chronic abnormal perturbations or mutations (Kauffman 1971; Huang 1999; Huang 2009; Huang 2012). The co-expression of markers from different cell lineage in these attractor states (Figure 12.4c) in fact is an often observed feature of cancer cells (Huang 2013).

Relative stability of attractors. The eight-state cycle attractor of the CNS precursor cell (basin 1) would correspond to the promiscuous expression of the stem cell (Qiu et al. 2012). We now investigate the relative stability and the transition probability between different attractors by randomly switching the state of a gene (bit-flips) in the attractors. The results are summarized in the attractor transition graph (Figure 12.4d) which represents the transition probability between attractors. It demonstrates that the trajectories corresponding to normal development map on to transitions of a high probability (evident as thickness of the direct links between the *CNS precursor* and the *neuron*, *astrocyte* and *oligodendrocyte* attractors. (However, backwards differentiation to the CNS precursor are also likely according to the model, indicating that some feature is still missing that would prevent the "backflow"—such as downstream maturation steps in the differentiated cell types.)

By contrast, the "trans-differentiation" events between differentiated cell types have lower transition probabilities. For example, there are no directed links between *astrocyte* and *oligodendrocyte*. We also find that the three differentiated cell types have almost equal attracting basin as indicated by the size of the circle. Furthermore, our result shows that transition into the putative "cancer attractors" is not frequent.

7 BOOLEAN NETWORK MODEL FOR PANCREAS DEVELOPMENT AND REPROGRAMMING

7.1 Biology of pancreas differentiation

The pancreas is a gland that secrets various digestion enzymes into the intestinal lumen. But in addition to this *exocrine* function the pancreas is an *endocrine* organ: the beta cells in the pancreas islets secret the insulin into the circulation that regulates blood glucose levels and metabolism. Deficiency of beta cells leads to diabetes. Thus much effort is being spent in developing cell type reprogramming to produce beta-cells as a regenerative therapy for diabetes. This has stimulated characterization of cell lineage determining factors in the pancreas (Gittes 2009) and reprogramming experiments (Zhou and Melton 2008; Collombat et al. 2009; Ber et al. 2003). *Pdx1* is the first gene in embryonic development that marks the onset of the pancreas cell lineage (Offield et al. 1996). The cells with high *Ptf1a* expression are fated to the *exocrine* pancreas. The few cells which display temporarily high Ngn3 expression will form the *endocrine* cell lineages. The expression of *Pax4* in some cells further specifies the β, δ lineages while *Arx* specifies the α, γ lineages). To build the network, the interactions between these five genes were again derived from the literature (largely based on CHIP-chip or knockout/overexpressing experiments (Gittes 2009; Zhou et al. 2011)). More details of network topology can be found in our paper (Zhou et al. 2011).

7.2 Boolean network model for pancreas development

Again, with the network topology established (now including some information on the signs of the directed edges) we need to assign the Boolean functions onto the five nodes, given virtually complete lack of information about the molecular details that map the inputs to the target gene outputs. Here we take a different strategy for this task, reversing the question: We use information from the known dynamics of cell fates to constrain the space of Boolean functions by using a statistical ensemble approach to examine if functional constraints can help narrow down the space of network architecture (with respect to Boolean functions).

Thus, the dynamic constraint requirement is that the resulting network has at least three attractors with the gene expression patterns as defined above the structural constraints is to explicitly adopt the known signs of regulation and use the canalizing, nested-canalizing, and sign-compatible Boolean functions (see Section 3.1). The known topology drastically constrains the number of possible functions. Except for *Pdx1* which has only one input, all other genes have three inputs. With these constrains, the number of sets of Boolean functions which have at least three known attractors is 1,048,576. Among these combinations, there were 78,400 networks with canalyzing functions, among which there were only 9216 with nested canalyzing functions. Among the latter we found only 3600 sets of Boolean functions which are sign-compatible.

Determining global ordering. From the experiments of perturbations, the exocrine cells are the least stable among three pancreas cell types. The β, σ progenitor is more stable than α, γ, PP progenitor (Zhou et al. 2011). With the goal of studying relative stability in mind we require not only that the Boolean network model recapitulates the correct (observed) gene expression patterns associated with each lineage cell types but also that it reproduces the correct "ordering" of the cell phenotypes with respect to relative stability during of pancreas development. Thus we have one additional functional constraint for network determination: Concretely, transition probabilities should reflect the direction of development.

How to obtain the cell type (attractor) ordering of a network? In Section 5.6, we defined the ordering of cell attractors based on the mean first passage time (MFPT). In this ensemble approach we asked whether imposing increasing constraints on the set of Boolean networks as discussed in the previous section will increase the probability of obtaining attractor landscapes with the correct ordering. To evaluate the effect of constraining the Boolean functions, we calculate the cell ordering according to the MFPT for each of the different sets of Boolean functions imposed. The results clearly show that by imposing an increasing number of biologically meaningful constrains on the network structure (usage of Boolean functions), including canalizing functions, nested canalizing functions, and sign-compatible function, we narrow down the ensemble of networks that can produce the correct biological ordering of attractor states (Zhou et. al. in press).

This example shows that Boolean network models are useful tools to integrate loose biological facts regarding regulatory interactions between genes and can be used to construct dynamical networks that recapitulate not only the correct cell expression patterns but also an attractor landscape that models the hierarchy in cell-type development.

On the pragmatic side, with the measure of transition barrier height between different cell-type attractors, we have a tool for identifying the key genes that need to be perturbed to achieve a cell reprogramming. Determining the set of genes in the network whose activity change most sensitively affects the transition barriers between the attractors A and B, and determining the initial direction of the path of least action for exiting attractor A toward B, can offer hints for designing the optimal gene perturbation protocol for cell-type reprogramming.

TABLE 12.3 A summary of the recent transdifferentiation experiments.

Starting cell type(s)	Reprogrammed cell type(s)	Factor(s) used	Combination(s) of factor(S) used	Delivery mode(s)	Latency until observation of first colonies	Efficiency
Fibroblasts (embryonic)	Myoblasts	MyoD	NA	NA	NA	NA
Common lymphoid progenitor	Myeloid lineage cells	GM-CSF; IL-2	NA	Retrovirus	NA	NA
B cell precursors (primary)	Macrophages	C/EBPalpha; C/EBPbeta	NA	Retrovirus	NA	NA
T cell progenitors	Macrophages	C/EBPalpha; C/EBPbeta; PU.1	NA	Retrovirus	NA	NA
B cells	T cells	Pax5 deletion	NA	NA	NA	NA
Fibroblasts (NIH 3T3 line)	Macrophage-like cells	C/EBPalpha; PU.1	C/EBPalpha, PU.1	Retrovirus	NA	NA
Exocrine cells (from adult pancreas)	Beta-cells	Mafa; Ngn3; Pdx1	Mafa, Ngn3, Pdx1	Adenovirus	NA	Up to 20%
Embryos E6.5-7.5	Cadiac myocytes	Baf60c; Gata4; Tbx5	Baf60c, Gata4, Tbx5	Expression plasmid	NA	NA
Pre-B cells	Macrophages	C/EBPalpha	NA	Retrovirus	NA	NA
Fibroblasts (MEF from TauEGFP knock in mice)	Functional neurons	Ascl1; Brn2; Myt1 l; Olig2; Zic1	Ascl1, Brn2, Myt1 l	Lentivirus	NA	5F: 1.8-7.7%
Fibroblasts (cardiac, postnatal)	Cardiomyocyte-like cells	Gata4; Mef2c; Tbx5	Gata4, Mef2c, Tbx5	Retrovirus	NA	NA

This table summarizes recent experiments of cell fate conversion which associates with more than 10 distinct cell types. As it shows, the efficiency of trans-differentiation (>1%) is at least 100 times larger than that of the iPSs, which is less than 0:01%. In addition, the conversion between two cell types can be achieved by different reprogramming factors.

8 CONCLUSION—TOWARD A LA CARTE CELL REPROGRAMMING

The dogma held by "mainstream" biologists of differentiation as an irreversible process has been reshaped by the discovery of induced Pluripotent Stem Cells (iPS) and other experiments of cell trans-differentiation. These experiments lend new credence to the old ideas of cell types as attractor states in which no cell type switch is absolutely impossible but switching types is only a matter of probability. With the advanced models of network dynamics that consider the relative stability of states and the increasing availability of information on GRN structure, cell reprogramming is evolving from an art of empirical trial-and-error experiments to an engineering process that can be rationally designed based on a wiring diagram. To date more than ten (still counting) major cell types in human and mouse have been successfully reprogrammed to a less mature stem-like state. As shown in Table 12.3, an obvious characteristic of reprogramming is that the reprogramming efficiency is much higher between developmentally close cell types than between distant ones.

Another discovery, stunning to biologists but readily predicted by the theory of network dynamics, is that the reprogramming can be achieved by distinct sets of genes (for the same reprogramming) (Shu et al., 2013). In the light of "epigenetic landscape" we can conceptualize development and reprogramming within the same framework, as shown in Figure 1b. Both development and reprogramming can be considered as a set of transitions from one valley (attractors) to another, Since (in the continuous case) there exists infinite transition paths (state space trajectories) between any two cell attractors, reprogramming can be achieved through many different combinations of the genetic perturbations, among which some are better than others, if not optimal to have highest reprogramming efficiency. The recent achievement of reprogramming iPS without overexpression of the canonical set of pluripotency factors (Yamanaka protocol) but instead using a combination of fate determining factors is also in line with predictions from dynamical systems model of GRNs (Shu et al. 2013).

In post-genome era, understanding of biological processes has shifted from the notion of causation embodied by a single linear molecular pathway to the high-dimensional dynamics of complex non-linear systems epitomized by regulatory networks. Many higher-level biological functions of cells, such as cell differentiation, cell cycle, immune responses, or neuronal activities can only be explained by the dynamics of biological networks. In this chapter, we introduced the basic concepts of cell attractors and showed that Waddington's metaphoric epigenetic landscape has a formal basis in the attractor landscape. This conceptual framework helps to understand core properties of cell differentiation and ultimately, multicellularity. Specifically, we developed the concept of relative stability of network states on the epigenetic landscape, thus providing the elevation in the landscape picture a formal, quantifiable basis. We proposed methods to quantify the relative stability of attractor states in discrete gene networks models. We show in two examples that even with incomplete information about network structures, the use of Boolean networks can capture the essential outlines of cell fate dynamics and more importantly, permit the estimation of relative stability and the attractor transition barriers. These measures hold great promise for the rational design of the perturbation protocols for cell reprogramming in regenerative medicine. As the knowledge of the structure of GRNs for the development of various tissues will undoubtedly increase in the next decade, the utilization of such network information for therapeutic reprogramming may benefit from the concepts developed here. But conversely the new knowledge about the biology of regulatory networks and cell fate behavior, obtained through novel gene expression profiling at the resolution of single-cells, including the identification of rare (intermediate) subtypes and rare trans-differentiation events, will also stimulate the necessary improvement and refinement of the theory that we have outline here as a starting point.

References

Aldana-Gonzalez, M., Coppersmith, S., and Kadanoff, L.. In (E. Kaplan, J. E. Mardsen, and K. R. Sreenivasan, eds.), (2003). *Perspectives and Problems in Nonlinear Science*. In *A celebratory volume in honor of Lawrence Sirovich*. New York: Springer.

Aldana, M., and Cluzel, P. (2003). A natural class of robust networks. *Proc. Nat. Acad. Sci.* **100**:8710–8714.

Álvarez-Buylla, E. R., Chaos, Á., Aldana, M., Benítez, M., Cortes-Poza, Y., Espinosa-Soto, C., Hartasánchez, D. A., Lotto, R. B., Malkin, D., and Santos, G. J. E. (2008). Floral morphogenesis: stochastic explorations of a gene network epigenetic landscape. *PLoS ONE* **3**:e3626.

Amaral, L. a. N., Scala, A., Barthélémy, M., and Stanley, H. E. (2000). Classes of small-world networks. *Proc. Nat. Acad. Sci.* **97**:11149–11152.

Balleza, E., Alvarez-Buylla, E. R., Chaos, A., Kauffman, S., Shmulevich, I., and Aldana, M. (2008). Critical dynamics in genetic regulatory networks: examples from four kingdoms. *PLoS ONE* **3**:e2456.

Barabási, A.-L. and Albert, R. (1999). Emergence of scaling in random networks. science, 286, 509–512.

Ber, I., Shternhall, K., Perl, S., Ohanuna, Z., Goldberg, I., Barshack, I., Benvenisti-Zarum, L., Meivar-Levy, I., and Ferber, S. (2003). Functional, persistent, and extended liver to pancreas transdifferentiation. *J. Biol. Chem.* **278**:31950–31957.

Bertrand, N., Castro, D. S., and Guillemot, F. (2002). Proneural genes and the specification of neural cell types. *Nat. Rev. Neurosci.* **3**:517–530.

Bouvier, M. (1990). Cross-talk between second messengers. *Ann. NY Acad. Sci.* **594**:120–129.

Brown, K. S., Hill, C. C., Calero, G. A., Myers, C. R., Lee, K. H., Sethna, J. P., and Cerione, R. A. (2004). The statistical mechanics of complex signaling networks: nerve growth factor signaling. *Phys. Biol.* **1**:184.

Cheng, D.-Z., Qi, H., and Li, Z. (2011). *Analysis and control of Boolean networks: a semi-tensor product approach*. Springerverlag London Limited.

Collombat, P., Xu, X., Ravassard, P., Sosa-Pineda, B., Dussaud, S., Billestrup, N., Madsen, O. D., Serup, P., Heimberg, H., and Mansouri, A. (2009). The Ectopic Expression of< i> Pax4</i> in the Mouse Pancreas Converts Progenitor Cells into α and Subsequently β Cells. *Cell* **138**:449–462.

Cordell, H. J. (2009). Detecting gene-gene interactions that underlie human diseases. *Nat. Rev. Genet.* **10**:392–404.

Derrida, B., and Pomeau, Y. (1986). Random networks of automata: a simple annealed approximation. *Europhys. Lett.* **1**:45.

Efe, J. A., Hilcove, S., Kim, J., Zhou, H., Ouyang, K., Wang, G., Chen, J., and Ding, S. (2011). Conversion of mouse fibroblasts into cardiomyocytes using a direct reprogramming strategy. *Nat. Cell Biol.* **13**:215–222.

Elowitz, M. B., Levine, A. J., Siggia, E. D., and Swain, P. S. (2002). Stochastic gene expression in a single cell. *Science* **297**:1183–1186.

Fox, J. J., and Hill, C. C. (2001). From topology to dynamics in biochemical networks. *Chaos: An Interdisciplinary Journal of Nonlinear Science* **11**:809–815.

Freidlin, M. I., and Wentzell, A. D. (2012). *Random perturbations of dynamical systems*. Springer.

Galloway, J. L., Wingert, R. A., Thisse, C., Thisse, B., and Zon, L. I. (2005). Loss of gata1 but not gata2 converts erythropoiesis to myelopoiesis in zebrafish embryos. *Dev. Cell* **8**:109–116.

Gittes, G. K. (2009). Developmental biology of the pancreas: a comprehensive review. *Develop. Biol.* **326**:4–35.

Goldberg, A. D., Allis, C. D., and Bernstein, E. (2007). Epigenetics: a landscape takes shape. *Cell* **128**:635–638.

Graf, T. (2002). Differentiation plasticity of hematopoietic cells. *Blood* **99**:3089–3101.

Graf, T. (2011). Historical origins of transdifferentiation and reprogramming. *Cell Stem Cell* **9**:504–516.

Greil, F., Drossel, B., and Sattler, J. (2007). Critical Kauffman networks under deterministic asynchronous update. *New J. Phys.* **9**:373.

Gurdon, J. B., Elsdale, T. R., and Fischberg, M. (1958). Sexually mature individuals of Xenopus laevis from the transplantation of single somatic nuclei. *Nature* **182**:64–65.

Hopfield, J. J. (1984). Neurons with graded response have collective computational properties like those of two-state neurons. *Proc. Nat. Acad. Sci. USA* **81**:3088–3092.

Hsiao, L. L., Dangond, F., Yoshida, T., Hong, R., Jensen, R. V., Misra, J., Dillon, W., Lee, K. F., Clark, K. E., Haverty, P., Weng, Z., Mutter, G. L., Frosch, M. P., Macdonald, M. E., Milford, E. L., Crum, C. P., Bueno, R., Pratt, R. E., Mahadevappa, M., Warrington, J. A., Stephanopoulos, G., and Gullans, S. R. (2001). A compendium of gene expression in normal human tissues. *Physiol. Genom.* **7**:97–104.

Huang, S. (1999). Gene expression profiling, genetic networks, and cellular states: an integrating concept for tumorigenesis and drug discovery. *J. Mol. Med.* **77**:469–480.

Huang, S. (2009). Reprogramming cell fates: reconciling rarity with robustness. *BioEssays* **31**:546–560.

Huang, S. (2012). The molecular and mathematical basis of Waddington's epigenetic landscape: A framework for post-Darwinian biology?. *BioEssays* **34**:149–157.

Huang, S. (2013). Genetic and non-genetic instability in tumor progression: link between the fitness landscape and the epigenetic landscape of cancer cells. *Cancer Metastasis Rev.* 1–26.

Huang, S., Eichler, G., Bar-Yam, Y., and Ingber, D. E. (2005). Cell fates as high-dimensional attractor states of a complex gene regulatory network. *Phys. Rev. Lett.* **94**:128701.

Huang, S., Guo, Y.-P., May, G., and Enver, T. (2007). Bifurcation dynamics in lineage-commitment in bipotent progenitor cells. *Develop. Biol.* **305**:695–713.

Huang, S., and Ingber, D. E. (2000). Shape-dependent control of cell growth, differentiation, and apoptosis: switching between attractors in cell regulatory networks. *Exp. Cell Res.* **261**:91–103.

Huang, S., and Kauffman, S. (2009). Complex gene regulatory networks-from structure to biological observables: cell fate determination. In (R. A. Meyers (Ed.), *Encyclopedia of Complexity and Systems Science*, pp. 1180–1293. Springer.

Jarrah, A. S., Raposa, B., and Laubenbacher, R. (2007). Nested Canalyzing, Unate Cascade, and Polynomial Functions. *Physica D* **233**:167–174.

Joy, M. P., Brock, A., Ingber, D. E., and Huang, S. (2005). High-betweenness proteins in the yeast protein interaction network. *BioMed Res. Int.* **2005**:96–103.

Kauffman, S. (1969). Homeostasis and differentiation in random genetic control networks. *Nature* **224**:177–178.

Kauffman, S. (2004). A proposal for using the ensemble approach to understand genetic regulatory networks. *J. Theor. Biol.* **230**:581–590.

Kauffman, S., Peterson, C., Samuelsson, B., and Troein, C. (2003). Random Boolean network models and the yeast transcriptional network. *Proc. Nat. Acad. Sci.* **100**:14796–14799.

Kauffman, S. A. 1971. Cellular homeostasis, epigenesis and replication in randomly aggregated macromolecular systems.

Kauffman, S. A. (1993). *The origins of order: Self organization and selection in evolution.* USA: Oxford University Press.

Kubicek, S., and Jenuwein, T. (2004). A crack in histone lysine methylation. *Cell* **119**:903–906.

Larue, L., and Delmas, V. (2006). The WNT/Beta-catenin pathway in melanoma. *Front Biosci.* **11**:733–742.

Mali, P., and Cheng, L. (2012). Concise review: Human cell engineering: cellular reprogramming and genome editing. *Stem Cells* **30**:75–81.

Marcotte, E. M. (2001). The path not taken. *Nat. Biotechnol.* **19**:626–628.

Maskos, U., and Southern, E. M. (1992). Oligonucleotide hybridisations on glass supports: a novel linker for oligonucleotide synthesis and hybridisation properties of oligonucleotides synthesised in situ. *Nucl. Acids Res.* **20**:1679–1684.

Matache, M. T., and Heidel, J. (2004). Random Boolean network model exhibiting deterministic chaos. *Phys. Rev. E Stat. Nonlin. Soft Matter Phys.* **69**:056214.

May, R. M. (1972). Will a large complex system be stable?. *Nature* **238**:413–414.

Milo, R., Itzkovitz, S., Kashtan, N., Levitt, R., Shen-Orr, S., Ayzenshtat, I., Sheffer, M., and Alon, U. (2004). Superfamilies of evolved and designed networks. *Science* **303**:1538–1542.

Monod, J. and Jacob, F. (1961) General conclusions: teleonomic mechanisms in cellular metabolism, growth, and differentiation. Cold Spring Harbor Symposia on Quantitative Biology. Cold Spring Harbor Laboratory Press, 389–401.

Mortazavi, A., Williams, B. A., Mccue, K., Schaeffer, L., and Wold, B. (2008). Mapping and quantifying mammalian transcriptomes by RNA-Seq. *Nat. Methods* **5**:621–628.

Murtaugh, L. C. (2008). The what, where, when and how of Wnt/beta-catenin signaling in pancreas development. *Organogenesis* **4**:81–86.

Nykter, M., Price, N. D., Aldana, M., Ramsey, S. A., Kauffman, S. A., Hood, L. E., Yli-Harja, O., and Shmulevich, I. (2008a). Gene expression dynamics in the macrophage exhibit criticality. *Proc. Nat. Acad. Sci.* **105**:1897–1900.

Nykter, M., Price, N. D., Larjo, A., Aho, T., Kauffman, S. A., Yli-Harja, O., and Shmulevich, I. (2008b). Critical networks exhibit maximal information diversity in structure-dynamics relationships. *Phys. Rev. Lett.* **100**:058702.

Offield, M. F., Jetton, T. L., Labosky, P. A., Ray, M., Stein, R. W., Magnuson, M. A., Hogan, B., and Wright, C. (1996). PDX-1 is required for pancreatic outgrowth and differentiation of the rostral duodenum. *Development* **122**:983–995.

Oliveri, P., Carrick, D. M., and Davidson, E. H. (2002). A regulatory gene network that directs micromere specification in the sea urchin embryo. *Dev. Biol.* **246**:209–228.

Oliveri, P., and Davidson, E. H. (2004a). Gene regulatory network analysis in sea urchin embryos. *Methods Cell. Biol.* **74**:775–794.

Oliveri, P., and Davidson, E. H. (2004b). Gene regulatory network controlling embryonic specification in the sea urchin. *Curr. Opin. Genet. Dev.* **14**:351–360.

Orkin, S. H., and Zon, L. I. (2008). SnapShot: hematopoiesis. *Cell* **132**:712.e1–712.e2.

Perou, C. M., Sørlie, T., Eisen, M. B., Van De Rijn, M., Jeffrey, S. S., Rees, C. A., Pollack, J. R., Ross, D. T., Johnsen, H., and Akslen, L. A. (2000). Molecular portraits of human breast tumours. *Nature* **406**:747–752.

Qiu, X., Ding, S., and Shi, T. (2012). From Understanding the Development Landscape of the Canonical Fate-Switch Pair to Constructing a Dynamic Landscape for Two-Step Neural Differentiation. PLoS One, 7.

Ravasz, E., Somera, A. L., Mongru, D. A., Oltvai, Z. N., and Barabási, A.-L. (2002). Hierarchical organization of modularity in metabolic networks. *Science* **297**:1551–1555.

Ravin, R., Hoeppner, D. J., Munno, D. M., Carmel, L., Sullivan, J., Levitt, D. L., Miller, J. L., Athaide, C., Panchision, D. M., and Mckay, R. D. (2008). Potency and fate specification in CNS stem cell populations in vitro. *Cell Stem Cell* **3**:670–680.

Shen-Orr, S. S., Milo, R., Mangan, S., and Alon, U. (2002). Network motifs in the transcriptional regulation network of Escherichia coli. *Nat. Genet.* **31**:64–68.

Shmulevich, I., Dougherty, E. R., Kim, S., and Zhang, W. (2002). Probabilistic Boolean networks: a rule-based uncertainty model for gene regulatory networks. *Bioinformatics* **18**:261–274.

Shmulevich, I., and Kauffman, S. A. (2004). Activities and sensitivities in Boolean network models. *Phys. Rev. Lett.* **93**:048701.

Shu, J., Wu, C., Wu, Y., Li, Z., Shao, S., Zhao, W., Tang, X., Yang, H., Shen, L., and Zuo, X. (2013). Induction of Pluripotency in Mouse Somatic Cells with Lineage Specifiers. *Cell* **153**:963–975.

Smith, J., Theodoris, C., and Davidson, E. H. (2007). A gene regulatory network subcircuit drives a dynamic pattern of gene expression. *Science* **318**:794–797.

Southan, C. (2004). Has the yo-yo stopped? An assessment of human protein-coding gene number. *Proteomics* **4**:1712–1726.

Strang, G. (2003). *Introduction to linear algebra*. Wellesley Cambridge Pr.

Swain, P. S., Elowitz, M. B., and Siggia, E. D. (2002a). Intrinsic and extrinsic contributions to stochasticity in gene expression. *Proc. Nat. Acad. Sci. USA* **99**:12795–12800.

Takahashi, K., and Yamanaka, S. (2006). Induction of pluripotent stem cells from mouse embryonic and adult fibroblast cultures by defined factors. *Cell* **126**:663–676.

Thomas, R. (1978). Logical analysis of systems comprising feedback loops. *J. Theor. Biol.* **73**:631–656.

Torres-Sosa, C., Huang, S., and Aldana, M. (2012). Criticality Is an Emergent Property of Genetic Networks that Exhibit Evolvability. *PLoS Comput. Biol.* **8**:e1002669.

Vaquerizas, J. M., Kummerfeld, S. K., Teichmann, S. A., and Luscombe, N. M. (2009). A census of human transcription factors: function, expression and evolution. *Nat. Rev. Genet.* **10**:252–263.

Von Bertalanffy, L. (1956). General System Theory. *Gen. Syst.* **1**:1–10.

Waddington, C. H. (1957). The strategy of the genes. A discussion of some aspects of theoretical biology. With an appendix by H. Kacser., ix+-262.

Wang, R.-S., Saadatpour, A., and Albert, R. (2012). Boolean modeling in systems biology: an overview of methodology and applications. *Phys. Biol.* **9**:055001.

Watts, D. J., and Strogatz, S. H. (1998). Collective dynamics of 'small-world' networks. *Nature* **393**:440–442.

Wuensche, A. (1998) Genomic regulation modeled as a network with basins of attraction. Pacific Symposium on Biocomputing, 44.

Wuensche, A. (2010). DDLab-Discrete Dynamics Lab.

Zanudo, J. G., Aldana, M., and Martínez-Mekler, G. (2011). Boolean Threshold Networks: Virtues and Limitations for Biological Modeling. Information Processing and Biological Systems. Springer.

Zhou, J. X., Aliyu, M., Aurell, E., and Huang, S. (2012). Quasi-potential landscape in complex multi-stable systems. *J. R. Soc. Interface* **9**:3539–3553.

Zhou, J. X., Brusch, L., and Huang, S. (2011). Predicting pancreas cell fate decisions and reprogramming with a hierarchical multi-attractor model. *PLoS ONE* **6**:e14752.

Zhou, J.X., Samal, A., d'Herouel,A.F., Price,D.N., Huang, S. (in press). Relative Stability and Global Ordering Of Boolean Network Landscape for the Pancreas Cell Differentiation and Reprogramming.

Zhou, Q., Brown, J., Kanarek, A., Rajagopal, J., and Melton, D. A. (2008). In vivo reprogramming of adult pancreatic exocrine cells to beta-cells. *Nature* **455**:627–632.

Zhou, Q., and Melton, D. A. (2008). Extreme makeover: converting one cell into another. *Cell Stem Cell* **3**:382–388.

CHAPTER

13

Stochastic Simulations of Cellular Processes: From Single Cells to Colonies

John Cole, Michael J. Hallock, Piyush Labhsetwar, Joseph R. Peterson, John E. Stone, Zaida Luthey-Schulten

The University of Illinois at Urbana-Champaign, USA

CONTENTS

Abstract

All chemical reactions are inherently random discrete events; while large numbers of reacting species in well-stirred vessels my appear to be governed by deterministic expressions, the biochemistry at the heart of the living cell—which may involve only a single copy of a gene or only a handfull of proteins—can exhibit significant fluctuations from mean behavior. Here we describe the **Lattice Microbes** software for the stochastic simulation of biochemical reaction networks within realistic models of cells, and explore its application to two model systems. The first is the *lac* genetic switch, which illustrates how stochastic gene expression can drive identical cells in macroscopically identical environments toward very different cell fates, and the second

http://dx.doi.org/10.1016/B978-0-12-405926-9.00013-7

is the MinDE system, whose oscillatory behavior along the length of the *E. coli* cell illustrates the necessity of detailed spatial resolution in accurately modeling cellular biochemistry. We conclude by describing the use of a hybrid methodology that couples the Lattice Microbes' reaction-diffusion modeling capability with a genome-scale flux-balance model of metabolism in order to describe the collective metabolism of a dense colony of cells.

1 INTRODUCTION

Reaction-diffusion processes are ubiquitous in biological systems. Nutrients in the medium may be taken up or secreted via passive transport, by diffusing through the membrane, or active transport through membrane-bound transporters. Once inside the cell, metabolites interact with other cellular components including proteins and nucleic acids in order to take part in an extensive network of biochemical reactions, generating in the process the multitude of building blocks that add up to life. Cellular processes like gene expression and regulation are dependent on proteins and nucleic acids that are found in relatively low copy numbers, and consequently can exhibit large fluctuations due to the stochasticity (or noise) intrinsic to all chemical processes. A series of pioneering single molecule experiments which monitored the fluorescence of proteins labeled with reporter systems capable of capturing these stochastic effects at the single cell level have been reviewed in several recent articles (Munsky et al. 2012; Taniguchi et al. 2010). In addition to the *intrinsic* noise of the reaction, there are several sources of long-time scale *extrinsic* noise that give rise to gene expression variability. Enzyme, polymerase, and ribosome counts, as examples, can all change over the course of a cell cycle and during cell division; because they are all integral parts of the gene expression machinery, they can impart correlated variability to all gene expression. In general, extrinsic variability dominates among genes expressed in relatively high copy numbers whereas intrinsic variability dominates in the low copy number regime.

Variations in protein copy numbers and phenotypic behaviors observed among isogenic cells growing under macroscopically identical conditions motivate a probabilistic rather than deterministic formulation of the underlying biochemistry involved. Reaction schemes occurring in a well-stirred environment can be treated by solving the chemical master equation (CME), which governs the time evolution of the probability, $P(\mathbf{x}, t)$, for the system to be in a state $\mathbf{x}$, specified by the number of molecular species. Unfortunately, a spatially homogenous volume is often a poor approximation to a living cell.

Cellular volumes can range from a few cubic microns to thousands, and reactions are often highly localized to certain parts of the cell (e.g. membrane, cytoplasm, nucleoid) and separated from each other by densely crowded regions teeming with diffusing obstacles such as proteins or ribosomes. The cellular volume occupied by proteins and RNA is estimated to be approximately 30% for a fast growing *Escherichia coli* (*E. coli*) (Sundararaj et al. 2004); adding in the entire chromosome brings this number closer to 40%. Stochastic modeling of a system of biochemical reactions inside a cell therefore must handle this type of spatial inhomogeneity, and should be able to efficiently simulate time scales on the order of the cell cycle (minutes to hours). To account for spatial organization and molecular crowding, the cell is divided into discrete subvolumes, v, and molecules are allowed to diffuse between adjacent subvolumes but are excluded from subvolumes occupied by an obstacle. Molecules occupying the same local subvolume are allowed to react with each other according to their given rate laws. The probability of being in a given state, $P(\mathbf{x}_v, t)$, obeys the so-called reaction-diffusion master equation (RDME), and varies according to position within the cell. Except for some simple cases, neither the CME or the RDME formulations can be solved analytically; rather, one must carry out stochastic simulations of the processes such that the underlying Markovian processes and transition probabilities are obeyed. In our previous studies of stochastic gene expression of the *lac* genetic switch in *E. coli*, we developed the graphics processing unit (GPU)-based **Lattice Microbes** software (Roberts et al. 2011, 2013) to efficiently sample trajectories from both the CME and RDME treatment on workstations and high-performance computers (HPC). By spatially decomposing the cell across multiple GPUs, our approach has recently been extended to dividing bacterial cells, larger eukaryal cells, and small colonies of interacting bacterial cells. The performance speedup over other methods for simulating cells with realistic molecular crowding is due in large part to the GPU architecture (Roberts et al. 2013; Hallock et al. in revision).

Complete kinetic descriptions of cellular reaction networks can require tens of thousands of kinetic parameters, many of which are as yet unknown. Stochastic simulations of the metabolic and translational networks in *E. coli*, for example, would require kinetic parameters for over 30,000 reactions, many of which are currently unavailable in the literature. Nevertheless, for several model organisms, decades of work have provided systems of balanced reaction networks describing several key cellular processes including metabolism and translation (Schellenberger et al. 2010). A method known as flux balance analysis (FBA) requires only reaction stoichiometry and constraints based on substrate availability, enzyme copy numbers, or thermodynamics, to name a few, in order to predict steady-state fluxes throughout the various pathways in the networks (for a review, see Lewis et al. (2012)). FBA poses the reaction network as a linear programming problem and searches for the set of reaction fluxes—subject to the condition that all metabolite concentrations are at steady state—that optimize some objective function. An example objective function useful for studying a model of metabolism is the production of biomass—a reaction in the model that requires several "building block" metabolites from around the network (lipids, amino acids, nucleic acids, *etc.*) in the approximate proportions that make up cells. Such a biomass objective is applicable when assuming cells are trying to maximize their growth rate.

Many interesting applications have been found for FBA-based modeling approaches. For instance, recent studies have coupled multiple FBA models to study nutrient exchange between different species in a community (Zomorrodi and Maranas 2012; Zhuang et al. 2012). In the case of *Mycoplasma genitalium*, Covert et al. were able to iteratively couple the dynamic response of kinetic models of several cellular reaction modules over short times with a flux balance model of metabolism in order to obtain a time-dependent description of a complete organism (Karr et al. 2012). Even in the case of the small pathogen studied, over 20,000 parameters were required to develop the model, and the study was instrumental in checking the consistency of the kinetic and turnover parameters as well as the protein distributions observed by a variety of experiments.

In this chapter we aim to further discuss these whole cell modeling strategies and provide examples where we have successfully applied them to cellular processes. We start off discussing the CME and RDME treatments in **Lattice Microbes**. We then present an example study of the *lac* genetic switch in *Escherichia coli* (*E. coli*) under the assumption of spatial homogeneity (i.e. we use a CME-sampling simulation approach). We then highlight the Min protein system in *E. coli* in which regions of high membrane-bound protein concentration that arise through the exchange of proteins between the membrane and cytoplasm oscillate along the length of the cell, necessitating the spatial resolution offered by RDME-sampling simulation. Finally, we present a simple study of a hybrid RDME/FBA methodology applied to a more complex growth scenario. In analogy to input-output models used in economics, we use hybrid RDME/FBA simulations of cellular networks to demonstrate how a small colony of interacting bacterial cells might respond to the competition for resources.

2 CME AND RDME SIMULATIONS IN LATTICE MICROBES

The **Lattice Microbes** software is capable of approximating the CME and RDME through a number of methods. It uses the standard stochastic simulation algorithm of Gillespie Gillespie (2007) to solve the CME. For solving the RDME, **Lattice Microbes** uses a lattice-based approach and operator splitting to calculate the reaction and diffusion operations separately. Each lattice site is allowed to contain up to a certain number of particles which may react with each other or diffuse to neighboring sites. Lattice sites are ascribed a "type" which provides structure to the domain (for example a cell membrane, the cellular cytosol, or the extracellular space, etc.) and the reactive or diffusive properties of each type of particle can specified separately on each site.

Diffusion is accounted for by random transitions of molecular species between neighboring subvolumes at a predetermined time according to their macroscopic diffusion coefficients. Because diffusion rates are most commonly much larger than reaction rates, diffusion sets the smallest time step that captures the system statistics. This time step is related to the lattice spacing, λ and the diffusion coefficient, D, through:

$$\tau \leq \frac{\lambda^2}{2D}$$

The software combines the multiparticle (MP) method for diffusion developed by Chopard and Droz (1998) in lattice gas automata for reaction diffusion systems with Gillespie's stochastic simulator algorithm for reactions within the subvolumes (Gillespie, 2007). Reactions occur only between molecules within a subvolume and each subvolume is considered to be well stirred such that reactions within it follow standard kinetic theory and can be described by the CME. This approach is most similar to the Gillespie multiparticle (GMP) method first introduced by Rodríguez et al. (2006). Using the multiparticle diffusion (MPD) method, the diffusion operator of the RDME is parallelized for efficient calculation on a GPU at a per-subvolume granularity (Roberts et al. 2009). Uniquely, our MPD-RDME approach is of sufficient performance to permit the inclusion of *in vivo* crowding into the model, by constructing an approximation of the crowded cytoplasm using reflective sites.

The time evolution of the probability for the system to be in a specific state $\mathbf{x}$ (where $\mathbf{x}_\nu$ contains the number of molecules of each of N species in the $\nu \in V$ subvolume) is the sum of the rates of change due to reaction and diffusion, as described by the operators $\mathcal{R}$ and $\mathcal{D}$, respectively:

$$\mathcal{R}P(\mathbf{x},t) = \sum_{\nu}^{V}\sum_{r}^{R}[-a_r(\mathbf{x}_\nu)P(\mathbf{x}_\nu,t) + a_r(\mathbf{x}_\nu - \mathbf{S}_\mathbf{r})P(\mathbf{x}_\nu - \mathbf{S}_\mathbf{r},t)]$$

$$\mathcal{D}P(\mathbf{x},t) = \sum_{\nu}^{V}\sum_{\xi}^{\pm\hat{i},\hat{j},\hat{k}}\sum_{\alpha}^{N}[-d^\alpha x_\nu^\alpha P(\mathbf{x},t) + d^\alpha(x_{\nu+\xi}^\alpha + 1)P(\mathbf{x} + 1_{\nu+\xi}^\alpha - 1_\nu^\alpha,t)]$$

$$\frac{dP(\mathbf{x},t)}{dt} = \mathcal{R}P(\mathbf{x},t) + \mathcal{D}P(\mathbf{x},t)$$

The reaction operator is simply the CME applied to each subvolume independently, where $a_r(\mathbf{x})$ is the reaction propensity for reaction r of R and S is the $N \times R$ stoichiometric matrix describing the net change in molecule number when a reaction occurs. The diffusion operator describes the rate of change of the probability due to the molecules' propensity to diffuse between the subvolumes. x_ν^α is the number of molecules of species $\alpha \in N$ in subvolume ν and d^α is the diffusive propensity for a molecule of species α to jump from subvolume ν to neighboring subvolume $\nu + \xi$, which is related to its macroscopic diffusion coefficient by $d = \frac{D}{\lambda^2}$. The first part of the diffusion operator then is probability flux out of the current state due to molecules diffusing from subvolume ν to subvolume $\nu + \xi$, where ξ is a neighboring subvolume in the $\pm x$, $\pm y$, or $\pm z$ direction, as indicated by the $\hat{i}, \hat{j}$, and $\hat{k}$ units vectors. The second part of the diffusion operator describes probability flux into the current state due to molecules diffusing into the current subvolume from a neighboring subvolume. The 1_ν^α syntax represents a single molecule of type α in subvolume ν.

3 SIMULATING THE *lac* GENETIC SWITCH IN *E. COLI*

The *lac* genetic switch is an inducible, bistable genetic system used by *E. coli* to sense the presence of lactose and produce proteins to utilize it. In the absence or presence of low concentrations of external inducer (I_{ex}—a lactose analog that is not metabolizable) few copies of the *lacY* permease gene are expressed resulting in few copies of the LacY permease protein and the cell is said to be in the "uninduced state," whereas in the presence of high concentrations of I_{ex}, the cell expresses high numbers of the *lac* operon and is said to be in the "induced state." The system relies on a positive feedback loop wherein the inducer that is transported into the cell up-regulates the production of more transporters, which, in turn, take up more inducer. Under uninduced conditions, repressor protein dimers, R_2, bind to the operator region upstream of the *lac* operon genes, preventing docking of the polymerase and therefore transcription. Cytoplasmic inducer, I, can bind the repressors, preventing them from binding the operator, and thus allow the transcription of LacY—the lactose transporter protein encoded by one of the genes in the *lac* operon. For details on this genetic switch see (Figure 13.1). All of the processes in this genetic system can be represented by a set of 23 biochemical reactions among 12 species (Table 13.1). These reactions along with their rate laws and kinetic parameters are stored in a file called `lac.sbml` (SBML is a popular file format for encoding systems biology data, and it can be read by the *Lattice Microbes* software), which can be found in the compressed `LatticeMicrobesWorkflowFiles.zip` directory available free for download by clicking the "Tutorial files" link at http://www.scs.illinois.edu/schulten/lm/index.html.

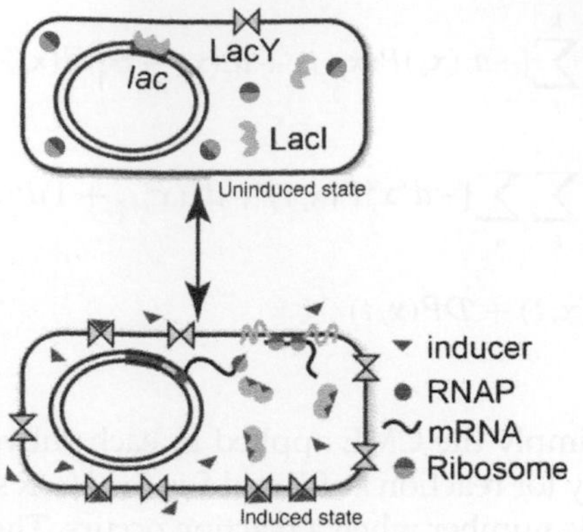

FIGURE 13.1 Two possible states of *E. coli* in presence and absence of inducer (Roberts et al. 2011) are shown. In the absence of inducer, the lac repressor (LacI) binds to the lac operator preventing transcription of genes in the lac operon. Following an increase in the extracellular inducer concentration, inducer enters the cell via both diffusion across the membrane and active transport by lactose permease (LacY). Once inside, inducer binds free LacI molecules preventing them from binding to the operator. After the intracellular inducer concentration reaches a threshold, any bound repressor is knocked-off the operator leading to expression of the lac genes. At high intracellular inducer concentrations the genes for lactose metabolism are fully induced. After inducer is removed, repressor rebinds to the operator preventing further expression of the lac operon and the enzymes for lactose metabolism are either degraded or diluted through cellular division.

TABLE 13.1 Rate constants used for simulating lac genetic switch in *E. coli* Roberts et al. (2011).

Reaction	Parameter	Rate (source[a])	Propensity
Lac operon regulation			
$R_2 + O \rightarrow R_2O$	k_{ron}	2.43×10^6 M^{-1}s^{-1}(M)	$\frac{k_{ron}}{N_A V} \cdot R_2 \cdot O$
$IR_2 + O \rightarrow IR_2O$	k_{iron}	1.21×10^6 M^{-1}s^{-1}(M)	$\frac{k_{iron}}{N_A V} \cdot IR_2 \cdot O$
$I_2R_2 + O \rightarrow I_2R_2O$	k_{i2ron}	2.43×10^4 M^{-1}s^{-1}(M)	$\frac{k_{i2ron}}{N_A V} \cdot I_2R_2 \cdot O$
$R_2O \rightarrow R_2 + O$	k_{roff}	6.30×10^{-4} s^{-1}(S[b])	$k_{roff} \cdot R_2O$
$IR_2O \rightarrow IR_2 + O$	k_{iroff}	6.30×10^{-4} s^{-1}(S[b])	$k_{iroff} \cdot IR_2O$
$I_2R_2O \rightarrow I_2R_2 + O$	k_{i2roff}	3.15×10^{-1} s^{-1}(M)	$k_{i2roff} \cdot I_2R_2O$
Transcription, translation, and degradation			
$O \rightarrow O + mY$	k_{tr}	1.26×10^{-1} s^{-1}(M)	$k_{tr} \cdot O$
$mY \rightarrow mY + Y$	k_{tn}	4.44×10^{-2} s^{-1}(S)	$k_{tn} \cdot mY$
$mY \rightarrow \varnothing$	k_{degm}	1.11×10^{-2} s^{-1}(S)	$k_{degm} \cdot mY$
$Y \rightarrow \varnothing$	k_{degp}	2.10×10^{-4} s^{-1}(M)	$k_{degp} \cdot Y$

(*Continued*)

TABLE 13.1 (Continued)

Reaction	Parameter	Rate (source[a])	Propensity
Lac inducer–repressor interactions			
$I + R_2 \rightarrow IR_2$	k_{ion}	2.27×10^4 $M^{-1}s^{-1}$(M)	$\frac{k_{ion}}{N_A V} \cdot I \cdot R_2$
$I + IR_2 \rightarrow I_2R_2$	k_{i2on}	1.14×10^4 $M^{-1}s^{-1}$(M)	$\frac{k_{i2on}}{N_A V} \cdot I \cdot IR_2$
$I + R_2O \rightarrow IR_2O$	k_{iopon}	6.67×10^2 $M^{-1}s^{-1}$(M)	$\frac{k_{iopon}}{N_A V} \cdot I \cdot R_2O$
$I + IR_2O \rightarrow I_2R_2O$	k_{i2opon}	3.33×10^2 $M^{-1}s^{-1}$(M)	$\frac{k_{i2opon}}{N_A V} \cdot I \cdot IR_2O$
$IR_2 \rightarrow I + R_2$	k_{ioff}	2.00×10^{-1} s^{-1}(K[c])	$k_{ioff} \cdot IR_2$
$I_2R_2 \rightarrow I + IR_2$	k_{i2off}	4.00×10^{-1} s^{-1}(K[c])	$k_{i2off} \cdot I_2R_2$
$IR_2O \rightarrow I + R_2O$	k_{iopoff}	1.00 s^{-1}(K[c])	$k_{iopoff} \cdot IR_2O$
$I_2R_2O \rightarrow I + IR_2O$	$k_{i2opoff}$	2.00 s^{-1} (K[c])	$k_{i2opoff} \cdot I_2R_2O$
Inducer transport			
$I_{ex} \rightarrow I$	k_{id}	2.33×10^{-3} s^{-1}(K[d])	$k_{id} \cdot I_{ex}$
$I \rightarrow I_{ex}$	k_{id}	2.33×10^{-3} s^{-1}(K[d])	$k_{id} \cdot I$
$Y + I_{ex} \rightarrow YI$	k_{yion}	3.03×10^4 $M^{-1}s^{-1}$(K)	$\frac{k_{yion}}{N_A V} \cdot Y \cdot I_{ex}$
$YI \rightarrow Y + I_{ex}$	k_{yioff}	1.20×10^{-1} s^{-1}(K)	$k_{yioff} \cdot YI$
$YI \rightarrow Y + I$	k_{it}	1.20×10^1 s^{-1}(K[e])	$k_{it} \cdot YI$

[a]*S = in vivo single molecule experiment, K = in vitro (kinetic) experiment, M = model parameter fit to single molecule distributions.* [b]*Goeddel et al. (1977).* [c]*O'Gorman et al. (1980), Dunaway et al. (1980).* [d]*Maloney and Wilson (1973), Chung and Stephanopoulos (1996).* [e]*Dornmair et al. (1989).*

Our studies of the *lac* system were simulated using the **Lattice Microbes** software (Roberts et al., 2011). Each replicate was performed on a single GPU independently of all other replicates. These simulations were performed in two very different spatial model systems of *E. coli*: a fast growing model system of approximate length 2 μm and radius 0.5 μm, and a slow growing model system of approximate length 3 μm and radius 0.25 μm. These models were packed with on the order of half a million obstacles representing a range of cellular components varying in size from small proteins to polymerases to ribosomes. These obstacles' relative distributions were based on proteomics data and, in the case of the slow growing model, cryoelectron tomography data which show locations within the cell of individual ribosomes and a condensed nucleoid region. In all, roughly 1 million active species were simulated at any given time. Under crowded conditions, the simulation is of considerable computational complexity and approximating the RDME requires more physical time and is best carried out on a computing cluster; without molecular crowding and assuming well-stirred conditions, the time-dependent behavior of LacY and mRNA production can be easily studied as a function of the inducer concentrations on a consumer desktop computer.

3.1 Simulating the *lac* genetic switch under well-stirred conditions: a brief tutorial

Due to the long time and computational requirements of the RDME for spatially resolved systems, this tutorial will use a CME version of the *lac* system. We will simulate the *lac* genetic switch for 10 h which is the time taken for count of LacY protein to stabilize. One hundred different trajectories (replicates), each representing a unique cell in the population, will be simulated at I_{ex} concentrations of 10, 15, 20, and 30 μM. At the low I_{ex} concentration of 10 μM few cells transition to the induced state and most cells express LacY at levels below 400–600 proteins per cell. At a high I_{ex} concentration of 30 μM almost all cells transition to the induced state and express LacY at levels above 1,750 per cell. In the intermediate I_{ex} concentrations (15 and 20 μM), bimodal populations emerge in which both induced and uninduced phenotypes are simultaneously present. In order to investigate this directly, the reaction network and kinetic parameters will be imported from the `lac.sbml` file, and a set of simulations of the *lac* genetic switch will be performed.

For each I_{ex} concentration to be studied, the contents of the `lac.sbml` file will need to be edited, and its file name changed (e.g. `lac_10.sbml`, `lac_15.sbml`, *etc.*). Note that the units used are particle number rather than concentration; assuming a cell volume of 8×10^{-16} L, the particle numbers corresponding to I_{ex} concentrations of 10, 15, 20 and 30 μM are 4,816, 7,224, 9,632, and 14,448 respectively. In the interest of time, both I_{ex} and I concentrations can be changed to avoid simulating the time taken for them to equilibrate (because their volumes are identical, simply set both internal and external inducer counts equal).

A list of the necessary software includes:

1. **Lattice Microbes** http://www.scs.illinois.edu/schulten/lm/index.html—**Lattice Microbes** is a software capable of calculating the CME and RDME via various approximation methods. The software was designed from the ground up to utilize the incredible performance of current graphics processing units (GPUs), though allows for some methods to be solved on the CPU. Several tutorials are available as well as binaries for Mac OSX and Linux. In addition, the source code is available under an open source license.
2. **MATLAB**—This common commercial analysis software used as a post-processing the simulation output of Lattice Microbes.
3. **HDFView** http://www.hdfgroup.org/hdf-java-html/hdfview/—A free graphical program for viewing the contents of the simulation output of Lattice Microbes.
4. **VMD 1.9.1** 64-bit version www.ks.uiuc.edu/Research/vmd/—A free visualization program used to generate many of the images in this chapter. It is able to animate of the output from **Lattice Microbes** and perform various post-processing via a scripting language interface.

After installing **Lattice Microbes** and downloading the tutorial files, the following commands may be used to perform the simulation for the 10 μM I_{ex} concentration. Create a simulation file from the SBML file:

```
[userhostqs/bimol]$./lm_sbml_importlac – cme – sbml_10.lmlac_10.sbml
```

Next, set the frequency, `writeInterval`, at which simulation data is written to the output file to be 1 second and the duration, `maxTime`, of the simulation to be 10 h:

```
[userhost qs/bimol]$./lm_setp lac – cme – sbml_10.lm
writeInterval = le0 maxTime = 3.6e4
```

Finally, launch 100 replicates, or in other words cells, of the simulation to be run:

```
[userhost qs/bimol]$./lm – r 1 – 100 – ws – f lac – cme – sbml_10.lm
```

We can identify if a cell has transitioned into an induced state by investigating the final LacY copy number from its simulated trajectory. Histograms of these data can be generated using the matlab script `laccme.m` included with the downloaded compressed directory (see Figure 13.2):

```
inputFilename='lac-cme-sbml_10.lm';
ts=cast(permute(hdf5read(inputFilename,sprintf('/Simulations/%07d/. . .
    SpeciesCountTimes',1)),[2,1]),'double');
```

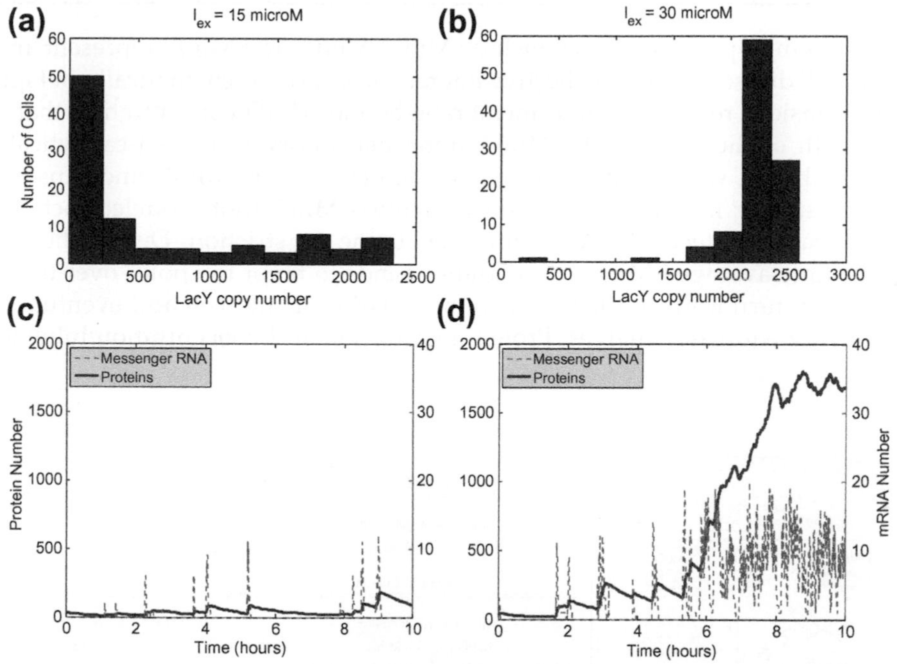

FIGURE 13.2 A demonstration of a colony the CME applied to a colony of cells with two levels of *lac* inducer. (a) After 10 h in a relatively low inducer concentration of 15 μM there is a bimodal distribution of cells where a small portion has been induced into the LacY protein producing state while the majority remain in the uninduced state. (b) After 10 h in a high inducer concentration of 30 μM virtually all of the cells have been induced into a state that produces significant LacY. Time traces for cells that have been grown in 15 μM inducer that (c) was in the uninduced during the 10 h and (d) one that switched into the induced state. The time traces demonstrate the stochastic expression of messenger RNA, shown in green, and the accumulation of protein over the course of the simulation. The loss of protein over each hour period is due to largely to dilution as the cell grows and divides, where in the simulations is due to the rate ascribed to protein degradation. It can be seen that once a cell is induced, the frequency of RNA transcription increases drastically and the average RNA number goes from essentially 0 to about 10 copies per cell.

```
numberReplicates=100;
finalLacY = zeros(numberReplicates,1);
for R=[1:numberReplicates]
 counts=cast(permute(hdf5read(inputFilename,sprintf('/. . .
     Simulations/%07d/SpeciesCounts'R)),[2,1]),'double');
 finalLacY(R) = counts(length(ts),9);
end
hist(finalLacY);
axis([0 3000 1e0 6e1]); xlabel('LacY count number'); ylabel('Number of
Cells');
```

Repeat this step for 15, 20, and 30 μM.

4 SIMULATING MinDE OSCILLATIONS IN *E. COLI*

The Min system of proteins, which include MinC, MinD, and MinE, represent an integral part of the *E. coli* divisome. Their collective interactions, shown schematically in Figure 13.3, give rise to transient regions of high membrane-bound MinD concentration that oscillate along the length of the cell. Briefly, MinD, upon phosphorylation, self-catalytically binds to the cell membrane, while MinE attaches to membrane-bound MinD and causes dephosphorylation, resulting in detachment. MinD-recruited MinC (not modeled) acts to inhibit FtsZ polymerization, effectively preventing membrane constriction. Due to the oscillatory behavior, the time-averaged MinC concentration tends to favor the poles over the center of the cell, which in turn leads to the localization of FtsZ near mid-cell and eventual cell division into roughly equivalent halves. Protein localization and concentration inhomogeneity

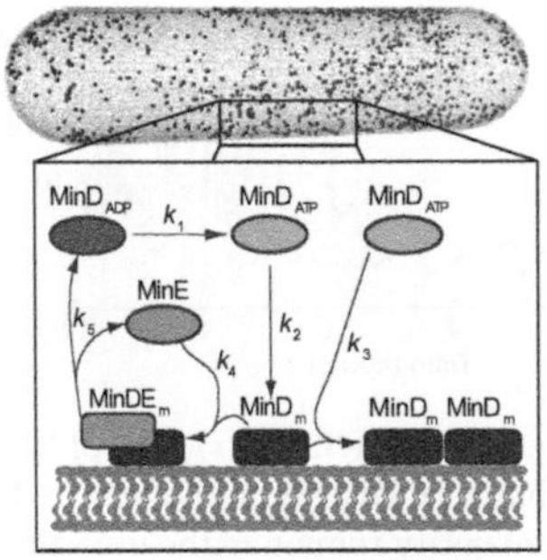

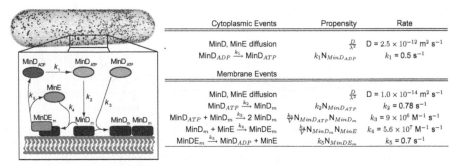

Cytoplasmic Events	Propensity	Rate
MinD, MinE diffusion	$\frac{D}{\lambda^2}$	D = 2.5×10^{-12} m^2 s^{-1}
$\text{MinD}_{ADP} \xrightarrow{k_1} \text{MinD}_{ATP}$	$k_1 N_{MinD_{ADP}}$	$k_1 = 0.5$ s^{-1}
Membrane Events		
MinD, MinE diffusion	$\frac{D}{\lambda^2}$	D = 1.0×10^{-14} m^2 s^{-1}
$\text{MinD}_{ATP} \xrightarrow{k_2} \text{MinD}_m$	$k_2 N_{MinD_{ATP}}$	$k_2 = 0.78$ s^{-1}
$\text{MinD}_{ATP} + \text{MinD}_m \xrightarrow{k_3} 2\ \text{MinD}_m$	$\frac{k_3}{V} N_{MinD_{ATP}} N_{MinD_m}$	$k_3 = 9 \times 10^6$ M^{-1} s^{-1}
$\text{MinD}_m + \text{MinE} \xrightarrow{k_4} \text{MinDE}_m$	$\frac{k_4}{V} N_{MinD_m} N_{MinE}$	$k_4 = 5.6 \times 10^7$ M^{-1} s^{-1}
$\text{MinDE}_m \xrightarrow{k_5} \text{MinD}_{ADP} + \text{MinE}$	$k_5 N_{MinDE_m}$	$k_5 = 0.7$ s^{-1}

FIGURE 13.3 The Min protein system schematic and simulation parameters for the kinetic model. Diffusion and reaction rates, as well as initial particle numbers, are shown in the table below. The proteins are allowed to sit in either the membrane or the cytoplasm, and rates of diffusion to and from the membrane are taken into account. Each species also has a specific rate of diffusion inside the membrane and within the cytoplasm which are different. In addition reactions progress at different rates (or not occur at all) depending on where the interacting proteins live. For example the MinD is only allowed to dimerize when the two particles are attached to the membrane.

represent an integral part of the proper functioning of this system, and as such its study is uniquely amenable to RDME simulation. This protein system has been well studied using both experimental and computational methods (Raskin and de Boer 1999; Fange and Elf 2006; Tostevin and Howard 2006).

Immediately prior to division, the volume of a simulated cell can exceed that which can be represented by a lattice capable of fitting into the memory of many commercial GPUs. This necessitated the development of a version of **Lattice Microbes** capable of distributing a single simulation volume across multiple GPUs, allowing for both larger and longer simulations than ever before (Hallock et al. in revision). The simulation of the MinDE system (MinC has been omitted for simplicity) requires a 4 μm long *E. coli* cell undergoing cell division. The cell membrane geometry is constructed from a 3 μm long cylinder intersecting hemispheres of 1 μm in diameter at either end. The model is discretized to a simulation lattice of dimensions 64 × 64 × 256 sites with 16 nm spacing, and simulated with a time step of 50 μs. After the cell is discretized, obstacles representing ribosomes and other membrane proteins such as transporters are randomly placed in the cell membrane and cytoplasm as seen in Figure 13.4a. When the simulation starts, MinD and MinE are randomly distributed within the cytoplasmic space, and no proteins are initially on the membrane. The amount of MinD present is equally split between $MinD_{ADP}$ and $MinD_{ATP}$ with 1758 particles each. MinE has an initial count of 914 particles.

The Min system involves reactions both on the membrane surface as well as the cytoplasm interior necessitating treatment of these lattice sites differently. The outermost layer of lattice sites are designated as a distinct type (membrane) from the inner region of the cell. Unbound

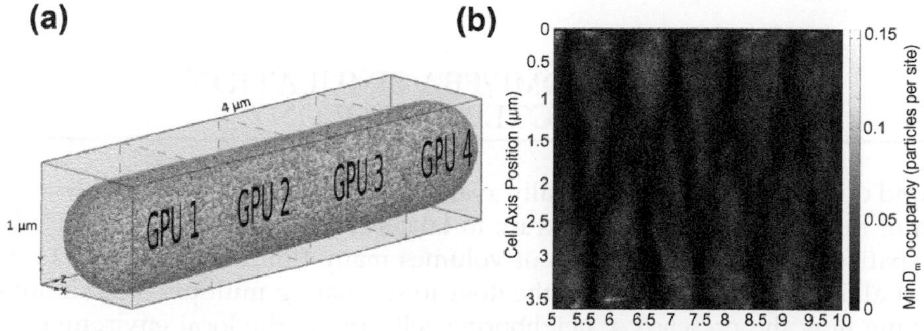

FIGURE 13.4 (a) A representation of the whole cell volume with obstacles in the membrane. The membrane is shown in green and the obstacles as the orange blobs. These obstacles represent membrane-bound proteins that hinder the diffusion of MinD and slow the rate of oscillation. For simulation purposes, this cell is distributed over 4 GPUs along its longest dimension z, as shown. (b) A space-time plot of the average occupancy of a lattice site showing periodic oscillations of the membrane-bound $MinD_m$ species. The occupancy is calculated from the number of proteins present within a plane along the z-axis divided by the number of membrane sites in that plane. The streaks show high localization of MinD at the poles of the cell and relatively lower probability at the center of the cell. The oscillations in the original model (Fange and Elf 2006) were close to 30s while in the new model containing membrane-bound obstacles the oscillations are closer to the experimentally observed 1 min (Hu and Lutkenhaus 1999) highlighting the utility of explicitly including obstacles in the RDME. (For interpretation of the references to color in this figure legend, the reader is referred to the web version of this book.)

proteins can freely move between the two site types, but complexes on the membrane (designated with a subscript *m*) may only diffuse between membrane sites. With the exception of MinD phosphorylation which occurs in cytoplasmic sites, all other reactions occur within the membrane sites of the lattice. Because the membrane is considerably more viscous—in addition to being a two-dimensional construct—the diffusion of proteins on the membrane is significantly slower than their diffusion through the cytosol. In addition, diffusion of membrane-bound species into the cytosol and *vice-versa* is slower than free diffusion in the cytosol. This necessitates diffusion rates for the proteins in different regions of the cell, as highlighted in Figure 13.3.

The kinetic model of the Min system includes only experimentally known interactions between the proteins and is adapted from Fange and Elf (2006). The reactions involved can be seen in Figure 13.3 with their corresponding rate constants and diffusion coefficients. The model is capable of replicating the characteristic features of the Min system although the original rates resulted in oscillations that occur at about twice the experimentally measure frequency. Addition of obstacles slowed the oscillations by a factor of approximately 1.5, bringing the simulations into closer agreement with values measured experimentally (Hu and Lutkenhaus 1999). This highlights the importance of explicitly modeling obstacles in biological reaction-diffusion systems.

Even though the simulation is purely stochastic, the expected macroscopic time evolution of the system with the oscillatory behavior of the membrane-bound species is observed. In Figure 13.4b, we track the location of $MinD_m$ proteins along the cell over time, and present the average occupancy in terms of number of particles present versus the number of membrane lattice sites. The end-to-end oscillations are clearly visible. With the multiple GPU enabled **Lattice Microbes** software running on 4 NVIDIA GTX680 GPUs, we obtained 384 s of simulation time per hour of wall clock time.

5 HYBRID RDME/FBA SIMULATIONS OF A BACTERIAL COLONY

The rapid development of commercially available GPU hardware coupled with the recent extension of the **Lattice Microbes** software to take advantage of multiple GPUs has made possible spatially resolved simulations of volumes many times larger than a bacterial cell (Hallock et al. in revision). This opens the door to simulating multiple cells simultaneously and studying how the presence of neighboring cells affects the local environments and, in turn, behaviors of individual cells within a dense cluster or colony. Recent work using flux balance analysis (FBA) (Schellenberger et al. 2011; Lewis et al. 2012) to model metabolism in *E. coli* has suggested that enzyme expression variability gives rise to a diverse set of metabolic phenotypes within clonal populations (Labhsetwar et al. 2013). By integrating an FBA description of metabolism within the cell with realistic reaction-diffusion modeling of substrates outside the cell (see Figure 13.5), we can extend our understanding of how cells vary behaviorally to include spatial effects and the presence of neighboring cells.

Attempts have been made in the past to use FBA—a technique that solves for optimal sets of *steady-state* biochemical reaction fluxes—in a time-resolved manner (Covert et al. 2008; Karr et al. 2012). Attempts have also been made to use FBA to study the interaction of multiple cells and even multiple species (Zomorrodi and Maranas 2012; Zhuang et al.

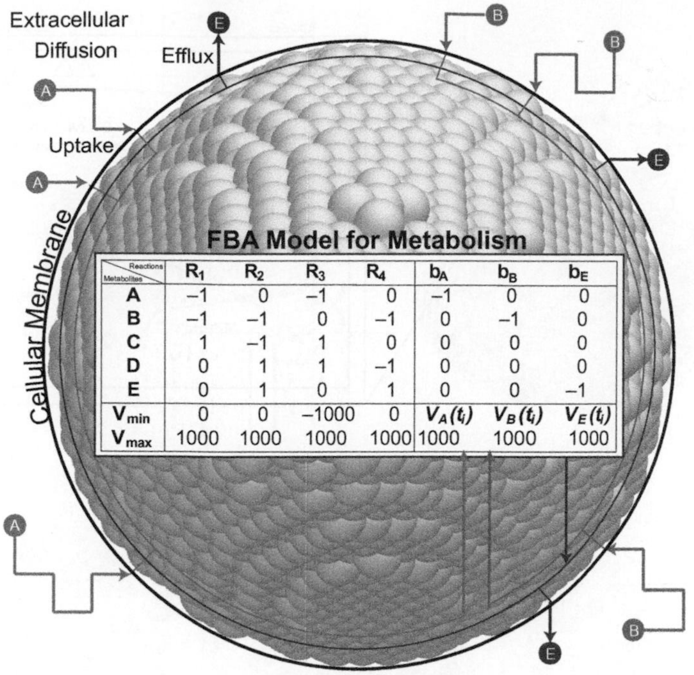

FIGURE 13.5 Schematic representing how FBA can be integrated into a reaction-diffusion modeling framework. During a short diffusion simulation, particles of types A and B are allowed to diffuse into the cell (approximated here as a yellow sphere discretized to a lattice). The rate at which these particles are taken up is used to set upper bounds on exchange reactions in the FBA model. Particles of type E are generated as metabolic byproducts, and are allowed to diffuse out of the cell. (For interpretation of the references to color in this figure legend, the reader is referred to the web version of this book.)

2012). Here we incorporate elements of these approaches and draw on our own expertise in spatially resolved whole-cell modeling to simulate a population of 100 cells in a solution of substrates. These simulations are intentionally simplified in order to illustrate how spatial heterogeneity within bacterial colonies can be modeled, as well as to showcase the power of GPU computing—although it is already feasible to distribute the colony simulation across several GPUs, the results presented here were performed on a commercial desktop computer with a single NVIDIA Quadro 4000 GPU. The model is fairly simple. Substrates—in this case glucose and oxygen—diffuse from a constant concentration boundary outside a cluster of randomly placed spherical cells of volume 10^{-15} L each (see Figure 13.6a). The diffusion is performed stochastically on a lattice (with 64 nm resolution to ensure that the entire $16.3 \times 16.3 \times 16.3\ \mu m^3$ lattice would fit in the device memory) using the **Lattice Microbes** software (see Table 13.2). After 1 ms of diffusion time (chosen to be significantly longer than the diffusion time step), the simulation is halted, and the results are returned to host memory. Whatever substrates have diffused into each cell are tallied and considered "available" to that cell. The time-averaged rates of accumulation of these substrates are used to set upper bounds on their respective exchange reactions, and parsimonious FBA (computed using the freely available python implementation

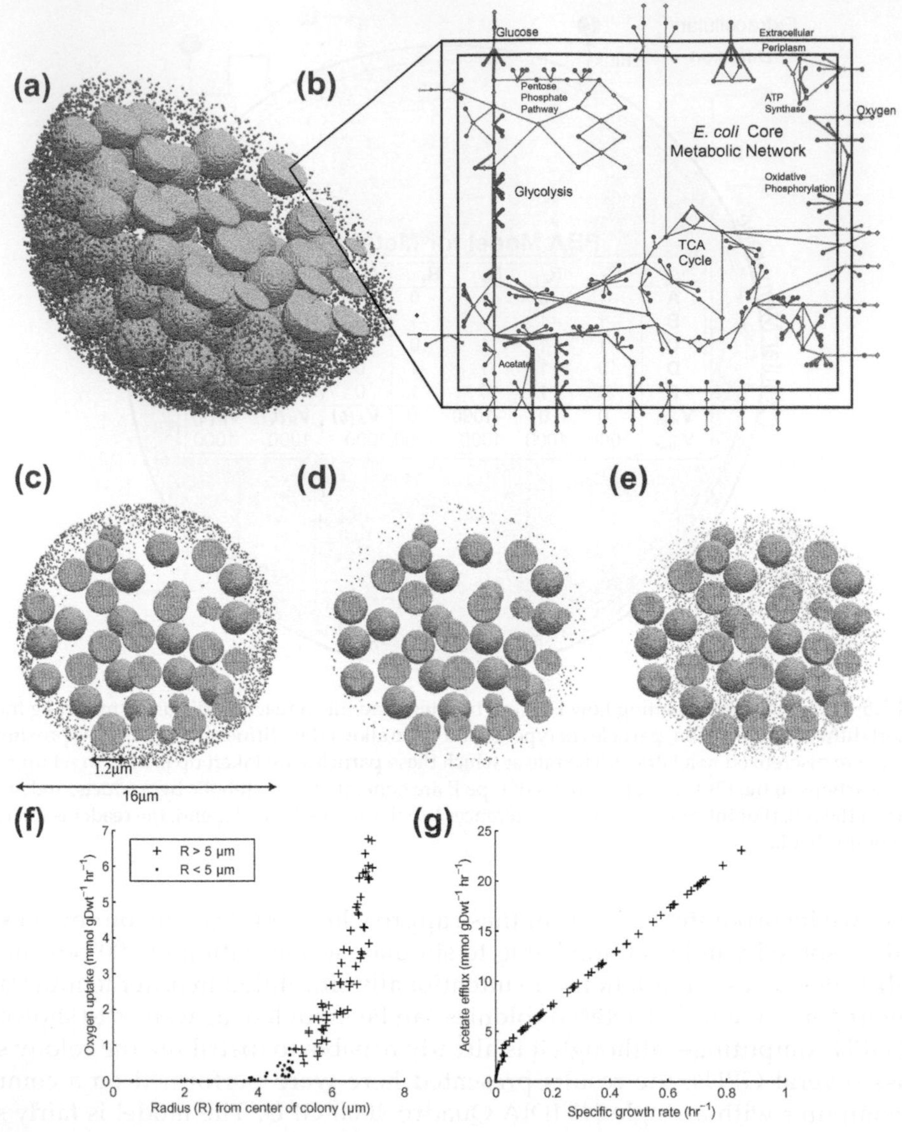

FIGURE 13.6 Cut-away view (a) of a cluster of 100 randomly placed cells (yellow) shown in a solution of glucose (gray). The metabolism (b) of each cell is independently described by FBA; the time-dependent uptake rate of each diffusing substrate for each cell is set based on the rate of substrate accumulation over the preceding time step, and parsimonious FBA is used to solve for the reaction flux throughout the metabolic network. Uptake rates for other substrates not explicitly modeled in the extracellular space such as ammonia or phosphate ions are left unconstrained. Substrates available to each cell, including glucose (c) and oxygen (d) and (f), and byproducts produced by the cell such as acetate (e), can be highly dependent on the cell's location within the colony. This location-dependance of substrate availability can give rise to metabolic variability (g) between cells within the colony. The popular VMD molecular dynamics visualization software (Humphrey et al. 1996) can be used to render and animate all **Lattice Microbes** trajectories. (For interpretation of the references to color in this figure legend, the reader is referred to the web version of this book.)

TABLE 13.2 Diffusion rates for substrates in the colony simulation.

Substrate	D ($\mu m^2\ s^{-1}$ at 25 °C)	Reference
Oxygen (O_2)	2,000	Han and Bartels (1996)
Glucose	670	Longsworth (1955)
Acetate	1,210	Cussler (1997)

of the COBRA toolbox Schellenberger et al. (2011)) is used to predict the reaction flux throughout the cell's metabolic network (the Core *E. coli* metabolic model (Palsson, 2006) was used; see Figure 13.6b). Following this FBA step, the spatial lattice is updated by removing the substrate particles predicted to be used by each cell and adding substrate particles predicted to be produced by each cell as metabolic byproducts (in both cases rounded to the nearest whole particle). **Lattice Microbes** is then launched again, and the cycle repeats. Care should be taken in interpreting the results of this type of simulation. The resulting time course of metabolic fluxes within each cell should be averaged over windows long enough that the cell can be assumed to be at steady state (values on the order of a second to minutes have been used in the past (Covert et al. 2008; Karr et al. 2012). The basic modeling algorithm is outlined below:

```
Data: Substrate concentrations on the boundary, diffusion rates, metabolic model
Result: Metabolic flux trajectories, spatial simulation trajectory
Initialization: Randomly place cells and discretize to lattice, import metabolic model;
while t < maxT do
    Perform diffusion simulation of duration Δt in Lattice Microbes;
    for cell ∈ Colony do
        for substrate ∈ SimulatedSubstrates do
            availableParticles ← # of substrate particles that diffused into the cell during Δt;
            Upper bound on substrate exchange reaction ← availableParticles / Δt;
        end
        Use parsimonious flux balance analysis to predict reaction flux through the constrained
        metabolic model;
        for substrate ∈ SimulatedSubstrates do
            particleFlux ← substrate exchange reaction flux × Δt;
            if particleFlux is into the cell then
                Randomly remove particleFlux particles from the lattice sites inside the cell;
            else
                Randomly add particleFlux particles to the lattice sites on the periphery of the cell;
            end
        end
        t ← t + Δt;
    end
end
```

Algorithm 1: Pseudocode describing the simulation of a colony of cells in a solution of substrates.

Due to intentionally low oxygen availability, the modeled cells pursue an anaerobic acetogenic metabolism, with the cells at the periphery taking up more substrates and growing faster than those buried toward the center of the colony (see Figure 13.6c–e). Interestingly, despite a relatively smooth increase in substrate availability going from the center to the edge of the colony, there nonetheless exists an abrupt change in acetate production with growth rate (see Figure 13.6f–g). Cells within roughly 5 μm of the center of the colony are highly anaerobic and produce large amounts of acetate relative to their low growth rates. Cells closer to the periphery, whose oxygen availability tends to be at least 1 mmol $gDwt^{-1}$ h^{-1}, exhibit significantly faster growth with respect to their acetate production.

This type of methodological synthesis offers new insight into how local cellular environments can both alter and be altered by cellular behavior. The methodology can also naturally be extended to include models of quorum sensing and chemical signal exchange, as well as various forms of uptake and/or regulatory control.

Acknowledgments

Lattice Microbes development is supported by the Department of Energy Office of Science (BER) under grant DE-FG02-10ER6510, National Science Foundation under grant NSF MCB 08-44670 and NSF Center for Physics of Living Cells PHY-0822613.

References

Chopard, B., and Droz, M. (1998). *Cellular Automata Modeling Of Physical Systems*. Cambridge, UK: Cambridge University Press.

Chung, J., and Stephanopoulos, G. (1996). On physiological multiplicity and population heterogeneity of biological systems. *Chem. Eng. Sci.* **51**:1509–1521.

Covert, M., Xiao, N., Chen, T., and Karr, J. (2008). Integrating metabolic, transcriptional regulatory and signal transduction models in *Escherichia coli*. *Bioinformatics* **24**:2044–2050.

Cussler, EL. (1997). *Diffusion: mass transfer in fluid systems*. Cambridge university press.

Dornmair, K., Overath, P., and Jähnig, F. (1989). Fast measurement of galactoside transport by lactose permease. *J. Biol. Chem.* **264**:342–346.

Dunaway, M., Olson, J. S., Rosenberg, J. M., Kallai, O. B., Dickerson, R. E., and Matthews, K. S. (1980). Kinetic studies of inducer binding to lac repressoroperator complex. *J. Biol. Chem.* **255**:10115–10119.

Fange, D., and Elf, J. (2006). Noise-induced Min phenotypes in *E. coli*. *PLoS Comput. Biol.* **2**:e80.

Gillespie, D. T. (2007). Stochastic simulation of chemical kinetics. *Annu. Rev. Phys. Chem.* **58**:35–55.

Goeddel, D. V., Yansura, D. G., and Caruthers, M. H. (1977). Binding of synthetic lactose operator DNAs to lactose represessors. *Proc. Natl. Acad. Sci.* **74**:3292–3296.

Hallock, MJ, Stone, JE, Roberts, E, Fry, C, Luthey-Schulten, Z (in revision, Journal of Parallel Computing). Simulation of reaction diffusion processes over biologically-relevant size and time scales using multi-GPU workstations.

Han, P., and Bartels, D. M. (1996). Temperature dependence of oxygen diffusion in H2O and D2O. *J. Phys. Chem.* **100**:5597–5602.

Hu, Z., and Lutkenhaus, J. (1999). Topological regulation of cell division in *Escherichia coli* involves rapid pole to pole oscillation of the division inhibitor MinC under control of MinD and MinE. *Mol. Microbiol.* **34**:6419–6424.

Humphrey, W., Dalke, A., and Schulten, K. (1996). VMD: visual molecular dynamics. *J. Mol. Graph* **14**(33–8):27–28.

Karr, J., Sanghvi, J., Macklin, D., Gutschow, M., Jacobs, J., Bolival, B., Assad-Garcia, N., Glass, J., and Covert, M. (2012). A whole-cell computational model predicts phenotype from genotype. *Cell* **150**:389–401.

Labhsetwar, P., Cole, J. A., Roberts, E., Price, N. D., and Luther-Schulten, Z. (2013). Heterogeneity in protein expression induces metabolic variability in a modeled E. coli population. *Proc. Natl. Acad. Sci* **110**:14006–14011.

Lewis, N., Nagarajan, H., and Palsson, B. O. (2012). Constraining the metabolic genotype-phenotype relationship using a phylogeny of in silico methods. *Nat. Rev. Microbiol.* **10**:291–305.

Longsworth, L. (1955). *Electrochemistry in biology and medicine*. New York: John Wiley & Sons Inc.

Maloney, P. C., and Wilson, T. H. (1973). Quantitative aspects of active transport by the lactose transport system of *Escherichia coli*. *Biochim. Biophys. Acta*. **330**:196–205.

Munsky, B., Neuert, G., and van Oudenaarden, A. (2012). Using gene expression noise to understand gene regulation. *Science* **336**:183–187.

O'Gorman, R. B., Rosenberg, J. M., Kallai, O. B., Dickerson, R. E., Itakura, K., Riggs, A. D., and Matthews, K. S. (1980). Equilibrium binding of inducer to lac repressoroperator DNA complex. *J. Biol. Chem*. **255**:10107–10114.

Palsson, Bernhard (2006). *Systems Biology: Properties of Reconstructed Networks*. New York: Cambridge University Press. Hardcover.

Raskin, D. M., and de Boer, P. A. J. (1999). Rapid pole-to-pole oscillation of a protein required for directing division to the middle of *Escherichia coli*. *Proc. Natl. Acad. Sci. USA* **96**:4971–4976.

Roberts, E., Stone, J. E., Sepúlveda, L., Hwu, W. M., and Luthey-Schulten, Z. (2009). Long time-scale simulations of in vivo diffusion using GPU hardware. *Parallel & Distributed Processing, 2009, IPDPS 2009. IEEE International Symposium on (IEEE)* 1–8.

Roberts, E., Magis, A., Ortiz, J. O., Baumeister, W., and Luthey-Schulten, Z. (2011). Noise contributions in an inducible genetic switch: A whole-cell simulation study. *PLoS Comp. Bio*. **7**:e1002010.

Roberts, E., Stone, J. E., and Luthey-Schulten, Z. (2013). Lattice microbes: High-performance stochastic simulation method for the reaction-diffusion master equation. *J. Comp. Chem*. **34**:245–255.

Rodríguez, JV., Kaandorp, JA., Dobrzyński, M., and Blom, JG. (2006). Spatial stochastic modelling of the phosphoenolpyruvate-dependent phosphotransferase (PTS) pathway in *Escherichia coli*. *Bioinformatics* **22**:1895–1901.

Schellenberger, J., Park, JO., Conrad, TM., and Palsson, B. (2010). BiGG: a Biochemical Genetic and Genomic knowledgebase of large scale metabolic reconstructions. *BMC Bioinformatics* **11**

Schellenberger, J., Que, R., Fleming, R. M. T., Thiele, Ines, Orth, JD., Feist, AM., Zielinski, DC., Bordbar, A., Lewis, NE., Rahmanian, S., Kang, J., Hyduke, DR., and Palsson, BO. (2011). Quantitative prediction of cellular metabolism with constraint-based models: the COBRA Toolbox v2.0. *Nat. Protoc*. **6**:1290–1307.

Sundararaj, S., Guo, A., Habibi-Nazhad, B., Rouani, M., Stothard, P., Ellison, M., and Wishart, D. S. (2004). The CyberCell Database (CCDB): a comprehensive, self-updating, relational database to coordinate and facilitate in silico modeling of *Escherichia coli*. *Nucl. Acids Res*. **32**:D293–D295.

Taniguchi, Y., Choi, P. J., Li, G. W., Chen, H., Babu, M., Hearn, J., Emili, A., and Xie, X. S. (2010). Quantifying *E. coli* Proteome and Transcriptome with Single-Molecule Sensitivity in Single Cells. *Science* **329**:533–538.

Tostevin, F., and Howard, M. (2006). A stochastic model of Min oscillations in *Escherichia coli* and Min protein segregation during cell division. *Phys. Biol*. **3**:1.

Zhuang, K., Ma, E., Lovley, D. R., and Mahadevan, R. (2012). The design of long-term effective uranium bioremediation strategy using a community metabolic model. *Biotechnol. Bioeng*. **109**:2475–2483.

Zomorrodi, A. R., and Maranas, C. D. (2012). OptCom: a multi-level optimization framework for the metabolic modeling and analysis of microbial communities. *PLoS Comp. Bio*. **8**:e1002363.

CHAPTER

14

Advances in Machine Learning for Processing and Comparison of Metagenomic Data

Jean-Luc Bouchot[a], *William L. Trimble*[b], *Gregory Ditzler*[c], *Yemin Lan*[d], *Steve Essinger*[c], *Gail Rosen*[c]

[a]Department of Mathematics, Drexel University, PA, Philadelphia, USA

[b]Institute for Genomics and Systems Biology, Argonne National Laboratory, University of Chicago, Chicago, IL, USA

[c]Department of Electrical and Computer Engineering, Drexel University, PA, Philadelphia, USA

[d]School of Biomedical Engineering, Science and Health, Drexel University, PA, Philadelphia, USA

CONTENTS

http://dx.doi.org/10.1016/B978-0-12-405926-9.00014-9

Abstract

Recent advances in next-generation sequencing have enabled high-throughput determination of biological sequences in microbial communities, also known as microbiomes. The large volume of data now presents the challenge of how to extract knowledge—recognize patterns, find similarities, and find relationships—from complex mixtures of nucleic acid sequences currently being examined. In this chapter we review basic concepts as well as state-of-the-art techniques to analyze hundreds of samples which each contain millions of DNA and RNA sequences. We describe the general character of sequence data and describe some of the processing steps that prepare raw sequence data for inference. We then describe the process of extracting features from the data, assigning taxonomic and gene labels to the sequences. Then we review methods for cross-sample comparisons: (1) using similarity measures and ordination techniques to visualize and measure differences between samples and (2) feature selection and classification to select the most relevant features for discriminating between samples.

Finally, in conclusion, we outline some open research problems and challenges left for future research.

1 INTRODUCTION

Metagenomics is the study of nucleic acids extracted from the environment, as opposed to genomics, which studies the nucleic acids derived from single organisms.

In a metagenomic study, a sample is collected from the environment, which can be a gram of soil (Rousk et al. 2010; Bowers et al. 2011), milliliter of ocean (Williamson et al. 2008), swab from an object (Caporaso et al. 2011), or a sample of the microbes associated with a larger organism, such as humans (Caporaso et al. 2011; Costello et al. 2009), sometimes termed the "microbiome." Until now, microbes were usually studied in isolation, whereby researchers literally isolated and cultured the organism to sequence and study its genome and gene functions. However microbes actually live in communities, cooperating with and competing against each other. While found commonly in soil, water, buildings, etc. in our everyday lives, microbes are also found in unusual places like extremely cold Antarctica (Varin et al. 2012), extremely hot springs (Jiménez et al. 2012), and the hypersaline Dead Sea (Bodaker et al. 2009). They regulate the global carbon and nitrogen cycles (Hunter et al. 2006; McCarren et al. 2010) of the Earth and are thought to be responsible for half the oxygen on the Earth (Rocap et al. 2003).

It is now thought that these communities of microbes not only play a large role in the environment but also human health. Microbes are found at almost every interface of the body, including skin, mouth, airways, and even places like the lungs and amniotic fluid once thought to be sterile (Koren et al. 2013; Pragman et al. 2012). It is thought that like environmental ecosystems, the more diverse the human ecosystem, the better we can ward off disease (van Elsas et al. 2012; Findley et al. 2013). The concept of microbiome has additionally spurred the hypothesis that human hosts entertain multiple stable ecological community types, termed enterotypes, (Arumugam et al. 2011) and has been suggested as a forensics tool (Fierer et al. 2010). Though many groups are pursuing metagenomic sequence data, the computational metagenomic methods used to study the communities are underdeveloped, so we discuss recent methods in the paper. However, almost no one has scratched the surface to use the findings of these studies to engineer microbiomes to improve the environment, generate biofuels, and cure disease. This leaves to the imagination—how can personal omics profiling revolutionize medicine (Chen et al. 2012)?

Currently to profile a metagenomic sample, DNA or RNA is extracted chemically and turned into purified DNA. This is prepared and fed into a machine that determines the sequence of information-containing monomers in DNA fragments. This process is called "sequencing" and has, thanks to technological improvements in the recent decade, become much faster and much cheaper, producing millions of short strings of data, called sequencing **reads**, representing millions of biological molecules at once.

From this digitization of DNA, biologists can address the questions "Who is there?" and "What are they doing?" (Handelsman 2007; Raes et al. 2007; Eisen, 2007; Valdivia-Granda 2008). The answer to the "who" question, obtained by inferring the name or position in the taxonomy of the organism from which a sequence was likely derived, is called taxonomic classification. The answer to the "what" question, the process of recognizing the biochemical functions of the sampled genes, is called functional annotation. The current algorithms to solve these problems (Xiao et al. 2003; Bazinet and Cummings 2012) fall short of the speed and accuracy required to process and compare the volumes of data currently being generated. In addition, algorithmic procedures to study how environmental factors affect microbial populations are under active development.

Sequence data comes in two broad kinds—the sequencing of targeted genetic loci, selected by PCR, called **amplicon sequencing**, and the sequencing of random genetic loci, called **shotgun sequencing**. Specific subsets of the 16S ribosomal subunit gene in prokaryotes and the ribosomal spacer ITS in fungi have been popular targets for amplicon metagenomics. For both sequencing methodologies, sequences are filtered, transformed, and interpreted by explicit or implicit comparison to a database of sequences that are presumed known. This approach is called "closed-reference annotation." The number of possible sequences is extremely large: $4^{100} = 10^{60}$ possible 100-basepair(bp) reads. Annotation provides a first round of dimensionality reduction, mapping from this extremely highly dimensional space to the merely large dimensionality ($10^6 - 10^8$) vector space of annotations.

Sequencing techniques naturally divide into targeted and shotgun sequencing. Shotgun data are more complex, require greater sequencing depth, and have thousands more possible annotations. Targeted sequencing, called amplicon sequencing, are generally less expensive and permit larger numbers of samples to be sequenced for similar cost, but are confined to providing examples of sequences of a specific gene, potentially answering only the "Who" question. Shotgun sequences are able to address the "What" question because they consist mostly of protein-coding sequence which has biochemical functions, but cost much more to analyze. Though amplicon and shotgun sequence data products are dramatically different, the analytical techniques for comparing samples and drawing inferences post-annotation are very similar.

We describe the process of generating sequence data, a variety of procedures to extract features from the sequence data, the mathematical procedures for sample comparison, visualization, and feature selection, and describe future challenges for the interpretation of sequence data. Since metagenomic data comprise sequences from unknown mixtures of unknown organisms, the field is challenging indeed.

2 PREPROCESSING

Nucleic acid sequences are inferred from highly-multiplexed data acquisition systems which, in batches, capture signals that reveal the sequence of $10^5 - 10^9$ individual molecules, often called templates. Data from sequencing instruments passes through a number of steps before comparison to existing annotated biological sequence data. Collectively called preprocessing, the steps of base calling, sequence filtering, vector removal, sequence compression and assembly, and gene prediction are steps to filter, condition, and compress sequence data before annotation.

2.1 Base calling

All modern sequencing techniques use spatial separation to multiplex the large number of templates and have an analog-to-digital conversion that converts the chemical information into digital data. Depending on the particular sequencing technology, the raw signals can be single-color images (pyrosequencing), four-color images (Illumina, PacBio, ABIsolid), or arrays of potential sensors (Iontorrent). The initial stage of recognizing the sequence of bases from the raw instrument output is called **base calling**; this is usually done with vendor-provided software. The basecallers produce the symbols A, C, G, and T, to indicate the four bases, and the symbol N to indicate complete uncertainty in the identity of the underlying base. Sequences containing N (the **ambiguous base symbol**) require special handling and interpretation. Base calling produces a set of short (25–600 bp) sequences, called reads, and a per-base-pair indication of the base-caller's posterior probability of having reported an accurate base. The per-base quality score is sometimes called a Phred score after an early automated base-calling program that established the encoding standard (Ewing et al. 1998). The standard format for data from the base caller is FASTQ. FASTQ files have a variety of encoding schemes produced by different vendors; the oldest, "Sanger-style" encoding is preferred for data sharing (Cock et al. 2010).

2.2 Demultiplexing

It is possible to simultaneously sequence multiple samples by attaching artificial sequences which are recognized as sample identifier labels. Called "multiplex identifiers" or more commonly **barcodes**, these are synthetic sequences that are not part of the biological signal, but permit many samples to be run at lower per-sample depth and cost. The recognition of barcodes and separation of a mixture of samples into sequence data for individual samples is called **demultiplexing** and is an essential part of sequencing protocols which use pooled samples.

2.3 Quality filtering

Sequence quality data can be used to filter the raw instrument output to improve the signal-to-noise characteristics of the sequence data. Filtering can be applied to whole reads (accepting or rejecting each read), can selectively discard low-quality basepairs from the ends of reads, or can remove reads with characteristics that suggest sequencing artifacts.A number of recipes for sequence quality filtering exist (Minoche et al. 2011; Huse et al. 2007; Cox et al. 2010), and these generally lower the rate of erroneous sequence recovery without removing large fractions of the sequence data. Some sequence analysis methods analyze sequences in a quality-aware way (Kelley et al. 2010), but most of them depend only on the sequence, not on the qualities. Some workflows discard the quality values at this stage.

2.4 Contaminant screening

The template DNA usually requires chemical modifications to correctly interface with the sequencing instrument; kits for these steps are provided by the instrument vendors. These modifications include shearing and size-selecting the template molecules and ligating artificial sequences containing the barcodes, primers for in-instrument PCR, and other artificial nucleic acid constructs that make sequencing possible. These sequences, called **adapters** are not intended to be part of the sequencing output, but occur in a minority of output sequences, ranging from 0.1% to 5%. These unwanted sequences can be removed by similarity searching and filtering; the significance of their effect as signal contaminants is not known.

When metagenomic samples are extracted to study the microbial communities associated with animals and plants, considerable amounts of the eukaryotic host DNA may end up being sequenced. This "host" DNA must be analyzed separately, and it is standard to remove DNA which matches (by similarity) the genome of the host organism before annotation.

2.5 Clustering and assembly

After quality filtering, clustering and assembly are two approaches to reduce the size and redundancy of the set of sequences. Clustering and assembly are lossy compression approaches that identify redundancy in the input sequences and use this redundancy to reduce the amount of computational effort on similarity searching. Clustering (using, CD-HIT (Li and Godzik, 2006) or UCLUST (Edgar, 2010)) is performed for improved speed, replacing a set of similar sequences with one representative. Assembly, on the other hand, both reduces sequence volume and replaces short sequences with inferred longer sequences. The compression afforded by clustering or assembly depends on the sequence-level redundancy of the input data. Some data sets with dominant genomes that comprise a majority of the sequence data have assemblies that reduce to 1% of the input sequence bulk, while others fail to compress significantly. These longer, derived sequences are called **contigs** and represent data from multiple instrument reads. If neither of these approaches is used, the filtered short reads can be annotated.

2.6 Gene prediction

Unlike clustering and assembly, which are principally technologically-inspired steps, gene prediction is a computational step which attempts to identify a biological pattern, mimicking the patterns recognized by transcription and translation machinery. Gene predictors take DNA sequences as their input, predict the start and stop sites of genes contained on those sequences, and produce in-silico translations of the genes so identified.

This translation step converts nucleic acid sequences into amino acid sequences, reducing the length of the sequences by a factor of about three. Since individual reads are shorter than typical microbial gene sizes (ca. 900 bp (Konstantinidis and Tiedje 2004)), individual-read gene prediction produces mostly incomplete predicted protein sequences. This factor-of-three reduction in sequence length reflects the fact that gene prediction is a lossy compression step.

Gene prediction tools were developed for the annotation of complete or near-complete genomes, and were later adapted to handle short-read data. GLIMMER uses interpolated Markov models whose parameters are trained on long coding regions and smoothed to give predictions on shorter coding regions (Salzberg et al. 1998). It is well suited for assemblies from single organisms.

For short reads or contigs from mixtures of organisms, one-size-fits-all gene prediction tools are indicated. MetaGeneMark (Besemer and Borodovsky 1999; Zhu et al. 2010) and MetaGeneAnnotator (Noguchi et al. 2008) were early applications of Markov models to gene prediction; they deliver good results on error-free data. More recent and more elaborate gene predictors are FragGeneScan(FGS) (Rho et al. 2010), which uses a hidden-Markov model, and Prodigal (Hyatt et al. 2010), which uses dynamic programming, are engineered to perform well on short reads. FGS and Prodigal have more robustness against sequencing error.

Gene prediction accuracy in complete genomes is reported as better than 95%; for short reads (or short contigs) the accuracy is lower. It should be mentioned that gene prediction is not equally sensitive across taxa; some organisms have genes which the gene prediction tools miss 20% of the time. The loss of sensitivity for some organisms is more severe for shorter reads (less than 200 bp). The increased bias and reduced sensitivity of short-reads drives many researchers to perform assembly of short-reads prior to annotation; this exchanges the biases caused by short reads for yet-uncharacterized biases caused by assembly.

3 ANNOTATION OF GENES

At this stage, the biologist's central questions, "Who" and "What" are addressed by classifying the sequences. Annotation is the process of assigning biological meaning to the sequences, usually after gene sequences are identified from bulk reads or from partially-assembled contigs. Annotation consists of comparison, either explicit (similarity searching against a database of sequences) or implicit (searching against models or profiles derived from sets of sequences) against a database of sequences that have already been named. These databases include previously annotated and/or manually curated sequences. Comparing new sequences to existing ones allows each sequence to be associated with the name of the organism, of the protein, of the function, or of the pathways associated with the protein in the database. **Taxonomic classification** refers to annotation that produces inferences about organism name; **functional classification** concerns itself with identifying biochemical function from protein sequences.

3.1 Taxonomic classification

To answer the "Who is there" question (and its quantitative counterpart, "how much of each"), methods are needed that are capable of classifying newly-observed sequences using information from an existing database of sequences and annotations.

Factors which can impact the classifier's accuracy include read length and sequence novelty. Classifiers are expected to act on short (less than 200 bp) reads and on variable-length, but longer, assembled contigs. Short reads, however, can fail to be unique within the sequence database, thus yielding ambiguous classification. Some of this ambiguity can be overcome by longer reads but some reflects fundamental similarity between annotated sequences. In the opposite direction, sequences can be ambiguous because they lack a good match in the database. The appropriate annotation and interpretation of these novel sequences remains a serious challenge for taxonomic classification and annotation in general.

There are four primary methods (see Table 14.1) to perform taxonomic classification of genome fragments: *homology*, *mapping*, *composition*, and *phylogeny* based methods. A fifth category is emerging that combines two or more of these types. However, hybrid methods typically take longer to run (Bazinet and Cummings 2012; Segata et al. 2012).

Many current approaches align sequenced fragments to known genomes using sequence similarity. This approach has a rich history from BLAST (Altschul et al. 1990), one of the first

TABLE 14.1 Summary of the homology-based and composition-based methods for WGS taxonomic classification.

Features	Classifier	Published method
Similarity-based	Alignment	BLAST (Altschul et al. 1990), CARMA3 (Gerlach and Stoye 2011), MetaPhyler(Liu et al. 2010), MetaPhlan (Segata et al. 2012)
	Alignment + Last common ancestor	MEGAN (Huson et al. 2007), MARTA (Horton et al. 2010), MTR (Gori et al. 2011), SOrt-ITEMS (Monzoorul et al. 2009)
	Clustering + Alignment	jMOTU (Jones et al. 2011)
Composition-based	Naïve Bayesian	NBC (Rosen et al. 2011; Rosen and Lim 2012)
	Support Vector Machines	PhyloPythiaS (Patil et al. 2011)
	Interpolated Markov Models (IMM)	Phymm (Brady and Salzberg 2009), Scimm (Kelley and Salzberg 2010)
	Miscellaneous	TACOA (Diaz et al. 2009), RAIphy (Nalbantoglu et al. 2011), and MetaCluster(Leung et al. 2011)
Mapping	Bloom Filter	FACS (Stranneheim et al. 2010)
	Burrows-Wheeler Transform	Bowtie2 (Langmead and Salzberg 2012), BWA (Li and Durbin 2009), SOAP (Li et al., 2009)
	Miscellaneous	CLC (CLCBio, XXX), MAP (Reumers et al. 2012), SMALT (SMALT XXX)
Phylogeny	Maximum-Likelihood	EPA (Berger et al. 2011), pplacer(Matsen et al. 2010), FastTree(Price et al. 2009)
	Miscellaneous	SAP (Munch et al. 2008)
Hybrid	IMMs + BLAST	PhymmBL(Brady and Salzberg 2009)
	NBC + BLAST	RITA (Macdonald et al. 2012)
	k-mer Clustering + BLAST	SPHINX (Mohammed et al. 2010)
	Alignment + Phylogeny	PaPaRa(Berger and Stamatakis 2011),AMPHORA (Wu and Eisen 2008), MLTreeMap (Stark et al. 2010), TreePhyler (Schreiber et al. 2010), (NAST, Simrank) (DeSantis et al. 2006)

optimized alignment tools. While homology-based techniques perform well in identifying protein families and gene homology (Bateman et al. 2008; Koski and Golding 2001), this computation takes longer and can be more costly than sequencing itself, as noted by Huson et al. (2011), Gilbert et al. (2011). Also, the e-values provided by these tools signify that the sequence does not match by chance, but they do not indicate a particular confidence to the chosen class-label (e.g. if the sequence may belong to two protein families above random chance, which family's assignment is more confident?)

New methods have emerged that perform similarity searches using dramatically fewer computational resources than BLAST and FASTA. Called read mappers, these employ data structures including the Burrows-Wheeler Transform (Langmead and Salzberg 2012; Li and Durbin 2009; Li et al. 2009) and Bloom filters (Martin et al. 2012). The Burrows-Wheeler transform (BWT) is a type of transform that makes the sequence compressible and fast to search. Read mappers based on BWT have quite fast mapping times with high sensitivity and low false positive rates. These techniques promise to be fast but as noted, the false positive rate must be optimized. Bloom filters are probabilistic data structures based on hashing that have efficient lookup times, have no false negatives, and have "manageable" false positive rates.

Composition-based classification approaches use features of length-*k* motifs, or *k*-mers, and usually build models based on the motif frequencies of occurrence. Intrinsic compositional structure has had many applications in sequence analysis: Markov models (Lukashin and Borodovsky 1997) tandem repeat detection (Rosen 2006; Akhtar et al. 2008), inference of evolutionary relationships based on di-, tri-, and tetra-nucleotide compositions (Karlin and Burge 1995; Mrázek and Campbell 1997; Nakashima and et al. 1998; Pride et al. 2003; Abe and et al. 2003; Abe and et al. 2005; Fertil et al. 2005; Teeling et al. 2004), and the examination of longer oligomers for genomic signatures (Deschavanne et al. 1999). Wang et al. (2007) use a naive Bayes classifier with 8-mers (*k*-mers of length 8) for 16S recognition. Sandberg et al. pioneered work for whole-genome shotgun sequencing (Sandberg et al. 2001). However, taxonomic classification of WGS sequences has been developed since, with a few naive Bayes classifier implementations, support vector machines, interpolated Markov models, and probabilistic analyses of *k*-mers (see Table 14.1). The advantage of composition-based methods is that they are fast, but they have difficulty assessing the true confidence of their assignments.

Phylogenetic methods attempt to classify a sequence and infer its placement on a phylogenetic tree. These programs aim to address a common question in biology: how is the sequence under study related to the known sequences? These methods infer the position of the new sequence in a tree describing inferred evolutionary relationships between sequences. Note, however, that not all programs compute the branch length. The advantages of phylogenetic methods are to assign taxonomy at upper-level and lower-level ranks, making "novelty-detection" inherent. However, these methods are very computationally intensive.

In addition, many "hybrid" techniques are now emerging that attempt to combine usually composition and homology based methods, since they often complement each other. These techniques often combine the fine resolution of composition-based methods with the more general similarity measures of homology. There are some phylogenetic algorithms that do a pre-processing alignment against a precomputed reference alignment of marker genes before phylogenetic placement (see Hybrid Alignment + Phylogeny in Table 14.1).

3.2 Protein similarity searches and databases

The "Who is there" question can be approached using either protein sequences or nucleic acid sequences, but the "What are they doing" question is best answered with proteins. Starting from predicted protein sequences from a measured dataset, protein annotation tries to infer the most likely function of the gene sampled. This has been an extremely prolific area with homology searches being used to identify function from similar protein domains. However, proteins are complicated: similar sequences sometimes have different function and distant sequences sometimes have similar functions. Consequently, much effort has been placed not only in the methods to identify function but also into development of comprehensive databases. Protein similarity searching is a step that usually requires the most computation-owing to the size of the databases used for comparison.

Researchers can infer the function of unknown metagenomic sequences from the functions of known sequences in the databases that they resemble the most. A variety of functional databases has enabled researchers to view gene composition from various angles. The databases are built upon reference sequences and have different types and different levels of detail of additional information about the sequences. Some organize protein functions into hierarchies at different resolutions, while others emphasize proteins in particular specialties. This section describes some of the databases used to annotate protein-coding genes, which constitute a major part of most metagenomic samples.

Two of the largest reference sequence collections are **the Universal Protein Resource (UniProt) databases** (Consortium 2012), and **NCBI's RefSeq database** (Pruitt et al. 2007). The former are a set of protein databases developed to provide comprehensive knowledge on various protein functions. The UniProtKB/Swiss-Prot database, which is probably the most popular among UniProt databases, has manually curated annotations by expert reviewers and covers a variety of protein functions. The latest release of UniProtKB/Swiss-Prot in November 2012 contains 538,585 sequence entries coming from 12,930 species. There is also a database specifically developed for metagenomic and environmental data called the UniProtMetagenomic and Environmental Sequences (UniMES). It is composed of metagenomic sequences clustered into groups (functional features) using CD-HIT algorithm (Li and Godzik 2006). RefSeq contains a variety of non-redundant and curated DNA, RNA and protein sequences. While annotations are mainly available for a subset of the database, especially human sequences, RefSeq also profiles conserved domains from NCBI's Conserved Domain Database and protein features from UniProtKB/Swiss-Prot. The database now includes 17,977,767 proteins comprised of 6,003,283,860 amino acids, and includes the complete genomes of 18,512 organisms (release 56 in November 2012). Refseq is continually updated with newly sequenced organisms.

Although tens of millions of genes have now been annotated, the variety of descriptions of these genes can still be hard to summarize or interpret. With this concern in mind, the **Gene Ontology** database (Ashburner et al. 2000) strives to standardize the representation of gene and gene product attributes across species and databases. The annotation of unknown sequences falls into a well-controlled vocabulary, consequently, it is widely used for interpreting gene functions. While Gene Ontology started out as a database for all eukaryotes, it now contains a prokaryote-specific subset.

The **Clusters of Orthologous Groups of proteins (COGs)** (Tatusov et al. 2003) database categorizes the conserved sequences across complete genomes based on orthologous relationships between them. Each COG contains either a single protein or an orthologous group of proteins from multiple genomes, and is classified into one of 23 functional categories. Such high-level classification provides a general view of metagenomic constitutions, and allows for low-resolution comparison between samples. The latest COGs in 2003 contain 4,873 entries, covering proteins from 66 prokaryote and unicellular eukaryote genomes. The eukaryotic version of it, **eukaryotic orthologous groups (KOGs)** (Tatusov et al. 2003), includes 7 eukaryotic genomes. To further improve the orthologous groups database by adding more annotated genomes, **eggNOG** (Powell et al. 2012) inherits the functional categories from COGs/KOGs but has expanded to contain 721,801 orthologous groups of 4,396,591 proteins, covering 1,133 species (as of January 2013). This database is constructed through identification of reciprocal best BLAST matches and triangular linkage clustering. Compared to COGs/KOGs, eggNOG has a finer phylogenetic resolution and a hierarchical classification of protein function, as well as offers more frequent database updates.

Separating orthologous groups, however, is not the only way to explore the diversity of functional roles. Analyzing all biological reactions that can possibly be completed by the gene content is another quest popular among bioinformaticians. The **Kyoto Encyclopedia of Genes and Genomes (KEGG)** (Ogata et al. 1999) provides manually drawn pathways that map genes and other molecules into chains of reactions. It is a good way to examine and compare the functional composition of metagenomes, and to identify genes playing a role in specific biological processes. As of January 2013, the KEGG Pathway has 435 pathway maps in total. The **Metacyc** (Caspi et al. 2012) database is a different pathway database belonging to the **BioCyc** database collection (Caspi et al. 2012). It contains more than 1,928 experimentally elucidated metabolic pathways from 2,362 organisms (version 16.5 released in November 2012). About 38% of the reactions can be linked to KEGG. However, compared to KEGG pathways that are constructed typically based on reactions from multiple species, Metacyc pathways are often smaller and picture reactions within single organisms. To view the pathways in a different way, **SEED** (Overbeek et al. 2005) provides an annotation environment that generalizes pathways into 891 subsystems (as of January 2013). Each subsystem is a set of functions that piece together a specific pathway, biological process, or structural complex. As one of the initial attempts to address comprehensive, expert-curated metabolic subsystems for genomic analysis, SEED annotation has been included by almost all of the large-scale analysis pipelines.

3.3 Protein domain annotation

Protein domain annotation is an alternative approach to sequence similarity searches. Rather than relying on pairwise sequence alignments, domain annotation uses models that represent conserved protein regions. These conserved regions are inferred from multiple sequence alignments (of database proteins) and have higher theoretical sensitivity than sequence comparisons lacking weights informed by biological conservation. Conserved protein regions, or domains/families, are represented by Hidden Markov Models (HMMs) built from multiple sequence alignment. Instead of sequence similarity, which searches for local alignments, protein domain annotation scans for small functional regions the genes may carry.

The Pfam database (Punta et al. 2012) is a large collection of protein domains/families containing 13,672 entries (Release 26.0 in November 2011). It is mainly comprised of sequences from UniProt Knowledge Database (Consortium 2012), NCBI GenPept Database (Sayers et al. 2012), and Protein Data Bank (Rose et al. 2013). Because of its wide coverage of proteins and intuitive naming strategies, Pfam has become a preferable annotation resource for protein domains/families. **TIGRFAMs** (Haft et al. 2013) are a similar set of models designed to be complementary to Pfam. The development of this database aims to provide functionally accurate names for genes being annotated, so that a well-informed annotator would assign the same protein name across different species with good confidence (Bateman and Haft 2002). HMMER3 (Eddy 2009) is a software package that applies accurate probabilistic models for searching the HMM profile, and can be used to annotate sequences with Pfam or TIGRfam-derived clusters.

FIGfam (Meyer et al. 2009) is another collection of protein families. Unlike Pfam's sensitive identification of all possible domains on the given sequences, FIGfam strictly requires full-length sequence similarity and common domain structure within a protein family, sacrificing sensitivity for more accurate sequence binning. It currently contains more than 100,000 entries, coming from over 950,000 manually annotated proteins of many hundred bacteria and archaea. Two other multiple sequence alignment bases, TIGRFAM (Haft et al. 2013) and PIRSF (Nikolskaya et al. 2006), have a similar requirement for binning proteins into families. However, these two databases cannot compete with FIGfam in the number of manually curated sequences, coverage of families, and computation time (Meyer et al. 2009).

It should be mentioned that there are many other protein family databases similar to the ones above but that focus on maintaining annotations for particular classes of proteins, such as **PROSITE** (Sigrist et al. 2013) that focuses on the biological functions of domains, **BLOCKS+** (Henikoff et al. 1999) that focuses on the family's characteristic and distinctive sequence features and **SMART** (Letunic et al. 2012) that focuses on domains found in signaling proteins, extracellular and nuclear domains. Additionally, some databases use protein secondary structure in characterizing protein functions, such as in **SCOP** (Andreeva et al. 2008) and **CATH** (Knudsen and Wiuf, 2010) databases, aiming to provide a comprehensive description of the structural and evolutionary relationships between all proteins whose structure is known. There are also databases that take into consideration both sequence alignment and secondary protein structural information, such as **SUPFAM** (Pandit et al. 2004) and **ProDom** (Bru et al. 2005).

3.4 ID mapping and computational complexity

As functional databases become more diverse, considerable effort has been made to connect similar entries of various databases, in order to gain comprehensive understanding of numerous gene annotations and avoid non-necessary repeat of annotation work.

Some databases incorporate annotations from other databases, such as **InterPro** (Mulder et al. 2007) that integrates protein signatures from a variety of sources including Pfam, PROSITE, ProDom, PIRSF, CATH, TIGRFAM, etc., and the **M5NR database** (Wilke et al. 2012) that integrates Gene Ontology, KEGG, SEED, UniProt, eggNOG, etc. About 80% of the proteins in UniProtKB/Swiss-Prot have Pfam matches. Also, the entry mapping between many functional databases is made available on the UniProt website, including the mapping between most entries in UniProt, PIRSF, RefSeq, KEGG, eggNOG, BioCyc, etc. In addition, the UniProt Gene Ontology Annotation (UniProt-GOA) database (Dimmer et al. 2011) provides high-quality Gene Ontology annotations to proteins in the UniProt Knowledgebase.

While gene annotation provides direct insight into the functional composition of metagenomes, the proportion of sequences that can be annotated is relatively limited. A gene annotation example for human gut metagenomes published in a comparative metagenomics study shows that most functional annotations are only able to assign fewer than 50% of the samples

TABLE 14.2 Percentage of metagenome samples covered by gene annotation resources.

Metagenomic sample	Sequences annotated	Gene annotation resource
MetaHit dataset (124 samples)	77.1%	Taxonomic annotation
	50.2%	Pfam
	40.7%	KEGG Ontology
	18.7%	KEGG Pathway
A multi-source dataset (52 samples)	52.0%	Pfam
	47.5%	Gene Ontology

(Table 14.2) (Lan et al. 2013), revealing a need to improve current annotation methods and characterize genes with yet unknown functions.

Another challenge for similarity searching is the high computational cost compared with taxonomy classification, using searching tools either against reference sequences or HMMs. Using the dataset 6-19-DNA-flx(MG-RAST accession 4440276.3) as an example, a marine metagenomic sample collected from coastal waters in Norway. This dataset represents 68Mbases of metagenomic sequence data which reduces to 255,702 predicted protein sequences. It takes 34.0 CPU hours on a local machine (single 800 MHz AMD Phenom(tm) II X6 1045T processor) to BLAST it against UniProtKB/Swiss-Prot database, resulting in 28.8% of the sequences annotated (e-value 10^{-5}), while it takes 59.9 CPU hours to search Pfams, annotating 30.4% of the sequences.

Shotgun metagenomic datasets at present comprise between 10^7 and 10^{11} base pairs per sample, sometimes amounting to billions of reads. The databases to be searched have typically 10^9–10^{10} amino acids. Searching ever-larger sets of sequences for matches against growing databases of "known" sequences makes annotation the most computationally expensive step in sequence analysis (Wilkening et al. 2009). With more metagenomic data made available by the use of high-throughput sequencing, faster annotation procedures are urgently needed.

3.5 Existing pipelines for metagenomic annotation

Several large-scale pipelines provide gene annotation for metagenomic data across various functional databases. MG-RAST (Meyer et al. 2008), for example, is a fully automated analysis pipeline designed specifically for metagenomic data. It provides functional annotation on KEGG, eggNOG, COG, and SEED subsystems on multiple levels of resolution. IMG/M (Markowitz et al. 2008) is another automated annotation pipeline. It can be used for annotating COGs, Pfams and KEGG pathways, with a preference for larger assembled contigs compared to MG-RAST. RAMMCAP (Rapid Analysis of Multiple Metagenomes with a Clustering and Annotation Pipeline) (Li 2009) provides implementation of HMMER for Pfam, and TIGRFAM annotation, as well as BLAST for COG annotation.

4 CROSS SAMPLE ANALYSIS

This section focuses on the last building blocks (from Figure 14.1) of metagenomic sample analysis. Here we are concerned with inferring information based on the community data matrix, as detailed in Figure 14.2

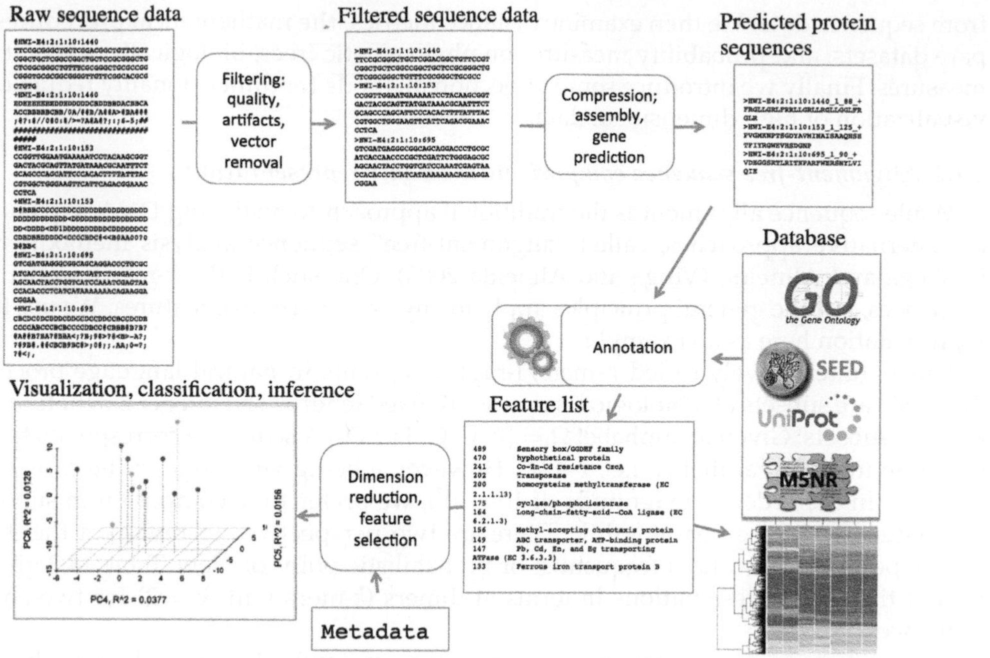

FIGURE 14.1 Diagram of generic sequence analysis workflow from raw data to visualization and classification. Each analytical step removes information; this results in a smaller volume and smaller dimensionality of data at later stages of processing.

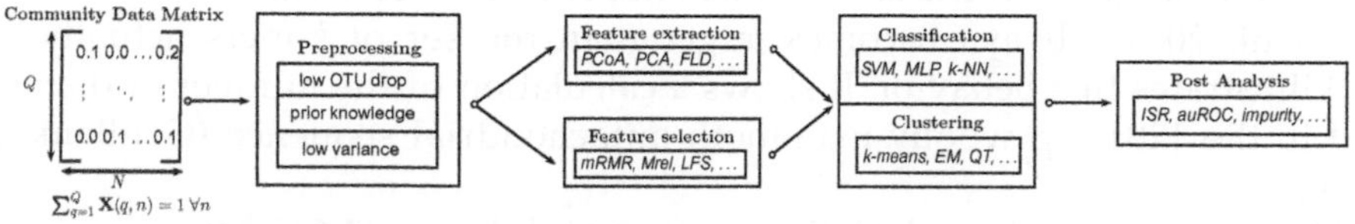

FIGURE14.2 As a last step in the analysis of metagenomic data, feature selection methods are important in understanding microbial communities. This corresponds to a zoom in on the two last boxes of Figure 14.1.

We will first review some ways to compare data and project them for visualization purposes and then introduce methods to select a subset of features that should be the most useful for further processing.

4.1 Initial manipulation of annotation

In cross sample analysis, one is interested in comparing samples and finding the features that make different samples and samples with different mutatants distinct. Samples represent mixtures of microorganisms; these mixtures might contain slightly different lineages of a particular species of organisms, might contain the same organisms in different proportions, or might contain completely different organisms over varying environments. We will first examine the k-mer representation, an annotation-independent approach to creating features from sequence data. We then examine distance metrics, the mathematical procedures to compare datasets, and probability measures on phylogenetic trees, biologically-relevant distance measures. Finally we introduce some projection methods for dimensionality reduction for the visualization of high dimensional data.

4.1.1 Alignment-free sequence comparison: the k-mer representation

While sequence alignment is the traditional approach to analyzing DNA sequences, there are alternative approaches, called "alignment-free" sequence analysis methods, reviewed in Vinga and Almeida (Vinga and Almeida 2003). One such is the *k*-mer representation of sequences, but the general principles apply to any vector space of features. We use the *k*-mer representation here as an example.

k-mers (alternatively called n-mers, l-tuples, n-grams in natural language processing, or "words") are subsets of a biological sequence of fixed length. The integer k denotes the length of these subsets. Given an alphabet $\Omega = \{A, C, G, T\}$ a DNA sequence corresponds to a word x of length n on that alphabet, i.e., $x \in \Omega^n$. However, n being very large in the case of genome analysis (in the order of magnitude of 10^6–10^7), we prefer to decompose it in sub-words or sub-sequences of a given length k. There are two perspectives to represent the data: a set theory point of view and a frequentist or probabilistic point of view. Table 14.3 gives examples of the two representations in terms of dimers (*k*-mers with $k = 2$) for two short DNA sequences.

Assume an input sequence x of size n and let us denote by $V_k(x) = \{\omega \in \Omega^k : \exists\, l \in \{1, \ldots, n\}, x_{l \ldots l+k-1} = \omega\}$. This is the set of all *k*-mers found anywhere in the read x.

k is a parameter which can be chosen by the researcher. As k increases the set of possible *k*-mers (numbering 4^k) increases exponentially. Since biological sequences are finite, for large enough k (in the range 8–14) the set of *k*-mers not encountered (which are called nullomers (Fofanov et al. 2004) always becomes larger than the set of *k*-mers actually observed. Table 14.3 illustrates this behavior. It shows a calculation of the number of distinct *k*-mers contained in the 12817 bp woolly mammoth mitochondrial sequence (GenBank accession DQ188829).

Table 14.4 shows a similar calculation on the much larger (4.645 Mbase) genome of the bacterium *Escherichia coli* K-12 MG1655 (Refseq accession NC_000913). As we can see from these two tables, the larger the size of the *k*-mers, the less likely a random *k*-mer is to occur. The probability distribution of these subsequences, and of numbers in the *k*-mer representation, is an area of current study useful for interpreting comparisons between these representations.

TABLE 14.3 Evolution of the set of found *k*-mers with *k* getting bigger for a small sequence.

Mammoth (12,817 nucleotides)	$\lvert V_k(x)\rvert$	Max	Ratio
$k = 4$	256	256	100%
$k = 6$	3,460	4,096	84.47%
$k = 9$	15,276	262,164	5.83%

TABLE 14.4 Evolution of the set of found k-mers for a larger sequence.

E.coli (4,639,675 nucleotides)	$\|V_k(x)\|$	Max (= 4^k)	Ratio
$k = 4$	256	256	100.0%
$k = 6$	4,096	4,096	100.0%
$k = 8$	65,361	65,536	99.7%
$k = 10$	898,108	1,048,576	85.6%
$k = 15$	4,517,622	1.1×10^9	4.2×10^{-3}
$k = 20$	4,561,225	1.1×10^{12}	4.1×10^{-6}
$k = 40$	4,575,486	1.2×10^{24}	3.8×10^{-18}

4.1.2 Distances and divergences

Once features (whether from taxonomic classification, protein annotation, or k-mer analysis) have been extracted from a set of sequences, the next most fundamental operation is the pairwise comparison of samples.

A straightforward tool for comparing two set-based representations x and y is known as the Jaccard index (Jaccard 1901) and defined as

$$J(x,y) = \frac{|V_k(x) \cap V_k(y)|}{|V_k(x) \cup V_k(y)|} \tag{14.1}$$

This represents the fraction of common elements over the set of all elements in these two sequences. We clearly have that $J(x,y) = 0$ if no k-mer from x is found in y and $J(x,y) = 1$ if all the k-mers of both sequences are found in the other. Note that this index only indicates if x and y contain similar sets of k-mers but does not imply similar ordering of the two sequences. Another well-known similarity based on set representations is the Sørensen similarity index. It is defined as:

$$S(x,y) = \frac{2|V_k(x) \cap V_k(y)|}{|V_k(x)| + |V_k(y)|} \tag{14.2}$$

It can be seen as ratio of the number of k-mers in common to the (potentially doubled) number of different k-mers found. Once again a 1 corresponds to the case where the sets of k-mers are exactly the same and 0 happens when there are no common elements. This similarity is also used in the context of frequency representation and known as the Bray-Curtis index in this case (see Equation (14.3) for the details).

Another remark about the Jaccard (or the Sørensen) index is that it lacks information regarding the frequency of each k-mer which implies that we have to work on largest sub-sequences and hence makes it harder to process. Clearly a probabilistic representation of such k-mers overcomes that problem. A sequence of length n has up to $m = n - k + 1$ k- mers taken from the 4^k different options. Denote by $m_j(x), j \in \{1, \ldots, 4^k\}$ the number of occurrences of k-mer j then the frequency representation of x is given by the 4^k dimensional vector $\vec{x} = \{m_j(x)/m\}_{j=1\cdots 4^k}$.

TABLE 14.5 Set and probabilistic description of two DNA subsequences when considering only dimers. The last column counts the occurrences of each possible dimer, including unobserved dimers not present in the sequences.

Sequence x	*k-mer set* $V_2(x)$	**Probability vector** $\vec{x}$
GTACGTACACACA	{GT, TA, AC, CG, CA}	1/12(0,4,0,0,3,0,1,0,0,0,0,2,2,0,0,0)
ATAGACATAGATA	{AT, TA, AG, GA, AC, CA}	1/12(0,1,2,3,1,0,0,0,2,0,0,0,3,0,0,0)

This representation can also be viewed as a probability distribution over the set of words of size k. It tells us *that the probability of picking k-mer j by randomly picking a sub-sequence of size k in the DNA sequence x is* $\vec{x}_j$ (see Table 14.5).

Another similarity coefficient often used for sequence comparison (and later for sample comparison) is known as the Bray-Curtis dissimilarity, sometimes inaccurately called a "distance." The Bray-Curtis dissimilarity is not a metric; it does not satisfy the triangle inequality, but is symmetrical. It is defined as

$$BC(x,y) = \frac{2\sum_{i=1}^{4^k} \min(m_i(x), m_i(y))}{m(x) + m(y)} \tag{14.3}$$

It can be seen as the proportion of common k-mers given the sum of k-mers contained in either of the reads. Two DNA sequences (or two entire datasets) can be compared by evaluating the divergence of two probability measures. f-divergences, introduced independently in Csiszár (1963), Ali and Silvey (1966), are particularly appropriate for this task. Divergences are reviewed in Liese and Vajda (Liese and Vajda 2006). Basseville (Basseville 1996) (in French) offers a quite exhaustive survey of such measures as well.

Definition 14.1 f—divergence measures

Given two probability distribution P and Q absolutely continuous with respect to a reference measure μ over the set Ω and denote by p and q their probability density; moreover, let f be a convex function such that $f(1) = 0$ then the f-divergence of P given Q is defined as

$$D_f(P||Q) = \int_{\Omega} f\left(\frac{p(x)}{q(x)}\right) q(x) d\mu(x) \tag{14.4}$$

For discrete probability distributions (as are the case in bioinformatics) the previous formulation is equivalent to the following:

$$D_f(P||Q) = \sum_i f\left(\frac{p(i)}{q(i)}\right) q(i) \tag{14.5}$$

TABLE 14.6 Some examples of *f*-divergence measures.

Name	Formula	*f*	Reference
Kullback-Leibler	$D_{KL}(P\|\|Q) = \sum_i q(i) ln\left(\frac{q(i)}{p(i)}\right)$	$t \mapsto -ln(t)$	(Kullback 1997)
Hellinger	$D_H(P\|\|Q) = \sum_t(\sqrt{p(i)} - \sqrt{q(i)})^2$	$t \mapsto (\sqrt{t} - 1)^2$	(Lin 1991)
Bhattacharyya	$D_{BC}(P\|\|Q) = -\sum_t \sqrt{p(i)q(i)}$	$t \mapsto -\sqrt{t}$	(Bhattacharyya 1943)

This framework includes many of the metrics often used in DNA comparison such as the Hellinger distance and Kullback-Leibler divergence as special cases. Table 14.6 gives some examples of such *f*-divergences. Such divergence measures usually lack symmetry.

4.1.3 *Unifrac distances*

The distances and divergences so far have been mathematical (Sørensen, Hellinger) and information-theoretic (Kullback-Leibler) in origin, but not biological. When the features represent organisms with known taxonomic relationships (that is, the samples have been projected onto a common phylogenetic tree), distances between samples can be constructed with awareness of the phylogenetic relationships. (The procedure for building a phylogenetic tree is not developed in this section, as it would bring us far beyond the scope of this chapter.) The first widely-adopted metric using the phylogenetic tree is the **UniFrac** measure (Lozupone and Knight 2005). This metric can be formulated as follows.

Consider a phylogenetic tree T, that can either be taken as a universal reference or built from the samples themselves. It can be seen as a set of nodes $\{n_i\}_i$ and a hierarchical relationship $\{t_i\}_i$. Now, let A and B denote respectively the first and second samples. Both can be represented as a set of branches $\{a_j\}_j$ (respectively $\{b_j\}_j$) assumed to be in T. We will abusively write A and B for both the samples and the branches representing them in the phylogenetic tree but the meaning should be clear in the context. The uniform fraction (a.k.a. UniFrac) of similarity is defined as the fraction of branches belonging to only a single sample over the overall length based on both of them. Figure 14.3 illustrates this. Assume you are given two samples, one containing species 1–5 (represented as the leaves on the tree) and another one containing species 3–9. The tree shows a potential phylogenetic relation between all the species where the dashed blue connections correspond to phylogenetic relation that are present in both of the samples. The UniFrac similarity distance between these two samples can be seen as the proportion of solid lines given the whole tree (or in other words, the size of the tree without the dashed part over the size of the whole tree).

Formally, we have:

$$UniFrac(A, B) = \frac{|A| + |B| - 2|A \cap B|}{|A| + |B| - |A \cap B|} \tag{14.6}$$

Unifrac can be generalized by considering that each t_j has a given length l_j (depending on the inferred time between two branches or any phylogenetic related metrics) and by weighting the branches by their frequencies or abundances. The yields the weighed UniFracmeasure (Lozupone et al. 2007):

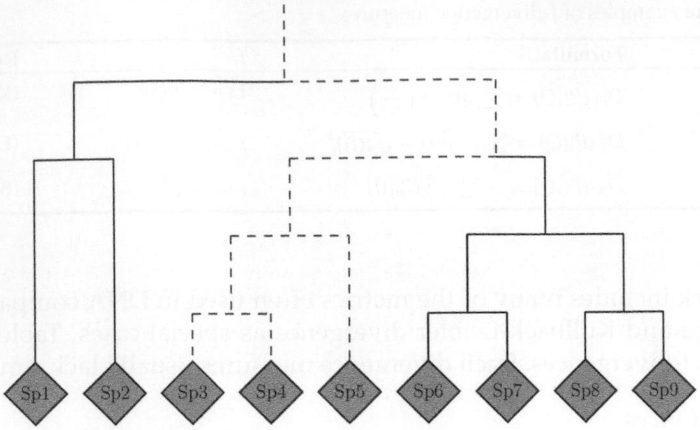

FIGURE 14.3 Example of a basic phylogenetic tree and how to compute the UniFrac distance (See text for details).

$$\mathrm{wUF}(A,B) = \sum l_i \left| \frac{A_i}{m} - \frac{B_i}{n} \right| \tag{14.7}$$

where A_i (respectively B_i) is the number of descendant of branch i in A (respectively B), i.e., $A_i = |\{t_j : t_i \in Parents_A(t_j)\}|$. m and n denote the respective number of reads in sample A and B. This formulation corresponds to weighting a certain branch by its relative importance in the total length of the tree. The original UniFrac metric can be recovered by assuming that A_i/m and B_i/n take values in $\{0,1\}$ whether the current branch is in the analyzed sample or not.

With this new approach, we can generalize even further by noticing that a sample corresponds to a probability distribution on the phylogenetic tree (Evans and Matsen 2010). We can understand this distribution as *What is the probability that picking a random read from a sample corresponds to this particular taxa?* Now keeping this probabilistic view in mind opens new perspectives towards phylogenetic tree-based sample comparison as we can now use any similarity or divergence measures between probability distributions and adapt them to work on a tree structure.

In their novel work, (Evans and Matsen 2010) showed that applying the Kantorovitch-Rubinstein metric (also known as the Earth Mover's Distance in computer science or the Wasserstein distance in mathematics) yields a generalization of the previous weighted and unweighted UniFrac. We refer to (Evans and Matsen 2010) for the mathematical derivations and only give its formulation:

$$Z(P,Q) := \int_T \left| P\left(\tau(y)\right) - Q\left(\tau(y)\right) \right| \lambda(dy) \tag{14.8}$$

In this expression, P and Q represent both probability measures of A and B respectively on the phylogenetic tree T. The notation $\tau(y)$ denotes the subgraph starting at node y (part of the tree that is below y). λ denotes the equivalent to the Lebesgue measure on the tree T (which contains a distance metric derived from the length of the branches).

This generalization can even go one step further by integrating any pseudo-metric f instead of the absolute value:

$$\hat{Z}_f(P,Q) := \int_T f\left(P\left(\tau(y)\right) - Q\left(\tau(y)\right)\right) \lambda(dy) \tag{14.9}$$

It is clear that this definition yields the classical UniFrac metric if f takes the value one when exactly one of the probabilities P and Q is greater than 0.

4.1.4 Dimensionality reduction for visualization purposes

Ecologists employ ordination methods when a visual relation is desired based on similarity of a set of multivariate objects (Jongman et al. 1987; TerBraak and Prentice 2004). Typically, each object represents a sample site and is a table representing the abundances of organisms within the community. This composition generally varies among the sites and may be structured by environmental variables termed gradients. An ideal ordination technique would display all sample sites in the same order, as they exist along the environmental gradient, with inter-sample distances proportional to their separation along the gradient (Legendre and Legendre 2012). Various ordination methods are available for both direct (constrained) and indirect (unconstrained) analyses. The difference between the classes of methods depends on whether environmental gradient measurements are included (direct) or omitted (indirect). Popular methods discussed below include PCA, PCoA, NMDS, CA, CCA, RDA, and DCA (Jongman et al. 1987; TerBraak and Prentice 2004; Legendre and Legendre 2012; Fasham 1977; Kuczynski et al. 2010; Gauch et al. 1977).

Metagenomic annotations are a class of high-dimensional data that can be explored and examined using dimension reduction. In such cases we are given a set of n samples (e.g., samples that are collected from different regions of the body). Each sample, which we call x, is described by a certain number K of features (e.g., the frequencies or abundances of annotated microbial species) and all of them are gathered in what is called a **data matrix**: $X = [x^{(1)}, x^{(2)}, \ldots, x^{(n)}] \in \mathbb{R}^{K \times n}$. The number of features can be between 10 and 10^7, making visualization impossible (since displaying more than three dimensions is challenging at best). Picking just three variables to display randomly is not a good choice-it throws away most of the data without attempting to identify and preserve aspects of the data that may prove interesting. For concreteness, consider the case where the features are the abundances of each of $K = 150$ types of known bacteria. If we decide to choose a subset of these dimensions of size $m = 3$ for visualization or further investigation, there are $\frac{K!}{m!(K-m)!} = 551,300$ possible candidates to choose from. We will present two examples of data reduction techniques that try to choose "interesting" subsets of the feature space that are commonly used for visualization purposes: **Principal Component Analysis (PCA)** and **Principal Coordinate Analysis (PCoA)**. Both rely on projections onto orthogonal axes representing the most variance of the data as possible.

PCA is a method that projects the data onto axes which contain most of the variance. This is done by calculating the eigenvalue decomposition of the covariance matrix and keeping only the projections of the data onto the few most important eigenvectors. This procedure is called **spectral decomposition** and the eigenvectors corresponding to the largest eigenvalues are called the **principal components**. They point in the directions with the highest variability of the data. This method reduces the data to a sum of typical mixtures of the different bacteria in a sample, but it will not give the most relevant bacteria given an outside parameter. The whole PCA decomposition can be seen as a combination of an average microbiome mixture over all samples plus some small variations according to some calculated mixtures.

The large dimensionality of feature vectors makes spectral decomposition of the covariance matrix intractable in most cases. Consequently, PCA as a dimensionality reduction technique is applied to the analysis of $(n \times n)$ resemblance or distance matrices.

PCoA is yet another method for dimensionality reduction useful for visualization (Legendre and Legendre 2012). First introduced (Gower 1966) as a method that would preserve the distances between objects even when representing them using fewer components, it performs PCA on a modified version of the distance matrix. A main advantage of using PCoA over PCA is that it allows the user to tune the similarity of distance metric used for comparison; this fact yields a more flexible tool regarding the dynamics or range of the different variables. A resemblance matrix is built by comparing each element of the data matrix to one another using the chosen comparison metric d:

$$\forall i, j \in \{1, \ldots, n\}, D_{ij} = d\left(x^{(i)}, x^{(j)}\right)$$

This matrix is then squared and centered as follows:

$$A_{ij} = D_{ij}^2$$

$$B_{ij} = A_{ij} - \overline{A_i} - \overline{A_j} + \overline{A}$$

where $\overline{A_i}, \overline{A_j}$ and $\overline{A}$ denote the means taken of each rows, columns and the whole matrix, respectively. This matrix transformation does not affect the distance relationships between the samples and hence keeps the structure of the data. But on the other hand it centers the data on the centroid of the samples.

Finally, a spectral decomposition is applied to the B matrix and its eigenvectors are scaled by the square root of the eigenvalues. Usually only a few eigenvectors cover most the variability of the data. Note that when using the Euclidean distance as a metric for the resemblance matrix, PCoA yields equivalent result to the PCA approach based on the spectral decomposition of the covariance matrix.

Some care should be taken with this method. It works well when used with a metric distance measures (i.e. a binary positive definite form fulfilling the triangle inequality). Since some beloved discrepancies do not fulfill the triangle inequality, they should not be used in this framework if one wishes to transform the data into another space. This should not be a

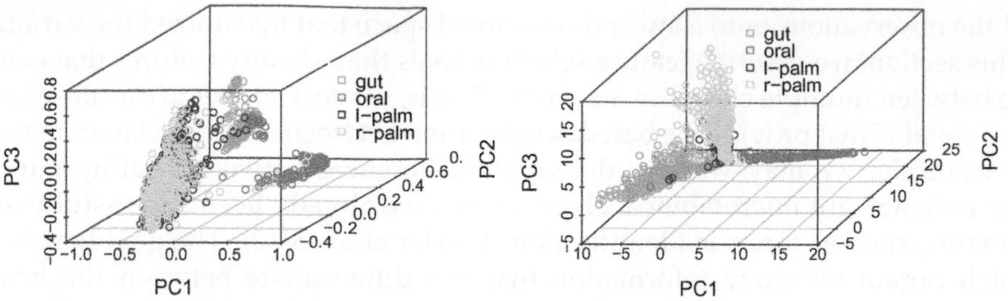

FIGURE 14.4 PCoA plots of the 15 month study of the human microbiome(G. Caporaso et al., 2011) *left* Hellinger and *right* Euclidean.

major concern if the only purpose of the transformation is the visualization of the data. Figure 14.4 shows some PCoA plots for the Human microbiome study, comparing visualizations based on Hellinger distance (left hand side) and Euclidean distance (to the right). Note that PCA would give similar results to the PCoA with the Euclidean distance.

4.1.5 Testing for differences

Once we can visually see that the sample groupings are separable, we may wish to test whether the visual differences are statistically significant or not. The **ANalysis Of SIMilarity (ANOSIM)** tool was first introduced in (Clarke 1993, Clarke and Warwick 1994) to solve this problem, as a hypothesis test based on the distance matrix used in PCoA.

Assume you are given labels associated to the different samples (for instance the site where they were taken from). We order the set of all different distances in an increasing order and replace the distance matrix D by the rank matrix R_D where the components of $\{R_D\}_{ij}$ correspond to the rank of D_{ij}. Then compute the **within site similarity** R_w as the average of all ranks between two samples coming from a same site on the one hand and the **between class similarity** as the average of all ranks between samples with different labels. The ANOSIM test calculates

$$R = 4\frac{R_b - R_w}{n(n-1)} \tag{14.10}$$

where n denotes the number of samples. The higher the value of this number the better it is. Moreover note that the value has to be in the range $[-1, 1]$ where values closer to 1 mean that the data are highly separable.

To compare the significance of the data to a null hypothesis, we can construct the null hypothesis by permuting randomly the labels of the samples and then comparing the significance of the original R against the null hypothesis R to see if the original R has greater significance.

4.2 Feature selection

The previous section discussed several dimensionality reduction techniques, all of which are based on the projection of observations onto a lower dimensional space. For example, PCA projected the observations onto a lower dimensional space that maximized the variation in the data. In this section, we describe **feature selection** tools that identify features that can best discriminate between multiple classes in a dataset. That is, we seek to identify a subset of features $\mathcal{F}_\theta$ of the original $\mathcal{F}$ that provide the best discrimination between multiple classes in the dataset.

As an example, we may want to determine differences between healthy patients' and unhealthy patients' gut microbiomes. These ideas have already been successfully applied in other domains, such as forensic identification (Ditzler et al. 2012). The goal here is to determine which organisms carry information that can differentiate between the healthy and unhealthy populations. From a machine learning perspective, this is a feature selection problem; however, from a biological perspective, the selection of organisms allows the biologist the opportunity to identify a set of species that is responsible for differentiating healthy and unhealthy patients. It is important to note that there may be additional factors that influence the results, but may not be in the feature set.

Selecting highly informative features is the primary objective of any feature selection method; however, other objectives are typically used in feature selection as well. Clearly, selecting features that are relevant is of top priority, but many feature selection methods have redundancy tools integrated into their selection objective as well. That is, they select informative features that are not redundant with respect to one another. Many biologists may not be worried about redundancy if the sole purpose of their data analysis is to find the most informative features, because they simply do care that they may be redundant. Classification scenarios generally need to have some form of redundancy built into the feature selection algorithm to boost the prediction accuracy.

In this section and its subsections, we have solely focused on filter-based feature selection methods, rather than wrapper-based feature selection. The interested reader is encouraged to pursue recent literature for the differences between various feature selection methods (Guyon et al. 2006; Guyon and Elisseeff 2003; Brown et al. 2012; Saeys et al. 2007).

4.2.1 *A forward selection algorithm*

In feature selection, we have an objective function $\mathcal{J}$ that we seek to maximize, and this function is dependent upon a subset of features $\mathcal{F}_\theta$. The goal of the forward selection algorithm is to find k features in $\mathcal{F}$ that maximize the objective function. A simple forward selection algorithm to achieve such a task is shown in Figure 14.5.

The algorithm begins by initializing $\mathcal{F}_\theta$ to an empty set, and the method takes in a number of features to select (k) and the original feature set ($\mathcal{F}$). Let X_j be a random variable for feature j and Y be the variable that determines the class label (e.g., healthy vs. unhealthy). The first step is to find the feature X_j which maximizes the objective function $\mathcal{J}$ that takes in the arguments X_j, Y, and $\mathcal{F}_\theta$. The feature X_j that maximizes the objective function is added to $\mathcal{F}_\theta$ and removed from $\mathcal{F}$. This process is repeated until the cardinality of $\mathcal{F}_\theta$ is k.

The feature selection algorithm in Figure 14.5 is a simple method to select the k features that maximize the objective function; however, the algorithm makes a key assumption that is often not true—feature independence. This algorithm assumes that all features are independent of each other, which is generally not the case with many real-world data sources. Nevertheless, this approach has been shown to be quite robust to a number of problems even when the assumptions are violated in practice (Duch et al. 2002; Brown et al. 2012; Ditzler et al. 2012; Peng et al. 2005).

Input: Feature set $\mathcal{F}$, an objective function $\mathcal{J}$, k features to select, and initialize an empty set $\mathcal{F}_\theta$

1. Maximize the objective function

$$X_j = \arg\max_{X_j \in \mathcal{F}} \mathcal{J}(X_j, Y, \mathcal{F}_\theta)$$

2. Update relevant feature set such that $\mathcal{F}_\theta \leftarrow \mathcal{F}_\theta \cup X_j$
3. Remove relevant feature from the original set $\mathcal{F} \leftarrow \mathcal{F} \backslash X_j$
4. Repeat until $|\mathcal{F}_\theta| = k$

FIGURE 14.5 Forward selection algorithm.

4.2.2 Information-theoretic feature selection

The feature selection algorithm presented above relied on an objective function; however, such a function has not yet been discussed in detail.

So far the objective function depends on X_j, Y, and $\mathcal{F}_\theta$, but what is the form of the function? Intuitively, it should promote features that are capable of describing the Y. That is, find the features that carry the most information about Y. In this section we focus solely on *information-theoretic* objective functions.

The fundamental unit of information is entropy,[1] which measures the level of uncertainty in a random variable X. Mathematically, this is given by,

$$H(X) = -\sum_{x \in \mathcal{X}} p_X(x) log(p_X(x)) \tag{14.11}$$

where p_x is the marginal probability distribution on the random variable X with possible outcomes in the set $\mathcal{X}$. The antilog of the entropy, an information metric, can be interpreted as the number of equiprobable outcomes in a distribution with the same information content. Different outcomes in the set $\mathcal{X}$ contribute different amounts to the overall entropy. Datasets that are evenly distributed have higher entropy than datasets that are skewed toward a handful of values.[2] Maximum entropy is achieved with a uniform distribution on $p_x(x)$. Figure 14.6 shows that this is the case for a Bernoulli random vaJriable. Similar to standard probabilities, entropy can be conditioned on a second random variable Y, which gives us conditional entropy.

$$H(X|Y) = -\sum_{y \in \mathcal{Y}} p_Y(y) \sum_{x \in \mathcal{X}} p_{X|Y}(x|y) log(p_{X|Y}(x|y)) \tag{14.12}$$

[1] Entropy is measured in bits, nats, or bans depending on whether a base 2, natural, or base 10 logarithm is used in the calculation, respectively.

[2] Imagine flipping a coin such that $\mathbb{P}(X = \text{heads}) = 0.99$ and $\mathbb{P}(X = \text{tails}) = 0.01$. Such a random variable has low entropy because there is little uncertainty in the outcome of X.

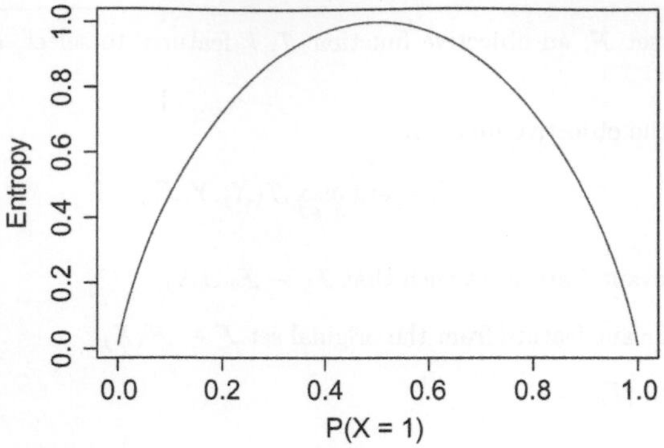

FIGURE 14.6 Entropy of a Bernoulli random variable. Maximum entropy, measured in bits, is achieved when the distribution on X is uniform.

Conditional entropy can be interpreted as the amount of information that is left in X after the outcome of the random variable Y is observed. Using the definitions of entropy and conditional entropy gives rise to mutual information, which is given by,

$$I(X;Y) = \sum_{x\in\mathcal{X}}\sum_{y\in\mathcal{Y}} p_{X,Y}(x,y) log\left(\frac{p_{X,Y}(x,y)}{p_X(x)p_Y(y)}\right) = H(X) - H(X|Y) \tag{14.13}$$

where $I(X;Y)$ is the remaining uncertainty in X after the uncertainty about X given what we known about Y is removed. Note that $I(X;Y) = 0$ if the random variables X and Y are independent of each other. This should be quite intuitive since J+15independent variables would be expected to share any information about each other. Lastly, define the **conditional mutual information**,

$$I(X;Y|Z) = \sum_z p_z(z) \sum_{x,y} p_{X,Y|Z}(x,y|z) log\left(\frac{p_{X,YZ}(x,y|z)}{p_{X|Z}(x|z)p_{Y|Z}(y|z)}\right) = H(X|Z) - H(X|Y,Z) \tag{14.14}$$

which is the amount of information left between X and Y after Z is observed. We now have discussed the appropriate tools in information theory that can allow us to design an objective function for the forward selection algorithm presented in Figure 14.5 that accounts for feature relevancy and redundancy (both conditional and unconditional). As an example, Equation (14.15) presents the objective function for the **Joint Mutual Information** feature selection method.

$$\mathcal{J}_{\text{JMI}}(X_t, Y, \mathcal{F}_\theta) = \text{I}(X_t; Y) - \frac{1}{|\mathcal{F}_\theta|} \sum_{X_j \in \mathcal{F}_\theta} [I(X_t; X_j) - I(X_t; X_j|Y)] \tag{14.15}$$

There are three terms in $\mathcal{J}_{\text{JMI}}(X_t, Y, \mathcal{F}_\theta)$ that controls the features that are selected. The first term $I(X_t; Y)$ is simply the amount of information shared between X_t (i.e., the feature under test), and the class label Y. The second term $I(X_t; X_j)$ is a measure of redundancy and since $I(X_t; X_j) \geq 0$, the quantity decreases $\mathcal{J}_{\text{JMI}}(X_t, Y, \mathcal{F}_\theta)$. Hence, a measure of removing redundant features. The third term shows that the $\mathcal{J}_{\text{JMI}}(X_t, Y, \mathcal{F}_\theta)$ can be increased by having some level of conditional redundancy between features.

4.2.3 *Measuring feature consistency*

The reliability or consistency of a feature selection method remains an important question. Would the feature selection algorithms always return the same relevant features if we were to use the forward selection method on cross-validation or bootstrap datasets? To answer this question, a simple consistency index may be applied to measure the similarity between multiple sets.

Typically some form of cross-validation or bootstrapping is applied to a dataset and feature selection algorithm to determine the relevant features; however, what if the features selected vary slightly over each of the validation/bootstrap trials? In such situations, we need a way to quantify the **consistency** of the relevant feature set. Kuncheva developed a consistency index that meets three primary criteria for an index: (*a*) the consistency index is a monotonically increasing function of increasing elements in common with two sets union, (*b*) the index is bounded, and (*c*) the index should have a constant value for independently drawn subsets of features of the same cardinality (Kuncheva 2007). Using these criteria, Kuncheva derived the following definition of consistency.

Definition 14.2 Consistency (Kuncheva 2007) The consistency index for two subsets $\mathcal{A} \subseteq \mathcal{F}$ and $\mathcal{B} \subseteq \mathcal{F}$ such that $r = |\mathcal{A} \cap \mathcal{B}|$ and $|\mathcal{A}| = |\mathcal{B}| = k$, where $1 \leq k \leq |\mathcal{F}| = K$, is

$$\mathfrak{I}_{\mathcal{F}}(\mathcal{A}, \mathcal{B}) = \frac{rK - k^2}{k(K - k)} \tag{14.16}$$

What Does All This Mean?

This section has described the information theoretic tools to select or design an objective function for a feature selection method. If the end goal is to strictly find highly informative features than maximizing $I(X_j|Y)$ is sufficient. However, for many classification problems incorporating redundancy and conditional redundancy is quite beneficial over methods that do not use redundancy, though using redundancy terms does not guarantee improved performance.

5 UNDERSTANDING MICROBIAL COMMUNITIES

In the section above, we have described the methods used for comparing metagenomic samples and identifying relevant features. These machine learning techniques, when applied to real metagenomic problems, provide us with more opportunities to understand the lives of microbes in their natural, highly-connected environments.

For example, by assessing the biodiversity across metagenomes, we can learn about the functional capabilities of microbes in a community and evaluate hypotheses about survival strategies under environmental shift. Systems investigated already with these tools include the redundancy of microbes in infected human lungs of cystic fibrosis patients (Stressmann et al. 2012), the role of microbes in human breast milk in colonization of the infant gastrointestinal tract and maintenance of mammary health (Hunt et al. 2011), and the communities of microbes on human skin to examine how antibiotic exposure and lifestyle changes alter the skin microbiomes electively (Grice et al. 2009).

Moreover, the use of metagenomic methods allows a window into the interaction between microbes. One study (Faust et al. 2012) compared human metagenomes across different body sites and identified 3,005 significant co-occurrence and co-exclusion relationships between bacterial branches. This is an informative way for us to learn about potential microbial interactions. There are also a slew of on-going studies that link microbes by similar genes or pathways they share, in search of microorganism cooperation and competition. Another tool has been developed for analyzing the topology of metabolic networks and calculating the metabolic overlap between species, which provides a way of estimating the competitive potential between bacterial species (Kreimer et al. 2012). Although this is not readily a tool for metagenomes, it shows us that extracting metabolic information has potential to answer more biological questions than we currently do.

In addition to the comparison between microbes, many people are interested in the symbiosis between microbes and their human host. By comparing the functional capability of microbiomes and their host, we can learn about microbes' strategy to maintain the symbiosis, such as providing nutrients, degradation of toxins and immune enhancement (Dethlefsen et al. 2007).

We are glad to observe the increase of not only metagenomic studies, but also the increase of metatranscriptomic, metaproteomic, and metabolomic data. The incorporation of microbial genomes, transcripts, proteins, and metabolites into the machine learning techniques introduced provides more information and can possibly lead to personalized medicine (Chen et al. 2012).

6 OPEN PROBLEMS AND CHALLENGES

There are a plethora of open problems in metagenome analysis. We will highlight several that we believe are important to fully exploit the information in the sequence of a sample and its relationship to its environment.

Metagenomic annotation can typically provide only an approximate estimate of the taxonomic (Koslicki et al. in press; Bazinet and Cummings 2012; Wang et al. 2007) and functional content (Meyer et al. 2008; Huson et al. 2011; Fizzy 2013) of an environmental sample (e.g., 16S rRNA surveys and "light-sequencing" whole-genome shotgun (WGS) studies). The high coverage of deep WGS sequencing offers the promise of providing the identity and relative abundance of even low-abundance organisms, rather than that of just the most-abundant organisms. Currently, low abundance taxa cannot be studied rigorously, due to lack of effective confidence estimation procedures in taxonomic/gene identification: reads originating from known organisms or gene families can be falsely labeled due to sequencing errors causing techniques to miss their presence all-together; conversely, reads from novel low-abundance organisms or genes can be mistaken as errors. *Therefore, it is important to be able to assign a confidence to the probability of detecting an organism in a sample.*

High coverage also enables the sampling of genetically novel organisms as well as informing how these organisms interact with their environment. However, while ~18000 genomes have been sequenced and their annotation nearly completed, many more—in fact vast majority of—species have not been sequenced. This makes deciphering whether a metagenomic read originates from "novel" organism a formidable task. In fact, due to the pangenome and the flexible definition of a species, strain classification is practically impossible. *A very important open problem is to identify strains by comparing the assigned gene and taxonomic labels to previously-known and annotated data about an environment, and offer suggestions about possible horizontal-gene transfer, genetic modification/evolution, and level of error that might have affected a read.*

Metagenomes are described using thousands of features; features are explanatory variables that represent species, metabolic pathways, orthologous protein groups, protein families or other functional categories. Methods are needed to exclude features whose abundance/expression remains stable over certain physiologies, or those that have little or very indirect impact on physiological changes of interest. *An interesting open problem is to develop a computationally-identifiable set of metagenome features that are predictive of physiologies.* We hypothesize that different metagenomic datasets will require different feature selection methods which makes assumptions about the underlying biology.

When comparing multiple samples, dimensionality reduction techniques are used to visualize the data.

However, due to loss of information from dimension reduction, distortion occurs. In particular, ordination methods suffer from the "arch effect," a mathematical artifact that has no real relationship to community structure (Gauch et al. 1977). It arises because the second ordination axis is constrained to be uncorrelated with the first axis, but is not constrained to be independent of it. To circumvent the arch effect it is necessary to ensure that subsequent axes do not have a systematic relation to the first axis. Detrended correspondence Analysis (DCA) has been developed to address the arch effect, but in turn destroys information in higher axes that could be related to additional environmental gradients (Hill and Gauch 1980). While this technique may be useful for single gradient ordination, the arch effect prohibits the ordination of multiple gradients since axes must be independent in order to be interpreted separately. Given that many communities are structured by multiple gradients the development of corresponding methods is fertile ground for research. Adjacently, the selection of proper ordination techniques given the sampling depth and magnitude of the gradient (effect size) is also an open area of research. It has been shown in simulation that an improper choice of method can lead to erroneous results (Kuczynski et al. 2010). Therefore, analysis of methods for discerning samples that are clustered tightly versus those that are differentiated by a continuum would be most welcome to the field.

Acknowledgments

This work was supported in part by the National Science Foundation (NSF) CAREER award number 0845827, NSF award number 1120622, and Department of Energy (DOE) Office of Science (BER) award DE-SC0004335.

References

Abe, T. et al. (2003). Informatics for unveiling hidden genome signatures. *Genome Res.* **13**:693–702.

Abe, T. et al. (2005). Novel phylogenetic studies of genomic sequence fragments derived from uncultured microbe mixtures in environmental and clinical samples. *DNA Res.* **12**:281–290.

Akhtar, M., Epps, J., and Ambikairajah, E. (2008). Signal processing in sequence analysis: Advances in eukaryotic gene prediction. *IEEE Select. Topics Sig. Proces.* **2**(3):310–321.

Ali, S., and Silvey, S. (1966). A general class of coefficients of divergence of one distribution from another. *J. R. Stat. Soc. B (Methodological)* 131–142.

Altschul, S., Gish, W., Miller, W., Myers, E., and Lipman, D. (1990). Basic local alignment search tool. *J. Mol. Biol.* **215**:403–410.

Andreeva, A., Howorth, D., Chandonia, J.M., Brenner, S.E., Hubbard, T.J., Chothia, C., and Murzin, A.G. (2008) Data growth and its impact on the scop database: new developments, 36 D419–D425. Available: http://www.ncbi.nlm.nih.gov/pubmed/18000004.

Arumugam, M., Raes, J., Pelletier, E., Le Paslier, D., Yamada, T., Mende, D. R., Fernandes, G. R., Tap, J., Bruls, T., Batto, J.-M., et al. (2011). Enterotypes of the human gut microbiome. *Nature* **473**:174–180.

Ashburner, M., Ball, C.A., Blake, J.A., Botstein, D., Butler, H., Cherry, J.M., Davis, A.P., Dolinski, K., Dwight, S.S., Eppig, JT., Harris, M.A., Hill, D.P., Issel-Tarver, L., Kasarskis, A., Lewis, S., Matese, J.C., Richardson, J.E., Ringwald, M., Rubin, G.M., and Sherlock, G. (2000). Gene ontology: tool for the unification of biology. the gene ontology consortium, 25:25–29. Available: http://www.ncbi.nlm.nih.gov/pubmed/1080.

Basseville, M. (1996). FrançaisInformation: entropies, divergences et moyennes. Rapport de recherche PI-1020. Available: http://hal.inria.fr/inria-00490399.

Bateman A., and Haft D.H. (2002). Hmm-based databases in interpro, 3:236–245. Available: http://www.ncbi.nlm.nih.gov/pubmed/12230032.

Bateman, A., Coin, L., Durbin, R., Finn, R., Hollich, V., Griffiths-Johns, S., Khanna, A., Marshall, M., Moxon, S., Sonnhammer, E., Studholme, D., Yeats, C., and Eddy, S. R. (2008). The Pfam protein families database. *Nucleic Acids Res.* **36**:281–288.

Bazinet, A., and Cummings, M. (2012). A comparative evaluation of sequence classification programs. *BMC Bioinformatics*.

Berger, S. A., and Stamatakis, A. (2011). Aligning short reads to reference alignments and trees. *Bioinformatics* **27**(15):2068–2075.

Berger, S. A., Krompass, D., and Stamatakis, A. (2011). Performance, accuracy, and web server for evolutionary placement of short sequence reads under maximum likelihood. *Syst. Biol.* **60**(3):291–302.

Besemer, J., and Borodovsky, M. (1999). Heuristic approach to deriving models for gene finding. *Nucleic Acids Res.* **27**(19):3911–3920. http://dx.doi.org/10.1093/nar/ 27.19.3911.

Bhattacharyya, A. (1943). On a measure of divergence between two statistical populations defined by their probability distributions. *Bull. Calcutta Math. Soc.* **35**:99–109.

Bodaker, I., Sharon, I., Suzuki, M. T., Feingersch, R., Shmoish, M., Andreishcheva, E., Sogin, M. L., Rosenberg, M., Maguire, M. E., Belkin, S., et al. (2009). Comparative community genomics in the dead sea: an increasingly extreme environment. *ISME J.* **4**(3):399–407.

Bowers, R. M., McLetchie, S., Knight, R., and Fierer, N. (2011). Spatial variability in airborne bacterial communities across land-use types and their relationship to the bacterial communities of potential source environments. *ISME J.* **5**:601–612.

Brady, A., and Salzberg, S. (2009). Phymm and Phymmbl: metagenomic phylogenetic classification with interpolated Markov models. *Nat. Methods* **6**(9):673–676.

Brown, G., Pocock, A., Zhao, M.-J., and Luján, M. (2012). Conditional likelihood maximisation: A unifying framework for information theoretic feature selection. *J. Mach. Learn. Res.* **13**:27–66.

Bru, C., Courcelle, E., Carrere, S., Beausse, Y., Dalmar, S., and Kahn, D. (2005). The prodom database of protein domain families: more emphasis on 3d, 33:D212–D215. Available: http://www.ncbi.nlm.nih.gov/pubmed/15608179.

Caporaso, J. G., Lauber, C. L., Costello, E. K., Berg-Lyons, D., Gonzalez, A., Stombaugh, J., Knights, D., Gajer, P., Ravel, J., Fierer, N., Gordon, J. I., and Knight, R. (2011). Moving pictures of the human microbiome. *Genome Biol.* **12**(5).

Caspi, R., Altman, T., Dreher, K., Fulcher, C.A., Subhraveti, P., Keseler, I.M., Kothari, A., Krummenacker, M., Latendresse, M., Mueller, L.A., Ong, Q., Paley, S., Pujar, A., Shearer, A.G., Travers, M., Weerasinghe, D., Zhang,

P., and Karp, P.D. (2012). The metacyc database of metabolic pathways and enzymes and the biocyc collection of pathway/genome databases, 40:D742–D74253. Available: http://www.ncbi.nlm.nih.gov/pubmed/22102576.

Chen, R., Mias, G. I., Li-Pook-Than, J., Jiang, L., Lam, H. Y., Chen, R., Miriami, E., Karczewski, K. J., Hariharan, M., Dewey, F. E., et al. (2012). Personal omics profiling reveals dynamic molecular and medical phenotypes. *Cell* **148**(6):1293–1307.

Clarke, K. (1993). Non-parametric multivariate analyses of changes in community structure. *Aust. J. Ecol.* **18**(1):117–143.

Clarke, K., and Warwick, R. (1994). Change in marine communities: an approach to statistical analysis and interpretation. Plymouth marine laboratory, Natural environment research council.

CLCBio (Last accessed in 2013), http://www.clcbio.com/desktop-applications/features/. [Online]. Available: http://www.clcbio.com/ desktop-applications/features/.

Cock, P. J., Fields, C. J., Goto, N., Heuer, M. L., and Rice, P. M. (2010). The sanger FASTQ file format for sequences with quality scores, and the Solexa/Illumina FASTQ variants. *Nucleic Acids Res.* **38**(6):1767–1771. http://dx.doi.org/10.1093/nar/gkp1137.

Consortium, T. U. (2012). Reorganizing the protein space at the universal protein resource (uniprot). *Nucleic Acids Res.* **40**(D1):D71–D75. http://dx.doi.org/10.1093/nar/gkr981.

Costello, E. K., Lauber, C. L., Hamady, M., Fierer, N., Gordon, J. I., and Knight, R. (2009). Bacterial community variation in human body habitats across space and time. *Science* **326**:1694–1697.

Cox, M., Peterson, D., and Biggs, P. (2010). SolexaQA: At-a-glance quality assessment of Illumina second-generation sequencing data. *BMC Bioinformatics* **11**(1):485+. http://dx.doi.org/10.1186/1471-2105-11-485.

Csiszár, I. (1963). EineinformationstheoretischeUngleichung und ihreanwendung auf den Beweis der ergodizität von MarkoffschenKetten. *Publ. Math. Inst. Hungar. Acad.* **8**:95–108.

DeSantis, T., Hugenholtz, P., Keller, K., Brodie, E., Larsen, N., Piceno, Y., Phan, R., and Andersen, G. (2006). NAST: A multiple sequence alignment server for comparative analysis of 16S rRNA genes. *Nucleic Acids Res.* **34**:W394 –W399.

Deschavanne, P. J., Giron, A., Vilain, J., Fagot, G., and Fertil, B. (1999). Genomic signature: characterization and classification of species assessed by chaos game representation of sequences. *Mol. Biol. Evol.* **16**:1391–1399.

Dethlefsen, L., McFall-Ngai, M., and Relman, D. A. (2007). An ecological and evolutionary perspective on human-microbe mutualism and disease. *Nature* **449**(7164):811–818.

Diaz, N. N., Krause, L., Goesmann, A., Niehaus, K., and Nattkemper, T. W. (2009). TACOA—taxonomic classification of environmental genomic fragments using a kernelized nearest neighbor approach. *BMC Bioinformatics*

Dimmer, E.C., Huntley, R.P., Alam-Faruque, Y., Sawford, T., O'Donovan, C., Martin, M.J., Bely, B., Browne, P., Mun Chan, W., Eberhardt, R., Gardner, M., Laiho, K., Legge, D., Magrane, M., Pichler, K., Poggioli, D., Sehra, H., Auchincloss, A., Axelsen, K., Blatter, M.C., Boutet, E., Braconi-Quintaje, S., Breuza, L., Bridge, A., Coudert, E., Estreicher, A., Famiglietti, L., Ferro-Rojas, S., Feuermann, M., Gos, A., Gruaz-Gumowski, N., Hinz, U., Hulo, C., James, J., Jimenez, S., Jungo, F., Keller, G., Lemercier, P., Lieberherr, D., Masson, P., Moinat, M., Pedruzzi, I., Poux, S., Rivoire, C., Roechert, B., Schneider, M., Stutz, A., Sundaram, S., Tognolli, M., Bougueleret, L., Argoud-Puy, G., Cusin, I., Duek-Roggli, P., Xenarios, I., and Apweiler, R. (2012) The uniprot-go annotation database in 2011, 40:D565–D570. Available: http://www.ncbi.nlm.nih.gov/pubmed/22123736.

Ditzler, G., Polikar, R., Rosen, G. (2012) Forensic identification with environmental samples. In IEEE Intl. Conference on Acoustics, Speech, and, Signal Processing.

Ditzler, G., Polikar, R., Rosen, G. (2012). Information theoretic feature selection for high dimensional metagenomic data. In IEEE Gen. Sig. Proc. and Stat. Workshop (GENSIPS).

Duch, W., Grqbczewski, K., Winiarski, T., Biesiada, J., Kachel, A.(2002). Feature selection based on information theory, consistancy, and separability indices. In International Conference on Neural Information Processing, pp. 1951–1955.

Eddy, S.R. (2009) A new generation of homology search tools based on probabilistic inference, 23:205–211. Available: http://www.ncbi.nlm.nih.gov/pubmed/20180275.

Edgar, R. C. (2010). Search and clustering orders of magnitude faster than BLAST. *Bioinformatics (Oxford, England)* **26**(19):2460–2461. http://dx.doi.org/10.1093/bioinformatics/btq461.

Eisen, J. A. (2007). Environmental shotgun sequencing: Its potential and challenges for studying the hidden world of microbes. *PLoS Biol.* **5**(3).

Evans, S. N., and Matsen, F. A. (2010). The phylogenetic kantorovich-rubinstein metric for environmental sequence samples. *J. R. Stat. Soc.*

Ewing, B., Hillier, L., Wendl, M. C., and Green, P. (1998). Base-calling of automated sequencer traces using phred i accuracy assessment. *Genome Res.* **8**(3):175–185. http://dx.doi.org/10.1101/gr.8.3.175.

Fasham, M. (1977). A comparison of nonmetric multidimensional scaling, principal components and reciprocal averaging for the ordination of simulated coenoclines, and coenoplanes. *Ecology* **58**(3):551–561.

Faust, K., Sathirapongsasuti, J. F., Izard, J., Segata, N., Gevers, D., Raes, J., and Huttenhower, C. (2012). Microbial co-occurrence relationships in the human microbiome. *PLoS Comput. Biol.* **8**(7):e1002606.

Fizzy feature selection tool. (Last accessed in 2013) https://github.com/gditzler/qiime/tree/fizzy.

Fertil, B., Massin, M., Lespinats, S., Devic, C., Dumee, P., and Giron, A. (2005). GENSTYLE: exploration and analysis of DNA sequences with genomic signature. *Nucleic Acids Res.* **33.**

Fierer, N., Lauber, C. L., Zhou, N., McDonald, D., Costello, E. K., and Knight, R. (2010). Forensic identification using skin bacterial communities. *Proc. Nat. Acad. Sci.* **107**(14):6477–6481.

Findley, K., Oh, J., Yang, J., Conlan, S., Deming, C., Meyer, J. A., Schoenfeld, D., Nomicos, E., Park, M., Sequencing, N. I. S. C. C., et al. (2013). Topographic diversity of fungal and bacterial communities in human skin. *Nature* advance online, publication, p. 2013/05/22/online.

Fofanov, Y., Luo, Y., Katili, C., et al. (2004). How independent are the appearances of n-mers in different genomes? *Bioinformatics*.

Gauch, H., Whittaker, R., and Wentworth, T. (1977). A comparative study of reciprocal averaging and other ordination techniques. *J. Ecol.* **65**(1):157–174.

Gerlach, W., and Stoye, J. (2011). Taxonomic classification of metagenomic shotgun sequences with CARMA3. *Nucleic Acids Res.* **39**(14):e91.

Gilbert, J., Meyer, F., and Bailey, M. (2011). The future of microbial metagenomics (or is ignorance bliss?). *ISME J.* **5**:777–779.

Gori, F., Folino, G., Jetten, M., and Marchiori, E. (2011). MTR: taxonomic annotation of short metagenomic reads using clustering at multiple taxonomic ranks. *Bioinformatics* **27**(2):196–203.

Gower, J. (1966). Some distance properties of latent root and vector methods used in multivariate analysis. *Biometrika* **53**(3–4):325–338.

Grice, E. A., Kong, H. H., Conlan, S., Deming, C. B., Davis, J., Young, A. C., Bouffard, G. G., Blakesley, R. W., Murray, P. R., Green, E. D., et al. (2009). Topographical and temporal diversity of the human skin microbiome. *Science* **324**(5931):1190–1192.

Guyon, I., and Elisseeff, A. (2003). An introduction to variable and feature selection. *J. Mach. Learn. Res.* **3**:1157–1182.

Guyon, I., Gunn, S., Nikravesh, M., and Zadeh, L. A. (2006). *Feature Extraction: Foundations and Applications*. Springer.

Haft, D.H., Selengut, J.D., Richter, R.A., Harkins, D., Basu, M.K., and Beck, E. (2013). Tigrfams and genome properties in 2013, 41:D387–D395. Available: http://www.ncbi.nlm.nih.gov/pubmed/23197656.

Handelsman, J. (2007). *Committee on Metagenomics: Challenges and Functional Applications*. The National Academies Press.

Henikoff, S., Henikoff, J.G., and Pietrokovski, S. (1999). Blocks+: a non-redundant database of protein alignment blocks derived from multiple compilations, 15:471–479. Available: http://www.ncbi.nlm.nih.gov/pubmed/10383472.

Hill, M., and Gauch, H. (1980). Detrended correspondence analysis: An improved ordination technique. *Plant Ecol.* **42**(1):47–58.

Horton, M., Bodenhausen, N., and Bergelson, J. (2010). MARTA: a suite of java-based tools for assigning taxonomic status to DNA sequences. *Bioinformatics* **26**(4):568–569.

Hunt, K. M., Foster, J. A., Forney, L. J., Schütte, U. M., Beck, D. L., Abdo, Z., Fox, L. K., Williams, J. E., McGuire, M. K., and McGuire, M. A. (2011). Characterization of the diversity and temporal stability of bacterial communities in human milk. *PLoS One* **6**(6):e21313.

Hunter, E. M., Mills, H. J., and Kostka, J. E. (2006). Microbial community diversity associated with carbon and nitrogen cycling in permeable shelf sediments. *Appl. Environ. Microbiol.* **72**(9):5689–5701.

Huse, S. M., Huber, J. A., Morrison, H. G., Sogin, M. L., and Welch, D. M. M. (2007). Accuracy and quality of massively parallel DNA pyrosequencing. *Genome Biol.* **8**(7):R143+. http://dx.doi.org/10.1186/gb-2007-8-7-r143.

Huson, D. H., Auch, A. F., Qi, J., and Schuster, S. C. (2007). MEGAN analysis of metagenomic data. *Genome Res.* **17**(3):377–386.

Huson, J. H., Mitra, S., Ruscheweyh, H. J., Weber, N., and Schuster, S. C. (2011). Integrative analysis of environmental sequences using megan 4. *Genome Res.* **21**(9):1552–1560.

Hyatt, D., Chen, G.-L.L., Locascio, P. F., Larimer, M. L. L., Larimer, F. W., and Hauser, L. J. (2010). Prodigal: Prokaryotic gene recognition and translation initiation site identification. *BMC Bioinformatics* **11**(1):119+. http://dx.doi.org/10.1186/ 1471-2105-11-119.

Jaccard, P. (1901). *Etude Comparative De La Distribution Floraledansune Portion Des Alpeset Du Jura.* Impr Corbaz.

Jiménez, D. J., Andreote, F. D., Chaves, D., Montaña, J. S., Osorio-Forero, C., Junca, H., Zambrano, M. M., and Baena, S. (2012). Structural and functional insights from the metagenome of an acidic hot spring microbial planktonic community in the colombianandes. *PLoS One* **7**(12):e52069.

Jones, M., Ghoorah, A., and Baxter, M. (2011). JMOTU and Taxonerator: turning DNA barcode sequences into annotated operational taxonomic units. *PLoS One* **6**(4):e19259.

Jongman, R. H., TerBraak, C. J., and van Tongeren, O. F. (1987). *Data Analysis in Community and Landscape Ecology.* Wageningen: Pudoc.

Karlin, S., and Burge, C. (1995). Dinucleotide relative abundance extremes: a genomic signature. *Trends Genet.* **11**:283–290.

Kelley, D. R., and Salzberg, S. L. (2010). Clustering metagenomic sequences with interpolated Markov models. *BMC Bioinformatics* **11**(544).

Kelley, D. R., Schatz, M. C., and Salzberg, S. L. (2010). Quake: quality-aware detection and correction of sequencing errors. *Genome Biol.* **11**(11):R116+. http://dx.doi.org/10.1186/gb-2010-11-11-r116.

Knudsen M., and Wiuf, C., (2010) The cath database, 4:207–212. Available: http://www.ncbi.nlm.nih.gov/pubmed/20368142.

Konstantinidis, K. T., and Tiedje, J. M. (2004). Trends between gene content and genome size in prokaryotic species with larger genomes. *Proc. Natl. Acad. Sci. USA* **101**(9):3160–3165. http://dx.doi.org/10.1073/pnas.0308653100.

Koren, O., Knights, D., Gonzalez, A., Waldron, L., Segata, N., Knight, R., Huttenhower, C., and Ley, R. E. (2013). A guide to enterotypes across the human body: Meta-analysis of microbial community structures in human microbiome datasets. *PLoS Comput. Biol.* **9**(1):e1002863.

Koski, L., and Golding, G. B. (2001). The closest BLAST hit is often not the nearest neighbor. *J. Mol. Evol.* **52**(6):540–542.

Koslicki, D., Foucart, S.,Rosen, G. (in press). Quikr: A method for rapid reconstruction of bacterial communities via compressive sensing, Bioinfomatics.

Kreimer, A., Doron-Faigenboim, A., Borenstein, E., and Freilich, S. (2012). NetCmpt: a network-based tool for calculating the metabolic competition between bacterial species. *Bioinformatics* **28**(16):2195–2197.

Kuczynski, J., Liu, Z., Lozupone, C., McDonald, D., Fierer, N., and Knight, R. (2010). Microbial community resemblance methods differ in their ability to detect biologically relevant patterns. *Nat. Methods* **7**(10):813–821.

Kullback, S. (1997). *Information theory and statistics.* Dover Pubns.

Kuncheva, L.I. (2007). A stability index for feature selection. In International Conference on Artifical Intelligence and Application, pp. 390–395.

Lan, Y., Kriete, A., and Rosen, G. (2013). Selecting age-related functional characteristics in the human gut microbiome. *BMC Microbiome* **1**(1):1–12.

Langmead, B., and Salzberg, S. (2012). Fast gapped-read alignment with Bowtie 2. *Nat. Methods* **9**:357–359.

Legendre, P., and Legendre, L.. In Numerical Ecology, vol. 20. Elsevier.

Letunic, I., Doerks, T., and Bork, P. (2012). Smart 7: recent updates to the protein domain annotation resource. *Nucleic Acids Res.* **40**(D1):D302–D305.http://www.ncbi.nlm.nih.gov/pubmed/22053084.

Leung, H. C. M., Yiu, S., Yang, B., Pend, Y., Wang, Y., Liu, Z., Chen, J., Qin, J., Li, R., and Chin, F. (2011). A robust and accurate binning algorithm for metagenomic sequences with arbitrary species abundance ratio. *Bioinformatics* **27**(11):1489–1495.

Li, W.Z. (2009). Analysis and comparison of very large metagenomes with fast clustering and functional annotation, 10. Available: http://www.ncbi.nlm.nih.gov/pmc/articles/PMC2774329/.

Li, H., and Durbin, R. (2009). Fast and accurate short read alignment with Burrows-Wheeler Transform. *Bioinformatics*(25):1754–1760.

Li, W., and Godzik, A. (2006). Cd-hit: a fast program for clustering and comparing large sets of protein or nucleotide sequences. *Bioinformatics* **22**(13):1658–1659. http://dx.doi.org/10.1093/bioinformatics/ btl158.

Li, W., and Godzik, A. (2006) Cd-hit: a fast program for clustering and comparing large sets of protein or nucleotide sequences, 22:1658–1659. Available: http://www.ncbi.nlm.nih.gov/pubmed/16731699.

Li, R., Yu, C., Li, Y., Lam, T., Yiu, S., Kristiansen, K., and Wang, J. (2009). SOAP2: an improved ultrafast tool for short read alignment. *Bioinfomatics* **25**(15):1966–1967.

Liese, F., and Vajda, I. (2006). On divergences and informations in statistics and information theory. *Inform. Theory IEEE Trans.* **52**(10):4394–4412. http://dx.doi.org/10.1109/TIT.2006.881731.

Lin, J. (1991). Divergence measures based on the Shannon entropy. *IEEE Trans. Inform. Theory* **37**(1):145–151. http://dx.doi.org/10.1109/18.61115.

Liu, B., Gibbons, T., Ghodsi, M., Pop, M. (2010). Metaphyler: Taxonomic profiling for metagenomic sequences. In IEEE BIBM.

Lozupone, C., and Knight, R. (2005). UniFrac: A new phylogenetic method for comparing microbial communities. *Appl. Environ. Microbiol.* **71**(12).

Lozupone, C., Hamady, M., Kelley, S., and Knight, R. (2007). Quantitative and qualitative β diversity measures lead to different insights into factors that structure microbial communities. *Appl. Environ. Microbiol.* **73**(5).

Lukashin, A. V., and Borodovsky, M. (1997). Genemark.hmm: new solutions for gene finding. *Nucleic Acids Res.* **26**(4):1107–1115.

Macdonald, N. J., Parks, D. H., and Beiko, R. G. (2012). RITA: Rapid identification of high-confidence taxonomic assignments for metagenomic data. *Nucleic Acids Res.* http://dx.doi.org/10.1093/nar/gks335.

Markowitz, V.M., Ivanova, N.N., Szeto, E., Palaniappan, K., Chu, K., Dalevi, D., Chen, I.M., Grechkin, Y., Dubchak, I., Anderson, I., Lykidis, A., Mavromatis, K., Hugenholtz, P., and Kyrpides, N.C., Img/m: a data management and analysis system for metagenomes, 36:D534–D5348. Available: http://www.ncbi.nlm.nih.gov/pubmed/17932063.

Martin, J., Sykes, S., Young, S., Kota, K., Sanka, R., Sheth, N., Orvis, J., Sodergren, E., Wang, Z., Weinstock, G. M., and Mitreva, M. (2012). Optimizing read mapping to reference genomes to determine composition and species prevalence in microbial communities. *PLoS One* **7**(6):e36427.

Matsen, F. A., Kodner, R. B., and Armbrust, E. V. (2010). pplacer: linear time maximum-likelihood and Bayesian phylogenetic placement of sequences onto a fixed reference tree. *BMC Bioinformatics* **11**(538).

McCarren, J., Becker, J. W., Repeta, D. J., Shi, Y., Young, C. R., Malmstrom, R. R., Chisholm, S. W., and DeLong, E. F. (2010). Microbial community transcriptomes reveal microbes and metabolic pathways associated with dissolved organic matter turnover in the sea. *Proc. Natl. Acad. Sci. USA* **107**(38):16420–16427.

Meyer, F., Paarmann, D., D'Souza, M., Olson, R., Glass, E. M., Kubal, M., Paczian, T., Rodriguez, A., Stevens, R., Wilke, A., Wilkening, J., and Edwards, R. A. (2008). The metagenomics RAST server—a public resource for the automatic phylogenetic and functional analysis of metagenomes. *BMC Bioinformatics* **9**(386).

Meyer, F., Overbeek, R., and Rodriguez, A. (2009) Figfams: yet another set of protein families, 37:6643–6654. Available: http://www.ncbi.nlm.nih.gov/pubmed/19762480.

Minoche, A., Dohm, J., and Himmelbauer, H. (2011). Evaluation of genomic high-throughput sequencing data generated on illuminaHiSeq and genome analyzer systems. *Genome Biol.* **12**(11):R112+. http://dx.doi.org/10.1186/gb-2011-12-11-r112.

Mohammed, M. H., Ghosh, T. S., Singh, N. K., and Mande, S. S. (2010). SPHINX—an algorithm for taxonomic binning of metagenomic sequences. *Bioinformatics* **27**(1):22–30.

Monzoorul, H. M., Ghosh, T. S., Komanduri, D., and Mande, S. S. (2009). Sort-items: Sequence orthology based approach for improved taxonomic estimation of metagenomic sequences. *Bioinformatics* **25**(14):1722–1730.

Mrázek, S. K. J., and Campbell, A. M. (1997). Compositional biases of bacterial genomes and evolutionary implications. *J. Bacteriol.* **179**:3899–3913.

Mulder, N.J., Apweiler, R., Attwood, T.K., Bairoch, A., Bateman, A., Binns, D., Bork, P., Buillard, V., Cerutti, L., Copley, R., Courcelle, E., Das, U., Daugherty, L., Dibley, M., Finn, R., Fleischmann, W., Gough, J., Haft, D., Hulo, N., Hunter, S., Kahn, D., Kanapin, A., Kejariwal, A., Labarga, A., Langendijk-Genevaux, P.S., Lonsdale, D., Lopez, R., Letunic, I., Madera, M., Maslen, J., McAnulla, C., McDowall, J., Mistry, J., Mitchell, A., Nikolskaya, A.N., Orchard, S., Orengo, C., Petryszak, R., Selengut, J.D., Sigrist, C.J., Thomas, P.D., Valentin, F., Wilson, D., Wu, C.H., and Yeats, C. (2007). New developments in the interpro database, 35:D224–D228. Available: http://www.ncbi.nlm.nih.gov/pubmed/1720.

Munch, K., Boomsma, W., Huelsenbeck, J. P., Willerslev, E., and Nielsen, R. (2008). Statistical assignment of DNA sequences using Bayesian phylogenetics. *Syst Biol.* **57**(5):750–757.

Nakashima, H. et al. (1998). Genes from nine genomes are separated into their organisms in the dinucleotide composition space. *DNA Res.* **5**:251–259.

Nalbantoglu, O. U., Way, S. F., Hinrichs, S. H., and Sayood, K. (2011). RAIphy: Phylogenetic classification of metagenomics samples using iterative refinement of relative abundance index profiles. *BMC Bioinformatics* **12**(1).

Nikolskaya, A.N., Arighi, C.N., Huang, H., Barker, W.C., and Wu, C.H. (2006). Pirsf family classification system for protein functional and evolutionary analysis, 2:197–209. Available: http://www.ncbi.nlm.nih.gov/pubmed/19455212.

Noguchi, H., Taniguchi, T., and Itoh, T. (2008). MetaGeneAnnotator: Detecting species-specific patterns of ribosomal binding site for precise gene prediction in anonymous prokaryotic and phage genomes. *DNA Res.* **15**(6):387–396. http://dx.doi.org/10.1093/dnares/ dsn027.

Ogata, H., Goto,S., Sato, K., Fujibuchi, W., Bono, H., and Kanehisa, M. (1999). Kegg: Kyoto encyclopedia of genes and genomes, 27:29–34. Available: http://www.ncbi.nlm.nih.gov/pubmed/9847135.

Overbeek, R., Begley, T., Butler, R.M., Choudhuri, J.V., Chuang, H.Y., Cohoon, M., de Crecy-Lagard, V., Diaz, N., Disz, T., Edwards, R., Fonstein, M., Frank, E.D., Gerdes, S., Glass, E.M., Goesmann, A., Hanson, A., Iwata-Reuyl, D., Jensen, R., Jamshidi, N., Krause, L., Kubal, M., Larsen, N., Linke, B., McHardy, A.C. Meyer, F., Neuweger, H., Olsen, G., Olson, R., Osterman, A.,Portnoy, V., Pusch, G.D., Rodionov, D.A., Ruckert, C., Steiner, J., Stevens, R., Thiele, I., Vassieva, O., Ye, Y., Zagnitko, O., and Vonstein, V. (2005). The subsystems approach to genome annotation and its use in the project to annotate 1000 genomes, 33:5691–5702. Available: http://www.ncbi.nlm.nih.gov/pubmed/16214803.

Pandit, S.B., Bhadra, R., Gowri, V.S., Balaji, S., Anand, B., and Srinivasan, N. (2004). SUPFAM: a database of sequence superfamilies of protein domains, 5:28. Available: http://www.ncbi.nlm.nih.gov/pubmed/15113407.

Patil, K. R., Haider, P., Pope, P. B., Turnbaugh, P. J., Morrison, M., Scheffer, T., and McHardy, A. C. (2011). Taxonomic metagenome sequence assignment with structured output models. *Nat. Methods* **8**:191–192.

Peng, H., Long, F., and Ding, C. (2005). Feature selection based on mutual information: criteria of max-dependency, max-relevance, and min-redundancy. *IEEE Trans. Pattern Anal. Mach. Intell.* **27**(8):1226–1238.

Powell, S., Szklarczyk, D., Trachana, K., Roth, A., Kuhn, M., Muller, J., Arnold, R., Rattei, T., Letunic, I., Doerks, T., Jensen, L.J., von Mering, C., and Bork, P., (2012). eggnog v3.0: orthologous groups covering 1133 organisms at 41 different taxonomic ranges, 40:D284–D2849. Available: http://www.ncbi.nlm.nih.gov/pubmed/22096231.

Pragman, A. A., Kim, H. B., Reilly, C. S., Wendt, C., and Isaacson, R. E. (2012). The lung microbiome in moderate and severe chronic obstructive pulmonary disease. *PLoS One* **7**(10):e47305.

Price, M. N., Dehal, P. S., and Arkin, A. (2009). Fasttree: computing large minimum evolution trees with profiles instead of a distance matrix. *Mol. Biol. Evol.* **26**(7):1641–1650.

Pride, D., Meinersmann, R. J., Wassenaar, T. M., and Blaser, M. J. (2003). Evolutionary implications of microbial genome tetranucleotide frequency biases. *Genome Res.* **13**:145–158.

Pruitt, K.D., Tatusova, T., and Maglott, D.R. (2007). Ncbi reference sequences (refseq): a curated non-redundant sequence database of genomes, transcripts and proteins 35:D61–D65. Available: http://www.ncbi.nlm.nih.gov/pubmed/17130148.

Punta, M., Coggill, P.C., Eberhardt, R.Y., Mistry, J., Tate, J., Boursnell, C., Pang, N., Forslund, K., Ceric, G., Clements, J., Heger, A., Holm, L., Sonnhammer, E.L., Eddy, S.R., Bateman, A., and Finn, R.D. (2012). The pfam protein families database, 40:D290–D301. Available: http://www.ncbi.nlm.nih.gov/pubmed/22127870.

Raes, J., Foerstner, K. U., and Bork, P. (2007). Get the most out of your metagenome: computational analysis of environmental sequence data. *Curr. Opin. Microbiol.* **10**:1–9.

Reumers, J., Rijk, P. D., Zhao, H., Liekens, A., and Smeets, D. (2012). Optimized filtering reduces the error rate in detecting genomic variants by short-read sequencing. *Nat. Biotechnol.* **30**:61–68.

Rho, M., Tang, H., and Ye, Y. (2010). FragGeneScan: predicting genes in short and error-prone reads. *Nucleic Acids Res.* **38**(20):e191. http://dx.doi.org/10.1093/nar/ gkq747.

Rocap, G., Larimer, F. W., Lamerdin, J., Malfatti, S., Chain, P., Ahlgren, N. A., Arellano, A., Coleman, M., Hauser, L., Hess, W. R., et al. (2003). Genome divergence in two prochlorococcus ecotypes reflects oceanic niche differentiation. *Nature* **424**(6952):1042–1047.

Rose, P.W., Bi, C., Bluhm, W.F., Christie, C.H., Dimitropoulos, D., Dutta, S., Green, R.K., Goodsell, D.S., Prlic, A., Quesada, M., Quinn, G.B., Ramos, A.G., Westbrook, J.D., Young, J., Zardecki, C., Berman, H.M., and Bourne, P.E. (2013). The rcsb protein data bank: new resources for research and education, 41:D475–D482. Available: http://www.ncbi.nlm.nih.gov/pubmed/23193259.

Rosen, G. L. (2006). Examining coding structure and redundancy in DNA. *IEEE Eng. Med. Biol. Mag.* **Special Issue on Communication Theory, Coding Theory, and, Molecular Biology**:62–68.

Rosen, G., and Lim, T. Y. (2012). NBC update: The addition of viral and fungal databases to the nave bayes classification tool. *BMC Res. Notes.*

Rosen, G. L., Reichenberger, E. R., and Rosenfeld, A. M. (2011). NBC: the nave bayes classification tool webserver for taxonomic classification of metagenomic reads. *Bioinfomatics* **27**(1):127–129.

Rousk, J., Bååth, E., Brookes, P. C., Lauber, C. L., Lozupone, C., Caporaso, J. G., Knight, R., and Fierer, N. (2010). Soil bacterial and fungal communities across a pH gradient in an arable soil. *ISME J.* **4**:1340–1351.

Saeys, Y., Inza, I., and Larra naga, P. (2007). A review of feature selection techniques in bioinformatics. *Oxford Bioinformatics* **23**(19):2507–2517.

Salzberg, S. L., Delcher, A. L., Kasif, S., and White, O. (1998). Microbial gene identification using interpolated Markov models. *Nucleic Acids Res.* **26**(2):544–548. http://dx.doi.org/10.1093/nar/ 26.2.544.

Sandberg, R., Winberg, G., Bränden, C.-I., Kaske, A., Ernberg, I., and Cöster, J. (2001). Capturing whole-genome characteristics in short sequences using a nave Bäyesian classifier. *Genome Res.* **11**(8):1404–1409.

Sayers, E.W., Barrett, T., Benson, D.A., Bolton, E., Bryant, S.H., Canese, K., Chetvernin, V., Church, D.M., Dicuccio, M., Federhen, S., Feolo, M., Fingerman, I.M., Geer, L.Y., Helmberg, W., Kapustin, Y., Krasnov, S., Landsman, D., Lipman, D.J., Lu, Z., Madden, T.L., Madej, T., Maglott, D.R., Marchler-Bauer, A., Miller, V., Karsch-Mizrachi, I., Ostell, J., Panchenko, A., Phan, L., Pruitt, K.D., Schuler, G.D., Sequeira, E., Sherry, S.T., Shumway, M., Sirotkin, K., Slotta, D., Souvorov, A., Starchenko, G., Tatusova, T.A., Wagner, L., Wang, Y., Wilbur, W.J., Yaschenko, E., and Ye, J. (2012) Database resources of the national center for biotechnology information, 40:D13–D25. Available: http://www.ncbi.nlm.nih.gov/pubmed/2214.

Schreiber, F., Gumrich, P., Daniel, R., and Meinicke, P. (2010). Treephyler: fast taxonomic profiling of metagenomes. *Bioinformatics (Oxford, England)* **26**(7):960–961.

Segata, N., Waldron, L., Ballarini, A., Narasimhan, V., Jousson, O., and Huttenhower, C. (2012). Metagenomic microbial community profiling using unique clade-specific marker genes. *Nat. Methods.*

Sigrist, C.J., de Castro, E., Cerutti, L., Cuche, B.A., Hulo, N., Bridge, A., Bougueleret, L., and Xenarios, I. (2013). New and continuing developments at prosite, 41:D344–D3447. Available: http://www.ncbi.nlm.nih.gov/pubmed/23161676.

SMALT(Last accessed in 2013), http://www.sanger.ac.uk/resources/software/smalt/. [Online]. Available: http://www.sanger.ac.uk/resources/software/smalt/.

Stark, M., Berger, S. A., Stamatakis, A., and von Mering, C. (2010). MLTreeMap—accurate maximum likelihood placement of environmental DNA sequences into taxonomic and functional reference phylogenies. *BMC Genomics* **11**(461).

Stranneheim, H., Kaller, M., Allander, T., Andersson, B., Arvestad, L., and Lundeberg, J. (2010). Classification of DNA sequences using bloom filters. *Bioinformatics* **26**(13):1595–1600.

Stressmann, F. A., Rogers, G. B., van der Gast, C. J., Marsh, P., Vermeer, L. S., Carroll, M. P., Hoffman, L., Daniels, T. W., Patel, N., Forbes, B., et al. (2012). Long-term cultivation-independent microbial diversity analysis demonstrates that bacterial communities infecting the adult cystic fibrosis lung show stability and resilience. *Thorax* **67**(10):867–873.

Tatusov, R.L., Fedorova, N.D., Jackson, J.D., Jacobs, A.R., Kiryutin, B., Koonin, E.V., Krylov, D.M., Mazumder, R., Mekhedov, S.L., Nikolskaya, A.N., Rao, B.S., Smirnov, S., Sverdlov, A.V., Vasudevan, S., Wolf, Y.I., Yin, J.J., and Natale, D.A. (2003). The cog database: an updated version includes eukaryotes, 4:41. Available: http://www.ncbi.nlm.nih.gov/pubmed/12969510.

Teeling, H., Waldmann, J., Lombardot, T., Bauer, M., and Glockner, F. O. (2004). Tetra: a web-service and a stand-alone program for the analysis and comparison of tetranucleotide usage patterns in DNA sequences. *BMC Bioinformatics* **5**(163).

TerBraak, C. J., and Prentice, I. C. (2004). A theory of gradient analysis. *Adv. Ecol. Res.* **34**:235–282.

Valdivia-Granda, W. (2008). The next meta-challenge for bioinformatics. *Bioinformation* **2**(8):358–362.

van Elsas, J. D., Chiurazzi, M., Mallon, C. A., Elhottovā, D., Krištufek, V., and Salles, J. F. (2012). Microbial diversity determines the invasion of soil by a bacterial pathogen. *Proc. Nat. Acad. Sci.* **109**(4):1159–1164.

Varin, T., Lovejoy, C., Jungblut, A. D., Vincent, W. F., and Corbeil, J. (2012). Metagenomic analysis of stress genes in microbial mat communities from antarctica and the high arctic. *Appl. Environ. Microbiol.* **78**(2):549–559.

Vinga, S., and Almeida, J. (2003). Alignment-free sequence comparison—a review. *Bioinformatics* **19**(4):513–523. http://dx.doi.org/10.1093/bioinformatics/btg005.

Wang, Q., Garrity, G., Tiedje, J. M., and Cole, J. (2007). Nave Bäyes classifier for rapid assignment of rRNA sequences into the new bacterial taxonomy. *Appl. Environ. Microbiol.* 5261–5267.

Wilke, A., Harrison, T., Wilkening, J., Field, D., Glass, E. M., Kyrpides, N., Mavrommatis, K., and Meyer, F. (2012). The M5nr: a novel non-redundant database containing protein sequences and annotations from multiple sources and associated tools. *BMC Bioinformatics* **13**(1):141.http://www.ncbi.nlm.nih.gov/pubmed/22720753.

Wilkening, J., Wilke, A., Desai, N., and Meyer. F. (2009). Using clouds for metagenomics: a case study. In IEEE International Conference on Cluster Computing (Cluster 2009), Aug 31–Sep 04, 2009 New Orleans, LA. IEEE, pp. 1–6. http://dx.doi.org/10.1109/CLUSTR.2009.5289187.

Williamson, S., Rusch, D., Yooseph, S., Halpern, A., Heidelberg, K., Glass, J., Andrews-Pfannkoch, C., Fadrosh, D., Miller, C., Sutton, G., Frazier, M., and Venter, J. C. (2008). The Sorcerer II global ocean sampling expedition: Metagenomic characterization of viruses within aquatic microbial samples. *PLoS Biol.*(1).

Wu, M., and Eisen, J. A. (2008). A simple, fast, and accurate method of phylogenomic inference. *Genome Biol.* **9**(10):R151.

Xiao, X., Dow, E.R., Eberhart, R., Miled, Z.B., Oppelt, R.J. (2003). Gene clustering using self-organizing maps and particle swarm optimization. In International Parallel and Distributed Processing, Symposium.

Zhu, W., Lomsadze, A., and Borodovsky, M. (2010). Ab initio gene identification in metagenomic sequences. *Nucleic Acids Res.* **38**(12):e132. http://dx.doi.org/10.1093/ nar/gkq275.

CHAPTER

15

Systems Biology of Infectious Diseases and Vaccines

Helder I Nakaya[a,b,c]

[a]Department of Pathology, Emory University, Atlanta, GA, USA
[b]Vaccine Research Center, Emory University, Atlanta, GA, USA
[c]Department of Clinical Analyses and Toxicology, University of Sao Paulo, Sao Paulo, SP, Brazil

CONTENTS

Abstract

Pathogens and vaccines stimulate the immune system through an intricate and elaborate network of specialized cells and organs. Immune activation triggers several biological activities that require spatial and dynamic coordination. These activities range from recognition of pathogen-derived factors to cell intercommunication to cell differentiation. Systems biology approaches provide a comprehensive way of dissecting the complex interactions within these processes, and can lead to a better understanding of vaccine-induced immunity and disease pathogenesis. In recent years, systems biology has been successfully applied in analyzing the immune response to a wide range of vaccines and infectious agents. However, dealing with the large amount of data generated from high-throughput techniques and the inherent complexity of the immune system represent major computational and biological challenges. This chapter highlights the recent technological and methodological advances in the field and shows how systems biology can be applied to unraveling novel insights into the molecular mechanisms of immunity.

http://dx.doi.org/10.1016/B978-0-12-405926-9.00015-0

1 INTRODUCTION

The immune system is a complex defense system whose main function is to provide immunity, which is the body's protection from infection and disease. To achieve this, the immune system utilizes a vast number of cell types, each having a specialized role in recognizing and eliminating foreign pathogenic invaders. Although a great number of pathogens are naturally eliminated by the immune system, some evade the host defenses and proliferate, establishing infection that may result in hospitalization and death. In immunocompromised populations, non-pathogenic microorganisms can also result in severe infection. It is how the immune cells respond and interact with each other and the pathogens that determine the disease outcome. So far, very little is known about the dynamic network of cells and molecules behind such responses. Similarly, we have a limited knowledge of the molecular mechanisms that mediate vaccine-induced immunity. Despite their undisputed successes, most vaccines were designed empirically, with the gene networks and pathways associated to immunity remaining largely unknown (Nakaya et al. 2012).

Major technological breakthroughs of high-throughput technologies now allow scientists to study entire genomes, sets of transcripts (transcriptome), proteins (proteome), and metabolites (metabolome) of cells and tissues (Nakaya et al. 2012). As these technologies become more accessible and cost-efficient, their use has expanded, creating a unique opportunity for scientists to profile immune responses of large cohorts and in clinical trials (Chaussabel et al. 2010). Systems biology utilizes the enormous amount of data generated by these techniques to describe the complex interactions between all the parts of a biological system under different types of perturbations, and to construct mathematical models to predict the behavior of the system (Ideker et al. 2001; Kitano 2002). This powerful approach promises to revolutionize our understanding of biological systems.

The application of systems biology to vaccinology and infectious disease may potentially fill many fundamental gaps in basic immunology, as well as enable the rational design and testing of novel vaccines (Nakaya et al. 2012). Also, the exploration of the interconnected networks that control and drive the immune response to infection may shed some light on the understanding of infectious diseases (Casadevall and Pirofski 2003) and identify therapeutic targets and improve clinical outcomes (Aderem et al. 2011). However, the inherent complexity of immune system and the technical difficulties associated with the computational analyses of large datasets imposes great challenges for the field. In this chapter I describes how systems biology is re-shaping the study of immune responses and the many challenges associated with this exciting enterprise.

2 A BRIEF OVERVIEW OF THE IMMUNE RESPONSE

The capacity to respond to as well as to clear and/or control an invading pathogen is the primary goal of the immune system. This is achieved by two different but complementary arms: the innate immune system, which quickly (few hours to few days) recognizes and responds to pathogens, and the adaptive immune system, which is responsible for mounting a late response, but one that can persists for years (memory). Both arms form a remarkably versatile defense system (Kuby et al. 2002) that involves a myriad of cells and molecules that act together in a dynamic and complex fashion. This section provides a simplified description of the main effectors of immune responses.

The recognition of a pathogen by specialized cells can trigger a broad range of effector responses, each uniquely suited to eliminate a particular type of pathogen (Kuby et al. 2002). More importantly, if a memory response is induced, a later exposure to the same pathogen will result in a rapid resolution by the immune system, eliminating the pathogen and preventing disease (Kuby et al. 2002). Vaccines attempt to mimic these naturally induced memory responses (or immunity) by exposing the immune system to altered forms of a pathogen or components of a pathogen which does not cause disease. Since adaptive immunity is contingent upon an effective innate immune response, a successful vaccine must be able to induce both arms of immune responses.

In addition to anatomic and humoral barriers, the innate immune system utilizes a great variety of specialized cells and complex biological processes. Neutrophils and macrophages are able to engulf and kill certain types of pathogens, whereas Natural Killer (NK) cells can non-specifically kill cells that have been infected by viruses. Dendritic cells can process and present antigens (i.e., foreign substances that evoke the production of antibodies) to cells of the adaptive immune system. All these processes involve an intricate number of chemical molecules (RNAs, proteins, metabolites) being produced, released, and detected by these innate cells. Among the soluble products of innate immunity, we can cite many cytokines and chemokines, as well as antimicrobial peptides and complement fragments.

Adaptive immunity protects the body against infection with antibodies and T cells. Antibodies (or immunoglobulins) are proteins produced and secreted by B cells, which can bind to antigens on invading pathogens. This interaction can directly inactivate the pathogen or activate a variety of inflammatory mediators that will destroy the pathogen (Rote 2009). T cells, during an immune response, can differentiate into several subpopulations of effector T cells that have an effect on many other cells (Rote 2009). Cytotoxic T cells (usually expressing the surface protein CD8) will attack and kill cells infected by viruses. T helper cells, which express the protein CD4 on their surface upon maturation, can stimulate the activities of other leukocytes through cell-to-cell contact or through the secretion of cytokines (Rote 2009). Thus, the appropriate interactions between T and B cells and the functions of both types of responses are critical for the success of an acquired immune response (Rote 2009).

The main effectors of vaccine response are becoming gradually unveiled in the last decades. Figure 15.1 summarizes the major events that may be involved in this response. Upon exposure to antigen, cells from the innate immune system, such as immature dendritic cells (DCs) and monocytes become activated and migrate to lymph nodes. During this migration, these antigen presenting cells process the antigen into small peptides and display them at the cell surface to B, CD4+ T, and CD8+ T cells. DC-activated CD4+ T cells can differentiate into mutually exclusive differentiation pathways (Figure 15.1). T helper type 1 (Th1) CD4+ T cells support CD8+ T cell activation and can also participates in the elimination of intracellular pathogens. T helper type 2 (Th2) CD4+ T cells (and Th1 cells) support B cell activation and differentiation into short-live antibody secreting plasma cells (plasmablasts), whereas follicular CD4+ helper T cells (Tfh) and follicular DCs (fDC) provide help to germinal center (GC) B cells. Vaccines may instead elicit regulatory CD4+ CD25+ T cells (Treg). DCs that capture antigen in the absence of "danger" signals remain immature in their migration to lymph nodes, inducing naïve T cells to differentiate into Tregs and not effector T cells. These Tregs can suppress Th1 and Th2 responses. CD8+ T cells activated by DCs become cytotoxic T cells which are capable of killing infected cells or pathogens. These cytotoxic T cells can differentiate into two types of memory T cells: effector memory T cells or central memory T cells. If the latter cells recognize antigens transported by activated DCs, they can quickly proliferate and differentiate into the former cells. Vaccine antigen-specific B cells when activated by DCs and CD4+ T cells rapidly differentiate into plasmablasts. If sufficient help from antigen-specific T cells is received, the B cells proliferate in the

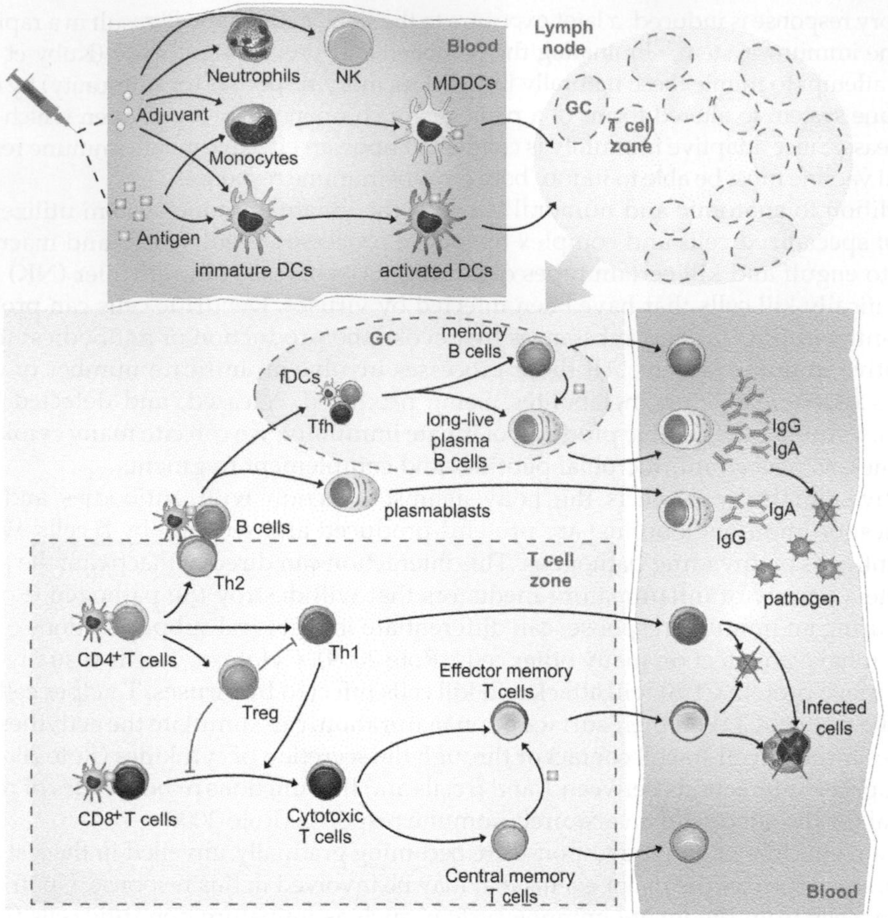

FIGURE 15.1 Main effectors of vaccine response. Vaccine-induced immune effectors include antibodies, produced by B lymphocytes, and cytotoxic CD8+ T lymphocytes. The generation and maintenance of specific B and CD8+ T cell responses is supported by CD4+ T helper lymphocytes. Cells from the innate immune system, such as dendritic cells and monocytes play a pivotal role in regulating the quantity, quality, and longevity of the adaptive immune response induced by the vaccine. DC, dendritic cell; fDC, follicular dendritic cells; Tfh, follicular CD4+ helper T cells; Treg, regulatory CD4+ CD25+ T cells; NK, natural killer cells; GC, germinal center.

germinal centers and can differentiate into memory or long-live antibody secreting plasma B cells. The secreted antibodies (mostly IgG and IgA) can neutralize the pathogen and protect the body from infection if their affinity (quality) and abundance (titers) are sufficiently high and sustained on mucosal surfaces (Figure 15.1). Finally, adjuvants play their role by stimulating different innate immune cells, improving the potency of the immune response to co-administered antigens (Kwissa et al. 2007).

Although the main cellular players of immune responses have been identified, the genetic and signaling programs that control their differentiation, activation status, proliferation, or death are poorly characterized. For instance, which genes should be activated in plasma B cells to increase the quality and quantity of antibodies? What is the genetic program of activated DCs that will contribute to a strong CD8+ cytotoxic T cell response? Which genes determine the fate of CD4+ T cells after its contact with activated DCs? The road for answering these questions remains long but systems biology can increase our pace toward discovery.

3 SYSTEMS IMMUNOLOGY TOOLS AND DATABASES

3.1 The arsenal of modern immunologists

Conventional immunology and reductionist methods of cellular and molecular biology have identified most of the known components of the immune system (Ricciardi-Castagnoli and Granucci 2002). Methods such as ELISA (Enzyme-linked immunosorbent assay), flow-cytometry, and real-time quantitative PCR are still invaluable in describing and analyzing specific cell subsets, proteins, or genes during an immune response. However, they have limited power when it comes to analyzing several features of a system in parallel, and focus instead on parts of the immune system rather than the whole (Nakaya et al. 2012). A more holistic biological approach is required in order to reassemble these parts and their connections and dynamics during an immune response.

With the revolution in nanotechnology, robotics, optics, and electronics, immunologists have now an arsenal of high-throughput technologies at their disposal. A wide range of molecular and cellular profiling assays, such as next-generation sequencing, CyTOF® and Luminex®, are easily accessible to laboratories investigating human health and disease. Global changes in metabolites or protein levels are assessed by mass spectrometry and nuclear magnetic resonance. Even the phosphorylation state of intracellular proteins, which is an important regulator of signal transduction pathways, can also be measured through phospho-specific flow cytometry. This method named phospho flow has been successfully applied to the characterization of signaling pathways after a microbial challenge and after antigenic stimulation (Hotson et al. 2009; Krutzik et al. 2005).

Among the so-called 'omics' technologies, DNA microarrays are still the preferable high-throughput screening tool for most systems immunologists (Haining and Wherry 2010). Representing thousands of distinct genes or genomic regions, microarrays can be used to profile a wide range of cellular and molecular processes: gene transcription, alternative splicing, DNA methylation, single-nucleotide polymorphisms (SNPs), proteins binding to DNA– and RNA–elements (ChIP-on-chip), microRNA and noncoding RNA transcription and genomic copy number variations. In addition to its flexibility, the availability of many easy-to-use analytical software and programs, allied to its relative low cost, DNA microarrays are being vastly applied in immunology, from measuring the global transcriptional changes of dendritic cell during differentiation (Le Naour et al. 2001) to assessing the global changes in STAT-target genes upon interferon treatments (Hartman et al. 2005). Many more examples can be found investigating the global expression changes of genes and microRNAs during infection (Jenner and Young 2005; Zeiner et al. 2010) or after vaccination (Gaucher et al. 2008; Nakaya et al. 2011; Querec et al. 2009).

The analysis of genomes (DNA-seq) and DNA elements (ChIP-seq), as well as transcriptomes (RNA-seq) and gene regulatory networks can also be achieved through next-generation sequencing technologies (Zak and Aderem 2009). This powerful approach generates millions of sequence reads per run and is able to measure the transcriptome of cells with high genome

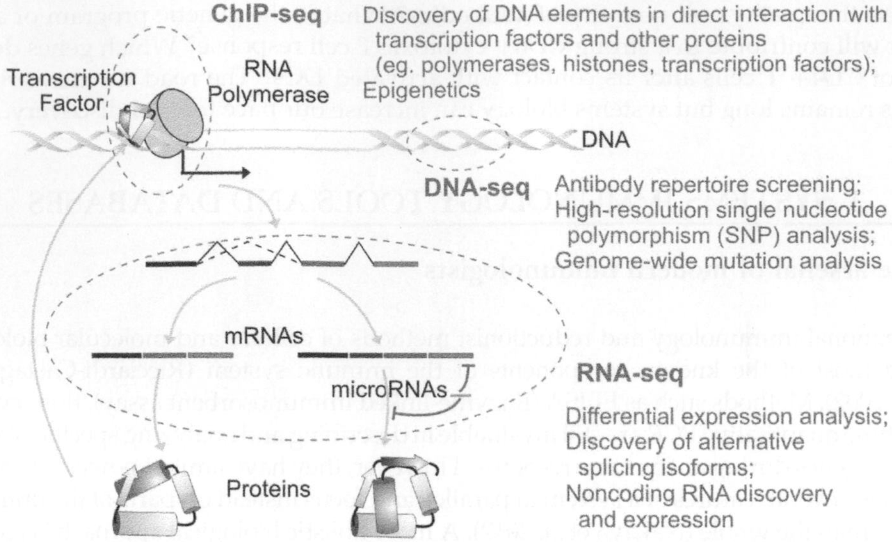

FIGURE 15.2 Applications of next-generation sequencing technology to study immune responses. Next-generation sequencing techniques can be used to analyze genomes or DNA (DNA-seq), DNA elements (ChIP-seq), and transcriptomes (RNA-seq) in the context of immune regulation.

coverage. As the cost of next-generation sequencing goes down, it will potentially replace hybridization-based technologies such as DNA microarrays (Nakaya et al. 2012). Next-generation sequencing has many potential applications for studying immune responses (Figure 15.2). For example, RNA-seq experiments revealed that RIG-I, a key player in the recognition of RNA viruses, preferentially associates with shorter viral RNA molecules in infected cells (Baum et al. 2010), or that long noncoding RNAs are differentially induced during the course of viral (Peng et al. 2010). A variation of RNA-seq method, called genome-wide nuclear 'run-on' analysis (GRO-seq), and chromatin immunoprecipitation combined with next-generation sequencing (ChIP-seq) were used to determine the impact of the Influenza virus NS1 gene on the dynamics of host gene transcription, demonstrating how the H3N2 influenza A virus interferes with antiviral gene expression by exploiting the very basic principles of the epigenetic control of gene regulation (Marazzi et al. 2012). And finally, DNA-seq can be used to characterize natural antibody repertoires induced by infection or vaccination, and may significantly improve antibody discovery (Fischer 2011).

At the cellular level, two-photon microscopy is the method that best captures the dynamic nature of how the cells behave in their native environment (Bullen et al. 2009). This technology allows the real–time visualization of immune cells during differentiation, migration, death, and interactions with other cells and microbes, and has shed important light on T cell development, antigen recognition, cell trafficking, and effector functions (Mirsky et al. 2011). The integration of cellular behavior data with the molecular data generated by microarrays and high-throughput sequencing technologies may have a huge impact on identifying the functional regulatory circuits associated to maturation, survival, and pathogen-recognition of immune cells.

A novel single cell detection technology, named cytometry by time-of-flight, or CyTOF®, promises to revolutionize the field. This technique is much more powerful than the Fluorescence Activated Cell Sorting (FACS) tool because it allows simultaneous measurement of up to 100 surface markers and signaling proteins of immune cells (Bendall et al. 2011). It employs antibodies labeled with transition element isotopes and a time-of-flight mass spectrometer. By analyzing the expression of many more surface markers and cytokines, Newell et al were able to observe an intriguingly diverging phenotypes in $CD8^+$ T cell populations (Newell et al. 2012).

Genome-wide RNA interference-based screening represents one of the most powerful approaches of functional genomics. It generally utilizes small interfering RNA (siRNA) libraries constructed in 96/384-well plates where, on each well, a single gene should be silenced. Cells are then exposed to the same conditions (e.g. virus infection) and distributed on the plates. The effect of knocking down the expression of these genes on a given cellular process is evaluated by a subsequent screening readout (Houzet and Jeang 2011). This method was successfully applied to identify cellular factors implicated in HIV replication (Konig et al. 2008; Brass et al. 2008; Zhou et al. 2008), as well as influenza virus replication (Konig et al. 2010; Karlas et al. 2010).

New high-throughput multiplex immunoassays, such as antibody microarrays, are available for diagnostic discovery, biomarker-assisted drug development, or "simply" quantitative proteomics studies (Kingsmore 2006). In addition to common proteomics and metabolomics technologies that rely on quantitative mass spectrometry, antibody microarrays consist of ordered, immobilized capture antibodies paired with mixtures of detector antibody that allows highly parallel measurement of protein levels (Kingsmore and Patel 2003). This sensitive protein microarray technique that incorporated rolling-circle amplification technology was used to elucidate the cytokine response signature of systemic adverse events following smallpox immunization (McKinney et al. 2006).

3.2 Databases

Fortunately, the enormous amount of information derived from both reductionist and holistic approaches is being systematically deposited into public databases. More than simply data repositories, most of the databases are excellent tools for data mining and functional analysis. Certain databases contain a broad range of immune-related data, from gene expression data of macrophages to 3D protein structures of influenza viruses; some of them are summarized in Table 15.1.

Equally broad are the many applications of such databases to systems biology analyses. When available, high-quality data can be downloaded from the databases and used on a particular analysis or meta-analysis. For example, the comprehensive information on gene functions, manually curated pathways and transcription factor and microRNA regulation can be extremely useful for interpreting the findings of large–scale analyses. Additionally, gene expression and co-expression data of specific cell types under different conditions or the experimentally validated interactome (protein–protein, protein–DNA, microRNA–RNA) data can be a valuable resource for network analysis and pathway enrichment analysis. Also, many of these databases include data of animal models and *in vitro* experiments facilitating the design and translation to functional validation experiments.

The InnateDB (http://www.innatedb.com) represents a state-of-the-art platform that can facilitate systems-level analyses of mammalian innate immunity. It contains publicly available data of genes, proteins, networks, and signaling pathways involved in the innate immune response of mammals to microbial infection (Lynn et al. 2008). To date, the InnateDB team has

TABLE 15.1 Immunological databases and tools.

Name	Purpose	Data type	Reference or website
Macrophages.com	Macrophage biology	*GE; P; NET*	http://www.macrophages.com
DC-ATLAS	Dendritic cell biology	*GE; NET*	http://www.dc-atlas.net/
Immunome	Genes and proteins of the human immune system	*PD; GF*	http://bioinf.uta.fi/Immunome
Innate Immune Database (IIDB)	Genes and proteins of the mouse immune system	*GF; NET; GR*	http://www.innateimmunity-systemsbiology.org/
Immunological Genome Project	Gene expression data of well-defined cell types	*GE; NET; GR*	http://www.immgen.org/
Influenza Research Database	Resource for the influenza virus research community	*S; PD*	http://www.fludb.org
SystemsInfluenza.org	Immune system response and interaction with the influenza virus	*GE; I*	http://www.systemsinfluenza.org/
InnateDB	Innate immune response to infection	*GF; NET; I*	http://www.innatedb.com
Systems Virology Center	Molecular processes related to progression of infectious diseases	*GE; P*	https://www.systemsvirology.org
TB Database	Integrated platform for Tuberculosis research	*GF; GE; NET; P*	http://www.tbdb.org/
miR2Disease	miRNA deregulation in various human diseases	*miR*	http://www.mir2disease.org/
ImmunoDeficiency Resource	Compendium of information on the immunodeficiencies	*GF*	http://bioinf.uta.fi/idr/
IMGT	Sequence data of immune-related genes	*PD; S*	http://www.imgt.org/
Interferome	Interferon regulated genes	*GE; GF; GR; S*	http://www.interferome.org/
LymphTF DB	B and T Lymphocyte Transcription Factor Activity in Mouse	*GR*	http://www.iupui.edu/~tfinterx/
ImmPort	Data warehouse of immunological data	*GE; GF;*	https://immport.niaid.nih.gov
PHISTO	Comprehensive pathogen-human protein-protein interaction	*I*	http://www.phisto.org

GE = Gene expression data; P = Protein level data; NET = Pathways, gene networks and co-expressed genes data; PD = Protein domains and 3D structures; GF = Gene annotation or function; GR = Gene regulation data; S = sequence data; I = Interactome data; miR = micro RNA data.

manually curated more than 18 thousands molecular interactions related to innate immunity, and more recently to allergy and asthma. The platform can also be used as a tool for Gene Ontology analysis, network visualization, and Transcription Factor Binding Site analysis.

Another benchmark platform for systems immunology analyses was developed by the Immunological Genome Project team (http://www.immgen.org/). The database contains a large collection of gene expression profiles of well-defined cell types in different states of differentiation, maturation, and activation responses. This huge amount of information (publicly available for downloading) supports the computational reconstruction of the genetic circuitries underlying several immune-related processes and can be used to reveal the gene signatures of specific immune cell populations. The platform also contains user-friendly tools for generating interactive heatmaps of gene families, displaying gene modules of coregulated genes, visualization of RNA-seq data of two cell lineages, and for revealing the differences in gene expression between different cell populations.

4 BLOOD TRANSCRIPTOMICS

Blood is the main channel for migration and trafficking of immune cells between lymphoid organs and other sites of the body, and therefore provides a comprehensive view of the status of the immune system in health and disease (Chaussabel et al. 2010). In addition, blood can be extracted, stored and processed easily, making it one of the most favorable tissues for studying human immunity at the systems-level. To date, hundreds of blood transcriptomic experiments were performed and many more are underway. However, due to its inherent heterogeneity, the analysis of gene expression data from blood is challenging.

A common dilemma when designing blood transcriptomic studies involves the choice of sample types to be screened (Nakaya and Pulendran 2012). Blood (e.g. whole blood or peripheral blood mononuclear cells, PBMCs) is composed of multiple cell lineages in different states of activation and differentiation (Pulendran et al. 2010). In response to a stimulus (e.g. infection or vaccination), different cell subsets can proliferate, migrate, and die in a dynamic and interdependent fashion. Therefore, transcriptional profiling of this mixed population tissue will capture the changes of both cellular and transcript abundance, making results difficult to interpret (Chaussabel et al. 2010). An alternative solution would be to measure the transcriptome of isolated cell subsets, which can provide valuable mechanistic insights of specific cells (Nakaya et al. 2011; Grigoryev et al. 2010). Notwithstanding, the high cost and great amount of work associated with isolating and screening cell subsets make this approach unpractical and prohibitive to most clinical studies (Nakaya and Pulendran 2012).

Deconvolution methods can offer a good solution to deal with the cell-type composition problem of blood samples. They can be applied to accurately quantify the constituents of blood samples (Abbas et al. 2009) or, when cell subset frequency is known, to identify subset-specific differential expression (Shen-Orr et al. 2010). In order to quantify the proportions of cells in blood, the expression signatures of each immune cell subset must be known. Assuming that the expression of genes in a given sample can be modeled as a linear combination of the expression of those genes in each of the cells in the sample, linear equations can then be used to fit the fractions of cell subsets to the whole blood sample's expression (Lu et al. 2003). Gene signatures of immune cell subsets were collected or analyzed by many groups and can be used to deconvolute blood transcriptomic data (Abbas et al. 2005; Palmer et al. 2006; Miller et al. 2012; Shaffer et al. 2001). The second deconvolution method requires known or estimated frequencies of cell types in order to perform cell type–specific differential expression analysis

(Shen-Orr et al. 2010). Two caveats of these methods are that (1) the immune cell types are ambiguously defined, and (2) flow cytometry data and microarray expression were shown to be poorly correlated (Hyatt et al. 2006).

Other methods developed to analyze blood microarray data compare blood signatures to previously defined gene sets or modules of particular a cell type (Nakaya et al. 2011; Berry et al. 2010; Chaussabel et al. 2008). Transcriptional modules defined by genes coordinately expressed in multiple blood transcriptomic studies were successfully used to classify disease activity (Berry et al. 2010; Chaussabel et al. 2008). Using an alternative approach, our group first identified the gene signatures of the main peripheral blood mononuclear cells (i.e. monocytes, myeloid dendritic cells, plasmacytoid dendritic cells, B cells, T cells, and NK cells) and then compared these immune signatures to the genes identified in our blood transcriptomics analysis in order to find significant enrichment of specific cell types (Nakaya et al. 2011). Another computational method, developed by Bolen et al. (2011) attempts to predict the most likely cellular source for a predefined gene expression signature using only the transcriptional profiling data from total PBMCs.

5 SYSTEMS BIOLOGY OF INFECTIOUS DISEASES

Investigating the complex interactions and changes that occur during infection or exposure to a pathogen can help us answer many questions about microbes and the immune system. What are the factors and mechanisms that protect cells from being infected or that prevent a virus from efficiently replicating inside a cell? Which signaling pathways need to be activated or repressed to mount an effective T cell response? How do pathogens successfully avoid host recognition or their destruction by host immune cells? Why are some individuals susceptible to certain pathogens while others are not? The list of questions is long and many others will arise once we start unraveling the mechanisms of infectious diseases.

Systems-biology provides the most straightforward approach for global modeling of microbial pathogenesis. Figure 15.3 shows examples of experimental designs and strategies. In general, high-throughput technologies are used to measure the behavior of all the components of immune system cells or tissues during an infection. Computational and mathematical models are then constructed, validated, and analyzed using this data, and key networks of interactions are identified. At last, this approach can suggest novel functional properties and be able to predict the most informative sets of future experiments (Young et al. 2008).

Investigating the molecular interactions between a pathogen and the host can also be performed at systems-level. To be able to sense viruses, bacteria, parasites, or fungi, the cells of the innate immune system express the so-called pattern recognition receptors (Pulendran et al. 2010). In an elegant example of network modeling performed by Amit et al. (2009), the authors reconstructed, in an unbiased way, the transcriptional networks triggered by five pathogen-derived components, including the adjuvant CpG, a synthetic single-stranded DNA that binds to toll-like receptor 9. They also constructed a model that associated regulators with their targets by systematically silencing the expression of most of the candidate regulators in combination with gene expression profiling (Amit et al. 2009). Using a perfect example of systems-biology approach (i.e. the systematic perturbation of the system, the measurements of its effect on global

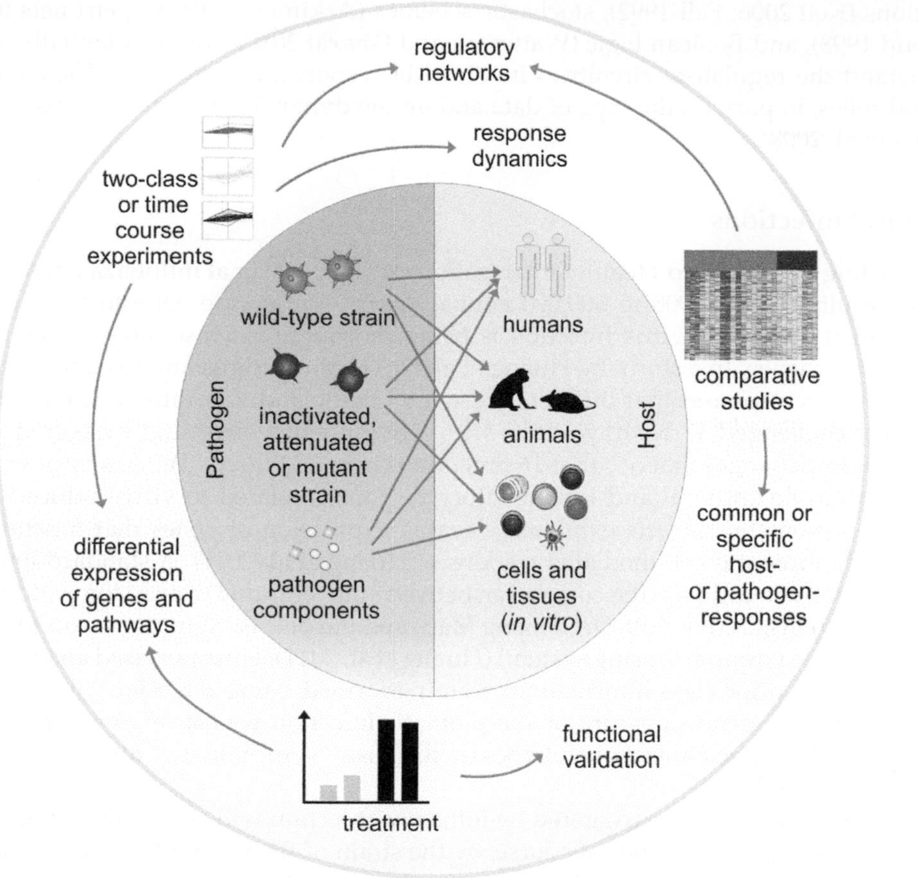

FIGURE 15.3 Systems-biology approaches applied to investigate host-pathogen interactions. Different host-pathogen models of infection or vaccination are shown in the central circle. The various types of analyses that can be exploited to holistically assess and predict these interactions are shown in the outer circle.

scale, and the mathematical modeling to explain or predict the data), Amit et al. found that different regulatory arms control two key programs related to inflammatory response and antiviral response (Amit et al. 2009).

Modeling infections at the population-level poses a great challenge to epidemiologists, immunologists, and computational scientists. The underlying assumption of most studies of host–pathogen and host-host interactions is that the human population can be treated as a homogenous group. However, models generated under such assumption tend to provide a poor fit to observed data and many times fail to make correct predictions (Young et al. 2008). Therefore, it is critical that individual variation be taken into account when modeling host responses.

As we will see in the following sections, the appropriate mathematical or computational model can vary greatly. Modeling methods, such as ordinary and partial differential equations (Kell 2006; Fell 1992), stochastic schemes (Arkin et al. 1998), petri nets (Goss and Peccoud 1998), and Boolean logic (Watterson and Ghazal 2010) can be potentially applied to understand the regulatory circuitries involved in response to infections. The choice of the method relies, in part, on the type of data and on the dynamics that are under consideration (Young et al. 2008).

5.1 Viral infections

According to the World Health Organization (WHO), seasonal influenza epidemics occur yearly, resulting in 250,000 to 500,000 annual deaths worldwide. Due to this great public health threat, influenza virus infection is being thoroughly investigated through systems biology approaches. In a study by Huang et al. (2011), the authors analyzed the dynamics of host molecular responses that differentiate symptomatic and asymptomatic influenza infection. They challenged 17 healthy adults with live influenza virus and measured the blood transcriptomic changes that occur at 16 timepoints over 132 hours. While symptomatic hosts invoked multiple antiviral and inflammatory responses related to virus-induced oxidative stress, asymptomatic subjects exhibited elevated expression of genes that function in antioxidant responses and cell-mediated responses (Huang et al. 2011). A standard linear mixed model was used to estimate the correlation between the temporal expression patterns of clusters of genes (clustered by Self-Organizing Map) and the disease symptom scores (defined by a standardized symptom scoring system) (Huang et al. 2011). Unsupervised analyses (i.e. that did not require prior class information) were performed using Bayesian Linear Unmixing, revealing that the gene signature of symptomatic infection was strong enough to separate subjects into these two clinical phenotypes (in this case, "symptomatic" and "asymptomatic") (Huang et al. 2011).

However, host responses triggered by influenza infection will be contingent upon the cell type that is being infected and, of course, by the strain of the virus. One of these strains (the "1918 influenza virus strain") killed an estimated 50 million people during the "Spanish influenza" pandemics of 1918 and was recently reconstructed by modern reverse genetics techniques (Billharz et al. 2009). Billharz et al. performed systems-level analyses of human lung epithelial cells infected *in vitro* with 1918 virus to define the global host transcriptional response to this influenza strain (Billharz et al. 2009). Differentially expressed genes were identified by creating ratio profiles by combining replicates and applying error weighting (consisting in adjusting for additive and multiplicative noise) (Billharz et al. 2009). For that, they utilized the Rosetta Resolver system, a multi-user system for storage and analysis of gene expression microarray data (http://www.lgtc.nl/rosetta/). This approach revealed that the protein NS1 of the 1918 virus must block host interferon and lipid metabolism signaling pathways, both of which important for host antiviral response (Billharz et al. 2009).

Systems biology of influenza infection was also studied in animal models. In order to determine the factors responsible for the increased virulence of the 1918 influenza strain, Kash et al. performed a comprehensive genomic analysis of mice infected with the reconstructed 1918 influenza virus (Kash et al. 2006). Among their findings, they discovered that the increased and accelerated activation of host immune response genes caused by influenza infection were associated with severe pulmonary pathology (Kash et al. 2006). The pathogenicity of 1918 virus was also assessed in primates by gene expression microarrays (Kobasa et al. 2007). In their work, they showed the severity and outcome of infection by the 1918 virus can be associated to a dysregulation of the antiviral response genes, such as *DDX58* and *IFIH1* (Kobasa et al. 2007).

Infection by the human immunodeficiency virus (HIV) has also been heavily studied by systems biology approaches. A common theme for several of these studies was toward the understanding of HIV disease progression, utilizing for that cohorts of rare individuals who could naturally control HIV infection. These so-called elite controllers, despite detectable viral loads could prevent the progression of the disease for long periods of time even in the absence of treatment (Peretz et al. 2012). Distinct transcriptional profiles were identified in T cell subsets and intestinal mucosal tissue of elite controllers compared to disease progressors (the main findings of these studies were extensively reviewed by Peretz et al. (2012) and Fonseca et al. (2011)).

Genome-scale RNAi screens were also conducted by independent groups to discover the cellular factors associated with HIV replication (Konig et al. 2008; Brass et al. 2008; Zhou et al. 2008). Although many of the cellular factors identified by each group were previously implicated in HIV replication, a surprisingly low overlap was found between any pair of screens (Bushman et al. 2009). Nevertheless, when host factors that participate in similar cellular processes were grouped, the overlap between pair of screens increased (Bushman et al. 2009). This indicates that functional analysis approaches can provide a less biased and less noisy representation of global changes than traditional single gene analysis. Additionally, network analyses were performed by Bushman et al. (2009) and Konig et al. (2008) in order to reveal how the host cellular factors interact with each other and with the HIV-encoded proteins. The interaction networks were elucidated based upon protein-protein binding data derived from databases containing experimental and literature-curated data (e.g. Bind, MINT, Reactome, Y2H, NIAD, etc.) (Konig et al. 2008; Bushman et al. 2009). To further identify densely connected sub-networks within this interactome map, MCODE (Bader and Hogue 2003), a graph theoretic clustering algorithm, was utilized.

Genomic studies of lesser known viruses can indicate potential application of alternative drugs and biologic therapies. Transcriptomic analysis of mice infected with Chikungunya virus, a mosquito-borne alphavirus that causes a chronic debilitating polyarthralgia/polyarthritis in humans, was recently performed by our group (Nakaya et al. 2012). Our goal was to determine whether the inflammatory gene expression signature of Chikungunya arthritis showed any similarities with human rheumatoid arthritis (RA) or with a mouse model of RA. The rationale behind this was to assess whether drugs developed for rheumatoid arthritis might be useful in the treatment of alphavirus-induced arthritis, for which current treatments are often inadequate. First, genes significantly induced or repressed post-infection were identified by a statistical framework described by Ling et al. (2010). Their method relies on an iterative procedure to perform robust estimation of the null hypothesis (assuming that the gene expression background difference is normally distributed), and allowing the identification of differentially expressed genes as outliers (Ling et al. 2010). Next, gene set enrichment analysis (Subramanian et al. 2005) was used to show a highly significant overlap in the differentially expressed genes in the Chikungunya arthritis model and in RA, suggesting that RA, a chronic autoimmune arthritis, and Chikungunya disease, indeed share multiple inflammatory processes (Nakaya et al. 2012).

Finally, a systematic comparison of published transcriptional-profiling data from 32 studies that involved 77 interactions between different host and pathogens (mostly viruses) were performed by (Jenner and Young 2005). This meta-analysis yielded not only novel and unique insights about microbial pathogenesis, but also revealed a common host-transcriptional-response, comprised of genes that seem to be similarly induced in many different cell types exposed to several pathogen species (Jenner and Young 2005). As expected, this common host response was enriched for genes associated with inflammatory processes, interferon response and genes that are known to activate or limit the immune responses (Jenner and Young 2005). However, the host–pathogen interactions described there, combined with further interactome data can be extremely useful to reconstruct the regulatory networks that underlie the transcriptional response to infection (Jenner and Young 2005).

5.2 Bacterial infections

Each pathogenic bacterium interacts with the host in a unique and specific way. Ramilo et al. addressed this issue by analyzing the gene expression profiles of subjects with acute infections caused by four common pathogens: *Escherichia coli*, *Staphylococcus aureus*, *Streptococcus pneumonia*, and influenza A virus (Ramilo et al. 2007). Applying nonparametric univariate tests, such as Mann-Whitney U or Fisher exact test, they first ranked genes on the basis of their ability to discriminate between groups of patients infected with the same pathogen, and then used a K-Nearest Neighbors method to determine the discriminatory power of the top ranked (i.e. classifier) genes (Ramilo et al. 2007). Using this strategy, they were able to identify discriminative blood transcriptional signatures, and demonstrate the potential clinical application of gene signatures in the diagnosis of infectious diseases (Ramilo et al. 2007).

Banchereau et al. also characterized the whole blood transcriptome of patients infected with *S. aureus* (Banchereau et al. 2012). In this work, however, they examined how the diverse clinical manifestations of the disease impact the blood gene signatures. To examine the heterogeneity in the blood signatures and then identify the factors associated with such variation, the authors calculated a "Molecular Distance To Health" score (MDTH) for each individual patient (Banchereau et al. 2012). The MDTH was introduced by Pankla et al. (2009) while analyzing the blood transcriptomics of patients with septicemic melioidosis (caused by the gram-negative bacillus *Burkholderia pseudomallei*). Figure 15.4 summarizes how the MDTH can be calculated. Using the MDTH score and blood transcription modules, Banchereau et al provided a new understanding of the relation/interaction between host response and clinical disease manifestations to *S. aureus* (Banchereau et al. 2012).

Of the clinically relevant bacterial infections, tuberculosis (TB), caused by *Mycobacterium tuberculosis* is by far among the top ones. The WHO estimated that, in 2011, 1.4 million people died from TB and 8.7 million fell ill. A much greater number of people are infected with *M. tuberculosis* but remain asymptomatic (latent TB). Since current tests fail to identify subjects with latent TB that will develop the disease, Berry et al tried to address if blood transcript signatures could perform this task (Berry et al. 2010). In their work, they defined a distinct 393-transcript signature in patients with active TB that was then applied to predict if latent TB patients, from two independent cohorts would develop active disease (Berry et al. 2010). The k-nearest neighbor class prediction method they used gave sensitivity and specificity rates higher than 60% and 90%, respectively for both test and validation cohorts (Berry et al. 2010). Additionally, they utilized blood co-transcriptional gene modules (Chaussabel et al. 2008) to

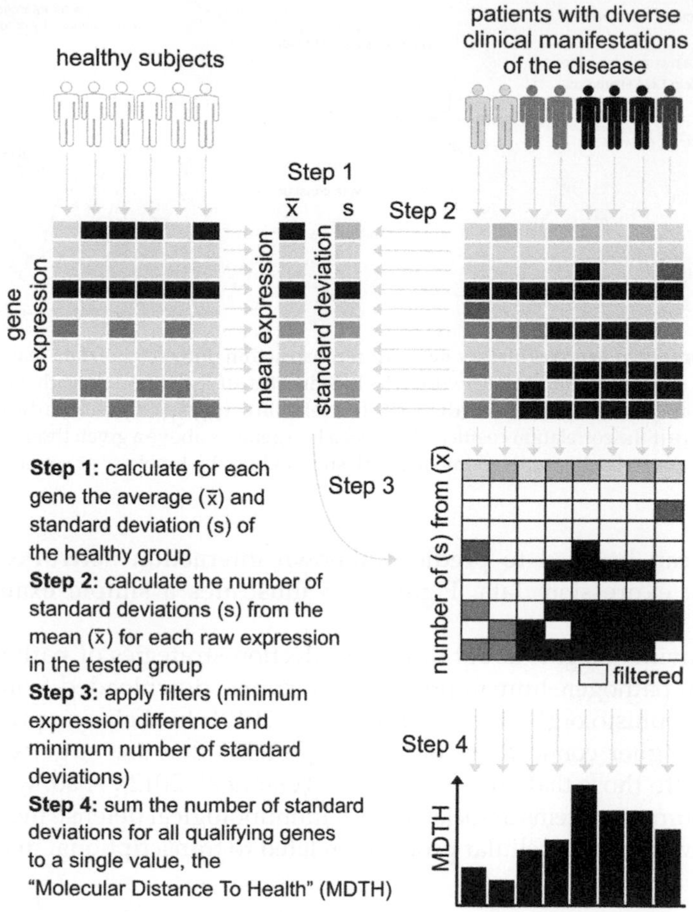
patients with diverse clinical manifestations of the disease
healthy subjects
Step 1
x̄
s
Step 2
gene expression
mean expression
standard deviation
Step 1: calculate for each gene the average (x̄) and standard deviation (s) of the healthy group
Step 2: calculate the number of standard deviations (s) from the mean (x̄) for each raw expression in the tested group
Step 3: apply filters (minimum expression difference and minimum number of standard deviations)
Step 4: sum the number of standard deviations for all qualifying genes to a single value, the "Molecular Distance To Health" (MDTH)
Step 3
number of (s) from (x̄)
filtered
Step 4
MDTH

FIGURE 15.4 **Molecular distance to health (MDTH).** This score measures the global transcriptional perturbation in each patient compared to the median of healthy controls.

identify functional components of the transcriptional host response during active TB (Berry et al. 2010). Combining the modular TB signature with flow cytometry data, they revealed that the TB signature detected a neutrophil-driven interferon-inducible gene profile and that it also includes changes in cellular composition (Berry et al. 2010).

Additionally, Magombedze and Mulder investigated the TB latency dynamics through a meta-analysis with publicly available gene expression data from time course experiments (Magombedze and Mulder 2012). They utilized reverse network engineering techniques to predict gene dependencies and regulatory interactions, and constructed a mathematical model for the inferred gene regulatory networks. Their systems biology approach predicted interesting key TB genes, such as *Rv1370c* and *Rv3131* in the latency/dormancy program that could be targeted as potential latency drug candidates (Magombedze and Mulder 2012). Hecker et al. (2009) and Marbach et al. (2010) nicely reviewed reverse engineering

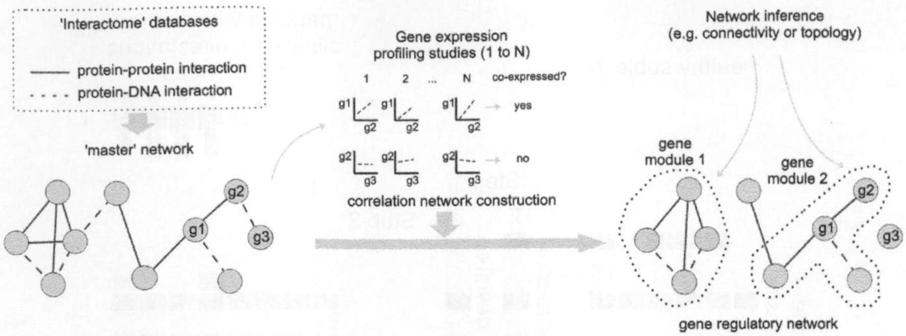

FIGURE 15.5 **Example of gene regulatory network reconstruction.** Interactome data (e.g. protein-protein, protein-DNA) is used to construct a 'master' network which delineates all the connections that exist between components. These connections are then confirmed on the basis of correlation network analysis from different gene-expression profiling studies, where if the correlation coefficient between two genes is above a given threshold they are predicted to interact. The network can be decomposed into network sub-modules by topology or connectivity.

techniques that can be used to predict unknown interaction networks based on high-throughput gene expression data. Figure 15.5 illustrates a simple example of network reconstruction.

In order to provide insights about different infection strategies of pathogens, Tekir et al. analyzed > 23,000 pathogen–human protein interactions, downloaded from PHISTO search tool (http://www.phisto.org) (Durmus Tekir et al. 2012). In their comprehensive analysis, they observed a higher connectivity of human proteins that are targeted by bacteria and viruses compared to those that are not (Durmus Tekir et al. 2012). Also, while bacteria seem to interact with human proteins associated with immunological defense mechanisms, viruses seem to interact with human cellular processes related to transcriptional machinery (Durmus Tekir et al. 2012).

5.3 Infection caused by other organisms

Malaria is one of the greatest public health problems worldwide and has been extensively studied by systems biology approaches. The transcriptional activity of Plasmodium genome, the parasite protozoan that causes malaria, was assessed during human blood stage by next-generation sequencing (Otto et al. 2010), tiling microrrays (Broadbent et al. 2011), and custom-made Affymetrix chips (Daily et al. 2007). Daily et al. (2007) compared the expression profiles of parasites derived directly from venous blood samples of patients to the ones obtained *in vitro* by other groups. Using a non-negative matrix factorization algorithm, they clustered the *in vivo* expression profiles into three distinct groups, and discovered that only one of them was similar to early ring-stage *in vitro* profiles (Daily et al. 2007). The other two clusters were not similar to those of either early or late *in vitro* stages, and therefore could represent novel transcriptional states (Daily et al. 2007). Their work has shown that the molecular signatures of the parasite *in vivo* can be different from the ones found in *in vitro* models, and that this can influence the development of novel drug targets or alternative therapies for malaria (Daily et al. 2007).

Most host-pathogen studies have focused on monitoring the changes that occur either on the host side or on the pathogen side. Tierney et al approached this differently (Tierney et al. 2012). The authors quantified the gene expression dynamics of both *Candida albicans* (fungal pathogen) and *Mus musculus* (host) during phagocytosis by dendritic cells using RNA-seq (Tierney et al. 2012). In order to generate the inferred regulatory network, they combined the expression kinetics of candidate genes (prioritized with a specific set of criteria) and the putative regulatory interactions obtained from different data sources (and scored based on the "confidence" of the prior knowledge source) (Tierney et al. 2012). As a result, they were able to identify novel interspecies host-pathogen interactions, and validate experimentally some of them (Tierney et al. 2012).

6 SYSTEMS VACCINOLOGY

The emerging field of systems vaccinology represents a stepping stone for understanding how vaccine-induced immunity works. This would be of paramount importance in the rational design of future vaccines (Pulendran et al. 2010), breaking up several centuries of empirically designed vaccines. The major goals are to unravel the molecular mechanisms of vaccines and to identify signatures that correlate or predict vaccine immunogenicity and/or disease protection (Nakaya et al. 2012). These can only be achieved through the use of high-throughput technologies to monitor all the parts of immune system and with computational modeling to analyze the complex interactions between these parts (Nakaya and Pulendran 2012).

Recently, systems vaccinology has been successfully applied to study empirically designed vaccines and is beginning to yield mechanistic insights about immune regulation (Nakaya and Pulendran 2012). However, the successful integration of systems approaches with vaccine development still faces several challenges and potential pitfalls. The biological complexity underlying the immune system itself, and the intrinsic noise, bias, and errors of data generated by high-throughput techniques cause major challenges (Nakaya and Pulendran 2012). Others factors, such as prior immunological history and ethics, represent different challenges that are inherent (and sometimes unique) to this field of research.

6.1 Yellow fever vaccine

The Yellow Fever YF-17D vaccine is a live attenuated virus vaccine, and is one of the most successful vaccines ever developed. A single immunization confers protection in nearly 90% of vaccinees and results in strong T cell response (both cytototoxic T cells and helper T cells) and in robust neutralizing antibody response that can persist for nearly 40 years (Pulendran et al. 2010). Therefore, it is no surprise that YF-17D is among the first vaccines to be studied by systems vaccinology (Gaucher et al. 2008; Querec et al. 2009). In order to obtain biological insights about the mechanism of action of this vaccine, our group (Querec et al. 2009) and others (Gaucher et al. 2008) independently analyzed the gene expression profiles induced in the blood of individuals a few days after YF-17D vaccination. These analyses revealed innate gene signatures composed of type I interferon, inflammasome, and complement genes (Gaucher et al. 2008; Querec et al. 2009). We also identified two key transcription factors that mediate type I interferon responses, *IRF7* and *STAT1* as being up-regulated post-YF-17D vaccination (Querec et al. 2009). Additional analyses revealed statistically over-represented frequencies of IRF7 transcription factor binding sites in the promoters region of differentially expressed genes, indicating its importance and central role in YF-17D vaccine response (Querec et al. 2009).

The second goal of our study with YF-17D vaccine was to identify early innate signatures that predict adaptive immune outcomes (i.e. neutralizing antibody and CD8+ T cell responses). However, for the YF-17D vaccine, these outcomes were not clearly defined. For instance, what is the minimum level of neutralizing antibody titers induced by the vaccine that is necessary to confer protection against subsequent exposure to the wild-type yellow fever virus? In addition, how much of an increase in cell frequency is considered a "sufficient" CD8+ T cell response? Thus, before proceeding with the predictive analyses, we should first deal with the lack of such well-defined "correlates of protection" for YF-17D vaccine (i.e. the level of a given immune parameter that needs to be reached or exceeded after vaccination in order to assume protection). We addressed this issue by performing unsupervised principal component analyses (using selected genes), which segregated the subjects into two distinct subgroups (Querec et al. 2009). A cutoff of 3% for CD8+ T cell responses and a neutralizing antibody titer cutoff of 170 were used to define the "correlates of immunogenicity" for YF-17D vaccine (Querec et al. 2009).

The challenge was to identify gene signatures that could correctly classify a second and independent YF-17D vaccine trial, which was collected more than 1 year after the first trial. Using the trial 1 as a training set and the trial 2 as a validation set, we tested two different classification methods: the classification to the nearest centroid, or ClaNC (Dabney 2005) and the discriminant analysis via mixed integer programming, or DAMIP (Lee 2007). While both methods correctly classified >80% of the vaccinees according to their CD8+ T cell response, DAMIP program achieved this precision using gene sets comprised of very few genes (called as 'classification rules') (Querec et al. 2009). DAMIP also correctly predicts the magnitude of B cell neutralizing antibody responses with very high accuracy (Querec et al. 2009). These provided a proof-of-concept demonstration that systems biology approaches can indeed be used to predict the immunogenicity of vaccines (Nakaya and Pulendran 2012). It also demonstrated that the DAMIP model is a very powerful supervised-learning classification approach (Lee 2007), that generates classification rules with high prediction accuracy even among small training sets (Brooks and Lee 2010).

Potentially novel mechanistic insights of vaccine action emerged from our study with YF-17D vaccine (Querec et al. 2009). The gene *EIF2AK4* (also known as *GCN2*) was frequently found in the DAMIP classification rules that predict CD8+ T cell responses. When the cell is under certain types of cellular stresses (e.g. amino acid starvation), it phosphorylates GCN2, triggering a signaling pathway that results in the shutdown of housekeeping mRNA genes and the formation of stress granules (Kedersha et al. 2007). Mechanistic studies using *GCN2* knockout mice are being conducted by our group to investigate the role of GCN2 in regulating CD8+ T cell responses (Nair et al., manuscript in preparation).

6.2 Influenza vaccines

Investigating the molecular mechanism of action of influenza vaccines proved to be even more challenging than the YF-17D study. In the United States, there are two types of licensed vaccines for seasonal influenza: trivalent inactivated influenza vaccine (TIV), given by intramuscular injection; and live attenuated influenza vaccine (LAIV), administered intranasally. Each vaccine contains three strains of influenza viruses which are selected each year on the basis of the results of the Global Influenza Surveillance and Response System (more information can be found at http://www.influenzacentre.org). Therefore, depending on the antigenic match between the vaccine and the circulating influenza strains, the vaccine efficacy can significantly vary from one year to the next (Nakaya et al. 2011). Additionally, unlike the subjects used in the YF-17D study, most individuals vaccinated against seasonal influenza have already been exposed to the virus through previous infections or vaccinations (Nakaya et al. 2011). It is unclear how the preexisting levels of antibody in these non-naïve subjects would impact the search for predictors of vaccine immunogenicity.

To determine on a genome-wide scale the expression changes induced by TIV or LAIV vaccination, we did microarray analysis using peripheral blood mononuclear cells (PBMCs) collected from 56 vaccinees on days 0, 3, and 7 after vaccination. Pathway analyses revealed that the expression of genes from inflammasome and antimicrobial pathways was similarly altered by both influenza vaccines (Nakaya et al. 2011). LAIV induced the expression of several interferon-related genes, similar to that observed with the other live attenuated virus vaccine YF-17D. TIV, however, induced a signature that was characteristic of plasma B cell response (Nakaya et al. 2011).

The DAMIP method was used to identify innate gene signatures that predict the antibody responses induced one month after vaccination (Nakaya et al. 2011). To train the program to establish an unbiased estimate of correct classification, we utilized the expression profiles of subjects vaccinated with TIV during the 2008-2009 influenza season (Figure 15.6). A second trial (the test set) consisting of gene-expression profiles of TIV vaccinees from 2007-2008 influenza season was used to evaluate the predictive accuracy of the classification rules identified in the first trial. With this approach, DAMIP model generated signatures with a tenfold cross-validation accuracy of > 90% in the training trial and a "blind prediction" accuracy also > 90% for the testing trial (Nakaya et al. 2011). To validate the utility of these gene signatures in predicting the magnitude of antibody response, we included a third trial comprised of TIV vaccinees from the 2009-2010 influenza season. Again, DAMIP was able to generate signatures that classify with 85% accuracy the vaccinees with high (i.e. four-fold or higher increase in antibody titers 30 days after vaccination) or low (less than four-fold) antibody responses (Nakaya et al. 2011).

To demonstrate that systems vaccinology can be used to generate new hypotheses, we selected one gene from our classification rules, *CAMK4*, for functional confirmation experiments. Using *in vitro* experiments and mice deficient in CAMK4, we demonstrated an unappreciated role of CAMK4 in B-cell responses (Nakaya et al. 2011). Thus, by using a knockout mouse model to validate the signatures identified from vaccinated humans, our study was the first to complete the iterative systems vaccinology cycle (Zak and Aderem 2012).

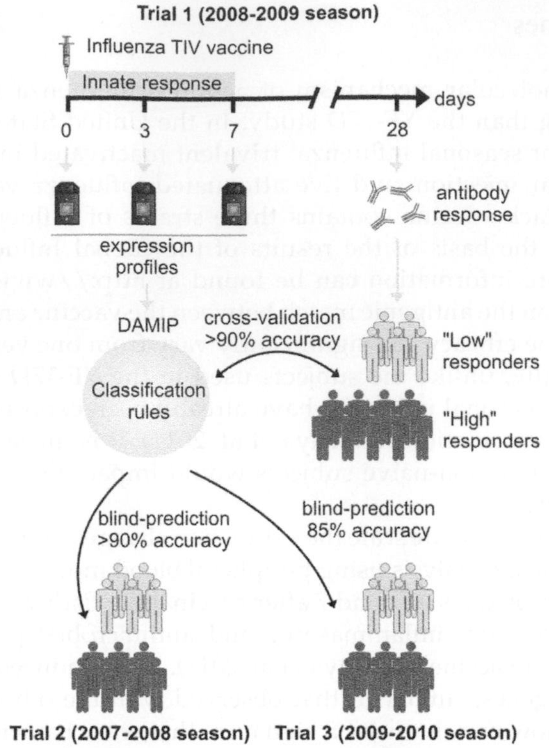

FIGURE 15.6 Signatures that predict the antibody response induced by TIV influenza vaccine. The top part shows the experimental design used in our previous work (Nakaya et al. 2011). The DAMIP method was used to identify innate gene signatures, called 'classification rules' that could predict the antibody responses induced 28 days after vaccination. DAMIP was performed using the 2008–2009 trial as the training set and the 2007–2008 and 2009–2010 trials as the validation sets. The accuracy represents the number of subjects correctly classified as "low" or "high" antibody responders.

Analyses of the global transcriptional response to influenza vaccination were also performed by others (Bucasas et al. 2011; Zhu et al. 2010). Zhu et al. conducted a study with 85 children 12–35 months of age vaccinated either with TIV or LAIV, and found that among the genes induced by the vaccines, several of them were type 1 interferon genes (Zhu et al. 2010). Bucasa et al. also identified interferon-related genes being induced 24 hours post-TIV immunization (Bucasas et al. 2011). Their findings suggest that even an inactivated virus vaccine (TIV) can elicit a type of immune response that is usually activated by innate cells during viral infections (Bucasas et al. 2011).

6.3 Other vaccines

Global gene expression profiling was used to investigate the molecular mechanisms of RTS,S candidate malaria vaccine (Vahey et al. 2010). This vaccine which is administered in 3 doses at 1-month interval showed that the risk of vaccinated children experiencing clinical malaria is reduced by 56% (Agnandji et al. 2011). The work performed by Vahey et al. assessed the patterns of expressed genes in the PBMCs of 39 volunteers on the day of the third vaccination followed by 24 hours, 72 hours, 2 weeks after vaccination, and on day 5 after challenge (determined by experimental challenge with mosquito-borne *Plasmodium falciparum* malaria) (Vahey et al. 2010). The authors perform class prediction analyses using the "prediction analysis of microarrays with R" tool (PAM-R), which uses a "nearest shrunken centroids" method to identify subsets of genes that best characterize each class (Tibshirani et al. 2002). Using the expression data from day 5 after challenge, PAM-R identified a 393-gene signature that correctly classified all vaccine recipients into protected, delayed in the onset of parasitemia, and not delayed in the onset of parasitemia (Vahey et al. 2010). Next, using gene set enrichment analysis (GSEA, http://www.broadinstitute.org), the authors identified a 32-gene set related to proteasome degradation pathway that was up-regulated in persons in the protected group at 2 weeks after the third vaccination but before challenge (Vahey et al. 2010). The involvement of these genes with the efficient processing of the MHC peptides suggests a potential role of the vaccine in conferring major histocompatibility complex class 1–mediated protection (Vahey et al. 2010).

7 CHALLENGES AND LIMITATIONS

The application of systems biology approaches to any field, especially that of immunology, faces many challenges and potential limitations. These challenges, which have been extensively reviewed elsewhere (Nakaya et al. 2012; Nakaya and Pulendran 2012; Pulendran et al. 2010; Young et al. 2008), are in part related to confounding factors generally found in studying immune responses. These factors can be divided into different levels, from working with highly heterogeneous human cohorts to reconstructing networks using specific experimental data (Figure 15.7). This section will not focus on the inherent problems associated with high-throughput technologies, such as errors, noise, and biases that, if not corrected, may affect downstream analyses (Nakaya and Pulendran 2012). Nor will it focus on the intrinsic variation introduced by the stochasticity of many biological processes, such as transcription initiation, translation, and posttranscriptional regulation mechanisms inside cells. Instead, this section will address some of the challenges associated with analyzing the system behavior of immune responses.

One of the first and most critical steps is the experimental design itself. In general, due to the high costs of performing high-throughput experiments, systems biology studies are comprised of relatively small cohorts and limited number of samples (and time points). In addition to minimal sample sizes for achieving statistical power, the challenge consists of selecting volunteers that will be part of the cohort. The human population, and therefore their immune responses, is incredibly heterogeneous. Of the many factors that could impact someone's immunological outcome, we can cite gender, ethnicity, age, stress status, vaccination history, prior and current disease conditions, genetic background, and baseline levels of immune parameters (Figure 15.7). Therefore, systems biology studies should be performed on cohorts that are relatively uniform with respect to such variables (Nakaya and Pulendran 2012).

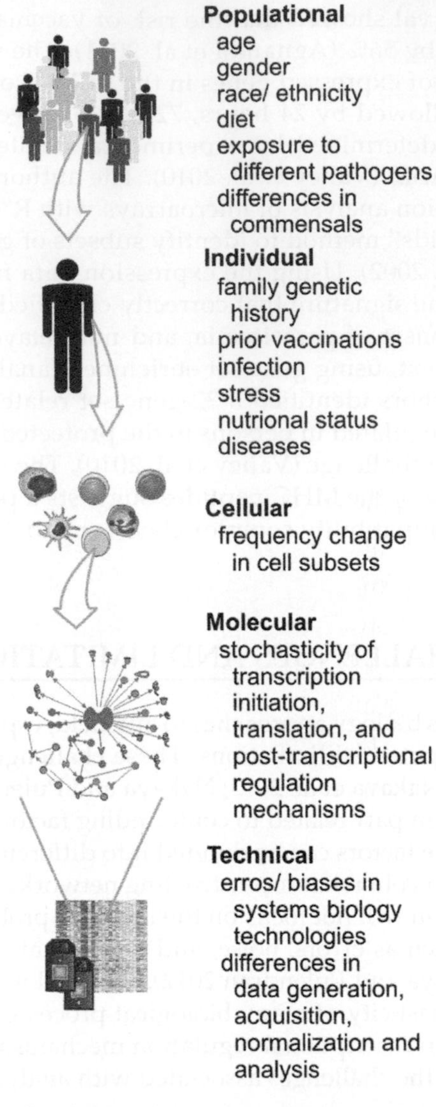

FIGURE 15.7 Potential confounding factors when investigating immune responses at systems-level.

Conversely, if the goal of the study is to examine immune responses that differ with regard to specific age groups (e.g. young adults versus elderly versus infants), or geographical or ethnic origins, or disease states (e.g. healthy subjects versus those with autoimmune diseases or HIV), then the design must carefully control all the other variables (Nakaya and Pulendran 2012).

The choice of time points at which to track the kinects of immune responses can be a very difficult task. Innate responses can be detected a few hours after encountering a pathogen and may be comprised of waves of genes expressed in a tightly regulated time-frame (Granucci et al.

2001). Similarly, during adaptive immune responses, the levels and frequencies of genes and cell types constantly and specifically change over the course of a few days to years (Perelson 2002). Therefore, the choice of time points for an experimental design may considerably impact the applicability of mathematical models created to describe the dynamics of immune responses.

Finally, a better understanding of the functional principles and dynamics of cellular systems can only be achieved with the integration of multiple layers of information, derived. from distinct 'omics' analyses (genomics, transcriptomics, proteomics, interactomics etc.) (Nakaya et al. 2012). However, the integration of genome-scale data types is not a trivial task. Many software packages were developed for this purpose, and some of them were summarized by (Joyce and Palsson 2006). The integration is generally approached by (1) delineating all the connections that exist between cellular components and constructing a 'master' network scaffold; (2) decomposing the network scaffold into network sub-modules; and (3) developing models to simulate and predict the network behavior under specific conditions (Joyce and Palsson 2006). After the many technical, computational, and biological issues are overcome, multi'omics' analyses can provide a bigger picture of the intricate and complex mechanisms of immune responses (Nakaya et al. 2012).

8 CONCLUSIONS

This chapter showed how systems biology can be used to understand and predict the complex mechanisms underlying immune responses. The development of testable predictive models of infectious diseases can potentially lead to improvements in diagnosis and disease therapy. When applied to vaccinology, it could enable the rational design of vaccines or to improvements on existing ones. However, the next big step lies not in the acquisition of additional data but in how to transform it into meaningful knowledge.

With the continuous development of computational and informatics tools to integrate and to analyze 'omics' data, and combined with the large amount of information shared in public databases, systems biology analysis is becoming increasingly accessible to immunologists with no computational training. This may have a profound impact on data interpretation and on the design of innovative experiments. More importantly, it will reduce the gap between discovery-based science and translational science.

References

Abbas, A. R., Baldwin, D., Ma, Y., Ouyang, W., Gurney, A., Martin, F., Fong, S., Campagne, M. V., Godowski, P., Williams, P. M., Chan, A. C., and Clark, H. F. (2005). Immune response in silico (IRIS): immune-specific genes identified from a compendium of microarray expression data. *Genes Immun.* 6:319–331.

Abbas, A. R., Wolslegel, K., Seshasayee, D., Modrusan, Z., and Clark, H. F. (2009). Deconvolution of blood microarray data identifies cellular activation patterns in systemic lupus erythematosus. *PLoS One* 4:e6098.

Aderem, A., Adkins, J. N., Ansong, C., Galagan, J., Kaiser, S., Korth, M. J., Law, G. L., McDermott, J. G., Proll, S. C., Rosenberger, C., Schoolnik, G., and Katze, M. G. (2011). A Systems Biology Approach to Infectious Disease Research: Innovating the Pathogen-Host Research Paradigm. *Mbio* 2.

Agnandji, S. T., Lell, B., Soulanoudjingar, S. S., Fernandes, J. F., Abossolo, B. P., Conzelmann, C., Methogo, B. G. N. O., Doucka, Y., Flamen, A., Mordmuller, B., Issifou, S., Kremsner, P. G., Sacarlal, J., Aide, P., Lanaspa, M., Aponte, J.

J., Nhamuave, A., Quelhas, D., Bassat, Q., Mandjate, S., Macete, E., Alonso, P., Abdulla, S., Salim, N., Juma, O., Shomari, M., Shubis, K., Machera, F., Hamad, A. S., Minja, R., Mpina, M., Mtoro, A., Sykes, A., Ahmed, S., Urassa, A. M., Ali, A. M., Mwangoka, G., Tanner, M., Tinto, H., D'Alessandro, U., Sorgho, H., Valea, I., Tahita, M. C., Kabore, W., Ouedraogo, S., Sandrine, Y., Guiguemde, R. T., Ouedraogo, J. B., Hamel, M. J., Kariuki, S., Odero, C., Oneko, M., Otieno, K., Awino, N., Omoto, J., Williamson, J., Muturi-Kioi, V., Laserson, K. F., Slutsker, L., Otieno, W., Otieno, L., Nekoye, O., Gondi, S., Otieno, A., Ogutu, B., Wasuna, R., Owira, V., Jones, D., Onyango, A. A., Njuguna, P., Chilengi, R., Akoo, P., Kerubo, C., Gitaka, J., Maingi, C., Lang, T., Olotu, A., Tsofa, B., Bejon, P., Peshu, N., Marsh, K., Owusu-Agyei, S., Asante, K. P., Osei-Kwakye, K., Boahen, O., Ayamba, S., Kayan, K., Owusu-Ofori, R., Dosoo, D., Asante, I., Adjei, G., Kwara, E., Chandramohan, D., Greenwood, B., Lusingu, J., Gesase, S., Malabeja, A., Abdul, O., Kilavo, H., Mahende, C., Liheluka, E., Lemnge, M., Theander, T., Drakeley, C., Ansong, D., Agbenyega, T., Adjei, S., Boateng, H. O., Rettig, T., Bawa, J., Sylverken, J., Sambian, D., Agyekum, A., Owusu, L., Martinson, F., Hoffman, I., Mvalo, T., Kamthunzi, P., Nkomo, R., Msika, A., Jumbe, A., Chome, N., Nyakuipa, D., Chintedza, J., Ballou, W. R., Bruls, M., Cohen, J., Guerra, Y., Jongert, E., Lapierre, D., Leach, A., Lievens, M., Ofori-Anyinam, O., Vekemans, J., Carter, T., Leboulleux, D., Loucq, C., Radford, A., Savarese, B., Schellenberg, D., Sillman, M., Vansadia, P., and Partnership, S. C. T. (2011). First results of phase 3 trial of RTS, S/AS01 malaria vaccine in African children. *N. Engl. J. Med.* 365:1863–1875.

Amit, I., Garber, M., Chevrier, N., Leite, A. P., Donner, Y., Eisenhaure, T., Guttman, M., Grenier, J. K., Li, W., Zuk, O., Schubert, L. A., Birditt, B., Shay, T., Goren, A., Zhang, X., Smith, Z., Deering, R., McDonald, R. C., Cabili, M., Bernstein, B. E., Rinn, J. L., Meissner, A., Root, D. E., Hacohen, N., and Regev, A. (2009). Unbiased reconstruction of a mammalian transcriptional network mediating pathogen responses. *Science* 326:257–263.

Arkin, A., Ross, J., and McAdams, H. H. (1998). Stochastic kinetic analysis of developmental pathway bifurcation in phage lambda-infected *Escherichia coli* cells. *Genetics* 149:1633–1648.

Bader, G. D., and Hogue, C. W. (2003). An automated method for finding molecular complexes in large protein interaction networks. *Bmc Bioinformatics* 4.

Banchereau, R., Jordan-Villegas, A., Ardura, M., Mejias, A., Baldwin, N., Xu, H., Saye, E., Rossello-Urgell, J., Nguyen, P., Blankenship, D., Creech, C. B., Pascual, V., Banchereau, J., Chaussabel, D., and Ramilo, O. (2012). Host immune transcriptional profiles reflect the variability in clinical disease manifestations in patients with *Staphylococcus aureus* infections. *PLoS One* 7:e34390.

Baum, A., Sachidanandam, R., and Garcia-Sastre, A. (2010). Preference of RIG-I for short viral RNA molecules in infected cells revealed by next-generation sequencing. *Proc. Natl. Acad. Sci. USA* 107:16303–16308.

Bendall, S. C., Simonds, E. F., Qiu, P., Amir el, A. D., Krutzik, P. O., Finck, R., Bruggner, R. V., Melamed, R., Trejo, A., Ornatsky, O. I., Balderas, R. S., Plevritis, S. K., Sachs, K., Pe'er, D., Tanner, S. D., and Nolan, G. P. (2011). Single-cell mass cytometry of differential immune and drug responses across a human hematopoietic continuum. *Science* 332: 687–696.

Berry, M. P. R., Graham, C. M., McNab, F. W., Xu, Z. H., Bloch, S. A. A., Oni, T., Wilkinson, K. A., Banchereau, R., Skinner, J., Wilkinson, R. J., Quinn, C., Blankenship, D., Dhawan, R., Cush, J. J., Mejias, A., Ramilo, O., Kon, O. M., Pascual, V., Banchereau, J., Chaussabel, D., and O'Garra, A. (2010). An interferon-inducible neutrophil-driven blood transcriptional signature in human tuberculosis. *Nature* 466:973–977.

Billharz, R., Zeng, H., Proll, S. C., Korth, M. J., Lederer, S., Albrecht, R., Goodman, A. G., Rosenzweig, E., Tumpey, T. M., Garcia-Sastre, A., and Katze, M. G. (2009). The NS1 Protein of the 1918 Pandemic Influenza Virus Blocks Host Interferon and Lipid Metabolism Pathways. *J. Virol.* 83:10557–10570.

Bolen, C. R., Uduman, M., and Kleinstein, S. H. (2011). Cell subset prediction for blood genomic studies. *Bmc Bioinformatics* 12.

Brass, A. L., Dykxhoorn, D. M., Benita, Y., Yan, N., Engelman, A., Xavier, R. J., Lieberman, J., and Elledge, S. J. (2008). Identification of host proteins required for HIV infection through a functional genomic screen. *Science* 319:921–926.

Broadbent, K. M., Park, D., Wolf, A. R., Van Tyne, D., Sims, J. S., Ribacke, U., Volkman, S., Duraisingh, M., Wirth, D., Sabeti, P. C., and Rinn, J. L. (2011). A global transcriptional analysis of *Plasmodium falciparum* malaria reveals a novel family of telomere-associated lncRNAs. *Genome Biol.* 12:R56.

Brooks, J. P., and Lee, E. K. (2010). Analysis of the consistency of a mixed integer programming-based multi-category constrained discriminant model. *Ann. Operations Res.* 174:147–168.

Bucasas, K. L., Franco, L. M., Shaw, C. A., Bray, M. S., Wells, J. M., Nino, D., Arden, N., Quarles, J. M., Couch, R. B., and Belmont, J. W. (2011). Early Patterns of Gene Expression Correlate With the Humoral Immune Response to Influenza Vaccination in Humans. *J. Infect. Dis.* 203:921–929.

Bullen, A., Friedman, R. S., and Krummel, M. F. (2009). Two-Photon Imaging of the Immune System: A Custom Technology Platform for High-Speed, Multicolor Tissue Imaging of Immune Responses. *Visualizing Immun.* 334:1–29.

Bushman, F. D., Malani, N., Fernandes, J., D'Orso, I., Cagney, G., Diamond, T. L., Zhou, H. L., Hazuda, D. J., Espeseth, A. S., Konig, R., Bandyopadhyay, S., Ideker, T., Goff, S. P., Krogan, N. J., Frankel, A. D., Young, J. A. T., and Chanda, S. K. (2009). Host cell factors in HIV replication: Meta-analysis of genome-wide studies. *Plos Pathog.* 5.

Casadevall, A., and Pirofski, L. A. (2003). The damage-response framework of microbial pathogenesis. *Nat. Rev. Microbiol.* 1:17–24.

Chaussabel, D., Quinn, C., Shen, J., Patel, P., Glaser, C., Baldwin, N., Stichweh, D., Blankenship, D., Li, L., Munagala, I., Bennett, L., Allantaz, F., Mejias, A., Ardura, M., Kaizer, E., Monnet, L., Allman, W., Randall, H., Johnson, D., Lanier, A., Punaro, M., Wittkowski, K. M., White, P., Fay, J., Klintmalm, G., Ramilo, O., Palucka, A. K., Banchereau, J., and Pascual, V. (2008). A modular analysis framework for blood genomics studies: Application to systemic lupus erythematosus. *Immunity* 29:150–164.

Chaussabel, D., Pascual, V., and Banchereau, J. (2010). Assessing the human immune system through blood transcriptomics. *Bmc Biol.* 8.

Dabney, A. R. (2005). Classification of microarrays to nearest centroids. *Bioinformatics* 21:4148–4154.

Daily, J. P., Scanfeld, D., Pochet, N., Le Roch, K., Plouffe, D., Kamal, M., Sarr, O., Mboup, S., Ndir, O., Wypij, D., Levasseur, K., Thomas, E., Tamayo, P., Dong, C., Zhou, Y., Lander, E. S., Ndiaye, D., Wirth, D., Winzeler, E. A., Mesirov, J. P., and Regev, A. (2007). Distinct physiological states of *Plasmodium falciparum* in malaria-infected patients. *Nature* 450:1091–1095.

Durmus Tekir, S., Cakir, T., and Ulgen, K. O. (2012). Infection strategies of bacterial and viral pathogens through pathogen-human protein-protein interactions. *Front Microbiol.* 3:46.

Fell, D. A. (1992). Metabolic control analysis - a survey of its theoretical and experimental development. *Biochem. J.* 286:313–330.

Fischer, N. (2011). Sequencing antibody repertoires the next generation. *Mabs* 3:17–20.

Fonseca, S. G., Procopio, F. A., Goulet, J. P., Yassine-Diab, B., Ancuta, P., and Sekaly, R. P. (2011). Unique features of memory T cells in HIV elite controllers: a systems biology perspective. *Curr. Opin. HIV/AIDS* 6:188–196.

Gaucher, D., Therrien, R., Kettaf, N., Angermann, B. R., Boucher, G., Filali-Mouhim, A., Moser, J. M., Mehta, R. S., Drake, D. R., Castro, E., Akondy, R., Rinfret, A., Yassine-Diab, B., Said, E. A., Chouikh, Y., Cameron, M. J., Clum, R., Kelvin, D., Somogyi, R., Greller, L. D., Balderas, R. S., Wilkinson, P., Pantaleo, G., Tartaglia, J., Haddad, E. K., and Sekaly, R. P. (2008). Yellow fever vaccine induces integrated multilineage and polyfunctional immune responses. *J. Exp. Med.* 205:3119–3131.

Goss, P. J. E., and Peccoud, J. (1998). Quantitative modeling of stochastic systems in molecular biology by using stochastic petri nets. *Proc. Natl. Acad. Sci. USA* 95:6750–6755.

Granucci, F., Vizzardelli, C., Pavelka, N., Feau, S., Persico, M., Virzi, E., Rescigno, M., Moro, G., and Ricciardi-Castagnoli, P. (2001). Inducible IL-2 production by dendritic cells revealed by global gene expression analysis. *Nat. Immunol.* 2:882–888.

Grigoryev, Y. A., Kurian, S. M., Avnur, Z., Borie, D., Deng, J., Campbell, D., Sung, J., Nikolcheva, T., Quinn, A., Schulman, H., Peng, S. L., Schaffer, R., Fisher, J., Mondala, T., Head, S., Flechner, S. M., Kantor, A. B., Marsh, C., and Salomon, D. R. (2010). Deconvoluting post-transplant immunity: cell subset-specific mapping reveals pathways for activation and expansion of memory T, monocytes and B cells. *PLoS One* 5:e13358.

Haining, W. N., and Wherry, E. J. (2010). Integrating genomic signatures for immunologic discovery. *Immunity* 32:152–161.

Hartman, S. E., Bertone, P., Nath, A. K., Royce, T. E., Gerstein, M., Weissman, S., and Snyder, M. (2005). Global changes in STAT target selection and transcription regulation upon interferon treatments. *Genes Dev.* 19:2953–2968.

Hecker, M., Lambeck, S., Toepfer, S., van Someren, E., and Guthke, R. (2009). Gene regulatory network inference: Data integration in dynamic models-A review. *Biosystems* 96:86–103.

Hotson, A. N., Hardy, J. W., Hale, M. B., Contag, C. H., and Nolan, G. P. (2009). The T cell STAT signaling network is reprogrammed within hours of bacteremia via secondary signals. *J. Immunol.* 182:7558–7568.

Houzet, L., and Jeang, K. T. (2011). Genome-wide screening using RNA interference to study host factors in viral replication and pathogenesis. *Exp. Biol. Med.* 236:962–967.

Huang, Y. S., Zaas, A. K., Rao, A., Dobigeon, N., Woolf, P. J., Veldman, T., Oien, N. C., McClain, M. T., Varkey, J. B., Nicholson, B., Carin, L., Kingsmore, S., Woods, C. W., Ginsburg, G. S., and Hero, A. O. (2011). Temporal dynamics of host molecular responses differentiate symptomatic and asymptomatic influenza a infection. *Plos Genet*. 7.

Hyatt, G., Melamed, R., Park, R., Seguritan, R., Laplace, C., Poirot, L., Zucchelli, S., Obst, R., Matos, M., Venanzi, E., Goldrath, A., Nguyen, L., Luckey, J., Yamagata, T., Herman, A., Jacobs, J., Mathis, D., and Benoist, C. (2006). Gene expression microarrays: Glimpses of the immunological genome. *Nat. Immunol.* 7:686–691.

Ideker, T., Galitski, T., and Hood, L. (2001). A new approach to decoding life: Systems biology. *Annu. Rev. Genomics Hum. Genet*. 2:343–372.

Jenner, R. G., and Young, R. A. (2005). Insights into host responses against pathogens from transcriptional profiling. *Nat. Rev. Microbiol*. 3:281–294.

Joyce, A. R., and Palsson, B. O. (2006). The model organism as a system: Integrating 'omics' data sets. *Nat. Rev. Mol. Cell Biol.* 7:198–210.

Karlas, A., Machuy, N., Shin, Y., Pleissner, K. P., Artarini, A., Heuer, D., Becker, D., Khalil, H., Ogilvie, L. A., Hess, S., Maurer, A. P., Muller, E., Wolff, T., Rudel, T., and Meyer, T. F. (2010). Genome-wide RNAi screen identifies human host factors crucial for influenza virus replication. *Nature* 463:818–822.

Kash, J. C., Tumpey, T. M., Proll, S. C., Carter, V., Perwitasari, O., Thomas, M. J., Basler, C. F., Palese, P., Taubenberger, J. K., Garcia-Sastre, A., Swayne, D. E., and Katze, M. G. (2006). Genomic analysis of increased host immune and cell death responses induced by 1918 influenza virus. *Nature* 443:578–581.

Kedersha, N., and Anderson, P. (2007). Mammalian stress granules and processing bodies. *Transl. Initiation Cell Biol. High-Throughput Methods Chem-Based App*. 431:61.

Kell, D. B. (2006). Systems biology, metabolic modelling and metabolomics in drug discovery and development. *Drug Disco. Today* 11:1085–1092.

Kingsmore, S. F. (2006). Multiplexed protein measurement: Technologies and applications of protein and antibody arrays. *Nat. Rev. Drug Discov.* 5:310–320.

Kingsmore, S. F., and Patel, D. D. (2003). Multiplexed protein profiling on antibody-based microarrays by rolling circle amplification. *Curr. Opin. Biotechnol.* 14:74–81.

Kitano, H. (2002). Computational systems biology. *Nature* 420:206–210.

Kobasa, D., Jones, S. M., Shinya, K., Kash, J. C., Copps, J., Ebihara, H., Hatta, Y., Kim, J. H., Halfmann, P., Hatta, M., Feldmann, F., Alimonti, J. B., Fernando, L., Li, Y., Katze, M. G., Feldmann, H., and Kawaoka, Y. (2007). Aberrant innate immune response in lethal infection of macaques with the 1918 influenza virus. *Nature* 445:319–323.

Konig, R., Zhou, Y. Y., Elleder, D., Diamond, T. L., Bonamy, G. M. C., Irelan, J. T., Chiang, C. Y., Tu, B. P., De Jesus, P. D., Lilley, C. E., Seidel, S., Opaluch, A. M., Caldwell, J. S., Weitzman, M. D., Kuhen, K. L., Bandyopadhyay, S., Ideker, T., Orth, A. P., Miraglia, L. J., Bushman, F. D., Young, J. A., and Chanda, S. K. (2008). Global analysis of host-pathogen interactions that regulate early-stage HIV-1 replication. *Cell* 135:49–60.

Konig, R., Stertz, S., Zhou, Y., Inoue, A., Hoffmann, H. H., Bhattacharyya, S., Alamares, J. G., Tscherne, D. M., Ortigoza, M. B., Liang, Y. H., Gao, Q. S., Andrews, S. E., Bandyopadhyay, S., De Jesus, P., Tu, B. P., Pache, L., Shih, C., Orth, A., Bonamy, G., Miraglia, L., Ideker, T., Garcia-Sastre, A., Young, J. A. T., Palese, P., Shaw, M. L., and Chanda, S. K. (2010). Human host factors required for influenza virus replication. *Nature* 463:813–817.

Krutzik, P. O., Hale, M. B., and Nolan, G. P. (2005). Characterization of the murine immunological signaling network with phosphospecific flow cytometry. *J. Immunol.* 175:2366–2373.

Kuby, J., Kindt, T. J., Osborne, B. A., and Goldsby, R. A. (2002). *Immunology*. (5th ed.). W. H. Freeman.

Kwissa, M., Kasturi, S. P., and Pulendran, B. (2007). The science of adjuvants. *Expert Rev. Vaccines* 6:673–684.

Le Naour, F., Hohenkirk, L., Grolleau, A., Misek, D. E., Lescure, P., Geiger, J. D., Hanash, S., and Beretta, L. (2001). Profiling changes in gene expression during differentiation and maturation of monocyte-derived dendritic cells using both oligonucleotide microarrays and proteomics. *J. Biol. Chem.* 276:17920–17931.

Lee, E. K. (2007). Large-scale optimization-based classification models in medicine and biology. *Ann. Biomed. Eng.* 35:1095–1109.

Ling, Z. Q., Wang, Y., Mukaisho, K., Hattori, T., Tatsuta, T., Ge, M. H., Jin, L., Mao, W. M., and Sugihara, H. (2010). Novel statistical framework to identify differentially expressed genes allowing transcriptomic background differences. *Bioinformatics* 26:1431–1436.

Lu, P., Nakorchevskiy, A., and Marcotte, E. M. (2003). Expression deconvolution: A reinterpretation of DNA microarray data reveals dynamic changes in cell populations. *Proc. Natl. Acad. Sci. USA* 100:10370–10375.

Lynn, D. J., Winsor, G. L., Chan, C., Richard, N., Laird, M. R., Barsky, A., Gardy, J. L., Roche, F. M., Chan, T. H. W., Shah, N., Lo, R., Naseer, M., Que, J., Yau, M., Acab, M., Tulpan, D., Whiteside, M. D., Chikatamarla, A., Mah, B.,

Munzner, T., Hokamp, K., Hancock, R. E. W., and Brinkman, F. S. L. (2008). InnateDB: Facilitating systems-level analyses of the mammalian innate immune response. *Mol. Syst. Biol.* 4.

Magombedze, G., and Mulder, N. (2012). Understanding TB latency using computational and dynamic modelling procedures. *Infec. Genet. Evol.* 13:267–283.

Marazzi, I., Ho, J. S. Y., Kim, J., Manicassamy, B., Dewell, S., Albrecht, R. A., Seibert, C. W., Schaefer, U., Jeffrey, K. L., Prinjha, R. K., Lee, K., Garcia-Sastre, A., Roeder, R. G., and Tarakhovsky, A. (2012). Suppression of the antiviral response by an influenza histone mimic. *Nature* 483:428–433.

Marbach, D., Prill, R. J., Schaffter, T., Mattiussi, C., Floreano, D., and Stolovitzky, G. (2010). Revealing strengths and weaknesses of methods for gene network inference. *Proc. Natl. Acad. Sci. USA* 107:6286–6291.

McKinney, B. A., Reif, D. M., Rock, M. T., Edwards, K. M., Kingsmore, S. F., Moore, J. H., and Crowe, J. E. (2006). Cytokine expression patterns associated with systemic adverse events following smallpox immunization. *J. Infect. Dis.* 194:444–453.

Miller, J. C., Brown, B. D., Shay, T., Gautier, E. L., Jojic, V., Cohain, A., Pandey, G., Leboeuf, M., Elpek, K. G., Helft, J., Hashimoto, D., Chow, A., Price, J., Greter, M., Bogunovic, M., Bellemare-Pelletier, A., Frenette, P. S., Randolph, G. J., Turley, S. J., Merad, M., and Consortium, I. G. (2012). Deciphering the transcriptional network of the dendritic cell lineage. *Nat. Immunol.* 13:888–899.

Mirsky, H. P., Miller, M. J., Linderman, J. J., and Kirschner, D. E. (2011). Systems biology approaches for understanding cellular mechanisms of immunity in lymph nodes during infection. *J. Theor. Biol.* 287:160–170.

Nakaya, H. I., and Pulendran, B. (2012). Systems vaccinology: Its promise and challenge for HIV vaccine development. *Curr. Opin. HIV/AIDS* 7:24–31.

Nakaya, H. I., Wrammert, J., Lee, E. K., Racioppi, L., Marie-Kunze, S., Haining, W. N., Means, A. R., Kasturi, S. P., Khan, N., Li, G. M., McCausland, M., Kanchan, V., Kokko, K. E., Li, S., Elbein, R., Mehta, A. K., Aderem, A., Subbarao, K., Ahmed, R., and Pulendran, B. (2011). Systems biology of vaccination for seasonal influenza in humans. *Nat. Immunol.* 12:786–795.

Nakaya, H. I., Li, S., and Pulendran, B. (2012). Systems vaccinology: Learning to compute the behavior of vaccine induced immunity. *Wiley Interdiscip. Rev. Syst. Biol. Med.* 4:193–205.

Nakaya, H. I., Gardner, J., Poo, Y. S., Major, L., Pulendran, B., and Suhrbier, A. (2012). Gene profiling of chikungunya virus arthritis in a mouse model reveals significant overlap with rheumatoid arthritis. *Arthritis Rheum.* 64:3553–3563.

Newell, E. W., Sigal, N., Bendall, S. C., Nolan, G. P., and Davis, M. M. (2012). Cytometry by time-of-flight shows combinatorial cytokine expression and virus-specific cell niches within a continuum of CD8(+) T cell phenotypes. *Immunity* 36:142–152.

Otto, T. D., Wilinski, D., Assefa, S., Keane, T. M., Sarry, L. R., Bohme, U., Lemieux, J., Barrell, B., Pain, A., Berriman, M., Newbold, C., and Llinas, M. (2010). New insights into the blood-stage transcriptome of *Plasmodium falciparum* using RNA-seq. *Mol. Microbiol.* 76:12–24.

Palmer, C., Diehn, M., Alizadeh, A. A., and Brown, P. O. (2006). Cell-type specific gene expression profiles of leukocytes in human peripheral blood. *BMC Genomics* 7.

Pankla, R., Buddhisa, S., Berry, M., Blankenship, D. M., Bancroft, G. J., Banchereau, J., Lertmemongkolchai, G., Chaussabel, D., et al. (2009). Genomic transcriptional profiling identifies a candidate blood biomarker signature for the diagnosis of septicemic melioidosis. *Genome Biol.* 10:R127.

Peng, X. X., Gralinski, L., Armour, C. D., Ferris, M. T., Thomas, M. J., Proll, S., Bradel-Tretheway, B. G., Korth, M. J., Castle, J. C., Biery, M. C., Bouzek, H. K., Haynor, D. R., Frieman, M. B., Heise, M., Raymond, C. K., Baric, R. S., and Katze, M. G. (2010). Unique signatures of long noncoding RNA expression in response to virus infection and altered innate immune signaling. *Mbio* 1.

Perelson, A. S. (2002). Modelling viral and immune system dynamics. *Nat. Rev. Immunol.* 2:28–36.

Peretz, Y., Cameron, C., and Sekaly, R. P. (2012). Dissecting the HIV-specific immune response: A systems biology approach. *Curr. Opin. HIV/AIDS* 7:17–23.

Pulendran, B., Li, S., and Nakaya, H. I. (2010). Systems vaccinology. *Immunity* 33:516–529.

Querec, T. D., Akondy, R. S., Lee, E. K., Cao, W., Nakaya, H. I., Teuwen, D., Pirani, A., Gernert, K., Deng, J., Marzolf, B., Kennedy, K., Wu, H., Bennouna, S., Oluoch, H., Miller, J., Vencio, R. Z., Mulligan, M., Aderem, A., Ahmed, R., and Pulendran, B. (2009). Systems biology approach predicts immunogenicity of the yellow fever vaccine in humans. *Nat. Immunol.* 10:116–125.

Ramilo, O., Allman, W., Chung, W., Mejias, A., Ardura, M., Glaser, C., Wittkowski, K. M., Piqueras, B., Banchereau, J., Palucka, A. K., and Chaussabel, D. (2007). Gene expression patterns in blood leukocytes discriminate patients with acute infections. *Blood* 109:2066–2077.

Ricciardi-Castagnoli, P., and Granucci, F. (2002). Interpretation of the complexity of innate immune responses by functional genomics. *Nat. Rev. Immunol.* 2:881–888.

Rote, N. S. (2009). Pathophysiology: The Biologic Basis for Disease in Adults and Children. In (Kathryn L. McCance, and Sue E. Huethe, eds.), 6th ed. Mosby.

Shaffer, A. L., Rosenwald, A., Hurt, E. M., Giltnane, J. M., Lam, L. T., Pickeral, O. K., and Staudt, L. M. (2001). Signatures of the immune response. *Immunity* 15:375–385.

Shen-Orr, S. S., Tibshirani, R., Khatri, P., Bodian, D. L., Staedtler, F., Perry, N. M., Hastie, T., Sarwal, M. M., Davis, M. M., and Butte, A. J. (2010). Cell type-specific gene expression differences in complex tissues. *Nat. Methods* 7:287–289.

Subramanian, A., Tamayo, P., Mootha, V. K., Mukherjee, S., Ebert, B. L., Gillette, M. A., Paulovich, A., Pomeroy, S. L., Golub, T. R., Lander, E. S., and Mesirov, J. P. (2005). Gene set enrichment analysis: A knowledge-based approach for interpreting genome-wide expression profiles. *Proc. Natl. Acad. Sci. USA* 102:15545–15550.

Tibshirani, R., Hastie, T., Narasimhan, B., and Chu, G. (2002). Diagnosis of multiple cancer types by shrunken centroids of gene expression. *Proc. Natl. Acad. Sci. USA* 99:6567–6572.

Tierney, L., Linde, J., Muller, S., Brunke, S., Molina, J. C., Hube, B., Schock, U., Guthke, R., and Kuchler, K. (2012). An interspecies regulatory network inferred from simultaneous RNA-seq of candida albicans invading innate immune cells. *Front Microbiol.* 3:85.

Vahey, M. T., Wang, Z. N., Kester, K. E., Cummings, J., Heppner, D. G., Nau, M. E., Ofori-Anyinam, O., Cohen, J., Coche, T., Ballou, W. R., and Ockenhouse, C. F. (2010). Expression of genes associated with immunoproteasome processing of major histocompatibility complex peptides is indicative of protection with adjuvanted RTS, S malaria vaccine. *J. Infect. Dis.* 201:580–589.

Watterson, S., and Ghazal, P. (2010). Use of logic theory in understanding regulatory pathway signaling in response to infection. *Future Microbiol.* 5:163–176.

Young, D., Stark, J., and Kirschner, D. (2008). Systems biology of persistent infection: tuberculosis as a case study. *Nat. Rev. Microbiol.* 6:520–528.

Zak, D. E., and Aderem, A. (2009). Systems biology of innate immunity. *Immunol. Rev.* 227:264–282.

Zak, D. E., and Aderem, A. (2012). Overcoming limitations in the systems vaccinology approach: a pathway for accelerated HIV vaccine development. *Curr. Opin. HIV/AIDS* 7:58–63.

Zeiner, G. M., Norman, K. L., Thomson, J. M., Hammond, S. M., and Boothroyd, J. C. (2010). Toxoplasma gondii infection specifically increases the levels of key host microRNAs. *PLoS One* 5:e8742.

Zhou, H. L., Xu, M., Huang, Q., Gates, A. T., Zhang, X. H. D., Castle, J. C., Stec, E., Ferrer, M., Strulovici, B., Hazuda, D. J., and Espeseth, A. S. (2008). Genome-Scale RNAi Screen for Host Factors Required for HIV Replication. *Cell Host Microbe* 4:495–504.

Zhu, W., Higgs, B. W., Morehouse, C., Streicher, K., Ambrose, C. S., Woo, J., Kemble, G. W., Jallal, B., and Yao, Y. H. (2010). A whole genome transcriptional analysis of the early immune response induced by live attenuated and inactivated influenza vaccines in young children. *Vaccine* 28:2865–2876.

CHAPTER

16

Computational Modeling and Simulation of Animal Early Embryogenesis with the MecaGen Platform

Julien Delile[a,c], *René Doursat*[a,b], *Nadine Peyriéras*[c]

[a]Institut des Systèmes Complexes Paris Ile-de-France (ISC-PIF), CNRS, Paris, France

[b]School of Biomedical Engineering, Drexel University, Philadelphia, PA, USA

[c]Neurobiology and Development Lab, Terrasse, Gif-sur-Yvette Cedex, France

CONTENTS

Computational Systems Biology, Second Edition

http://dx.doi.org/10.1016/B978-0-12-405926-9.00016-2

Abstract

We propose a theoretical, yet realistic agent-based model and simulation platform of animal embryogenesis, called MecaGen,[1] centered on the physico-chemical coupling of cell mechanics with gene expression and molecular signaling. This project aims to investigate the multiscale dynamics of the early stages of biological morphogenesis. Here, embryonic development is viewed as an emergent, self-organized phenomenon based on a myriad of cells and their genetically regulated, and regulating, biomechanical behavior. Cells' mechanical properties (such as division rate, adhesion strength, or intrinsic motility) are closely correlated with their spatial location and temporal state of genetic and molecular dynamics (such as internal protein and external ligand concentrations) and affect each other concurrently. In a second part, we illustrate our model on artificial data (gene regulation motifs and cell sorting), then demonstrate a customization and application to a real biological case study in the zebrafish early development. We use as an example the episode of intercalation patterns appearing during the first phase of epiboly and the movements of the deep cells between the yolk and the enveloping layer. A domain of the model's multidimensional parameter space is explored systematically, while experimental data obtained from microscopy imaging of live embryos is used to measure the "fitness" of the virtual embryo and validate our hypotheses.

1 INTRODUCTION

The spontaneous making of an entire multicellular organism from a single cell ranks among the most exquisitely complex phenomena in nature. Through a precise spatiotemporal interplay of genetic switches, chemical signals, and mechanical constraints, an elaborate form is created without any of its myriad of cells containing the explicit map of the resulting architecture. An eternal source of fascination for generations of philosophers, artists, and scientists, biological morphogenesis is the epitome of what can be called today a *self-organizing complex system*. To follow the metaphor proposed by Enrico Coen in his book *The Art of Genes* (Coen 1999), it could be said that the embryo is similar to a "canvas that paints itself " (where colors represent differentiated cell types) at the same time that it is growing and sculpting itself —both patterning and shaping affecting each other in a tight feedback loop.

Schematically, it means that the *mechanical* properties of cells, such as their division rate, adhesion strength, or intrinsic motility, are closely correlated with their current spatial location and temporal state of *genetic* and molecular dynamics, such as concentrations of internal

[1] available at http://mecagen.org.

proteins and external ligands, and affect each other concurrently. The genetic dynamics forms distinct *morphogenetic fields* (an emergent "hidden geography" on the embryo (Coen 1999)), while the mechanical dynamics causes these fields to expand, fold, and deform. The mechano-genetic coupling operates at the scale of individual cells, but has consequences at multiple scales across the entire embryo and throughout the whole developmental process. It creates a cascade of (non-self-similar) "fractal" re-patterning and re-shaping of the morphogenetic fields, which, as they are expanding, segment themselves again into subfields by further spatial rearrangements and differentiation of cells.

In this introductory part, we propose a brief historical summary of developmental biology, born from classical embryology (Section 1.1), followed by a review of a few important families of embryogenetic models, such as reaction-diffusion, morphogen gradients, cell shaping, and differential adhesion (Section 1.2). Then, we identify the common modeling challenges and principles that will constitute the basis of our generic model and platform, called MecaGen (Section 1.3). Its purpose is to contribute to the understanding of the coupled mechanical-genetic dynamics that drives the growth of a multicellular organism, through agent-based modeling and computational experiments.

1.1 Developmental biology

Biological development, also referred to as "embryogenesis" in the earlier stages, can be generally defined as a dynamical process leading a given organism to a certain morphological state. In that sense, studying development means investigating the mechanisms that preside over the coordination of cellular differentiation in an organism through space and time. The dynamics of morphogenesis, or "morphodynamics," is far from steady, however, as embryos often alternate phases of drastic transformations with uniform periods dedicated to growth only. The most dramatic events occur in the beginning, when the egg divides into a great number of cells within a short time. These cells soon begin to perform a collective ballet of complex movements precisely coordinated by a complex web of physico-chemical interactions. It is interesting to note that this process never ends, the morphology of an organism undergoing constant change, albeit at smaller levels of detail, until senescence and death.

The definition of development has its own embryogenesis: it has also changed and reformed itself through the numerous discoveries and practical methods that have punctuated the history of the field. Four major periods are conventionally distinguished (Hopwood 2008): (a) pre-1880: classical descriptive embryology, (b) 1880–1930: classical experimental embryology; (c) 1930–1960: reconciling genetics and embryology, leading to developmental genetics; (d) 1960-today: modern developmental biology, molecular genetics, and biomechanics.

Descriptive and experimental embryology: According to the old theory of *preformation*, organisms were believed to simply unfold and expand from miniature versions of themselves, but not create new structures. In the 1820s, Christian Pander explained that development was actually based on the transformation of primitive sheets of tissue, called the *germ layers*. During the first half of the 19th century, under the influence of Johannes Müller, the *cell theory* attempted to unify the development of various observed eggs. Cells had then become the fundamental building blocks of every living species in the minds of the scientists. Additionally, Robert Remak stated that every cell was produced by a preexisting cell, and introduced the concept of *germ-layer specificity* in vertebrates, i.e. the fact that each layer (endoderm, mesoderm, and ectoderm) specified the type or *fate* of the cells originating from it (e.g. intestine, muscle, or skin cells). In the 1880s, with the discipline of *Entwicklungsmechanik* (developmental mechanics), Wilhem Roux and others applied to embryos various kinds of perturbations (mechanical, thermal, chemical, or electrical) to study their effects. The key question was whether the differentiation of embryo parts was endogenous, calling it *autonomous*, or whether it was under external influence, i.e. *dependent*. Later, it was recognized that this debate had no definitive answer and reality was somewhere in the middle. Neither totally mosaic nor totally regulative, developmental principles strike a balance between both principles (Lawrence and Levine 2006). The early 20th-century embryologists refined these questions with new experiments such as grafts, in particular on the newt embryo, aimed at deciphering what determined cell fates. Ross Harrison introduced the concept of *morphogenetic fields*, then Hans Spemann and Hilde Mangold observed that a piece of tissue, the blastopore lip, when transplanted from the gastrula to another embryo, *induced* a neurulating process and the formation of a secondary embryonic axis. They called this tissue the primary embryonic *organizer*.

Developmental genetics: During the rise of genetics, Conrad Hal Waddington stressed the importance of genes in development as "controllers" of cellular fate. By comparing mutated *Drosophila* embryos, he observed that a presumptive tissue (the imaginal disc) could transform into either a leg or an antenna. He illustrated his view by the concepts of *epigenetic landscape* and *canalization*, which he compared to grooves and bumps guiding a rolling "ball" symbolizing cell fate on a hilly terrain. We will use these Waddingtonian operational concepts when coupling the mechanic and genetic parts of our model in Part 4. Developmental genetics established a new methodology for the study of embryology. Instead of perturbing tissues, *mutant* phenotypes were generated by modifying their genetic expression, especially by "knocking out" genes one by one and inferring their role in absentia. Such experiments were most systematically conducted during the 1980s by Christiane Nüsslein-Volhard and Eric Wieschaus in *Drosophila* (Nüsslein-Volhard and Wieschaus 1980) and several other model organisms, more recently in the zebrafish (Nüsslein-Volhard 2012).

Molecular genetics: The discovery of the operon-lactose mechanism by Jacob and Monod in 1961 marked the start of the molecular genetic trend in embryology. It applied the idea of induction at the subcellular level by introducing genetic determinants, the *regulator* and *operator genes*, which explain how the rate of protein synthesis was controlled by the action of *repressors*. This crucial discovery reconciled the embryological orchestration of cell behavior with the molecular paradigm. The modern view systematized the role of genetic regulators by casting them into arrays of target sites for *transcription factors* (TFs) on the DNA (Arnone and Davidson 1997). Taken together, these arrays define a web of genetic interactions called a *gene regulatory network* (GRN), whose dynamics depends on the network topology and the various TF quantities. Since 2002 rapid progress in systematic sequencing and functional genetics has led to the publication of large-scale GRN maps, such as the one underlying the early patterning of the zebrafish embryo (Chan et al. 2009). GRN dynamics is initialized by various *maternal factors* (Pelegri 2003), which are TFs already present in the egg and whose anisotropic distribution is also an important cause of the patterning of the body plan (Gavis and Lehmann

1992). Critically, it also involves communication capabilities through secretion, diffusion, and binding of extracellular ligands, which trigger transduction processes and subsequent modification of the cytoplasmic dynamics. More recently, a growing number of *epigenetic* regulatory mechanisms have also been identified, such as mechanotransduction, methylation, and other epigenetic modifications, notably "gene silencing" by RNA interference.

Cell biomechanics: Today, the post-genomic era is bringing back the cell as the integrator of the molecular and genetic machinery. Understanding precisely how the cell *behaves physically* has become a major question. Cell motility, cell adhesion, and membrane deformation are all part of the *biomechanics* underlying morphogenetic processes and their emergent features at a macroscopic level. As reviewed by Keller (2012), this field remained quiet for a long period but was recently revived. Keller distinguishes two notions in the physical shaping of embryos, already envisioned by Johannes Holtfreter in the 1930s: *selective affinity* modulated by adhesion, and *physical integration* of multiple local cellular behaviors. In particular, Holtfreter observed that cells from different germ layers mixed together were still able to recognize their lineage origins and adopt different preferential association or "affinities" accordingly. In the 1960s, Malcom Steinberg refined this idea into the *Differential Adhesion Hypothesis* (DAH) (Steinberg 1962), stating that cells are both cohesive and mutually motile in such a way that the interfacial surface tension leads the ensemble toward the most stable configuration. These concepts form the basis of more recent quantitative approaches of cell biomechanics in culture and *in vivo* (von Dassow and Davidson 2011).

1.2 Models of embryonic development

Although the works cited above made important theoretical hypotheses and proposed key ideas to explain development, they did not propose formal models *per se*, whether of a mathematical-analytical or a computational type, i.e. they performed no symbolic or numerical processing. In recent years, however, an ever increasing number of theoretical and quantitative models and simulations of development have emerged. In this section, we provide a small sampler of studies that constitute typical illustrations of the most common modeling and simulation paradigms currently in practice.

Reaction-diffusion systems: A historical landmark in the advent of developmental models was established by Alan Turing in 1952 with his work on "The chemical basis of morphogenesis" (Turing 1952). He proved that ordered patterns, such as stripes and spots of alternating color, could spontaneously arise from the amplification of unstable fluctuations in an initially homogeneous substrate. This idea was further elaborated and popularized by Gierer and Meinhardt in the 1970s (Gierer and Meinhardt 1972). They showed that, by combining "a short-range positive feedback with a long-range negative feedback," they could generate all possible Turing patterns. Typically, a pigmented medium such as an animal coat could undergo spontaneous symmetry-breaking by diffusion and reaction of an activator substance with an inhibitor substance, called *morphogens*, characterized by two different decay rates and distances (Meinhardt and Gierer 1974). This was also demonstrated by abstract models of vertebrate skin patterning, such as the stripes of the angelfish, implemented in cellular automata (Young 1984; Kondo and Miura 2010).

However, this did not imply that the *in vivo* mechanisms were actually understood. Although reaction-diffusion models can theoretically account for all sorts of patterns, biological striping phenomena where this framework applies are much more rare. For example, it is now established that the gene expression patterns in the *Drosophila* segmentation cannot be explained by reaction-diffusion models (Bieler et al. 2011). The zebrafish pigmentation offers another contrasting example of pattern that does not form via reaction-diffusion *stricto sensu*, i.e. based on putative molecules diffusing at long range, but rather via a "combination of other signaling mechanisms that have long and short functional distances" (Inaba et al. 2012).

Morphogen gradients and positional information: Most biological systems distinguish themselves by strong morphological features, i.e. an elaborate shape and body plan *architecture*, which are much more sophisticated than texture-like pattern formation. The precisely arranged body shape of animals, made of articulated segments and subparts, is not the result of free-forming random instabilities, but rather a "genomically guided" morphogenesis process. This aspect can be better captured through the paradigm of *positional information* (PI) introduced by Lewis Wolpert in the 1960s (Wolpert 1969, 2011). At an abstract level, the key idea is simply that cells must establish long-range communication system that allows them to create different parts of the organism in different locations. It is inevitable that some form of PI should be at work in multicellular organism development, embodied in various ways, for example via passive diffusion of morphogens spreading throughout the tissue or cell-to-cell intermediate-messenger signaling (Lawrence 2001; Lander et al. 2002; Tabata and Takei 2004).

Several experimental techniques have been developed to study these modes of morphogen propagation (Kicheva et al. 2012). In any case, they all give rise to concentration *gradients*, either in the extracellular matrix (ECM) or in the cells' cytoplasm. In effect, PI is a genuine *coordinate system* that self-organizes by decentralized chemical signaling among cells. Recurring at multiple levels of details in a (non-self-similar) fractal fashion, it constitutes the basis of an entire "hidden geography" covering the embryo, following Enrico Coen's image (Coen 1999), and is also employed in abstract models of development and artificial life systems (Eggenberger 1997; Kumar and Bentley 2003; Doursat 2006). On the other hand, a major issue with concentration gradients is their robustness (Barkai and Shilo 2009). Since gradient diffusion and signal propagation are highly noisy and approximative, the stability of the emergent structures is believed to rather emerge from a combination of PI *and* gene regulation, in particular via some "attractor dynamics" in the GRN (Kauffman 1969; Reinitz and Sharp 1995), amidst the continually changing spatial environment of the growing organism (Rolland-Lagan et al. 2012).

Epithelial cell shaping and division patterns: A relatively recent interest in epithelial tissue modeling has generated a certain number of models focused on cell shaping, distribution of neighborhood sizes, and division axis fields. In (Gibson et al. 2006), the authors use a Markov chain model to explain the evolution of the distribution of cell shape in the *Drosophila* epithelium. They propose that cell proliferation, not cell packing, is responsible for the shaping of cells in monolayered epithelia. The model is generalized and compared to different organisms. Other investigators (Farhadifar et al. 2007) contend that physical forces, in addition to cell division, are also required to explain epithelial cell shape in the wing disc of *Drosophila*. They use a vertex-based model in which vertices represent intersections between the junctions linking wing cells. Forces are derived from an energy function that takes into account cell elasticity, cortical tension, and intercellular adhesion. The model is tested on experimental data obtained by laser ablation.

Sandersius et al. (2011) have investigated epithelium patterning before and during the primitive streak formation in the chick embryo. For them, against Gibson et al. (2006), non-spatial Markov models are not sufficient to explain the histogram of number of neighbors in proliferating-only epithelium. They argue that any attempt to improve biological plausibility of this type of model (e.g. with 3-sided cells or asynchronous division) induces a deviation from, instead of a refinement of, the "standard" histogram observed in various species. On the other hand, they show that their own geometrical epithelium model (based on a "Subcellular Element Model," Section 2.1) predicts the histogram with growth rate being the unique meaningful parameter.

Differential adhesion and cell sorting: The concept of patterning and compartment formation through cell sorting by differential adhesion, which was developed by Steinberg under the name of *Differential Adhesion Hypothesis* (DAH), is both powerful from a theoretical point of view and for its adequacy to describe the biological systems in agreement with typical biological observations at the tissular, cellular, and molecular level. Theoretical modeling and computer simulation in 2D and 3D of DAH-based cell sorting have been repeatedly carried out. In 1992, Graner and Glazier published their seminal cellular Potts model (Graner and Glazier 1992; Glazier and Graner 1993). Other theoretical frameworks were used to simulate similar processes: Broadland and Chen favored a finite element model (Brodland and Chen 2000), Landsberg et al. developed a vertex model for a network of adherens junctions to simulate the formation of compartments in *Drosophila* embryogenesis (Landsberg et al. 2009; Aliee et al. 2012), Beatrici and Brunnet explored the possibility to achieve cell sorting solely by motility differences in a model of self-propelled particles (Beatrici and Brunnet 2011).

The relevance of DAH has been reinforced by the characterization of cell adhesion molecules and their quantitative contribution to the surface tension in aggregates, thus providing a molecular basis to cell sorting (Foty and Steinberg 2005). The nature of the dependency between the surface tension of an aggregate and the cadherin expression level has also been explored theoretically (Zhang et al. 2011). More recent studies have tried to experimentally distinguish the respective contribution of cell adhesion and cortex tension in cell-cell contact formation, cell sorting, and tissue segregation. Heisenberg, Paluch, and colleagues approached these issues in zebrafish early development and the segregation of embryonic progenitors (Maitre et al. 2012).

1.3 Toward common modeling principles

Most of the models reviewed in the previous section were focused on specific aspects of development, whether certain episodes of embryogenesis localized in space and time, or particular mechanical or genetic components of the dynamics. The ambition of the MecaGen project is to integrate all these dimensions into one comprehensive, or *in toto*, framework.

In biological systems, three levels of organization are generally considered: the subcellular level (in which the individual elements are molecules), the cellular level (cells), and the organism level (tissues and organs). Even though cell-cell mechanical and chemical interactions are ultimately grounded in the same physics of molecular interactions (covalent, ionic, hydrogen, and electrostatic bonds), they seem to obey their own laws and "cell behavior ontology" on a higher phenomenological level. Therefore, designing a model of multicellular development requires identifying custom laws at each level—as the reductionist dream of a huge atom-based simulation is not conceivable or just completely impractical. This involves a mix of continuous and discrete approaches, bringing analytical, statistical, and agent-based computational models together. Several works have ventured proposing such integrated frameworks at various degrees of completion and with different emphasis: multiscale mechanical forces (Blanchard and Adams 2011; van Leeuwen et al. 2009), multiscale pattern formation (Grima 2008; Little and Wieschaus 2011), multimodel and simulation platforms such as CompuCell3D (Izaguirre et al. 2004; Cickovski et al. 2007; Swat et al. 2008), or multiscale abstract models and artificial life systems (Doursat 2008; Joachimczak and Wróbel 2008; Schramm et al. 2011; Doursat et al. 2012).

The two major groups of mesoscopic properties that appear in most of these studies, and constitute the foundation of our own model, are (a) biomechanical properties and (b) genetic regulation and molecular signaling properties. The key toward understanding the morphogenesis and systemic properties of the organism lies in the *coupling* of both. It concerns how (b) influences (a) through the production and modulation of the cytoskeleton, molecular motors, and cell adhesion, but also how (a) influences (b) through the transduction of mechanical stress. The modeling work should identify the appropriate level of schematization, i.e. capture the essential causal relationships without going into fine molecular details.

Typical systemic properties of living organisms, such as development, autopoiesis or homeostasis, can only be understood through a *complex systems* approach of their underlying biological processes. Complex systems are composed of a great number of small elements that interact locally and produce a collective behavior in a decentralized and self-organized fashion. Concerning embryogenesis, this perspective requires new experimental methods, in particular the use of animal models chosen for their accessibility, transparency, and phylogenetic position. The originality of MecaGen is to directly confront the level of the complexity of living processes, something that biology has so far partly evaded in its traditional attempts to address the "function" of single genes, or dissect subcellular processes in isolated cultured cells. Now that the pieces of the puzzle have been (more or less) well identified, it is time to try and *integrate* them all together at the level of thousands of genes and millions of cells in order to see the big picture of the growing organism.

In the remainder of this chapter, the two modules, MECA and GEN, are explained separately, then coupled in Parts 2–4 (Figure 16.7 for a preview of the main components of the model and their relationships). The resulting agent-based simulations create an "in silico" embryo, i.e. a virtual test object that can be manipulated and measured in ways impossible with a real embryo. Next, Part 5 shows two illustrations on artificial data: gene regulation motifs and cell sorting, and Part 6 demonstrates a custom application of MecaGen to a real biological case study: the zebrafish early development. We take as an example the intercalation patterns appearing during the first phase of epiboly and the movements of the deep cells. Measures from the simulated embryo are confronted to measures extracted from microscopy imaging. The goal is to show that the parameters of our model can be tuned to validate the simulations, hence draw biologically meaningful conclusions. Finally, Part 7 offers a critical discussion of the choices made and perspectives for future work.

2 MECA: MODEL OF CELL BIOMECHANICS

In this first part of the model, we formalize the mechanical interactions and behavioral properties of the cells. We begin with a brief review of various biomechanical models (Section 2.1), in continuous or discrete spaces, of geometrical or physical nature, paying closer attention to *off-lattice, particle-based methods,* which will be the basis of our own approach. Next, we present a *discrete-element model using one particle per cell*, driven by an overdamped equation of motion (Section 2.2) of the type $\lambda\vec{v}_i = \vec{F}_i^P + \vec{F}_i^A$, where $\vec{v}_i$ is the velocity of one cell i, $\vec{F}_i^P$ represents "passive" interaction forces controlling cell stiffness and adhesion (Section 2.3), and $\vec{F}_i^A$ represents "active" interaction forces, i.e. specific cell behavior, such as protrusive activity or apical constriction, based on polarization axes. (Section 2.4). These forces are calculated by adding contributions from cells j in the neighborhood $\mathcal{N}_i$ of cell i, defined by topological criteria.

2.1 Challenges in biomechanical modeling

Through his theory, Wilhelm Roux established the importance of mechanics in the study of developmental systems. Since then, a great number of theoretical models of biomechanics have been proposed at various levels of abstraction—and speculation. Depending on the researchers' background and their focus of interest, embryogenesis has been assimilated to differential geometry, pattern formation, fluid dynamics, material physics, systems architecture, cellular automata or collective motion, among many disciplines. In particular, the growth and shaping of cells, tissues and organs have been variously compared to manifolds, balloons, tensegrity structures, bubbles, swarms, and so on. This diversity is due to the extremely elusive nature of multicellular systems compared to the traditional objects studied by classical mechanics. Whereas the Newtonian framework is well suited to fixed objects presenting high spatiotemporal regularities, living matter is riddled with heterogeneity, irregularities, and ceaseless internal adaptivity. Local cell behaviors and global tissue properties can change rapidly as they rest upon a molecular structure in constant flux and state of self-reorganization. Therefore, this heterogeneity of behaviors gave rise to a heterogeneity of models, unfortunately not always compatible with each other. Nonetheless, these attempts are useful to help capture pieces of the puzzle and bring us closer to a more accurate and complete rendition of organism development.

We distinguish here between "macroscopic" models relying on continuous space and "microscopic" models relying on discrete elements. The latter will constitute the basis for the *particle-based* approach that we follow in our own model.

Macroscopic viewpoint: continuous-space laws: Macroscopic descriptions of the embryo set behavioral laws directly at the global tissular level without explicit underlying cellular or molecular components. They are generally based on macroscopic partial (spatial) differential equations, which have the benefit of compactness, as they offer an inclusive representation of development in one or a few formulas. On the other hand, the main disadvantage of grand formalisms is often too much generality or vagueness, with a consequent lack of operational tools. In any case, cell tissue in this paradigm is construed as a continuous mass, equivalent to an infinity of infinitesimal points. Mathematical biology (Murray 2003) epitomizes the continuum mechanics paradigm, which is broadly divided into *solid mechanics* and *fluid mechanics* approaches. A distinctive feature of solids and fluids is their unequal ability to resist the action of a tangential shearing force. Both fields distinguish different types of bulk behavior and both have been applied to biological matter and multicellular tissue. In the case of fluids, stresses are linked to velocity fields through a continuity equation and conservation laws. In the case of solids, stresses are linked to a deformation tensor (strain) (Fleury 2005).

Microscopic viewpoint: discrete-element rules: Microscopic descriptions of biological tissue consider the cells that constitute it (sometimes the subcellular structures and molecules, too) as autonomously acting components. It is their collective behavior that determines the mechanical properties of the tissue at the emergent level. As the elements of discrete models do not always coincide one-to-one with cells (being possibly subcellular or supracellular), they are alternatively called "particles." Their properties generally include spatial coordinates and geometric features, and optionally mechanical and physical properties. There are four main groups of discrete models, depending on whether particles are confined to a discrete grid or not, and whether cells are made of several particles or only one: (i) on-lattice models with one particle per cell, corresponding to *cellular automata* (extensively reviewed by Deutsch and Dormann (2005)); (ii) on-lattice models with multiple particles per cell, essentially represented by the *Cellular Potts Model* (introduced by Graner and Glazier (1992) and best exemplified by Marée and Hogeweg (2001)); (iii) off-lattice models with one particle per cell, composed of a 2D/3D irregular network whose vertices represent cells and edges represent cell-cell interactions (typically as in the *Delaunay-Object-Dynamics* model by Schaller and Meyer-Hermann (2004)); and (iv) off-lattice models with multiple particles per cell, in which the fine grain of subcellular particles is preserved (most notably the *Subcellular Element Model* (ScEM) of Newman (2005)). The framework we eventually adopted in MecaGen belongs to category (iii) and its specific features are explained below.

2.2 Central equation of cell motion

The biomechanical model presented here is a type of *particle-based physics*, meaning that cells are represented by "particles"—here, only one per cell. The classical Newtonian *equation of motion* describing a particle with mass m and acceleration $\vec{a}$ reads $m\vec{a} = \vec{F}(\vec{X}, \vec{v}, R)$, where the sum of forces $\vec{F}$ can depend on the particle's location $\vec{X}$, velocity $\vec{v}$, and/or radius R. Cells, however, are small, ambivalent fluid-solid entities, and their interactions are "sticky," which makes their inertial forces negligible with respect to viscosity (corresponding to a low Reynolds number). In that case, applied forces become proportional to velocity, not acceleration: if $m \ll \lambda$, then $m\vec{a} = -\lambda\vec{v} + \vec{F}$ yields $\lambda\vec{v} = \vec{F}$.

Generalizing to a multicellular swarm S, the motion of each cell i is governed by the sum of forces $\vec{F}_{ij}$ exerted by all other cells j belonging to its neighborhood $\mathcal{N}_i$:

$$\lambda_i \vec{v}_i = \sum_{j \in \mathcal{N}_i} \vec{F}_{ij} = \sum_{j \in \mathcal{N}_i} \vec{F}_{ij}^P + \vec{F}_{ij}^A = \vec{F}_i^P + \vec{F}_i^A \quad (16.1)$$

where $\vec{F}_i^P$ represents "passive" interaction forces, $\vec{F}_i^A$ represents "active" interaction forces (explained in Sections 2.3 and 2.4), and the damping coefficient is proportional to the surface

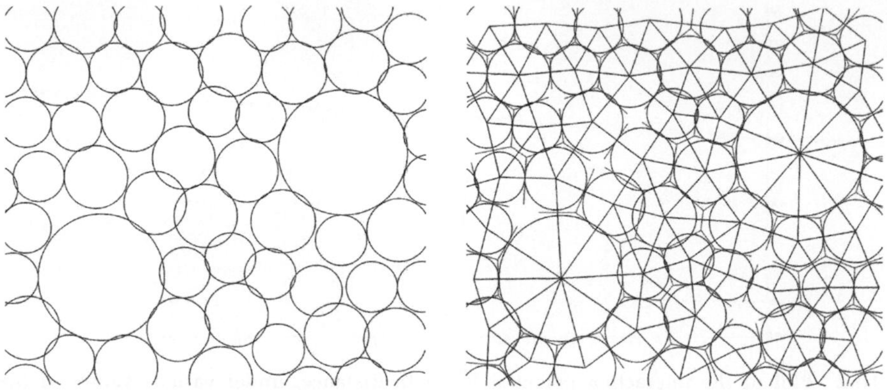

FIGURE 16.1 **Output of the neighborhood algorithm.** Left: A 2D swarm of cells characterized by various given positions and radii. Right: The neighborhood links (black edges, radiating from the centers) and contact areas (red edges, tangential to the circles) between cells calculated by the method described in this section. (For interpretation of the references to color in this figure legend, the reader is referred to the web version of this book.)

area of the cell: $\lambda_i = \lambda_0 R_i^{\,2}$. The neighborhood $\mathcal{N}_i$ is calculated in two steps: first, a preselection of potential neighbors that obey certain *metric* criteria, then a refinement of this list according to *topological* features (Figure 16.1). According to the metric criteria, two cells of radius R_i, R_j and locations $\vec{X}_i, \vec{X}_j$ are considered neighbors if their distance is smaller than a cutoff value:

$$\mathcal{N}_i^m = \left\{ j \in S : \left\| \vec{X}_i - \vec{X}_j \right\| \le c_{\max}(R_i + R_j) \right\}. \tag{16.2}$$

In the following, we denote $r_{ij} = \left\| \vec{X}_i - \vec{X}_j \right\|$ and $r_{ij}^{\max} = c_{\max}(R_i + R_j)$, i.e. $r_{ij} \le r_{ij}^{\max}$ for neighbor cells i and j. Although cells are "spheroidal," they also have the possibility to deform in order to interact with farther away neighbor cells. Radius $r_{ij}^{\max}$ sets the maximum distance of this deformation. To evaluate $c_{\max}$, we established an empirical law relating r_{ij} to the contact area between i and j, denoted by A_{ij}, such that it vanishes for $r_{ij} = r_{ij}^{\max}$:

$$A_{ij} = A(r_{ij}, R_i, R_j) = a(r_{ij} - r_{ij}^{\max})^2 \text{ iff } r_{ij} < r_{ij}^{\max}, \quad \text{otherwise } 0. \tag{16.3}$$

In the absence of real data, we constructed an artificial testbed experiment to infer an approximate relationship. It consisted of an ellipsoidal domain that was filled with three consecutive generations of dividing cells, then distorted in various ways to force the cells into different spatial rearrangements. We found the best empirical fit for values $a = 1.3697$ and $c_{\max} = 1.2414$, which are used throughout the model.

A purely metric neighborhood, however, is not viable as it often leads to collapsing volumes during simulation when adhesion between interacting cells is high. This is why we ultimately used a topological neighborhood denoted by $\mathcal{N}_i^t$, based on a variant of the Voronoi diagram and its dual, the Delaunay triangulation, called a *Gabriel graph*. In 2D, this method imposes that no node be found inside the circle whose diameter is a valid neighborhood edge. We generalized the Gabriel criterion to the 3D case using spheres as follows:

$$\mathcal{N}_i^t = \left\{ j \in \mathcal{N}_i^m : \forall k \in \mathcal{N}_i^m, \quad \left\| \vec{X}_k - \frac{1}{2}(\vec{X}_i + \vec{X}_j) \right\| \ge \frac{r_{ij}}{2} \right\}. \tag{16.4}$$

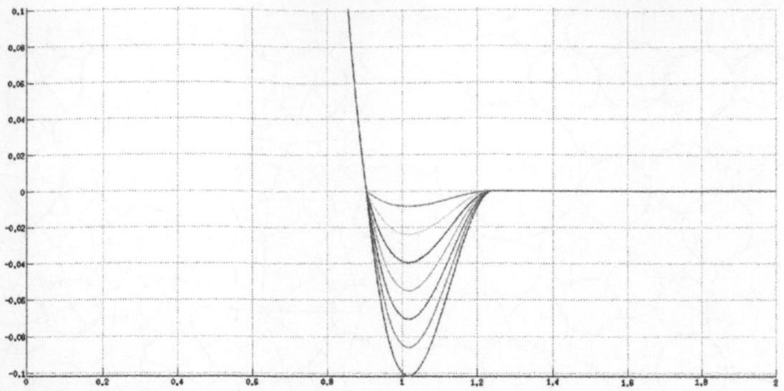

FIGURE 16.2 Plot of the interaction potential E^P with distance, under various values of the adhesion coefficient w_{adh}. The relaxation force $\vec{F}^P$ is derived from E^P. Curves are composed of three domains: repulsion at short range (until the minimum, i.e. $F = 0$), attraction at mid-range (after the minimum), and neutrality at long range (constant F). See text for details.

2.3 Interaction potential forces

For every pair of neighboring particles (i, j) we focus in this section on the interaction potential E^P_{ij} from which the "passive, or *relaxation*" force $\vec{F}^P_{ij}$ is derived. Like most particle-based interaction potential models, we distinguish three distance domains (Figure 16.2): (a) a *repulsion* domain (decreasing E) at distances shorter than an equilibrium distance defined by $r^{eq}_{ij} = c^{eq}_i R_i + c^{eq}_j R_j$, where c^{eq}_i is a coefficient that may depend on the cell; (b) an *attraction* domain (increasing E) at distances greater than r^{eq}_{ij}; and (c) a *neutral* domain (constant E) beyond the maximum limit of the interaction field $r^{max}_{ij} = c_{max}(R_i + R_j)$.

Toward short distances, as soon as two cells touch each other, adhesive forces tend to increase their contact area A_{ij} until inner resistance compensates the push. This implicitly defines an equilibrium surface area and distance. Accordingly, the expression of the relaxation force is made of three parts:

$$\vec{F}^P_{ij} = \begin{cases} -A_{ij} w_{rep}(r_{ij} - r^{eq}_{ij}).\vec{u}_{ij} & \text{if } r_{ij} < r^{eq}_{ij} \\ -A_{ij} w_{adh}(r_{ij} - r^{eq}_{ij}).\vec{u}_{ij} & \text{if } r_{ij} \geq r^{eq}_{ij} \text{ and } r_{ij} < r^{max}_{ij} \\ \vec{0} & \text{if } r_{ij} \geq r^{max}_{ij} \end{cases} \tag{16.5}$$

where $A_{ij} = a(r_{ij} - r^{max}_{ij})^2$ is the contact area introduced earlier, while the depth of the well is controlled by a repulsion coefficient w_{rep} until r^{eq}_{ij} and an adhesion coefficient w_{adh} beyond r^{eq}_{ij}.

In the previous section, we estimated a universal average value for coefficient c_{max} based on empirical statistics of the contact areas between neighboring particles. Here, we need to estimate the equilibrium coefficients c^{eq}_i of the relaxation forces. For this, we rely on the densest arrangement of sphere packing, in which each sphere touches 12 other spheres, as an approximation. In this scenario, we obtain a uniform value $c^{eq}_i \equiv c_{eq} = (\pi/(3\sqrt{2}))^{1/3} \simeq 0.904$.

2.4 Behavioral forces

Another crucial difference with solid objects is that surrounding cells are responsible not only for dampening motion but also for motion itself. To progress, a cell needs to cling and push back surrounding cells, somewhat like a swimmer pushes back water to move forward. Thus, in addition to the passive attraction/repulsion forces $\vec{F}_{ij}^{P}$, we introduce *proactive behavioral* forces $\vec{F}_{ij}^{A}$, composed of an "intrinsic" term $\vec{F}_{ij}^{A,\text{int}}$ and its "extrinsic" counterpart $\vec{F}_{ij}^{A,\text{ext}}$, whose purpose is to provide a schematic model of the cells' specialized biomechanics. During development and across numerous species, cells manifest a wide variety of mechanical properties and behavioral phenomena. We focus here on one such mechanism, *cellular protrusion*, which we believe is the main driving force in the zebrafish early gastrulation.

2.4.1 Protrusion behavior

Cell protrusion is essentially a *cyclic* activity, similar to the activity of tracked vehicles (such as tanks) except that, since inertia plays no part in cellular interactions, adhesion is regulated in a special way to avoid sliding between the cell surfaces in contact. Protrusive activity induces an *intercalation* of the cell between its neighbors. One condition is the presence of an *axis of polarization*, which is generally related to the diffusion of external ligand molecules and an asymmetrical distribution of internal substances (explained in Part 4). This axis can also be caused by mechanotransduction from neighboring cell-cell contacts, or feedback from the active forces themselves, but these aspects are not modeled here. In any case, it determines two regions of the cell, or *poles*, where protrusive activity occurs: if only one pole is active, the cell is called "monopolar"; if both are active, it is called "bipolar."

At the subcellular level, the main structure underlying protrusion is the cellular scaffolding of the *cytoskeleton*, whose three main components are microfilaments (similar to an "envelope" that contracts and dilates), intermediate filaments ("cables" exerting a tension), and microtubules ("beams" resisting compression). To explain protrusion, we focus on the microfilaments, which constitute most of the cell cortex, a mesh-like network made of actin and myosin molecules that lie just below the plasma membrane and are attached to it by catenin molecules. The active deformation of this acto-myosin network, essentially by (re)polymerization of actin, provides the driving mechanism of protrusion (Figure 16.3).

The coupled action of acto-myosin cortex and the focal adhesion points form a sort of "treadmill" originating at the tip of the protrusion (Figure 16.4). This movement induces a torque transmission between the protruding cell and each of the neighbor cells attached by focal adhesion points. The transfer of cell material in the bulge results from the "intrinsic" force generated by the acto-myosin cortex, while the "extrinsic" force is exerted on the adjacent cell through the focal adhesion points. In some cases, an additional mechanism of cellular contraction at the back of the cell (not included here) amplifies the intrinsic force. We assume that the distribution of focal adhesion points is homogeneous on the surface area of the cell, so the quantity of torque transmitted between two neighboring cells i and j is proportional to their contact area A_{ij}.

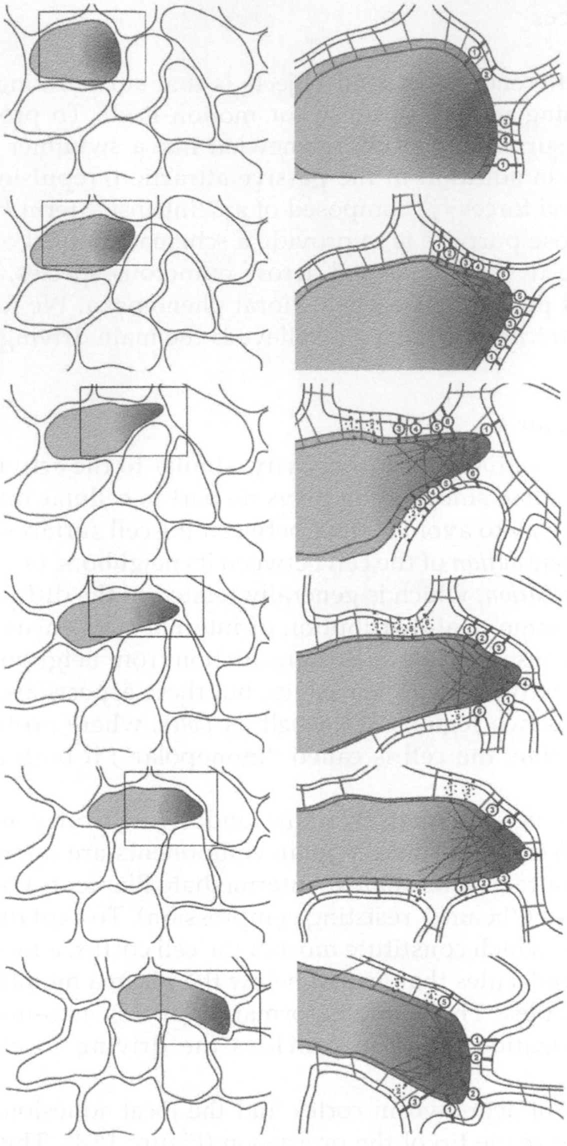

FIGURE 16.3 Cellular protrusion illustrated at the subcellular level. A cell is attached to its neighbors by molecular bridges (essentially cadherin molecules, symbolized by thin orange edges), which actively deform their internal acto-myosin cortical network in the direction of the polarization axis (blue mesh of lines and curves) indicated by the internal chemical gradient (yellow-green shades across the cell). A bulge eventually appears at the active pole, pushing away neighboring cells. No intercalation process would be observed, however, without a precise regulation of the adhesion contacts between the cells. Thus, in addition to the regular adhesion bonds, special *focal adhesion points* (thick red edges carrying numbers) also appear at the surface of the protruding region of the cell. These bonds bear extra load generated by the protrusive activity of the acto-myosin cortex. They become visible around the tip of the bulge and, as the cell is advancing, maintain spatial cohesion between neighboring cytoskeletons. Without them, the cell would slip on the surface and the efficiency of the protrusion would be greatly reduced. Focal adhesion points gradually disappear from the cell membrane as the cell advances relatively to the bonded neighbors. (For interpretation of the references to color in this figure legend, the reader is referred to the web version of this book.)

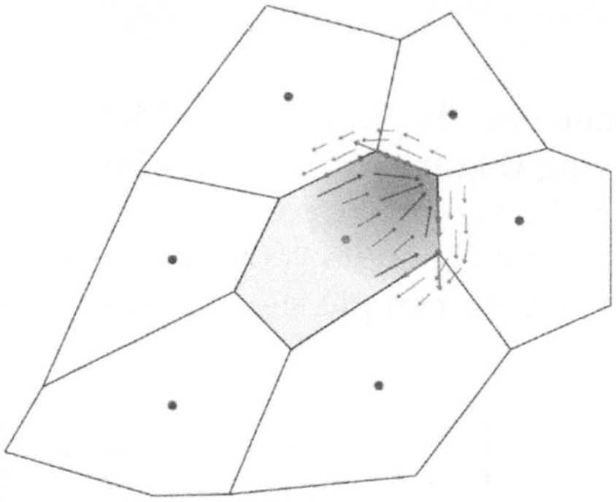

FIGURE 16.4 **Idealized view of the protrusive activity in MECA.** Internal arrows represent the cell interior flow and external arrows the cell neighborhood flow, as the central cell exerts a protrusion over its surroundings. The schematized focal adhesion points of Figure 16.3, which appear at the tip of the cell, move back then disappear as the cell moves forward.

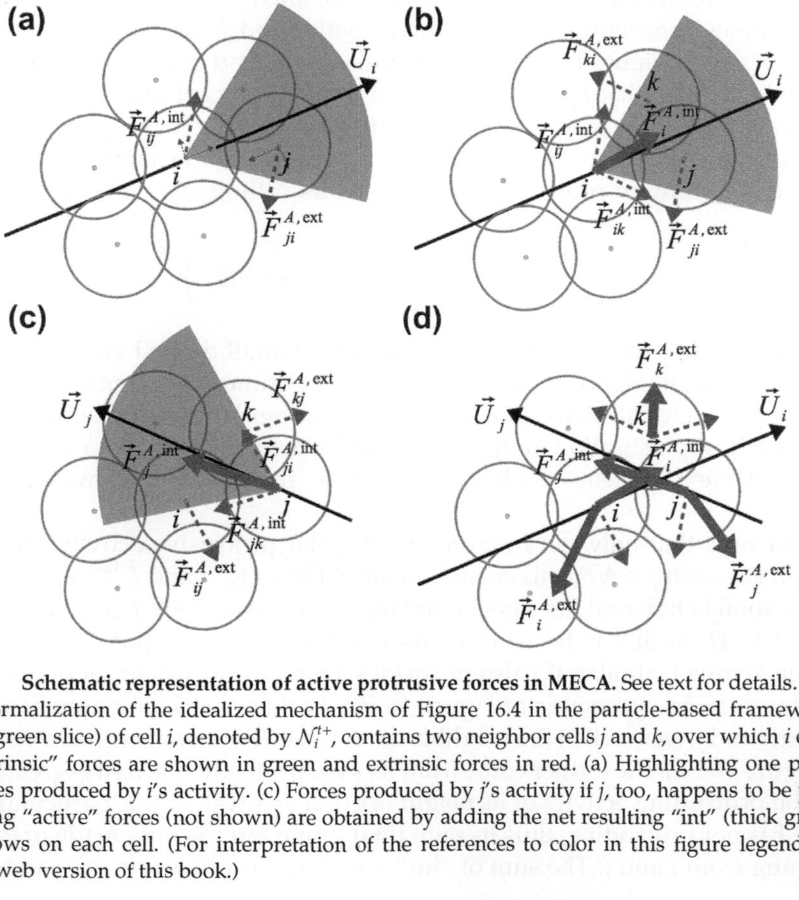

FIGURE 16.5 **Schematic representation of active protrusive forces in MECA.** See text for details. These schemas illustrate the formalization of the idealized mechanism of Figure 16.4 in the particle-based framework. (a, b) The polar domain (green slice) of cell i, denoted by $\mathcal{N}_i^{t+}$, contains two neighbor cells j and k, over which i exerts a protrusive force. "Intrinsic" forces are shown in green and extrinsic forces in red. (a) Highlighting one pair of opposite forces. (b) Forces produced by i's activity. (c) Forces produced by j's activity if j, too, happens to be protruding. (d) The net resulting "active" forces (not shown) are obtained by adding the net resulting "int" (thick green) and "ext" (thick red) arrows on each cell. (For interpretation of the references to color in this figure legend, the reader is referred to the web version of this book.)

2.4.2 *Active force model*

In our particle-based framework, the mathematical interpretation and representation of this mechanism is the following (Figure 16.5a): a cell i possesses a normalized *polarization axis* $\vec{U}_i$ (black arrow), considered given in this part. Inside $\mathcal{N}_i^t$, we denote by $\mathcal{N}_i^{t+}$ the sublist of neighbors that make contact with cell i on its "positive" pole, i.e. are positioned relative to i in the same general direction as $\vec{U}_i$ (green pie-slice domain, covering two cells j and k in the figure):

$$\mathcal{N}_i^{t+} = \left\{ j \in \mathcal{N}_i^t : \frac{\vec{X}_j - \vec{X}_i}{\left\| \vec{X}_j - \vec{X}_i \right\|} \cdot \vec{U}_i \geq \eta \right\} \tag{16.6}$$

A threshold value η controls the relative size of the protrusion (the opening of the pie slice). Similarly, we denote by $\mathcal{N}_i^{t-}$ the sublist of neighbors that share a contact area on the "negative" pole of the cell, i.e. away from the polarization vector. This opposite neighborhood is used in the case of an opposite monopolar or a bipolar protrusion behavior.

In the regular monopolar case illustrated here, for each neighbor $j \in \mathcal{N}_i^{t+}$, a pair of equal and opposite forces contribute to the motion of both i and j: an intrinsic force $\vec{F}_{ij}^{A,\text{int}}$ (larger dashed green arrow in Figure 16.5a) and its simultaneous and exact counterpart $\vec{F}_{ji}^{A,\text{ext}}$ (larger dashed red arrow), such that $\vec{F}_{ji}^{A,\text{ext}} = -\vec{F}_{ij}^{A,\text{int}}$. The common axis of these forces is designed to roughly emulate the profile of the contact area that can be seen in the polygonal representation of Figure 16.4 (but not in the disc-particle representation of Figure 16.5). It is a linear combination of the unitary protrusion axis $\vec{U}_i$ and its orthogonal complement $\vec{U}_i^{\perp j}$ passing through j:

$$\vec{F}_{ij}^{A,\text{int}} = f^A A_{ij} \cdot \left(\cos(\nu)\, \vec{U}_i + \sin(\nu)\, \vec{U}_i^{\perp j} \right) \tag{16.7}$$

where the angle ν tunes the profile of the contact area (small dashed arrows resulting in the larger dashed arrows in Figure 16.5a) and coefficient f^A tunes the intensity of the force. The angle could be precisely calculated as a function of the angular position of each neighbor, but we deemed such sophistication unnecessary and opted instead for a constant value of $\arctan(4/3) \approx 53°$ (experiments with other values around 45° showed no significant difference).

Suppose for now that only cell i exerts a monopolar protrusive activity on its neighbors (Figure 16.5b). For each $j \in \mathcal{N}_i^{t+}$, this creates a pair of forces $\vec{F}_{ij}^{A,\text{int}}$ and $\vec{F}_{ji}^{A,\text{ext}}$ as described above. Therefore, the total behavioral force generated by i's protrusion (solid green arrow, not necessarily parallel to $\vec{U}_i$ in 3D) is the sum of its neighbors' contributions: $\vec{F}_i^{A,\text{int}} = \vec{F}_{ij}^{A,\text{int}} + \vec{F}_{ik}^{A,\text{int}}$ (dashed green arrows). Similar, if j also protrudes, then an equivalent set of forces is created around it (Figure 16.5c, symmetric of Figure 16.5b). In that case, combining both protruding activities from i and j, each cell in the neighborhood can be the site of both intrinsic and extrinsic forces (Figure 16.5d): the former come from its own protruding activity (green arrows), the latter from the protruding activity of its neighbors (red arrows). In this particular illustration, the third cell k is not protruding, thus its own total active force is only made of extrinsic components coming from i and j. The sum of "int" and "ext" forces on i (resp. j and k) yields the net "active" force on this cell (not shown in Figure 16.5d), which corresponds to $\vec{F}_i^A$ (resp. $\vec{F}_j^A$ and $\vec{F}_k^A$) in its motion equation. Each net active force leads a cell to move alongside its neighbors and pass through.

Finally, at the scale of the whole embryo, the net global force resulting from this complex field of local intrinsic/extrinsic active forces is zero, due to their mutual compensation: $\vec{F}^A \equiv \sum_i \sum_{j \in N_i} \vec{F}_{ij}^A = \sum_i \vec{F}_i^A = \vec{0}$. This is a reasonable expectation, as the relative movements of cells with respect to each other (protrusion, constriction, migration, etc.) should not have the effect of moving the embryo but only reshaping it.

Summary: The biomechanical model MECA proposes basic rules that are sufficient to simulate the physics of a high number of cells in a deforming tissue. Among its original features, we have defined a new neighborhood based on an adaptation of the Gabriel rule to 3D sets of particles; we have obtained a new approximation of the classical inter-particles force potential (of the Morse or Lennard-Jones type) by scaling an elastic potential via an estimation of the contact area; we have also distinguished "passive" interaction forces, responsible for simple attraction and repulsion, from "active" interaction forces, responsible for more complex cell behaviors such as protrusion. Altogether, these modeling choices allow us to carry out massive computational simulations and explore large domains of parameter space relatively quickly (Part 6).

3 GEN: MODEL OF GENETIC REGULATION AND MOLECULAR SIGNALING

The goal of this part is to briefly review the principles of gene regulatory networks (GRNs) and chemical signaling, and describe the corresponding components of our model. The molecular and genetic interactions occurring during development are a subject of intense research (Wilczynski and Furlong 2010; Ben-Tabou and Davidson 2009; Giacomantonio and Goodhill 2010), at the crossroads between bioinformatics, systems biology, and chemical kinetics. Nonetheless, we believe that relevant insight can already be gained by adopting three simple and easily computable types of rules: (1) a set of rules driving the dynamics of *intracellular* gene/protein reactions (Section 3.1); (2) rules driving the dynamics of cellular secretion and transduction, linking the intracellular with the extracellular milieu (Section 3.2); and (3) rules driving the dynamics of *extracellular* reactions, transport, and diffusion (Section 3.3).

These rules are generally expressed in a chemical kinetic framework by ordinary differential equations (ODEs) of the type $dp/dt = f(p, g, q, r)$, where p represents protein concentrations, g gene expression levels, q external ligands, and r membrane receptors. Extracellular reactions, transport, and diffusion of ligands are also taken into account via partial differential equations (PDEs) involving $\partial q/\partial t$ and fluxes $\vec{J} = -D\vec{\nabla}q$.

3.1 Intracellular gene and protein reactions

Protein concentrations $\mathbf{p} = \{p_a\}$ representing the various protein types P_a inside the cell can evolve through (i) protein-protein reactions, (ii) synthesis by encoding genes, or (iii) degradation by the molecular environment. Conversely, gene activities $\mathbf{g} = \{g_b\}$ are regulated by the proteins (bypassing RNA) via Boolean functions representing a logical combination of promoters and repressors. For example, two protein reactants yielding one protein product can be formalized by the following reaction and rate equations:

$$P_0 + P_1 \xrightarrow{k} P_2 \quad \text{with} \quad \begin{cases} \dot{p}_1 = -k'p_1 + \gamma_1 g_1 - \kappa_1 \\ \dot{p}_2 = +k'p_1 + \gamma_2 g_2 - \kappa_2 \end{cases} \tag{16.8}$$

where $k' = kp_0$ is the linear "pseudo-coefficient" of the reaction, assuming that P_0 is predominant ($p_0 \gg p_1$) and its variations negligible, γ_a is a linear rate of P_a's synthesis by encoding gene G_a, and κ_a is a constant rate for P_a's degradation.

Conversely, the activity of a gene G_b can be enhanced by the presence of promoting transcription factors (TFs) and/or the absence of repressing TFs. Here, a TF is assumed to be one of the proteins P_a and we denote by $P_a \curvearrowright G_b$ its structural ability to bind one of the cis-regulatory sites of G_b (regions of DNA near the gene sequence). Since multiple TFs may simultaneously influence a single gene, a binary matrix $\mathbf{\Gamma} = \{\Gamma_{ab}\}$ is a well-suited schematization (Peter et al. 2012):

$$\Gamma_{ab}(t) = 1 \text{ iff } P_a \curvearrowright G_b \text{ and } p_a(t) \geq \theta_{ab}, \quad \text{otherwise } 0 \tag{16.9}$$

where θ_{ab} is the concentration threshold above which protein a effectively binds site b. Then, the activity of gene G_b is determined by the output of a logic function f_b, a combination of the Boolean operators AND, OR, and NOT: $g_b(t) = f_b(\mathbf{\Gamma}(t))$. For example, if f_b is a pure AND operator, then all promoters must be present and all repressors absent to activate G_b. If it is a pure OR operator, then a single promoter suffices.

3.2 Signal secretion and transduction

Cells in the developing embryo communicate chemically through various means. Two of the most common mechanisms are: (a) *secretion*, typically by exocytosis, of proteins or metabolites through the cell membrane, and (b) *transduction* via receptors in the membrane, by which a signal triggers a second messenger on the other side. The interfacing module connected to the GRN that exports and imports these molecules will be generically named here *ligands*. A ligand Q_a can be externalized from the cellular domain into the space between cells, called "interstitium," with a secretion rate σ_a. Conversely, an extracellular signal can be transduced into an intracellular protein through a *signal transduction* module, comprising a receptor protein R_{ab} on the membrane, to which Q_a can bind and trigger the intracellular synthesis of protein P_b. The corresponding kinetic equations are not detailed here.

3.3 Extracellular reactions, transport, and diffusion

Various models of the spatial configuration of the interstitium have been elaborated (Kojić et al. 2010), but we prefer using the graph of neighborhood relationships $\mathcal{N}_i$ derived from the Gabriel rule (Section 2.2) to serve as transport infrastructure. The diffusion dynamics is based on Fick's law, stating that ligands move from high- to low-concentration regions

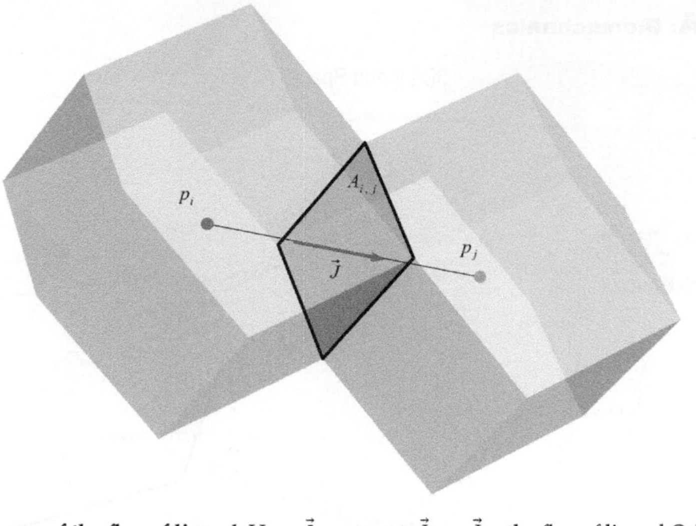

FIGURE 16.6 **Schema of the flux of ligand.** Here, $\vec{J}$ represents $\vec{J}_{a,ij} = \vec{J}_{a,ji}$, the flux of ligand Q_a between the cellular volumes occupied by neighboring particle-cells i and j.

proportionally to the *gradient* of concentration. Therefore, a discrete approximation of the flux of ligand Q_a on the edge between cell i and j, denoted by $\vec{J}_{a,ij}$, reads

$$\vec{J}_{a,ij} = -D_a \frac{q_{a,j} - q_{a,i}}{r_{ij}} \vec{u}_{ij} \tag{16.10}$$

where $q_{a,i}$ is the ligand's concentration near the surface of cell i, D_a a diffusion coefficient, $\vec{u}_{ij}$ the unit vector from i to j, and $r_{ij} = ||\vec{u}_{ij}||$ (Figure 16.6). Note that this expression is invariant by reversal of direction. Then, the temporal evolution of the concentration is determined by the *continuity equation*, which is a local form of conservation law. The divergence theorem gives the integral form of the continuity equation, applied to the volume of the cell. Its continuous expression is

$$\frac{\partial q_{a,i}}{\partial t} + \iint_O \vec{J}_{a,i}.\vec{dA} = s_{a,i} + d_{a,i} \tag{16.11}$$

where $\vec{J}_{a,i} = \sum_j \vec{J}_{a,ij}$ is the total flux of ligand a with respect to cell i, $\vec{dA}$ is the normal vector of the closed surface of the cell, $s_{a,i}$ is the "source" term corresponding to the rate of ligand produced by secretion, and $d_{a,i}$ is the "sink" term corresponding to the rate of extracellular ligand Q_a disappearing by transduction (terms from Section 3.2 not detailed here). Finally, importing the previous discrete approximation, we obtain

$$\frac{\partial q_{a,i}}{\partial t} = D_a \left(\sum_{j \in \mathcal{N}_i^t} \frac{A_{ij}}{r_{ij}} (q_{a,j} - q_{a,i}) \right) + s_{a,i} + d_{a,i} \tag{16.12}$$

Summary: The GEN model of genetic regulation and molecular signaling provides a new adaptation of the classical reaction-diffusion framework to a moving substrate. The

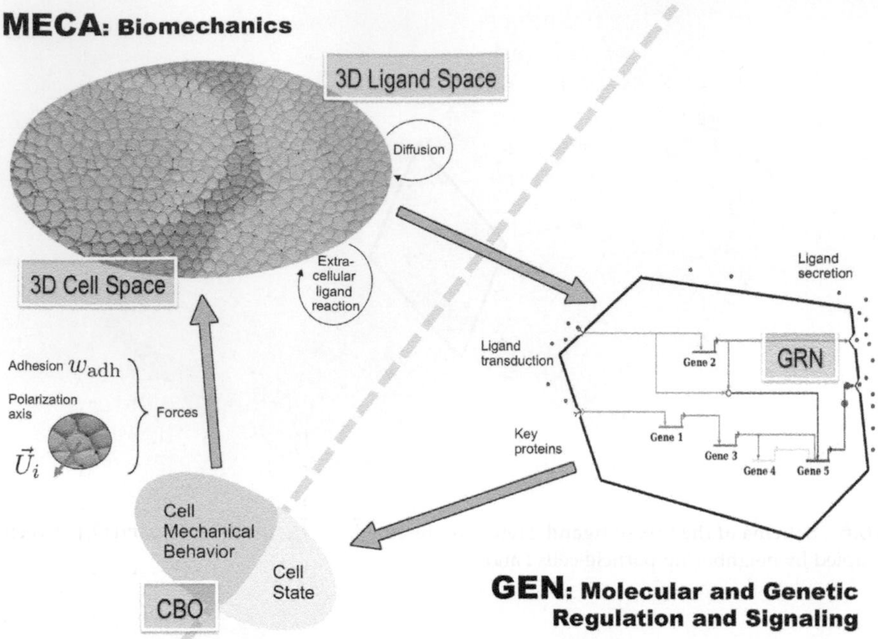

FIGURE 16.7 Flowchart of the complete MecaGen model, illustrating its core principles. Three modules are described in this chapter. (1) A particle-based framework supports both the biomechanics (3D cell space, Part 2) and the extracellular diffusion (3D ligand space, Section 3.3). (2) Intracellular molecular signaling and genetic regulation are modeled by a GRN via differential equations and Boolean operators (Section 3.1). (3) A cell behavior ontology (CBO) is also discussed in Section 4.1. Here, we temporarily simplify this diagram by introducing a custom cell differentiation tool, the Waddingtonian Timeline Specification (WTS, Section 4.2), which allows us to test the other mechanisms in artificial contexts (Part 5) as well as real biological scenarios (Part 6).

discretized form of the ligand diffusion equation relates the local concentrations of ligands to the cells' positions. As a consequence, the ligand patterns can be modified by deformation of the tissue. Moreover, each cell can independently harbor chemical "reactions" organized into genetic and molecular processes that are modeled by differential equations and Boolean operators. Communication between the intracellular protein quantities and the extracellular ligand quantities is achieved by transduction and secretion modules. Similarly to the MECA part, these features allow running simulations that involve thousands of cells in reasonable computing time.

4 MECAGEN: MODEL OF MECHANIC-GENETIC COUPLING

This last part lays out the foundations of an integrated morphogenetic model linking biomechanics (from Part 2) and genetic regulation/molecular signaling (from Part 3). To this goal, it proposes a "cell behavior ontology" (CBO) relating *cell states* to *cell behaviors*. Ideally, a complete model would "plug" the MECA and GEN modules into each other via this CBO, as illustrated in Figure 16.7. For the moment, however, we restrict ourselves to a simplified scheme bypassing the actual molecular and genetic processes on the GEN side. Kinetic equations are replaced with predefined cell states, or *cell types*, serving as entries into a "lookup table" containing one set of output values per cell type or pair of cell types. Only the diffusion dynamics of Section 3.3 is preserved here. This continuous-to-discrete abstraction has been commonly practiced (Thomas 1973) and will allow us to test the mechanical hypotheses introduced in MECA.

4.1 Cell behavior ontology

First, biological systems modeling requires the choice of an ontology, i.e. a hierarchy of predefined *categories* and relationships among them. Here, the appropriate candidates are the various cell behaviors that occur during a developmental process. In our model, we propose a simpler mapping between the dynamical rules of MECA and those of GEN. Ideally, mechanical properties should "emerge" from the regulative molecular microstructure, represented by a certain subset M of intracellular protein concentrations $\mathbf{p}_i = \{p_{a,i}\}_{a \in M}$. In particular, genetic output should determine the values of the two main mechanical parameters: the adhesion coefficient w_{adh} of the relaxation forces (Section 2.3), and the polarization axes $\vec{U}_i$ determining active protrusion (Section 2.4). In principle, such parameters are local functions of pairs of cells (i, j) via $(\mathbf{p}_i, \mathbf{p}_j)$. Instead, they depend here on pairs of *cell types*, denoted by $(\mathcal{T}, \mathcal{T}')$. For example, the adhesion coefficients become $w^{\text{adh}}_{\mathcal{T}\mathcal{T}'} = w_{\text{adh}}(\mathbf{p}_{\mathcal{T}}, \mathbf{p}_{\mathcal{T}'})$, where $\mathbf{p}_{\mathcal{T}}$ is typically an average over $\{\mathbf{p}_i\}_{i \in \mathcal{T}}$. Other features, such as cell cycle length and cell volume control, are always decoupled from genetic regulation, and receive fixed parameter values. Yet other mechanisms, such as cell death and the structure of the extracellular matrix (ECM), are not included for now.

4.2 Waddingtonian timeline specification

We "read out" behavioral parameters of the CBO directly from a new tool that we call a *Waddingtonian Timeline Specification* (WTS, Section 1.1), for which a dedicated graphical user interface was created (Figure 16.8a). The first step in setting up a WTS is to "carve the hillside" by specifying a temporal series of *cell types* $\{\mathcal{T}(i, t)\}$ that cells may adopt during the developmental process, along with the transition rules among these types. To this aim, we segment the timeline into *stages* delimited by particular points in time $\{t_1, t_2, \ldots\}$ at which new cell types may be introduced. For example, Stage 2 corresponds to the time interval $[t_2, t_3)$. During any given stage, cells may transition from one existing type to another type under the rules specified in a table (see next). The overall WTS structure can be represented by a pseudo-tree of cell types, with lateral transfers among the branches, expanding over time.

4.2.1 *Differentiation table* $\mathcal{D}$

To specify the conditions inducing a cell to change its type, we rely on the classical concept of *differentiation*. In our simplified model, cell differentiation depends on a Wolpertian *positional information* mechanism (Section 1.2). During stage S, corresponding to interval $[t_S, t_{S+1})$, if

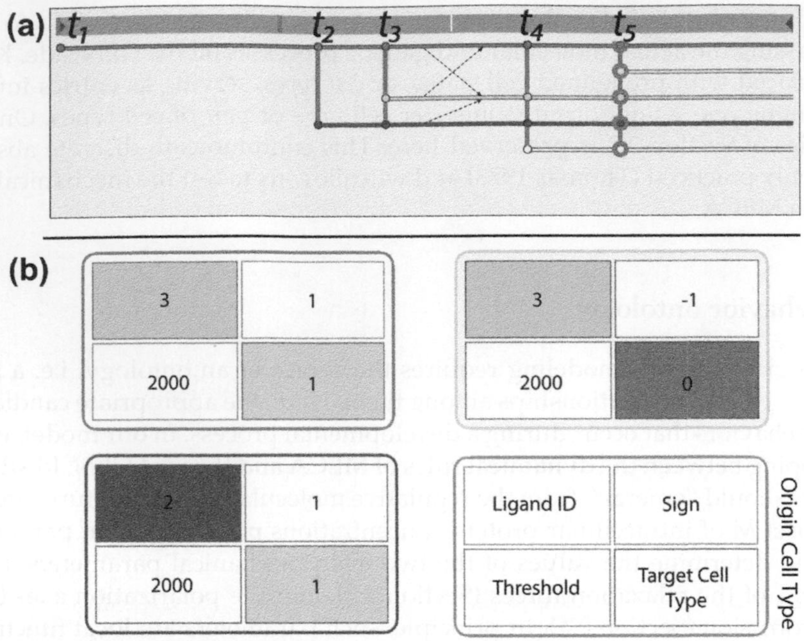

FIGURE 16.8 Waddingtonian timeline of cell types $\{\mathcal{T}(i,t)\}$ and differentiation table $\mathcal{D}$. (a) The gray bar at the top is the time axis (oriented left to right), segmented into stages $S = [t_S, t_{S+1})$. The colored horizontal branches symbolize the types that cells can potentially take, corresponding to the grooves of a Waddingtonian landscape. Here, five stages in the timeline indicate the onset of one type (red), two types (red and blue), …, until five types (red, cyan, green, blue, yellow). Differentiations, i.e. type transitions, may happen within each stage, for example shown here in Stage 3: the three thin dashed arrows represent the differentiation table ((b), see below), indicating that type red may become green, green may become red, and blue may become green. In this WTS graphical interface, stages can also be selected manually to specify their parameters (next figures): here, Stage 5 is selected by clicking on t_5, which is represented by gray circles on all the type nodes. (b) Differentiation table $\mathcal{D}_3$ representing the possible type transitions during Stage 3. It contains three differentiation modules displayed in one column, one module by origin type. In each module, the current cell type $\mathcal{T}(i,t)$ is represented by the round-corner frame color, the target cell type by the color (or id) of the bottom-right block, and the ligand-threshold-sign triplet $(Q_a, \theta_a, \epsilon_a)$ by the top-left block's color (or id), bottom-left block's value, and top-left block's value. Each cell changes its type depending on whether $\epsilon_a q_{a,i} \geq \epsilon_a \theta_a$. Bottom right: The generic template of one differentiation module inside one origin type, as followed by the other three modules. (For interpretation of the references to color in this figure legend, the reader is referred to the web version of this book.)

the local ligand concentration $q_{a,i}$ of molecular species Q_a on cell i crosses (i.e. either exceeds or sinks below) a given threshold θ_a, then cell i changes types. Generally, the new type is a function of the current type via a *differentiation operator* $\mathcal{D}$ represented by a ruleset or "lookup table" predefined for each stage S (Figure 16.8b), which we denote by $\mathcal{D}_S$. This table is organized in modules indexed by triplets composed of the ligand species, their differentiation thresholds, and the threshold signs. A module can be denoted by $\mathcal{T}(i,t) \leftarrow \mathcal{D}_S\big[\mathcal{T}(i,t), \{(Q_a, \theta_a, \epsilon_a)\}_{a \in M}\big]$, where the sign ϵ_a expresses whether the condition is about an exceeding or a sinking concentration, which can be written $\epsilon_a q_{a,i} \geq \epsilon_a \theta_a$.

4.2.2 *Passive adhesion table* $\mathscr{P}$

Once the differentiation backbone of the WTS has been established, the *adhesion coefficient* parameters of relaxation forces $\vec{F}_{ij}^{P}$ can be specified for each pair of cell types, thus we can denote them by $w_{TT'}^{\text{adh}}$ for $i \in T$ and $j \in T'$. Since passive adhesion forces are symmetrical, we have $w_{TT'}^{\text{adh}} = w_{T'T}^{\text{adh}}$ and these values can be organized into a triangular $T \times T'$ matrix, denoted here by $\mathscr{P}$. An example can be seen in Figure 16.11.

4.2.3 *Ligand sinks and sources table* $\mathscr{L}$

At each stage S, we define sources and sinks for each ligand through another table denoted $\mathscr{L}_S$. Each cell type can potentially secrete or absorb any ligand type Q_a. Additionally, the *spatial configuration* of the ligand sources must also be specified. The module used for this type of specification can be seen in the example of Figures 16.11 and 16.16. We define, per cell type, the id of the ligand and the geometrical border of the volume of secretion. Assuming a spherical embryo, an orthonormal coordinate frame is set up along the animal-vegetal (AV) axis, antero-posterior (AP) axis, and bilateral symmetry left-right (LR) axis. On each axis, we define two cutoff values to extract a slice, then take the intersection of all three slices to define the source region of ligand release. Several such source regions can be defined per cell type. Thus the spatial ligand source table is composed of sextuplets of cutoff coordinate values for each ligand inside each cell type module. External sources of ligands, such as the yolk (see example in Figure 16.16), may also be added.

4.2.4 *Active protrusion table* $\mathscr{A}$

Finally, once the ligand sources/sinks table $\mathscr{L}$ is defined, the "active" cell behavior can be set up by adding other behavioral modules for a given cell type at a given stage. To this aim, we define an active protrusion table $\mathscr{A}$ composed of modules associated to an origin cell type, whose parameters are explained below. Every "active" cell behavior exploited in MecaGen requires a *polarization axis*. In real cells, polarization correlates with an asymmetry of intracellular molecular concentrations. In our model, since we adopted one particle per cell, there can be no spatialization of intracellular material. Thus we chose to represent this asymmetry by 3D vectors $\vec{U}_i$ passing through the centers of the cells (Section 2.4). More precisely, a cell i can be potentially polarized by multiple mechanisms as the developmental process unfolds, corresponding to multiple "candidate" polarization axes. These modes of polarization determination can be: (a) a local gradient-based or "chemotactic" mode (one of the possible GEN-to-MECA coupling links), (b) a cell-cell contact propagation mode or (c) a force-induced mode (both of the MECA-to-MECA sort), and (d) a default mode used only if a polarized cell has no input to trigger any of the above three mechanisms, in which case the axis is randomly reoriented until another polarization mode takes over.

When a new polarization axis $\vec{U}_i'$ has been calculated via one of these four modes, the current axis is updated through an inertia coefficient ω according to $\vec{U}_i \leftarrow \omega\,\vec{U}_i + \vec{U}_i'$, followed by renormalization to keep the vectors unitary. In the remainder of this chapter, we only use the chemotactic mode (a) to modulate the dynamics of protrusion with ligand diffusion (beside the default mode (d), which is only a random reset). The hypothesis underlying mode (a) is that a cell is able to detect an asymmetry of extracellular ligand concentration in its local

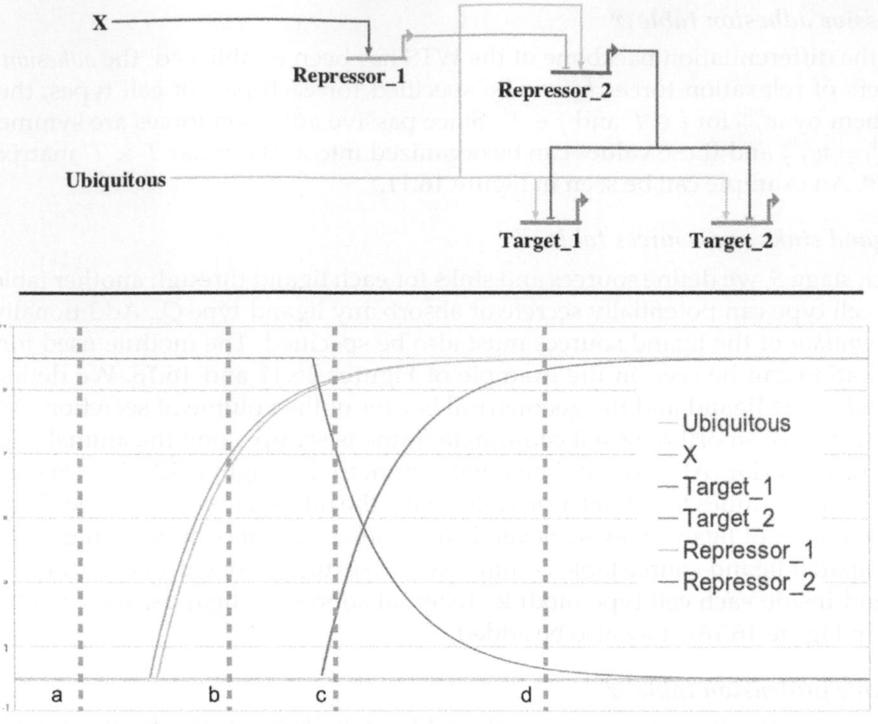

FIGURE 16.9 "Double negative gate" GRN subcircuit and protein concentration dynamics. Top: Network map. Bottom: Evolution of protein concentrations in the region where X is expressed. See text for the explanation of the curves' profile. The tagged vertical bars a, b, c, and d indicate the timing of the snapshots shown in Figure 16.10. The curve of Target1 (pink) is hidden by the curve of Target2 (blue) as their dynamics is exactly the same. (For interpretation of the references to color in this figure legend, the reader is referred to the web version of this book.)

vicinity. Accordingly, the candidate axis of polarization is calculated by a linear average of the neighborhood edges $\vec{u}_{ij}$, in which the weights are functions of the differences in ligand concentrations:

$$\vec{U}_i' = \sum_{j \in \mathcal{N}_i^t} (q_{a,j} - q_{a,i})^m \, \vec{u}_{ij} \tag{16.13}$$

where $q_{a,i}$ is the local quantity of extracellular ligand Q_a surrounding i (Section 3.3), and m is an integer controlling the sensibility of detection of local concentration differences (m must be odd to conserve vector directions, typically $m=3$).

Putting these features together, each module of the active protrusion table $\mathscr{A}$ is composed of four parameters (see example in Figures 16.11 and 16.16):

- the target cell type T' that the protrusion is affecting,
- the chosen index among all the various candidate axes of protrusion $\{\vec{U}_i\}$, which can be calculated here only by one of the ligand-based mode (a) or random mode (d),

- the intensity f^A of the protrusive force (Section 2.4; the length of the dashed arrows in Figure 16.5),
- a ternary value equal to +1 if the cell is monopolar in the direction of $\mathcal{N}_i^{t+}$, −1 if it is monopolar in the opposite direction $\mathcal{N}_i^{t-}$, or 0 if it is bipolar i.e. protruding in both directions.

Summary: The Waddingtonian timeline concludes our modeling framework. It is a novel, yet limited, method of specifying cell behaviors through space and time. It allows a partial exploitation of the principles involved in MecaGen but is sufficient to start exploring the mechanical space and coupling principles. We now illustrate this framework on artificial data (Part 5), then on a biological case study of intercalation patterns in the zebrafish early development (Part 6).

5 ILLUSTRATIONS ON ARTIFICIAL DATA

5.1 Gene regulation motifs

This section offers a glimpse of the possibilities of our genetic regulation and molecular signaling model through a simple, idealized example. We follow here Eric Davidson's article "Emerging properties of animal gene regulatory networks" (Davidson 2010), which describes various small GRN subcircuits, showing their involvement in embryonic development, and focus on one of them: the *double negative gate*. Our example is a small part of the sea urchin embryo's GRN (Peter and Davidson 2009; Davidson 2009) allowing the activation of a series of genes in a specific region of the embryo under the control of localized expression, represented by protein X (Figures 16.9, 16.10). The interesting feature of this circuit is that X does not directly promote the set of regulated genes (Target1 and Target2), but rather *inhibits inhibitors* of these genes (Repressor1 and Repressor2). The net effect is that the target genes are expressed in a particular region of the embryo and shut down everywhere else.

We illustrate the dynamics of this particular motif in an artificial cell population comprising 4,886 cells laid out in a thin 3D space delimited by two planes at a distance equivalent to two cell diameters (Figure 16.10). The cells are assumed immobile, in a mechanical equilibrium state, and no active forces are present.

- In the beginning, protein Ubiquitous (present in all cells) activates at the same time genes Target1 and Target2 *and* their repressor Repressor2, so that only the protein encoded by Repressor2 is expressed ubiquitously (Figures 16.9a and 16.10a).
- At a later point in time, protein X is introduced in one region of the cell population by switching its concentration rate in these cells to a constant value of 0.1 unit per time step. In parallel, all proteins have a similar degradation rate of 0.99 unit per time step, so that the concentration of X tends toward an equilibrium quantity of 10 units.
- As soon as the concentration of X exceeds a binding threshold $\theta_{X,Rep1} = 1$ on the cis-regulatory element of Repressor1, the corresponding protein is produced at a rate of 0.1 unit per time step. (Figures 16.9b and 16.10b).
- Once the concentration of protein Repressor1 exceeds in turn another threshold $\theta_{Rep1,Rep2} = 9$, the Repressor2 gene state is switched to 0 via the AND Boolean function relating the Repressor1 and Ubiquitous transcription factors.

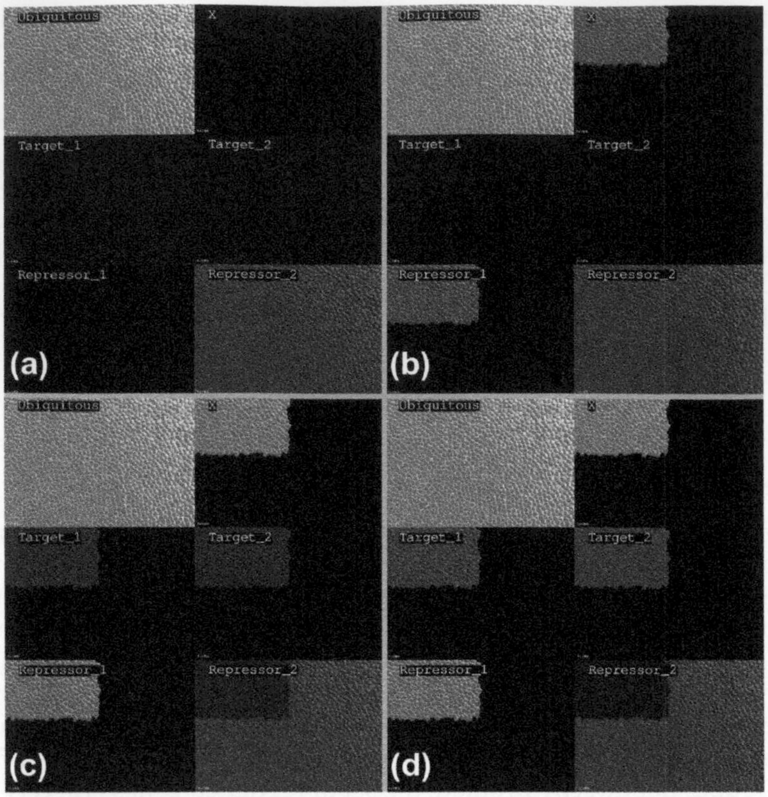

FIGURE 16.10 Spatial evolution of protein concentrations in the double negative gate experiment. The letters correspond to the bars of Figure 16.9. Each image is composed of six simultaneous views of the simulated cell population. View location (correlated with color) represents the protein type, from left to right and top to bottom: Ubiquitous, X, Target1, Target2, Repressor1, Repressor2. Shade represents the protein concentration (dark for low, bright for high). The top left corner of each image is the region where protein X is artificially secreted.

- Finally, the concentration of Repressor2 protein, which is no longer produced by its encoding gene, decreases by degradation. Once it passes below concentration thresholds $\theta_{\text{Rep2,Tar1}} = \theta_{\text{Rep2,Tar2}} = 9$ on the sites of genes Target1 and Target2 via another AND operator, the target genes start to be expressed in the spatial region of the X protein (Figures 16.9c and 16.10c).

The temporal evolution of all proteins is shown in Figure 16.9, and their spatial map in Figure 16.10.

5.2 Cell sorting

A main point of MecaGen is that a cell's motility is due to its protrusive activity. In this section, we illustrate this principle through an abstract simulation of *cell sorting*. Historically, spontaneous cell rearrangement is one of the multicellular phenomena most studied by

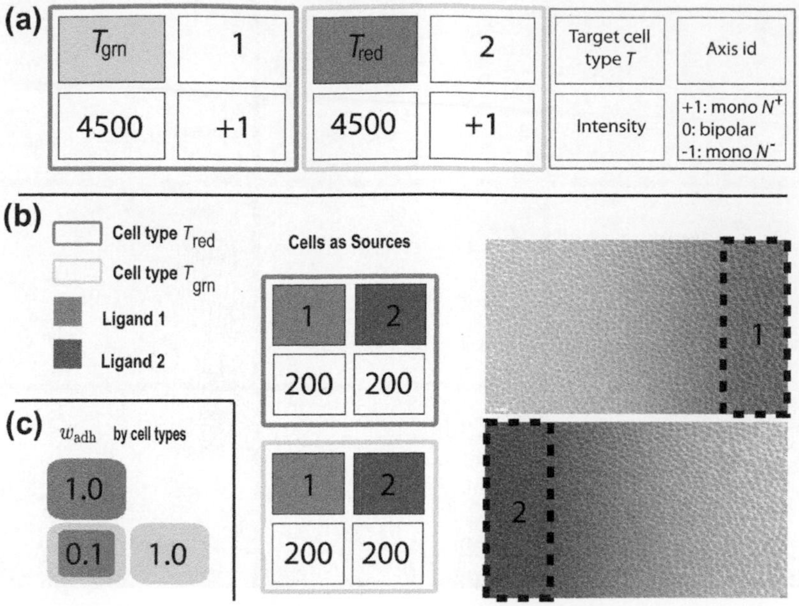

FIGURE 16.11 **Tables for the cell sorting experiment.** See definition in Section 4.2 and text for details. (a) Active protrusion table $\mathscr{A}$: protrusion behavior here is heterotypic, i.e. cells act only upon neighboring cells of a different type. Axis id 1 (resp. 2) is the gradient-based polarization mode (a) with ligand 1 (resp. 2). (b) Ligand diffusion table $\mathscr{L}$: both cell types secrete both ligand types Q_1 and Q_2 with the same rates $s_1 = s_2 = 200$, in simulation units. They do this, however, only if they enter one of the source regions on either vertical border of the domain. (c) Passive adhesion table $\mathscr{P}$.

theoretical models, notably the Differential Adhesion Hypothesis (DAH) (Steinberg 1962) and the Cellular Potts Model (Graner and Glazier 1992) (Section 1.2). These models often use a "temperature" parameter, derived by analogy from thermodynamics and corresponding to an intrinsic cell motility coefficient (Zhang et al. 2011), which controls membrane fluctuations and sorting efficiency. We perform here a similar experiment, but explore our own parameter ontology based on the orientation of the polarization axis. We start from the same cell tissue as Section 5.1 with the essential difference that cells can now move but not change types. In the WTS framework presented above, it means that we are zooming inside one stage S with only two horizontal cell type lines, one red and one green, and no transition arrows between them, i.e. no differentiation table $\mathscr{D}$. Initially, cells are randomly assigned one of two cell types: a "red" cell type $\mathcal{T}_{red}$ and a "green" cell type $\mathcal{T}_{grn}$, creating two populations of fixed size.

Passive adhesion table $\mathscr{P}$: Taking after the DAH, we postulate that both cell populations have a *strong homotypic adhesion*, i.e. a large adhesion coefficient w_{adh} for the passive forces exerted between cells of the same type, and a *weak heterotypic adhesion*, i.e. a small adhesion coefficient between cells of different type. Using our previous notations from Section 4.2, this results in a simple two-type table $\mathscr{P}$ (Figure 16.11c) with one high value $w^{adh}_{\mathcal{T}\mathcal{T}} = w^{adh}_{\mathcal{T}'\mathcal{T}'} = 1.0$ and one low value $w^{adh}_{\mathcal{T}\mathcal{T}'} = w^{adh}_{\mathcal{T}'\mathcal{T}} = 0.1$, where $\mathcal{T}, \mathcal{T}'$ stand for $\mathcal{T}_{red}, \mathcal{T}_{grn}$.

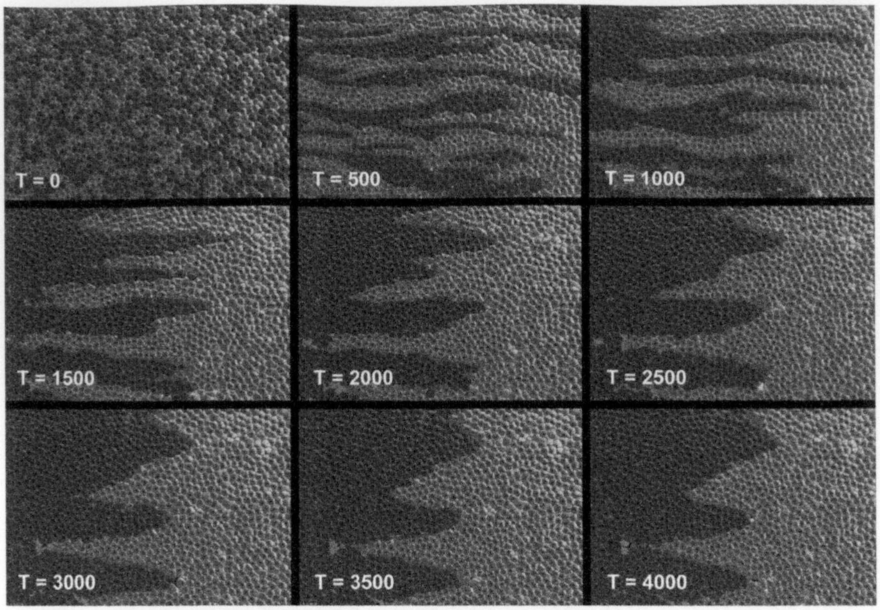

FIGURE 16.12 **Ligand-based heterotypic protrusion, planar diffusion sources.** See text for comments. Two hidden ligands are diffusing from the left and right borders of the cell bilayer. Green (right-half) cells' polarization axes are oriented toward the right source and red (left-half) cells' axes toward the left source. Each cell type is exerting monopolar protrusion over the other cell type (heterotypic contacts).

Ligand table $\mathscr{L}$: Polarization axes are specified by the ligand-based chemotactic mode (a) (Section 4.2). Two different ligand molecular species are secreted, Q_1 and Q_2, and both types of cells $\mathcal{T}_{red}$ and $\mathcal{T}_{grn}$ are potential sources for these ligands with the same secretion rates s_1 and s_2 (Figure 16.11b). No cell absorbs any ligand, so there is no boundary condition on the low concentration end. On the high concentration end, however, there is a spatial constraint on where the ligand sources are located: two rectangular domains are predefined on the left and right border of the frame, and whenever a cell of any type enters the right (resp. left) domain, it starts secreting Q_1 (resp. Q_2).

Active protrusion table $\mathscr{A}$: In this particular experiment, the protrusive behavior is heterotypic, i.e. red cells protrude on the green cells only, and vice versa. It means that the active mechanical interactions described in Figure 16.5 occur at the interface between the two populations, not within populations. Another rule is that $\mathcal{T}_{red}$ cells respond only to the gradient created by ligand Q_1, and $\mathcal{T}_{grn}$ cells only to Q_2. The rest of the active protrusion table $\mathcal{A}$ (Figure 16.11a) concerns the protrusion force intensity f^A and the polarity, which is +1 here for both cell types, meaning that all cells protrude in the uphill direction of their preferred gradient. The net effect is that red cells orient their polarization axis toward the left border (higher q_1 concentration values) and green cells toward the right border (higher q_2).

Results: Although cells collectively exhibit a clear sorting behavior (Figure 16.12), we observe that the boundary line between the two populations does not become flat, as would be expected from a classical DAH study. In the present experiment, all cell polarization axes $\vec{U}_i$ are roughly colinear and aligned with the horizontal direction. This is because at later stages (here, after time step 3500), the profile of the boundary line between the red and green populations is directly related to η, the dot-product limit determining the "positive" polar neighborhood $\mathcal{N}_i^{t+}$ centered around $\vec{U}_i$ (Section 2.4; pie slice in Figure 16.5). Due to this limit, a green cell near the boundary line, which protrudes toward the right side of the tissue, does not have any more red cells in its polar neighborhood, therefore the equilibrium state of tissue dynamics displays a jagged boundary line. In conclusion, the manner in which protrusion behavior is modeled here is not sufficient to obtain the smoother boundary of regular cell sorting phenomena, and would require additional mechanisms.

6 BIOLOGICAL CASE STUDY: INTERCALATION PATTERNS IN THE ZEBRAFISH EPIBOLY

The zebrafish early development is the site of multiple morphogenetic events that illustrate the links between microscopic cell behaviors and macroscopic deformations. We choose to examine more closely and treat one of these events by modeling and simulation in order to illustrate the applicability of the MecaGen framework to biological data.

6.1 Hypotheses and model

We focus here on the first phase of a major developmental event, the *epiboly*, occurring between 3.3 hours postfertilization (hpf) and 5.5 hpf. It is characterized by a flattening of the deep cell mass and its spreading over the yolk cell toward the vegetal pole (Figure 16.13). At 3.3 hpf, or "high stage," the deep cells lie on top of the yolk, sandwiched between the yolk syncytial layer (YSL) and a population of newly differentiated epithelial cells, called the enveloping layer (EVL). The interface between YSL and EVL is called the "margin." As flattening occurs, the deep cells start to *intercalate radially*, i.e. migrate from the depth of the blastoderm toward its surface. The qualitative description highlighted by the names of the developmental stages, "high," "oblong," and "sphere," refers to the flattening of the blastoderm and suggests that the overall shape of the embryo becomes gradually closer to spherical. Then, at 5.3 hpf, i.e. about 50% of the epiboly stage, the yolk bulges inside the blastoderm, forming a dome shape until the depth of the blastoderm is uniform over all latitudes.

While intrinsic deep cell behaviors are supposed to be responsible for most of the deformation of the embryo at these stages, we cannot exclude an active participation of the YSL or the newly differentiated EVL to the epiboly. In the present case study, we use two kinds of measures: macroscopic measures characterizing the doming phenomenon, and microscopic measures characterizing the intercalation patterns, in order to show that the intrinsic behavior of deep cells is sufficient to trigger upward yolk bulging (doming motion) and downward margin progression toward the yolk's equatorial latitude. In this context, we also evaluate how the YSL margin and the EVL's tangential stiffness modulate the deep cells' driving force.

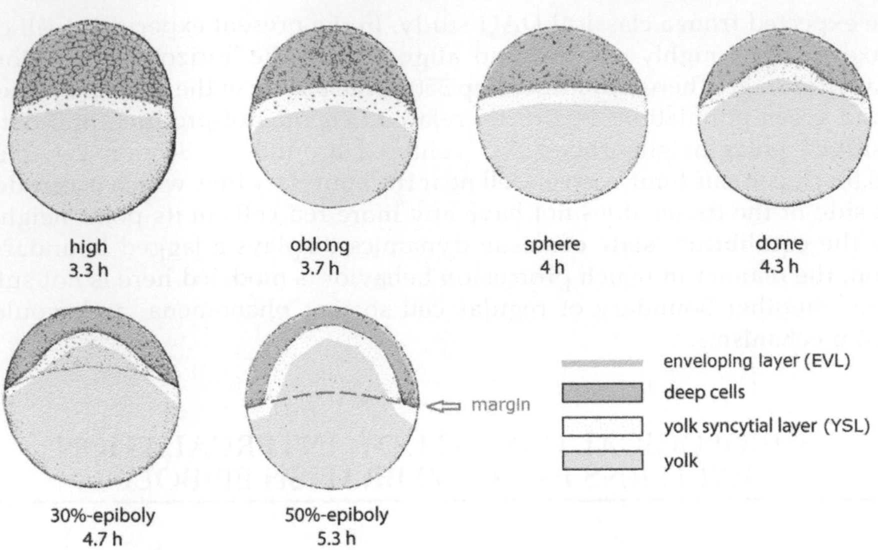

FIGURE 16.13 **Zebrafish early gastrula stages.** Adapted from Kimmel et al. (1995), with permission. From the high stage to the 50% epiboly stage: lateral views with animal pole to the top and dorsal side, identified by the shield stage, to the right. The enveloping layer (EVL) is in yellow, the yolk syncytial layer (YSL) in pale yellow, and deep cells in blue. The whole spatio-temporal sequence is expected to last 2 h at 28.5 ° C. (For interpretation of the references to color in this figure legend, the reader is referred to the web version of this book.)

6.1.1 Passive margin sliding scenario

We envision five possible, but non-exclusive scenarios explaining how the margin moves toward the vegetal pole (Figure 16.14): (i) the internal YSL (iYSL) actively spreads over the yolk (in its cortical region), carrying both the deep cells and the EVL margin with it; (ii) the EVL actively spreads over the blastoderm, carrying the margin with it; (iii) the margin is pulled downward by an active mechanism in the external YSL (eYSL); (iv) some active mechanism inside the yolk triggers the convex bulge inside the blastoderm area; and (v) the deep cells actively intercalate and their collective behavior induces a pressure at the marginal region, pushing the resisting margin toward the vegetal pole.

Scenarios (i) and (iii) would require some active mechanism in the network of microtubules linking the yolk syncytial nuclei (YSN), either by pushing from the iYSL or pulling from the vegetal eYSL. Disruption of the microtubules with nocodazole at the sphere stage is not sufficient, however, to stop the epibolic motion (Solnica-Krezel and Driever 1994). Scenario (ii) would require an active flattening of the EVL apico-basal thickness and conjugated extension of its lateral surface. It would imply that, at the margin, the EVL would move toward the yolk equatorial latitude ahead of the deep cells, but this is not what we observe in our imaging data (Figure 16.14). The inside of the yolk has also not been described to contain a well-structured cytoskeleton. This penalizes the possibility envisioned by scenario (iv) of an active mechanism occurring in this domain.

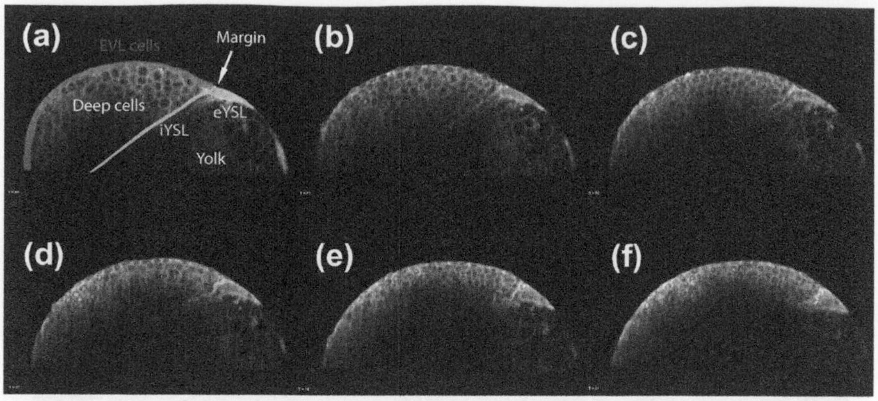

FIGURE 16.14 Wild type zebrafish embryo imaged live from the oblong stage to 30% epiboly. We observe here a slice passing approximately through the center and the animal pole of the embryo. a: oblong stage. b: transition between oblong and sphere stage. c: sphere stage. d: transition between sphere and dome stage. e: dome stage. f: transition from dome to 30% epiboly stage (dataset 071222bF from Nadine Peyriéras's lab).

All the experiments described in the literature indicate that epiboly is a robust process, probably relying on several redundant mechanisms. However, since the only scenario that has not been contradicted in the literature is (v), our goal will be to show by modeling and simulation in MecaGen that active intercalation of the deep cells is sufficient to drive epiboly during the studied period. This particular scenario requires *a mechanism that will convert the push exerted by the deep cells over the margin into a sliding movement of the margin toward the vegetal pole*. We describe here how this mechanism is modeled.

6.1.2 MECA: force model

The marginal deep cells are stuck in the corner formed by the YSL and the EVL. We expect that the margin will slide toward the vegetal pole if the norm of the tangential force exerted by the deep cells (DC) on the marginal yolk membrane particles (MYM), denoted by $\vec{F}_{ij}^{\text{m:D},\parallel}$, is larger than a given "resistance threshold" $\theta_{\text{m},\parallel}$ (Figure 16.15c). We call this force the "pushing force" as it expresses the localized quantity of force exerted by a DC particle j over an MYM particle i. Its equation reads:

$$\vec{F}_{ij}^{\text{m:D},\parallel} = \begin{cases} -w_{\text{rep}}^{\text{ym:D}}(r_{ij}^{\parallel} - r_{ij}^{\text{eq},\parallel}).\,A_{ij}(r_{ij}^{\parallel}, R_i, R_{\text{ym}}).\vec{U}_{\text{ym},i}^{\parallel} & \text{if } r_{ij}^{\parallel} < r_{ij}^{\text{eq},\parallel} \\ \vec{0} & \text{if } r_{ij}^{\parallel} \geq r_{ij}^{\text{eq},\parallel} \end{cases} \tag{16.14}$$

where the repulsion coefficient $w_{\text{rep}}^{\text{ym:D}}$ is the same as the one controlling the repulsion at the YM-DC interface, A_{ij} is the contact area, $r_{ij}^{\parallel}$ is the dot product of the relative position vector $r_{ij}\vec{u}_{ij}$ and the tangential vector $-\vec{U}_{\text{ym},i}^{\parallel}$ of the MYM particle i (Figure 16.15c,d), and $r_{ij}^{\text{eq},\parallel} = c_{\text{eq}}(R_i + R_{\text{ym}})$. Only the repulsive part of the force ($r < r^{\text{eq}}$) has a non-zero formulation because we do not consider here the reverse situation of marginal deep cells going back toward the animal pole of the yolk and pulling the margin with them.

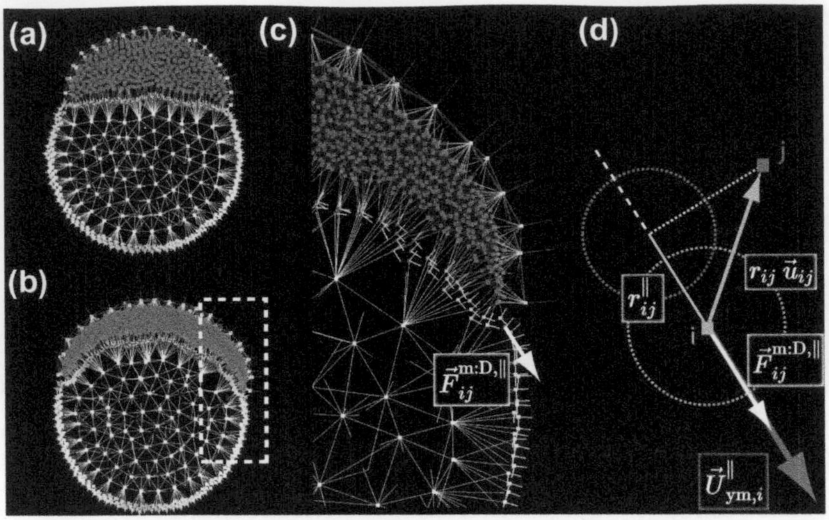

FIGURE 16.15 **Mechanism controlling the passive sliding of the blastoderm and EVL margin toward the vegetal pole.** a: Sagittal section of the simulated embryo at the onset of epiboly. b: Sagittal section at 30% epiboly. c: Zoom on the marginal region of the embryo at 30% epiboly. When a deep cell j (DC, in red) is in contact (green lines) with a margin yolk membrane (MYM, orange) particle i, a "pushing force" $F_{ij}^{m:D,\|}$ is calculated to estimate the mechanical pressure exerted by j on the margin at the cellular level. If this force exceeds a certain "resistance threshold" $\theta_{m,\|}$, the MYM particle loses its marginal properties, and transmits it to one or several regular YM particle(s) at a more vegetal latitude. c: Schema describing the pushing force exerted by DC particle j over MYM cell i. The pushing force is non-zero only if the distance between the positions of j and i projected on the tangential vector $\vec{U}_{ym,i}^{\|}$ (not shown) is smaller than the equilibrium distance $r_{ij}^{eq,\|} = c_{eq}(R_i + R_{ym})$. The orange and red circles highlight the radii of cells i and j respectively. (For interpretation of the references to color in this figure legend, the reader is referred to the web version of this book.)

6.1.3 GEN: chemical model

The objective of this study is to show that radial intercalation is sufficient to drive epiboly. At the cellular level, the mechanism attributed to the cells is *bipolar protrusion*. We propose two similar means of specifying radial polarization fields through the WTS described in Part 4:

- The first polarization field is specified by the ligand-based polarization mode (a), using a diffusive ligand Q_1 secreted by the EVL. For this ligand, the YSL acts as a sink (Figure 16.16, top embryo).
- The second polarization field is obtained by reversing the sink and source roles, based on another ligand Q_2 secreted by the YSL (Figure 16.16, bottom embryo).

If the interfaces between the EVL deep cells and the YSL deep cells were exactly parallel during epiboly, these two gradients would generate identical polarization fields. This is obviously not the case before 30% epiboly, justifying our choice of two different radial polarization fields. Using the ligand-based polarization mode (a), however, should not be interpreted as an explanation of how a polarization field is actually generated in the embryo. In this

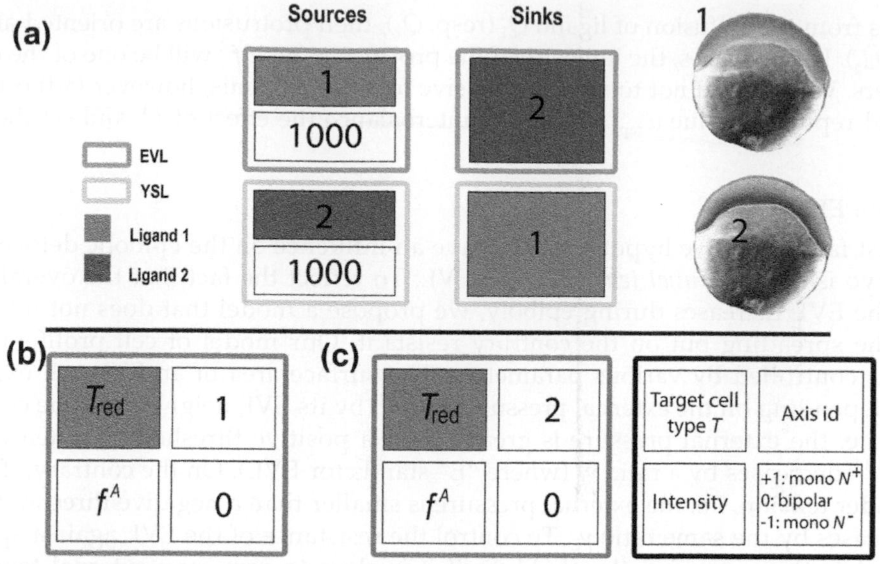

FIGURE 16.16 Tables for the "Intercalation" case study. (a) Ligand diffusion table $\mathscr{L}$. Two gradient fields are established by ligand diffusion across the dome region formed by the deep cells. They contribute to the specification of the axes of the polarization: a ligand Q_1 is secreted by the EVL with secretion rate $s_1 = 1000$ and absorbed by the yolk membrane particles, more precisely the YSL. Conversely, a ligand Q_2 is secreted by the YSL with rate $s_2 = 1000$ and absorbed by the EVL. (b,c) Active protrusion tables $\mathscr{A}$. (a) All the cells belonging to the T_{red} population exert bipolar protrusions over each other along the polarization axis $\vec{U}_1$ derived from the gradient field of ligand Q_1. (b) The same cells can exert another bipolar protrusion along $\vec{U}_2$ derived from Q_2. In both cases, the intensity of the protrusive force is f^A.

study, we are agnostic with respect to the detailed physico-chemical polarization mechanisms, and only interested in the effects that abstract fields have on cell movements and emerging morphogenetic processes at a macroscopic level.

The polarization fields specified above are highly regular, in any case much less fluctuating than would be the case biologically. To test the effect of a certain amount of stochasticity in these fields, we also introduce a parameter $\lambda_r \in [0, 1]$: if $\lambda_r = 0$, the polarization axes $\vec{U}_i$ are as specified above; if $\lambda_r = 1$, the polarization field is purely random, i.e. for each cell i a random vector $\vec{U}_{r,i}$ is generated every 15 mn of simulation time; intermediate values provide a mix. Thus the effective polarization axis is now $\vec{U}_i^e = \lambda_r \vec{U}_{r,i} + (1 - \lambda_r)\vec{U}_i$, followed by a renormalization step to keep the polarization vector unitary.

6.1.4 MecaGen: force-chemical coupling model

Once the polarization fields are established, the protrusive behavior of the cells must be parametrized. For the sake of simplicity, we subsume the deep cell population under one cell type T_{red}, and postulate homotypic, *bipolar* protrusion forces. Parallel to the pair of polarization fields, we also specify two protrusion rules (Figure 16.16): when the polarization field originates from the diffusion of ligand Q_1 (resp. Q_2), then protrusions are oriented along axis $\vec{U}_1$ (resp. $\vec{U}_2$). In both cases, the intensity of the protrusive force f^A will be one of the explored parameters. We decided not to vary the passive force coefficients, however (adhesive value $w^{adh}_{T_{red}T_{red}}$ and repulsive value w_{rep}), as they counterbalance the effect of f^A, and set them to 1.0 instead.

6.1.5 *Extra EVL module*

The last factor that we hypothesize to have an influence on the epibolic deformation of the embryo is the *tangential tension* in the EVL. To reflect the fact that the overall surface area of the EVL increases during epiboly, we propose a model that does not intrinsically trigger the spreading but on the contrary resists it. Our model of cell proliferation and growth is controlled by various parameters. The surface area of an EVL cell expands or shrinks depending on the external pressure exerted by its EVL neighbors. If the cell is compressed, i.e. the external pressure is greater than a positive threshold θ_E^+, then its lateral radius $R_i^{lat,E}$ decreases by a ratio γ_E (where "E" stands for EVL). On the contrary, if the EVL cell is under tension, i.e. the external pressure is smaller than a negative threshold θ_E^-, then $R_i^{lat,E}$ increases by the same ratio γ_E. To control the resistance of the EVL against spreading, we modulate the expansion threshold θ_E^-: if it is close to zero, any external tension will trigger expansion and potentially proliferation of the tissue, and the EVL will not resist spreading. Conversely, if the absolute value of θ_E^- is high enough, the EVL will not expand or proliferate but will resist spreading. Between these two extremes, we expect that the EVL will exhibit an intermediate degree of resistance, allowing us to decipher its influence on the whole epibolic motion.

6.2 Real embryo and measured data

A qualitative understanding of the macro-scale deformation of the embryo can be derived from Karlstrom and Kane's (1996) "flipbook" of embryogenesis (Karlstrom and Kane 1996) by measuring the macroscopic deformation occurring during epiboly. We extracted 12 images between the oblong stage and the 50% epiboly stage (Figure 16.17), and adjusted this timing in hpf units using the table provided in Karlstrom and Kane (1996) (top left of each frame, second line). We manually annotated the most important landmarks on each image using six dots (see caption).

6.2.1 *Real measures*

Macroscopic spatial measures were inferred from the singular landmarks described above and consist of the temporal evolution of four absolute *distances* (Figure 16.18, dashed lines): the embryo height from the vegetal pole to animal pole (red dashed line), the margin height from the vegetal pole to the central marginal position (green dashed line), the yolk height from the vegetal pole to the yolk animal pole (blue dashed line), and the margin width from the left to the right marginal positions (yellow dashed line). These measures provide an absolute macroscopic description of the deformation occurring during epiboly. However,

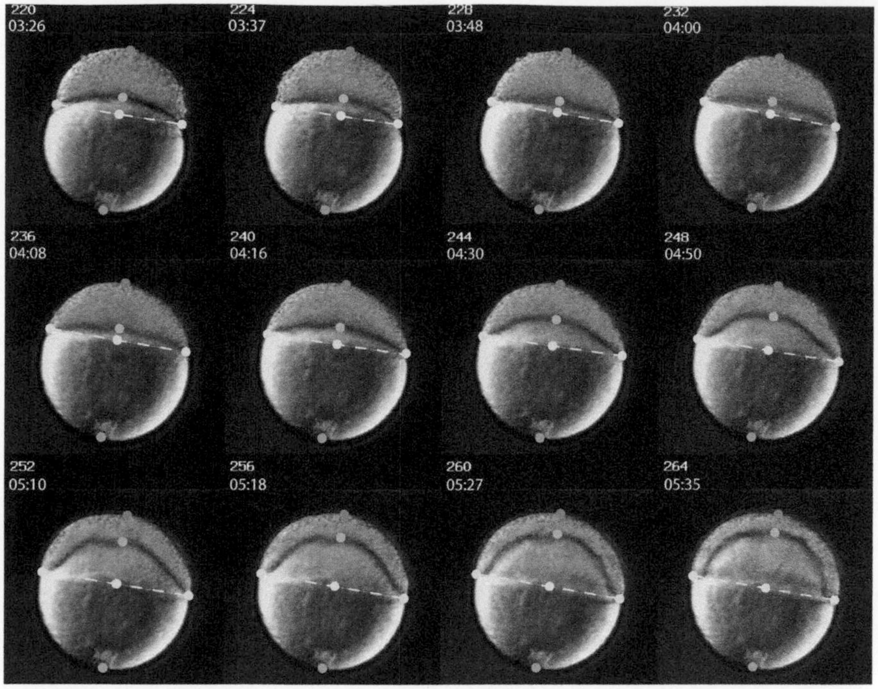

FIGURE 16.17 Macroscopic landmarks of the epibolic deformation from the "flipbook" specimen. Snapshots of the zebrafish development from the oblong stage to 50% epiboly extracted and adapted from the movie by Karlstrom and Kane (1996), with permission. We have manually added colored dots to estimate the macroscopic morphological characteristics of the embryo: red dots signal the animal pole of each embryo, green dots the vegetal pole, blue dots the animal-pole limit of the yolk, and triplets of yellow dots delineate the margin, where the left and right dots identify the external position of the margin and the central one correspond to their averaged projection on the AV axis. The time value displayed below the image id is in hpf units given by Karlstrom and Kane (1996). These timings do not scale linearly with the image ids and have been renormalized. (For interpretation of the references to color in this figure legend, the reader is referred to the web version of this book.)

comparing different embryos, real or simulated, required a normalization of the distances. We chose the embryo height as the baseline, leaving three measures ("e" stands for embryo in the notations):

- the normalized margin height H^{e}_{m}, obtained by dividing the margin height by the embryo height (green solid line): it characterizes the overall covering of the yolk by the cells, and tends to zero as the tail bud closure proceeds;
- the normalized yolk height H^{e}_{Y}, obtained by dividing the yolk height by the embryo height (blue solid line): it characterizes the doming of the blastoderm and the bulging of the yolk;
- the embryo *sphericity* coefficient C^{e}_{Φ}, obtained by dividing the margin width by the embryo height (yellow solid line): this value is 1.0 for a spherical embryo, and smaller (resp. greater) for an embryo elongated (resp. flattened) along the AV axis.

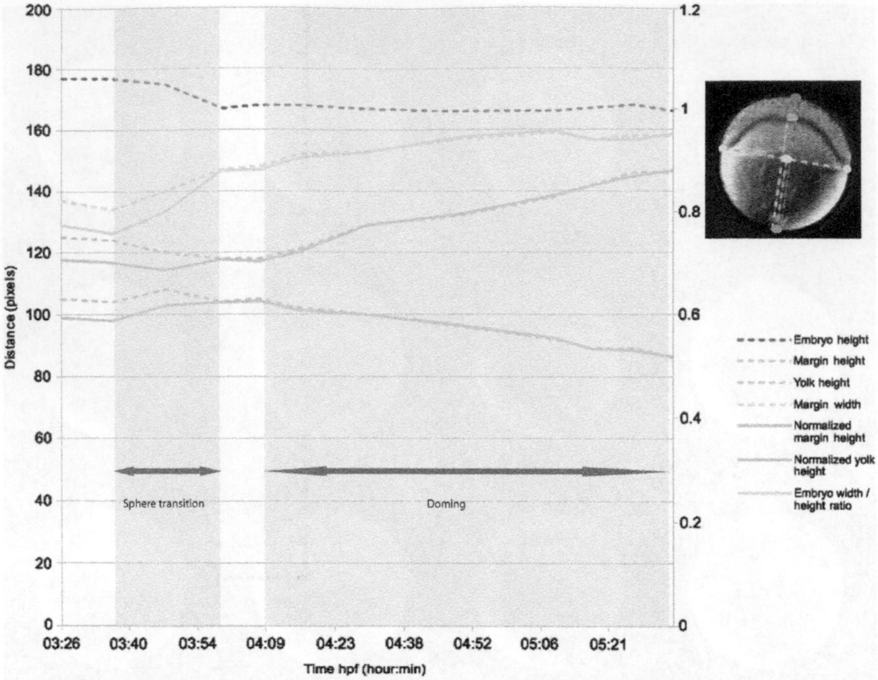

FIGURE 16.18 Macroscopic measures of the epibolic deformation in the "flipbook" specimen. The measures defined by the macroscopic landmarks displayed in Figure 16.17 are shown. The red (top) curve is the plot of the distance between the animal pole (AP) of the embryo and the vegetal pole (VP) of the yolk (embryo height). The green (bottom) curve is the plot of the distance between the projection of the margin on the animal-vegetal (AV) axis and the VP of the yolk (margin height). The blue (next to bottom) curve is distance between the AP of the yolk and the VP of the yolk (yolk height). The yellow (next to top) curve is the lateral distance between the margin positions (margin diameter). The dashed lines give the absolute distance between landmarks in pixels (left ordinate axis). The continuous lines give the normalized distances (right ordinate axis). The normalization is obtained by dividing each value by the current yolk height (i.e. dashed red line). The abscissa gives the time in hpf units. (For interpretation of the references to color in this figure legend, the reader is referred to the web version of this book.)

6.2.2 *Observations*

These simple measures allow distinguishing two macroscopic phases of deformation (gray areas in Figure 16.18): the sphere transition deformation, occurring between 3.6 hpf and 4 hpf in the flipbook, and the doming deformation, starting 8 min later and continuing until about 5.5 hpf. During the sphere transition, the absolute height of the embryo decreases, while its sphericity increases rapidly. The flattening at the sphere stage of the yolk cell-blastoderm interface appears moderate, and it is possible that other specimens behave somewhat differently in this respect (as in Figure 16.14c for example). Additional embryos would be useful to refine this measure (and the other measures as well). The doming transition is accompanied by an important move of the blastoderm margin toward the vegetal pole and an even more important relative displacement of the yolk cell's animal pole, while the overall sphericity slowly increases.

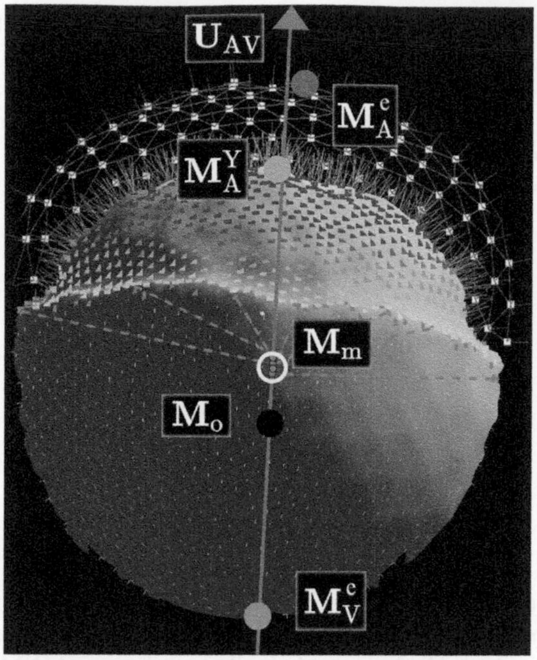

FIGURE 16.19 **Macroscopic landmarks of the epibolic deformation in simulated specimens.** Landmark dots have been manually added for the purpose of the illustration. They represent the macroscopic landmarks automatically calculated by the simulated measurements. The gray line is the animal-vegetal (AV) axis, *a priori* specified at initialization. The red dot is the embryo animal pole $\mathbf{M}_A^e$, the blue dot is the yolk animal pole $\mathbf{M}_A^Y$, the black dot is the embryo center $\mathbf{M}_o$, the green dot is the embryo vegetal pole $\mathbf{M}_V^e$, the orange dot is the margin "level" $\mathbf{M}_m$, i.e. the average of all the projections of margin yolk membrane particles (small orange circles) on the AV axis (only a few of these particles are displayed). Note that the positions of the yolk animal pole, embryo animal pole, and embryo vegetal pole are never exactly aligned on the AV axis as they must each coincide with a particle's center. The deep cells are not displayed here, leaving a carved out domain between the yolk cell and the EVL. (For interpretation of the references to color in this figure legend, the reader is referred to the web version of this book.)

6.3 Simulated embryo and first comparisons

6.3.1 Simulated measures

In contrast with 2D images of real specimens, the simulated embryo requires automated measurements adapted to its 3D structure. Here, they were calculated in reference to the AV axis and a particular point $\mathbf{M}_o$ in the center of the embryo (in this section, we use upright boldface notation for 3D coordinates and vectors). The unitary vector of the AV axis, denoted by $\mathbf{U}_{AV}$, was specified a priori in the initial conditions (Figure 16.19). The embryo's center $\mathbf{M}_o$ was calculated and updated at each simulation step by averaging the positions of the yolk membrane (ym) and yolk interior (yi) particles:

$$\mathbf{M}_o = \frac{1}{N_{yi} + N_{ym}} \left(\sum_{i=0}^{N_{yi}-1} \mathbf{X}_{yi,i} + \sum_{i=0}^{N_{ym}-1} \mathbf{X}_{ym,i} \right) \tag{16.15}$$

where $\mathbf{X}_{yi,i}$ (resp. $\mathbf{X}_{ym,i}$) is the position of yolk interior (resp. yolk membrane) particle i and N_{yi} (resp. N_{ym}) is the total number of yolk interior (resp. yolk membrane) particles.

The embryo vegetal pole $\mathbf{M}^{e}_{V}$, embryo animal pole $\mathbf{M}^{e}_{A}$, and yolk animal pole $\mathbf{M}^{Y}_{A}$ were obtained by calculating the dot product between $\mathbf{U}_{AV}$ and each ym or EVL particle's relative position with respect to the center, then selecting the position that realizes the maximum (farthest value in the positive direction) or minimum (farthest value in the negative direction) of this product:

$$\mathbf{M}^{e}_{V} = \underset{\mathbf{X}_{ym,i} \in \mathcal{S}_{ym}}{\arg\min} \left((\mathbf{X}_{ym,i} - \mathbf{M}_{o}) \cdot \mathbf{U}_{AV} \right) \quad (16.16)$$

$$\mathbf{M}^{e}_{A} = \underset{\mathbf{X}_{E,i} \in \mathcal{S}_{E}}{\arg\max} \left((\mathbf{X}_{E,i} - \mathbf{M}_{o}) \cdot \mathbf{U}_{AV} \right) \quad (16.17)$$

$$\mathbf{M}^{Y}_{A} = \underset{\mathbf{X}_{ym,i} \in \mathcal{S}_{ym}}{\arg\max} \left((\mathbf{X}_{ym,i} - \mathbf{M}_{o}) \cdot \mathbf{U}_{AV} \right) \quad (16.18)$$

where $\mathcal{S}_{ym}$ is the set of yolk membrane particles' position and $\mathcal{S}_{E}$ is the set of EVL cell particles' position. The projection of the margin on the AV axis, denoted by $\mathbf{M}_{m}$, was obtained by averaging the point projections of all the margin yolk membrane (MYM) particles onto the AV axis:

$$\mathbf{M}_{m} = \mathbf{M}_{o} + \frac{1}{N_{m}} \sum_{i=0}^{N_{m}-1} \left((\mathbf{X}_{m,i} - \mathbf{M}_{o}) \cdot \mathbf{U}_{AV} \right) \mathbf{U}_{AV} \quad (16.19)$$

where $\mathbf{X}_{m,i}$ is the position of MYM particle i and N_{m} is the number of MYM particles. Finally, the simulated embryo width W was set to twice the average of the radii defined by the distances between the MYM particles and their common projection $\mathbf{M}_{m}$:

$$W = \frac{2}{N_{m}} \sum_{i=0}^{N_{m}-1} \left\| \mathbf{X}_{m,i} - \mathbf{M}_{m} \right\| \quad (16.20)$$

Similarly to the real specimen, we could then define the same macroscopic measures of epibolic deformation on the simulated embryo (indicated by "s,") i.e. the normalized margin height H^{s}_{m}, the normalized yolk height H^{s}_{Y}, and the sphericity ratio C^{s}_{Φ}:

$$H^{s}_{m} = \frac{\left\| \mathbf{M}_{m} - \mathbf{M}^{e}_{V} \right\|}{\left\| \mathbf{M}^{e}_{A} - \mathbf{M}^{e}_{V} \right\|}, \quad H^{s}_{Y} = \frac{\left\| \mathbf{M}^{Y}_{A} - \mathbf{M}^{e}_{V} \right\|}{\left\| \mathbf{M}^{e}_{A} - \mathbf{M}^{e}_{V} \right\|}, \quad C^{s}_{\Phi} = \frac{W}{\left\| \mathbf{M}^{e}_{A} - \mathbf{M}^{e}_{V} \right\|} \quad (16.21)$$

6.3.2 Preliminary results

Judging by Figure 16.20, our first observation was that the deep cells' active protrusive behavior seemed sufficient to drive the embryo's deformation during epiboly in the context of the simulation. The temporal evolution of the above macroscopic measures fits reasonably

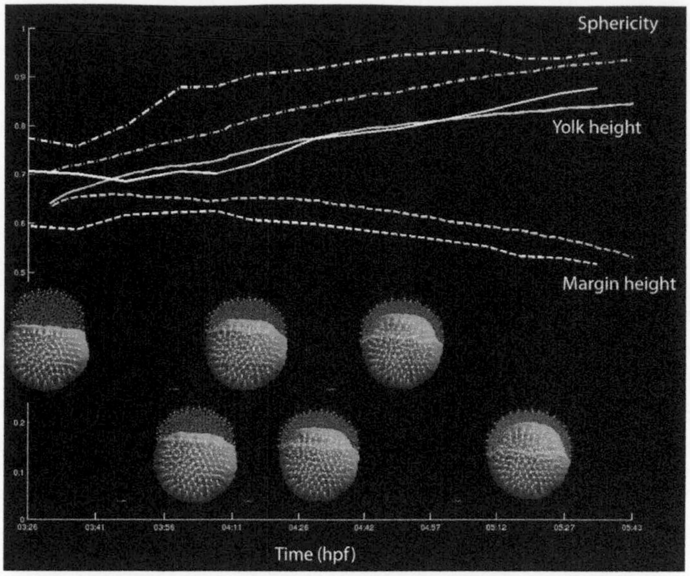

FIGURE 16.20 **Macroscopic measures of the epibolic deformation in a simulated specimen.** Six snapshots corresponding to different stages of a simulated embryo are displayed along with the temporal evolution of the corresponding macroscopic measures (blue), compared with the flipbook measures (white). Sphericity is represented by the dash-dot lines, normalized yolk height by the solid lines, and normalized margin height by the dashed lines. The embryos' positions correspond approximately to the snapshot times in abscissa. The simulated embryo parameters are: ligand source Q_2 on the yolk, $\theta_{m,\|} = 5.33, \lambda_r = 0, \theta_E^- = 56.67$, and $f^A = 3556$. (For interpretation of the references to color in this figure legend, the reader is referred to the web version of this book.)

well the data extracted from the flipbook. The main discrepancy is the apparent lack of sphere stage transition leading to a spherical morphology during the first hour. We did not observe the characteristic phase of increased sphericity concomitant with a *statu quo* for the normalized yolk and margin heights. In the simulated embryo's trajectory, the early increase of sphericity is always simultaneous with the decrease of at least one of the other macroscopic measures. A possible explanation could be that the initialization of the simulation is not close enough to the real high stage, with a yolk/deep cell interface already presenting a flat shape in the simulation.

6.4 Parameter exploration and validation

6.4.1 Fitness function and parameter space

After studying one virtual embryo under a fixed set of parameters, we proceeded to a broader exploration of parameter space to assess the validity of our simulations and model. For this, we designed a global *fitness function F* to fully automate the quantitative comparison between the simulated embryo and the flipbook specimen. Building upon the above measures, this function is the average of three objective subfunctions: a normalized margin height function F_m; a normalized yolk height function F_Y; and a sphericity function F_Φ:

$$F = \frac{1}{3}(F_m + F_Y + F_\Phi), \quad \text{with}$$
$$F_m = \sum_{t=t_1}^{t_{12}} \left|H_m^s(t) - H_m^e(t)\right|, \quad F_Y = \sum_{t=t_1}^{t_{12}} \left|H_Y^s(t) - H_Y^e(t)\right|, \quad F_\Phi = \sum_{t=t_1}^{t_{12}} \left|C_\Phi^s(t) - C_\Phi^e(t)\right| \tag{16.22}$$

where $t_1 \ldots t_{12}$ are the timings of the 12 images extracted from the flipbook specimen (Figure 16.17). The contribution of each objective function is not individually normalized as these functions represent differences of previously normalized measures.

We explored a five-dimensional parameter space with the following axes: (1) the type of polarization field: EVL-origin or YSL-origin; (2) the margin resistance $\theta_{m,\parallel}$; (3) the stochasticity of the polarization field controlled by λ_r; (4) the EVL resistance to external tension, controlled by θ_E^-; and (5) the intensity of the protrusion force f^A. This space was regularly sampled over the range and cardinalities shown in Figure 16.21.

6.4.2 *Results*

A number of insights could be gained from an analysis of the fitness landscape. A general trend is that the protrusive force intensity f^A and the randomness factor λ_r have counterbalancing effects. A higher protrusive force coupled with a higher random factor produces a fitness level similar to a lower force coupled with a lower randomness, as indicated by the isolines of Figure 16.22. The profile of the isolines reveals the relationship between both parameters: it appears to be supralinear, since an increase of f^A requires an exponential increase of λ_r to be counterbalanced.

For couples of parameters (f^A, λ_r) situated below the isoline passing through coordinates (2,000, 0.05), we did not observe any macroscopic epiboly behavior. We could however qualitatively distinguish different microscopic behaviors in this area: for low levels f^A, the lack of epibolic deformation is due to the lack of intercalating behavior at the cellular level; on the contrary, for high levels of f^A and λ_r, the cells start intercalating inefficiently, with cells sliding

	Min.	Max.	Cardinality	Unit
source	1	2	2	-
$\theta_{m,\parallel}$	1	40	10	N
λ_r	0	0.1	10	-
θ_E^-	10	150	10	$N.m^{-2}$
f^A	0	8000	10	N

FIGURE 16.21 **Range, cardinalities, and units of the five parameters explored in this case study.**

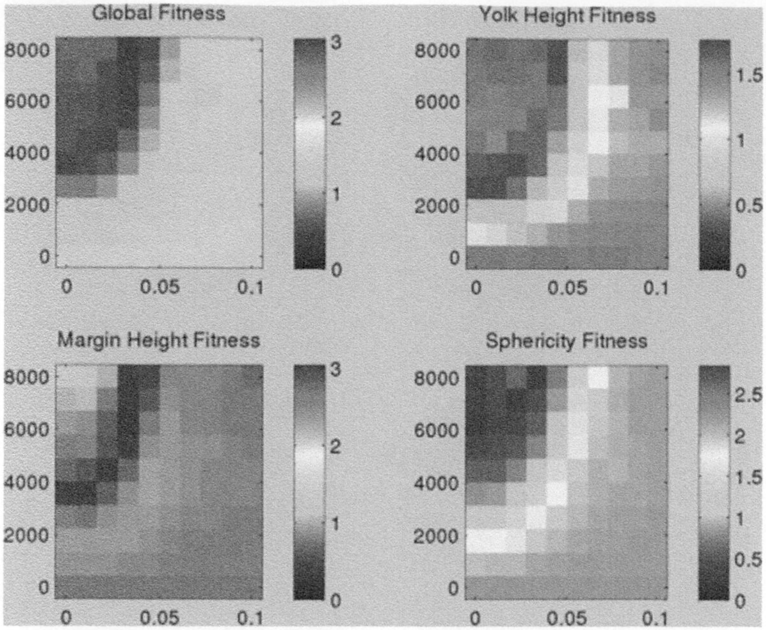

FIGURE 16.22 Fitness landscapes as a function of the random parameter λ_r and the protrusive force intensity parameter f^A. Top Left: global fitness function. Top Right: normalized yolk height objective function F_Y. Bottom Left: normalized margin height function F_m. Bottom Right: sphericity objective function F_Φ. On each plot, the random parameter λ_r is shown in abscissa and the protrusive force intensity f^A in ordinate. The color maps scale between zero and the maximum value of the fitness landscape that they are associated with (to the left).

on each other in a fluid-like manner, and tissue cohesion is lost. This behavior is due to an inequality between the active and passive forces in favor of the protrusive forces.

Further study of these mechanisms would require a preliminary calibration between both types of forces to ensure that these behaviors do not occur. In the following, we performed an a posteriori calibration of f^A at value 3555. Eliminating the f^A dimension allowed a 4D visualization of the fitness landscapes (Figure 16.23) and their mutual comparisons in both polarization scenarios.

Another noticeable general trend was the penalizing effect of the polarization field randomness: all objective functions perform poorly for high λ_r values (top slice of 3D charts). The only exception concerned the normalized margin height measure F_m, which tempered this effect when conjugated with low EVL resistance to tension θ_E^-, and low margin resistance to deep cells' pressure $\theta_{m,\parallel}$ (Figure 16.23a). Observations of the simulated phenotypes in this particular domain showed that the relaxed state of the EVL and margin, coupled with the low efficiency of the deep cells' protrusive activity (due to high randomness), produced a slight move of the margin toward the vegetal pole along with a de-flattening of the yolk/deep cells interface.

This observation stresses the importance of the embryo's external tension (EVL+Margin) in the shaping of the cellular domain. We also noted that in the scenario of the EVL as a ligand

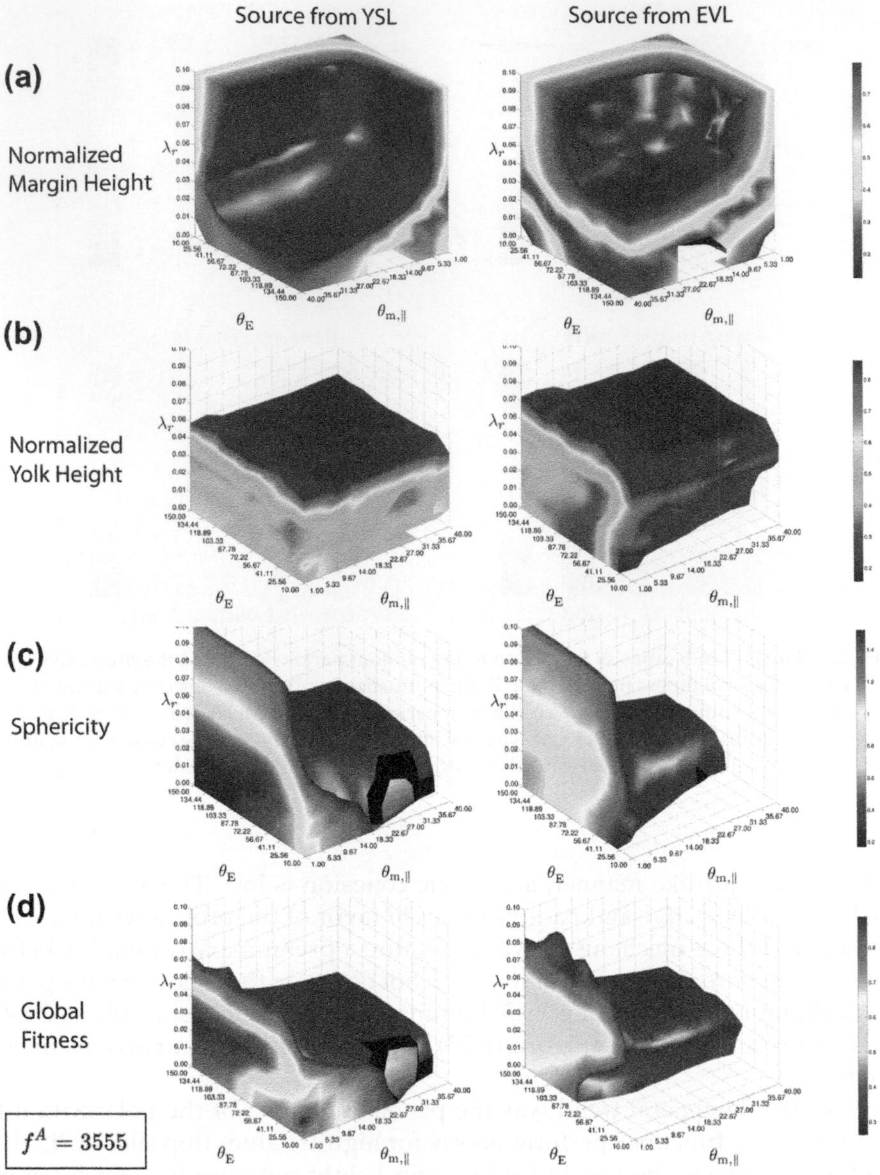

FIGURE 16.23 **3D plots of the objective and global fitness functions.** For all simulations, the protrusive force intensity f^A has been set to 3555. The vertical axis indicates the random parameter λ_r, the depth axis indicates the threshold controlling the EVL resistance θ_E^-, and the horizontal axis indicates the margin resistance threshold $\theta_{m,\|}$. (a) 3D plot of the normalized margin height objective function F_m. The isosurface represents the best fitness volume (threshold 0.79). This 3D objective function landscape has been rotated, unlike the following plots, to show a better angle of view. (b) 3D plot of the normalized yolk height objective function F_Y. The threshold of the isosurface is set to 0.86. (c) 3D plot of the sphericity objective function F_Φ. The threshold of the isosurface is set to 1.52. (d) 3D plot of the global fitness function F. The threshold of the isosurface is set to 0.88.

source (value 1), the EVL's topology became more irregular. There is feedback coupling between the perturbation of the polarization field, disorienting the deep cells, and the disorganization of the EVL, which in turn perturbs the polarization field. Both yolk height F_Y and sphericity measure F_Φ performed badly as yolk bulging did not occur.

At the opposite side of the parameter spectrum, i.e. low polarization randomness λ_r and high EVL and margin resistances, θ_E^- and $\theta_{m,\|}$, deep cell intercalation gains in efficiency but is blocked by the margin, preventing them to spread over the yolk. Interestingly, the two polarization scenarios offer alternative behaviors in response to this abnormal condition. In the YSL-based field, intercalation exerts a spreading force that deforms the overlying EVL, while this deformation is much more important in the EVL-based field, where the epiboly's spreading triggers a wrenching of the blastoderm from the yolk surface area. This pathological behavior was not expected and can be explained by an inadequacy of the intensity of the forces, without damping induced by random polarization. Obviously, both F_Y and F_Φ penalize the EVL ligand scenario, compared to the YSL one (Figure 16.23b and c, bottom right corner of the cubes).

Another dramatic effect was obtained if a perfectly efficient intercalation, i.e. with no axis randomness, was happening together with strong EVL resistance θ_E^- and weak margin resistance $\theta_{m,\|}$. The previous scenario happened again, i.e. the EVL blocked the spreading of the deep cells, except at some point when the margin still received pressure that made it move toward the vegetal pole, pulling the yolk membrane toward the animal pole. The accumulating yolk membrane ended up being rolled in a unrealistic fashion, stretching the inner yolk membrane particles, and finally allowing the strongly intercalating deep cells to perforate the yolk membrane and penetrate into the yolk.

The last example of aberrant development was detected by measure F_m, when the margin was located too far toward the vegetal pole (Figure 16.23a, bottom right). Yet, the other two measures, F_Y and F_Φ, evaluated the developmental trajectory of the embryo as excellent (Figure 16.23b and c, bottom left corner). This mischaracterization of an abnormal state highlights the difficulty of predicting the behavior of a simulated model.

6.5 Tentative conclusion

Altogether, the simulations conducted in this case study seem to validate the hypothesis that individual cell protrusive activity is sufficient to drive epiboly until the 50% stage. We have pointed out, however, the absence of sphere stage transition, i.e. from the so-called "high stage" to a more spherical shape presenting a flat interface between the yolk and the blastoderm. In the simulated embryos, early increasing sphericity always comes together with a progression of the embryo margin toward the yolk. This may be due to the fact that the initialization of the simulation does not sufficiently resemble the real high stage, as the yolk/deep-cell interface already presents a flat shape in the simulation.

Another interpretation is that additional mechanisms are missing in the explored parameter space, such as a different organization of the polarization field or new behavioral rules in the different compartments of the embryo. In particular, to better characterize the first epiboly episode and capture the effective properties of cell motility, we would need more precise measurements of the individual epibolic behaviors at the cellular level, not just global geometric criteria.

7 DISCUSSION

The "right" mesoscopic level: The most striking characteristic of multicellular systems is their extreme *heterogeneity* of properties and behaviors. As Henri Atlan metaphorically stated through his famous book title "Between Crystal and Smoke" (Atlan 1979), the structure of living matter is somewhere between a highly regularly organized state and a highly randomly disorganized state. Accordingly, the best level to model the morphogenesis of multicellular organisms resides between the macroscopic level, where global mathematical regularities are too constrained and not expressive enough, and the microscopic level, where molecular dynamics is too complex and uncontrollable. Continuous equations must be coupled with discrete local rules, and this necessitates a characterization of the diversity of the underlying cell types and behaviors. A hybrid approach requires a discrete representation of the tissue based on individual components. In our own study of early embryo development, we chose the single-cell level as it allows this local description of cell properties in relatively simple terms. Two criteria led us to make particular choices for the cell biomechanics and the genetic regulation and molecular signaling: the similarities between the variables involved in the model and the observations/concepts produced by the embryologists, on the one hand; and the simplicity of the description leading to a manageable number of parameters, on the other hand. This should not only allow computationally feasible simulations by today's standards but, most importantly, a biologically meaningful interpretation of their outcome.

Portability to other animal models: The MecaGen project was envisioned as a generic modeling platform for all types of animal development. Its foundational principles should be applicable to any multicellular system combining biomechanics with genetic regulation and molecular signaling. The next step in the development of this platform is to expand its cell behavior ontology (CBO) to integrate other types of epithelial and mesenchymal behaviors. In the epithelial case, not many improvements should be needed to fulfill this objective. The adhesion coefficient of "lateral" neighborhood links could be increased and epithelial behaviors, including apical constriction and active intercalation in epithelial layers, should allow the platform to simulate monolayered embryos such as *Drosophila* or sea urchin. This being said, the current MecaGen implementation is not compatible with every animal cell behavior either. Its major limitation resides in the single-particle cell abstraction, which is not adapted to cellular shapes that depart greatly from spheroids or cuboids. Other types of animal morphogenesis rely greatly on cell elongation, such as *Phallusia mammillata* or nematodes. In those cases, an ellipsoid particle model such as Palsson's (Palsson 2001) would provide a reasonable solution for asymmetric cells. In later stages of vertebrate development, too, cells differentiate into extremely stretched shapes such as muscle cells, for which the single-particle framework is clearly inappropriate.

Toward an "evo-devo" perspective: Once the MECA and GEN parts of the model are finally connected and their dynamics truly coupled, without WTS shortcut, a promising extension of this work will be its application to "evolutionary developmental" questions. Evo-devo does not generally aim at directly comparing simulated phenotypes and real embryos but rather asking how evolution is able to generate new structures and behaviors at the level of the whole embryo. This would involve modeling and simulating an even higher level of organization, in which the whole embryo behaves and potentially interacts with its environment. It can be seen as another way to explore the model's parameter space without isolating the developmental trajectories around a target phenotype (zebrafish in this chapter). The evaluation would emerge from a Darwinian selection process in an artificial environment—whether by survival or reproduction of particular behaviors. A particularly fascinating exploration would be to start from a simple individual organism such as the *urbilaterian*, a hypothetical ancestor of all animals exhibiting bilateral symmetry (Erwin and Davidson 2002; Hejnol and Martindale 2008), and guide its evolution through mutation of its gene regulatory networks toward multiple descendant species. To our knowledge, no computational evo-devo study has proposed a developmental model presenting as many similarities with real biological systems as MecaGen does. It would be a great opportunity to better decipher and understand the evolutionary forces that drive the diversity of life.

References

Coen, E. (1999). *The Art of Genes. How Organisms Make Themselves.* Oxford University Press on Demand.

Hopwood, N. (2008). Embryology. *Cambridge History of Science* **6**.

Lawrence, P. A., and Levine, M. (2006). Mosaic and regulative development: two faces of one coin. *Curr. Biol.* **16**(7):R236–R239.

Nüsslein-Volhard, C., and Wieschaus, E. (1980). Mutations affecting segment number and polarity in Drosophila. *Nature* **287**(5785):795–801.

Nüsslein-Volhard, C. (2012). The zebrafish issue of Development. *Development* **139**(22):4099–4103.

Arnone, M. I., and Davidson, E. H. (1997). The hardwiring of development: organization and function of genomic regulatory systems. *Development* **124**(10):1851–1864.

Chan, T.-M., Longabaugh, W., Bolouri, H., Chen, H.-L., Tseng, W.-F., Chao, C.-H., Jang, T.-H., Lin, Y.-I., Hung, S.-C., Wang, H.-D., and Yuh, C.-H. (2009). Developmental gene regulatory networks in the zebrafish embryo. *Biochim. biophys. Acta.* **1789**(4):279–298.

Pelegri, F. (2003). Maternal factors in zebrafish development. *Develop. Dyn. : An official publication of the American Association of Anatomists* **228**(3):535–554.

Gavis, E. R., and Lehmann, R. (1992). Localization of nanos RNA controls embryonic polarity. *Cell* **71**(2):301–313.

Keller, R. (2012). Physical biology returns to morphogenesis. *Science* **338**(6104):201–203.

Steinberg, M. S. (1962). On the mechanism of tissue reconstruction by dissociated cells. I. Population kinetics, differential adhesiveness. and the absence of directed migration. *Proc. Natl. Acad. Sci. USA* **48**:1577–1582.

von Dassow, M., and Davidson, L. A. (2011). Physics and the canalization of morphogenesis: a grand challenge in organismal biology. *Phys. Biol.* **8**(4):045002.

Turing, A. M. (1952). The chemical basis of morphogenesis. *Philos. Trans. R. Soc. Lond. B, Biol. Sci.* **237**(641):37–72.

Gierer, A., and Meinhardt, H. (1972). A theory of biological pattern formation. *Biol. Cybern.* **12**(1):30–39.

Meinhardt, H., and Gierer, A. (1974). Applications of a theory of biological pattern formation based on lateral inhibition. *J. Cell Sci.* **15**(2):321–346.

Young, D. A. (1984). A local activator-inhibitor model of vertebrate skin patterns. *Math. Biosci.* **72**(1):51–58.

Kondo, S., and Miura, T. (2010). Reaction-diffusion model as a framework for understanding biological pattern formation. *Science* **329**(5999):1616–1620.

Bieler, J., Pozzorini, C., and Naef, F. (2011). Whole-embryo modeling of early segmentation in Drosophila identifies robust and fragile expression domains. *Biophys. J.* **101**(2):287–296.

Inaba, M., Yamanaka, H., and Kondo, S. (2012). Pigment pattern formation by contact-dependent depolarization. *Science* **335**(6069):677.

Wolpert, L. (1969). Positional information and the spatial pattern of cellular differentiation. *J. Theor. Biol.* **25**(1):1.

Wolpert, L. (2011). Positional information and patterning revisited. *J. Theor. Biol.* **269**(1):359–365.

Lawrence, P. A. (2001). Morphogens: how big is the big picture?. *Nat. Cell Biol.* **3**(7):E151–4.

Lander, A. D., Nie, Q., and Wan, F. Y. M. (2002). Do morphogen gradients arise by diffusion?. *Develop. cell* **2**(6):785–796.

Tabata, T., and Takei, Y. (2004). Morphogens, their identification and regulation. *Development* **131**(4):703–712.

Kicheva, A., Bollenbach, T., Wartlick, O., Jülicher, F., and González-Gaitán, M. (2012). Investigating the principles of morphogen gradient formation: from tissues to cells. *Curr. opin. Genet. Develop.* 1–6.

Eggenberger, P. (1997). Evolving morphologies of simulated 3D organisms based on differential gene expression. In *Proceedings of the Fourth European Conference on Artificial Life*, pp. 205–213.

Kumar, S., and Bentley, P. (2003). Biologically inspired evolutionary development. In *Evolvable Systems: From Biology to Hardware*, pp. 57–68.

Doursat, R. (2006). The growing canvas of biological development: multiscale pattern generation on an expanding lattice of gene regulatory nets. *InterJournal: Complex Systems 1809*

Barkai, N., and Shilo, B.-Z. (2009). Robust generation and decoding of morphogen gradients. *Cold Spring Harb. Perspect. Biol.* **1**(5):a001990.

Kauffman, S. (1969). Homeostasis and differentiation in random genetic control networks. *Nature* **224**(5215):177–178.

Reinitz, J., and Sharp, D. (1995). Mechanism of eve stripe formation. *Mech. Develop.* **49**(1):133.

Rolland-Lagan, A., Paquette, M., Tweedle, V., and Akimenko, M. (2012). Morphogen-based simulation model of ray growth and joint patterning during fin development and regeneration. *Development* **139**:1–10.

Gibson, M. C., Patel, A. B., Nagpal, R., and Perrimon, N. (2006). The emergence of geometric order in proliferating metazoan epithelia. *Nature* **442**(7106):1038–1041.

Farhadifar, R., Röper, J., Aigouy, B., Eaton, S., and Jülicher, F. (2007). The influence of cell mechanics, cell-cell interactions, and proliferation on epithelial packing. *Curr. Biol.* **17**(24):2095–2104.

Sandersius, S., Chuai, M., Weijer, C., and Newman, T. (2011). Correlating Cell Behavior with Tissue Topology in Embryonic Epithelia. *PLoS One* **6**(4):e18081.

Graner, F., and Glazier, J. (1992). Simulation of biological cell sorting using a two-dimensional extended Potts model. *Phys. Rev. Lett.* **69**(13):2013–2016.

Glazier, J., and Graner, F. (1993). Simulation of the differential adhesion driven rearrangement of biological cells. *Phys. Rev. E* **47**(3):2128–2154.

Brodland, G. W., and Chen, H. H. (2000). The mechanics of heterotypic cell aggregates: insights from computer simulations. *J. Biomech. Eng.* **122**(4):402–407.

Landsberg, K. P., Farhadifar, R., Ranft, J., Umetsu, D., Widmann, T. J., Bittig, T., Said, A., Jülicher, F., and Dahmann, C. (2009). Increased cell bond tension governs cell sorting at the drosophila anteroposterior compartment boundary. *Curr. Biol.* **19**(22):1950–1955.

Aliee, M., Röper, J.-C., Landsberg, K. P., Pentzold, C., Widmann, T. J., Jülicher, F., and Dahmann, C. (2012). Physical mechanisms shaping the drosophila dorsoventral compartment boundary. *Curr. Biol.* 1–10.

Beatrici, C. P., and Brunnet, L. G. (2011). Cell sorting based on motility differences. *Phys. Rev. E* **84**(3 Pt 1):031927.

Foty, R., and Steinberg, M. (2005). The differential adhesion hypothesis: a direct evaluation. *Develop. Biol.* **278**(1):255–263.

Zhang, Y., Thomas, G. L., Swat, M., Shirinifard, A., and Glazier, J. A. (2011). Computer Simulations of Cell Sorting Due to Differential Adhesion. *PLoS One* **6**(10):e24999.

Maitre, J. L., Berthoumieux, H., Krens, S. F. G., Salbreux, G., Jülicher, F., Paluch, E., and Heisenberg, C.-P. (2012). Adhesion Functions in Cell Sorting by Mechanically Coupling the Cortices of Adhering Cells. *Science* **338**(6104):253–256.

Blanchard, G. B., and Adams, R. J. (2011). Measuring the multi-scale integration of mechanical forces during morphogenesis. *Curr. Opin. Genet. Develop.* 1–11.

van Leeuwen, I. M. M., Mirams, G. R., Walter, A., Fletcher, A., Murray, P., Osborne, J., Varma, S., Young, S. J., Cooper, J., Doyle, B., Pitt-Francis, J., Momtahan, L., Pathmanathan, P., Whiteley, J. P., Chapman, S. J., Gavaghan, D. J., Jensen, O. E., King, J. R., Maini, P. K., Waters, S. L., and Byrne, H. M. (2009). An integrative computational model for intestinal tissue renewal. *Cell Prolif.* **42**(5):617–636.

Grima, R. (2008). Multiscale modeling of biological pattern formation. *Curr. Top. Develop. Biol.* **81**:435–460.

Little, S. C., and Wieschaus, E. F. (2011). Shifting patterns: merging molecules, morphogens, motility, and methodology. *Develop. cell* **21**(1):2–4.

Izaguirre, J., Chaturvedi, R., Huang, C., Cickovski, T., Coffland, J., Thomas, G., Forgacs, G., Alber, M., Hentschel, G., and Newman, S. (2004). CompuCell, a multi-model framework for simulation of morphogenesis. *Bioinformatics* **20**(7):1129–1137.

Cickovski, T., Aras, K., Swat, M., Merks, R., Glimm, T., Hentschel, H., Alber, M., Glazier, J., Newman, S., and Izaguirre, J. (2007). From genes to organisms via the cell: a problem-solving environment for multicellular development. *Comput. Sci. Eng.* **9**(4):50–60.

Swat, M. H. M., Hester, S. D. S., Balter, A. I. A., Heiland, R. W. R., Zaitlen, B. L. B., and Glazier, J. A. J. (2008). Multicell simulations of development and disease using the CompuCell 3D simulation environment. *Methods Mol. Biol.* **500**:361–428. (Clifton, NJ).

Doursat, R. (2008). Programmable architectures that are complex and self-organized: From morphogenesis to engineering. In *Proceedings of Artificial XI*, pp. 181–188.

Joachimczak, M., and Wróbel, B. (2008). Evo-devo in silico: a model of a gene network regulating multicellular development in 3D space with artificial physics. In *Proceedings of the Eleventh International Conference on the Simulation and Synthesis of Living Systems, Artificial Life XI*, pp. 297–304.

Schramm, L., Jin, Y., and Sendhoff, B. (2011). Emerged coupling of motor control and morphological development in evolution of multi-cellular animats. *Advances in Artificial Life. Darwin Meets von Neumann* 27–34.

Doursat, R., Sánchez, C., Dordea, R., Fourquet, D., and Kowaliw, T. (2012). Embryomorphic engineering: emergent innovation through evolutionary development. In (R. Doursat, H. Sayama, and O. Michel, eds.), *Morphogenetic Engineering: Toward Programmable Complex Systems*. Springer.

Murray, J. D. (2003). *Mathematical biology II: spatial models and biomedical applications*. Springer.

Fleury, V. (2005). An elasto-plastic model of avian gastrulation. *Organogenesis* **2**(1):6–16.

Deutsch, A., and Dormann, S. (). Cellular Automaton Modeling of Biological Pattern Formation. In Characterization, Applications, and Analysis2005. Boston: Birkhauser.

Marée, A., and Hogeweg, P. (2001). How amoeboids self-organize into a fruiting body: multicellular coordination in *Dictyostelium discoideum*. *Proc. Natl. Acad. Sci.* **98**(7):3879.

Schaller, G., and Meyer-Hermann, M. (2004). Kinetic and dynamic Delaunay tetrahedralizations in three dimensions. *Comput. Phys. Commun.* **162**(1):9–23.

Newman, T. J. (2005). Modeling multicellular systems using subcellular elements. *Math. Biosci. Eng.* **2**(3):613–624.

Wilczynski, B., and Furlong, E. E. M. (2010). Challenges for modeling global gene regulatory networks during development: Insights from Drosophila. *Develop. Biol.* **340**(2):161–169.

Ben-Tabou de Leon, S., and Davidson, E. (2009). Modeling the dynamics of transcriptional gene regulatory networks for animal development. *Develop. Biol.* **325**(2):317–328.

Giacomantonio, C. E., and Goodhill, G. J. (2010). A Boolean Model of the Gene Regulatory Network Underlying Mammalian Cortical Area Development. *PLoS Comput. Biol.* **6**(9):e1000936.

Peter, I. S., Faure, E., and Davidson, E. H. (2012). Predictive computation of genomic logic processing functions in embryonic development. *Proc. Natl. Acad. Sci.* **109**(41):16434–16442.

Kojić, N., Huang, A., Chung, E., Ivanović, M., Filipović, N., Kojić, M., and Tschumperlin, D. J. (2010). A 3-D Model of Ligand Transport in a Deforming Extracellular Space. *Biophys. J.* **99**(11):3517–3525.

Thomas, R. R. (1973). Boolean formalization of genetic control circuits. *J. Theor. Biol.* **42**(3):563–585.

Davidson, E. H. (2010). Emerging properties of animal gene regulatory networks. *Nature* **468**(7326):911–920.

Peter, I. S., and Davidson, E. H. (2009). Modularity and design principles in the sea urchin embryo gene regulatory network. *FEBS Lett.* **583**(24):3948–3958.

Davidson, E. H. (2009). Network design principles from the sea urchin embryo. *Curr. Opin. Genet. Develop.* **19**(6):535–540.

Solnica-Krezel, L., and Driever, W. (1994). Microtubule arrays of the zebrafish yolk cell: organization and function during epiboly. *Development* **120**(9):2443–2455.

Karlstrom, R. O., and Kane, D. A. (1996). A flipbook of zebrafish embryogenesis. *Development* **123**:461.

Atlan, Henri (1979). *Entre le cristal et la fumée: essai sur l'organisation du vivant*. Éditions du Seuil.

Palsson, E. (2001). A three-dimensional model of cell movement in multicellular systems. *Future Gener. Comput. Syst.* **17**(7):835–852.

Erwin, D. H., and Davidson, E. H. (2002). The last common bilaterian ancestor. *Development* **129**(13):3021–3032.

Hejnol, A., and Martindale, M. Q. (2008). Acoel development supports a simple planula-like urbilaterian. *Phil. Trans. R. Soc. B: Biol. Sci.* **363**(1496):1493–1501.

Kimmel, C. B., Ballard, W. W., Kimmel, S. R., Ullmann, B., and Schilling, T. F. (1995). Stages of embryonic development of the zebrafish. *Develop. Dyn. : An official publication of the American Association of Anatomists* **203**(3):253–310.

CHAPTER

17

Developing a Systems Biology of Aging

Andres Kriete[a], *Mathieu Cloutier*[b]

[a]School of Biomedical Engineering, Science and Health Systems, Drexel University, Bossone Research Center, Philadelphia, PA, USA

[b]GERAD and Department of Chemical Engineering, Ecole Polytechnique de Montreal, Montreal, QC, Canada

CONTENTS

Abstract

What makes the study of aging particularly challenging is the wide spectrum of phenotypical changes that can be observed during its progression. While initial attention was paid to damage accumulation, dysfunction, and failure, it is now realized that aging, and associated diseases including dementias, are influenced by a multitude of interacting factors. Proximal mechanisms beyond passive accumulation of damage include regulatory mechanisms, stress responses, changes in networks, as well as genetic and stochastic effects. The application of computational systems biology in aging, which is in line with other attempts to overcome the study of isolated or compartmentalized mechanisms, has made initial progress allowing us to simulate partial aspects of the aging dynamics and to make new hypotheses about how these aging mechanism shape disease

http://dx.doi.org/10.1016/B978-0-12-405926-9.00017-4

progression. Here we provide examples for analysis of networks, regulatory mechanisms, and spatiotemporal effects in the study of proximal mechanisms of aging and Parkinson's Disease. In addition, we introduce complexity theories that may contribute to explain the ultimate causes of aging with an evolutionary view.

1 INTRODUCTION

For systems biology to be successful in deciphering aging and age-related diseases a powerful, flexible, and comprehensive computational approach is required to study a variety of mechanisms in an integrated fashion. While systems biology applications in aging are making some progress (Kirkwood, 2011; West and Bergman, 2009; Kriete et al., 2011), they are dependent on and limited by the availability of suitable data obtained under controlled conditions. For instance, we can sample proteomics and gene expression data at different chronological ages of cells and tissues to provide us with snapshots of the functional activities of metabolic, gene regulatory, and signaling pathways. While such studies have significantly contributed to the success of systems biology in other areas, aging phenotypes exhibit more complex pattern and states such as damage accumulation, protein oxidation and misfolding, dysfunction of organelles, which are not readily accessible by current omics-based examinations. Furthermore, allometric relationships between species, environmental conditions, stochastic effects, as well as environmental conditions and genetic variants also play a role in modulating aging (West and Bergman, 2009; Bergman et al., 2007; Herndon et al., 2002; Li et al., 2011; Kriete, 2006). In order to proceed, attempts addressing a combination of at least a subset of mechanisms are first steps toward the development of a more comprehensive model. In the following we provide examples to combine observations of damage progression with the study of regulatory mechanism, in networks as well as whole-cell models of Parkinson's Disease (PD), which are examples to overcome the study of compartmentalized mechanisms in isolation.

However, while these initial attempts address the proximal mechanisms of aging, the ultimate cause of aging cannot be fully explained without an evolutionary view, culminating in the question "Why do we age?" (Kirkwood, 2000). Theoretical-evolutionary theories have provided important insights into aging (Ljubuncic and Reznick, 2009; Kirkwood, 2005; Rose et al., 2008), but such theories appear to be difficult to be implemented into current computational modeling endeavors. We therefore have to overcome fundamental conceptional hurdles allowing us to combine evolutionary aspects, experimental observations, and mathematical modeling. Therefore, in another aspect of this contribution, we discuss how the complexity theory of robustness, and the "robust yet fragile" paradigm, can provide a broader framework for future systems biology oriented studies of the biology of aging.

2 AGING NETWORKS

When aging mechanisms are placed in context with organizational principles of biological systems, such as pathways and networks or in conjunction with evolutionary theories, new opportunities are opened, realizing the contribution that regulatory mechanisms play in the

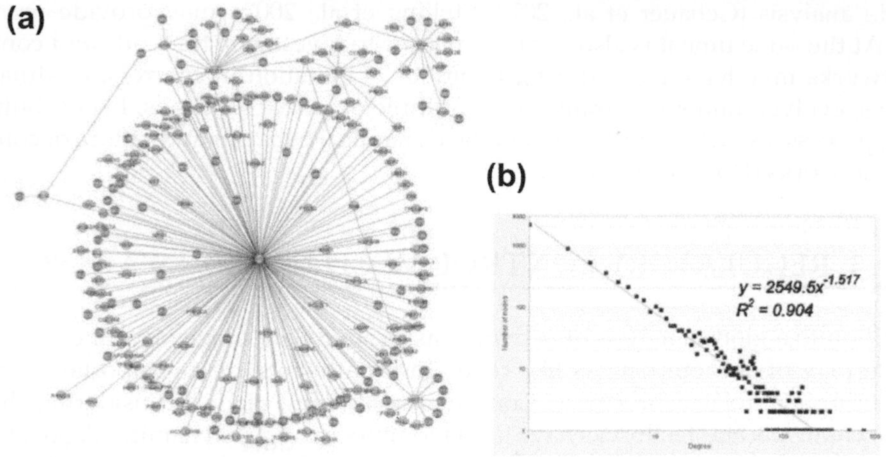

FIGURE 17.1 (a) Chromatin network of proteins involved in aging. (b) The network has a scale-free property.

progression of aging. Examination of networks is one of the directions systems biology can take in aging research. Assembly of aging-associated networks from proteins known to be influential for the aging process if perturbed, demonstrates the broad spectrum of protein function (signaling, mitochondrial, metabolism) and distribution over most cellular compartments belonging to this network as shown by Budovsky et al. (2007). During evolution proteins can take multiple roles in multiple traits, i.e. they become pleiotropic, which keeps growing complexity at bay. Proteins associated with aging show a higher degree of pleiotropy as well as higher connectivity (Criollo et al., 2012; Dong et al., 2010; Kriete et al., 2010; Witten and Bonchev, 2007; Fortney et al., 2010). The role of modular structures of protein networks and changes of protein connectivity with age have been investigated (Xue et al., 2007; Soltow et al., 2010; Yucel, 2011), but is currently not known if these networks are a complete representation of all proteins involved in aging, since higher connectivity may render these proteins experimentally more noticeable (Criollo et al., 2012). The most connected genes of the aging network compiled by Budovsky et al. (2007) include BCL2, ESR1, MYC, NFKB1, STAT3, SYK, and UBE2I, comprising stress-response genes also known to play roles in age-related diseases. Furthermore, the network contains highly connected, evolutionary conserved hubs eliciting pro-survival responses if activated, such as caloric restriction (Wuttke et al., 2012).

Figure 17.1a shows a subnetwork specifically developed for chromatin-related genes (Lo, 2007). It contains a major hub protein p53, an important regulator of chromosomal integrity, as well as associated FOXO genes, which variants have been found as a potential contributor to lifespan in humans by association studies (Willcox et al., 2008; Kleindorp et al., 2011). The topology of subnetworks, like other longevity-related subnetworks, shows a typical scale-free distribution (Figure 17.1b). While higher connectivity of proteins is a sign of conservation and preferred attachments they received during evolution, the analysis of topological features and prediction of stability resulting from these networks, such as attack tolerance, currently offer limited insights to elucidate the aging process. It appears that a functionally oriented analysis of these networks, with respect to feedbacks, control, dynamics, including metabolic flux mode analysis (Gebauer et al., 2012; Stelling et al., 2002), may provide more useful insights. At the same time it is also of great interest to investigate tradeoffs and competition these networks may have faced during evolution. Limitation in controls, modularity and hierarchies, evolved under constraints and multiple objective functions, likely contribute to the aging process, as they are influential in the dynamical behavior and failure of comparable technical networks (Doyle et al., 2005).

3 REGULATORY CONTROL MECHANISMS IN AGING

In addition to a global analysis of networks associated with longevity, functional analysis in the interplay of subcomponents like regulatory pathways are an important component in deciphering age-related processes. Computational aging models considering the role of control mechanisms and feedbacks have targeted mitochondrial dynamics (Figge et al., 2012; Kowald and Kirkwood, 2011), protein homeostasis (Proctor and Lorimer, 2011), as well as the modularity of protein networks changing with age (Xue et al., 2007; Soltow et al., 2010; Yucel, 2011). To fully decipher the aging dynamics, functional aging models should target a cellular level, in order to consider interdependent mechanisms like accumulating damage by oxidation of proteins, damage to nuclear and mitochondrial DNA, dysfunctional mitochondria, and alterations in biosynthesis. All these mechanisms occur simultaneously and in context with regulatory mechanisms, such as increase in stress signaling, adaptive changes in gene expressions, and epigenetic alterations. Cells in proliferative tissues can arrest in a state of replicative senescence, while more severely damaged cells may enter mitochondrial induced apoptosis limiting their detrimental effect to the organism, and these mechanisms are reviewed in depth elsewhere (Kirkwood, 2005; Johnson et al., 1999; Navarro and Boveris, 2007; Kenyon, 2010; Kourtis and Tavernarakis, 2011; Kujoth et al., 2005).

One comprehensive aging model, which included mitochondria, aberrant proteins, free radicals, and scavengers (MARS model), was developed by Kowald and Kirkwood to study the interplay between metabolism, damage, and repair predicting the progression of aging (Kowald and Kirkwood, 1996). In a similar way, an adaptive response model was suggested (Kriete et al., 2010) using fuzzy logic to integrate oxidative phosphorylation in mitochondria, biosynthesis in the endoplasmic reticulum, and negative feedbacks activated upon cellular stress. In this model, feedbacks downregulate mitochondria and biosynthesis, but promote glycolysis, thus containing ROS (Kriete et al., 2010). Feedbacks in this model can be interpreted as barriers preventing a sudden breakdown, whereby the combination of positive damage-accumulation cycles and negative stress-response feedbacks shape the overall behavior of cellular and physiological decline by a progressive adaptation.

The molecular mechanisms behind age-related stress responses and their feedbacks are well investigated, both in bacterial eukaryotes like yeast, as well as in higher organisms. In yeast, asymmetric cell division causes damage to be unequally sequestered between mother and daughter cells (Figure 17.2). The damage retained by the mother cell causes a spectrum of dysfunctions. In response to mitochondrial dysfunction a feedback mechanism termed retrograde response involving RTG-genes changes the gene expression adaptively and extends lifespan (Butow and Avadhani, 2004; Jazwinski, 2000). It has been proposed that feedback architectures always have fragilities (Csete and Doyle, 2002), and the RTG pathway causes accumulation of

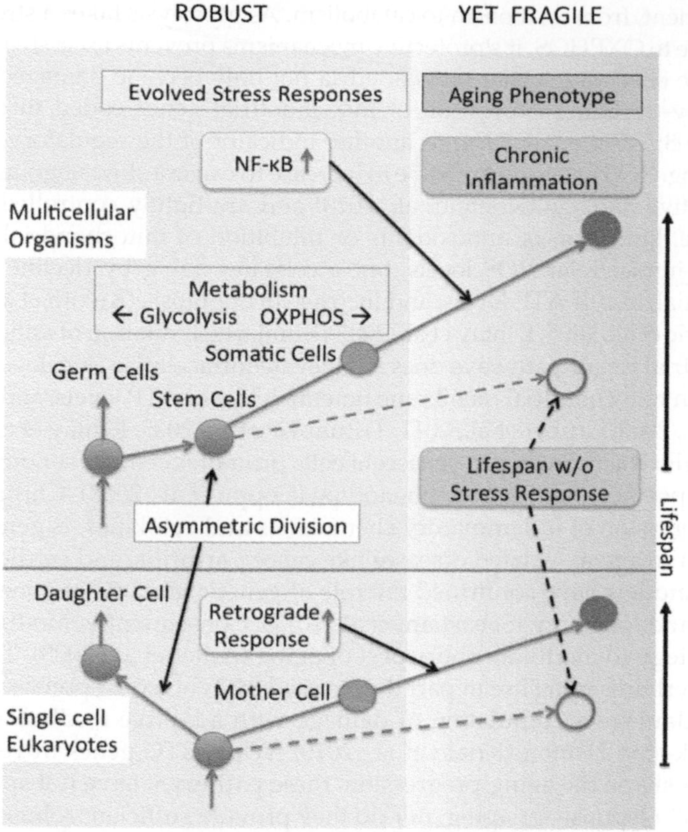

FIGURE 17.2 Key signatures of the "robustness-yet fragile" paradigm. Asymmetric cell division in bacteria predates specialization of cells in higher organism. In multicellular organisms asymmetry has contributed to the development of powerful somatic cells, at the cost of fragility introduced by oxidative phosphorylation as a major and effective source of energy generation, while germ and stem cells mostly rely on glycolysis. Evolved feedbacks, such as the retrograde response in yeast and NF-κB in higher organisms, become active during aging and shape the aging process adaptively in response to mitochondrial dysfunction and accumulating damage, but show tradeoffs such as chronic inflammation.

extrachromosomal circles. In higher organisms, the damage is similarly distributed by an asymmetric cell division, which leads to a separation between germ, pluripotent, and specialized somatic cells (Figure 17.2). While germ cells remain intact, somatic cells age. With increasing oxidation and mitochondrial dysfunction the Nuclear Factor kappa B (NF-κB), at the core of a bow-tie architecture of an autoimmunity protein network (Kitano et al., 2006), elicits a pro-survival response in pre-senescent cells, similar to the RTG pathway in yeast. The response is known to keep intracellular levels of free radicals low by activating the expression of scavenger molecules, which contributes to improvement in protein quality (Rivas and Ullrich, 1992). Furthermore, the chronic low-grade activity of the NF-κB pathway, activated by cell-intrinsic "atypical" mechanisms (Kriete and Mayo, 2009; Evans et al., 1995), may also contribute to a metabolic adjustment, from anabolism to catabolism. As glycolysis takes a stronger role in ATP generation relative to OXPHOS, it's protective mechanisms prevents excessive protein oxidation (Brand, 1997). The observation that mitochondria not only become damaged, but are actively downregulated by declining expression of mitochondrial genes coded in the nuclear DNA (Preston et al., 2008; Zahn et al., 2006), is another indicator of the regulatory, adaptive mechanisms during aging. ROS levels do not have to increase to cause a slow ongoing accumulation of permanent oxidative damage (Kriete et al., 2010) and are tightly controlled in pre-senescent cells. For instance, limitation of antioxidants or inhibition of mitochondrial repair pathways does not elevate intracellular ROS levels, but accelerates aging by decline in mitochondrial membrane potential, loss of ATP levels, and increase in apoptosis (Kujoth et al., 2005; Gruber et al., 2011; Trifunovic et al., 2005; Echtay et al., 2002). Similarly, limitation of antioxidants or inhibition of mitochondrial repair pathways does not elevate intracellular ROS levels, but accelerates aging by decline in mitochondrial membrane potential, loss of ATP levels, and increase in apoptosis (Kujoth et al., 2005; Gruber et al., 2011; Trifunovic et al., 2005; Echtay et al., 2002).

Constitutive NF-κB activity in pre-senescent cells promotes cellular senescence (Rovillain et al., 2011) with a specific inflammatory phenotype (Coppe et al., 2008). Chronic inflammation, including the expression of inflammatory chemokines and cytokines, is generally considered a major risk factor in age-associated diseases like cancer, arthritis, and cardiovascular disease, and genetic risk models have confirmed the role of genetic variants of genes associated with NF-κB networks and longevity (Sebastiani et al., 2012). Consequently, modulation of NF-κB is considered a strategy to modulate one aspect of aging (Adler et al., 2008). Thus, the dynamic mechanisms underlying aging are in part determined by evolved responses and the combination of ongoing damage accumulation of damage with adaptive feedbacks allows aging to progress in a lock-step fashion (Kriete et al., 2010). While RTG genes in yeast and NF-κB in higher organisms shape the aging progression, these pathways have not specifically evolved to be an "optimal" response for aging, nor do they provide sufficient robustness to revert the aging phenotype. Instead, they introduce new vulnerabilities. The antagonistic activity of the pro-survival mechanism NF-κB and the pro-apoptotic function of p53 is an example. The activity of the p53 pathway is essential for base excision repair and modulation of apoptosis, but competes with NF-κB over a common pool of transcriptional co-activators (Ak and Levine, 2010). In aging, the pro-survival mechanism dominates the repair and apoptotic pathway, so that no only cytosolic, but also nuclear damage can progress. Chronic inflammation, change in metabolism and reduced repair mechanisms expose the organism to fragilities such as cancer, diabetes, or dementias on the long term. These diseases have aspects of an accelerated aging phenotype, demonstrating the loss of regulatory mechanisms. The underlying dynamics can be modeled at increasing levels of detail as shown in the next section for Parkinson's Disease.

4 CELL MODELS OF PARKINSON'S DISEASE

4.1 Modeling PD-related pathways

PD is the second most prevalent neurodegenerative disease after Alzheimer's and affects up to 1% of the population aged 65 or more. Some cases (between 5 and 10%) have a known genetic component and can result in early onset PD (Lotharius and Brundin, 2002). However, a large majority of cases have no known cause and are labeled as idiopathic PD. For these, it is assumed that a combination of factors, including age, is involved.

Although the root causes of PD are poorly understood, the associated physiological and cellular changes are relatively homogenous. More specifically, the dopaminergic neurons of the substantia nigra pars compacta are affected, showing elevated ROS levels, accumulation of misfolded α-synuclein (αS) and mitochondrial damage (Malkus et al., 2009). This results in a failure to sustain dopamine levels and motor symptoms ensue. Even though each of the aforementioned mechanisms is relatively well understood, dynamical feedback interactions are present and this complicates the analysis. Thus, the etiopathology of PD is often referred to as a "vicious cycle" (Malkus et al., 2009). PD is thus caused by a physiological system (i.e. the brain) that exhibits some systematic failure caused by a wide array of age-related processes. In that regard, PD is a good case study to develop a systems understanding of an age-related ailment.

In the context of a systems approach to PD, mathematical models complement experimental data by providing more abstract and generalized insights. We recently developed Ordinary Differential Equations (ODE) models of cellular metabolism in the context of PD (Cloutier et al., 2012a; Cloutier et al., 2012b; Cloutier and Wellstead, 2012) and used them to propose that a positive feedback might be an important mechanism both in terms of disease susceptibility and progression. Figure 17.3a presents an overview of this model, with a sample simulation (Figure 17.3b) comparing experimental and predicted lactate (LAC) levels on a short time-scale (minutes). This model is then used to produce valuable hypotheses on PD, as described in the next section.

4.2 Feedback interactions

The vicious cycle of PD is described in the model through the critical feedback interaction between ROS generation and protein misfolding. More specifically, when ROS causes damage to αS, the misfolded polymers of the protein tend to form porous structures that attach to membranes, including the mitochondrial membrane. This leads to more ROS generation by the mitochondria, thus closing the positive feedback loop. We synthesized this observation with a simplified feedback model, as shown in Figure 17.3c. Simulations show that the system can exhibit an irreversible transition after exposure to ROS inducing toxin (Figure 17.3d), with one stable state representing a "healthy" cellular system (labeled "1" in Figure 17.3), and another stable state with elevated ROS and misfolded αS (i.e. the "disease" state, labeled "3"). The complete bifurcation diagram is shown in Figure 17.3e. This simplified model (Cloutier and Wellstead, 2012), as well as the more descriptive model (Cloutier et al., 2012b), both showed to be extremely coherent with a wide range of experimental observations on PD cellular physiology. More specifically, the presence of a positive feedback loop explains two important phenomenon: i-a transient exposure to ROS can irreversibly induce the disease (as done in animal models); and ii-slow changes associated with aging could push the system toward the "tipping point" shown in Figure 17.3e and rapid changes could result from the transition.

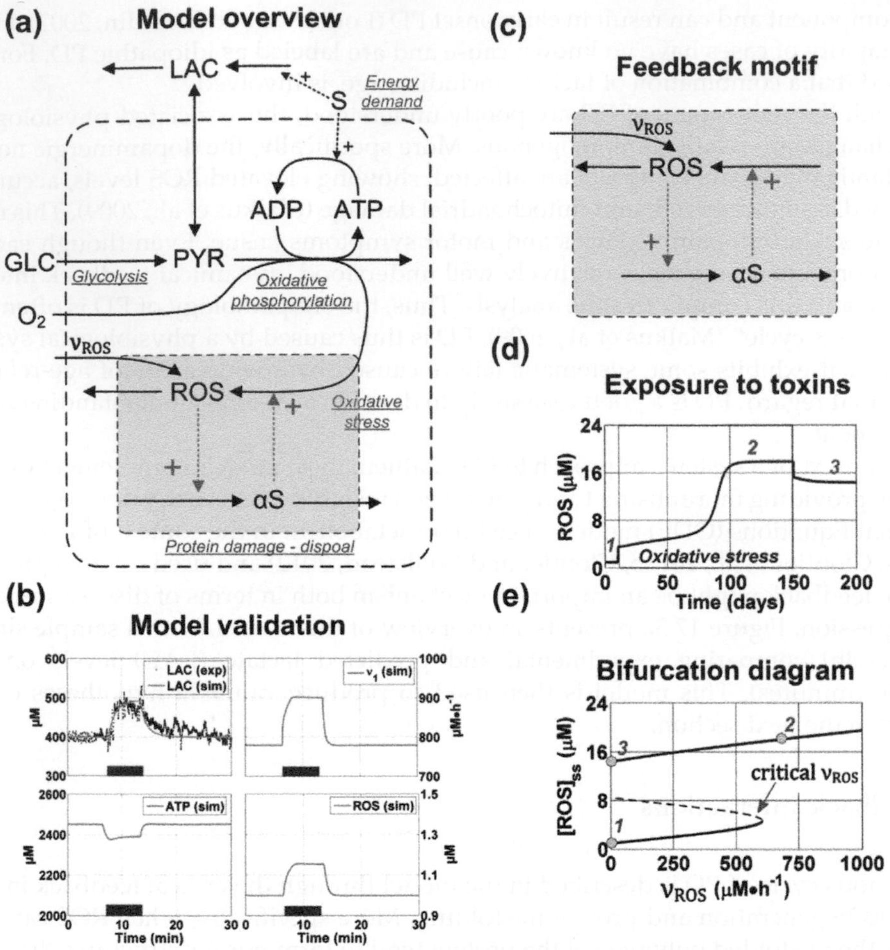

FIGURE 17.3 Modeling and simulations of PD-related pathways. (a) Model overview, with the major pathways of energy metabolism and implication in PD. The model describes the dynamics for glucose (GLC), pyruvate (PYR), adenosine di- and tri-phosphate (ADP, ATP), extracellular lactate (LAC), reactive oxygen species (ROS), and misfolded α-synuclein (αS). An external oxidative stress can be applied (v_{ROS}). (b) Model validation with experimental LAC data. (c) Extraction of a core feedback motif between ROS and αS. (d) Simulation for a transient exposure to ROS inducing toxins (i.e. increase in v_{ROS} over the gray area). (e) Complete bifurcation diagram for steady-state values of ROS with regard to v_{ROS}. Further details on this model and additional simulation results can be found in Cloutier et al. (2012a), Cloutier et al. (2012b), and Cloutier and Wellstead (2012).

5 SIMULATIONS AND PREDICTIONS

In addition to describing known cellular processes involved in PD, the model can be used as an *in silico* platform to perform preliminary analysis of important research hypotheses. In this section, we will briefly present two research hypotheses for which the model can rapidly provide critical insight and complement experimental approaches. First, spatiotemporal

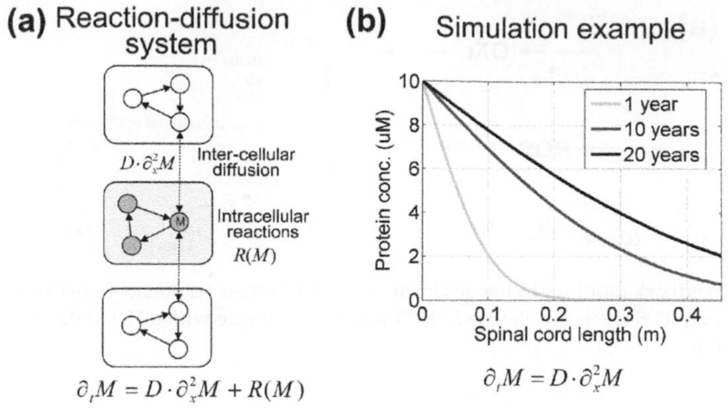

FIGURE 17.4 (a) Overview of a reaction-diffusion system for PD. (b) Simulation example for one dimensional diffusion in the spinal cord without feedback reactions. In the simulation, we assume a constant protein concentration of 10 μM at one end (enteric nerves with high level of damage) and $D = 1 \times 10^{-10}$ m^2/s.

considerations will be presented, highlighting the fact that a feedback motif in PD might be necessary to explain PD progression over time and space. Then, gene expression and negative feedback mechanisms will be considered, showing that a wide range of dynamical response is to be expected in PD cellular physiology.

5.1 Spatiotemporal considerations

A very important observation about PD came from Braak et al. (2004), who noticed that the disease's biomarkers (i.e. misfolded αS and its associated damage) spreads from the enteric nerve system through the spinal cord, reaching the brain, and affecting different regions in a specific temporal sequence. This process obviously takes years to reach its course, but it is still sufficient to cause significant damage to the brain within the normal lifespan.

One important research question in that context is the possibility that diffusion might be an important mechanism in PD. And more specifically, is diffusion the major mechanism for the disease spatial progression, or are other mechanisms involved? For example, it has been known since the seminal work of Alan Turing on morphogenesis (Turing, 1952) that spatiotemporal properties in biology can be described by reaction-diffusion systems. More recently, it was also suggested that simple feedback motifs within a diffusive system can exhibit important emergent properties in terms of pattern formation (Cotterell and Sharpe, 2010). In PD, the question would thus revolve around the possibility that a feedback motif, such as the one presented in Figure 17.3, could be involved in the disease's spatiotemporal progression. As shown in Figure 17.4a, this could be simulated by considering an array of feedback motifs, representing different nerve cells or different parts of a nervous tissue, connected by intercellular diffusion. Thus, future modeling efforts will revolve around a mathematical description (in terms of reaction-diffusion) of the Braak staging hypothesis. Interestingly, a preliminary simulation for diffusion only (Figure 17.4b) shows that the diffusion process by itself may be

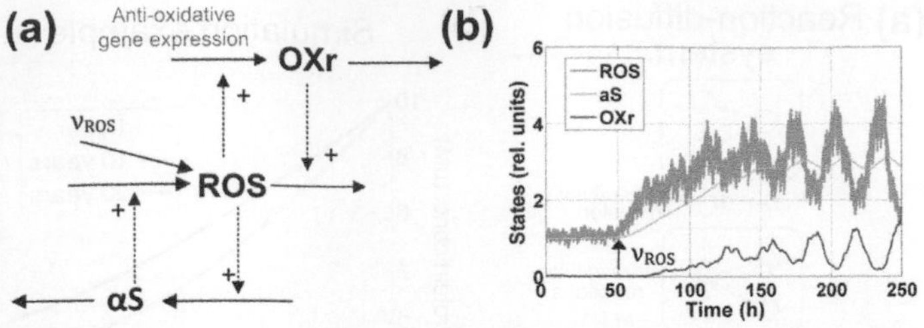

FIGURE 17.5 (a) Feedback motif with changes in anti-oxidative stress response. Genes related to oxidative stress (OXr) are activated when ROS levels are elevated. (b) Simulation example with a 12 h delay and 20% pseudorandom noise in gene expression.

too slow to explain how the disease could spread through the spinal cord within a normal lifespan. Even with conservative estimates for the diffusion constant, it would take many decades for damaged proteins to spread through the spinal cord. In that context, it is probable that a positive feedback motif, such as the one presented here, locally increases the generation of cellular damage. The example shown in Figure 17.4 is for 1-dimension diffusion, but more detailed geometries could also be considered within a finite element modeling approach.

5.2 Modeling gene expression and negative feedback in PD

Another important question with regard to PD is the influence of gene expression and more specifically the anti-oxidative stress response and age-related changes in gene expression. In Figure 17.5a, starting from the positive feedback motif presented in Figure 17.3c, we add reactions for the anti-oxidative mechanisms that are activated both in normal stress response and over the course of age-related changes in metabolism. Interestingly, the simulations (Figure 17.5b) show that a complex, oscillatory regime can develop over a short timescale, especially if we consider that gene expression can be noisy and delayed. In PD, this timescale is important as it represents the rapid response to toxin exposure in animal models. Our simulations thus show that obtaining good temporal data might extremely important for PD research (i.e. as a complement to single time point "-omics" data). Also, these simulation results suggest that complex dynamical changes in cellular physiology are important in PD and thus the slow changes associated with aging could make the system reach a "tipping point" at which more rapid changes are observed.

As the models presented in this section are descriptive of the cellular processes associated with PD, it will be important to incorporate the known changes in gene expression in order to obtain a phenomenological modeling of PD with regard to the aging process. More specifically, and as was briefly discussed elsewhere (Cloutier et al., 2012a; Cloutier et al., 2012b; Cloutier and Wellstead, 2012), the kinetic parameters in the model can be directly linked to specific genes, whereas an increase in gene expression would lead to a higher reaction capacity, and inversely. The resulting changes in systems properties (bistability, oscillations, etc.) as shown here in Figures 17.3–17.5 will be of critical importance both in terms of data analysis and hypotheses generation.

6 ROBUSTNESS IN THE CONTEXT OF THEORIES AND MODELS OF AGING

Attempts to explain the ultimate cause of aging have produced a number of different theories, as reviewed elsewhere (Ljubuncic and Reznick, 2009; Kirkwood, 2005; Rose et al., 2008; Longo et al., 2005). Of specific interest are theories considering tradeoffs. Such a tradeoff was originally proposed by Williams (1957), who described how the selection of some pleiotropic genes benefiting the young organism become detrimental in late life. Hereby genes contributing to aging are being actively kept in the gene pool due to their beneficial role in the young. Another theory was explored by Kirkwood and Holliday and became known as the "disposable soma" theory, postulating a specific class of energy-related pleiotropic gene mutations which increase energy expenditure for reproductive tasks, while cutting down on energy required for molecular proofreading and repair in somatic cells (Kirkwood and Holliday, 1979). Related computational models have considered optimization aspects in dynamical population models demonstrating repair–growth–reproduction tradeoffs (Chu and Lee, 2006; Mangel, 2001) or life-history optimization through distribution of limited resources for growth, reproduction, and repair (Vaupel et al., 2004; Schaffer, 1974; Cichon, 1997; Perrin and Silby, 1993). Similarly, cell population models have targeted optimization of fitness in asymmetric cell division and survival rates (Ackermann et al., 2007; Erjavec et al., 2008; Evans and Steinsaltz, 2007; Chao, 2010). However, a thorough experimental validation of aging theories has been limited (Kirkwood, 2005; Flatt and Promislow, 2007; de Magalhaes, 2005), and prevented the broader acceptance of a specific aging theory.

More recently, complexity concepts like self-organized criticality (SOC), which focus on the boundary of disorder and order (Bak and Paczuski, 1995; Bak et al., 1987), have gained interest to explain fundamental biological properties. The theory of SOC predicts attractors for stable system states and the concept is useful to describe how cells and organism organize themselves and can exist in a complex multiparameter state space defined by quantities such as gene transcription, protein activities, metabolic fluxes or organelle phenotypes. The existence of such attractors provides robust phenotypes or cell fates, and cells switch between these states or return to such points when perturbed. The underlying theoretical concepts hint to self-organization and can be explored by Boolean network models (Huang et al., 2005; Kauffman, 1969), as discussed in Chapter 12. But in contrast to well-defined attractors in normal cellular operations, aging phenotypes trace elongated and widening clusters in state space (Figure 17.6). As described in earlier sections, slowly changing parameters include oxidation of proteins, damage to nuclear and mitochondrial DNA, accumulation of dysfunctional mitochondria, declining metabolism, and biosynthesis, along with an increase in stress signaling and epigenetic alterations. Aging cells may also enter cell fates limiting the spread of damage in tissues and organs. Furthermore, cells in proliferative tissue can arrest in a state of replicative senescence, while more severely damaged cells may enter mitochondrial induced apoptosis limiting their detrimental effect to the organism. Slow changes in parameter space found in aging, accompanied by transitions into new states (including age-related diseases like cancer) and loss of coherency away from stable attractors, is perhaps better explained by the hypothesis that cells have limited robustness. While points of stability are provided by sophisticated control mechanisms and homeostatic regulations in response to

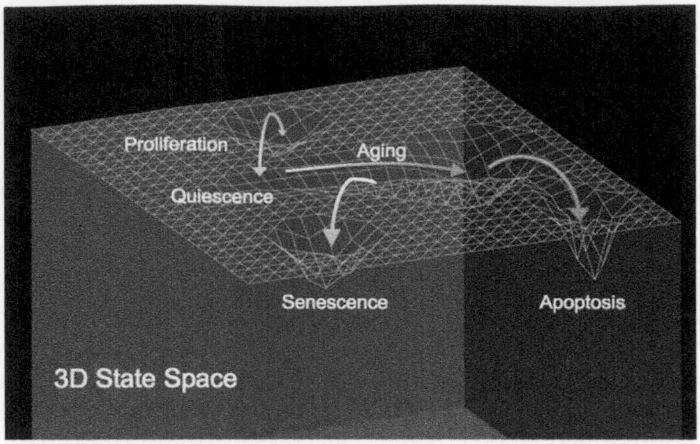

FIGURE 17.6 Schematic of aging in cellular state space. Normal young cells can switch between well-defined cell states, due to self-organization and control mechanisms as shown by Huang and co-workers (Huang et al, 2005). However, in aging cells change many conditions rather slowly, accumulate damage, upregulate stress responses, and their decline demonstrates limited robustness. Aged cells can enter a new stable state, such as replicative senescence, or apoptose.

most internal and external perturbations in young biological systems, these mechanisms are insufficient to prevent the occurrence of aging.

A theory considering limitations in control, regulation and "evolutionary" design flaws builds on the idea that evolutionary systems are highly optimized and evolved to tolerate the most common stressors and fluctuations, but are fragile to others. That is, they exhibit a "robustness-yet-fragile" property (Csete and Doyle, 2002; Carlson and Doyle, 2002; Kitano, 2007; Carlson et al., 1999). In addition, complex systems reside in highly optimized tolerance (HOT) state, but since robustness is a limited resource for designed technical or evolved biological systems, improvement of performance in one area is compensated by fragilities in another (Csete and Doyle, 2002). This systems concept has been successfully applied to elucidate robustness of cellular functions (Stelling et al., 2004), metabolic networks (Stelling et al., 2002), also see Chapter 3, biochemical reactions (Morohashi et al., 2002), evolvability (Wagner, 2005), immunosenescence (Stromberg and Carlson, 2006) and host-pathogen interactions (Kitano, 2007), and has been suggested as a theoretical model for aging (Kriete, 2013). Since robustness tradeoffs are fragilities with respect to unexpected perturbations, the declining forces of natural selection in adult organisms give rise to aging phenotypes exposing these limitations due to a lack of adaptation. Specifically, the weakening of evolutionary forces has prevented the development of mechanisms to provide adequate control and responses to the aged phenotype. Although evolved responses such as the retrograde response (RTG) in yeast and the Nuclear Factor kappa-B (NF-κB) pathway become active as markers of elevated energetic stress and redox state (Srinivasan et al., 2010), they can only provide adequate responses and robustness in acute episodes of stress and mitochondrial dysfunction in young organisms, but reveal tradeoffs if chronically activated in aging (see Figure 17.2). Thus, they are inadequate to provide appropriate responses or even revert the aging process.

7 DISCUSSION AND OUTLOOK

Biological systems, reside in a state of highly optimized tolerance providing robustness in many traits and stability to most common perturbations. At the same time, the "robust, yet fragile" duality neglects others areas including limited damage control causing fragility and aging. While increase in robustness and specialization drives internal complexity by adding feedback and control mechanisms, a high degree of specialization and distribution of performance and robustness of limited resources causes vulnerabilities to uncommon stressors. This is particularly evident for brain tissues, with highly specialized, dynamic neuronal cells requiring an efficient and elevated metabolism. When such cells become compromised during aging, they are at risk to fall into a vicious cycle of decline and dysfunction. Related stress responses are barriers evolved to protect against rapid breakdowns in young organisms, and shape the aging dynamics in cellular networks into the evolutionary shadow after reproduction. While these evolved control mechanisms support the system to regain stability during acute episodes of external stress, their chronic activation in aging "lock" the system into a slow decline. This causes conditions for fragilities such as age-related diseases. Additional environmental risk factors, stochastic effects, and genotype constitute additional accelerating factors. Furthermore, spatiotemporal effects promote the decline regionally. Taken together, these mechanisms exhibit a vicious cycle, rather a slow decline in normal aging.

These examples demonstrate how a tight combination of theoretical biology, experimental data with computational systems biology offers the best opportunities in aging research. It is likely that many age-associated diseases can only be properly studied and treated by keeping in mind the underlying aging mechanisms, and systems biology can help building bridges between the different angles of investigation.

References

Ackermann, M. et al. (2007). On the evolutionary origin of aging. *Aging Cell* **6**(2):235–244.

Adler, A. S. et al. (2008). Reversal of aging by NF-kappa B blockade. *Cell Cycle* **7**(5):556–559.

Ak, P., and Levine, A. J. (2010). P53 and NF-kappaB: different strategies for responding to stress lead to a functional antagonism. *Faseb J.* **24**(10):3643–3652.

Bak, P., and Paczuski, M. (1995). Complexity, contingency, and criticality. *Proc. Natl. Acad. Sci. USA* **92**(15):6689–6696.

Bak, P., Tang, C., and Wiesenfeld, K. (1987). Self-organized criticality: An explanation of the 1/f noise. *Phys. Rev. Lett.* **59**(4):381–384.

Bergman, A. et al. (2007). Buffering mechanisms in aging: a systems approach toward uncovering the genetic component of aging. *PLoS Comput. Biol.* **3**(8):e170.

Braak, H. et al. (2004). Stages in the development of Parkinson's disease-related pathology. *Cell Tissue Res.* **318**(1):121–134.

Brand, K. (1997). Aerobic glycolysis by proliferating cells: protection against oxidative stress at the expense of energy yield. *J. Bioenerg. Biomembr.* **29**(4):355–364.

Budovsky, A. et al. (2007). Longevity network: construction and implications. *Mech. Ageing Dev.* **128**(1):117–124.

Butow, R. A., and Avadhani, N. G. (2004). Mitochondrial signaling: the retrograde response. *Mol. Cell.* **14**(1):1–15.

Carlson, J. M., and Doyle, J. (1999). Highly optimized tolerance: a mechanism for power laws in designed systems. *Phys. Rev. E Stat. Phys. Plasmas. Fluids Relat. Interdiscip. Topics* **60**(2 Pt A):1412–1427.

Carlson, J. M., and Doyle, J. (2002). Complexity and robustness. *Proc. Natl. Acad. Sci. USA* **99**(Suppl 1):2538–2545.

Chao, L. (2010). A model for damage load and its implications for the evolution of bacterial aging. *PLoS Genet.* **6**(8)

Chu, C. Y., and Lee, R. (2006). The co-evolution of intergenerational transfers and longevity: an optimal life history approach. *Theor. Popul. Biol.* **69**(2):193–201.

Cichon, M. (1997). Evolution of longevity through optimal resource allocation. *Proc. R. Soc. Lond. B Biol. Sci.* **264**:1383–1388.

Cloutier, M., and Wellstead, P. (2012). Modelling protein and oxidative metabolism in Parkinson's disease. In (P. Wellstead, and M. Cloutier, eds.), *Systems Biology of Parkinson's Disease*. New York: Springer.

Cloutier, M., and Wellstead, P. (2012). Dynamic modelling of protein and oxidative metabolisms simulates the pathogenesis of Parkinson's disease. *Syst. Biol. IET* **6**(3):65–72.

Cloutier, M., Middleton, R., and Wellstead, P. (2012b). Feedback motif for the pathogenesis of Parkinson's disease. *Syst. Biol. IET* **6**(3):86–93.

Coppe, J. P. et al. (2008). Senescence-Associated Secretory Phenotypes Reveal Cell-Nonautonomous Functions of Oncogenic RAS and the p53 Tumor Suppressor. *PLoS Biol.* **6**(12):e301.

Cotterell, J., and Sharpe, J. (2010). An atlas of gene regulatory networks reveals multiple three-gene mechanisms for interpreting morphogen gradients. *Mol. Syst. Biol.* **6**:425.

Criollo, A. et al. (2012). Autophagy is required for the activation of NF kappa B. *Cell Cycle* **11**(1):194–199.

Csete, M. E., and Doyle, J. C. (2002). Reverse engineering of biological complexity. *Science* **295**(5560):1664–1669.

de Magalhaes, J. P. (2005). Open-minded scepticism: inferring the causal mechanisms of human ageing from genetic perturbations. *Ageing Res. Rev.* **4**(1):1–22.

Dong, J. et al. (2010). Constitutively active NF-kappaB triggers systemic TNFalpha-dependent inflammation and localized TNFalpha-independent inflammatory disease. *Genes Dev.* **24**(16):1709–1717.

Doyle, J. C. et al. (2005). The "robust yet fragile" nature of the Internet. *Proc. Natl. Acad. Sci. USA* **102**(41):14497–14502.

Echtay, K. S. et al. (2002). Superoxide activates mitochondrial uncoupling proteins. *Nature* **415**(6867):96–99.

Erjavec, N. et al. (2008). Selective benefits of damage partitioning in unicellular systems and its effects on aging. *Proc. Natl. Acad. Sci. U.S.A.* **105**(48):18764–18769.

Evans, S. N., and Steinsaltz, D. (2007). Damage segregation at fissioning may increase growth rates: a superprocess model. *Theor. Popul. Biol.* **71**(4):473–490.

Evans, W. J., Cui, L., and Starr, A. (1995). Olfactory event-related potentials in normal human subjects: effects of age and gender. *Electroencephalogr. Clin. Neurophysiol.* **95**(4):293–301.

Figge, M. T. et al. (2012). Deceleration of fusion-fission cycles improves mitochondrial quality control during aging. *PLoS Comput. Biol.* **8**(6):e1002576.

Flatt, T., and Promislow, D. E. (2007). Physiology. Still pondering an age-old question. *Science* **318**(5854):1255–1256.

Fortney, K., Kotlyar, M., and Jurisica, I. (2010). Inferring the functions of longevity genes with modular subnetwork biomarkers of *Caenorhabditis elegans* aging. *Genome Biol* **11**(2):R13.

Gebauer, J. et al. (2012). Detecting and investigating substrate cycles in a genome-scale human metabolic network. *FEBS J.* **279**(17):3192–3202.

Gruber, J. et al. (2011). Mitochondrial changes in ageing *Caenorhabditis elegans*–what do we learn from superoxide dismutase knockouts?. *PLoS One* **6**(5):e19444.

Herndon, L. A. et al. (2002). Stochastic and genetic factors influence tissue-specific decline in ageing *C. elegans*. *Nature* **419**(6909):808–814.

Huang, S. et al. (2005). Cell fates as high-dimensional attractor states of a complex gene regulatory network. *Phys. Rev. Lett.* **94**(12):128701.

Jazwinski, S. M. (2000). Metabolic control and ageing. *Trends Genet.* **16**(11):506–511.

Johnson, F. B., Sinclair, D. A., and Guarente, L. (1999). Molecular biology of aging. *Cell* **96**(2):291–302.

Kauffman, S. A. (1969). Metabolic stability and epigenesis in randomly constructed genetic nets. *J. Theor. Biol.* **22**(3):437–467.

Kenyon, C. J. (2010). The genetics of ageing. *Nature* **464**(7288):504–512.

Kirkwood, T. (2000). Why do we age?. *Nature* 408.

Kirkwood, T. (2005). Understanding the odd science of aging. *Cell* **120**:437–447.

Kirkwood, T. B. (2011). Systems biology of ageing and longevity. *Philos. Trans. R Soc. London B: Biol. Sci.* **366**(1561):64–70.

Kirkwood, T. B., and Holliday, R. (1979). The evolution of ageing and longevity. *Proc. R. Soc. Lond. B Biol. Sci.* **205**(1161):531–546.

Kitano, H. (2007). Towards a theory of biological robustness. *Mol. Syst. Biol.* **3**:137.

Kitano, H. (2007). Biological robustness in complex host-pathogen systems. *Prog. Drug Res.* **64**(239):241–263.

Kitano, H., and Oda, K. (2006). Robustness trade-offs and host-microbial symbiosis in the immune system. *Mol Syst Biol.* **2**:2006 0022.

Kleindorp, R. et al. (2011). Candidate gene study of FOXO1, FOXO4, and FOXO6 reveals no association with human longevity in Germans. *Aging Cell* **10**(4):622–628.

Kourtis, N., and Tavernarakis, N. (2011). Cellular stress response pathways and ageing: intricate molecular relationships. *Embo J.* **30**(13):2520–2531.

Kowald, A., and Kirkwood, T. B. (1996). A network theory of ageing: the interactions of defective mitochondria, aberrant proteins, free radicals and scavengers in the ageing process. *Mutat. Res.* **316**(5–6):209–236.

Kowald, A., and Kirkwood, T. B. (2011). Evolution of the mitochondrial fusion-fission cycle and its role in aging. *Proc. Natl. Acad. Sci. USA* **108**(25):10237–10242.

Kriete, A. (2006). Systems approaches to the networks of aging. *Ageing Res. Rev.*

Kriete, A. (2013). Robustness and aging - a systems biology perspective. *Biosystems* **112**(1):37–48.

Kriete, A., and Mayo, K. L. (2009). Atypical pathways of NF-kappaB activation and aging. *Exp. Gerontol.* **44**(4):250–255.

Kriete, A., Bosl, W. J., and Booker, G. (2010). Rule-based cell systems model of aging using feedback loop motifs mediated by stress responses. *PLoS Comput. Biol.* **6**(6):e1000820.

Kriete, A. et al. (2011). Computational systems biology of aging. *Wiley Interdiscip. Rev. Syst. Biol. Med.* **3**(4):414–428.

Kujoth, G. C. et al. (2005). Mitochondrial DNA mutations, oxidative stress, and apoptosis in mammalian aging. *Science* **309**(5733):481–484.

Li, Y., and de Magalhaes, J. P. (2011). Accelerated protein evolution analysis reveals genes and pathways associated with the evolution of mammalian longevity. *Age (Dordr)*

Ljubuncic, P., and Reznick, A. Z. (2009). The evolutionary theories of aging revisited–a mini-review. *Gerontology* **55**(2):205–216.

Lo, A. (2007). *A Knowledge Based Systems Model of the Chromatin Protein Interactome.* Thesis: Drexel University.

Longo, V. D., Mitteldorf, J., and Skulachev, V. P. (2005). Programmed and altruistic ageing. *Nat. Rev. Genet.* **6**(11):866–872.

Lotharius, J., and Brundin, P. (2002). Pathogenesis of Parkinson's disease: dopamine, vesicles and alpha-synuclein. *Nat. Rev. Neurosci.* **3**(12):932–942.

Malkus, K. A., Tsika, E., and Ischiropoulos, H. (2009). Oxidative modifications, mitochondrial dysfunction, and impaired protein degradation in Parkinson's disease: how neurons are lost in the Bermuda triangle. *Mol. Neurodegener.* **4**:24.

Mangel, M. (2001). Complex adaptive systems, aging and longevity. *J. Theor. Biol.* **213**(4):559–571.

Morohashi, M. et al. (2002). Robustness as a measure of plausibility in models of biochemical networks. *J. Theor. Biol.* **216**(1):19–30.

Navarro, A., and Boveris, A. (2007). The mitochondrial energy transduction system and the aging process. *Am. J. Physiol. Cell. Physiol.* **292**(2):C670–C686.

Perrin, M., and Silby, R. M. (1993). Dynamic models of energy allocation and investment. *Annu. Rev. Ecol. Syst.* **24**:379–410.

Preston, C. C. et al. (2008). Aging-induced alterations in gene transcripts and functional activity of mitochondrial oxidative phosphorylation complexes in the heart. *Mech. Ageing Dev.* **129**(6):304–312.

Proctor, C. J., and Lorimer, I. A. (2011). Modelling the role of the Hsp70/Hsp90 system in the maintenance of protein homeostasis. *PLoS One* **6**(7):e22038.

Rivas, J. M., and Ullrich, S. E. (1992). Systemic suppression of delayed-type hypersensitivity by supernatants from UV-irradiated keratinocytes. An essential role for keratinocyte-derived IL-10. *J. Immunol.* **149**(12):3865–3871.

Rose, M. R. et al. (2008). Evolution of ageing since Darwin. *J. Genet.* **87**(4):363–371.

Rovillain, E. et al. (2011). Activation of nuclear factor-kappa B signalling promotes cellular senescence. *Oncogene* **30**(20):2356–2366.

Schaffer, W. M. (1974). Selection for optimal life histories: the effects of age structure. *Ecology* **55**:291–303.

Sebastiani, P. et al. (2012). Genetic signatures of exceptional longevity in humans. *PLoS One* **7**(1):e29848.

Soltow, Q. A., Jones, D. P., and Promislow, D. E. (2010). A network perspective on metabolism and aging. *Integr. Comp. Biol.* **50**(5):844–854.

Srinivasan, V. et al. (2010). Comparing the yeast retrograde response and NF-kappaB stress responses: implications for aging. *Aging Cell* **9**(6):933–941.

Stelling, J. et al. (2002). Metabolic network structure determines key aspects of functionality and regulation. *Nature* **420**(6912):190–193.

Stelling, J. et al. (2004). Robustness of cellular functions. *Cell* **118**(6):675–685.

Stromberg, S. P., and Carlson, J. (2006). Robustness and fragility in immunosenescence. *PLoS Comput. Biol.* **2**(11):e160.

Trifunovic, A. et al. (2005). Somatic mtDNA mutations cause aging phenotypes without affecting reactive oxygen species production. *Proc. Natl. Acad. Sci. USA* **102**(50):17993–17998.

Turing, A. M. (1952). The chemical basis of morphogenesis. *Philos. Trans. R. Soc. Lond. B Biol. Sci.* **237**(641):37–72.

Vaupel, J. W. et al. (2004). The case for negative senescence. *Theor. Popul. Biol.* **65**(4):339–351.

Wagner, A. (2005). Robustness, evolvability, and neutrality. *FEBS Lett.* **579**(8):1772–1778.

West, G. B., and Bergman, A. (2009). Toward a systems biology framework for understanding aging and health span. *J. Gerontol. A Biol. Sci. Med. Sci.* **64**(2):205–208.

Willcox, B. J. et al. (2008). FOXO3A genotype is strongly associated with human longevity. *Proc. Natl. Acad. Sci. USA* **105**(37):13987–13992.

Williams, G. (1957). Pleiotropy, natural selection, and the evolution of senescence. *Evolution* **11**:398–411.

Witten, T. M., and Bonchev, D. (2007). Predicting aging/longevity-related genes in the nematode *Caenorhabditis elegans*. *Chem. Biodivers.* **4**(11):2639–2655.

Wuttke, D. et al. (2012). Dissecting the gene network of dietary restriction to identify evolutionarily conserved pathways and new functional genes. *PLoS Genet.* **8**(8):e1002834.

Xue, H. et al. (2007). A modular network model of aging. *Mol. Syst. Biol.* **3**:147.

Borklu Yucel, E., and Ulgen, K. O. (2011). A network-based approach on elucidating the multi-faceted nature of chronological aging in *S. cerevisiae*. *PLoS One* **6**(12):e29284.

Zahn, J. M. et al. (2006). Transcriptional profiling of aging in human muscle reveals a common aging signature. *PLoS Genet.* **2**(7):e115.

CHAPTER

18

Molecular Correlates of Morphometric Subtypes in Glioblastoma Multiforme

Hang Chang[a], *Ju Han*[a], *Gerald V. Fontenay*[a], *Cemal C. Bilgin*[a], *Nandita Nayak*[a], *Alexander Borowski*[b], *Paul Spellman*[c], *Bahram Parvin*[a]

[a]**Life Sciences Division, Lawrence Berkeley National Laboratory, Berkeley, CA, USA**

[b]**Center for Comparative Medicine, University of California, Davis, CA, USA**

[c]**Department of Biomedical Engineering, Oregon Health Sciences University, Portland, Oregon, USA**

CONTENTS

Computational Systems Biology, Second Edition
http://dx.doi.org/10.1016/B978-0-12-405926-9.00018-6

Abstract

Integrated analysis of tissue histology with the genome-wide array and clinical data has the potential to generate hypotheses as well as be prognostic. However, due to the inherent technical and biological variations, automated analysis of whole mount tissue sections is impeded in very large datasets, such as The Cancer Genome Atlas (TCGA), where tissue sections are collected from different laboratories. We aim to characterize tumor architecture from hematoxylin and eosin (H&E) stained tissue sections, through the delineation of nuclear regions on a cell-by-cell basis. Such a representation can then be utilized to derive intrinsic morphometric subtypes across a large cohort for prediction and molecular association. Our approach has been validated on manually annotated samples, and then applied to a Glioblastoma Multiforme (GBM) cohort of 377 whole slide images from 146 patients. Further bioinformatics analysis, based on the multidimensional representation of the nuclear features and their organization, has identified (i) statistically significant morphometric sub types; (ii) whether each subtype can be predictive or not; and (iii) that the molecular correlates of predictive subtypes are consistent with the literature. The net result is the realization of the concept of pathway pathology through analysis of a large cohort of whole slide images.

1 INTRODUCTION

The interaction between underlying molecular defects and environmental factors can be captured by tumor histopathology; thus, we hypothesize that quantification of histology sections on a cell-by-cell basis in terms of morphological features and organization, leads to a new systems biology approach for the characterization and identification of molecular markers of tumor composition. As opposed to genome-wide array data, the large-scale quantitative characterization of tumor morphology from standard hematoxylin and eosin (H&E) stained tissue sections can offer alternative views for subtyping and survival analysis. Furthermore, computed morphometric indices can be tested against outcome. Meanwhile, derived representations (e.g., meta-features), from cellular level quantitative analysis, can also be utilized to probe for tumor heterogeneity and its underlying molecular basis. To answer the questions about morphometric indices that are predictive of the outcome, we have developed a computational pipeline to process large cohorts of whole mount tissue sections, which have been collected through The Cancer Genome Atlas (TCGA).

The computational pipeline consists of advanced algorithms for nuclear delineation (Chang et al. 2013-b) and tissue classification (classifying tissue into different component, e.g., tumor, necrosis), which are implemented efficiently to operate in a high performance computing environment on decomposed tissue blocks of 1k-by-1k pixels. The net result is a multidimensional representation of the tissue block that captures features at both nuclear level (e.g., size, shape, cellular density) and patch level (e.g., necrosis ratio). To tackle the large amount of technical and biological variations, expert annotated images with corresponding image-derived features (e.g., shape, intensity) are used for the construction of prior knowledge based on the Gaussian Mixture Model (GMM). In this context, the key contribution is to (i) utilize a dictionary of images for the characterization of technical variations and biological heterogeneity, and (ii) label each nucleus in the context of tumor histopathology, subjecting to spatial continuity with a graphcut formulation (Demir 2009; Latson et al. 2003). Nuclear architecture and organization are then constructed per patient as equal probability histograms that are normalized across all patients. A total of 377 GBM tumor sections from 146 patients are initially include a morphometric index, is examined for subtyping at patient level. Organization of the book chapter is as follows. Section 2 reviews prior literature. Section 3 summarizes nuclear segmentation and patch-based classification. Section 4 presents subtyping analysis and the characterization of heterogeneity. Section 5 describes the soft ware architecture. Section 6 concludes the chapter.

2 BACKGROUND

Histology sections are typically visualized with H&E stains that label DNA and protein contents, in various shades of color. Generally, these sections are rich in content since various cell types, cell states and health, cellular secretion, and cellular organization can be characterized by a trained pathologist with the caveat of inter and intra-observer variations (Dalton et al. 2000). Several reviews for the application and analysis of H&E sections can be found in Chang et al. (2011-a, 2013-b), Gurcan et al. (2009), Demir (2009). From our perspective, the trend and direction of the research community focuses on the following three key concepts.

The first key concept involves tumor grading through either rough or accurate nuclear segmentation (Latson et al. 2003) followed by cellular organization characterization (Doyle et al. 2011) and classification. In some cases, tumor grading has been associated with progression, recurrence, and invasion carcinoma (e.g., breast DCIS), where outcome is highly dependent on mixed grading (e.g., presence of more than one grade) and tumor heterogeneity. Since mixed grading appears to be present in 50% of patients (Miller et al. 2001), it introduces significant challenges to the pathologists. A recent study indicates that DCIS recurrence (Axelrod et al. 2008) in patients with more than one nuclear grade can be predicted through detailed segmentation and multivariate representation of nuclear features from H&E stained sections. In this study, nuclear regions were manually segmented from H&E stained samples, and each nucleus was profiled with a multidimensional representation. The significance of this particular study is that it has been repeated quantitatively to indicate prognostic outcome. In other related studies, nuclear features have also been shown to contribute to diagnosis and prognosis values for carcinoma of the colorectal mucosa (Verhest et al. 1990), prostate (Veltri et al. 2004), and breast (Mommers et al. 2001).

The second concept focuses on the patch-based (e.g., region-based) analysis of tissue sections based on features either engineered by human (Bhagavatula et al. 2010; Kong et al. 2010; Han et al. 2011; Kothari et al. 2012) or generated through automatic feature learning (Le et al. 2012; Huang et al. 2011). Automatic feature learning, in its simplest form, is based on independent component analysis (ICA), which computes kernels corresponding to oriented edge detectors. Another example is the independent subspace analysis (ISA), which learns invariant kernels from the data through non-linear mapping (Le et al. 2012). Yet, one of the shortcomings of ISA is that it lacks the ability to reconstruct original data, which can be attributed to its strict feed forward nature. However, this ability can be offered by some other techniques, such as Restricted Boltzmann Machines (RBM) (Hinton 2006) and Predictive Sparse Decomposition (PSD) (Kavukcuoglu 2008).

The last key concept suggests utilizing the detection of specific cells in the autoimmune system (e.g., lymphocytes) as a prognostic tool for breast cancer (Fatakdawala et al. 2010). As part of the adaptive immune response, the presence of lymphocytes has been correlated with nodal metastasis and HER2-positive breast cancer, GBM, and ovarian cancer (Zhang et al. 2003).

3 MORPHOMETRIC REPRESENTATION

Morphometric representation is in the context of nuclear segmentation and classification of tumor histopathology. Each component is summarized below.

3.1 Nuclear segmentation

The main barriers in nuclear segmentation are biological heterogeneity (e.g., cell type) and technical variations (e.g., fixation), which are visible in the dataset provided by TCGA. Present techniques have focused on thresholding with a subsequent morphological operation (Phukpattaranont et al. 2007; Ballaro et al. 2008; Petushi et al. 2006); fuzzy techniques (Latson et al. 2003; Land et al. 2008); geodesic active contour models (Fatakdawala et al. 2010; Glotsos et al. 2004); color separation followed by optimum thresholding and learning (Chang et al. 2009; Cosatto et al. 2008); hierarchical self-organizing map (Datar et al. 2008); and spectral clustering (Doyle et al. 2008). Several examples are given below. In Bunyak et al. (2011), multiphase level sets (Nath et al. 2006; Chang and Parvin 2010) were used for nuclear segmentation based on seeds detected through iterative radial voting (Parvin et al. 2007). In Al-Kofahi et al. (2010), the input image was initially classified into foreground and background regions with graph cut. The seeds were then collected from the foreground regions via a constrained multiscale *Laplacian of Gaussian (LoG)* filter and final segmentation was generated by coupling the classification along with seeds within graph cut framework. Similarly, in Kong et al. (2011), color texture extracted from the most discriminant color space was used to binarize the normalized input image into foreground and background regions; this was followed by an iterative operation, based on concave points and radial-symmetry, to split touching nuclei. Recently, a spatially constrained expectation maximization algorithm (Monaco et al. 2012) was proposed to address the "color nonstandardness" in histological sections in the HSV color space; however, the evidence shown in Section 3.1.7 B (MRGC vs MRGC-CF) indicates that strict incorporation of color and spatial information will not be sufficient. Another related work (Kothari et al. 2011) was built upon a consensus concept, where the labels were determined by multiple classifiers constructed from different reference images; we will refer to this method as MCV (multiclassifier voting), for short, in the rest of the book chapter. Although, MCV provides a better handler for the variation in the data; however, it is still possible to have noisy and erroneous classification (as shown in Figure 18.7), which is due to the lack of local statistical information and smoothness constraint.

In summary, the techniques above are often specific to small datasets that originate from a single laboratory, and ignore both the cellular heterogeneity (e.g., variation in chromatin patterns) and the technical variations manifested in both nuclear and background signals. As shown in Figure 18.1, our goal is to enable the processing of whole mount tissue sections, from multiple laboratories, to construct a large database of morphometric features, and to enable subtyping and genomic association.

Figure 18.2 shows the details of the proposed approach, where several key observations are leveraged for classifying nuclear regions: (i) global variations, across a large cohort of tissue

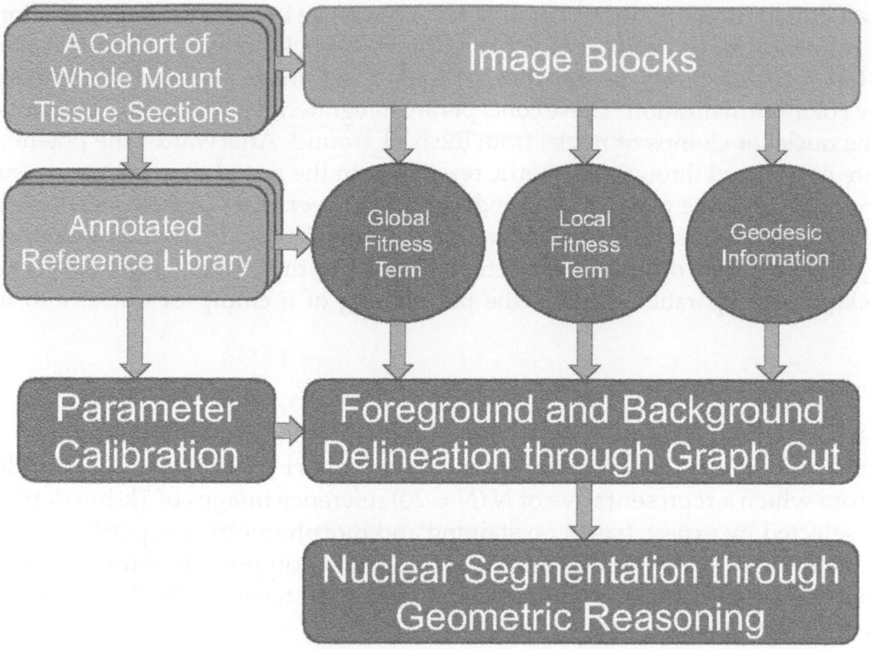

FIGURE 18.1 Work flow in nuclear segmentation for a cohort of whole mount tissue sections.

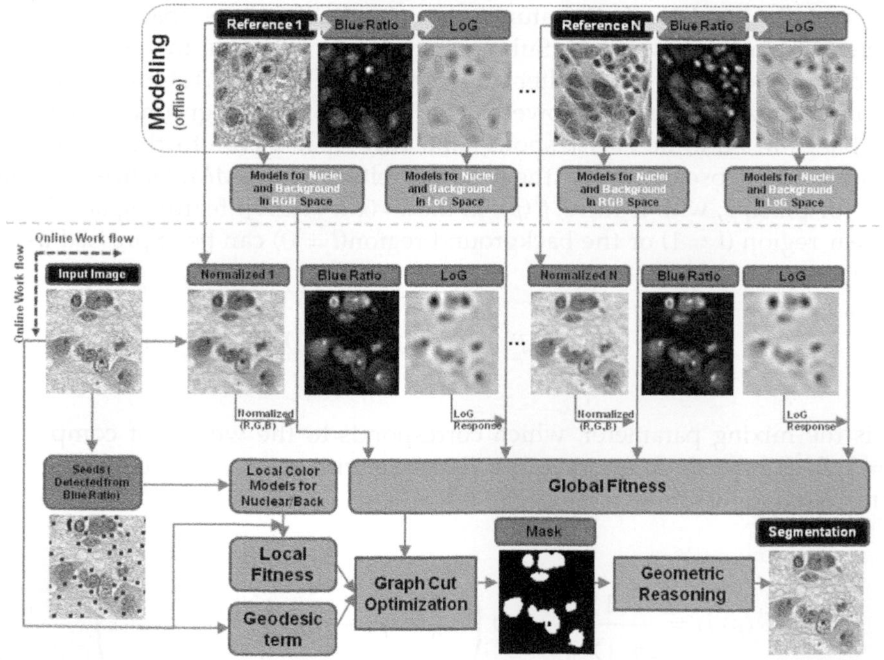

FIGURE 18.2 Steps in nuclear segmentation.

sections, can be captured by a representative set of reference images, (ii) local variations, within an image, can be captured by local foreground (nuclei)/background samples detected by *LoG* filter, and (iii) variations in image statistics, between a test image and a reference image, can be reduced by color normalization. These concepts are integrated within a graph cut framework, to separate the nuclei or clumps of nuclei from the background. Afterwards, the potential clumps of nuclei are partitioned through geometric reasoning. In the rest of this section, we summarize (a) the construction of the global prior models from a diverse set of reference images, (b) the strategy for color normalization, (c) the strategy for dimension reduction based on color transformation, (d) the details of feature extraction, (e) the multireference graph cut formalism for nuclei/background separation, and (f) the partitioning of a clump of nuclei into individual nucleus.

3.1.1 Construction and representation of priors

This step aims to capture the global variations for an entire cohort based on a well-constructed reference library. In our analysis, the target cohort consists of 377 individual tissue sections, from which a representative of N ($N = 20$) reference images of 1k-by-1k pixels at 20X have been selected by expert, based on staining and morphometric properties, in such a way that each one of them is a unique exemplar of tumor phenotypes. Therefore, we suggest that each reference image possesses a unique feature space, in terms of *RGB* and *LoG* responses, that leads to 2N feature spaces for the reference set:

$$\{F^1_{RGB_1}, F^2_{RGB_2}, \ldots, F^1_{RGB_N}, F^{N+1}_{LOG_1}, F^{N+2}_{LOG_2}, \ldots, F^{2N}_{LOG_N}\} \tag{18.1}$$

where $F^{N+i}_{LoG_i}$ and $F^i_{RGB_i}$ and are *LoG* feature space and *RGB* feature spaces, respectively, for the ith referencee image, $1 \leq i \leq N$. Subsequently, each reference image is manually segmented and processed with a *LoG* filter (please refer to Section 3.1.3 for the details on our *LoG* integration), at a fixed scale, followed by the collection of foreground (nuclei) and background statistics in both the *LoG* response and *RGB* space. Due to the distinct modes in feature spaces, we choose to capture the heterogeneities with *GMM*. Hence, the conditional probability for pixel, p, with feature, $f^k(p)$, in the kth ($k \in [1,2N]$) feature space, belonging to either nuclear region ($l = 1$) or the background region($l = 0$) can be expressed as a mixture with D component densities:

$$GMM^k_l(p) = \sum_{j=1}^{D} \tilde{p}(f^k(p)|j)p(j) \tag{18.2}$$

Here $p(j)$ is the mixing parameter, which corresponds to the weight of component j, and $\sum_{j=1}^{D} P(j) = 1$. Each mixture component is a Gaussian with mean μ and covariance matrix Σ, in the corresponding feature space:

$$\tilde{p}(f^k(p)|j) = \frac{1}{2\pi^{\frac{3}{2}}|\sum|_j^{\frac{1}{2}}} \cdot \exp\left(-\frac{1}{2}(f^k(p) - \mu_j)^T \sum_j^{-1} (f^k(p) - \mu_j)\right) \tag{18.3}$$

where $P(j)$ and (μ_j, Σ_j) for $\tilde{p}(C_p|j)$ are estimated by expectation maximization (*EM*) algorithm (Tomasi).

3.1.2 Color normalization

The purpose of color normalization is to reduce the variations between an input test image and a reference image in image statistics. Thus, the prior models, constructed from each reference image, can be applied. Here, we adopted the color map normalization (Kothari et al. 2011) for its effectiveness on histological images. Let

- input image, I, and reference image, Q, have K_I and K_Q unique color triplets, respectively, in terms of (R, G, B);
- $\mathbb{R}_C^{I/Q}$ be a monotonic function, which maps the intensity of a specific color channel, $C \in \{R, G, B\}$, from Image I or Q to a rank that is in the range $[0, K_I)$ or $[0, K_Q)$;
- (r_p, g_p, b_p) be the color of pixel p, in image I, and $(\mathbb{R}_R^I(r_p), \mathbb{R}_G^I(G_p), \mathbb{R}_B^I(b_p))$ be the ranks for intensities in each color channel; and
- the intensity values r_{ref}, g_{ref}, and b_{ref} in each color channel, from image Q, have ranks:

$$\begin{aligned}
\mathbb{R}_R^Q(r_{ref}) &= \left\lfloor \frac{\mathbb{R}_R^I(r_p)}{K_I} \times K_Q + \frac{1}{2} \right\rfloor \\
\mathbb{R}_G^Q(g_{ref}) &= \left\lfloor \frac{\mathbb{R}_G^I(g_p)}{K_I} \times K_Q + \frac{1}{2} \right\rfloor \\
\mathbb{R}_B^Q(b_{ref}) &= \left\lfloor \frac{\mathbb{R}_B^I(b_p)}{K_I} \times K_Q + \frac{1}{2} \right\rfloor
\end{aligned} \tag{18.4}$$

As a result, the color for pixel, p: (r_p, g_p, b_p), will be normalized as $(r_{ref}, g_{ref}, b_{ref})$. Different from standard quantile normalization, which utilizes all pixel values in the image, color map normalization is based on the unique colors in the image, thereby, excludes color frequencies as a result of technical variations and tumor heterogeneity. Figure 18.2 shows some examples of color map normalization.

3.1.3 Color transformation

For more efficient integration of the *LoG* responses, a color transformation step is preferred to transform *RGB* space into a gray-level image for the accentuation of the nuclear stain and attenuation of background. Since present techniques in color decomposition (Rabinovich et al. 2003; Ruifork and Johnston 2001) are either very time-consuming or do not yield favorable outcomes, a more efficient strategy, which we refer to as blue ratio transformation, is proposed as follows: $BR(x,y) = \frac{100*B(x,y)}{1+R(x,y)+G(x,y)} \times \frac{256}{1+B(x,y)+R(x,y)+G(x,y)}$, where $B(x,y)$, $R(x,y)$, and $G(x,y)$ are the respective blue, red, and green intensities at position (x,y). In this formulation, the first and second terms accentuates nuclear stain while, the second term attenuates the background signals. Subsequently, the *LoG* responses are always computed at a single scale from the blue ratio image. In Figure 18.3 , we demonstrates the improvements resulting from the blue ratio transformation compared to color decomposition (Ruifork and Johnston 2001).

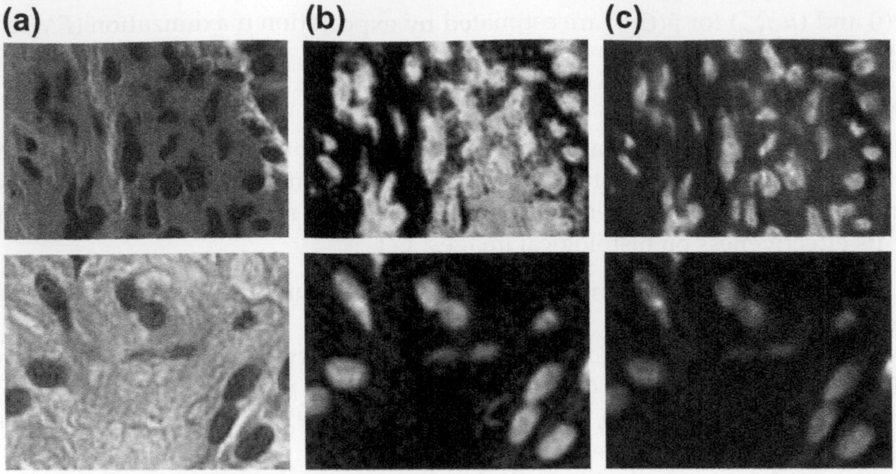

FIGURE 18.3 (a) Two diverse pinhole of tumor signatures; (b) decompositions by Ruifork and Johnston (2001); (c) blue ratio images. (For interpretation of the references to color in this figure legend, the reader is referred to the web version of this book.)

3.1.4 *Feature extraction*

We integrate both color and scale information, where the color information is directly from the *RGB* space, and the scale information is encoded by the *LoG* response. The following are steps for feature extraction:

1. Normalize the input image against every reference image, as described in Section 3.1.2;
2. Transform each normalized image into a blue ratio image, as described in Section 3.1.3;
3. Apply the *LoG* filter to each blue ratio image, at a fixed scale; and
4. Represent each pixel, in the test image, by its *RGB* color in each of the normalized images and the *LoG* response, from each of the blue ratio images.

As a result, each pixel in the test input image, where the first N features are normalized *RGB* colors, and the last N features are *LoG* responses extracted from the blue ratio of the normalized images. All $2N$ features are assumed to be independent of each other, per the selection of reference images. The rational for our feature extraction strategy is that: (1) color information is insufficient for the delineation of nuclear regions from the background due to large variations in the data; (2) the scales of the nuclear region and background structure are typically different; and (3) the nuclear region responds well to *LoG* filter (Al-Kofahi et al. 2010).

3.1.5 *Multi-reference graph cut model*

Since the intrinsic and extrinsic variations in a cohort are incorporated within a graph cut framework, the image is represented as a graph, $G = \langle \bar{V}, \bar{E} \rangle$, where $\bar{V}$ is the set of all nodes, and $\bar{E}$ is the set of all arcs connecting adjacent nodes. Though the nodes and edges typically correspond to the pixels (P) and their adjacency relationships, respectively, there are special nodes known as terminals, which correspond to the set of labels to be assigned to the pixels.

For graphs with two terminals, the terminals are generally referred to as the source (S) and the sink (T). The labeling problem is to assign a unique label x_p (1 for foreground, and 0 for background) for each node, $p \in \bar{V}$, which is performed by minimizing the Gibbs energy E (Geman et al. 1984):

$$E = \sum_{p \in \bar{V}} E_{fitness}(x_p) + \beta \sum_{(p,q) \in \bar{E}} E_{smoothness}(x_p, x_q) \tag{18.5}$$

where $E_{fitness}(x_p)$ encodes the data fitness cost for assigning x_p to p, and $E_{smoothness}(x_p, x_q)$ denotes the cost when the labels of adjacent nodes, p and q, are x_p and x_q, respectively; additionally, β is the weight for $E_{smoothness}$. For more information regarding the Goldberg-Tarjan "push-relabel" methods (Goldberg and Tarjan 1988), and Ford-Fulkerson "augmenting paths" (Ford and Fullkerson 1962), the two groups of algorithms utilized in the graph cut optimization, please see Cook et al. (1998).

To capture the intrinsic variations of the nuclear signature, we expressed, the data fitness term as a combination of the global property map and intrinsic local probability map, where the former captures the global variations of the cohort, and the latter captures local intrinsic image property in the absence of color map normalization. Equation 18.5 is then rewritten as

$$E = \sum_{p \in \bar{V}} (E_{gf}(x_p) + E_{lf}(x_p)) + \beta \sum_{(p,q) \in \bar{E}} E_{smoothness}(x_p, x_q) \tag{18.6}$$

where E_{gf} and E_{lf} are the global and local data fitness terms, respectively, encoding the fitness cost for assigning x_p to p. Below, we discuss each of the terms together with the optimization process.

3.1.5.1 GLOBAL FITNESS TERM

The global fitness is constructed based on manually annotated reference images. Assume that there are N reference images: Q_i, $i \in [1,N]$. Additionally, for each reference image, *GMMs* are used to model the nuclear signal and background in both *RGB* space and *LoG* response space, respectively: GMM^k_{Nuclei}, $GMM^k_{Background}$, in which $k \in [1,2N]$, and the first N *GMMs* are for the *RGB* space, and the last N *GMMs* are for *LoG* response space.

A normalized image, U_i, is first generated for the input test image, I, with respect to every reference image, Q_i. Subsequently, color and *LoG* responses of U_i are collected to construct $2N$ features per pixel, where the first N features are from the normalized color space, and the second N features are from *LoG* responses. Let,

- p be a node corresponding to a pixel;
- $f^k(p)$ be the kth feature of p;
- α be the weight of *LoG* response;
- p^k_l be the probability function of f^k being nuclei ($l = 1$)/background ($l = 0$):

$$p^k_l(p) = \frac{GMM^k_l(p)}{\sum_{j=0}^{1} GMM^k_j(p)} \tag{18.7}$$

- λ_i be the weight for Q_i:

$$\lambda_i = \frac{1}{3}\sum_{c}^{C\in\{R,G,B\}} \lambda_i^C \qquad (18.8)$$
$$\lambda_i^C = H^C(Q_i)H^C(U_i)/(||H^C(Q_i)||||H^C(U_i)||)$$

where $||\cdot||$ is L_2 norm, $H^C(\cdot)$ is the histogram function on a specific color channel $C \in \{R,G,B\}$ of an image. Intuitively, λ measures similarity between two histograms derived from Q_i and U_i. It weighs the fitness for the application of the prior model, constructed from Q_i, onto the features extracted from the normalized image U_i.

Thus, the global fitness term is then defined as

$$E_{gf}(x_p = i) = -\sum_{k=1}^{N} \lambda_k \log(p_i^k(f^k(p))) - \alpha \sum_{k=N+1}^{2N} \lambda_{k-N} \log(p_i^k(f^k(p))) \qquad (18.9)$$

where the first and second terms integrate normalized color features, and the second integrates the *LoG* responses.

3.1.5.2 LOCAL FITNESS TERM

At the cohort level, the global fitness term is designed through the utilization of both color and *LoG* information in the feature spaces of the references. However, the incorporation of information in the original color space of the input image is also important due to the local variations for a number of reasons, i.e., local lesions, non-uniformity in the tissue sections, etc. Taking this into consideration, the local data fitness of pixel, p, is constructed from the foreground and background samples in the neighborhood around p. These samples are detected by a *LoG* filter on the blue ratio image, where positive and negative peaks of the *LoG responses* often, but not always, correspond to the background and foreground (nuclear region), respectively. The following are details of the construction of the local fitness term:

1. Samples collection: This step aims to provide local foreground and background samples for further modeling of local image statistics. Figure 18.4 gives an example of the typical positive and negative peak responses associated with the *LoG* filter. To further improve the accuracy of the detected samples we've implemented the protocol outlined below:
   a. Create a blue ratio image (Section 3.1.3): In this transformed space, the preferred frequency of the background intensity always corresponds to the peak of the intensity histogram.
   b. Construct distributions of the foreground and background: here, we apply the *LoG* filter on the blue ratio image, and construct distributions of the blue ratio intensity at the detected peaks corresponding to the negative and positive *LoG* responses, respectively. Accuracy of detected samples can be improved in the following step.
   c. Constrain the sample selection: Three criteria are applied to improve the accuracy of detected samples: (i) the *LoG* responses must be above a minimum conservative threshold to remove noise introduced by artifacts; (ii) the intensity associated with

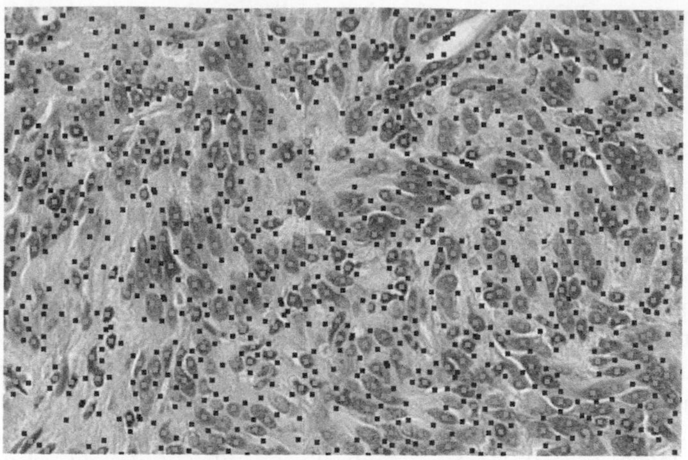

FIGURE 18.4 An example of the *LoG* response for detection of foreground (green dot) and background (blue dot) signals indicates an excellent performance on the initial estimate. (For interpretation of the references to color in this figure legend, the reader is referred to the web version of this book.)

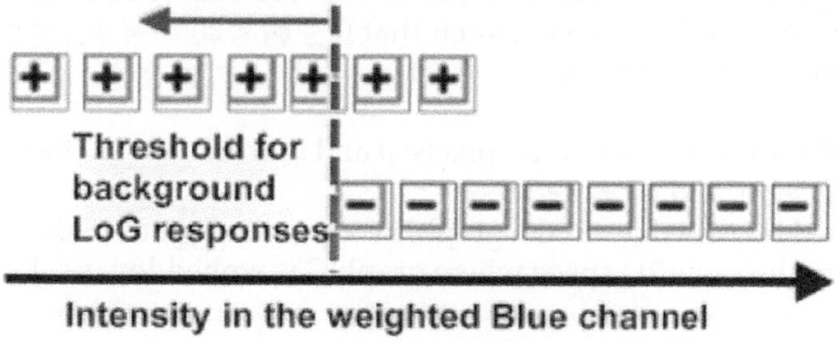

FIGURE 18.5 *LoG* responses can be either positive (e.g. potential background) or negative (e.g. foreground or part of foreground) in the transformed blue ratio image. In the blue ratio image with the most negative *LoG* response, the threshold is set at the minimum intensity. (For interpretation of the references to color in this figure legend, the reader is referred to the web version of this book.)

foreground samples must concur with the background peak, specified in step (a); and (iii) within a small neighborhood of $w_1 \times w_1$, the minimum blue ratio intensity, at the location of negative seeds, is set as the threshold for background peaks, as shown in Figure 18.5.

2. Local foreground and background color modeling: Foreground and background statistics, for each pixel, p, within a local neighborhood, $w_2 \times w_2$, are represented by two GMMs in the original color space, which correspond to the nuclei and background models, GMM_{Nuclei}^{Local} and $GMM_{Background}^{Local}$, respectively.

Then the definition of the local fitness term is:

$$E_{lf}(x_p = i) = -\gamma \log(p_l(f(p))) \quad (18.10)$$

where $f(p)$ refers to the RGB feature of node (pixel), p, in the original color space; γ weights the local fitness term; p_l is the probability function of f being Nuclei ($l = 1$)/background ($l = 0$), which results in

$$p_l(p) = \frac{GMM_l^{Local}(p)}{\sum_{j=0}^{1} GMM_j^{Local}(p)} \tag{18.11}$$

3.1.5.3 SMOOTHNESS TERM

While both global and local data fitness terms encode the likelihood of a pixel being foreground/background, the smoothness term ensures the smoothness of labeling between adjacent pixels. In the graph configuration, fitness and smoothness are encoded by t-links (links between node and terminals) and n-links (links between adjacent nodes), respectively. Therefore, in order to utilize geodesic information, we follow the setup in Boykov and Kolmogorov (2003) for n-links. As a result, the max-flow/min-cut solution for the graph corresponds to a local geodesic or, in a continuous case, to a minimal surface. Given the weighted graph, $G = \langle \bar{V}, \bar{E} \rangle$, constructed in Section 3.1.5. Let,

- $\{e_k \mid 1 \le k \le n_G\}$ be a set of vectors for the neighborhood system, where n_G is the order of the neighborhood system, and the vectors are ordered by their corresponding angle ϕ_k with respect to the $+x$ axis, such that $0 \le \phi_1 < \phi_2 \cdots < \phi_{nG} < \pi$. For example, when $n_G = 8$, we have $e_1 = (1, 0)$, $e_2 = (1, 1)$, $e_3 = (0, 1)$, $e_4 = (-1, 1)$, as shown in Figure 18.6(a);
- w_k be the weight for the edge between pixels: p and q, which are in the same neighborhood system, and $\vec{pq} = \pm e_k$;
- L be a line formed by the edges in the graph, as shown in Figure 18.6(c);
- C be a contour in the same 2D space where graph G is embedded, as shown in Figure 18.6(b);
- $|C|_G$ be the cut metric of C, as in

$$|C|_G = \sum_{e \in \bar{E}_C} W_e \tag{18.12}$$

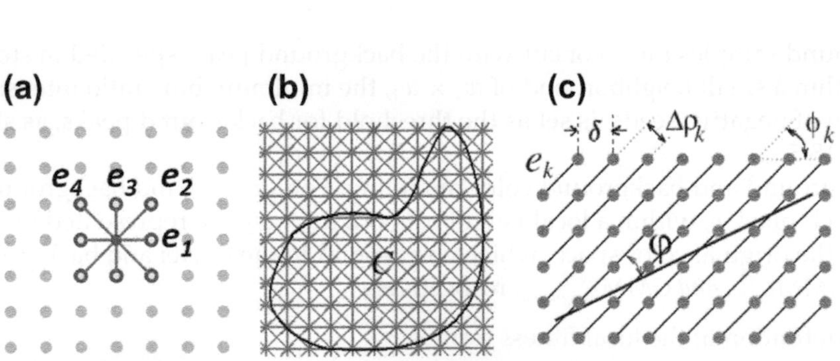

FIGURE 18.6 (a) Eight-neighborhood system: $n_G = 8$; (b) contour on eight-neighborhood 2D grid; (c) one family of lines formed by edges of the graph.

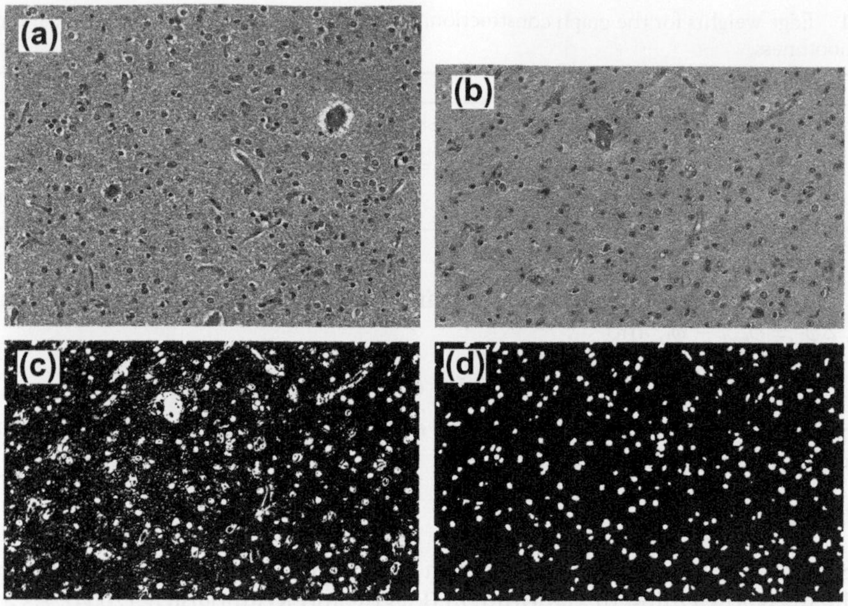

FIGURE 18.7 A comparison between MCV and MRGC (as shown in (c) and (d), respectively) based on the same reference image, as shown in (a). Even though the test image and the reference image are slightly different in color space, compared with MCV, MRGC still produces (1) more accurate classification, due to the encoding of statistics from test image's color space via local probability map; (2) less noisy classification due to the smoothness constrain.

where $\bar{E}_C$ is the set of edges intersecting contour C;

- $|C|_R$ be the Riemannian length of contour C;
- $D(p)$ be the metric(tensor), which continuously varies over point, p, in the 2D Riemannian space;

Based on Integral Geometry (Santalo 1979), the Crofton-style formula for the Riemannian length, $|C|_R$ of contour C, can be written as,

$$\int \frac{\det D(p)}{2(u_L^T \cdot D(p) \cdot u_L)^{\frac{3}{2}}} n_c dL = 2|C|_R \tag{18.13}$$

where u_L is the unit vector in the direction of the line L, and n_C is a function that specifies the number of intersections between L and C. According to Boykov and Kolmogorov (2003), the local geodesic can be approximated by the max-flow/min-cut solution ($|C|_G \rightarrow |C|_R$) with the following edge weight setting:

$$W_k(p) = \frac{\delta^2 \cdot |e_k|^2 \cdot \Delta\phi_k \cdot \det D(p)}{2 \cdot (e_k^T \cdot D(p) \cdot e_k)^{\frac{3}{2}}} \tag{18.14}$$

TABLE 18.1 Edge weights for the graph construction, where N is the neighborhood system, and β is the weight for smoothness.

Edge	Weight	For
$p \to S$	$E_{gf}(x_p = 1) + E_{lf}(x_p = 1)$	$p \in P$
$p \to T$	$E_{gf}(x_p = 0) + E_{lf}(x_p = 0)$	$p \in P$
$w_e(p, q)$	$\beta \cdot W_k(p)$	$\{p, q\} \in N, \phi_{\vec{pq}} \in \{\phi_k, \pi + \phi_k\}$

where δ is the cell-size of the grid, $\Delta\phi_k$ is the angular difference between the kth and $(k+1)^{\text{th}}$ edge lines, $\Delta\phi_k = \phi_{k+1} - \phi_k$, and

$$D(p) = g(|\nabla|) \cdot \mathbf{I} + (1 - g(|\nabla|)) \cdot \mathbf{u} \cdot \mathbf{u}^{\text{T}} \tag{18.15}$$

Here $\mathbf{u} = \frac{\nabla I}{|\nabla I|}$ is a unit vector in the direction of image gradient at point p, $\mathbf{I}$ is the identity matrix, and $g(x) = \exp(-\frac{x^2}{2\sigma^2})$.

3.1.5.4 OPTIMIZATION

Table 18.1 provides the details of the graph construction; the graph is further partitioned based on the max-flow/min-cut algorithm in Boykov and Kolmogorov (2004). As a result, the input test image is labeled into foreground and background. Details about the optimization can be found in Boykov and Kolmogorov (2004).

3.1.6 *Nuclear mask partitioning*

After the separation of foreground and background, the next step is to partition potential clumps of nuclei. Due to the fact that nuclear shape is typically convex, concavity detection and geometric reasoning (Wen et al. 2009) are applied to address the ambiguities associated with the delineation of overlapping nuclei. Details can be found in Wen et al. (2009).

3.1.7 *Experimental results and discussion*

In this section, we (i) discuss parameter setting, and (ii) evaluate performance of the system against previous methods.

3.1.7.1 EXPERIMENTAL DESIGN AND PARAMETER SETTING

Our experiment was carried out at 20X, where 20 reference images with size 1k-by-1k pixels were manually selected and annotated by an expert to capture the technical variations and biological heterogeneities in the target cohort. During nuclear segmentation, only the top $M = 10$ reference images with the highest weight of λ were used as a trade-off between computational complexity and performance. The number of components for *GMM* was evaluated and selected to be $D = 20$, while the parameters of *GMM* were estimated via *EM* algorithm. The other parameter were set at: $\alpha = 0.1$, $\beta = 10.0$, $\gamma = 0.1$, $w_1 = 100$, $w_2 = 100$, and $\sigma = 4.0$ (the scale for both seeds detection and *LoG* feature extraction), where w_1 was selected to minimize the seeds detection error on the annotated reference images; σ was determined based

TABLE 18.2 Comparison of average classification performance among our approach(MRGC), our previous approach (Chang et al., 2011-a), MCV approach in Kothari et al. (2011), and random forest. For MCV, only color in *RGB* space is used, which is identical to Kothari et al. (2011). For random forest, the same features are used: {R, G, B, *LoG*}, and the parameter settings are: *ntree* = 100, *mtry* = 2, *node* = 1.

Approach	Precision	Recall	F-Measure
MRGC-MS (Multi-Scale LoG)	0.77	0.82	0.794
MRGC	0.79	0.78	0.785
MRGC-CF (Color Feature Only)	0.72	0.83	0.771
MRGC-GF (Global Fitness Only)	0.80	0.71	0.752
Our Previous Approach	0.78	0.65	0.709
MCV	0.69	0.75	0.719
Random Forest	0.59	0.76	0.664

on the preferred nuclear size at 20X; and all other parameters were selected through cross validation.

3.1.7.2 EVALUATION

A two-fold cross validation, with optimized parameter settings, was applied to the reference images, followed by a comparison of average classification performance between our approach, MCV (Kothari et al. 2011), and random forest (Breiman 2001). As summarized in Table 18.2, our approach exhibits a superior performance.

The effectiveness of the local probability map is demonstrated with an intuitive example, as shown in Figure 18.8, where the characterization of the nuclei with low chromatin content

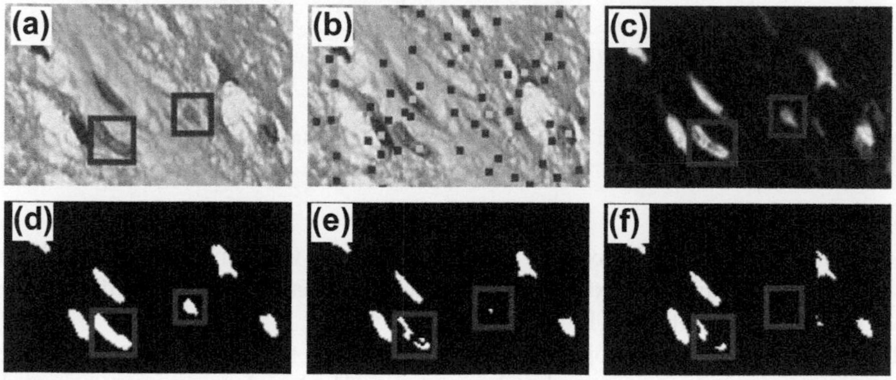

FIGURE 18.8 A comparison among our approach, MCV, and random forest. (a) Original image patch; (b) detected seeds, green: nuclei region; blue: background; (c) local nuclei probability established based on seeds; (d) classification by our approach; (e) classification by MCV; (f) classification by random forest. (For interpretation of the references to color in this figure legend, the reader is referred to the web version of this book.)

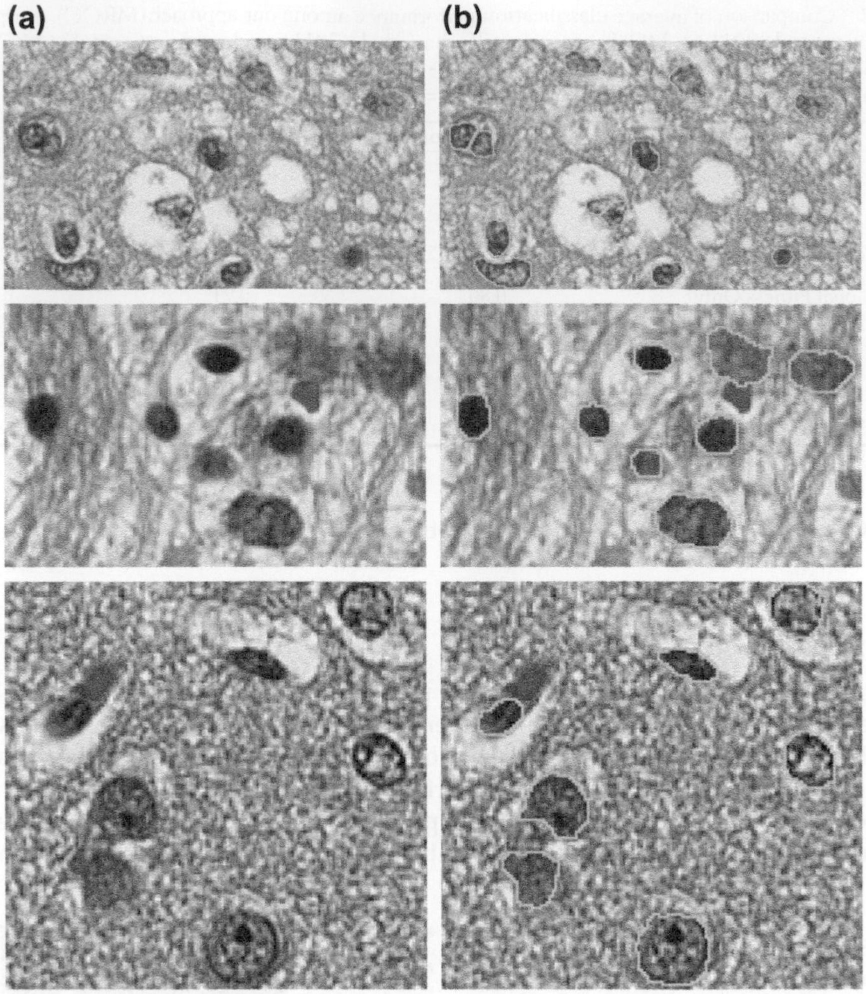

FIGURE 18.9 Segmentation on nuclei with low chromatin patterns. (a) Original image patch; (b) segmentation results.

(shown in the blue bounding boxes) is clearly improved with the help of local probability map. Figure 18.9 gives another example for further demonstration of the effectiveness of our approach on the segmentation of low chromatin nuclei.

Finally, Table 18.3 gives an object level comparison of the nuclear segmentation performance between our previous approach (Chang et al. 2011-a) and our current approach (Chang et al. 2011-a). Let,

- *MaxSize*(a, b) be the maximum size of nuclei a and b,
- *Overlap*(a, b) be the amount of overlap between nuclei, a and b.

TABLE 18.3 Comparison of average segmentation performance between our current approach (MRGC), and our previous approach (Chang et al. 2011-a), in which $precison = \frac{\#correctly\_segmented\_nuclei}{\#segmented\_nuclei}$, and $recall = \frac{\#correctly\_segmented\_nuclei}{\#manually\_segmented\_nuclei}$.

Approach	Precision	Recall	F-Measure
MRGC	0.75	0.85	0.797
Our Previous Approach	0.63	0.75	0.685

Subsequently, given any manually annotated nucleus, n_G, as ground truth, if there is one and only one segmented nucleus, n_S, that satisfies $\frac{Overlap(n_G,n_S)}{MaxSize(n_G,n_S)} > T$, then n_S is considered to be the correct segmentation for n_G. In our experiment, the threshold was set to be $T = 0.8$ empirically.

3.2 Patch-based analysis

The flip side of morphometric analysis is to quantify composition of each tissue section in terms of distinct histopathology, such as tumor or necrosis regions. This allows each nucleus can be tracked to its specific compartment. It is our suggestion that, compared to human engineered features (Lowe 1999; Dalal and Triggs 2005), unsupervised feature learning is more tolerant to batch effect (e.g., technical variations associated with sample preparation) and can learn pertinent features without user intervention. In our case, features are learned using PSD [74]. It contains both a feed-forward stage (e.g., encoding) and a feed backward stage (e.g., decoding), where the decoding step reconstructs the original patch through a sparse activation of an over-complete dictionary, and the encoding step efficiently produces the sparse code directly from the the original patch. The learned features are then summarized utilizing some pooling strategies for improved robustness of the representation, which will eventually be used towards the construction of classifier. Figure 18.10 indicates the overall recognition framework of our approach.

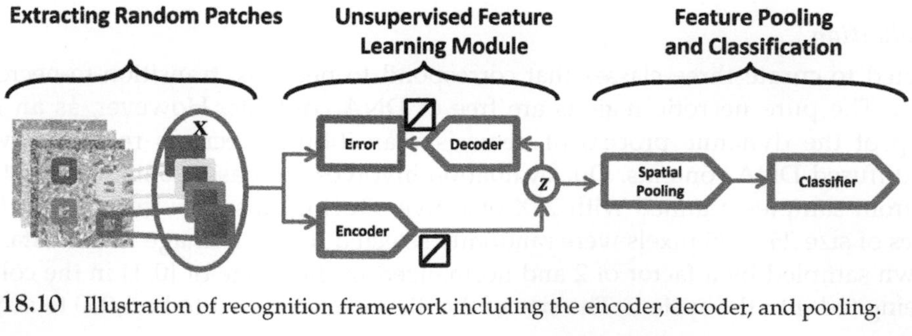

FIGURE 18.10 Illustration of recognition framework including the encoder, decoder, and pooling.

3.2.1 *Unsupervised feature learning*

Randomly selecting from the cohort, the sparse auto encoder takes a set of vectorized image patches, X, as input, with the objective is to constructing a sparse representation, Z, for each input, X, with a highly efficient feed forward fashion. Meanwhile, the feedback mechanism minimizes the reconstruction error of the original signal based on an over-complete dictionary, D. The objective function is as follows:

$$F(X) = ||WX - Z||_F^2 + \lambda||Z||_1 + ||DZ - X||_F^2 \quad (18.16)$$

where $X \in \mathcal{R}^n$, $Z \in \mathcal{R}^k$, the dictionary is $D \in \mathcal{R}^{n\times k}$, and the encoder is $W \in \mathcal{R}^{k\times n}$. The first and last terms are for encoding and decoding, respectively, whereas the second term denotes the sparse constraint with λ as the weighting parameter for sparsity, i.e., sparsity is increased with a higher value of λ.

In our experiment, to achieve the best performance in classification, λ is set to be 0.3 empirically.

The optimal D, W, and Z are learned through the minimization of $F(X)$, which is iterative by fixing one set of parameters while optimizing others and vice versa, i.e., iterate over steps (2) and (3) below:

1. Randomly initialize D and W.
2. Fix D and W and minimize Equation 18.16 with respect to Z, where Z for each input vector is estimated via the gradient descent method.
3. Fix Z and estimate D and W, then approximate D *and* W through stochastic gradient descent algorithm. This is used to improve the scalability of the optimization, which is necessary due to the large scale of training samples.

Figure 18.11 shows a few examples of the dictionary elements, computed from GBM dataset, which captures color and texture information in the cohort. Generally, this information is difficult to obtain using hand engineered features.

3.2.2 *Classification*

During classification, every image, in the training dataset, is divided into non-overlapping image patches, which are further processed with the feed forward encoding operation, $Z = WX$, followed by the max-pooling strategy upon the sparse codes forming the features for training. Here, a multi-class regularized SVM is used for classification with a regularization parameter 1 and a polynomial kernel of degree 3.

3.2.3 *Evaluation*

We opted to curate three classes that correspond to necrosis, transition-to-necrosis, and to tumors. The pure necrotic regions are free of DNA contents. However, as an intermediate step of the dynamic process of necrosis, transition-to-necrosis regions have punctated or diffused DNA contents. Our evaluation involves a dataset containing 1400 images curated from samples scanned with 20X objective. During unsupervised feature learning, 50 patches of size 25×25 pixels were randomly selected for each image in the dataset. They were down sampled by a factor of 2 and normalized in the range of $[0,1]$ in the color space before being fed into the system. The size of the dictionary was set to be 1,000 to achieve the

(a)

(b)

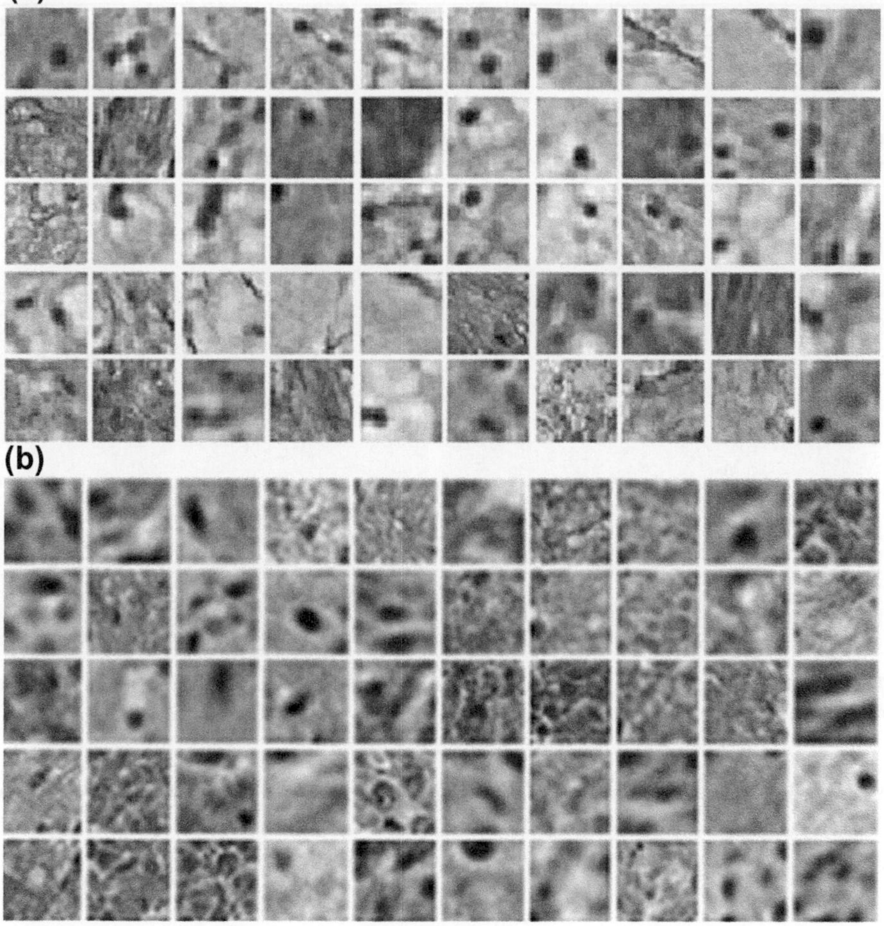

FIGURE 18.11 Representative set of computed basis function, D, for (a) the KIRC dataset and (b) the GBM dataset.

best classification performance during cross-validation, and the max-pooling strategy was performed on a 4-by-4 neighboring patch of the learning step. During classification, the total number of necrosis, transition-to-necrosis, and tumor patches were 12,000, 8,000, and 16,000, respectively. From, amongst those, 4,000 patches per category were randomly selected for training, and another 4,000 per category were randomly selected for testing. We repeated the classification for 100 times, and reported the performance in Table 18.4. Figure 18.12 shows an example of the reconstruction of a heterogeneous image with the tumor region on the right and transition-to-necrosis on the left. Based on the dictionary derived above, this indicates that the transition-to-necrosis region is visually distinguishable from the tumor during reconstruction.

TABLE 18.4 Confusion matrix for classifying three different morphometric signatures in GBM.

Tissue type	Necrosis	Tumor	Transition to necrosis
Necrosis	77.6	7.7	14.6
Tumor	0.5	93.3	6.0
Transition to Necrosis	10.9	6.3	82.8

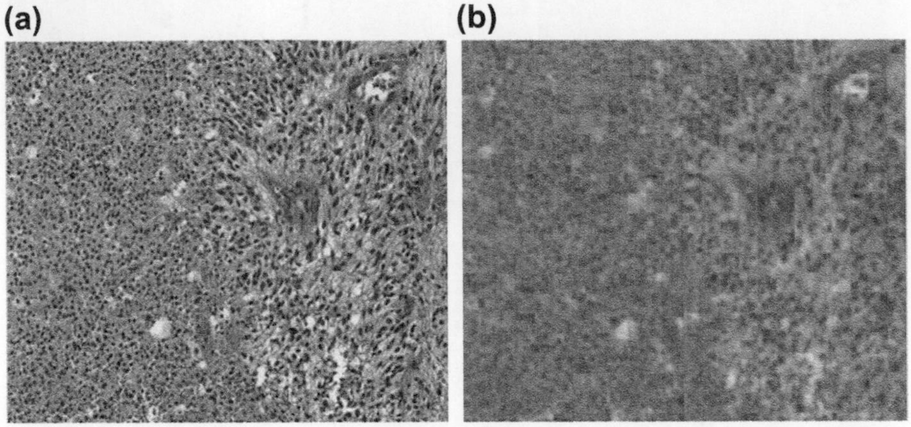

FIGURE 18.12 (a) A heterogeneous tissue section with transition to necrosis on the left and tumor on the right, and (b) its reconstruction after encoding and decoding.

Figure 18.13 shows some examples of classification on whole slide tissue sections with size 20k × 20k pixels. The examples are consistent with the evaluation and annotation from our pathologist, and further demonstrate the efficacy of our system.

4 BIOINFORMATICS ANALYSIS

Integrated analysis of tissue histology with the genome-wide array (e.g., OMIC) and clinical data has the potential to generate hypotheses as well as be prognostic. Different from typical subtyping analysis at patient level (Chang et al. 2011a, 2013b), we focus on subtypes that correspond to tumor composition, and evaluate every morphometric index or pairs of morphometric indices that are predictive of the outcome. Meanwhile, indices for morphometric heterogeneity are also derived in order to identify the molecular basis of tumor heterogeneity.

4.1 Morphometric summarization and subtyping at the block level

Morphometric summarization and subtyping on tissue patches provide a way for tissue compositional analysis. In this study, each tissue section is decomposed into non-overlapping patches (blocks) of 1k × 1k pixels. Distributions of each computed morphometric index are then

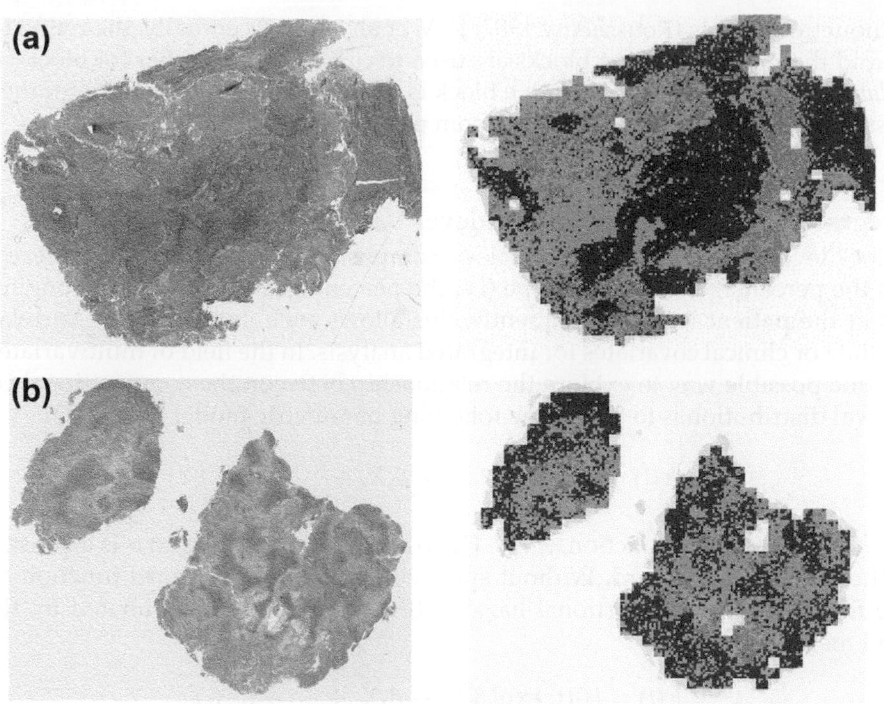

FIGURE 18.13 Two examples of classification results of a heterogeneous GBM tissue sections. The left and right images correspond to the original and classification results, respectively. Color coding is black (tumor), pink (necrosis), and green (transition to necrosis). (For interpretation of the references to color in this figure legend, the reader is referred to the web version of this book.)

constructed per block and normalized across all tissues within the same tumor type, thereby enabling morphometric subtyping at block level for a given tumor type as well as subsequent survival and compositional analysis. However, prior to the analyses, several problems will first need to be solved: (i) undesired effects on subtyping caused by background/border blocks in the tissue section; (ii) extremely large number of blocks per tissue section, e.g., 2500; (iii) imbalanced number of blocks per tissue section due to the variation of tissue size. To address the issues above, a computational pipeline with four major steps has been developed:

1. *Block filtering:* Any blocks containing background regions, where the background is detected at low resolution of the tissue section, are removed from subsequent analysis.
2. *Block Sampling:* Representative blocks for each tissue section are identified and selected as the centroids of the morphometric clusters, then they are computed through a *k*-means algorithm on all the blocks within the tissue section. As a result, the number of selected blocks is the same as the number of clusters, k, which is set to be proportional to the total number of blocks in the tissue section (e.g., 1%).
3. *Block Clustering:* Consensus clustering (Monti et al. 2003) is performed on representative blocks across different tissue sections for the identification of subtypes of a given tumor type, where the derived subtypes are further refined by removing the outliers through

the silhouette analysis (Rousseeuw 1987; R. V. et al. 2010). Eventually, the refined subtypes and their corresponding blocks are used to construct a classifier for block labeling.

4. *Block labeling*: Each non-representative block is assigned to a subtype through the nearest-neighbor classifier, which built from previous step.

4.2 Integrated analysis at the patient level

The block level subtyping, which enables a compositional representation for each patient, indicates the percentage of each subtype (i.e. the percentage of the blocks belonging to each subtype) at the patient level. Subsequently, this allows each subtype to be correlated with genomic data or clinical covariates for integrated analysis. In the field of multivariate survival analysis, one possible way to explore the relationship between the compositional covariates and survival distribution is to utilize the following parametric model (Fox 2002):

$$h\,(t) = \exp(\alpha + \beta_1 X_1 + \beta_2 X_2 + \cdots + \beta_k X_k) \tag{18.17}$$

where $h(t)$ is the hazard function, $X_i (i \in [1, k])$ are the covariates, and α is a constant representing the log-baseline hazard. Without specifying the baseline hazard function $\alpha(t) = \log h0(t)$, the following Cox proportional hazards (PH) model can be estimated by the partial likelihood method,

$$h\,(t) = h0(t)\exp(\beta_1 X_1 + \beta_2 X_2 + \cdots + \beta_k X_k) \tag{18.18}$$

To further explore the relationship between compositional covariates and survival distribution in the presence of important clinical covariates (e.g., age at initial pathologic diagnosis), the Cox PH model can be rewritten as:

$$h\,(t) = h0(t)\exp(\beta_1 C_1 + \beta_2 C_2 + \cdots + \beta_{N-1} C_{N-1} + \beta_N Age) \tag{18.19}$$

Here, C_i is the percentage of the ith subtype derived at the patient level. Due to the linear correlation among all the compositional covariates, $\sum_{i=1}^{N} C_i = 1$, only $N - 1$ of them are included in the model. From amongst these, the ones with small p-values (those under a certain threshold) are identified as statistically significant predictors of survival distribution.

Consequently, the identified histological predictor can now be used to infer the best correlated molecular candidates through correlation analysis. To this end, we adopted Pearson's product-moment correlation coefficient for this study. The significance of computed correlation between the histological predictor and expression values of each probe set for all available patients were further assessed by a two-tailed *t-test* with *n-2* degrees of freedom (*n* is the number of patients), where p-values for all probe sets were computed and corrected for multiple testing using a false discovery rate (FDR) Hochberg 1995.

4.3 Clustering results

Our representation for each block is a concatenated vector, from two 25-bin equal probability histograms, for nuclear size and cellularity, respectively. During the block filtering

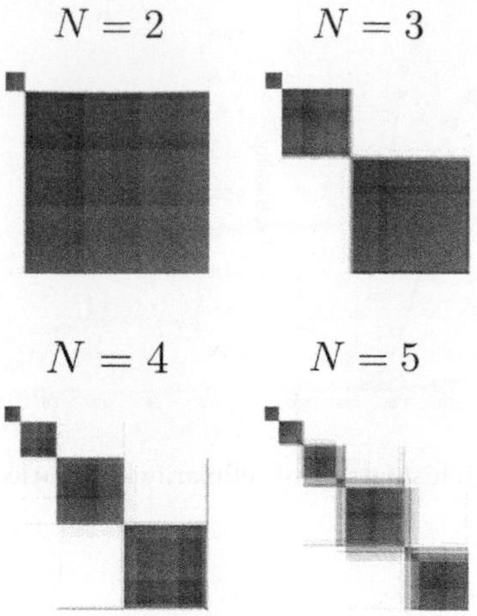

FIGURE 18.14 Consensus clustering matrix of 146 TCGA patients with GBM for cluster number $N = 2$ to $N = 5$.

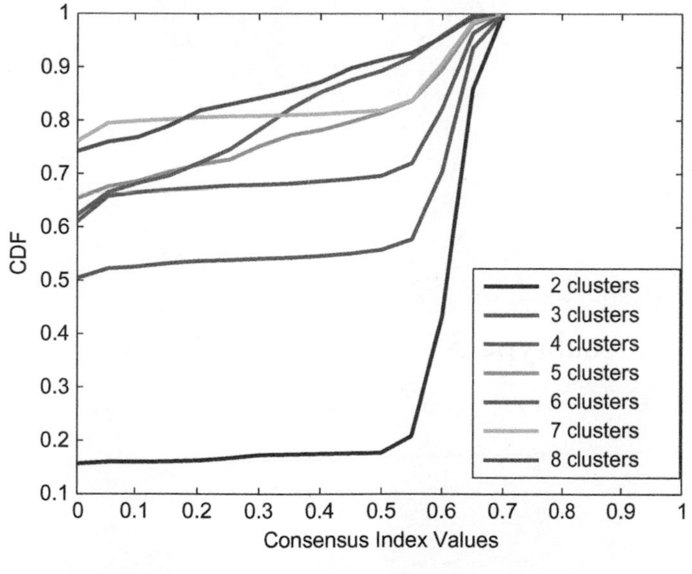

FIGURE 18.15 Consensus clustering CDF for cluster number $N = 2$ to $N = 8$.

step, a total of 162,510 tissue blocks (non-background/non-border) were identified, among which 1,582 representative ones were selected for consensus clustering. In the consensus clustering step, the k-means algorithm, with squared Euclidean distance as the distance metric, was repeated for 200 iterations with a sampling rate of 0.8. As shown in Figures 18.14 and 18.15, respectively, the derived consensus matrix and CDFs (cumulative density function)

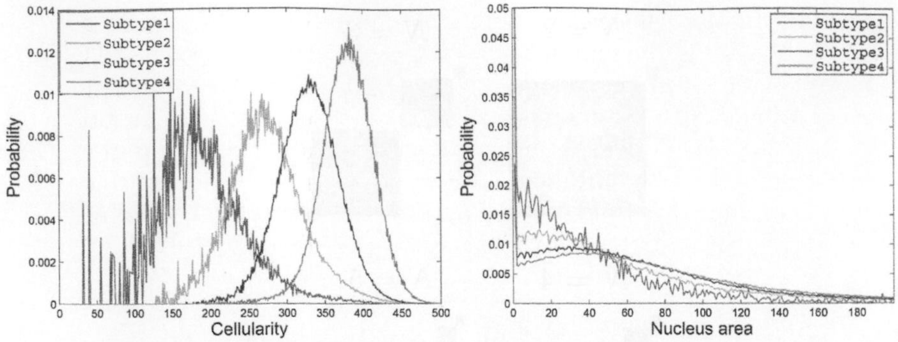

FIGURE 18.16 Average equal-bin-width histograms of cellularity and nuclear size for each block-level subtype ($N = 4$).

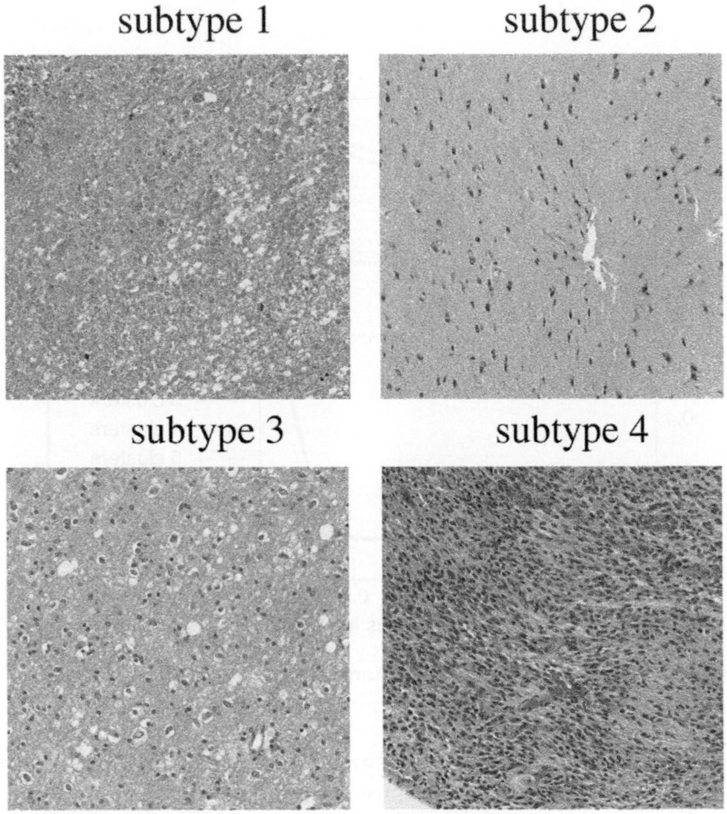

FIGURE 18.17 Representative blocks for each morphometric subtype. Each block is of 1000-by-1000 pixels at 20× resolution.

reveal four robust clusters (clustering stability significantly decrease for $N > 4$). Among all the representative blocks in the four subtypes (clusters) identified above, 1535 of them with positive silhouette value were retained as training samples for the construction of classifier. The average equal-bin-width histograms for each base block, from each subtype, are shown in Figure 18.16. Figure 18.17 gives examples of representative blocks from each one of the four subtypes, which exhibit significantly different signatures in cellularity (i.e., subtypes 1 to 4 correspond to extremely low, mid and high cellularity, respectively) and nuclear size (i.e., subtypes 1 to 4 exhibits a monotonically increasing trend in nuclear size).

4.4 Survival analysis and genomic association

Block labeling leads to a compositional representation at patient level, indicating the percentage of each subtype per patient. In the presence of age, the relationship between the patient level tumor composition and survival distribution, is then modeled as independent prognostic factors in Equation 18.19.

The implementation of survival analysis is based on the R survival package. Due to the linear dependence among all four compositional covariates, as mentioned in Section 4.2, we evaluate all possible combinations of the three covariates for survival analysis. The results, summarized in Table 18.5, indicates that both age and C_1 (Subtype1 composition) have consistently high hazard ratio with p-values < 0.1 (i.e., these covariates are negatively correlated with survival). As shown in Figures 18.16 and 18.17, subtype1 reveals a necrotic-like signature of small nuclear size and extremely low cellularity. Consistent with previous literature, this result indicates a negative correlation between the extent of necrosis and survival in GBM (Pierallini et al. 1998). Figure 18.18 shows a heat map of 48 probe sets that are significantly correlated with the subtype1 composition, with FDR adjusted p-value < 0.02. These probe sets were mapped into genes for further analysis.

Pathway and subnetwork enrichment analysis (see Figure 18.19) are then performed on the identified genes determined to have a significant correlation to the subtype1 composition. Pathway enrichment revealed STAT3, which is known to be a master regulator in GBM (Liu et al. 2010; Rahman et al. 2002), while the subnetwork enrichment identified AGT, PKC, PDGF, CEBPA, and TNF as the major hubs.

Temozolomide (TMZ), as a part of treatment for the patients in this cohort, interferes with DNA replication through methylation. However, some tumor cells are able to

TABLE 18.5 Multivariate survival analysis results by fitting the Cox PH model.

	Covariates in the Cox PH model							
	C1 + C2 + C3 + Age		**C1 + C2 + C4 + Age**		**C1 + C3 + C4 + Age**		**C2 + C3 + C4 + Age**	
	Hazard ratio	*p-value*	*Hazard ratio*	*p-value*	*Hazard ratio*	*p-value*	*Hazard ratio*	*p-value*
C1	1.0184	**0.0652**	1.0168	**0.0856**	1.030	**0.0631**	NA	NA
C2	0.9885	0.2342	0.9869	0.2771	NA	NA	0.9706	**0.0631**
C3	1.0016	0.7303	NA	NA	1.013	0.2771	0.9834	**0.0856**
C4	NA	NA	0.9984	0.7303	1.012	0.2342	0.9819	**0.0652**
Age	1.0283	**7.37e-5**	1.0283	**7.37e-5**	1.028	**7.37e-5**	1.0283	**7.37e-5**

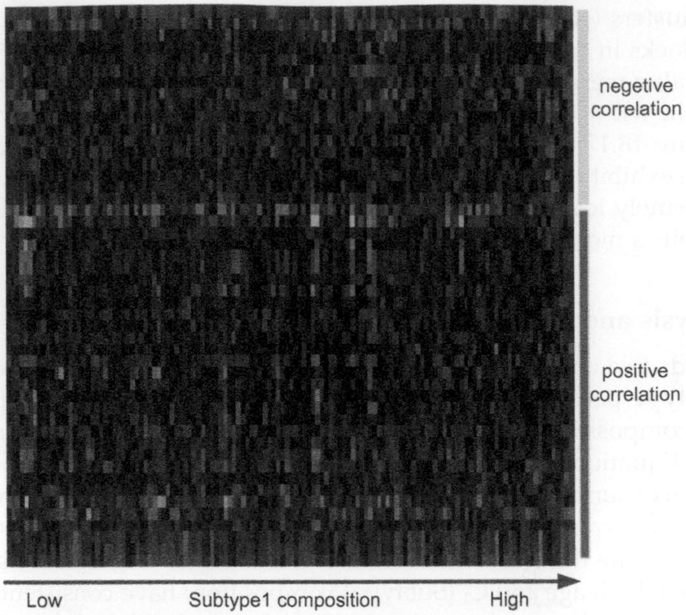

FIGURE 18.18 Heatmap of top 48 probesets (rows) that best correlate with the subtype1 composition, with FDR adjusted p-value < 0.02.

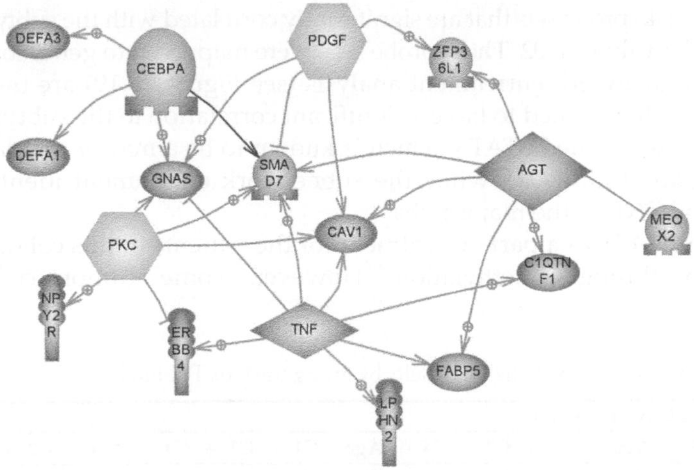

FIGURE 18.19 Subnetwork enrichment analysis for Subtype 1 reveals AGT, PDGF, PKC, TNF, and CEBPA as dominant regulators with p-value of less than 0.05.

repair the damage through the expression of AGT. In GBM, AGT maintains normal function of vasculature (Kakinuma et al. 1997), and cellular concentration of AGT enzyme is a primary determinant of the cytotoxicity of TMZ (Stupp et al. 2001) *in vitro*. Whereas PKC (Protein Kinase C) is well established in cancer signaling and therapy, as it is involved in proliferation, migration, and malignant transformation (Kazanietz 2010), and its isozyme has been suggested for chemotherapeutic targets in GBM (Martin and JHussanini 2005). TNF, on the other hand, refers to a group of cytokines that induce proliferation, inflammation, and apoptosis, depending upon the adaptor proteins. TNF is part of the anti-tumor strategy in which human glioma cell lines express its proteins. Manipulation of these proteins has shown to induce apoptosis in glioma cells (Chen et al. 1997). Other hubs are highly ranked in the TCGA gene tracker.

5 COMPUTATIONAL PIPELINE

The significance of our computational pipeline is its capacity of large-scale data analysis, which meets the TCGA requirements on data processing. As shown in Figure 18.20, the pipeline has the following four components: (I) consistency maintaining between the local and remote registries, (II) tissue section visualization, (III) data processing and feature importing, and (IV) data summarization through normalization. Details of each component are as follows:

I. Consistency of images between a local registry and TCGA registry (at the National Cancer Institute (NCI)) is constantly maintained. Images newly imported into TCGA's registry are synchronized with the local registry for processing. At present,

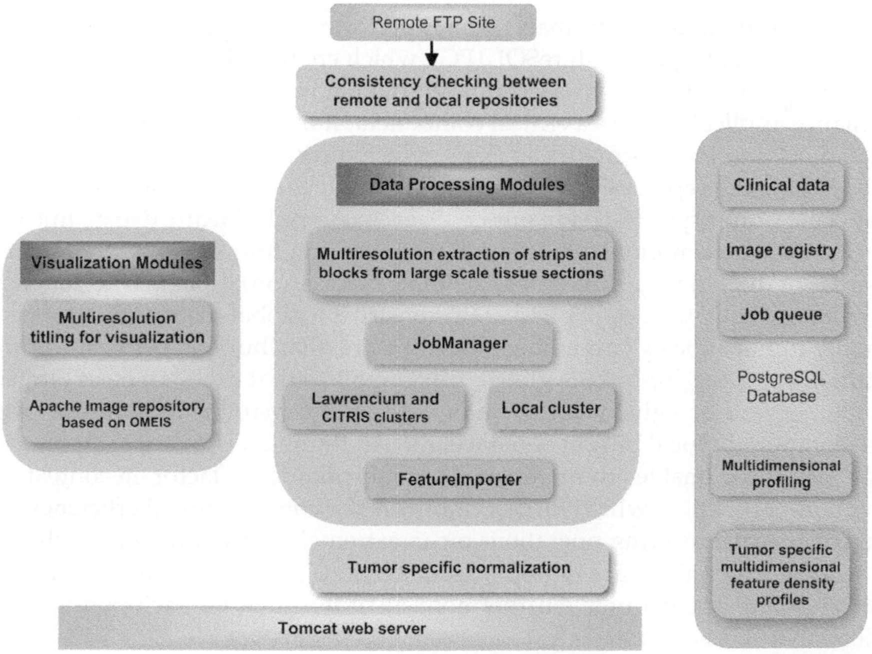

FIGURE 18.20 Computational pipeline consists of four modules: downloads images from the NIH repository. Each image is partitioned into strips of (1k-by-number of columns), stored in the OMEIS image server. Each strip is partitioned into blocks of 1k-by-1k pixels, where each block is submitted to one of the two clusters at Berkeley lab. Computed representations are then imported into a PostgreSQL database.

both frozen sections and those from paraffin embedded blocks are provided; both types of images are registered and displayed through our system, but only paraffin embedded blocks are analyzed. Each image is partitioned and stored as strips of 1k-by-number of columns on the OME image server (Goldberg et al. 2005; Parvin et al. 2000).

II. Visualization of each whole mount tissue section is provided with a GoogleMaps™-like interface, which is realized through tiling and the utilization of Flash technology. Prior to visualization, each tissue section is partitioned and stored as tiles of 256-by-256 pixels at various resolutions. When a user interaction (e.g., drag and zoom) with the interface in an effort to view the tissue section in a browser, the required tiles are immediately downloaded from the server and assembled for display. All data and images are publicly available on the following website: http://tcga.lbl.gov.

III. During data processing, each strip is partitioned into 1k-by-1k blocks, and submitted for cluster computing, where the block size is optimized with respect to processing time and wait time in the queue. Currently, it takes four days to process the entire GBM data set, which consists of 344 tissue sections. To further reduce the computational cost, a multithread implementation of the computational methods has been developed to utilize the multiple CPU cores of each node in the cluster. After processing, extracted features are then imported back into BioSig (Han et al. 2010; Monti et al. 2003), an imaging bioinformatics system, for (1) quality control by overlaying original image with the representation (e.g., nuclear segmentation) and (2) further bioinformatics analysis.

IV. The feature representation summarization is performed through procedural programming. BioSig is built upon PostgreSQL (PG), which enables the transparent transformation of SQL queries, through its server programming interface (SPI), for high performance applications. As a critical component, it increases the flexibility for feature manipulation, and bioinformatics analysis, which directly leads to an increased productivity by saving the reprocessing step when alternative representations need to be tested. For a specific tumor type (GBM in our case), each computed feature (e.g., nuclear size, cellularity, texture) is normalized through the following four steps before further analysis is conducted (e.g., subtyping, genomic association): (i) construct a density distribution for each feature per tissue; (ii) construct a global distribution for each feature per tumor type by combining all the feature distributions per tissue within the same tumor type; (iii) Re-bin the global distribution so that each bin has a similar population of cells of a given feature value; and (iv) Re-map the local density distributions to computed global bins of equal weight. All the steps above are implemented through SPI, and it enables the comparison of morphometric factor, in context, through its distribution function, which further improves the computational efficiency by avoiding classical clustering operations on an extremely large number of cells in the tissue section. When there are multiple tissue sections per patient, an average distribution is computed and archived. Furthermore, all of the data, for each tissue section, are downloadable and is visualizable.

6 CONCLUSION

This chapter introduced the concept of tumor heterogeneity in the context of nuclear morphology and organization. However, nuclear morphology is a complex segmentation problem subject to batch effect and biological variations. We proposed a dictionary based approach that captures intrinsic diversities in tumor signature for nuclear segmentation. Consequently, subtyping based on cellularity (e.g., rate of proliferation) was shown to be one of the better morphometric indices that correlate with the outcome. By performing subtyping, at the block level instead of a cohort of while slide images, we were able to identify four clusters that ultimately form the basis of representation for each histology section. Additionally, the molecular correlates of morphometric subtypes revealed molecular markers that are consistent with the literature for targeted therapy. The end result of the realization of one of the concepts in pathway pathology for revealing outcome based on computed morphometric indices and molecular correlates of computed indices.

References

Al-Kofahi, Y., Lassoued, W., Lee, W., and Roysam, B. (2010). Improved automatic detection and segmentation of cell nuclei in histopathology images. *IEEE Trans. Biomed. Eng.* **57**(4):841–852.

Axelrod, D., Miller, N., Lickley, H., Qian, J., Christens-Barry, W., Yuan, Y., Fu, Y., and Chapman, J. (2008). Effect of quantitative nuclear features on recurrence of ductal carcinoma in situ (dcis) of breast. *Cancer Inform.* **4**:99–109.

Ballaro, B., Florena, A., Franco, V., Tegolo, D., Tripodo, C., and Valenti, C. (2008). An automated image analysis methodology for classifying megakaryocytes in chronic myeloproliferative disorders. *Med. Image Anal.* **12**:703–712.

Bhagavatula, R., Fickus, M., Kelly, W., Guo, C., Ozolek, J., Castro, C., and Kovacevic, J. (2010). Automatic identification and delineation of germ layer components in H&E stained images of teratomas derived from human and nonhuman primate embryonic stem cells. In *ISBI*, pp. 1041–1044.

Boykov, Y., and Kolmogorov, V. (2003). Computing geodesics and minimal surfaces via graph cuts. In *Proceedings of IEEE ICCV*, vol. 1, pp. 26–33.

Boykov, Y., and Kolmogorov, V. (2004). An experimental comparison of min-cut/max-flow algorithms for energy minimization in vision. *IEEE Trans. PAMI* **26**(9):1124–1137.

Breiman, L. (2001). Random forests. *Mach. Learn.* **45**(1):5–32.

Bunyak, F., Hafiane, A., and Palanippan, K. (2011). Histopathology tissue segmentation by combining fuzzy clustering with multiphase vector level set. *Adv. Exp. Med. Biol.* **696**:413–424.

Chang, H., and Parvin, B. (2010). Multiphase level set for automated delineation of membranebound macromolecules. In *ISBI*, pp. 165–168.

Chang, H., Defilippis, R., Tlsty, T., and Parvin, B. (2009). Graphical methods for quantifying macromolecules through bright field imaging. *Bioinformatics* **25**(8):1070–1075.

Chang, H., Fontenay, G., Han, J., Cong, G., Baehner, F., Gray, J., Spellman, P., and Parvin, B. (2011-a). Morphometric analysis of TCGA Glioblastoma Multiforme. *J. BMC Bioinform.* **12**(1).

Chang, H., Han, J., Borowsky, A., Loss, L., Gray, J., Spellman, P., and Parvin, B. (2013-b). Invariant delineation of nuclear architecture in glioblastoma multiforme for clinical and molecular association. *IEEE Trans Med Imaging.*

Chen, T., Hinton, D., Sippy, B., and Hoffman, F. (1997). Soluble TNF-alpha receptors are constitutively shed and down regulate adhesion molecule expression in malignant gliomas. *Neuropathology* **56**:541–550.

Cook, W. J., Cunningham, W. H., Pulleyblank, W. R., and Schrijver, A. (1998). *Combinatorial Optimization.* John Wiley & Sons.

Cosatto, E., Miller, M., Graf, H., and Meyer, J. (2008). Grading nuclear pleomorphism on histological micrographs. In *International Conference on Pattern Recognition*, pp. 1–4.

Dalal, N., and Triggs, B. (2005). Histograms of oriented gradient for human detection. In *Proc. of CVPR*, pp. 886–893. Berlin: Springer.

Dalton, L., Pinder, S., Elston, C., Ellis, I., Page, D., Dupont, W., and Blamey, R. (2000). Histological grading of breast cancer: linkage of patient outcome with level of pathologist agreements. *Mod. Pathol.* **13**(7):730–735.

Datar, M., Padfield, D., and Cline, H. (2008). Color and texture based segmentation of molecular pathology images using HSOMs. In *ISBI*, pp. 292–295.

Demir, C., and Yener, B. (2009). Automated cancer diagnosis based on histopathological images: a systematic survey.

Doyle, S., Agner, S., Madabhushi, A., Feldman, M., and Tomaszewski, J. (2008). Automated grading of breast cancer histopathology using spectral clustering with textural and architectural image features. In *ISBI*, pp. 496–499.

Doyle, S., Feldman, M., Tomaszewski, J., Shih, N., and Madabhushu, A. (2011). Cascaded multiclass pairwise classifier (CASCAMPA) for normal, cancerous, and cancer confounder classes in prostate histology. In *ISBI*, pp. 715–718.

Fatakdawala, H., Xu, J., Basavanhally, A., Bhanot, G., Ganesan, S., Feldman, F., Tomaszewski, J., and Madabhushi, A. (2010). Expectation-maximization-driven geodesic active contours with overlap resolution (EMaGACOR): application to lymphocyte segmentation on breast cancer histopathology. *IEEE Trans. Biomed. Eng.* **57**(7):1676–1690.

Ford, L., and Fullkerson, D. (1962). *Flows in Networks*. Princeton University Press.

Fox, J. (2002). Cox proportional-hazard regression for survival data. In (R. Fox (Ed.), *An R and S-PLUS Companion to Applied Regression*. Thousand Oaks, CA: Sage.

Geman, S., and Geman, D. (1984). Stochastic relaxation, Gibbs distribution and the Bayesian restoration of images. *IEEE Trans. PAMI* **6**(6):721–741.

Glotsos, D., Spyridonos, P., Cavouras, D., Ravazoula, P., Dadioti, P., and Nikiforidis, G. (2004). Automated segmentation of routinely hematoxylin-eosin stained microscopic images by combining support vector machine, clustering, and active contour models. *Anal. Quant. Cytol. Histol.* **26**(6):331–340.

Goldberg, A. V., and Tarjan, R. E. (1988). A new approach to maximum-flow problem. *J. Assoc. Comput. Mach.* **35**(4):921–940.

Goldberg, I., Allan, C., Burel, J., Creager, A., Falconi, H., Hochheiser, H., Johnston, J., Mellen, J., Sorger, P., and Swedlow, J. (2005). The Open Microscopy Environment (OME) data model and xml files: open tools for informatics and quantitative analysis in biological images. *Genome Biol.* **6**(5):R4.

Gurcan, M., Boucheron, L., Can, A., Madabhushi, A., Rajpoot, N., and Bulent, Y. (2009). Histopathological image analysis: a review. *IEEE Trans. Biomed. Eng.* **2**:147–171.

Han, J., Chang, H., Andrarwewa, K., Yaswen, P., Barcellos-Hoff, M., and Parvin, B. (2010). Multidimensional profiling of cell surface proteins and nuclear markers. *IEEE Trans. Comput. Biol. Bioinform.* **7**(1):80–90.

Han, J., Chang, H., Loss, L., Zhang, K., Baehner, F., Gray, J., Spellman, P., and Parvin, B. (2011). Comparison of sparse coding and kernel methods for histopathological classification of glioblastoma multiforme. In *Proc. ISBI*, pp. 711–714.

Hinton, G. (2006). Reducing the dimensionality of data with neural networks. *Science* **313**:504–507.

Hochberg, Y. B. Y. (1995). Controlling the false discovery rate: a practical and powerful approach to multiple testing. *J. R. Stat. Soc. Ser. B* **57**:289–300.

Huang, C., Veillard, A., Lomeine, N., Racoceanu, D., and Roux, L. (2011). Time efficient sparse analysis of histopathological whole slide images. *Comput. Med. Imaging Graph.* **35**(7–8):579–591.

Kakinuma, Y., Hama, H., Syugiyama, F., Goto, K., Murakami, K., and Fukamizu, A. (1997). Antiapoptotic action of angiotensin fragments to neuronal cells from angiotensinogen knock-out mice. *Neurosci. Lett.* **232**:167–170.

Kazanietz, M. (2010). *Protein Kinase C in Cancer Signaling and Therapy*. Humana Press.

Kong, J., Cooper, L., Sharma, A., Kurk, T., Brat, D., and Saltz, J. (2010). Texture based image recognition in microscopy images of diffuse gliomas with multi-class gentle boosting mechanism. In *ICASSAP*, pp. 457–460.

Kong, H., Gurcan, M., and Belkacem-Boussaid, K. (2011). Partitioning histopathological images: an integrated framework for supervised color-texture segmentation and cell splitting. *IEEE Trans. Med. Imaging* **30**(9):1661–1677.

Kothari, S., Phan, J. H., Moffitt, R. A., Stokes, T. H., Hassberger, S. E., Chaudry, Q., Young, A. N., and Wang, M. D. (2011). Automatic batch-invariant color segmentation of histological cancer images. In *ISBI, IEEE*, pp. 657–660.

Kothari, S., Phan, J., Osunkoya, A., and Wang, M. (2012). Biological interpretation of morphological patterns in histopathological whole slide images. In *ACM Conference on Bioinformatics, Computational Biology and Biomedicine.*

Land, W., McKee, D., Zhukov, T., Song, D., and Qian, W. (2008). A kernelized fuzzy support vector machine CAD system for the diagnostic of lung cancer from tissue. *Int. J. Funct. Inform. Personal. Med.* **1**(1):26–52.

Latson, L., Sebek, N., and Powell, K. (2003). Automated cell nuclear segmentation in color images of hematoxylin and eosin-stained breast biopsy. *Anal. Quant. Cytol. Histol.* **26**(6):321–331.

Le, Q., Han, J., Gray, J., Spellman, P., Borowsky, A., and Parvin, B. (2012). Learning invariant features from tumor signature. In *ISBI*, pp. 302–305.

Liu, Y., Li, C., and Lin, J. (2010). Stat3 as a therapeutic target for glioblastoma. *Anticancer Agents Med. Chem.* **10**(7):512–519.

Lowe, D. (1999). Distinctive image features from local scale-invariant features. In *ICCV*, pp. 1150–1157.

Martin, P., and JHussanini, I. (2005). PKC eta as a therapeutic target in glioblastoma multiforme. *Expert Opin. Ther. Targets* **9**(2):299–313.

Miller, J. C., and Fish, N. E. (2001). In situ duct carcinoma of the breast: clinical and histopathologic factors and association with recurrent carcinoma. *Breast J.* **7**:292–302.

Mommers, E., Poulin, N., Sangulin, J., Meiher, C., Baak, J., and van Diest, P. (2001). Nuclear cytometric changes in breast carcinogenesis. *J. Pathol.* **193**(1):33–39.

Monaco, J., Hipp, J., Lucas, D., Smith, S., Balis, U., and Madabhushi, A. (2012). Image segmentation with implicit color standardization using spatially constrained expectation maximization: detection of nuclei. In *Medical Image Computing and Computed-assisted Intervention-MICCAI*, pp. 365–372.

Monti, S., Tamayo, P., Mesirov, J., and Golub, T. (2003). Consensus clustering – a resampling-based method for class discovery and visualization of gene expression microarray data. In *Mach. Learn. Funct. Genomics Special Issue*, pp. 91–118.

Nath, S., Palaniappan, K., and Bunyak, F. (2006). Cell segmentation using coupled level sets and graph-vertex. In *Medical Image Computing and Computed-assisted Intervention-MICCAI*, pp. 101–108.

Parvin, B., Cong, G., Fontenay, G., Taylor, J., Henshall, R., and Barcellos-Hoff, M. (2000). Biosig: a bioinformatic system for studying the mechanism of inter-cell signaling. In *IEEE International Symposium on Bio-Informatics and Biomedical Engineering*, pp. 281–288.

Parvin, B., Yang, Q., Han, J., Chang, H., Rydberg, B., and Barcellos-Hoff, M. H. (2007). Iterative voting for inference of structural saliency and characterization of subcellular events. *IEEE Trans. Image Process.* **16**(3):615–623.

Petushi, S., Garcia, F., Haber, M., Katsinis, C., and Tozeren, A. (2006). Large-scale computations on histology images reveal grade-differentiation parameters for breast cancer. *BMC Med. Imaging* **6**(14):1070–1075.

Phukpattaranont, P., and Boonyaphiphat, P. (2007). Color based segmentation of nuclear stained breast cancer cell images. *ECTI Trans. Electr. Eng. Commun.* **5**(2):158–164.

Pierallini, A., Bonamini, M., Pantano, P., Palmeggiani, F., Raguso, M., Osti, M., Anaveri, G., and Bozzao, L. (1998). Radiological assessment of necrosis in glioblastoma: variability and prognostic value. *Neuroradiology* **40**(3):150–153.

R.V. et al. (2010). Integrated genomic analysis identifies clinically relevant subtypes of glioblastoma characterized by abnormalities in PDGFRA, IDH1, EGFR, and NF1. *Cancer Cell* **17**(1):98–110.

Rabinovich, A., Agarwal, S., Laris, C., Price, J. H., and Belongie, S. (2003). Unsupervised color decomposition of histologically stained tissue samples. In *NIPS*, pp. 667–674.

Rahman, S., Harbor, P., Chernova, O., Barnett, G., Vogelbaum, M., and Haque, S. (2002). Inhibition of constitutively active Stat3 suppresses proliferation and induces apoptosis in glioblastoma multiforme cells. *Oncogene* **21**(55):8404–8413.

Rousseeuw, P. (1987). Silhouettes: a graphical aid to the interpretation and validation of cluster analysis. *J. Comput. Appl. Math.* **20**:53–65.

Ruifork, A., and Johnston, D. (2001). Quantification of histochemical staining by color decomposition. *Anal. Quant. Cytol. Histol.* **23**(4):291–299.

Santalo, L. A. (1979). *Integral Geometry and Geometric Probability*. Addison-Wesley.

Stupp, R., Gander, M., Leyvraz, S., and Newland, E. (2001). Current and future development in the use of temozolomide for the treatment of brain tumours. *Lancet Oncol.* **2**:552–560.

Tomasi, C. Estimating Gaussian Mixture Densities with EM—A Tutorial, www.cs.duke.edu/courses/spring04/cps196.1/handouts/EM/tomasiEM.pdf.

Veltri, R., Khan, M., Miller, M., Epstein, J., Mangold, L., Walsh, P., and Partin, A. (2004). Ability to predict metastasis based on pathology findings and alterations in nuclear structure of normal appearing and cancer peripheral zone epithelium in the prostate. *Clin. Cancer Res.* **10**:3465–3473.

Verhest, A., Kiss, R., d'Olne, D., Larsimont, D., Salman, I., de Launoit, Y., Fourneau, C., Pastells, J., and Pector, J. (1990). Characterization of human colorectal mucosa, polyps, and cancers by means of computerized mophonuclear image analysis. *Cancer* **65**:2047–2054.

Wen, Q., Chang, H., and Parvin, B. (2009). A Delaunay triangulation approach for segmenting clumps of nuclei. In *ISBI*, pp. 9–12.

Zhang, L., Conejo-Garcia, J., Katsaros, P., Gimotty, P., Massobrio, M., Regnani, G., Makrigiannakis, A., Gray, H., Schlienger, K., Liebman, M., Rubin, S., and Coukos, G. (2003). Intratumoral T cells, recurrence, and survival in epithelial ovarian cancer. *N. Engl. J. Med.* **348**(3):203–213.

CHAPTER

19

Applications in Cancer Research: Mathematical Models of Apoptosis

Stefan M. Kallenberger[a], *Stefan Legewie*[b], *Roland Eils*[a]

[a]Department for Bioinformatics and Functional Genomics, Division of Theoretical Bioinformatics, German Cancer Research Center (DKFZ), Institute for Pharmacy and Molecular Biotechnology (IPMB) and BioQuant, Heidelberg University, Heidelberg, Germany,
[b]Institute of Molecular Biology, Mainz, Germany

CONTENTS

Computational Systems Biology, Second Edition
http://dx.doi.org/10.1016/B978-0-12-405926-9.00019-8

Abstract

Apoptosis is a form of cellular suicide central to various aspects in biology including tissue homeostasis and embryonic development. It is typically dysregulated in cancer. Understanding the apoptotic signal transduction network is thus a central goal of cancer research. Quantitative modeling approaches provided valuable insights into determinants of cell fate decisions, and promise to become a valuable tool to optimize therapeutic strategies. In this chapter, we summarize modeling approaches used in systems biology of apoptosis. In addition, we give an overview of apoptosis-related research questions that can be addressed by modeling. Moreover, we review top-down and bottom-up modeling approaches applied to apoptosis, and particularly focus on ordinary differential equation (ODE) modeling. We describe bistability, temporal switching, cross-talk between death and survival, and discuss approaches to model cell-to-cell variability.

1 THE PERSPECTIVE OF APOPTOSIS MODELS IN CANCER RESEARCH

Apoptosis is a regulated signal transduction process leading to self-destruction of cells. While apoptosis is essential for embryogenesis and regulation of the immune system, its dysregulation can be the cause for cancer, immune system diseases, and neurodegenerative disorders (Hanahan and Weinberg 2011). Two signaling cascades initiate apoptosis, namely extrinsic and intrinsic apoptosis, which combine in a common final path. Extrinsic apoptosis is initiated by cell death ligands binding to their specific receptors. Important members of the death receptor (DR) family that belongs to the TNF-R superfamily are the receptors TNFR1 (DR1), CD95 (DR2, Fas, APO-1) and DR 4/5 (TRAILR1/2), which specifically initiate extrinsic cell death (Lavrik et al. 2005). Upon ligand binding to death receptors, death inducing signaling complexes (DISCs) are formed that serve as a platform for the activation of caspase-8 and -10 (Kischkel et al. 1995; Medema et al. 1997; Muzio et al. 1996). Caspase enzymes are aspartate-specific cysteine proteases and act as main executioners of apoptosis by cleaving specific target proteins (Fuentes-Prior and Salvesen 2004). The initiator caspases caspase-8 and -10 cleave and activate effector caspases-3 and -7 as well as the pro-apoptotic Bcl-2 family member Bid to tBid, which leads to mitochondria outer membrane permeabilization (MOMP) after stimulating pore formation by the proteins Bax or Bak (García-Sáez 2012; Deng et al. 2002). MOMP irreversibly triggers activation of effector caspases: the pro-apoptotic proteins Smac and cytochrome c are released from mitochondria. Together with the cytosolic protein Apaf-1, cytochrome c forms apoptosomes, serving as platform for the activation of procaspase-9 which then cleaves and activates effector caspases, while Smac blocks the inhibition of caspase-9 and effector caspases by XIAP (Verhagen et al. 2000; Du et al. 2000; Liu et al. 1996; Zhang et al. 2001; Sun et al. 2002; Li et al. 2002; Kluck et al. 1997). Active effector caspases cleave a variety of proteins including components of the cytoskeleton, and cause activation of the nuclease CAD (caspase-activated DNase) thus leading to chromosome fragmentation (Fuentes-Prior and Salvesen 2004; Samejima and Earnshaw 2005). Dependent on the requirement of effector caspases activation, two types of extrinsic apoptosis are distinguished: In type I cells initiator caspases are sufficiently active to *directly* activate effector caspases. In type II cells, amplification of the cell death signal through Bid cleavage and MOMP is required for undergoing apoptosis (Algeciras-Schimnich et al. 2003; Scaffidi et al. 1998).

Intrinsic apoptosis is directly initiated at the level of mitochondria. Different influences such as cellular stress, accumulation of reactive oxygen species (ROS) or DNA damage change the ratios between pro- and anti-apoptotic Bcl-2 family member proteins which leads to pore formation and MOMP, again leading to apoptosome formation and the activation of caspase-3 and -7 (Danial and Korsmeyer 2004; Galluzzi et al. 2012).

Apoptosis is a cellular process that can be readily observed under the microscope. However, understanding its mechanistic basis is challenging owing to complex interactions of a large number of signaling proteins and emergent behavior at the systems level. After applying a sufficiently strong death-inducing stimulus to a population of cells irreversible signaling events are initiated leading to the characteristic appearance of an apoptotic cell: Membrane blebbing proceeds, the cell shrinks and organelles disintegrate. Apoptosis occurs for extrinsic stimuli on a timescale of hours and for intrinsic stimuli of days, and is accessible to several experimental techniques allowing for the acquisition of quantitative data. The classical techniques of western blotting and immunoprecipitation enable coincidental acquisition of time-resolved population data for proteins and their intermediate processing stages. Fluorescence-based flow cytometry techniques allow measuring the protein concentrations at the single-cell level. A major disadvantage of flow cytometry is the inability of tracking time-dependent behavior of individual cells. This problem is overcome by fluorescence-based microscopic methods that were developed to obtain quantitative data of single cells with high temporal resolution: The activity of caspases can be monitored with FRET reporters or smart probes that harbor caspase cleavage sites (Tyas et al. 2000; Rehm et al. 2002; Beaudouin et al. 2013). Moreover, the mitochondrial pathway of apoptosis can be monitored by measuring Bax translocation, outer membrane permeabilization and Smac release (Albeck et al. 2008). The wide range of available experimental techniques and the detailed knowledge about molecular events render apoptosis a system suitable for modeling analyses. Apoptosis induced by death ligands is one of the few cell fate decisions known to proceed by purely post-transcriptional mechanisms, thus further simplifying the formulation of mathematical models.

Even though individual steps of the apoptotic signal transduction cascades are well understood, we lack insights into the system properties and the dynamics of the death decision. Questions to be addressed in apoptosis by systems biology approaches include:

(i) How do cells ensure that apoptosis robustly occurs in all-or-none manner? What is the "point-of-no-return" representing irreversibility in apoptosis? Which signaling motifs are responsible for such digital and context-specific behavior? As detailed below, mechanisms proposed using kinetic modeling include bistability due to positive feedback and sigmoidal responses arising from competitive inhibition.

(ii) How is specificity in the apoptosis *vs.* survival responses ensured? A topic of particular interest for apoptosis modeling is that apoptotic stimuli trigger survival or death signaling depending on initial conditions and the stimulus strength. At least in some cases, the inhibitory crosstalk between survival and cell death signaling pathways appears to be mutually exclusive at the single-cell level (Nair et al. 2004), implying that death and survival represent different attractor states for the cell. Modeling can be employed to identify critical nodes of signaling crosstalk that tip the balance between cell death and survival. Furthermore, the interlocked regulation of cell cycle is a topic followed by modelers. In this context the characterization of attractors, of fixed points and limit cycles is of interest.

(iii) What are the principles underlying cell-to-cell variability in the apoptosis response of a cell population? Why do cell types differ widely in their sensitivity to death-inducing stimuli? Currently, several new therapeutic agents are tested to stimulate apoptosis in cancer cells, to decelerate tumor growth, or to prevent cells, preferentially neurons or cardiomyocytes, from undergoing programmed cell death. Modeling approaches could help to plan therapies and to predict the outcome on a population of cells. Particularly by distinguishing cell death kinetics and the behavioral heterogeneity of different cell types, and predicting drug sensitization by co-treatments, modeling is a valuable tool. We will describe and review strategies to predict cell death kinetics of single cells and of heterogeneous cell populations.

(iv) How can models be used to predict the responsiveness of cancer cell populations toward cancer therapy? Starting from a certain model topology and measured numbers of pro- or anti-apoptotic signaling species, predictions of cell fates resulting from concentration trajectories at given input stimulus, represented e.g., by a drug concentration, can be obtained. In the context of cell-to-cell variability of initial protein concentrations one is reminded of the problem of fractional killing by chemotherapies: while applying a certain chemotherapeutic protocol stimulates apoptosis in a fraction of cancer cells, the surviving fraction will continue dividing. In the future, characterizing the variability of initial protein concentrations in a tumor cell population combined with mathematical modeling might support optimization of drug concentration trajectories or support the choice of efficient drug combinations to facilitate the eradication of a heterogeneous population of cancer cells. We will review applications of apoptosis models to predict the response of patients to cell death targeting therapies.

In the following, we will first give an overview of different modeling approaches and then review successful application of ODE apoptosis models to resolve biological questions. This chapter is an updated version of a previous chapter in "Systems Biology of Apoptosis" (Kallenberger and Legewie 2013) with a particular focus on applications of ODE models in cancer research.

2 OVERVIEW OF MATHEMATICAL FORMALISMS

Analyzing the cell on a systems view can be done by top-down and bottom-up approaches. Detailed mechanistic mathematical models constructed from the molecular characteristics of individual proteins ("bottom-up models") have so far only been developed for metabolic and signaling networks. In contrast, transcriptional regulatory networks, and the link between signaling networks and ultimate cellular decisions are best tackled by statistical methods which integrate huge amounts of data but are mostly phenomenological ("top-down modeling").

Top-down approaches examine the cell on a global level, treating individual regulatory modules as black boxes that are not analyzed mechanistically but only characterized with respect to input-output behavior. Thus, top-down methods typically do not require much prior knowledge about the system, so that many signaling and/or metabolic pathways can be studied at once. Most top-down approaches are solely data-driven and rely on high throughput screens of cellular behavior (gene expression profiling, proteomics, siRNA screening, sequencing, and affinity assays). Typically, the ultimate goal of top-down approaches is to identify biologically relevant patterns and correlations to the data (e.g., disease marker gene identification) or to predict new molecular interactions (e.g., reverse engineering algorithms).

Bottom-up approaches focus on well-characterized parts of the biochemical regulatory network, and are typically based on the assumption that the properties of these subnetworks (or "modules") can be studied in isolation. Based on prior knowledge and on time-resolved experimental data, mechanistic mathematical models describing the interactions of individual proteins in the module are constructed (e.g., by using sets of coupled differential equations). The goal of bottom-up modeling is to identify physiologically relevant systems-level properties emerging from complex interactions within the network (e.g., feedback).

Apoptosis-inducing signaling cascades, especially those induced by death ligands, were mainly studied using bottom-up modeling approaches, since: (i) the molecular events are well characterized; (ii) transcriptional events can be neglected; (iii) the ultimate death decision often closely correlates with all-or-none activation of effector caspases, implying that statistical methods are not required to link signaling to cellular phenotypes. However, bottom-up approaches to apoptosis are diverse and the methodology of choice depends on the complexity of the signaling network under study, the available experimental data, and the question to be addressed by modeling. Boolean approaches are typically employed to qualitatively analyze the (quasi-)static behavior of large apoptosis-survival crosstalk networks which comprise many molecular species. Ordinary differential equation (ODE) models allow for the quantitative description of network dynamics but typically require knowledge about many kinetic parameters which either limits the network size and/or requires huge amounts of experimental data. Standard ODE modeling may even not be sufficient if spatiotemporally resolved single-cell data is available: (i) spatial gradients within the cell can be modeled using subcellular compartment ODE models or partial differential equations (PDEs), (ii) cell-to-cell variability may arise due to stochastic dynamics of the apoptotic signaling cascade ("intrinsic noise") or due to cell-to-cell variability in the expression of pathway components ("extrinsic noise"). While ODE models with randomly sampled initial protein concentrations can be employed to simulate extrinsic noise, stochastic simulation algorithms are required to understand intrinsic noise. In the following, we will give an overview of top-down and bottom-up modeling approaches applied to apoptosis signaling, before discussing applications of ODE models in more detail.

2.1 Linear regression models

To systematically analyze how the pro- and anti-apoptotic cytokines TNF, EGF and insulin impinge on the cellular apoptosis decision, Janes et al. (2005) generated a compendium of co-stimulation measurements. Based on the assumption that simple linear combinations of signaling activity profiles account for apoptosis initiation, they employed a top-down modeling approach known as partial least-squares regression (PLSR) which does not require prior knowledge. PLS modeling calculates super axes as an orthogonal set of "principal components", which contain linear combinations of the original signaling protein activities weighted by their contribution to the apoptotic outputs. Thereby, the dimension of the data matrix is reduced to a small set of informative super axes, which can be used to predict apoptosis initiation for any experimental condition provided that measurements of signaling species used for model training are available. PLSR has been successfully applied to large-scale apoptosis datasets, and provided insights into complex phenomena such as autocrine amplification loops (Janes et al. 2005) or cytokine-modulated inter-relationships between different signaling pathways following DNA damage (Tentner et al. 2012). A major drawback of PLSR is the lack of mechanistic insights into (i) how signaling activity patterns are generated and (ii) how signaling activities are integrated, e.g., at the level of caspases, to control the death decision. Therefore, the next section will be devoted to bottom-up approaches applied to apoptosis which take into account mechanisms of apoptosis initiation.

2.2 Boolean models

Recent biomedical research revealed a plethora of protein-protein and enzymatic interactions, and thus extensively characterized the topology of the intracellular signaling network. However, quantitative information characterizing the affinity of protein-protein interactions or enzyme kinetic parameters is still scarce. Moreover, quantitative characterization is often performed using recombinant proteins *in vitro*, with questionable relevance to the *in vivo* situation. Simulations of large-scale networks is therefore often performed using Boolean or logic modeling, a qualitative approach that is based on network topology, but does not take into account quantitative features of individual reactions. Instead protein activities are represented by nodes which can either be on or off (activity 0 or 1), depending on the activities of upstream input nodes. Logic rules are applied at each iteration: For example, in a so-called *AND-gate*, the node Z will be activated if and only if *both* input nodes X and Y are active. In contrast, an *OR-gate* simply requires either X or Y to be active. Thus, Boolean rules can be used to qualitatively represent real biochemical mechanisms such as functional redundancy (*OR-gate*) or coincidence detection (*AND-gate*), the latter, arising from sequential processing by two distinct enzymes. Since logical rules are applied iteratively, the approach can be used to study temporal phenomena such as adaptation. Moreover, Boolean networks can exhibit nonlinear dynamic phenomena such as oscillations, and stable *vs*. unstable attractors.

A number of Boolean modeling studies have been presented in the context of apoptosis (Calzone et al. 2010; Mai and Liu 2009; Philippi et al. 2009; Schlatter et al. 2009; Zhang et al. 2008). All these studies analyzed the crosstalk of apoptosis signaling *via* caspases and survival pathways such as NF-kB signaling. The main goal was the identification of stable states in the systems, representing cell fates such as apoptosis, necrosis, and survival. Calzone et al. (2010) and Mai and Liu (2009) focused on signaling upon death receptor engagement. They showed that the stable states of the apoptosis network are robust and investigated the requirements for irreversibility in the apoptosis decision. Schlatter et al. (2009) and Philippi et al. (2009) took into account co-stimulation with pro-death and pro-survival ligands, and experimentally confirmed key model predictions. Zhang et al. (2008) analyzed antigen-induced survival signaling network in T cell large granular lymphocyte (T-LGL) leukemia cells including transcriptional induction of cytokines and autocrine stimulation events. Model predictions could be confirmed in leukemic cells isolated from patients, thus contributing to our understanding of signaling deregulation in the disease. Taken together, Boolean modeling approaches provided valuable insights into apoptosis at multiple timescales and for various experimental settings.

2.3 Quantitative modeling approaches

Although helpful to understand principles of network topologies, Boolean models are inherently limited in their capability of quantitatively describing the temporal dynamics of biochemical networks. In the context of perturbation analysis, Boolean approaches are restricted to the simulation of complete elimination of network nodes and/or reactions; thus, gradual phenomena such as dosage compensation cannot be studied. Moreover, the qualitative effects of perturbations as revealed by Boolean modeling are often intuitively clear. Thus, in many cases, nontrivial and experimentally testable predictions require quantitative modeling approaches such as ODE and PDE modeling, as well as stochastic simulations.

An ODE model comprises a network of coupled rate equations for every involved signaling species. The kinetics of each involved reaction is described with reaction rates dependent on the concentrations of educts and products. Specifically, one typically assumes that the number of product molecules synthesized in a certain time interval is linearly dependent on the concentrations of educt molecules (law of mass action). The net influx or efflux arising from all participating reactions determines the rate of change in each molecular species. Thus, ODE modeling is based on the assumption that the temporal derivatives of molecule concentrations equal the sum of all relevant reaction rates. Larger biochemical signal transduction networks are therefore reflected using coupled ODEs (see Chapter 3 by Westerhoff et al. for details).

Figure 19.1 illustrates the process of working with ODE models that are calibrated with experimental data, as it is typically applied in studies on apoptosis models. Conflicting hypotheses on biochemical mechanisms that are translated to alternative model topologies can be tested by assessing, which model variant can explain a set of experimental data sufficiently well. Kinetic parameters and initial protein concentrations are estimated, as well as scaling factors between model variables and experimental data, by fitting an ODE model to experimental data. An identifiability analysis can show if estimated parameters can be successfully determined from the given set of experimental data or are unidentifiable (Raue et al. 2009, 2010; Hengl et al. 2007). An unidentifiable parameter can have different values without reducing the fit quality, eventually being correlated with another unidentifiable parameter, which decreases the predictive power of the model. For model validation, experimental observable trajectories under different starting conditions as in the training data set (e.g., changed protein levels by knock-down or overexpression), can be predicted and tested by recording further experimental data under these conditions. After fitting alternative model variants, the most likely model can be determined by comparing values of the maximum likelihood estimator χ^2, using methods as the likelihood ratio test or the Akaike information criterion (AIC) (Burnham and Anderson 2010). If clear discrimination between alternative models is not possible, experimental conditions can be chosen, in which predictions from different candidate models differ the most. After having validated a model, its kinetic properties can be analyzed by a sensitivity analysis. The relevance of model reactions on the concentration of a model species at a certain time point can be determined by calculating derivatives to kinetic parameters, as applied in different apoptosis modeling studies (Bentele et al. 2004; Ho and Harrington 2010; Neumann et al. 2010). Furthermore, Direct Lyapunov Exponent (DLE) analysis has been used in apoptosis models to characterize functional roles of signaling

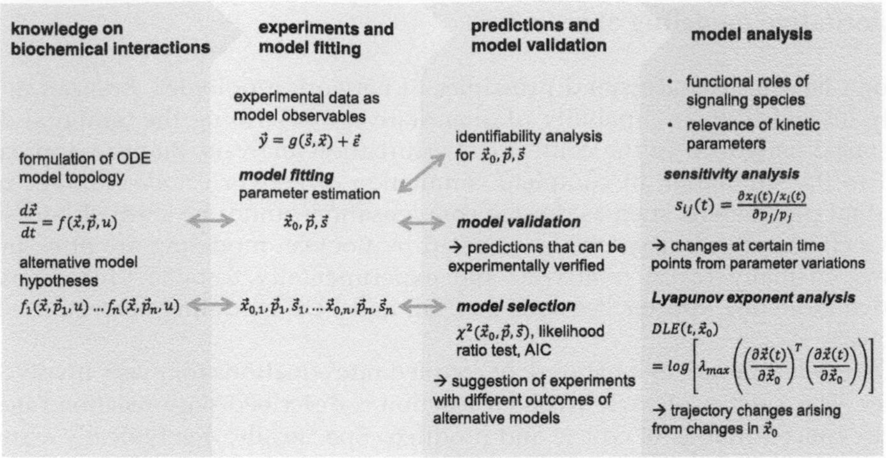

FIGURE 19.1 Overview of ODE modeling used in several apoptosis modeling studies. Biochemical knowledge on a signal transduction network can be translated to a system of coupled ODEs with variables $\overrightarrow{x}$, parameters $\overrightarrow{p}$ and an external stimulus u, which could be a cell death ligand or drug concentration. Conflicting mechanistic hypotheses can be translated to alternative model topologies. By model fitting to experimental data represented by observables $\overrightarrow{y}$ with experimental errors $\overrightarrow{\varepsilon}$, initial concentrations $\overrightarrow{x_0}$, parameters $\overrightarrow{p}$, and scaling factors $\overrightarrow{s}$ are estimated. After fitting of model variants, a model selection can be carried out based on methods as the likelihood ratio test or the Akaike information criterion (AIC). Identifiability of estimated parameters can be analyzed and experiments can be predicted for model validation or further model discrimination. To characterize kinetic properties of the underlying biochemical signal transduction network a sensitivity analysis can be conducted. Direct Lyapunov exponents (DLE), calculated from the maximum eigenvalue $\overrightarrow{\gamma}$ of a matrix containing derivatives of the variables $\overrightarrow{x_n}$ against initial values $\overrightarrow{x_0}$, can be used to characterize the dependency of model trajectories on initial concentrations (Aldridge et al. 2006).

species. By this method, trajectory changes of model species due to changes in initial concentrations of involved signaling proteins can be determined to analyze consequences for cellular fates (Aldridge et al. 2006, 2011).

ODE approaches assume that large numbers of signaling molecules are present within the cell, so that random fluctuations in reaction events can be neglected by averaging over the whole molecule population. Moreover, in ODE modeling it is assumed that the cell represents a well-stirred reactor, implying that diffusion effects do not matter and that special gradients, which are described in PDEs, can be neglected. In apoptosis networks, these assumptions are likely to be fulfilled, as caspases and their regulators are typically expressed at the number of several hundred thousand molecules per cell (Svingen et al. 2004). Furthermore, the time scale of apoptosis induction (hours) is slow relative to the time scale of protein diffusion within a cell (milliseconds to seconds); therefore, spatial gradients of apoptosis signaling molecules are unlikely to play a decisive role in apoptosis initiation.

Nonetheless, reaction-diffusion models allowed investigating molecular mechanisms of apoptosis induction: Using live-cell imaging with high temporal resolution, Rehm and colleagues observed that cytochrome c release from mitochondria during apoptosis occurs in spatial waves that propagate from a subcellular mitochondrial pool to the remainder of the mitochondrial population (Rehm et al. 2009). Partial differential equation (PDE) modeling was employed to investigate the dynamics of non-steady-state diffusion. This approach revealed that localized release and diffusion of inducers of mitochondrial outer membrane permeabilization (MOMP) alone was insufficient to explain the data. However, then the authors took into account that MOMP inducers bind to mitochondria, and modeling indicated that this absorption shapes the dynamics of cytochrome c release, thus providing insights into molecular mechanisms controlling apoptosis induction.

Owing to low molecule numbers of Bcl-2 family members, stochastic simulations using cellular automaton approaches were performed by Chen et al. (2007a), Siehs et al. (2002), and Düssmann et al. (2010) to describe the dynamics of mitochondrial outer membrane permeabilization (MOMP). Chen et al. (2007a) focused on bistability and concluded that the stochastic system attained two distinct stable states much like the deterministic case; thus robustness of switching toward molecular noise could be confirmed. Düssmann et al. (2010) compared their model to measurements in cells expressing Bax-FRET probes monitoring Bax oligomerization. Their model could provide an explanation for pore formation upon Bax accumulation and oligomerization in the outer mitochondria membrane. A further study making use of cellular automaton approaches explained the stoichiometry of DISC components that was observed in mass spectrometry experiments (Schleich et al. 2012). These experiments showed that in immunoprecipitates of DISCs, the number of procaspase-8 and c-FLIP molecules exceeds the number of FADD molecules several-fold, suggesting that chains of procaspase-8 and c-FLIP are formed on DISC-bound FADD molecules. A cellular automaton model was used to reproduce the observed protein ratios, and to test further hypotheses on chain lengths and chain formation kinetics. This approach facilitated handling the large combinatorial complexity arising from possible compositions of larger protein chains of FADD, c-FLIP, and procaspase-8, in comparison to an ODE model that would require a large number of equations for each possible oligomer state.

Live-cell imaging tools are increasingly important and allow the analysis of apoptosis at the single cell level or even with subcellular resolution. Thus, stochastic and reaction-diffusion modeling are likely to become central to apoptosis modeling. For example, death receptors are frequently expressed at low levels and form localized (nano-) clusters on the cell membrane (Dumitru and Gulbins, 2006), implying that deterministic ODE approaches will fail, especially upon weak stimulation. Stochastic and reaction-diffusion modeling will reveal underlying mechanisms and, more importantly, predict strategies for intervention for testing the functional relevance of such phenomena.

3 MECHANISTIC ODE MODELS DESCRIBING APOPTOSIS NETWORKS

The first mechanistic apoptosis model of coupled differential equations, presented by Fussenegger et al. (2000), described sequential activation of caspase-8, caspase-9, and caspase-3 by intrinsic or extrinsic stimuli. The model accounted for a positive feedback from caspase-3 promoting the release of cytochrome c from mitochondria and thus promoting the additional activation of caspase-9 in apoptosomes. As this model was not trained against quantitative data, it provided only predictions on activated fractions of initiator and executioner caspases dependent on initial concentrations of apoptosis promoting or inhibiting proteins. A lot of progress has been made since this first apoptosis model, and different aspects have been studied in detail.

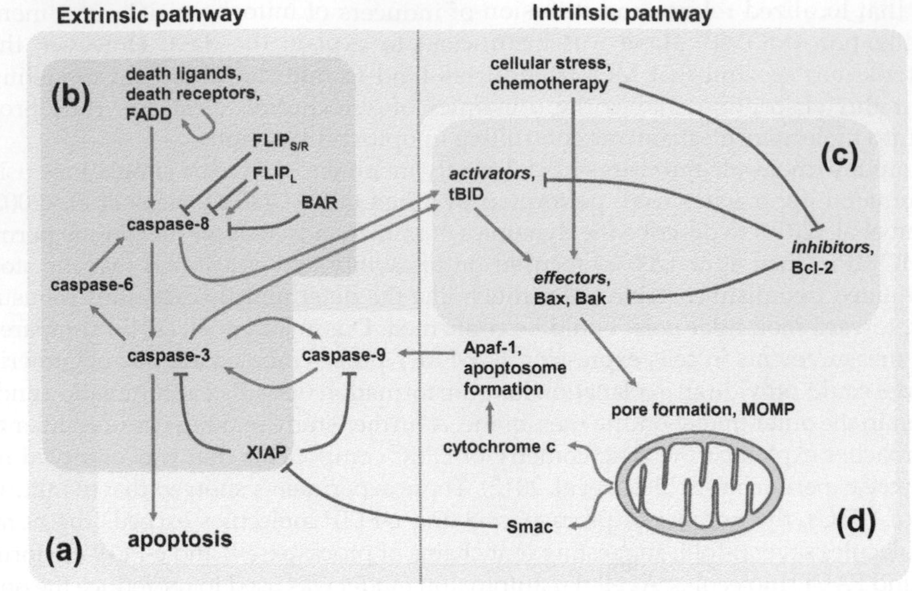

FIGURE 19.2 Overview of the extrinsic and intrinsic parts of the apoptotic signaling network. Subareas are indicated that were investigated by current modeling studies. (a) Modeling studies that captured extrinsic and intrinsic pathways (Bentele et al. 2004; Fussenegger et al. 2000; Bagci et al. 2006; Hua et al. 2005; Albeck et al. 2008; Harrington et al. 2008; Okazaki et al. 2008). (b) Modeling studies with main focus on the level of death receptors, DISC assembly and caspase activation processes (Ho and Harrington 2010; Neumann et al. 2010; Eissing et al. 2004; Laussmann et al. 2012; Würstle et al. 2010; Fricker et al. 2010). (c) Modeling studies that described interactions between members of the Bcl-2 family prior to mitochondria outer membrane permeabilization (MOMP) Chen et al. 2007a,b; Siehs et al. 2002; Düssmann et al. 2010; Lindner et al. 2013; Cui et al. 2008. (d) Modeling studies with main focus on intrinsic apoptosis and caspase inhibition (Rehm et al. 2006; Legewie et al. 2006; Stucki and Simon 2005; Huber et al. 2011; Zhang et al. 2009).

In the following, we will review the current literature on ODE-based apoptosis modeling. Figure 19.2 shows an overview about subareas of the apoptotic signaling network that were investigated by current models. First, we will describe models which understand apoptosis as a bistable process. Second, we will summarize studies investigating the temporal dynamics of apoptosis. Third, crosstalk models describing apoptosis and survival networks will be discussed. The final focus of our review will be cell-to-cell variability.

3.1 Origins of a robust all-or-none behavior—models characterized by bistability and feedback mechanisms

Bistability may play an important role for all-or-none and irreversible decision making, thus allowing the suppression of noise and prevention from accidental apoptotic stimuli. In the following, we will review models exhibiting bistability due to positive feedback in the intrinsic or extrinsic apoptosis pathways.

3.1.1 *Extrinsic apoptosis pathway*

Understanding bistability in the process of apoptosis initiation was the focus of the study of Eissing et al. (2004). Their model described the bistability in extrinsic apoptosis within the context of caspase-mediated positive feedback. Caspase-8 activated by receptor-induced apoptosis in type I cells activates caspase-3, while caspase-3 promotes positive feedback by caspase-8 activation. A stability analysis showed, which kinetic parameter values allowed bistability, and therefore a stable steady state for survival. It could be shown that bistability was only possible at parameter values far off the experimentally measured kinetic parameters. By extending the model topology, the authors concluded that bistable caspase activation within the physiologically reasonable parameter range required the consideration of inhibitors of activated caspase-8. Specifically, it was suggested that caspase-8 inhibitory proteins such as the bifunctional apoptosis regulator protein (BAR) (Zhang et al. 2000), and caspase-8 and -10-associated RING proteins (CARPs) (McDonald and El-Deiry 2004) play a central role for establishing bistability. The important anti-apoptotic role of the protein BAR was further investigated in the study of Pace et al. (2010).

Bistability on the ligand/receptor level was proposed upon theoretical considerations of a positive feedback in receptor oligomerization reactions (Ho and Harrington 2010). These were motivated by new insights into the structure and function of CD95 (APO-1/Fas) molecules (Scott et al. 2009). Protein crystallization experiments on receptor/FADD-clusters had shown that receptors in the absence of ligands favor a closed form where FADD cannot bind. Upon ligand binding an open form is favored, allowing FADD binding, DISC formation, and signal progression. The conformation of open receptors leads to the mutual stabilization of the receptors in their open state, which may cause receptor oligomerization and positive feedback amplification. An ODE model was formulated in a continuum approximation where molecule numbers were treated as local protein concentrations (Ho and Harrington, 2010). At high receptor densities, which could be potentially induced locally inside lipid rafts, reactions can take place where several open receptors stabilize each other. In the model these events could be approximated by higher order reactions. Rate equations for reactions that contain terms with an order of three or larger can have two stable steady states and one unstable steady state in between, which causes bistable behavior. Therefore, depending on the local receptor densities, reversible or irreversible bistability can result. This leads to an all-or-none response on the level of DISCs, resulting in a gradual response, integrated over all clusters on the cell level.

3.1.2 *Intrinsic apoptosis pathway*

The theoretical study by Bagci et al. (2006) addressed origins of bistability on the level of mitochondrial outer membrane permeabilization (MOMP) and apoptosome formation. Two positive feedback mechanisms contribute to bistability: First, caspase-3 cleaves and inactivates the MOMP inhibitor Bcl-2, and thereby amplifies its own production. A second feedback arises from the cleavage of the MOMP inducer Bid by caspase-3; thus Bid cleavage, initially triggered by caspase-8, can be enhanced by caspase-3. Their mass-action model describes oligomerization of Apaf-1 bound to cytochrome c to the heptameric complexes of apoptosomes. As this cooperative oligomerization process leads to higher order terms in the corresponding rate equation, the positive feedback interactions can result in bistable regimes corresponding to either survival or apoptosis. As the model of Bagci et al. (2006) does not consider reactions upstream of initiator caspases, initial doses of caspase-8 and caspase-3 serve as stimulus. Their considerations were motivated by experimental studies that had shown a survival mechanism of cancer cells based on elevated Bax degradation (Li and Dou 2000), decreased Bax expression in human breast cancers (Schorr 1999) or overexpression of Bcl-2 (Reed 1999). In the model of Bagci et al., bifurcation points in the caspase-3 activity were investigated, that are dependent on the production or degradation of Bax and their relation to inhibitory Bcl-2 proteins. Above a certain threshold for the degradation rate of Bax or below a certain threshold for the Bax production rate, the bistable behavior is changed into a monostable survival state. In this state an initiator caspase stimulus cannot trigger the apoptosome-mediated feedback anymore.

In a subsequent study the model was expanded to investigate the modulation of bistable switching by nitric oxide (NO) signaling which plays a dual role in the regulation of apoptosis and survival (Bagci et al. 2008): Several nitric oxide species such as NO or dinitrogen trioxide (N_2O_3) prevent apoptosis by inactivating both caspase-8 and caspase-3 (Li et al. 1997; Mannick et al. 1999; Rössig et al. 1999). In contrast, the NO species peroxynitrite (ONOO-) promotes apoptosis by triggering mitochondrial pore formation (Vieira et al. 2001). The model of Bagci et al. (2008) quantitatively describes the metabolism of nitric oxide species, and their effect on apoptosis. While NO species that exclusively inhibit caspase-8 only delay apoptosis, such species that inhibit caspase-3 as well as caspase-8 can prevent the bistable feedback from apoptosome formation, and cause survival. Bagci et al. also investigated the impact of glutathione which acts as a regulator of nitric oxide metabolism (Hu et al. 2006). Their model suggested that the pro-apoptotic effect of glutathione by inhibiting anti-apoptotic NO species is stronger than its anti-apoptotic effect by inhibiting NO species that facilitate mitochondria permeabilization.

Current studies on Bcl-2 family members show even more complicated relations on the level of mitochondria among proteins that act as sensitizers (as Bad, Noxa or Puma), activators (Bid, Bim), or effectors (Bax, Bak). To characterize the vulnerability of tumors to apoptosis effectors, the impacts of different Bcl-2 family members on mitochondria isolated from tumor samples were investigated (Certo et al. 2006; Deng et al. 2007). For more detailed reviews see (Brunelle and Letai 2009; Ni Chonghaile and Letai 2008; Vo et al. 2010).

Recently, models of intrinsic cell death were applied to predict the responsiveness of patient tumors to chemotherapies (Hector et al. 2012; Lindner et al. 2013; Murphy et al. 2013). Two studies applied a model describing activation of caspase-9 and caspase-3 after MOMP, cytochrome c and Smac release and inhibition of XIAP, which was originally developed based on experiments in common lab cell lines (Rehm et al. 2006). Measurements of Apaf-1, XIAP, Smac, procaspase-3 and -9 levels in patient tumor samples of colorectal cancers (Hector et al. 2012) and glioblastoma multiforme brain tumors (Murphy et al. 2013) were used as initial concentrations for model simulations. In the study on colon cancer samples, model simulations were used to predict if effector caspases activity could be effectively evoked by applying chemotherapy, and model predictions were significantly correlated with observed clinical outcomes (Hector et al. 2012). Similarly, the study on brain tumor samples showed that model simulations were correlated with progression free survival durations in patients (Murphy et al. 2013). A model describing interactions between pro- and anti-apoptotic Bcl-2 family members was developed by Lindner et al. to predict responses of colon cancers to chemotherapy with 5-FU and oxaliplatin, based on the quantification of Bak, Bax, Bcl-2, Bcl-xL, and Mcl-1 in tumor samples compared to normal tissue (Lindner et al. 2013). Similar to the study focused on signaling species downstream of MOMP, knowledge of Bcl-2 family member levels facilitated model predictions of responses to chemotherapy that were highly correlated with observed clinical outcomes. Furthermore, their model enabled predictions, which patients may be successfully co-treated with BH3-mimetic drugs as ABT-263, ABT-737 or ApoG2 that mimic natural inhibitors of anti-apoptotic Bcl-2 family members (Lessene et al. 2008).

Taken together, models of intrinsic cell death could successfully reveal mechanisms of interactions between pro- and anti-apoptotic Bcl-2 family members and show promising results with regard to chemotherapy optimization.

3.1.3 *Implicit feedback mechanisms in the intrinsic apoptosis pathway*

In the modeling studies summarized so far, the positive feedback mechanisms known from the biomedical literature and their contribution to bistability were analyzed. Additionally, mathematical modeling can provide valuable insights into non-obvious, hidden feedback loops that arise from the topology of the apoptosis network. This phenomenon has been referred to as implicit positive feedback regulation. The interplay of caspase-3, caspase-9, and inhibitors of apoptosis (IAPs) in the mitochondrial pro-apoptotic pathway was investigated in a model by Legewie et al. (2006): Cytochrome c released from mitochondria, triggers activation of caspase-9, which in turn cleaves procaspase-3 into active caspase-3. Both caspase-3 and caspase-9 are inhibited by XIAPs to prevent auto-reactive activation. Interestingly, an implicit positive feedback loop arises from the dual inhibition of both caspases by XIAPs: Once active caspase-3 is generated, it can bind to XIAPs, thus sequestering XIAPs away from caspase-9. This sequestration effect enhances caspase-9 activation, resulting in auto-amplification of caspase-3 cleavage. In the model by Legewie et al. the dependency of the concentration of active caspase-3 as the response to an Apaf-1 concentration shows different characteristics of either monostable, bistable reversible or bistable irreversible behavior. The authors concluded that implicit positive feedback alone brings a very small range of bistability; however, implicit feedback synergizes with other feedback mechanisms to establish a broad bistable range and irreversibility in the life-death decision.

The studies of Chen et al. (2007a,b) combined ODE, stochastic, and cellular automaton modeling to further understand signaling processes that potentially lead to MOMP. In these studies interactions between pore forming *effectors* (Bax, Bak), *activators* and *enablers* (tBid and several others), and *inhibitors* (Bcl-2 among others) that lead to or prevent mitochondria outer membrane permeabilization are analyzed. After translocation to mitochondria, inactive Bax and Bak are catalyzed to their active form by an *activator*. Subsequently, activated Bax and Bak lead to membrane pore formation and cell death. In the study of Cui et al. (2008) models involved in the bistability of MOMP were further developed. Questions on the possible model topology led to hierarchical considerations in the studies of Chen et al. (2007a,b) as well as Cui et al. (2008): Do activators and enablers *indirectly* induce apoptosis by sequestering Bcl-2 away from Bax, or are activators *directly* pro-apoptotic by catalyzing the reaction of Bax to its active form that can cause pore formation and cytochrome c release? This question led to an indirect model recapturing the inhibition of Bcl-2 by activators and topologies describing direct Bax activation. Inhibitors as Bcl-2 in the indirect topology interfere by inhibiting Bax and thereby preventing its oligomerization at the pores. In direct topologies they inhibit activators from catalyzing Bax activation. Direct topologies were favored in this study, as they involve two possible feedback mechanisms that could contribute to a bistability in Bax activation. These considerations were motivated by experimental studies that showed a bimodal distribution of cells that had low or high amounts of activated Bax and Bak monitored by flow cytometry (Fischer et al. 2004; Gómez-Benito et al. 2005; Willis et al. 2005). The first described feedback mechanism is facilitated by activated Bax that can sequester Bcl-2, leading to an increase of free activators and thereby providing increased Bax activation. This mechanism is similar to the role of XIAP as discussed in the study of Legewie et al. (2006), since Bcl-2 acts as a dual inhibitor of upstream activators and their downstream effector Bax. Furthermore, the model of Cui et al. (2008) considers a feedback mechanism, in which activated Bax itself provides further Bax activation. In their study the signal response behavior is characterized by the dependency of active Bax and Bcl-2 steady-state levels as dependent on the production rate of activators. In a model containing both feedback mechanisms the interval of activator production rates that lead to bistability of active Bax and Bcl-2 concentrations is significantly enlarged compared to a variant with only one feedback mechanism. Therefore, the combination of both feedback mechanisms would provide a higher robustness for the bistable behavior of Bax activation and mitochondria pore formation.

3.2 Origins of a robust all-or-none behavior—Switching and threshold mechanisms other than bistability

Biochemical signaling networks may exhibit switching mechanisms other than bistability arising from positive feedback. In such cases, the system exhibits a single steady state which increases in a steep, nonlinear manner with increasing input concentration. Such sigmoidal, all-or-none dose-response behavior has been termed ultrasensitivity. One ultrasensitivity mechanism with particular relevance to apoptosis is inhibitor ultrasensitivity: here, a protein inhibitor strongly binds to its target, implying that the target remains completely inactive unless the total concentration exceeds the total inhibitor concentration (Ferrell 1996). Thus, the stoichiometry between inhibitor and target determines the system behavior, explaining why the mechanism is also known as stoichiometric switch.

The critical roles of c-FLIP$_L$ and c-FLIP$_S$, which potentially act as stoichiometric inhibitors in the death-inducing signaling complex, were investigated in a model of Bentele et al. (2004). The dependence of the ligand concentration threshold on the concentrations of both splicing variants of c-FLIP was characterized, and it was concluded that c-FLIPs establish a stoichiometric switch. A large-scale model comprising DISC assembly, caspase activation, MOMP, interference from caspase inhibitors, and degradation processes was derived. The model could be fitted to quantitative western blot data (caspase-8, -2, -7, -3, -9, Bid, PARP) representing population measures of protein concentrations under different ligand concentrations using hierarchical parameter estimation. By a global sensitivity analysis clusters of modeled signaling proteins with high mutual sensitivities of protein concentrations were defined, which lead to functional subsystems. By disregarding parameters that had low sensitivities to parameters in one cluster the dimensionality of the parameter estimation problem could be decreased. Predictions of the reduced model were subsequently verified experimentally. Most importantly, it could be shown that the threshold ligand concentration was highly sensitive to the c-FLIP concentration, which is consistent with a stoichiometric switch mechanism.

A refined version of the Bentele model was presented in the theoretical study of Toivonen et al. (2011), which took into account fast turnover of c-FLIP variants that could be relevant for their anti-apoptotic effect. It could be shown that the concentration of c-FLIP at the time of ligand addition is central to apoptosis timing. Recently, accumulation of c-FLIP due to proteasome inhibition was investigated in a study by Laussmann et al. (2012). As a direct effect, c-FLIP overexpression delays caspase-8 activation. Changes in apoptosis kinetics, however, were not intuitive as proteasome inhibition simultaneously caused TRAIL receptor 2 accumulation. Therefore, pro- and anti-apoptotic effects of proteasome inhibition were investigated by a kinetic model.

Another ultrasensitivity mechanism with potential relevance to apoptosis is protein dimerization. For protein dimerization the steady state of the active dimer depends on the total protein concentration in a quadratic manner. Thus, weak input signals controlling the concentration of the monomer species can be suppressed, while stronger inputs are transmitted. This phenomenon, known as multistep ultrasensitivity, was analyzed by Würstle et al. (2010) as described in the following.

In the absence of death receptor ligands, the amplification loop from active caspase-8 to caspase-3, from activated caspase-8 to caspase-6 and back to caspase-8, has to be silenced to prevent apoptosis induction at low levels of active caspase-8. Würstle et al. compared different model variants to understand how efficient suppression of the amplification loop can be achieved (Würstle et al. 2010). First, they analyzed the role of well-known caspase inhibitors such as the caspase-8 inhibitor BAR and the caspase-3 inhibitor XIAP. Second, they took into account that only caspase-8 dimers are catalytically active, and considered de-dimerization of caspase-8 complexes released from the DISC. In this context, it had been shown experimentally that the caspase-8 dimerization equilibrium favors the formation of caspase-8 monomers (Pop et al. 2007). A core model describing the activation loop only was extended by either one of these three inhibiting mechanisms. Time series of caspase activation and substrate cleavage by caspase-3 caused by mild initial stimuli of caspase-8, -3, or -6, were calculated for each model variant, using experimentally measured kinetic constants for caspase activities and caspase-8 dimerization. Subsequently, time courses of the model variables were calculated under various initial concentrations of procaspases-3, -6, and -8, BAR and XIAP to assess the sensitivity of the system toward each inhibitory mechanism in a time interval of 24 h, respectively. Each parameter constellation leading to less than 20% substrate cleavage was classified as non-apoptotic, while more than 80% substrate cleavage was considered as effective apoptosis. Thereby, model variants could be compared regarding their potential to prevent apoptosis. A model was considered as more preventive if it caused weak cleavage in a larger fraction of the randomly chosen parameter sets than other model variants. As a result of an initial stimulus of caspase-8 the numbers of parameter constellations leading to hypothetic survival were slightly higher in the XIAP model than for the de-dimerization model, while the number was highest for the de-dimerization model in response to stimuli of caspase-3 or caspase-6. The apoptosis-preventing effect of the low affinity in a caspase-8 dimer becomes evident when considering that caspase-6 can only cleave monomers of procaspase-8 in absence of a dimerization inducer as the DISC. Because of the low affinity in the caspase-8 dimer the system is especially stable against a stimulus of caspase-8 monomers. Consequently, all three inhibitory mechanisms were included into one model to assess thresholds of the maximal caspase-8 stimulus strength that could be compensated. Threshold changes upon removal of one of the mechanisms were determined that showed again the strong perturbation resistance by caspase-8 dimerization and dissociation (Würstle et al. 2010). Thus, it was concluded that the caspase-8 dimerization equilibrium efficiently prevents accidental cell death initiation.

Another monostable model of the apoptosis threshold was introduced in the theoretical study of Stucki and Simon (2005). However, these authors did not focus on the mechanism of ultrasensitivity, but represented all-or-none caspase-3 activation phenomenologically using a Heaviside function in the caspase-3 production term. The major focus of the study was to analyze how the caspase-3 activation threshold could be modulated by the caspase-3 inhibitory XIAPs, the XIAP antagonist Smac, and Smac binding anti-apoptotic proteins such as survivin (Song et al. 2003). The potentially limiting role of caspase-3 degradation was addressed, and it was concluded that XIAPs efficiently suppress apoptosis by triggering the degradation of caspase-3 in a nonlinear manner.

3.3 Models characterized by a timing switch

Steady states, bistable switches, and ultrasensitivity govern long-term decision making within biochemical signaling networks. However, in the context of apoptosis, it is also important that the time course of effector caspase activation is abrupt. Such temporal switching ensures complete and coherent initiation of cellular demise. Single cell measurements using GFP-tagged cytochrome c and caspase FRET probes confirmed that mitochondrial permeabilization and subsequent effector caspase activation indeed occur in a temporally abrupt manner (Rehm et al. 2002; Goldstein et al. 2000). Accordingly, a more recent study concluded that the apoptosis timing in single cells consists of a variable lag time followed by the sudden switch-like effector caspase activation (Albeck et al. 2008). While the lag time varies within the range of one to several hours, dependent on the stimulus strength, the sudden switching time was shown to be relatively invariant around 30 minutes. This robustness of sudden switching can be interpreted as necessary to prevent from states of partial destruction that could cause genomic instability. The lag time is lengthened by proteins upstream of activated Bax, as c-FLIP, BAR or cytosolic Bcl-2, and shortened by TRAIL receptors, caspase-8, Bid and Bax. Moreover, the robustness of the switching time is determined on the level of Bax-Bcl-2 interaction leading to mitochondria pore formation (Albeck et al. 2008). Thus, most modeling studies characterizing the temporal dynamics of apoptosis initiation in type II cells employing the mitochondrial pathway were focused on regulation at the level of caspase-8 or Bcl-2. In the following we will review the systems biological literature on the temporal dynamics of apoptosis initiation.

In the study of Hua et al. (2005) different topologies reflecting possible interactions of Bcl-2 with Bid, tBid, or Bax were compared regarding their role in controlling the kinetics of caspase-3 activation and preventing apoptosis. Four topologies, including Bcl-2 binding to Bid, tBid or Bax only, or to tBid and Bax, were implemented into a large-scale model describing extrinsic apoptosis from ligand binding to caspase-3 activation. Specifically, their model describes DISC assembly, caspase-8 activation, Bid cleavage and subsequent mitochondrial reactions (i.e., binding reactions of Bcl-2, Bax oligomerization, Smac release, cytochrome c release and apoptosome formation). By comparing experimental data from wild type and Bcl-2 overexpressing cells with simulated trajectories of the model variants, model discrimination was possible: Their experimental data supported a mechanism where the caspase-3 time course reacts very sensitively to Bcl-2 overexpression, and the model suggested that this can only be realized if Bcl-2 can simultaneously inhibit both tBid and Bax. A global sensitivity analysis on initial concentrations of the model variables gave insight into effects of overexpression or suppression. In this context it was interesting that in the model of Hua et al. suppression of Bcl-2 under its basal level did not accelerate apoptosis, which could be experimentally verified (Hua et al. 2005). This indicates that Bcl-2 inhibitors could selectively sensitize Bcl-2 overexpressing tumor cells to apoptosis (Reed et al. 1996), while not affecting non-transformed cells expressing Bcl-2 at moderate levels. The sensitivity analysis by Hua et al. showed further asymmetric effects of overexpression or suppression: In some proteins an overexpression does not affect apoptosis timing, while their suppression causes significant changes (e.g., death receptors). Taken together, the model was able to predict dynamics of caspase-3 activation with high accuracy and provided insights into mechanisms of Bcl-2 action.

Albeck et al. (2008) presented a refined model which exhibits similar complexity as the Hua et al. (2005) model, but was based on a large body of data, mostly at the single-cell level. Specifically, the model was trained against population data acquired with flow cytometry and western blotting as well as single cell imaging data. These were measured at various TRAIL concentrations and under several conditions of overexpression or depletion of signaling proteins. In the study of Albeck et al. (2008) it was shown experimentally that MOMP timing and the kinetics of Smac/cytochrome c release were only dependent on the upstream signaling network controlling caspase-8 activation, while the contribution of positive feedback was negligible. Specifically, a role of three putative positive feedback mechanisms from caspase-3, caspase-6, or caspase-9 could be excluded. This suggests that some of the bistability mechanisms discussed above do not account for the temporal dynamics of apoptosis initiation at least in HeLa cells. In contrast to other apoptosis models the cell death decision was not dependent on bistability but explained apoptosis by the monostable trans-critical process of MOMP. The interaction of Bcl-2 family members with tBid and Bax, the process of Smac release followed by the reduction of effector caspase inhibition by XIAP, and the mitochondria membrane pore formation dynamics were identified as critical stages of the all-or-none behavior of effector caspase activation. Signal transduction from MOMP to effector caspases apparently proceeds in a redundant manner through Smac inactivating XIAP and apoptosome formation causing XIAP sequestration and activation of caspase-3. In conclusion, the study by Albeck et al. currently represents the most comprehensive and realistic large-scale model of apoptosis.

In a combined experimental and theoretical study, Rehm et al. analyzed the kinetics of temporally switch-like effector caspase activation downstream of mitochondria (Rehm et al. 2006). In particular, they focused on the control of effector caspase activation by XIAP. Their model described apoptosis signaling following MOMP induced by the drug staurosporine. The agent tetramethylrhodaminemethylester (TMRM) was used to experimentally measure changes of the mitochondria membrane potential to monitor the occurrence of MOMP. In their model, Smac and cytochrome c released from mitochondria served as stimuli. Subsequent events in the model include apoptosome formation, caspase-9 as well as caspase-3 activation and caspase inhibition by XIAP. Their modeling analyses focused on the inhibition of caspase-9 and caspase-3 auto-amplification loops by XIAP, and model predictions were confirmed using single cell experiments with cells stably expressing FRET probes that contained a cleavage site for caspase-3. Specifically, their model prediction that a reduction of XIAP levels would not affect apoptosis timing, while a XIAP overexpression would significantly delay effector caspase activation, could be experimentally verified in HeLa cells and in MCF7 cells, which are completely devoid of caspase-3. Similarly, another prediction that interference on the level of Smac has only weak influences on apoptosis timing was verified. In conclusion, the study of Rehm et al. provided detailed insights into the regulative function of XIAP on the timing of effector caspase activation (Rehm et al. 2006). Recently, the model was successfully applied to explain lack of effector caspase activation after MOMP in different cancer cell lines as a result from cell death impairing combinations of Apaf-1, procaspase-9, XIAP and procaspase-3 levels (Schmid et al. 2012). Huber et al. combined approaches from metabolic engineering with the model of Rehm et al. to study the crosstalk between reactions of the respiration chain and the intrinsic apoptosis pathway (Huber et al. 2011). Their model quantitatively characterized how an increased glucose level that increases cytosolic ATP production can stabilize the transmembrane potential, a mechanism that may support the cell death evasion of cancer cells.

We expect that future research will provide much more detailed insights into the kinetics of apoptosis initiation, since various tools are now available to monitor apoptosis on several signaling levels at the single-cell level: FRET reporters consisting of two fluorescent proteins linked with a cleavage sequence for caspase-8 or caspase-3 were used to monitor the activity of initiator and effector caspases (Tyas et al. 2000; Rehm et al. 2002; Albeck et al. 2008; Rehm et al. 2006). In the study of Albeck et al. a GFP-tagged form of Bax was used to measure the translocation of Bax into mitochondria upon Bid activation (Albeck et al. 2008). Furthermore, a reporter protein that contains the mitochondria import sequence of Smac and thus accumulates in the mitochondria inter-membrane space (IMS-RP) was used to indicate MOMP in single cells. Simultaneous and quantitative description of multiple signaling levels will be a major challenge for future modeling studies.

3.4 Modeling the ambiguity between cell death and survival

Experimental studies by Nair et al. suggested that the mechanisms of cell death and survival can be mutually exclusive (Nair et al. 2004). The behavior of a population of cells upon an oxidative stress (H_2O_2) stimulus was observed. While some cells underwent apoptosis, others clearly showed a successful overcoming of the stress stimulus and a proliferative response. However, the paradigm of mutually exclusive cell death or survival processes was challenged in the subsequent experimental and theoretical studies described in this section.

To understand the double-edged role of CD95 (APO-1/Fas) activation in apoptosis as well as in NF-κB activation, models describing the role of c-FLIP on both cell fates were established (Neumann et al. 2010; Fricker et al. 2010). A focus of the models is the balance between caspase activation and inhibitory processes at the DISC. Cleavage of homodimers of the two main procaspase-8 isoforms, procaspase-8a and b (p55 and p53), bound to FADD can result in two forms that possess catalytic activity: an intermediate form p43/p41 that remains bound to the DISC as a homodimer, and the completely processed

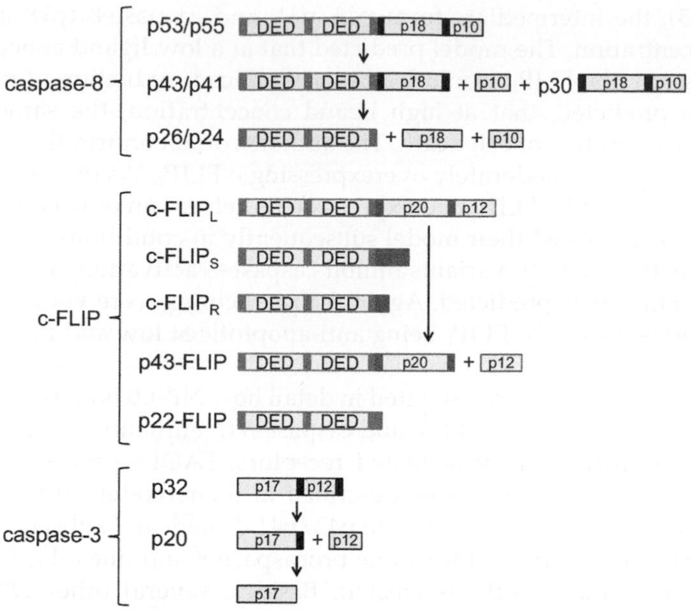

FIGURE 19.3 Forms of caspase-8, c-FLIP, and caspase-3. For caspase-8 activation the two isoforms of procaspase-8, p55 and p53, are cleaved to p43/p41 plus p18 or p26/p24 plus p30. The death effector domains (DEDs) of procaspase-8 can bind to FADD, to other procaspase-8 monomers or to the similar DEDs of c-FLIP proteins. These are c-FLIP$_L$, c-FLIP$_S$, c-FLIP$_R$, and the two cleaved forms p43-FLIP and p22-FLIP, containing catalytically inactive caspase-like domains p20 and p12 (Lavrik et al. 2005; Fricker et al. 2010). Caspase-3 exists as a pre-formed dimer and is activated by cleavage to p17 and p12.

form p18 that dissociates from the DISC as $p18_2p10_2$ heterotetramers (Hoffmann et al. 2009; Hughes et al. 2009) (Figure 19.3). Three splicing variants of the cellular FADD-like interleukin-1β-converting enzyme inhibitory protein (c-FLIP), c-FLIP short (c-FLIP$_S$), c-FLIP long (FLIP$_L$) and c-FLIP Raji (FLIP$_R$) can heterodimerize with a monomer of procaspase-8 bound to a FADD molecule at the DISC and interfere with caspase-8 activation. The two variants c-FLIP$_S$ and c-FLIP$_R$ block procaspase-8 autoprocessing in a heterodimer and therefore inhibit propagation of the apoptosis signal. In contrast, c-FLIP$_L$ can facilitate procaspase-8 cleavage to p43/p41 but not to p18. Therefore, c-FLIP$_L$ leads to heterodimers with p43/p41 at the DISC, and these complexes have a certain catalytic activity. While the two forms c-FLIP$_S$ and c-FLIP$_R$ clearly inhibit signal propagation, it was not obvious if c-FLIP$_L$ promotes or also inhibits apoptosis (Golks et al. 2005; Krueger et al. 2001; Scaffidi et al. 1999).

To resolve this question, a study of Fricker et al. on the signaling function of c-FLIP$_L$ combined experiments and modeling, and showed an ambiguous function of the protein as dependent on the stimulus strength (Fricker et al. 2010). Their model considered the formation of homodimers of procaspase-8 or heterodimers of procaspase-8 and c-FLIP variants at the DISC and either termination of further reactions or processing to caspase-8 or p43-FLIP by other active homo- or heterodimers. The model was trained against immunoblot data of procaspase-8 (p55), the intermediate form p43/p41, and caspase-8 (p18 in $p18_2$-$p10_2$) at a given ligand concentration. The model predicted that at a low ligand concentration a twentyfold overexpression of c-$FLIP_L$ would lead to a significant reduction of caspase-8 activity. Contrarily it was predicted, that at high ligand concentration, the same overexpression would lead to an acceleration of cell death. The authors could confirm these predictions with time lapse imaging of cells moderately overexpressing c-$FLIP_L$. As the processing of procaspase-8 is relatively fast, and c-$FLIP_L$ overexpression therefore can only cause small accelerating effects, Fricker et al. tested their model subsequently in conditions of c-$FLIP_S$ or c-$FLIP_R$ overexpression. As these c-FLIP variants inhibit caspase-8 activation, an even stronger activating effect of c-$FLIP_L$ was predicted. Again the predictions were verified, confirming the predicted ambiguous effect of c-$FLIP_L$ being anti-apoptotic at low and pro-apoptotic at high stimulus strengths.

The study by Neumann et al. investigated in detail how NF-κB is activated by CD95L, and how this process is modulated by c-FLIP and caspase-8 (Neumann et al. 2010). The different possibilities of DISC formation of activated receptors, FADD, procaspase-8, c-$FLIP_L$ and c-$FLIP_S$ and their processed forms were described in their model: (i) DISCs containing at least two procaspase-8 molecules give rise to p43/p41 dimers and subsequently mature caspase-8. (ii) At DISCs that contain at least one procaspase-8 and one c-$FLIP_L$ molecule a heterodimer of p43/p41 and c-$FLIP_L$ is created. Besides, several other DISC constitutions preventing further processing were considered. By immunoprecipitation experiments, it was shown that interaction of p43-FLIP with IKKα leads to the phosphorylation of IκB (NF-κB·IκB·P). Phosphorylation of IκB was previously shown to trigger degradation, thereby promoting NF-κB activation. The subsequent translocation of NF-κB into the nucleus after IκB·P degradation was monitored in live-cell experiments. The model matched the dynamics of these processes and the model complexity was iteratively reduced by summarizing or disregarding variables and modeled reactions. The simplification was supervised by means of the fitting accuracy in iterative parameter estimations. The balance between c-$FLIP_L$ and procaspase-8 was shown to be responsible for proliferative or apoptotic effects of CD95 stimulation. Regimes of predominant NF-κB activation or caspase-3 or of both processes could be predicted.

Systems biological studies on the ambiguity toward cell death or survival pathways revealed close interlinks between both processes. A more complicated overall image results when considering connections to other cellular signaling processes. Within the process of cell growth and mitosis, cell cycle regulatory mechanisms can determine pro- or anti-apoptotic conditioning as investigated in the cell cycle model of Pfeuty et al. (2008). Further interlinks exist between cell cycle repair mechanisms leading to cell cycle arrest or apoptosis execution (Zhang et al. 2009). Additionally, the apoptosis sensitivity is modulated by other cellular stress responses as theoretically analyzed in recent modeling studies (Bagci et al. 2008; Toivonen et al. 2011).

3.5 Understanding cell-to-cell variability

Several new experimental techniques and theoretical approaches were developed to investigate the origins and the role of cellular variability in cell death signaling. In several modeling studies, the effects of randomly choosing initial protein concentration sets from probability distributions to estimate consequences of variable initial protein concentrations were investigated (Eissing et al. 2004; Toivonen et al. 2011; Würstle et al. 2010; Albeck et al. 2008).

Eissing et al. reconciled contradictions in single-cell and cell population-based measurements: Caspase activation is temporally abrupt at the single-cell level, while it apparently takes several hours when assessed by western blot measurements summing up over millions of cells (Eissing et al. 2004). Using *in silico* simulations, Eissing et al. could demonstrate that cell-to-cell variability in the lag time before caspase activation could explain the slow and gradual western blot time course. Thus, owing to cell-to-cell variability, the fast kinetics of caspase-3 activation in single cells is masked in experimental observations of population data that show a gradual increase (Rehm et al. 2002).

In general, it is not clear whether cell-to-cell variability in cell signaling mainly arises from stochastic dynamics in biochemical reactions (intrinsic noise) or from the variability of initial protein levels (extrinsic noise). Combining modeling and single-cell experiments, it could be shown that heterogeneous apoptosis timing in a population of cells has its origin in the variable initial levels of apoptotic proteins (Spencer et al. 2009). In single-cell experiments using FRET reporters for initiator and effector caspase activity and the MOMP reporter protein IMS-RP, after cell divisions pairs of cells were observed. While the time of apoptosis was highly correlated in the first hours after cell division, correlation in cell death timing ceased in pairs of older sister cells. This correlation was sustained over a longer period of time by inhibition of protein synthesis. Thereby it was demonstrated that the variability of protein levels arising from noise in gene expression is responsible for cell-to-cell variability in apoptosis timing rather than genetic mutations or epigenetic differences that occur on a larger time scale. By combining single-cell experiments with the model of Albeck et al. it was verified that the time of apoptosis is dependent on the concentrations of several signaling proteins upstream of MOMP (Albeck et al. 2008). Thus, the control of apoptosis timing appears to be distributed over many protein expression levels. Only when overexpressing single signaling proteins as Bid, the dependency of single protein concentration increases. Based on the same model, Gaudet et al. simulated the effects of protein level changes on the variability of cell fates. Their study characterized to which degree variability in cell fate decisions dependents on the levels of involved signaling proteins, and how variances of initial protein levels and covariances between protein levels impact on the variability of characteristic features as the time of MOMP or the time when half of the effector caspase substrate PARP is cleaved (Gaudet et al. 2012). In particular, it was pointed out that altering the initial level of a certain model species can strongly change the influence of the variability of involved signaling species on cell death kinetics, termed contextual sensitivity.

As an alternative approach to link the possible behavior of heterogeneous single cells to their population level measures at certain time points of a dynamic process, Hasenauer et al. developed methods based on parameter probability densities (Hasenauer et al. 2011). These were demonstrated on a synthetic data set for a simple model of tumor necrosis factor (TNF) signaling (Chaves et al. 2008). The original parameter densities could successfully be estimated from simulated flow cytometric data.

Taken together, cell-to-cell variability is an inherently complex phenomenon that can only be tackled by quantitative approaches. ODE modeling combined with sensitivity analysis and stochastic modeling became valuable tools in this field of apoptosis research.

4 CONCLUSIONS

Apoptosis is a well-characterized biological process amenable to mathematical modeling. Mechanistic models provided valuable insights into nonlinear phenomena such as all-or-none switching and irreversible decision making. Modeling reconciled apparently contradictory observations at the single-cell and population level, and was employed to identify molecular mechanisms controlling whether a cell enters death via the type I or type II pathway of apoptosis (Aldridge et al. 2011; Hua et al. 2005; Harrington et al. 2008; Okazaki et al. 2008). In particular, the study by Hua et al. verified corresponding model predictions experimentally, and showed that the anti-apoptotic influence of Bcl-2 is completely lost in type II cells in the case of procaspase-8 overexpression (Hua et al. 2005). Lyapunov coefficients served as a tool to predict under which conditions changes in initial protein concentrations cells shift from a type I to a type II apoptosis behavior. Specifically, this method showed that the ratio between caspase-3 and XIAP determines the type of cell death (Aldridge et al. 2011). Non-intuitive feedback loops arising implicitly from the apoptosis network structure could be identified by simulation analysis (Legewie et al. 2006; Cui et al. 2008).

The crosstalk between cell death and survival signaling is much less understood; here, modeling was mostly restricted to top-down and qualitative approaches owing to crosstalk complexity. However, quantitative modeling and sensitivity analysis are required to predict effective co-treatment strategies for cancer cells that often harbor combined mutations in interdependent growth factor and apoptosis networks. Currently, a major limitation is our incomplete understanding of autophagy ("self eating") which shares many molecular components with the apoptosis machinery (e.g., Bcl-2 family members) (Choi et al. 2013; Rubinstein and Kimchi 2012). Depending on the cell type, autophagy protects cells from death by removing damaged organelles or it triggers another form of cell death, further complicating the apoptosis survival network.

Another limitation of current models is that they mainly focus on extrinsic apoptosis induced by death ligands. However, most pharmacologically relevant responses, e.g., during chemotherapy, proceed via the intrinsic mitochondrial pathway. The intrinsic pathway includes another layer of complexity, as it requires transcriptional regulation, e.g., of Bcl-2 protein family regulators (Puma, Noxa). Quantitative gene expression profiling and chromatin immunoprecipitation (ChIP) studies combined with systematic molecular perturbations are required to quantitatively model gene regulatory networks controlling intrinsic apoptosis. Antagonists inhibiting the Inhibitor of Apoptosis (IAP) proteins appear to be promising therapeutics, as they selectively kill cancer cells in the absence of further stimulation. Apoptosis models taking into account basal state signaling are required to understand and to optimize such therapeutic approaches.

Live-cell imaging and flow cytometric approaches led to insights into apoptosis at the single-cell level, and revealed principles of cell-to-cell variability (Rehm et al. 2006; Spencer et al. 2009). Further experimental and theoretical analyses are required to understand how complete eradication of tumor cell populations can be achieved. In principle, it might be possible that nonlinear phenomena such as bistability give rise to tumor cell sub-populations that are completely insensitive to therapy. Moreover, single cells may differ in the apoptosis pathways they employ, implying that combinatorial inhibition of multiple pathways is required for elimination of the whole tumor. This requires the development of new parameter estimation tools which take into account cell-to-cell variability, and integrate population-based as well as single-cell measurements.

References

Albeck, J. G., Burke, J. M., Aldridge, B. B., Zhang, M., Lauffenburger, D. A., and Sorger, P. K. (2008). Quantitative analysis of pathways controlling extrinsic apoptosis in single cells. *Mol. Cell* **30**:11–25.

Albeck, J. G., Burke, J. M., Spencer, S. L., Lauffenburger, D. A., and Sorger, P. K. (2008). Modeling a snap-action, variable-delay switch controlling extrinsic cell death. *PLoS Biol.* **6**:2831–2852.

Aldridge, B. B., Haller, G., Sorger, P. K., and Lauffenburger, D. A. (2006). Direct Lyapunov exponent analysis enables parametric study of transient signalling governing cell behaviour. *Syst. Biol. (Stevenage)* **153**:425–432.

Aldridge, B. B., Gaudet, S., Lauffenburger, D. A., and Sorger, P. K. (2011). Lyapunov exponents and phase diagrams reveal multi-factorial control over TRAIL-induced apoptosis. *Mol. Syst. Biol.* **7**:553.

Algeciras-Schimnich, A., Pietras, E. M., Barnhart, B. C., Legembre, P., Vijayan, S., Holbeck, S. L., and Peter, M. E. (2003). Two CD95 tumor classes with different sensitivities to antitumor drugs. *Proc. Natl. Acad. Sci. USA* **100**:11445–11450.

Bagci, E. Z., Vodovotz, Y., Billiar, T. R., Ermentrout, G. B., and Bahar, I. (2006). Bistability in apoptosis: roles of bax, bcl-2, and mitochondrial permeability transition pores. *Biophys. J.* **90**:1546–1559.

Bagci, E. Z., Vodovotz, Y., Billiar, T. R., Ermentrout, B., and Bahar, I. (2008). Computational insights on the competing effects of nitric oxide in regulating apoptosis. *PLoS ONE* **3**:e2249.

Beaudouin, J., Liesche, C., Aschenbrenner, S., Hörner, M., and Eils, R. (2013). *Caspase-8 cleaves its substrates from the plasma membrane upon CD95-induced apoptosis.* Cell Death Differ.

Bentele, M., Lavrik, I., Ulrich, M., Stösser, S., Heermann, D. W., Kalthoff, H., Krammer, P. H., and Eils, R. (2004). Mathematical modeling reveals threshold mechanism in CD95-induced apoptosis. *J. Cell Biol.* **166**:839–851.

Brunelle, J. K., and Letai, A. (2009). Control of mitochondrial apoptosis by the Bcl-2 family. *J. Cell. Sci.* **122**:437–441.

Burnham, K. P., and Anderson, D. R. (2010). *Model Selection and Multi-Model Inference: A Practical Information-Theoretic Approach*. New York, NY: Springer.

Calzone, L., Tournier, L., Fourquet, S., Thieffry, D., Zhivotovsky, B., Barillot, E., and Zinovyev, A. (2010). Mathematical modelling of cell-fate decision in response to death receptor engagement. *PLoS Comput. Biol.* **6**:e1000702.

Certo, M., Del Gaizo Moore, V., Nishino, M., Wei, G., Korsmeyer, S., Armstrong, S. A., and Letai, A. (2006). Mitochondria primed by death signals determine cellular addiction to antiapoptotic BCL-2 family members. *Cancer Cell* **9**:351–365.

Chaves, M., Eissing, T., and Allgower, F. (2008). Bistable biological systems: A characterization through local compact input-to-state stability. *IEEE Trans. Automat. Control* **53**:87–100.

Chen, C., Cui, J., Lu, H., Wang, R., Zhang, S., and Shen, P. (2007a). Modeling of the role of a Bax-activation switch in the mitochondrial apoptosis decision. *Biophys. J.* **92**:4304–4315.

Chen, C., Cui, J., Zhang, W., and Shen, P. (2007b). Robustness analysis identifies the plausible model of the Bcl-2 apoptotic switch. *FEBS Lett.* **581**:5143–5150.

Choi, A. M. K., Ryter, S. W., and Levine, B. (2013). Autophagy in human health and disease. *New Engl. J. Med.* **368**:651–662.

Cui, J., Chen, C., Lu, H., Sun, T., and Shen, P. (2008). Two independent positive feedbacks and bistability in the Bcl-2 apoptotic switch. *PLoS ONE* **3**:e1469.

Danial, N. N., and Korsmeyer, S. J. (2004). Cell death: critical control points. *Cell* **116**:205–219.

Deng, Y., Lin, Y., and Wu, X. (2002). TRAIL-induced apoptosis requires Bax-dependent mitochondrial release of Smac/DIABLO. *Genes Dev.* **16**:33–45.

Deng, J., Carlson, N., Takeyama, K., Dal Cin, P., Shipp, M., and Letai, A. (2007). BH3 profiling identifies three distinct classes of apoptotic blocks to predict response to ABT-737 and conventional chemotherapeutic agents. *Cancer Cell* **12**:171–185.

Du, C., Fang, M., Li, Y., Li, L., and Wang, X. (2000). Smac, a mitochondrial protein that promotes cytochrome c-dependent caspase activation by eliminating IAP inhibition. *Cell* **102**:33–42.

Dumitru, C. A., and Gulbins, E. (2006). TRAIL activates acid sphingomyelinase via a redox mechanism and releases ceramide to trigger apoptosis. *Oncogene* **25**:5612–5625.

Düssmann, H., Rehm, M., Concannon, C. G., Anguissola, S., Würstle, M., Kacmar, S., Völler, P., Huber, H. J., and Prehn, J. H. M. (2010). Single-cell quantification of Bax activation and mathematical modelling suggest pore formation on minimal mitochondrial Bax accumulation. *Cell Death Differ.* **17**:278–290.

Eissing, T., Conzelmann, H., Gilles, E. D., Allgöwer, F., Bullinger, E., and Scheurich, P. (2004). Bistability analyses of a caspase activation model for receptor-induced apoptosis. *J. Biol. Chem.* **279**:36892–36897.

Ferrell, J. E. Jr., (1996). Tripping the switch fantastic: how a protein kinase cascade can convert graded inputs into switch-like outputs. *Trends Biochem. Sci.* **21**:460–466.

Fischer, S. F., Vier, J., Kirschnek, S., Klos, A., Hess, S., Ying, S., and Häcker, G. (2004). Chlamydia inhibit host cell apoptosis by degradation of proapoptotic BH3-only proteins. *J. Exp. Med.* **200**:905–916.

Fricker, N., Beaudouin, J., Richter, P., Eils, R., Krammer, P. H., and Lavrik, I. N. (2010). Model-based dissection of CD95 signaling dynamics reveals both a pro- and antiapoptotic role of c-FLIPL. *J. Cell Biol.* **190**:377–389.

Fuentes-Prior, P., and Salvesen, G. S. (2004). The protein structures that shape caspase activity, specificity, activation and inhibition. *Biochem. J.* **384**:201–232.

Fussenegger, M., Bailey, J. E., and Varner, J. (2000). A mathematical model of caspase function in apoptosis. *Nat. Biotechnol.* **18**:768–774.

Galluzzi, L., Kepp, O., and Kroemer, G. (2012). Mitochondria: master regulators of danger signalling. *Nat. Rev. Mol. Cell Biol.* **13**:780–788.

García-Sáez, A. J. (2012). The secrets of the Bcl-2 family. *Cell Death Differ.* **19**:1733–1740.

Gaudet, S., Spencer, S. L., Chen, W. W., and Sorger, P. K. (2012). Exploring the contextual sensitivity of factors that determine cell-to-cell variability in receptor-mediated apoptosis. *PLoS Comput. Biol.* **8**:e1002482.

Goldstein, J. C., Waterhouse, N. J., Juin, P., Evan, G. I., and Green, D. R. (2000). The coordinate release of cytochrome c during apoptosis is rapid, complete and kinetically invariant. *Nat. Cell Biol.* **2**:156–162.

Golks, A., Brenner, D., Fritsch, C., Krammer, P. H., and Lavrik, I. N. (2005). c-FLIPR, a new regulator of death receptor-induced apoptosis. *J. Biol. Chem.* **280**:14507–14513.

Gómez-Benito, M., Marzo, I., Anel, A., and Naval, J. (2005). Farnesyltransferase inhibitor BMS-214662 induces apoptosis in myeloma cells through PUMA up-regulation, Bax and Bak activation, and Mcl-1 elimination. *Mol. Pharmacol.* **67**:1991–1998.

Hanahan, D., and Weinberg, R. A. (2011). Hallmarks of cancer: the next generation. *Cell* **144**:646–674.

Harrington, H. A., Ho, K. L., Ghosh, S., and Tung, K. C. (2008). Construction and analysis of a modular model of caspase activation in apoptosis. *Theor. Biol. Med. Model* **5**:26.

Hasenauer, J., Waldherr, S., Doszczak, M., Radde, N., Scheurich, P., and Allgöwer, F. (2011). Identification of models of heterogeneous cell populations from population snapshot data. *BMC Bioinformatics* **12**:125.

Hector, S., Rehm, M., Schmid, J., Kehoe, J., McCawley, N., Dicker, P., Murray, F., McNamara, D., Kay, E. W., Concannon, C. G., et al. (2012). Clinical application of a systems model of apoptosis execution for the prediction of colorectal cancer therapy responses and personalisation of therapy. *Gut* **61**:725–733.

Hengl, S., Kreutz, C., Timmer, J., and Maiwald, T. (2007). Data-based identifiability analysis of non-linear dynamical models. *Bioinformatics* **23**:2612–2618.

Ho, K. L., and Harrington, H. A. (2010). Bistability in apoptosis by receptor clustering. *PLoS Comput. Biol.* **6**:e1000956.

Hoffmann, J. C., Pappa, A., Krammer, P. H., and Lavrik, I. N. (2009). A new C-terminal cleavage product of procaspase-8, p30, defines an alternative pathway of procaspase-8 activation. *Mol. Cell. Biol.* **29**:4431–4440.

Hu, T.-M., Hayton, W. L., and Mallery, S. R. (2006). Kinetic modeling of nitric-oxide-associated reaction network. *Pharm. Res.* **23**:1702–1711.

Hua, F., Cornejo, M. G., Cardone, M. H., Stokes, C. L., and Lauffenburger, D. A. (2005). Effects of Bcl-2 levels on Fas signaling-induced caspase-3 activation: molecular genetic tests of computational model predictions. *J. Immunol.* **175**:985–995.

Huber, H. J., Dussmann, H., Kilbride, S. M., Rehm, M., and Prehn, J. H. M. (2011). Glucose metabolism determines resistance of cancer cells to bioenergetic crisis after cytochrome-c release. *Mol. Syst. Biol.* **7**:470.

Hughes, M. A., Harper, N., Butterworth, M., Cain, K., Cohen, G. M., and MacFarlane, M. (2009). Reconstitution of the death-inducing signaling complex reveals a substrate switch that determines CD95-mediated death or survival. *Mol. Cell* **35**:265–279.

Janes, K. A., Albeck, J. G., Gaudet, S., Sorger, P. K., Lauffenburger, D. A., and Yaffe, M. B. (2005). A systems model of signaling identifies a molecular basis set for cytokine-induced apoptosis. *Science* **310**:1646–1653.

Kallenberger, S., and Legewie, S. (2013). Modeling formalisms in systems biology of apoptosis. In (I. Lavrik (Ed.)), *Systems Biology of Apoptosis*, pp. 1–32. New York, NY: Springer.

Kischkel, F. C., Hellbardt, S., Behrmann, I., Germer, M., Pawlita, M., Krammer, P. H., and Peter, M. E. (1995). Cytotoxicity-dependent APO-1 (Fas/CD95)-associated proteins form a death-inducing signaling complex (DISC) with the receptor. *EMBO J.* **14**:5579–5588.

Kluck, R. M., Bossy-Wetzel, E., Green, D. R., and Newmeyer, D. D. (1997). The release of cytochrome c from mitochondria: a primary site for Bcl-2 regulation of apoptosis. *Science* **275**:1132–1136.

Krueger, A., Schmitz, I., Baumann, S., Krammer, P. H., and Kirchhoff, S. (2001). Cellular FLICE-inhibitory protein splice variants inhibit different steps of caspase-8 activation at the CD95 death-inducing signaling complex. *J. Biol. Chem.* **276**:20633–20640.

Laussmann, M. A., Passante, E., Hellwig, C. T., Tomiczek, B., Flanagan, L., Prehn, J. H. M., Huber, H. J., and Rehm, M. (2012). Proteasome inhibition can impair caspase-8 activation upon submaximal stimulation of apoptotic tumor necrosis factor-related apoptosis inducing ligand (TRAIL) signaling. *J. Biol. Chem.* **287**:14402–14411.

Lavrik, I., Golks, A., and Krammer, P. H. (2005). Death receptor signaling. *J. Cell Sci.* **118**:265–267.

Legewie, S., Blüthgen, N., and Herzel, H. (2006). Mathematical modeling identifies inhibitors of apoptosis as mediators of positive feedback and bistability. *PLoS Comput. Biol.* **2**:e120.

Lessene, G., Czabotar, P. E., and Colman, P. M. (2008). BCL-2 family antagonists for cancer therapy. *Nat. Rev. Drug Discov.* **7**:989–1000.

Li, B., and Dou, Q. P. (2000). Bax degradation by the ubiquitin/proteasome-dependent pathway: involvement in tumor survival and progression. *Proc. Natl. Acad. Sci. USA* **97**:3850–3855.

Li, P., Nijhawan, D., Budihardjo, I., Srinivasula, S. M., Ahmad, M., Alnemri, E. S., and Wang, X. (1997). Cytochrome c and dATP-dependent formation of Apaf-1/caspase-9 complex initiates an apoptotic protease cascade. *Cell* **91**:479–489.

Li, S., Zhao, Y., He, X., Kim, T.-H., Kuharsky, D. K., Rabinowich, H., Chen, J., Du, C., and Yin, X.-M. (2002). Relief of extrinsic pathway inhibition by the Bid-dependent mitochondrial release of Smac in Fas-mediated hepatocyte apoptosis. *J. Biol. Chem.* **277**:26912–26920.

Lindner, A. U., Concannon, C. G., Boukes, G. J., Cannon, M. D., Llambi, F., Ryan, D., Boland, K., Kehoe, J., McNamara, D. A., Murray, F., et al. (2013). Systems analysis of BCL2 protein family interactions establishes a model to predict responses to chemotherapy. *Cancer Res.* **73**:519–528.

Liu, X., Kim, C. N., Yang, J., Jemmerson, R., and Wang, X. (1996). Induction of apoptotic program in cell-free extracts: requirement for dATP and cytochrome c. *Cell* **86**:147–157.

Mai, Z., and Liu, H. (2009). Boolean network-based analysis of the apoptosis network: irreversible apoptosis and stable surviving. *J. Theor. Biol.* **259**:760–769.

Mannick, J. B., Hausladen, A., Liu, L., Hess, D. T., Zeng, M., Miao, Q. X., Kane, L. S., Gow, A. J., and Stamler, J. S. (1999). Fas-induced caspase denitrosylation. *Science* **284**:651–654.

McDonald, E. R., 3rd, and El-Deiry, W. S. (2004). Suppression of caspase-8- and -10-associated RING proteins results in sensitization to death ligands and inhibition of tumor cell growth. *Proc. Natl. Acad. Sci. USA* **101**:6170–6175.

Medema, J. P., Scaffidi, C., Kischkel, F. C., Shevchenko, A., Mann, M., Krammer, P. H., and Peter, M. E. (1997). FLICE is activated by association with the CD95 death-inducing signaling complex (DISC). *EMBO J.* **16**:2794–2804.

Murphy, Á. C., Weyhenmeyer, B., Schmid, J., Kilbride, S. M., Rehm, M., Huber, H. J., Senft, C., Weissenberger, J., Seifert, V., Dunst, M., et al. (2013). Activation of executioner caspases is a predictor of progression-free survival in glioblastoma patients: a systems medicine approach. *Cell Death Dis.* **4**:e629.

Muzio, M., Chinnaiyan, A. M., Kischkel, F. C., O'Rourke, K., Shevchenko, A., Ni, J., Scaffidi, C., Bretz, J. D., Zhang, M., Gentz, R., et al. (1996). FLICE, a novel FADD-homologous ICE/CED-3-like protease, is recruited to the CD95 (Fas/APO-1) death–inducing signaling complex. *Cell* **85**:817–827.

Nair, V. D., Yuen, T., Olanow, C. W., and Sealfon, S. C. (2004). Early single cell bifurcation of pro- and antiapoptotic states during oxidative stress. *J. Biol. Chem.* **279**:27494–27501.

Neumann, L., Pforr, C., Beaudouin, J., Pappa, A., Fricker, N., Krammer, P. H., Lavrik, I. N., and Eils, R. (2010). Dynamics within the CD95 death-inducing signaling complex decide life and death of cells. *Mol. Syst. Biol.* **6**:352.

Ni Chonghaile, T., and Letai, A. (2008). Mimicking the BH3 domain to kill cancer cells. *Oncogene* **27**(Suppl 1):S149–S157.

Okazaki, N., Asano, R., Kinoshita, T., and Chuman, H. (2008). Simple computational models of type I/type II cells in Fas signaling-induced apoptosis. *J. Theor. Biol.* **250**:621–633.

Pace, V., Bellizzi, D., Giordano, F., Panno, M. L., and De Benedictis, G. (2010). Experimental testing of a mathematical model relevant to the extrinsic pathway of apoptosis. *Cell Stress Chaperones* **15**:13–23.

Pfeuty, B., David-Pfeuty, T., and Kaneko, K. (2008). Underlying principles of cell fate determination during G1 phase of the mammalian cell cycle. *Cell cycle* **7**:3246–3257.

Philippi, N., Walter, D., Schlatter, R., Ferreira, K., Ederer, M., Sawodny, O., Timmer, J., Borner, C., and Dandekar, T. (2009). Modeling system states in liver cells: survival, apoptosis and their modifications in response to viral infection. *BMC Syst. Biol.* **3**:97.

Pop, C., Fitzgerald, P., Green, D. R., and Salvesen, G. S. (2007). Role of proteolysis in caspase-8 activation and stabilization. *Biochemistry* **46**:4398–4407.

Raue, A., Kreutz, C., Maiwald, T., Bachmann, J., Schilling, M., Klingmüller, U., and Timmer, J. (2009). Structural and practical identifiability analysis of partially observed dynamical models by exploiting the profile likelihood. *Bioinformatics* **25**:1923–1929.

Raue, A., Becker, V., Klingmüller, U., and Timmer, J. (2010). Identifiability and observability analysis for experimental design in nonlinear dynamical models. *Chaos* **20**:045105.

Reed, J. C. (1999). Dysregulation of apoptosis in cancer. *J. Clin. Oncol.* **17**:2941–2953.

Reed, J. C., Miyashita, T., Takayama, S., Wang, H. G., Sato, T., Krajewski, S., Aimé-Sempé, C., Bodrug, S., Kitada, S., and Hanada, M. (1996). BCL-2 family proteins: regulators of cell death involved in the pathogenesis of cancer and resistance to therapy. *J. Cell. Biochem.* **60**:23–32.

Rehm, M., Dussmann, H., Janicke, R. U., Tavare, J. M., Kogel, D., and Prehn, J. H. M. (2002). Single-cell fluorescence resonance energy transfer analysis demonstrates that caspase activation during apoptosis is a rapid process. Role of caspase-3. *J. Biol. Chem.* **277**:24506–24514.

Rehm, M., Huber, H. J., Dussmann, H., and Prehn, J. H. M. (2006). Systems analysis of effector caspase activation and its control by X-linked inhibitor of apoptosis protein. *EMBO J.* **25**:4338–4349.

Rehm, M., Huber, H. J., Hellwig, C. T., Anguissola, S., Dussmann, H., and Prehn, J. H. M. (2009). Dynamics of outer mitochondrial membrane permeabilization during apoptosis. *Cell Death Differ.* **16**:613–623.

Rössig, L., Fichtlscherer, B., Breitschopf, K., Haendeler, J., Zeiher, A. M., Mülsch, A., and Dimmeler, S. (1999). Nitric oxide inhibits caspase-3 by S-nitrosation in vivo. *J. Biol. Chem.* **274**:6823–6826.

Rubinstein, A. D., and Kimchi, A. (2012). Life in the balance - a mechanistic view of the crosstalk between autophagy and apoptosis. *J. Cell. Sci.* **125**:5259–5268.

Samejima, K., and Earnshaw, W. C. (2005). Trashing the genome: the role of nucleases during apoptosis. *Nat. Rev. Mol. Cell Biol.* **6**:677–688.

Scaffidi, C., Fulda, S., Srinivasan, A., Friesen, C., Li, F., Tomaselli, K. J., Debatin, K. M., Krammer, P. H., and Peter, M. E. (1998). Two CD95 (APO-1/Fas) signaling pathways. *EMBO J.* **17**:1675–1687.

Scaffidi, C., Schmitz, I., Krammer, P. H., and Peter, M. E. (1999). The role of c-FLIP in modulation of CD95-induced apoptosis. *J. Biol. Chem.* **274**:1541–1548.

Schlatter, R., Schmich, K., Avalos Vizcarra, I., Scheurich, P., Sauter, T., Borner, C., Ederer, M., Merfort, I., and Sawodny, O. (2009). ON/OFF and beyond–a Boolean model of apoptosis. *PLoS Comput. Biol.* **5**:e1000595.

Schleich, K., Warnken, U., Fricker, N., Oztürk, S., Richter, P., Kammerer, K., Schnölzer, M., Krammer, P. H., and Lavrik, I. N. (2012). Stoichiometry of the CD95 death-inducing signaling complex: experimental and modeling evidence for a death effector domain chain model. *Mol. Cell* **47**:306–319.

Schmid, J., Dussmann, H., Boukes, G. J., Flanagan, L., Lindner, A. U., O'Connor, C. L., Rehm, M., Prehn, J. H. M., and Huber, H. J. (2012). Systems analysis of cancer cell heterogeneity in caspase-dependent apoptosis subsequent to mitochondrial outer membrane permeabilization. *J. Biol. Chem.* **287**:41546–41559.

Schorr, K., Li, M., Krajewski, S., Reed, J. C., Furth, P. A., (1999). Bcl-2 gene family and related proteins in mammary gland involution and breast cancer. *J. Mammary Gland Biol. Neoplasia* **4**:153–164.

Scott, F. L., Stec, B., Pop, C., Dobaczewska, M. K., Lee, J. J., Monosov, E., Robinson, H., Salvesen, G. S., Schwarzenbacher, R., and Riedl, S. J. (2009). The Fas-FADD death domain complex structure unravels signalling by receptor clustering. *Nature* **457**:1019–1022.

Siehs, C., Oberbauer, R., Mayer, G., Lukas, A., and Mayer, B. (2002). Discrete simulation of regulatory homo- and heterodimerization in the apoptosis effector phase. *Bioinformatics* **18**:67–76.

Song, Z., Yao, X., and Wu, M. (2003). Direct interaction between survivin and Smac/DIABLO is essential for the anti-apoptotic activity of survivin during taxol-induced apoptosis. *J. Biol. Chem.* **278**:23130–23140.

Spencer, S. L., Gaudet, S., Albeck, J. G., Burke, J. M., and Sorger, P. K. (2009). Non-genetic origins of cell-to-cell variability in TRAIL-induced apoptosis. *Nature* **459**:428–432.

Stucki, J. W., and Simon, H.-U. (2005). Mathematical modeling of the regulation of caspase-3 activation and degradation. *J. Theor. Biol.* **234**:123–131.

Sun, X.-M., Bratton, S. B., Butterworth, M., MacFarlane, M., and Cohen, G. M. (2002). Bcl-2 and Bcl-xL inhibit CD95-mediated apoptosis by preventing mitochondrial release of Smac/DIABLO and subsequent inactivation of X-linked inhibitor-of-apoptosis protein. *J. Biol. Chem.* **277**:11345–11351.

Svingen, P. A., Loegering, D., Rodriquez, J., Meng, X. W., Mesner, P. W. Jr, Holbeck, S., Monks, A., Krajewski, S., Scudiero, D. A., Sausville, E. A., et al. (2004). Components of the cell death machine and drug sensitivity of the National Cancer Institute Cell Line Panel. *Clin. Cancer Res.* **10**:6807–6820.

Tentner, A. R., Lee, M. J., Ostheimer, G. J., Samson, L. D., Lauffenburger, D. A., and Yaffe, M. B. (2012). Combined experimental and computational analysis of DNA damage signaling reveals context-dependent roles for Erk in apoptosis and G1/S arrest after genotoxic stress. *Mol. Syst. Biol.* **8**:568.

Toivonen, H. T., Meinander, A., Asaoka, T., Westerlund, M., Pettersson, F., Mikhailov, A., Eriksson, J. E., and Saxén, H. (2011). Modeling reveals that dynamic regulation of c-FLIP levels determines cell-to-cell distribution of CD95-mediated apoptosis. *J. Biol. Chem.* **286**:18375–18382.

Tyas, L., Brophy, V. A., Pope, A., Rivett, A. J., and Tavaré, J. M. (2000). Rapid caspase-3 activation during apoptosis revealed using fluorescence-resonance energy transfer. *EMBO Rep.* **1**:266–270.

Verhagen, A. M., Ekert, P. G., Pakusch, M., Silke, J., Connolly, L. M., Reid, G. E., Moritz, R. L., Simpson, R. J., and Vaux, D. L. (2000). Identification of DIABLO, a mammalian protein that promotes apoptosis by binding to and antagonizing IAP proteins. *Cell* **102**:43–53.

Vieira, H. L., Belzacq, A. S., Haouzi, D., Bernassola, F., Cohen, I., Jacotot, E., Ferri, K. F., El Hamel, C., Bartle, L. M., Melino, G., et al. (2001). The adenine nucleotide translocator: a target of nitric oxide, peroxynitrite, and 4-hydroxynonenal. *Oncogene* **20**:4305–4316.

Vo, T.-T., and Letai, A. (2010). BH3-only proteins and their effects on cancer. *Adv. Exp. Med. Biol.* **687**:49–63.

Willis, S. N., Chen, L., Dewson, G., Wei, A., Naik, E., Fletcher, J. I., Adams, J. M., and Huang, D. C. S. (2005). Proapoptotic Bak is sequestered by Mcl-1 and Bcl-xL, but not Bcl-2, until displaced by BH3-only proteins. *Genes Dev.* **19**:1294–1305.

Würstle, M. L., Laussmann, M. A., and Rehm, M. (2010). The caspase-8 dimerization/dissociation balance is a highly potent regulator of caspase-8, -3, -6 signaling. *J. Biol. Chem.* **285**:33209–33218.

Zhang, H., Xu, Q., Krajewski, S., Krajewska, M., Xie, Z., Fuess, S., Kitada, S., Pawlowski, K., Godzik, A., and Reed, J. C. (2000). BAR: An apoptosis regulator at the intersection of caspases and Bcl-2 family proteins. *Proc. Natl. Acad. Sci. USA* **97**:2597–2602.

Zhang, X. D., Zhang, X. Y., Gray, C. P., Nguyen, T., and Hersey, P. (2001). Tumor necrosis factor-related apoptosis-inducing ligand-induced apoptosis of human melanoma is regulated by smac/DIABLO release from mitochondria. *Cancer Res.* **61**:7339–7348.

Zhang, R., Shah, M. V., Yang, J., Nyland, S. B., Liu, X., Yun, J. K., Albert, R., and Loughran, T. P. Jr., (2008). Network model of survival signaling in large granular lymphocyte leukemia. *Proc. Natl. Acad. Sci. USA* **105**:16308–16313.

Zhang, T., Brazhnik, P., and Tyson, J. J. (2009). Computational analysis of dynamical responses to the intrinsic pathway of programmed cell death. *Biophys. J.* **97**:415–434.

Author Index

B

C

D

E

G

L

X

Y

Subject Index

H

Q

Printed and bound by CPI Group (UK) Ltd, Croydon, CR0 4YY
03/10/2024
01040326-0006